The Management Body of Knowledge

By American Management Association

Published by American Management Association
1601 Broadway, New York, NY 10019
www.amanet.org

ISBN: 978-0-578-58526-0 (print)
ISBN: 978-0-578-59340-1 (ebook)

Contents

Beyond the Domains

Foreword

During my career, which has spanned three decades, I have been fortunate to have lived on four continents and have had the privilege to work with and for some incredible teams and leaders. My management style, is largely a result of how I have witnessed great managers effectively motivate their teams, deliver outstanding results, and shape the business environments and microcultures.

In contrast, I have also come across a few managers who have made some fundamental mistakes. The impact of their inability to manage teams, which affects other business units, often results in retention issues and toxic business environments.

As a functional title, "Manager" is so broad it can mean everything, anything, and nothing depending on the individual's respective level and organization. There are a few fundamental best practices of management that if understood can help improve consistency of results.

When a new manager transitions from being an individual contributor to managing a direct report or a team of people, it is no longer enough that the results derived from the individual's direct actions are well executed. It is now the collective actions of the team that drive the result. To gain credibility, a manager needs a fundamental understanding of the business and the ability to focus the actions of the team to drive results. Individual effort that worked in the past no longer seems to be effective. The rules have changed. I have personally seen great individual contributors struggle as they make this transition and lose credibility as a result.

There is an opportunity to provide a framework and approach to help new managers quickly assimilate to the new ways of working, managing collective tasks, paving the way forward, and motivating people. If any organization is going to put a stake in the ground and define the standards, at 95+ years of experience providing professional development for managers across the globe, the American Management Association (AMA) is in the perfect position to do so.

In a time when change is the only constant, and ambiguity and volatility are the norm, managers' competencies in the areas of business acumen and analytical intelligence are becoming increasingly important. The span of responsibility of a manager continues to increase in a flatter, global, and more matrixed business environment. AMA's approach using the Total Professional Model and its well researched and constructed Body of Knowledge includes the important aspects of Professional Effectiveness, Relationship Management, Business Acumen, and Analytical Intelligence, which are the essential toolkit for the modern manager.

Retention remains a significant challenge for organizations, and many employees do not/will not remain with one company for the duration of their careers. With this in mind, organizations are paying greater attention to helping employees identify career paths, cross-functional experiences, and more opportunities for promotability. In doing so, they are demonstrating to employees that the company has systems in place to recognize and reward superior performance.

In my experience, it is the people that define an organization's culture, and ultimately, its success. Equipping managers with a complete toolkit, develops the right level of competence and consistency of application and can lead to better employee retention, as well as improved motivation and team results.

The AMA's framework of the Total Professional Model and its well-researched and presented Body of Knowledge can help organizations sustain a position as an "Employer of Choice."

Brad Watt
Chief Learning Officer
Colgate-Palmolive Company

Acknowledgments

Name	Contributions
Susan Mason	1-Communication 2-Emotional Intelligence
Laura Smith Dunaief	3-Presentation Skills 4-Conflict Management 10-Managing Change
Haywood Spangler, PhD	5-Motivation 15-Critical Thinking 19-Ethics
Michael Kmetz, ABD	6-Collaboration 7-Influence
Joseph Reed, PhD	8-Delegation
Howard Jacobson, PhD Peter Bregman, CEO of Bregman Partners	9-Coaching for Performance
Lisa Mathews, MBA, PMP	11-Managing Projects
Miles Hutchinson, CGMA	12-Financial Acumen
Lior Arussy, CEO and Founder Strativity Group	13-Customer Focus
Russ Terry	14-Talent Management
Steven M. Rumery, PhD	16-Managing and Mastering Data
Dr. Kimbery Jarvis, CEO and Founder All Career Matters, Inc.	17-Work Style and Work Fit
José Pascal da Rocha, PhD, JD	18-Organizational Culture
Blade Kotelly	20-Managing Technology
Wendy Hirschberg, MA, Diversity Consultant	21-Diversity and Inclusion
Brad Watt, Chief Learning Officer, Colgate-Palmolive Company	Foreword Writer

Kalie Fiorenza	Content Editor
Andrew Ambraziejus	Content Editor
Louis Greenstein	Rewriter and Editor
Christopher Anzalone	Developmental Editor

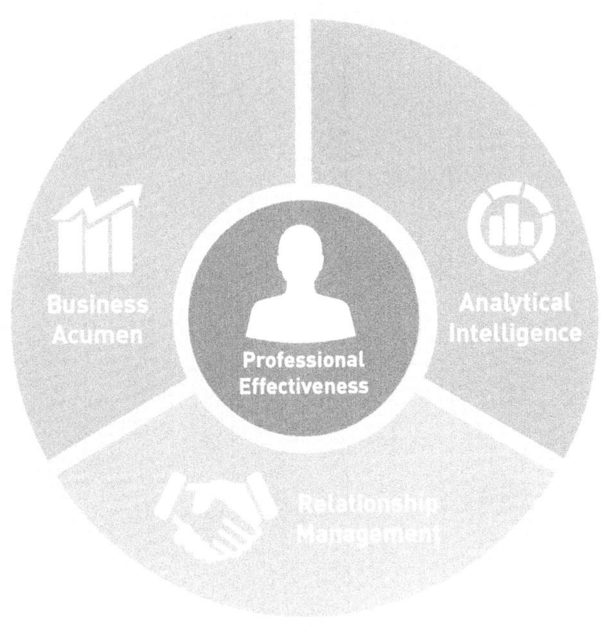

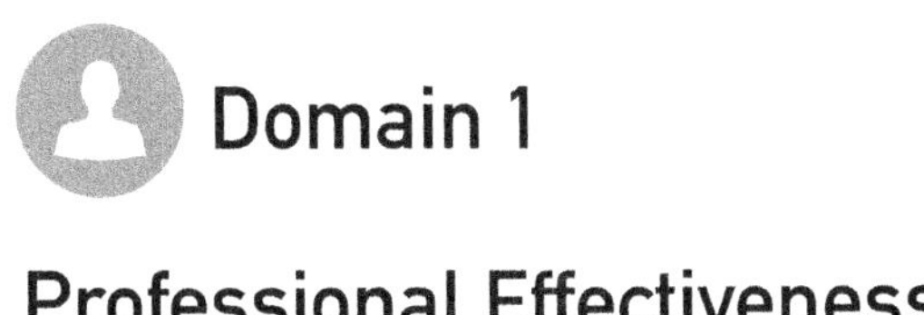

Domain 1

Professional Effectiveness

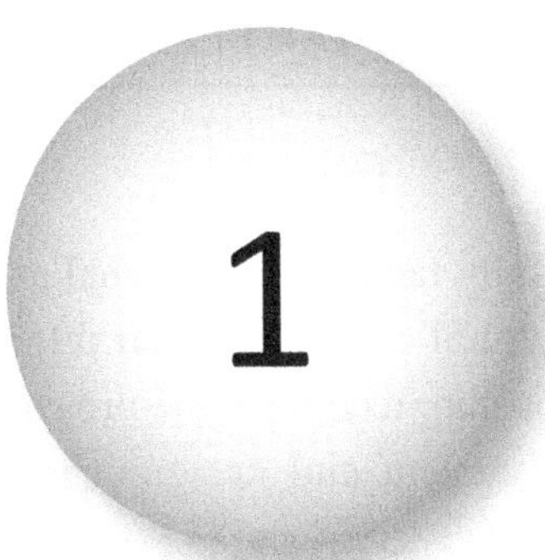

Communication

LEARNING OBJECTIVES

By the end of this chapter, you will be better equipped to:

- Identify the elements of communication that transcend communication channels or situations.
- Apply communication skills in managing team performance, member satisfaction, and innovation.
- Develop shared understanding of team's goals using various communication strategies.
- Deliver clear messages related to team and organizational vision, goals, and expectations.
- Manage emotionally charged communications through the use of strategies and techniques to minimize defensiveness and resistance.
- Identify verbal communication approaches to meet the needs and expectations of different audiences (for example, when delivering feedback to direct reports or contributing at meetings with the C-suite).
- Create clear and concise written communications in the form and manner best suited to the type of message and intended audience.
- Facilitate open conversations between and among supervisors, peers, and direct reports.

Communication is the complex and culturally bound process by which information is imparted or exchanged with the goal of creating shared meaning.

As noted in the learning objectives, to perform their job functions effectively managers need to know how to communicate for team performance; inform, influence, and motivate others by using strategic communication skills; successfully facilitate situational and challenging conversations; recognize and respectfully work with cross-cultural communication differences; adapt and flex personal preferences to facilitate rapport and relationship; recognize the pros and cons of virtual communication channel choices; and adjust messaging content and design when delivering up, down, and across the organization.

To investigate the complexity of managerial communication we address several critical topics in this chapter, as shown in Figure 1-1.

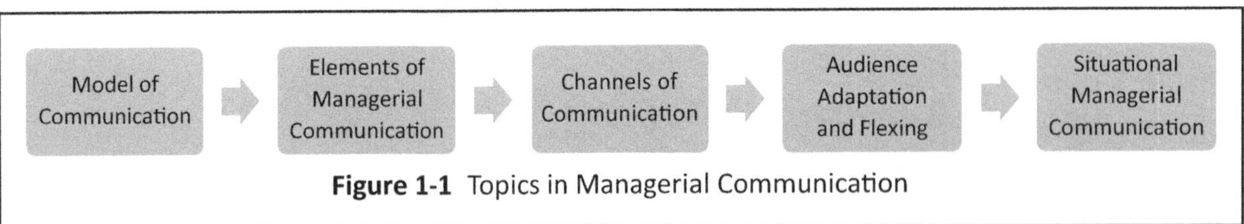

Figure 1-1 Topics in Managerial Communication

COMMUNICATION DEFINED

Managers at all career levels and across all organizational types must practice effective communication to achieve results with and through others.

Communication is the process by which information is imparted or exchanged. This process of creating shared meaning is shaped and affected by a speaker's and listener's culture, values, beliefs, gender, role, generation, profession, education, and other socioemotional factors. Effective managerial communication draws on a complex set of skills that incorporates critical thinking, analysis, and choice of appropriate signs and symbols to address a vast variety of human and organizational challenges.

As a transactional process, communication has managers acting simultaneously as senders and receivers. This process calls on them to evaluate how to best adapt to an audience and adjust a message accordingly to ensure content and purpose are interpreted as intended. This includes selecting the most appropriate channel of communication, whether that be written, face to face, or through mediated formats.

Managers use communication skills both to exhibit and to encourage emotional intelligence, critical thinking, coaching skills, customer focus, transformative change management, motivation, team collaboration, conflict management, relationship management, strategic action, performance management, ethical decision making, diversity, and so on. These are discussed in subsequent chapters.

Key Elements of Managerial Communication

- Effective managers use thoughtful, strategic, and self-aware communication that is audience, result, and emotional response driven.

- Managerial communication requires that one be culturally aware and take cultural norms into consideration when choosing words, phrases, voice, environment, body language, channel, and situation.
- Quality managerial communication involves being a consummate listener who uses questions to gain insights and to help listeners in the process of sharing quality information or acting with purpose.
- Interpersonal communication awareness and skills support a manager's ability to drive results while promoting team member satisfaction and employee retention. These one-on-one interactions show interest in the individual's work, performance successes and challenges, development opportunities, and ongoing well-being.
- Managers offer feedback that helps the team member strive to become an outstanding contributor. They seek and give feedback to influence, conduct performance appraisals, and provide coaching and mentoring.
- As effective communicators, managers are able to promote clear messages that proactively address expectations, goals, and vision.
- Effective managers approach situations with precision and purpose and are able to have critical conversations.
- Credible and trustworthy communication is foundational to getting work done with and through others. This form of communication encourages team buy-in and engagement.
- Creativity, innovation, and action are encouraged and supported when managers use inspiration, motivation, influence, persuasion, and team identity when communicating with their team(s). Inspirational, motivational, influential, and persuasive communication creates a robust environment for team members to act with creativity and innovation.

MODEL OF COMMUNICATION

As the model of communication shows, all communication is governed by culture (Figure 1-2). For managers, culture can manifest as geographic, organizational, and team-specific characteristics and tendencies that reflect beliefs, rules, and identity. Verbal, vocal, and body language communication practices carry and perpetuate these cultural markers. Meaningful cross-cultural communication is an essential part of being an effective manager.

Worldview is how we understand society—whether the society is our neighborhood, city, workplace, or country; it defines how that society should operate. Our worldview is governed by many pervasive and unconscious forces, such as how we conceive of time, interact with generations, use language, and define life and good work. Generally speaking, these and other forces shape the way we think, act,

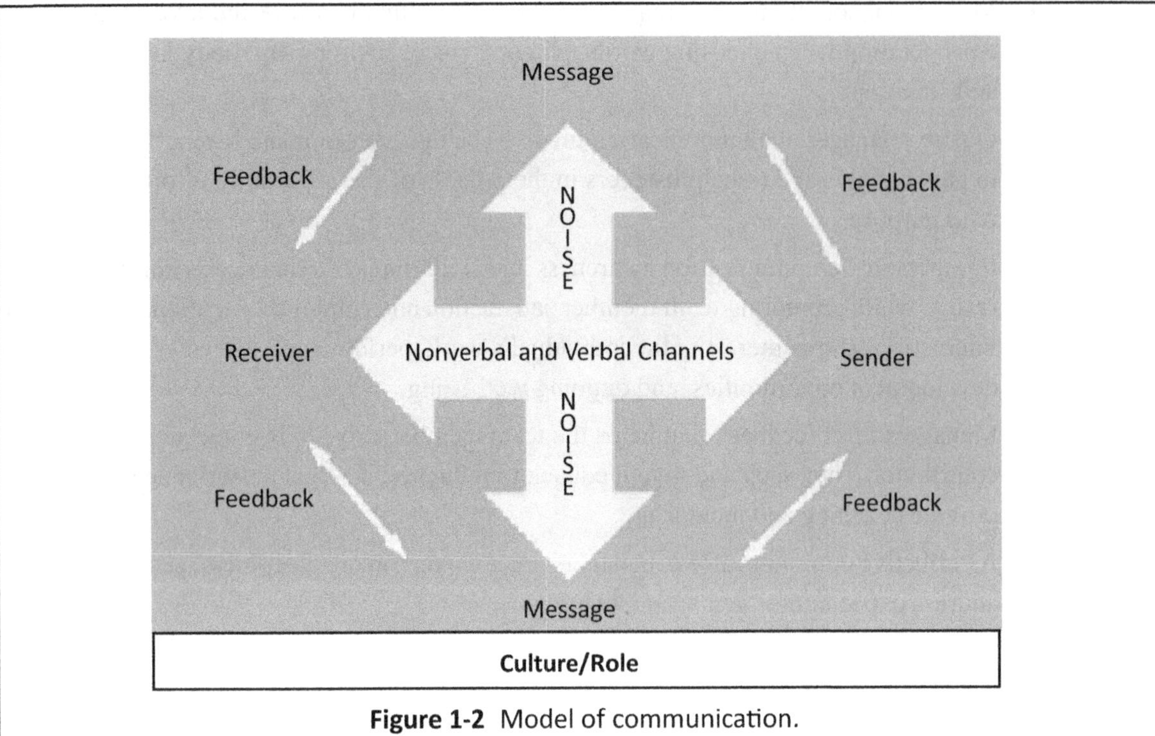

Figure 1-2 Model of communication.

and behave as members of a society. Collectively, these forces compose a checklist for defining ourselves, our behaviors, and what we expect of others.

All communication is also affected by perceptions of power and role. Based on your title and status as a manager, managerial power is evident when you communicate. Part of being a communicator is understanding how to work with others who perceive you as someone with authority. Managing these perceptions is the job of the manager.

Communication is a transactional process in which a speaker is also often a listener. Words, grammar, and structures of written communication are supplemented in oral communication through the use of vocal dynamics and body language. This demands using multisensory listening to decode messages and applying a focused message design to verbal and body language cues. The success of a message exchange then demands the giving and seeking—and receiving—of feedback. Without feedback a manager may incorrectly believe or assume communication has occurred and that the message was clearly understood. By asking questions that clarify messages and paraphrasing answers managers help build shared meaning, which is vital for creating workplace relationships with team members.

As in any open system in which elements affect each other and the environment, the impact of internal and/or external noise can and will break down messages. There is the noise of self-talk, which is the pervasive inner voice we all have that influences how we see the world, others, and ourselves. This noise within the open system of communication not only distracts but can also create faulty perceptions of situations and conversations. Managers must combat internal noise, such as feeling tired, hungry, or emo-

Myth: Your upbringing, education, exposure to a variety of communication styles, and past experiences aren't relevant and won't affect your core communication behaviors.

We are the total of our experiences, culture, society, and so much more. Worldview frames our thinking and communication. Self-knowledge and awareness of these variables will help us in being the type of communicator needed in any given workplace situation.

tionally charged. Room temperature, phones, computer screens, and texts are just a few of the external distractors that erode communication.

Being a conscious communicator is key to effective managerial messaging. This standard of interaction stresses self-awareness, emotional self-management, identification and acceptance of personal and professional responsibilities as a communicator, and skill and willingness to analyze interactions to maintain relationships. As a result, managers build credibility and trust with team members, which is essential for meeting goals and achieving business results.

Pro tip

Trust is an emotion that others give us when we have acted consistently and with credibility in what we do and say.

Trust is the basis of leadership, supervision, and management. It is also the essence of interdependency in teams and is at the core of risk taking. As a pivotal result of effective communication, trust can transcend diverse worldviews, perceptual patterns, position, power, authority, and culture of the organization or environment. Trustworthy communication and shared action are the hard-won prizes that fuel a manager's ability to get work done with and through team members.

THE HISTORY OF MANAGERIAL COMMUNICATION

During the latter part of the nineteenth century the field of communication shifted focus to the new findings of sociology, psychology, and anthropology. This evolution centered on communication as not just an exchange of information but also as a socioemotional event that affected how people perceived their lives, relationships, and work.

By the mid-1950s the study of management communication in the workplace was thriving. Books by Peter Drucker and other thinkers in the field had a profound effect on management thinking and practice. These management scholars studied how newer forms of mediated communication (television, audio and video recording/playback equipment, office telecommunications, primitive computing, in-office copiers, and the like) were changing business and a manager's role as communicator.

Major advancements in transportation and technology during the twentieth century also expanded the necessity for managers to become aware of and sensitive to intercultural and multicultural communication (see Chapter 20, Technology). Team-based initiatives and practices, agile organizations, self-directed teams, and a profusion of communication technologies have brought us to the present, in which how we manage is firmly centered on the uses of quality communication.

MANAGERIAL BEHAVIORS AND COMMUNICATION

A manager uses communication behaviors to effectively influence a wide variety of workplace settings and situations. In each interaction the manager should be honing communication behaviors to create productive working relationships and goal achievement with and among team members. The following sections focus on the key areas in which a manager must communicate with clarity, commitment, and authority.

Team Performance and Communication

As a manager you depend on your ability to work effectively with and through others to plan, organize, execute, and evaluate activities that enable you to achieve organizational goals. The most important resources managers have are the direct reports they oversee; thus one of their central managerial roles is gaining team member commitment by establishing a sense of affiliation with and satisfaction from shared projects and tasks.

The manager is responsible for using all forms of communication in pursuit of high-level results by encouraging reasonable risk taking, team player attitudes, healthy conflict, and empathy. Effective managerial communication and action helps create a team identity, binding the members together as a coherent whole, so they are ready to fill in for each other when needed for team results. In short, the primary managerial function is to drive excellence through communicating and developing shared understanding of and commitment to shared goals and objectives.

Whether a team meets physically or virtually, the manager communicates with the team, bringing it together as a unit and defining roles, responsibilities, working relationships and interactions, normative behaviors, and interdependent performance expectations. Team success critically depends on the steps managers take to ensure shared member-to-member communication. Whether these interactions are to problem solve, manage healthy conflict, achieve productivity, maintain respect, or take shared action, team member communication empowerment and accountability are cornerstones of a high-performing team.

Key Elements of Team Performance and Communication

- Develop a shared understanding of the team's goals using various communication strategies, including face-to-face and virtual interactions, meetings, and exchanges. Virtual teams present special communication challenges, and managers must be competent in using a diverse set of online tools (such as email, texts, social media, meeting software, videoconferencing, document sharing, and other apps) and communication skills (such as listening in sometimes unclear virtual channels, asking questions to establish meaning when there are limited visual and/or vocal communication cues, and using clear and succinct email).

- Use multisensory listening (see, hear, touch, taste, and smell) to collect as much meaningful communication data as possible. For example, consider the statement: "It is too hot for this to work." The meaning here depends on the environment/situation, vocal inflection, what "this" actually is, perhaps some shared tactile sense of "hot," and whether the team is discussing the taste of spicy food or the smell of hot metal. Multisensory listening does not mean that every situation will draw on all of the senses, but the willingness and ability to engage in a multisensory approach will benefit the building of shared meaning. Managers who become skilled in the nuances of communication that multisensory listening offers gain stronger work relationships and performance insights because they have more usable information to work with. Listening in this way takes into consideration all the signs, symbols, and cues offered verbally, vocally, and through body language to create meaning. Managers who model this sophisticated level of listening and encourage team members to do so create a more open team communication environment.
- Provide in-the-moment feedback on work well done or needing improvement. Regular and respectful feedback encourages performance improvement in a low-threat and motivating fashion.
- Develop team-based emotional intelligence that emphasizes empathy. Team members and the team as a whole benefit from working to understand each other. Agreement is not a requirement of empathy, which involves listening, using positive intentions, avoiding assumptions about intentions, and asking questions that lead to insights and the sense of walking in the other person's shoes.
- Use open-ended and targeted questions that guide achievement of tasks and team member empowerment and participation. Making statements and offering directives may sometimes be necessary yet generally achieve only team compliance. Committed team members achieve results, solve problems, and create and innovate when asked to engage. Empowerment of potential in each team member comes from guidance and questions that result in trust, ownership, respect of ideas, and participation.
- Engage team members through frequent individual, small-group, and large-group guided discussions directed toward goal achievement and team unity. Opening up communication lines to allow authentic sharing and rich idea generation is the ideal. Choosing the correct channel and format for these interactions is part of a manager's role.

Strategic Communication

When considering managerial communication, it is easy to get caught up in the day-to-day details of accomplishing work, and thus we can lose sight of the overarching necessity to set and follow a strategic view. This strategic view begins at the organizational level and filters through to each division, depart-

Myth: Humans make assumptions that should be honored when dealing across employee differences.

Humans make assumptions that should be recognized as assumptions and not fact. Unbridled assuming across differences has the potential to lead to perceptions and attitudes that bias our view of certain groups and individuals—stereotyping. Checking our assumptions will limit faulty conclusions about others.

ment, unit, and team in a progressively more granular fashion. No matter where you sit in the organization as a manager it is important to communicate how the work being pursued is directed toward pursuing team and organizational strategy. Through sharing a clear vision and goal that directs and guides others toward achieving results, a manager allows individual team members to coalesce into a high-performing, collaborative team.

In strategic communication, it is necessary to have a conversation about goals that encompass the desired result as well as how to achieve that result. This clear direction becomes the road map that links strategic objectives to work activities.

Managers are the pivot point between larger organizational goals and team action. Knowing how to translate strategy into a work plan calls for choosing language that is attuned to the listener's knowledge and role. In communication of this type, the manager must also help team members maintain motivation, even in stressful circumstances or during business downturns. Effectively planning and running team interactions and meetings that reinforce the strategic message helps the manager implement, reinvent, modify, and complete strategic goals.

Key Elements of Strategic Communication

- Set the direction to accomplish tasks. Bring value and support collaborative integrated organizational activity by delivering clear messages related to team and organizational vision, goals, and expectations. Even brainstorming in its free form is directed by a challenge, idea, or problem.
- Develop clear conversation goals that link strategic objectives to tasks. Knowing how to share the organization's strategy through plans and actions that will make sense to team members comes from having a clear communication goal, including the topic, the purpose for addressing the topic to a specific audience, and the drive toward a defined result.
- Use appropriate language and succinct structure. Industry, sector, and organizational culture will surround the specifics of how to effectively communicate. Guidelines include using respectful language, asking questions, being brief in regard to using another person's time, and having a clear conversation goal.
- Use complimentary body language and voice. Body language and vocal pitch, rate, and volume are the primary carriers of emotional data that help supplement the meaning created by the verbal elements. When determining the meaning of what is said, listeners seek coherence among all the signs and symbols used in the messaging. When they sense incongruity

(for example, words do not match the vocal tone used), listeners can be confused and may misunderstand. Confusion leads to suspicion, and listeners ask, "What does she really mean by that?"

- Employ motivation strategies. Managers need to know employee drivers. This information is generally available through observation and by practicing multisensory listening. Questions that focus on what the team member values and then figuring out what can be offered are part of retaining self-motivated employees.

Pro tip

When asked what motivates them, employees across sectors report being recognized, being well informed, and gaining new opportunities before they mention money.

- Use effective meeting communication. Good meeting management includes setting up meeting goals, providing a specific and action-oriented agenda with a timing plan, knowing how to engage all members and control the flow of sharing, engaging in active listening, and summarizing when needed. Modeling concise, specific, and emotionally well managed communication sets the expectations for all interactions.

Situational Managerial Communication

Managers face diverse situational communication on a daily basis, such as during team meetings, cross-functional conversations, client/customer briefings, updates to senior leaders, performance feedback, corrective feedback, coaching, motivating, directing activity, and conflict resolution. Some of these—like addressing poor performance or conflict resolution—are difficult, unique, and challenging. Whether typical or exceptional, whenever managers are called to communicate, they need to be emotionally well managed, assertive, adaptive, open, and attentive to the receiver of the communication.

An example of a successful situation involving conflict is when a high-performing manager creates and maintains a healthy environment in which team members can have robust exchanges without leading to defensiveness, resistance, demotivation, or poor working relationships. The aim of healthy conflict is collaborative action that arises from shared and open communication and goals that leads to creativity, innovation, and optimism. Trust grows and deepens in a healthy conflict environment.

When corrective performance conversations are necessary (discussed in Chapter 4, Conflict Management), a manager who has developed multisensory listening skills, assertive habits, clear and succinct messaging, and emotional self-management will stay on track. These sound communication practices during a corrective performance conversation will also prove helpful in termination-for-cause conversations, when emotions will run high and self-management is especially important for the manager. With a firm focus on the desired result, solid communication skills, and a respect for the other person, managers can effectively handle challenging situations.

Key Elements of Situational Communication

- Manage emotionally charged communications through the use of strategies and techniques to minimize defensiveness and resistance. By using empathy, multisensory listening, questions, paraphrasing, and so on, the manager shows interest in what the team member has to say and what the team member needs. Clear awareness of needs instead of assuming knowledge of needs is fundamental. Body language and particularly the use of a measured, calm, and low-threat voice complement such interactions.
- Apply assertiveness strategies and skills. Managers must express their needs, wants, and desires in a clear and respectful way that allows team members and others to cooperate. Asserting is not about always getting our way. It is about creating a culture of cooperation in which necessary tasks are done, improvements are made, and listening for content and feelings in communicating is a given.
- Ask insightful questions that promote empathy, understanding, and shared action. Managers succeed with and through the efforts of the team. Communication is the means through which this success is achieved. Words and actions communicate at all times, so managers must be always vigilant and honing their skills.
- Seek and give feedback that sets expectations, coaches for high-level performance, and develops effective working relationships. In-the-moment feedback, while the event is fresh for all, is best. Whether that exchange is face to face or remote, the timeliness and clarity of feedback and expectations make a difference in relational and bottom-line results.
- Use communication style preferences to adapt to the needs of others and achieve team results. Managers need to recognize and flex to the preferences of each team member to optimize communication clarity. Adapting does not need to be an odious task if we see it through the lens of creative differences being the starting place for innovation.
- Apply self-aware emotional intelligence to develop empathy. Managers need to identify their own emotional states and behaviors to begin the journey to understanding how emotions may impact others. Fully understanding another person's experiences and perceptions is impossible; however, by attempting to understand, managers show interest, helpful and appropriate curiosity, and signal interest in collaboration.
- Apply and encourage others to use multisensory listening. Managers in particular can be potent in achieving this type of listening behavior through their own practices. Questions, paraphrasing, listening for vocalics, and paying attention to posture and facial expressions will build clearer communication, empathy, and shared team commitment to achieve results.
- Manage with and through others by communicating a clear vision for change that all members of the team can relate to and support. This calls for listening to content and emotional information and making empowering choices to manifest ownership and responsibility for change. Managers can't avoid change; they need to lead change.

Myth: A manager must check for understanding in every exchange during the manager's day. Each communication is important no matter the priority. Correctness and comprehension should be sound.

No, we cannot and should not check for meaning around every exchange. Meaningful and important exchanges that will have consequence around correct performance of a task, attitudes around team action, and positions on solving issues are just a few of the types of communication that demand shared understanding.

Flexing Communication Styles to Achieve Results

Adapting and flexing communication style occurs when we engage in choosing the verbal, written, e-based and body language elements that will best position us to share meaning and connection with diverse team members, senior management, and customers. This approach is central to a manager's ability to influence and get heard.

When working to create shared meaning with others, a manager must consider individual differences in thinking and learning styles along with culture-based and generational predilections. Carefully consider the channels through which others prefer to receive information—such as email, texts, face-to-face talks, phone calls, conference calls, manuscripts, and memos.

The work of adapting and flexing to others' preferences is necessary to build rapport and a sense of similarity. When rapport exists, the exchange of ideas is facilitated. Openness and effective relations are created via multisensory listening and asking questions in tandem with adapting communication style. From this foundation you can more effectively facilitate change, inspire shared action, motivate others to reach for a shared vision, and influence behavior and thinking.

Key Elements of Flexing Communication Styles

- Tailor verbal communications to meet the needs and expectations of different audiences (for example, when delivering feedback to direct reports versus creating presentations to the C-suite leadership).
- Communicate up, down, and across the organization to achieve results. Managers must determine the responsibilities of team members given their organizational titles, roles, and assigned tasks. Managers must tune into this information and adapt and flex their language and content to fit these role and responsibility drivers. A new process pitch to senior management should be structured and delivered differently from that same topical pitch offered to midlevel managers. If managers want their colleagues to become active listeners, they must speak to their organizational responsibilities.
- Accommodate various communication styles to motivate and lead. For a message to be understood it needs to first be heard—that is, communicated and absorbed. That might mean a manager uses more emotive language and questions with listener X, whereas the manager is more direct and uses lower affect with listener Y. Flexing is adaptive communication and effective managers master this skill.

- Identify and use knowledge and insights into different thinking styles, cultures, and generations to accomplish results. Managers need to be adept at recognizing and adapting to differences created by geographical and demographic differences. They also need to be attuned to issues of race, class, sex, sexual orientation, and other cross-cultural factors.
- Use and encourage others to use multisensory listening techniques. Managers must model these behaviors and show the benefits of such actions for achieving team results.
- Develop and maintain high-level credibility and rapport with others in the organization. Find ways to engage in identification with others, fueling this with appropriate work-related self-disclosure and flexing to communication preferences. All these actions will result in establishing a sense of similarity that minimizes difference and develops credibility.
- Apply motivational language used to build strong team performance and individual team member satisfaction. Such language needs to be grounded in reality and adapted to the person or group being addressed and aligned to organizational values, mission, and strategy. Remember that success for a manager is achieving results while retaining productive team members. For both of those elements of success to occur, a manager needs to keep members engaged.
- Employ cross-cultural awareness and skill to communicate effectively with diverse team members. This form of communication adaptation is a study unto itself and is discussed in Chapter 20, Managing Technology.

Etiquette and Style

Written business communication has gone through many changes given the diverse channels managers now have for sharing messages. Informality may be the character of internal texting, but more formal interaction should always be the starting point with external customers. Consideration of the role, responsibility, communication channel preferences, position, and purpose for the communication will all inform the approach you take to written communication. Form and structure in written managerial interactions must follow the rules of grammar and punctuation, which create and maintain the credibility of the writer and the message. Promotability to the role of manager and beyond requires strong oral and written communication skills.

Managers are best served in all written work when they write in a fashion that is natural, succinct, and clear. Reports, emails, memos, legal briefs, and so on demand precision and a focus on

Myth: Because I said it, they understood it. The inability of others to receive and understand the intended meaning of my message is their processing issue.

Whether they should understand your intended meaning or not, your role and responsibility as manager calls for making communication clear and understood. That may mean repeating, adapting, flexing, and seeking feedback to achieve the necessary shared meaning.

correctness that can and will be meaningful across time, readers, leaders, and organizations. What managers write becomes record and documentation, directing team action toward goals, performance standards, personnel recommendations, and strategic plans. Care and attention to the structural demands of various types of writing (such as a business case, meeting notes, and performance appraisal) must be grasped and applied by any manager. Many organizations have established guidelines for such interactions.

Key Elements of Etiquette and Style

Managers need to observe the following fundamental considerations when they strive to achieve the proper formality, tone, and style in their written communication.

- Deliver clear and concise written communications in the form and manner best suited to the type of message and intended audience. Not unlike oral communication, written business interactions must be succinct. Simple sentences that adhere to written messaging conventions are expected.
- Apply motivational form and style to gain support of team initiatives. Whether co-located or in different sites, team members need managers to provide written comments, evaluations, feedback, and so on using the tools of motivation. Some of these tools are being sensitive to the team member's motivational drivers, using rapport and empathy, and showing how individual team members benefit from meeting expectations and accepting stretch goals.
- Gain credibility and visibility for self and team through clear message development. Managers may see their careers slowed or stalled due to poor written communication. Business writing is succinct, diplomatic, and sensitive to how the reader will interpret what is written and does not include emoticons or style embellishments, such as too many exclamation points.
- Guide strategic planning with accurate and well positioned ideas and data. Trust comes from offering information that is correct, fair, insightful, knowledgeable, and focused on bringing value by meeting strategic goals. Managers must offer clear value and strategic ideas to be seen as indispensable.
- Apply appropriate structures for the intended result and specific audiences (such as business cases, pitches, idea transfers, brainstorming). Credible managers stick to the topic and are aware that communication is often shared within the organization. They select the proper channel (printed memo, email, or text) and form (business case, pitch, status report, or proposal) for written exchanges. Their written messages have a clear central idea that covers topic, purpose, and intended result.
- Achieve goals by aligning communication behaviors to audience position and decision-making prerogatives.

Communicating Up, Down, and Across the Organization

The role of manager is pivotal to organizational communication, achievement of goals, profitability, and overall productivity. As the pivot point for so much activity, a manager must routinely use communication to inform, influence, direct, guide, and propose new ideas—up, down, and across the organization. With so much information and responsibility for results flowing through the managerial pivot point, managers are expected to be adept at clear, open, and collaborative communication.

Assessing and adapting any message to the role and responsibility of the listener(s) enhances meaning and motivation to attend to the communication. Managers must recognize the demands of every role in the organization and use those insights in tandem with assessment of other communication preferences to get their ideas heard. In meetings, keying-in on decision makers and thought/action leaders, while also satisfying the needs of all attendees, brings shared collaborative organizational action. Questions that generate insights are a vital tool for honing and refining a message that will speak to others' diverse needs. Whether motivating for shared action, seeking support to implement a business case, pitching a new idea, or offering a project update, managers ultimately find success by showing the listeners how the message is important to their role and responsibility.

Key Elements of Communicating Up, Down, and Across the Organization

A manager's day is filled with interactions with senior management, colleagues, customers, and team members. Often these interactions can be around the same topic, issue, or process. That means a manager must adapt communication to meet the needs of each listener. This up, down and across dynamic is best addressed by using the following points.

- Facilitate open conversations between and among supervisors, peers, and direct reports. Managers achieve results by encouraging team members to talk to each other about how to synergize and innovate rather than just bringing the ideas to them. In fact, value gets lost on a regular basis because managers are overwhelmed. Ideally they should not be at the hub of communication but rather they should be part of the rich and diverse network that dynamic and effective team-based communication can create. If a manager has a highly qualified team member ready to address a team process, she should put that person in front of senior management. If peers need to sort out issues, a manager who practices healthy conflict and collaboration can open up low-threat communication.
- Implement collaborative action to create benefits for the team and the whole organization. Collaboration is time consuming; depends on an attitude of positive intentions; demands multisensory listening; values relationship development; and calls for a willingness to achieve shared recognition, tactfulness, and a focus on business results. Collaboration builds ownership in the end product. Managers may believe that asking team members what they think is enough to achieve collaboration, but collaborative communication

Pro tip

When two people in apparent conflict paraphrase what they believe to be the other person's position and then refine those paraphrases until they both agree they understand each other, researchers find close to 50 percent of perceived conflict isn't real conflict.

involves asking good questions, listening attentively, having an ability to influence and be influenced, showing empathy, providing vision, and having concern for individual and team results.

- Effective meeting communication is essential for managing time and people resources efficiently. Managers must set meeting goals, detail a specific and action-oriented agenda with a timing plan, assign accountability to attendees, engage all attendees, control the flow of sharing, apply multisensory listening, keep the team on track, and summarize when needed. Managers generally benefit with better attendance and attention when they have fewer meetings and when the meetings they do have are well managed and productive. Banning distracting communications and focusing attention may be useful. Cutting meeting time in half will motivate attendees. As always, using concise, specific, and emotionally well managed communication sets the expectations for all interactions.
- Flex personal communication style to better align with specific team members. Communication is the complex process of creating shared meaning with others. By accepting broad diversity in communication preferences and by flexing verbal, vocal, and body language appropriately, managers show they are clearly seeking bridges to connect with diverse co-workers.
- Seek and give feedback that sets expectations, coaches for high-level performance, and develops effective working relationships. Managers are often compared to teachers. Both managers and teachers help people develop, learn, and achieve to their highest level. They achieve this by setting high expectations and offering feedback on how to perform in a better way; by paying attention to the unique ways those they address think, learn, communicate, express emotion, and so on; by contextualizing their interactions within a specific environment; and by seeking reflections on how they are doing, what they are doing that is effective, and where they need to step up their efforts.
- Apply active multisensory listening to better understand another person's drivers, communication preferences, and working style. Important information is freely available to managers who use multisensory listening to pay attention to team members. Managers who pay attention to a team member only when seeking something or directing work will miss large amounts of personal team member data that come up during simple exchanges. If a manager listens all the time to all the information that is available, he will find there is plenty of information about the needs and preferences of that team member. When working with remote team members, managers may need to be more proactive in creating time and space for this type of sharing.
- Ask insightful questions that promote empathy, understanding, and shared action. For managers, asking good questions is the very best way to get smart about people, processes, and innovations. Closed, open, probing, and hypothetical questions—when used appropriately and precisely—can streamline communication while building empowerment and shared vision.

Myth: We are who we are based on inborn traits. Socialization and learned behaviors can only marginally impact our effectiveness as a communicator.

No two brains have the exact same wiring and chemistry. Yet, the vast majority of how we use language and communication are learned behaviors. Neuroplasticity allows for learning throughout the lifespan, so improving communication behaviors is both possible and necessary.

- Apply motivational language and behaviors to encourage peak performance from individual team members for the benefit of the entire team. These messages need to be anchored in reality and adapted to the team member being addressed. Motivating, setting high expectations, coaching performance, and retaining team members are how a manager achieves results with and through their team members.

SCENARIOS FOR THE COMMUNICATION COMPETENCY

The following scenarios present two common types of communication challenges managers face.

Scenario 1

Jamal has been a manager at the Acme Company for three years. During a recent downsizing, two other managers were let go. Their teams were reassigned to Jamal. Though the new team members know and like each other, they struggle with articulating what they need from each other. Jamal really liked his original team and got them to work together in a highly collaborative way. With the new team members, however, he finds himself struggling to show empathy, listen to suggestions, and inspire shared action.

The possible managerial communication approaches Jamal can take include:

- Consider worldview
- Run a perception check
- Apply emotional intelligence
- Clarify using questions
- Communicate a shared vision
- Seek and give feedback

- Use team building communication
- Express clear goals and expectations
- Apply multisensory listening

Scenario 2

Kendra is a senior manager at the Electro Engineering Arm of the Department of Defense. As a government employee, Kendra has always needed to work with the civil service classifications and structures, and she has excelled in operating in this environment. Kendra now finds that her millennial employees want to have more involvement, influence, innovation, and impact than their titles allow for. She isn't sure how to respond in ways that will be effective, given the realities of her organization's culture and structure.

The possible managerial communication approaches Kendra can take include:

- Consider worldview
- Run a perception check
- Apply generational awareness
- Use emotional intelligence
- Seek feedback
- Use information building questions
- Apply multisensory listening
- Practice empathy

PROFICIENCY INDICATORS

How will you know if you are making progress in developing effective managerial communication? Table 1-1 provides a set of performance indicators that reflect managerial communication competence.

Table 1-1 Effective Managerial Communication Activity	
Communication The complex and culturally bound process by which information is imparted or exchanged with the goal of creating shared meaning	Effective managerial communication benefits the team and the organization. Managers do this when they: • Give clear directions and expectations toward the achievement of the team's and organization's goals and objectives. • Maintain effective relationships and team player attitudes that support motivation and innovation. • Use open and transparent communication to retain the brightest and best colleagues and team members, thus saving resources and organizational intelligence and know-how. • Deliver specific and objective feedback on team member performance and potential to enhance results and accomplish tasks. • Apply communication style adaptability to bring capacity to work with diverse employees, team members, senior management, and external customer groups. • Address difficult communication situations with empathy to resolve disruption to team performance. • Apply effective multisensory listening and emotional self-management to build trust, credibility, and shared accountability in achieving healthy conflict.

PERFORMANCE INDICATORS

It can be challenging for managers to know when they are achieving effective managerial communication performance. Insights can sometimes come from recognizing the behaviors that are ineffective and then knowing what can be done instead to achieve effective communication. Table 1-2 offers necessary points of assessment and effective behavioral choices.

Table 1-2 Characteristics of Effective and Poor Managerial Communication	
Effective Performance	**Poor Performance**
• Credible	• Dismissive
• Trustworthy	• Unavailable
• Multisensory listener	• Aggressive
• Skilled questioner	• Egotistical
• Appropriate and adaptive verbal and nonverbal communicator	• Inconsistent
• Empathetic	• Unclear
• Emotionally managed	• Disinterested
• Open, accessible, and approachable	• Incomplete sentences
• Motivating	• Flip-flopping on stated positions
• Inclusive	• Defensive

PERSISTENCE AND PRACTICE FOR EFFECTIVENESS

An unsuccessful attempt at better communication is not the end of the manager's work. When there has been a breakdown between two people the bridge building to reestablish a productive work relationship can take a good amount of effort and time. Persist with best practices, knowing you are on the right track. Though remember that managers can't make someone else cooperate, collaborate, or come to a mutual path forward.

They can, however, recognize their role and responsibility to achieve results with and through others. If managers stop their managerial work at just "achieve results," they will miss that the instruments for achieving such results are their team members. When managerial communication is executed with a task–relationship orientation in which the value and importance of each team member is recognized and respected, work progresses more efficiently, members are more satisfied, and commitment toward the achievement of goals meets or exceeds expectations. Managers can use authority to gain compliance from team members with average and often short-lived success. These points are a preface to the recognition that managers who consistently use effective communication realize time savings because team members are clear on the goal, plan, role, and value to the overall team results. When something in the plan doesn't work, they collaborate and fix it; when time pressures build, they help each other. Managers offer encouragement, motivation, recognition, and regular performance feedback—all directed toward continuous improvement. Listening is at the center of this shared process and shows respect for everyone's thoughts, concerns, and needs.

The expression of all these elements of communication can be presented directly or indirectly. For example, let's say a manager has come to an agreement with a team member that he will submit a client analysis report by 3:00 p.m. that day. Early that morning the manager might say directly and assertively, "Good morning, Frank. Quick reminder that the client report is due to me at three today." Or the manager might choose to go assertively indirect and say, "Good morning Frank. Are you on track to deliver the client report to me at three today?" The two messages are getting at the same point—the report is due and expected at 3:00 today—yet they might be heard differently. As manager you must always be thinking about the results you seek while executing your communication so that it makes sense and creates intended results with the other person.

Emotional Intelligence

LEARNING OBJECTIVES

By the end of this chapter, you will be better equipped to:

- Demonstrate a high level of Emotional Intelligence.
- Manage your own emotions and handle emotionally charged situations effectively and with empathy.
- Communicate with impact and promote clear messages of expectations, goals, and vision.
- Approach situations with emotional insights and purpose in order to conduct critical conversations.
- Adapt your message through planning, developing, and delivering clear and impactful presentations.
- Demonstrate confidence and create an engaging environment for the audience.
- Manage relationships with other stakeholders.
- Create a motivational climate through delegation and collaboration.
- Influence others to support an idea, agenda, or direction by understanding the listener's perspective and needs.
- Build trust and credibility to successfully negotiate for desired outcomes.
- Foster a culture of teamwork and accountability.
- Approach conflict in a direct and purposeful manner.
- Monitor employee performance through ongoing feedback, coaching, and goal setting.
- Lead your team through change.

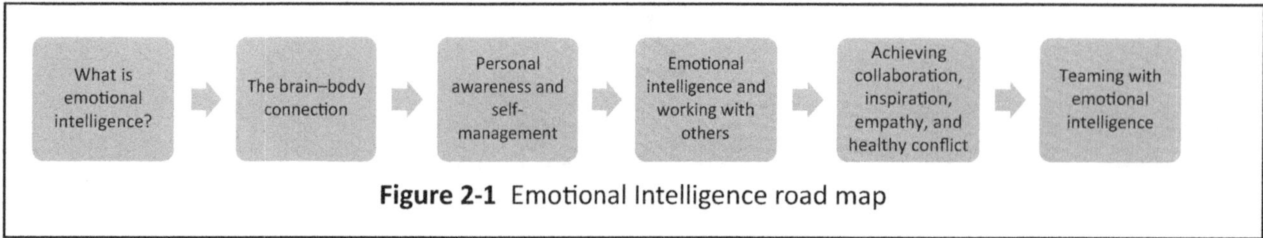

Figure 2-1 Emotional Intelligence road map

As noted in the list of outcomes, to perform their job functions effectively, managers need to know how to develop awareness of their thoughts and emotions, use self-awareness to guide their actions, hone their ability to assess others' emotional states, develop the ability to effectively use emotional expression, use emotionally intelligent strategies to manage situations, develop strategies to handle emotional triggers, and identify emotional language and behaviors.

This chapter addresses the key topics shown in Figure 2-1. By actively engaging in each of these topics a manager will have a well-grounded understanding of Emotional Intelligence in the workplace.

Pro tip

Feeling emotionally triggered? Try doing some math in your head, try reciting some poetry, start singing your favorite love song. These distractions will allow your brain to detach somewhat from the strong emotion and recover. Follow with some helpful self-talk!

IMPORTANCE OF EMOTIONAL INTELLIGENCE

Emotional Intelligence (EI) is the ability to identify and manage your own emotions and to observe and influence others' emotional states.

Emotions tell us important things about ourselves, others, and situations. Words, actions, and behaviors elicit emotional responses, such as satisfaction and dissatisfaction. Our emotions have physiological counterparts that help and sometimes hinder our emotional management and well-being. Emotional responses are communicated to others by what we say, but far more often, through our body language and vocal behaviors. Taken all together, emotions impact how we feel, respond, relate with others, and lead using EI (also known as *emotional quotient*, or EQ).

Strong, effective relationships are the currency of the fast-paced, team-based, and global working environments, and EI is the cornerstone of those impactful relationships. Managers must develop and exhibit EI competencies, such as personal awareness and impact, collaboration, and healthy conflict in order to achieve personal, team, and organizational success. With this set of behaviors and competencies, a manager possesses an engaged and consistent identity, appropriate for a high-performing organizational member.

EI is at the core of achieving personal awareness, connecting with others, managing stress, engaging in healthy conflict and collaboration, and exhibiting resilience and optimism.

Key Concepts of Emotional Intelligence

Managers who possess a high level of EI are able to manage their own emotions, create emotionally intelligent team environments, assist others with emotional self-management, and plan work activities with attention to team mood and disposition.

Identifying emotions is the first step toward managing your own emotions. It allows a manager to build self-awareness and be ready to objectively observe others' emotional information. Self-awareness takes skill, knowledge, and willingness to honestly self-examine your emotional makeup and behavior. This competency demands that, when observing others, managers avoid assuming and instead use listening and confirming interactions. As an example, when the team has encountered a performance failure, you and individual team members may feel frustration, disappointment, and confusion. Managers who gain emotional information derived from listening, observation, feedback, and questioning are better prepared to create empathy with and among team members.

What barriers do most managers face in developing emotional self-management? A primary challenge area involves emotional triggers, which are events that provoke strong knee-jerk reactions for individuals. For example, when a team member says "Whatever" in response to changing a way of doing a task, strong frustration can be triggered in the manager, who hears that word as dismissive or disrespectful. Or, for another example, when a manager is running a meeting and team members exchange smirks, the manager might feel challenged and angry or even fearful. Managers who are aware of their own emotional triggers can handle emotionally charged situations with empathy. Such insight is built on personal awareness and supported by regulating emotions, engaging in preemptive mindful activity, developing a capacity for optimism, and having systems for achieving resilience and healthy conflict.

Myth: Empathy is something like sympathy, right?

Yes and no. Yes, in that empathy and sympathy are both complex emotional states that are related to what we know and how we feel about someone else's circumstances. No, in that empathy can be experienced with all our workplace relationships at all times and sympathy is reserved for when someone has a significant personal loss. We can empathize with someone feeling loss and we can express sympathy, but the two emotional states are not one in the same.

Developing Your Emotional Intelligence: Cornerstones and Competencies

Conclusions from research in Emotional Intelligence can be summed up in the approach illustrated in Figure 2-2. The cornerstones of Emotional Intelligence are represented by the inner circle of the figure.

- *Aware*: Ability to understand your own emotions.
- *Connect*: Ability to perceive and understand the emotions of the people around you.
- *Manage*: Ability to monitor and assess your own emotions and adjust.
- *Achieve*: Ability to direct your emotions in a productive manner.

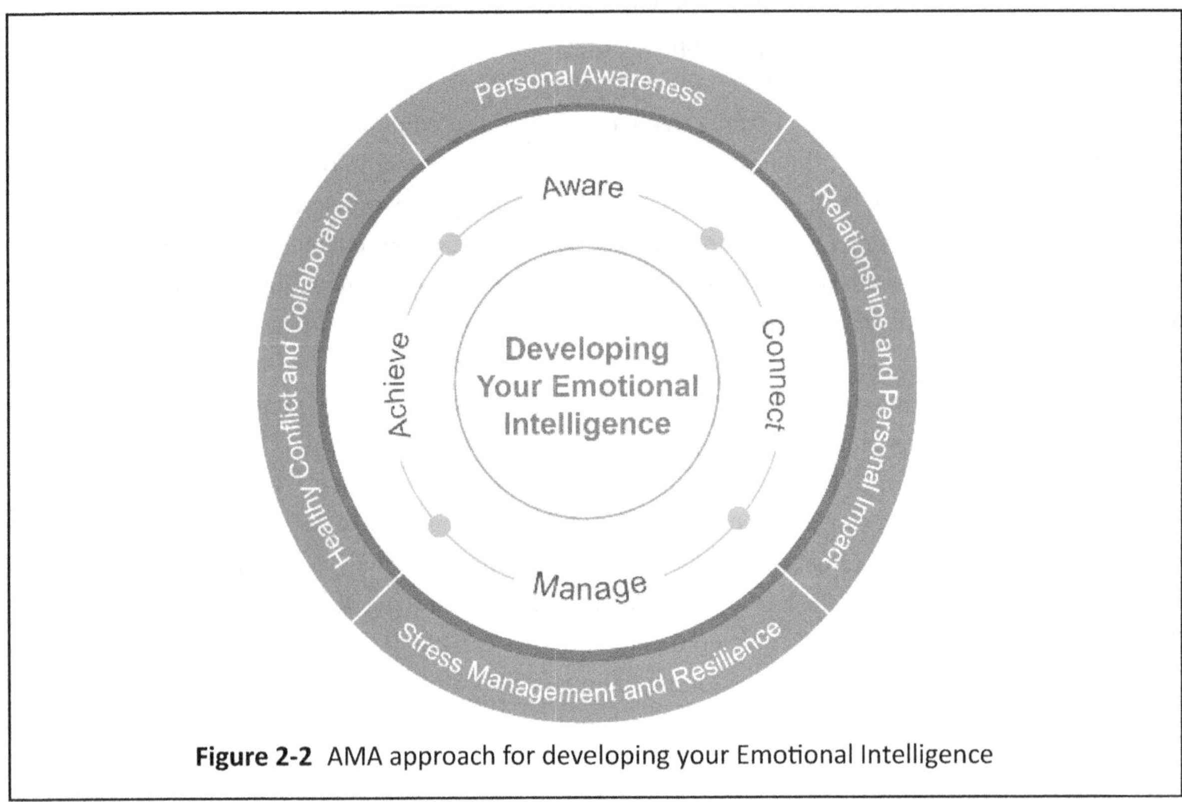

Figure 2-2 AMA approach for developing your Emotional Intelligence

Additional foundational skills include:

- *Personal Influence*: Building your personal credibility with others. Applying empathy as a powerful influencing strategy when coaching. Analyzing resistance through the lens of EI to identify alternative influencing approaches.
- *Inspiration*: Categorizing present strengths and liabilities to inspire colleagues. Applying skills to inspire others by using emotionally intelligent leadership stories.
- *Collaboration*: Identifying different types of leaders and colleagues to strengthen emotionally intelligent relationships and creativity.
- *Healthy Conflict*: Recognizing the central role of relationship development and maintenance in achieving healthy conflict. Identifying emotionally intelligent leadership communication strategies to create and maintain healthy conflict.

- *Team Leadership*: Assessing team performance, stress levels, and mood to remain optimistic and productive. Applying EI communication when a team or team member encounters failure. Building a culture of healthy conflict practices.

The outer circle of Figure 2-2 is focused on the four EI competencies that help managers improve workplace relationships and create the dynamic and creative working environments shown in Table 2-1.

Developing Managerial Emotional Intelligence: Cornerstones and Competencies

The cornerstones for developing managerial Emotional Intelligence are the same as those for personal Emotional Intelligence and are shown in Figure 2-3.

The outer circle of Figure 2-3 focuses on the six managerial and leadership Emotional Intelligence competencies. These competencies are defined in Table 2-2 and taken as a whole can drive results, increase satisfaction, and create dynamic and responsive organizational cultures.

HISTORICAL CONTEXT FOR THE DEVELOPMENT OF MANAGERIAL EMOTIONAL INTELLIGENCE

Emotional Intelligence can mistakenly be seen as a new science. Yet, the history of EI begins as far back as the ancient Greeks when the connections between emotion and cognition were discussed. Plato noted, "All learning has an emotional base."

In the twentieth century, the emergence of psychology, brain and behavior studies, and advances in data analysis from intellectual testing such as IQ prepared the way for a new interest in emotional information and work. In the 1930s, Edward Thorndike described the concept of *social intelligence* as the ability to get along with other people.

During the 1940s David Wechsler suggested that affective components of intelligence may be essential to success in life. Beginning in the 1950s humanistic psychologists such as Abraham Maslow focused on how people could build emotional strength. Education and parenting became further involved in teaching emotional awareness as a result of Howard Gardner's *The Shattered Mind*, and the concept of multiple intelligences, which include both interpersonal and emotional elements, was introduced.

Later, in the 1980s and into the 1990s, psychologists Peter Salovey and John Mayer published their brain-based studies of emotion in the journal *Imagination, Cognition, and Personality* under the title "Emotional Intelligence."

Building on all of this work, Daniel Goleman began researching EI in the workplace, and through multiple publications he has established EI as a fundamental twenty-first-century managerial skill that can be learned through pursuit of emotionally intelligent competencies and skill sets. Today, managers are expected to consistently practice emotionally intelligent behavior.

Table 2-1 Developing Emotional Intelligence Competencies	
Personal awareness	• Identifying your own emotions and behavioral responses • Categorizing present strengths and liabilities • Achieving emotional regulation
Relationships and personal impact	• Building your personal credibility with others • Applying empathy as a powerful relationship strategy • Identifying communication skills to build productive relationships • Identifying different types of inquiry that strengthen relationships • Analyzing resistance through the lens of Emotional Intelligence
Stress management and resilience	• Describing how emotions impact physiological responses and moods • Assessing stress levels and mood to remain optimistic and productive • Developing resilience and learning from failures
Healthy conflict and collaboration	• Recognizing the central role of relationship development and maintenance in achieving healthy conflict • Identifying emotionally intelligent communication strategies to create and maintain healthy conflict • Building a variety of healthy conflict practices • Describing collaboration as an emotionally intelligent relationship-based activity

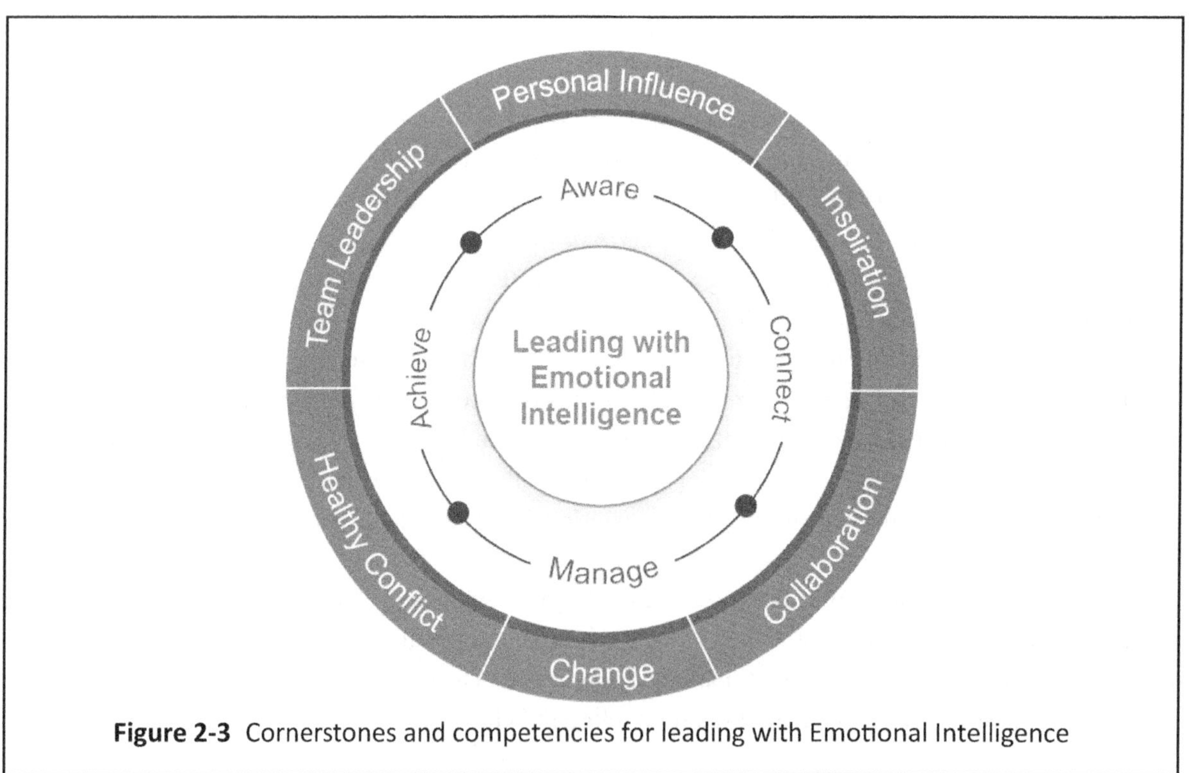

Figure 2-3 Cornerstones and competencies for leading with Emotional Intelligence

Table 2-2 Managing and Leading with Emotional Intelligence Competencies	
Personal influence	• Building your personal credibility with others • Applying empathy as a powerful influencing strategy when coaching • Analyzing resistance through the lens of EI to identify alternative influencing approaches
Inspiration	• Categorizing present strengths and liabilities to inspire colleagues • Applying skills to inspire using emotionally intelligent leadership stories
Collaboration	• Describing collaboration as an activity rooted in emotionally intelligent relationships • Identifying different types of leaders and colleagues to strengthen relationships and creativity
Change	• Describing how emotions impact attitudes toward change • Identifying communication skills that leaders can use to move past colleagues' resistance to change
Healthy conflict	• Recognizing the central role of relationship development and maintenance in achieving healthy conflict • Identifying emotionally intelligent leadership communication strategies to create and maintain healthy conflict
Team leadership	• Assessing team performance • Assessing team stress levels and mood to remain optimistic and productive • Applying emotionally intelligent communication when a team or team member encounters failure • Building a culture of healthy conflict practices

Myth: We all identify and respond to emotions in the same ways.

The majority of humans uniquely sense emotions due to differing brain-based structures, associations, experiences, models, and levels of awareness. The ability to observe emotional indicators differs from person to person. But don't let a perception of limited personal emotional self-awareness deter efforts from implementing emotionally intelligent managerial practices. A motivated manager can develop and learn to use emotionally intelligent approaches, such as positive intentions, empathy, and multisensory listening. This means employing a willingness to ask questions, seek and offer feedback, and practice open communication to strengthen interactions and working relationships.

MANAGERIAL BEHAVIORS ASSOCIATED WITH EMOTIONAL INTELLIGENCE

Presently none of us can read another person's mind. This reality leads to a recognition that how we understand much of our communication, and especially emotional information, comes through observable behaviors. EI managers are aware of how their behaviors communicate emotional information as well as how their team members' behaviors carry important emotional information.

Myth: There really isn't empirical proof that Emotional Intelligence works.

A number of qualitative and some quantitative studies have looked at relational benefits, team-based productivity, and results based on the application of managerial Emotional Intelligence. A consistent picture evolves from these studies to support managers' use of Emotional Intelligence to work effectively with and through others to achieve goals. Of special note are studies that have quantified the benefits of leading with Emotional Intelligence, including higher levels of employee retention, satisfaction, commitment, collaboration, team player attitude, optimal performance, and ongoing performance enhancements through professional development and growth.

Personal Awareness and Self-Management

Managers who are able to control their own emotions both model and promote this ability to their team members. Without personal awareness, it is more difficult to achieve empathy, collaboration, and healthy conflict because there is no means of relating your own emotional experiences and reactions to those of others.

Primary Managerial Function

Starting with a recognition of emotions, managers must be ready and able to identify the links among emotions, physiological changes, internalized subvocalizations or self-talk, and observable behaviors.

A robust emotions vocabulary helps with managing brain-based responses to emotions and encourages the sharing of feelings when such information is needed to create shared understandings. Various areas of the brain receive, process, and route data that inform cognitive and emotional functioning and behaviors. This mind–body connection creates a range of emotions, such as motivation, inspiration, satisfaction, defensiveness, and anger. These strong brain-based emotions can result in an emotional takeover, challenging a manager's ability to self-manage behaviors. Managers possessing Emotional Intelligence use mindfulness and self-awareness to proactively regulate their day-to-day interactions and better regulate their responses.

Managers must listen to their own self-talk and note how it either calms and neutralizes emotions or exasperates the helpful emotions they need in order to be monitored and controlled. Part of being a manager is knowing how to regulate behaviors and responses, even when faced with triggering language or actions. Emotional self-management and stress reduction includes understanding the physiological impact of all forms of emotional information.

As both a first and last step in personal awareness, the use of positive intentions and empathy help a manager keep a centered professional demeanor.

Pro tip

When you need to self-manage stress try taking one minute to do one thing: focusing on your breath. This mindfulness activity calls on you to push any distractions out of your brain and just fix your attention to the normal in and out of breathing. This activity refreshes the attention and offers the opportunity for an emotional reset.

Key Concepts of Personal Awareness and Self-Management

An emotionally intelligent manager and leader must develop a fundamental awareness of and ability to identify and name emotions and moods. Empathy for others is built through the recognition of the vast array of emotional states. Personal awareness is essential to foreground access to optimism and resilience. Self-awareness means recognizing and monitoring the persistent subvocalized talk inside our heads which reinforces and sustains the brain-based links between emotion and behavior. Self-talk can regulate and accelerate emotional states. In partnership with self-talk is the need to recognize and adapt our physiological responses to emotions. These responses are generated by the brain as chemical and behavioral responses to perceptions of threat, pleasure, calm, and so on.

Myth: Emotional Intelligence cannot really change the way someone thinks and behaves.

There are many aspects of managerial Emotional Intelligence that are intended to create a productive work environment in which employees become aware of their behaviors and, if necessary, modify or manage those behaviors. Most managers are not trained to analyze or assess employees' inner dynamics and should not attempt to do so. They are in a powerful place to share observations of helpful or unhelpful behaviors with team members, with the objectives of goal attainment, performance expectations, growth, collaboration, team player attitudes, and effective interpersonal communication. Because performance feedback or reflection on interactions has the potential to influence another person's behaviors, managerial Emotional Intelligence can change how others think and behave. That possible change is an individual choice, however, and managers cannot make it happen.

When practicing emotionally intelligent communication, start with positive intentions that give others the benefit of the doubt when facing challenging circumstances or actions. This mindset creates a low-threat environment that is more likely to lead to open and empathetic interactions.

It is important to choose words and phrasing that reflect self-management and professionalism and that are attuned to managerial relationships with colleagues, team members, customers, and senior leaders. For example, when a manager receives criticism that feels like a personal attack, he or she should avoid becoming defensive; instead the manager should speak assertively, saying "Thank you for that feedback, and I will consider it" or "That may be true, please offer me some specifics."

Other emotionally intelligent considerations for managers involve choosing the time and place when productive emotionally intelligent exchanges can be conducted. When speaking, be sure your voice elements

Pro tip
Emotional Intelligence and assertiveness are highly complementary. When you express your needs in a respectful way to others, you are also respecting yourself. This sense of value and worth go a long way to sustain solid self-esteem and well-being.

and tone complement your intentions and emotional level. In this regard, voice control becomes a vital skill for virtual managers as well as managers using any audio-based communications, such as conference calling, online meetings, and phone calls. Last, body language that aligns with and strengthens the vocal and verbal elements of the message helps maintain clarity of both content and emotion. When body language does not lineup with other cues, the consequences can be confusion, faulty assumptions, and potential distrust.

Emotional Intelligence and Working with Others

Beyond developing awareness of their own thoughts and emotions, managers must be ready to adapt to gain effectiveness with team members and with others across a variety of situations.

By observing and assessing the emotional data others share through verbal and nonverbal behavior, the manager gains some objectivity and can confirm or reevaluate what appears to be happening. In critical and difficult conversations, these observations and clarifications will keep the exchange healthy and will avoid the confusion associated with assuming.

Beyond handling challenging interactions, managers need to keep the team resilient and optimistic. At times this may mean emotional encouragement, helping the team feel hopeful, successful, interdependent, collaborative, motivated, and inspired. Creating a sense of membership, value, and empowerment is all part of the emotionally intelligent work of a manager.

Key Concepts of Emotional Intelligence and Working with Others

Everything we have covered thus far leads to several key concepts for a manager's use of Emotional Intelligence.

- Apply active multisensory listening at all times to pick up both the content and emotional data present in human interactions. Using all our senses to build understandings opens recognition of nonverbal emotional data that are carried through vocal and body language cues. For a fuller view of these aspects of Emotional Intelligence, see Chapter 21, Diversity and Inclusion, and Chapter 18, Organizational Culture.
- Achieve open communication that assists in honest and trusting exchanges. By illustrating true attention to the other, paraphrasing, and asking questions, managers build empathy and collaboration while minimizing defensiveness.
- Act as a model of an emotionally well-managed professional who encourages and supports EI in all team member relationships and interactions. Showing empathy that will encourage credibility, honesty, and respect not only enhances the relationship between manager and team member but creates an opportunity to learn more about each other and establish rapport.

- Use objectivity to plan and assess responses to situations and interactions to determine the appropriate emotional expression.
- Use positive intentions that assume the purposes of others are not meant to be difficult or problematic, but rather, positional. This is especially true when others do not express their ideas and intentions in an emotionally well-managed fashion. When managers acknowledge other people's positive intentions, it is easier for them to remain objective when assessing and reflecting on observed behaviors. Although this is challenging, it can help reframe the interaction and shared information, leading to more productive discussions instead of defensiveness.
- Read nonverbal behavior for emotional signs and symbols that add clarity and relational data to the interaction. Body language and voice are substantial carriers of emotive data in cultures in which emotional vocabulary is seldom used in business.

Achieving Empathy, Collaboration, and Healthy Conflict

A nondefensive exchange and an environment of trust, respect, and collaboration start with mutual positive intention for both parties. As a result, the manager, team member, and team have a safe group environment in which to operate, so that risk-taking, innovation, and creativity can occur. Several ingredients are needed to create a setting in which empathy leads the way to collaboration that uses healthy conflict.

Managerial empathy is the feeling that you understand another person's experiences and emotions: the ability to share someone else's feelings. For example, opportunities for workplace empathy occur when a colleague's project falls apart and thus appears uninspired or when a team member expresses satisfaction after being recognized for going above and beyond expectations. It both cases, the manager works to recognize and respond to the team members' emotions to achieve empathy.

To build collaboration, managers need to know what is going on; how people are feeling about assignments, processes, and goals; and what the team needs to move ahead with shared action. Managers need relational, tactical, emotional, and situational information to be able to collaborate. This means seeking and receiving feedback from colleagues, team members, customers, and others to improve practices and performance. Leading with self-awareness and assuredness results in trusting relationships among team members and between the manager and the team.

The competencies associated with Emotional Intelligence can be leveraged to obtain healthy conflict and an empowered and optimistic view of how teams and organizations can encourage creativity, diverse approaches, collaboration, and productivity.

Pro tip

When you need your team members to be creative, help them achieve this by having them use a no boundaries "what if . . ." approach. This resilience technique allows for brainstorming, nonjudgmental exchanges, and a focus on solutions instead of on the problem.

Key Concepts of Achieving Empathy, Collaboration, and Healthy Conflict

- Apply proactive and respectful language when interacting. Proactive language centers on action and begins with positive positioning: "You are doing this part of the project just as we discussed; let's look at what can be improved" versus "You aren't doing this the right way, I'll show you again what I want." Respectful language avoids any sense of name calling, stereotyping, belittling, overgeneralizing, or threatening. The goal is to reduce and deescalate defensiveness and maximize and optimize openness.
- Keep conflict productive by avoiding power plays, bullying, or personal attacks. A manager's authority is a given, and when it is unduly flaunted to exhibit power it can work in the short term but fail in building relationships or retention of strong employees. Similarly, sometimes managers fall into the trap of needing to be overly direct when providing honest feedback. At that point the team member may perceive a threat, and this will likely trigger emotions of aggression, fear, anxiety, or failure.
- Employ multisensory active listening, which is central for managers to better interpret the needs of others and to respond with empathy and professionalism. Managers minimize their abilities to motivate, inspire, support, or empathize with team members if they aren't perceiving and processing what the team member indicates as challenging, threatening, or satisfying. As a model of desirable emotionally intelligent behaviors, a manager demonstrates how to pay attention to each member's verbal, vocal, and body language signs and symbols to build more robust understanding.
- Use open communication to create trust, empowerment, inclusion, and value for all team members. Managers build a trusting environment when they themselves show trust. By giving team members a feeling of worth, support, autonomy, and respect, managers create self-monitoring and motivated team members. Clear, well-managed, authentic communication that respects the team, team members, and tasks at hand shows empathy and minimizes unhealthy conflict situations.
- Express positive intentions to model both empathy, openness, and respect of different experiences and cultures. By acting and speaking with emotional and content awareness, managers set the bar for team members. Emotional Intelligence can be contagious within the team.
- Use paraphrasing and questions to deepen understandings of others and avoid assumption of both content and emotional meanings. By using wording such as, "Are you saying . . . ?" or "I want to make sure I understand you correctly," you allow for validation of understanding. This ability to reflect on what people actually do or say rather than the conclusions you derive from their behaviors enhances the chances that shared meaning will be achieved. Managers who show authentic interest and curiosity will gain deeper insights and mutual respect.
- Read nonverbal behaviors for vocal and body language. This lets managers use the most emotionally telling aspects of shared communication to build deeper meaning. Successful managers use insights that are captured through culturally sensitive attention to

Pro tip

When a colleague is emotionally triggered, avoid saying, "Don't feel that way." A better approach is to listen, ask questions that might help the person process the event or problem, and empathize. Avoid trying to fix the situation or saying, "If I were you, I would . . ."

voice tone, pitch, rate, silence, posture, eye contact, and facial expressions along with verbal tools such as feedback, questions, and reflective paraphrasing to build team unity and emotional awareness.

Multisensory Listening, Feedback, and Questions

Employees want a manager to recognize and appreciate them as people and for the contribution and value they bring to the organization and team. They also seek socioemotional behaviors that respect their culture, beliefs, age, and so on. In short, they want a manager to treat them as the complex human beings they are and not just as cogs in a larger process. By honing multisensory listening that uses all the senses to take in cues, managers build and maintain relationships. Through active listening techniques, using paraphrasing and feedback, managers nurture effective work relationships, empathizing with the perspective of others and framing influence around what others need. These skills enhance a manager's informal power and personal influence. If team members resist a process or action, managers should ask active questions, building a solid foundation for understanding and productively addressing that resistance. Even if bad things happen along the way, team members will be less embittered by the perception that they are expendable if the manager has shown empathy. A vital managerial function is to seek and receive feedback to improve practices and performance. Managing from self-awareness and assuredness allows you to offer feedback that enhances trusting relationships among team members while looking at areas that need development.

Key Concepts of Multisensory Listening, Feedback, and Questions

- Be interested in others, as illustrated by focused listening and questions. Build valuable insights into performance and motivation by using questions that show interest in work-related activities without being intrusive. Such questions can build rapport, empathy, and a platform for shared understandings.
- Use and expect others to choose respectful language that encourages the giving and seeking of feedback and continuous improvement. Feedback that is stored up for a biannual review does little to achieve performance change and can create defensive or "gotcha" types of responses. Start with respect and positive intentions. Continuous feedback, without micromanaging or being perceived as one who is unable to delegate or trust others to make decisions on what is working and not working, allows the team and individual team members to see such communication as natural, helpful, and supportive.
- Practice active multisensory listening that captures the content and emotional data carried by words, phrasing, voice, body language, and situational dynamics. Along with nonverbal and verbal dynamics, the situation drives what content and which approach will manage emotional responses in a beneficial manner. Remember that emotive response does not always bring about positive, comfortable, or secure feelings. There are situations in which it is important to create concern, stress, and anxiety. Choosing the communication tools that are available and appropriate to the situation helps managers manage emotional dynamics.

- Practice professionally appropriate open communication by which others know that issues can be resolved, and resistance can be overcome. Managers sometimes see this as risky and avoid being open and transparent. Empathy, trust, shared vision, and mutual support are achieved through openness and visible vulnerability. When trust and respect are modeled by a manager, team members are more likely to interpret managerial actions as being for the good of the group, and support versus resistance is achieved.
- Ask questions to validate or correct perceptions. Paraphrasing expresses to a team member that building understanding is most important. That awareness lowers defensiveness and promotes clear thinking, problem solving, and shared action.

Myth: Emotions should stay outside of the workplace.

Work has never been separated from how we feel about it. With present-day insights into the competencies of Emotional Intelligence, managers are able to better manage and use insights offered through emotional data to align, motivate, and achieve results. Workplace Emotional Intelligence research concludes that managers who employ Emotional Intelligence gain higher levels of team commitment, achievement of results, and collaborative work.

Self-Control and Mindfulness

A manager is pressured from above and below to deal with personnel, solve problems, communicate, achieve team tasks, contribute to the strategic mission of the organization, innovate, and much more. In any given day, stress can occur. Stress at a manageable level helps performance, but when it becomes overwhelming stress can trigger unhelpful behaviors and conflict, contribute to burnout, and in general, disrupt a collaborative team model. Managers need to express emotion in a helpful yet honest fashion, and the behaviors they use create the tone and mood for the team. Modeling honesty begins with self-awareness and self-management and is followed by conscious communication choices that show emotional regulation and respect for team members. The hallmark of managers who demonstrate EI is the ownership of their emotions; they do not suggest that others made them feel or act in a particular way. Mindfulness is a mental state achieved by focusing one's awareness on the present moment while calmly acknowledging and accepting one's feelings. Practicing personal and team-based mindfulness activities (such as deep breathing, stretching, and breaks to walk around) help focus the brain and release stress. Managers need to help build a team environment that creates and sustains a sense of optimism, even when the situation is difficult or the team is facing a failure. When stressors such as timelines, insufficient resources, and difficult customers are present, managers must take the lead to create proactive stress management plans for team members and for themselves. Encouraging breaks, social exchanges, and exercise; providing healthy foods in the office area; and promoting mediation and other forms of mindfulness practices assist everyone in maintaining an optimal performance environment.

Myth: There really is no time to think about how people feel about doing their job.

The reality of the pressures of time and productivity sometimes lead us to believe that pushing through is our only option; on rare occasions, it is. Whatever our workplace worldviews, emotions are embedded in that personal reality. We have specific attitudes and beliefs around how work should be performed and what optimal performance represents. Highly effective managers in today's workplace recognize and manage their own perceptual frameworks for performance and appropriate emotional reactions in order to support high-level results from all team members.

Key Concepts of Self-Control and Mindfulness

As managers develop more emotional awareness, self-management, and capacity to authentically use emotionally intelligent behaviors, they become models of Emotional Intelligence for others. Starting with being able to identify their own emotions, managers discover the complexity of the multiple reactions they encounter daily. Recognition of the behaviors that are associated with their emotions allows for conscious decision making around emotional responses and emotional management. Managers must consider team members and specific situations when modeling Emotional Intelligence and emotional self-management.

These insights allow the manager to apply mindfulness and stress reduction activities, which in turn allow team members and managers to achieve optimal performance while maintaining health and well-being. Managing productive levels of stress on a personal and team level is the manager's job. Determining the appropriate mindful action with self and team members depends on the type of work being conducted.

Despite pursuing resilient thinking that encompasses use of optimism, helpful self-talk, and mindfulness, managers must be aware that failures will occur. Managers and teams distinguish themselves and their work by focusing on answers and solutions rather than on the problem. Speaking with hopefulness allows team members and managers to move to solutions rather than get mired in problems. Managers need to encourage, model, and take resilient action by expressing disappointment followed by a pivot to solution language and discussion. Critically, a manager must allow team members to express their emotions around a failure and then help them transition toward resilience by collaborating to set new goals, celebrating small successes, and staying engaged.

Myth: A lot of managers don't really seem authentic when they try to use EI.

When learning new behaviors or ways of performing, we may feel unnatural. Getting to "natural" is a result of learning, reinforcement, and unconscious integration of a behavior. Managers might initially fake emotional intelligent behaviors when learning how to make those behaviors a natural part of their style. This process from unnatural to natural is to be expected and is not a reason to stop promoting emotional intelligent growth.

Expressing feelings productively and under control creates an authentic, trusting, and cohesive working environment. All emotions are of value and, when expressed in an appropriate and professional manner, they can strengthen interpersonal relationships. The behaviors exhibited with any emotional response must be managed and chosen. For example, using "I" language when referencing personal emotions associated with a situation or another person's actions keeps the ownership with the speaker instead of blaming others. A statement such as "You make me frustrated because you are always showing up late for team meetings" shifts the ownership of the emotion to the other person. The truth is that the frustration is the speaker's emotional response to the situation. It is better for a manager to own the emotional response and link it to specific events and behaviors. "On Thursday, Friday, and now today you arrived fifteen minutes late for our team meeting. I am frustrated. Help me understand what is delaying you." Owning your emotion and linking it to a specific action keeps overgeneralization and accusations out of the exchange and reduces defensiveness.

This is what emotional self-management looks like.

CONTEXTUAL SCENARIOS FOR THE EMOTIONAL INTELLIGENCE COMPETENCY

The scenarios that follow illustrate two common types of EI challenges managers face.

Scenario 1

Silvia has been promoted to manager of the customer service team. She was an exceptional performer as a customer service representative and often took extra time to coach and support colleagues as they worked with their customer challenges. Managing the team is not without its challenges too. She now has to deal with people out sick, losing patience with customers, and snipping about others' habits. This was not what she signed on for. She wants to be helpful, supportive, likeable, and empathetic. But it seems she has to be an authoritarian manager instead. She is ready to quit!

The possible emotionally intelligent managerial approaches Silvia can take include:

- Self-awareness
- Self-management
- Active multisensory listening
- Information-building questions
- Personal influence
- Empathy
- Team stress awareness
- Stress awareness and action
- Coaching for resilience

- Inspiration and motivation
- Healthy conflict management

Though this list may seem daunting, the following analysis shows how naturally these skills can be used.

- Self-awareness—Is Silvia concerned with being successful in this new role? She is now managing people who were her co-workers and pals. There is so much pressure. Silvia starts with identifying her own emotions relative to the situation. Are they helpful given her own stress tolerance?
- Self-management—Silvia acts to manage her own reactions and identifies behavioral actions with emotional states. She will be better able to manage herself after understanding the common triggers that surround her. Team members replying with a "Whatever," when asked their reactions to changes is one. She doesn't need to be emotionally hijacked by that language or situation and so uses awareness and self-regulation.
- Active multisensory listening—What are the team members really telling her in their individual ways? She has been listening for content but ignoring emotional data. What can she glean from the way team members use eye contact, posture, vocal delivery, eye contact, and so on? Silvia also paraphrases key communication from team members to be sure she avoids assuming attitudes and positions; instead she verifies both the content and emotional information being shared. Interestingly, the team seems less defensive with her, but more important they are less defensive with customers.
- Information-building questions—Along the way Silvia finds insightful questions are helpful for gaining information as well as for showing interest in the situation and team member. "How are you feeling about trying this new approach with customers?" "What might we do to improve our results?" "In the future, what will be the best way to discuss these types of issues so that we can work collaboratively?"
- Personal influence—As team members gain a higher trust in Silvia and have a better sense of personal interest in each other's well-being, Silvia finds the team more open to opportunities to solve issues on their own. Team members are depending on each other to work through difficulties. When Silvia asks the team to step up their efforts, it is not seen as a treat or disciplinary action but rather as a positive belief in their capacity and competence.
- Empathy—Though it was work at first, modeling and stating positive intentions when interacting with team members has caused a shift in how Silvia perceives them and how they perceive her. A symbiotic awareness of shared and individual challenges has fueled higher levels of understanding.
- Team stress awareness—Through this process, it has become clear to Silvia that she is not alone in feeling burned out and demotivated. Even the team all-stars were faltering and calling in sick just to have a day to recover perspective. Silvia takes steps to reorganize the work flow, providing more frequent breaks, instituting several brief team activities a day to build interdependencies, and encouraging ten minutes of mindfulness practice each morning to help team members gain a more present startup for the day.

- Stress awareness and action—Silvia practices neutralizing self-talk and uses regulating physical behaviors, such as deep breathing and conscious muscle relaxation. She begins to consider what she wants for the team, and positions her vision around shared, positive, and empathetic action.
- Coaching for resilience—Things haven't always gone smoothly. Terri took another job, and a replacement has not been found. Also, the organization had a rough quarter, and earnings are down. Managers throughout the organization, including Silvia, are feeling more pressure to achieve their goals. Silvia has rallied team members with honesty and hopefulness.
- Inspiration and motivation—"This is not an easy situation, and we are facing a struggle. What can we do in our part of the business to improve results? Decide on our priorities? Alleviate noncritical activities? Reorganize to streamline what we do?" Silvia needs to understand what each team member finds inspiring and motivating and then adjust her style to meet those needs while making the situation mutually beneficial.
- Healthy conflict management—Though agreement with each other is not always possible, there is a clear sense of respect, which is desired and built on when solving problems or resolving interpersonal conflicts. Listening to each other, seeking the positive intention in each person's positions, and finding common ground are now exhibited.

Scenario 2

Vinny has been with the government his entire career and is now three years away from retirement. He enjoys his work and has mixed feelings about his upcoming retirement. Given his fluctuating feelings it isn't unusual for his colleagues to see him as sad, happy, remote, and the "same old Vinny" on any given day. Lizzy, his manager, has a solid relationship with Vinny and is aware of the struggle the next several years will bring for Vinny. Lizzy worries about him but also about the team that might be impacted by Vinny's shifting moods. She must maintain everyone's motivation and commitment, including Vinny's.

Lizzy's possible emotionally intelligent managerial approaches include:

- Self-awareness
- Self-management
- Stress awareness and action
- Active multisensory listening
- Information-building questions
- Empathy
- Collaboration
- Team mindfulness
- Resilience and optimism

- Inspiration and motivation
- Healthy conflict management

In the analysis that follows we see that what seems like an overwhelming set of considerations become achievable and logical.

- Self-awareness—Lizzy feels concern over the challenges she is facing. She has faith in her personal capacities to plan, organize, and execute within the structures and regulations of the government agency but struggles with managing people. Vinny presents a special challenge and this disconcerting. At times she is frustrated that she needs to deal with her emotional states and, at other times, appreciates that she is thoughtful around interpersonal relationships, which makes her approachable.
- Self-management—Lizzy has found that she becomes overly direct with her remarks when she feels she is losing control. Vinny's erratic emotional behavior leaves her feeling this way. To avoid souring her relationship with Vinny and to also model the self-managing behaviors she wants from the team, she is vigilant of this vulnerability. Lizzy now puts off responding in the moment to something Vinny asks or does until she is centered, working with positive intentionality, and self-managed.
- Stress awareness and action—Lizzy finds a network of other managers who are facing similar issues and reaches out to them when she needs support and guidance. She realizes that her concerns are not unusual. She also takes walks during her lunch break and twice a week attends a community yoga class in her apartment complex. Overall, she feels optimistic and empowered by these activities.
- Active multisensory listening—Lizzy pays close attention to the content and emotional data coming from Vinny and the rest of the team. She has found that if she catches disruptions, disagreements, or emotional fluctuations early, they are much easier to keep in the healthy resolution space. She is seeing that other team members are picking up on her modeling. They are keeping their focus on communicating clearly and respectfully working together. The overall effect is a better regulated working environment and sense of connectiveness.
- Information-building questions—Mere observation is not sufficient to keep Lizzy well informed. She has gotten in the habit of using many more questions to monitor the team's mood. "Before we get our day started, what do you need to do for yourself to be your best? How can I help?" This has replaced her statement format of the past, "Let's be our best today. Remember that we are all in this to serve the public." She also is using questions to observe and respond to Vinny's moods. "Vinny, were you aware that you just now slammed the phone down into its receiver? That's not okay, so help me understand what's up."
- Empathy—Asking questions and listening has led to understanding just how scared Vinny is of the new life he faces after retirement. Lizzy is struck by how her own fears mirror Vinny's. Lizzy and Vinny build a shared understanding that has enriched their relationship.

- Collaboration—Lizzy hosts monthly brown bag meetings with her team to discuss resources for mutual support, stress reduction, retirement planning, wellness, and other similar issues. These gatherings have broken down some of the walls the team believed existed. A new sense of openness, risk taking, and support to achieve results has emerged. Vinny has been a leader in planning these events and has a sense of long-term positive impact on the team.
- Team mindfulness—Lizzy's efforts are reducing the pieces of stress that she can influence. She looks out for the early warning signs of team member burnout: absences, lateness, vacillating emotions, isolation, and irritability. She takes early mindful action to help team members regulate and perform.
- Resilience and optimism—Given the nature of government employment and work, Lizzy finds that a pervasive attitude among her team is a feeling of hopelessness and not being able to change circumstances. Lizzy agrees that things are often frustrating but communicates that within their team they can make a difference for each other. They don't need to redefine the culture of government work to feel more successful, challenged, and satisfied by their work. This conversation is a daily activity now, and slowly members are taking on a hopeful attitude of making a difference where they sit.
- Inspiration and motivation—By creating options for team support and achievement Lizzy has achieved renewed attention, retention, and motivation within the team. She knows her team and is proactive using targeted messages of encouragement and feedback.
- Healthy conflict management—Collaboration means conflict. The team lives in a culture in which authority has directed them into compliance. As Lizzy encourages committed team action, there has been more conflict, particularly for Vinny who vacillates between "Who cares?" and "I have been at this a long time, and this is what to do." She recruits Vinny as an adviser, making it clear she is interested in his insights yet must ultimately work with the entire team to move ahead. Lizzy's relationship-building efforts with Vinny are paying off with his trust in her decision making. Lizzy models listening to everyone and paraphrasing to verify meaning and to seek the positive intention in each person's position and thus finds common ground.

Myth: EI's return on investment doesn't touch the bottom line.

Several studies have posited that Emotional Intelligence practices are directly tied to the bottom line. As with all research on human subjects, it is difficult to isolate one aspect of work relationships and processes and make factually irrefutable conclusions. Yet, the preponderance of the research to date backs up the multiple benefits of managing with Emotional Intelligence, including enhancement of the bottom line.

BENEFITS FROM MANAGING WITH EMOTIONAL INTELLIGENCE

When considering the managerial commitment needed to achieve proficiency in using Emotional Intelligence, it is motivating to consider the benefits such commitment will offer. Table 2-3 reminds us of what we mean by *managerial Emotional Intelligence* and further articulates several reasons for implementing EI practices

Table 2-3 Benefits of Managerial Emotional Intelligence

Emotional Intelligence	Effective managerial Emotional Intelligence benefits the team and the organization by:
The ability to identify and manage your own emotions and to observe and influence others' emotional states	• Creating more personal and professional satisfaction for self and team members • Encouraging higher levels of productivity and a greater sense of team commitment to exceed expectations • Developing higher levels of healthy conflict instead of destructive conflict • Modeling the skills for avoiding resistance to most decisions, changes, and work challenges • Inspiring team members and others to achieve results and meet goals • Supporting team members who know how to relate to each other and solve issues without the intervention of the manager

PERFORMANCE INDICATORS

It can be challenging for managers to know when they are achieving effective emotionally intelligent managerial performance. Insights can sometimes come from recognizing which behaviors are ineffective and then knowing what can be done instead to achieve emotionally intelligent effectiveness. Table 2-4 offers necessary points of assessment and effective behavioral choices.

Table 2-4 Emotional Intelligence: Strategies for Effective Performance and Outcomes of Poor Performance

Strategies for Effective EI Performance	**Outcomes of Poor EI Performance**
• Monitor emotions throughout the day or situation • Ask for feedback from others • Process feedback • Identify best time and location to address a situation	• Infighting and wasted time as team members work against each other • Team demotivation • Closed or infrequent communication • Dissatisfaction and poor retention • Poor long-term performance results

<table>
<tr>
<td>
<ul>
<li>Identify the best course of action (choice of words, time, tone, body language, delivery method, environment)</li>
<li>Observe others’ communication (words, tone, body language)</li>
<li>Ask questions to better understand others</li>
<li>Apply empathy</li>
<li>Clearly articulate the cause of the emotion</li>
<li>Clearly articulate the implications of own emotions within the setting</li>
<li>Explain point of view</li>
<li>Practice stress management techniques (breathing, mindfulness, meditation)</li>
<li>Practice active listening</li>
<li>Seek support from an objective party</li>
<li>Recognize emotional triggers</li>
<li>Step away from a negative situation to pause and reset</li>
<li>Identify emotional data in nonverbal cues</li>
<li>Engage the other party to confirm nonverbal cues</li>
<li>Seek to understand emotions and behaviors</li>
</ul>
</td>
<td>
<ul>
<li>Hostilities and disrespectful activity</li>
</ul>
</td>
</tr>
</table>

Presentation Skills

LEARNING OBJECTIVES

By the end of this chapter, you will be better equipped to:

- Identify a clear purpose for a presentation.
- Select the appropriate audience for a presentation.
- Design and prepare a presentation flow, visuals, and supporting materials that consider the audience needs, modality, and intended outcomes.
- Deliver an engaging presentation, using appropriate technology and tools, that achieves its intended purpose and enhances your credibility.
- Apply communication, emotional intelligence, and influencing skills during a presentation to achieve your purpose.

INTRODUCTION

Consider the last presentation you attended. Was the presentation's purpose clear? Was the presenter credible? Were your questions answered? Did you feel the time you spent at the presentation was valuable? Or were you tempted to multitask or to let your thoughts drift? Did you wonder why you were there?

Good presentations are meaningful; they engage us and accomplish a clear purpose, which makes it easier for us to assimilate and apply the content and ideas to our roles or responsibilities. Poorly planned or delivered presentations often leave us feeling like our time was wasted.

As managers, we are often called on to make presentations to an array of audiences. Whether the audience is a single person, such as a potential client or a senior executive; your staff; or a large group, such as a conference or town hall, it's crucial that you have the skills to interact and engage with your audience and to transmit your messages clearly.

Managers with strong presentation skills plan, develop, and deliver clear and effective presentations. They demonstrate confidence and create an engaging environment for the audience.

To accomplish this, effective presenters are clear about the purpose of their messages and their audiences' motivations and needs. They use this knowledge to customize all aspects of their planning, design, and delivery, including selecting the appropriate audience participants and delivery modality, when possible.

Of course, not all presentations can be planned. As a manager, you might be required to present a project, decision, or result unexpectedly, such as for an impromptu meeting or during a conference call. While these situations don't permit the same degree of preparation, strong presenters apply some of the same techniques to manage unplanned opportunities and deliver successful off-the-cuff presentations.

In this chapter, we explore the evolution of business presentations and present techniques for preparing an effective presentation that accomplishes your goals and meets your audience's needs. Our focus in this chapter is on oral presentations, where there is a live audience of either one or many people, either in person or connected digitally, rather than on written presentations. Note, however, that the techniques for understanding your audience and the methods for organizing information can also be applied to reports, memos, and other written presentations. See also Chapter 1, Communication.

In practice, the development of the presentation skills competency involves the activities displayed in Figure 3-1. We provide tactical guidance and examples to bring these to life, enabling you to present confidently and effectively and achieve your presentation goals.

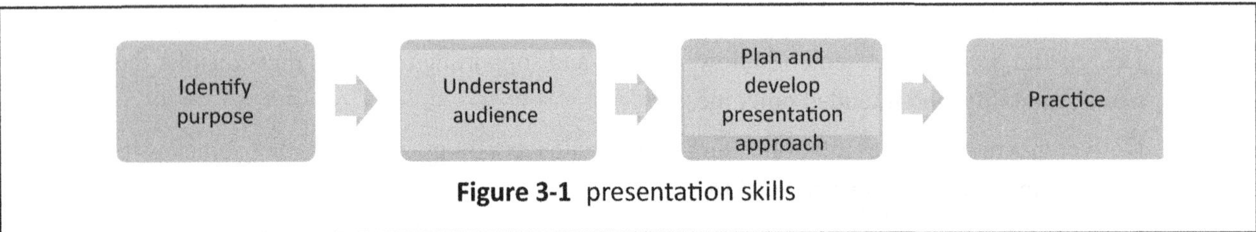

Figure 3-1 presentation skills

THE EVOLUTION OF BUSINESS PRESENTATIONS

To deliver effective presentations, it's not enough for us to mirror what we've seen in the past. Business presentations have fundamentally changed in the twenty-first century. What was once a formal endeavor that used limited technology has evolved considerably.

Whether the audience was large or small, most presentations used to be extremely formal, one-way performances. Presenters would deliver information, asking the audience to hold its questions and reactions until the presentation was finished. Often presenters would stand or sit separately from the audience in a power position, such as behind a podium or on a stage. Technology was stationary, such as overhead projectors and, later, desktop computers with projection capabilities. This was the *sage on the stage* approach and, as you can probably imagine, this format didn't foster much audience engagement or interaction.

Without audience engagement, it was hard for presenters to determine whether they had achieved their intended purpose. Often, they walked away wondering what the audience felt or thought.

While there are still occasions for formal presentations, technology and an increased awareness of the value of audience engagement have significantly shifted the presentation landscape. In many cases, presentations are less formal and more interactive, incorporating audience activities or dialogue with the presenter. Presenters now often take the role of facilitators, and well-executed presentations feel more like discussions or two-way interactions. Even in TED talks, where presenters are on a stage in front of an auditorium, presenters incorporate ways for the audience to interact by using polling, storytelling, or a conversational tone or humor.

The availability of new and constantly evolving portable technologies have expanded our expectations of digital elements that we can use when presenting. The first of these were PowerPoint and Prezi, both of which continually update their functionality to incorporate graphic, animation, video, and audio tools. In addition, widgets or supplemental technology allow even large audiences to interact with a presenter through polling, Q&A, and other real-time digital interaction tools.

At the most sophisticated levels, augmented and virtual reality have begun allowing presenters to alter the audience's perspective in real time. Imagine, rather than showing flat photos on a screen, being able to transport the audience with a three-dimensional (3D) experiential walk-through of a manufacturing site or even allowing them to immerse themselves in the experience of driving a vehicle—all while sitting in an office or auditorium.

As a result of these technological shifts, our expectations for presentations have also shifted. As audience members, we want to be engaged, either through interpersonal or digital means. We also anticipate that presenters will understand our needs and align their content with them so we can internalize, use, or react in meaningful ways.

The bar has certainly been raised for presenters. To establish credibility, we need to not only know our content but also anticipate our audience's needs as well as integrate and use technology effectively to support and supplement, but not distract from, our messages.

This requires preparation and focused practice.

What's New?

- Use of portable presentation technology
- Integration of digital interactive elements
- Expectation for audience engagement
- Level of formality
- Incorporation of storytelling
- Use of data visualization
- Use of neuroscience findings

TARGET YOUR MESSAGE TO YOUR AUDIENCE

The first step in the preparation process is to identify key and relevant content to deliver targeted information and a clear message. This is truly a multistep process that involves identifying your purpose, the content you need to include in your talking points to achieve your intended outcome, and your audience. Let's look at each in turn.

Table 3-1 Reasons for Making a Presentation

Primary Purpose for a Presentation	Key Elements to Achieve Your Purpose
Convey information	• Clear statement of the benefit of your audience knowing and paying attention to the information • Statements of information targeted to the audience's level and building off what they already know • Interaction and discussion opportunities for the audience to ask questions and for you to check their understanding • Visual aids to reinforce the information
Gain agreement or approval	• Clear statement of the benefit of your audience agreeing or providing approval • Organized articulation of the information they need to be comfortable with the decision you're seeking • Comparison to other alternatives under consideration or to the status quo • Supporting materials and data the audience needs to make a decision • Interaction and discussion opportunities for the audience to ask questions • Articulation of next steps in the approval and agreement process, if a decision can't be made at the time
Provide instructions	• Clear statement of the value and importance of the instructions for the audience in terms that are meaningful to them • Clear articulation of the instructions • Comparison to current processes, highlighting what is different (if applicable) • Visual aids that capture the instructions and can be used later to execute them • Interaction and discussion opportunities for the audience to identify resistance or potential obstacles and confirm understanding • Articulation of next steps
Solicit information	• Clear statement of the value and importance of providing the information • Overview of the specific information being sought and exactly how it will be used • Questions designed to elicit the information you need • Clear articulation of next steps and how and when the audience will see the results of their input

Identify Your Purpose

Without a clear purpose, it's likely you won't achieve the intent of your presentation. Your purpose provides a target to align all elements of your planning and, later, to influence your presentation delivery.

Let's look at an example: You are creating a presentation about your team's strategic plan for the next year. Your presentation objectives could include any one or a combination of the following:

- Convey information about the strategy details, obtain buy-in, and motivate others to action
- Seek agreement or approval for resources required to execute the plan
- Provide instructions to the audience who will need to execute the plan
- Solicit input to refine the plan

To achieve your goals, you will need to plan and structure your presentation with your target in mind.

Table 3-1 captures the primary reasons for making a presentation, along with key presentation elements that can help you achieve your purpose, regardless of the topic.

Primary Purposes for Presentations

Convey information

Seek agreement or approval

Provide instructions

Solicit input

RESEARCH AND DOCUMENT IDEAS AND TALKING POINTS

Once you've identified your clear purpose for the presentation, the next step in the preparation process is to gather the information and ideas you want to convey to accomplish your objectives. This process involves obtaining the data and resources you need and outlining the key points you plan to make.

Gather Data

Start gathering data by thinking about the information your audience will need to understand your messages. It can be helpful to consider the data you need in terms of background information and in terms of facts and supporting documentation to prove your points. You will need both.

First, capture data that establish or demonstrate your understanding of the audience's viewpoint or of the current state. What will you need to establish your credibility?

Then, consider what data will support the viewpoint you're presenting. Is there an alternate path or vision that you will share? What will be the outcome of pursuing this? Can you provide statistics or research to support your anticipated outcomes?

If your topic addresses issues internal to your organization, relevant information can often be gathered from internal departments or reports. For example, sales, financial, and operational data are frequently collected and reported. If you don't have regular access to the data you need, give yourself enough time to obtain and analyze the information before planning your talking points.

If data are not available, consider other means you might use to capture the current state. Options include interviewing experts or customers, observing work processes, and participating in meetings with those who can provide insight into the current state. Ask yourself what you could do to obtain this information and schedule time to follow through.

In other cases, the data you need will be external to your organization. For instance, you might need information about the competitive landscape, the economy, or future projections for a new technology that presents an opportunity or a threat to your organization. Identify where this information can be obtained. Industry associations, news articles, public financial reports and press releases, and vendors are all potential sources.

When possible, consider tapping an array of sources to validate the information you gather, especially if your starting point is not a primary source. An opinion piece from a trade journal about the industry outlook could be tainted by the author's bias, so it's important to dig deeper. Seek out the primary source the author is referencing to confirm his or her interpretations, if possible.

While you're collecting data, consider ways you can bring statistical information to life and help your audience connect with it. Neuroscience tells us that storytelling and providing examples can help accomplish this. What stories, examples, or experiences will support your data?

For example, consider a situation in which you've collected information demonstrating that your new suggested process will improve your product's durability. You plan to supplement this information with industry data that show this will make your product the most durable on the market. Although you intuitively know this will be good for business, you can bolster your case for the new process by also projecting the impact of increased product durability on near-term future sales.

To drive your point home, it can be helpful to relate why customers will care about durability by sharing a story. For example, provide a profile of a typical customer who needs to set aside money for two years so he can afford to replace the product. His increased confidence in your product's durability will allow that customer to use his savings to meet a pressing family need, like his child's college education.

Outline Your Presentation Flow

Once you have compiled your data, consider how you will organize the information to achieve your objective and create a high-level outline for developing your presentation.

While you are outlining your presentation flow, it can be helpful to have a guide to the methods of development (Table 3-2)—that is, the ways that you can organize information to effectively accomplish your purpose. The following discussion offers a high-level view of some effective ways to present information.

Depending on your goal, you might incorporate more than one method of development into your presentation. Let's consider an example of how that could look.

You will present an opinion about the need to change a current process and then will teach the proposed process. You decide to organize your overall presentation in a decreasing order of importance, starting with the most important reason to change and following with the less important reasons. At the point at which you plan to present your new solution, you insert a whole-by-whole comparison of the current process to the new process.

Myth: Include more content in your presentation than you need to achieve your purpose.

Content that doesn't serve your purpose should not be included in the presentation. This can include tangential information or deep technical detail. Instead of reinforcing your key points, such extraneous information distracts from your messaging and can confuse the audience.

Once you've crafted a high-level outline with an appropriate flow, you start annotating the outline, inserting key data, stories, and other talking points that will help your audience understand your message and ensure you achieve your presentation's purpose. This exercise helps you identify any holes in your data or available content. It also begins the culling process, whereby you eliminate content that doesn't serve your purpose.

KNOW YOUR AUDIENCE

It's tempting at this point, now that you've gathered information and drafted your high-level presentation outline, to dive immediately into preparing your final presentation, whether that involves creating visual aids or your own speaking notes. Before you do, though, you need to have a solid understanding of who your audience members will be.

Every audience—indeed, every individual in the audience—potentially has different needs that evolve from their roles, responsibilities, and areas of subject matter expertise. Understanding these motivations will provide insight into the depth and style of content they have an appetite for and what will drive their questions or concerns.

They will also have different preferred communication and decision-making styles. Knowing these can help you refine your outline and plan a presentation and support materials that specifically target your audience's preferences, which will help you accomplish your purpose.

Suppose your product presentation is designed to appeal to an audience of salespeople, who need to understand the nuances of the product's benefits to their prospective customers and who need to be equipped to answer technical questions. You could arrange for the salespeople to interact with the product and then provide them with a takeaway packet that includes key technical information and responses to frequently asked questions.

A presentation to senior management for budget approval will need to be different. The presentation itself could be crisp and high-level, providing comparisons of past and future revenues and expenditures and positioning your request in the context of market opportunities or threats. Your goal is to present a ten-thousand-foot view of the budget to orient management for the approval.

Table 3-2 Methods of Development

Purpose	**Method of Development**	**Explanation and Examples**
Explaining an unfamiliar subject	Comparison • Whole by whole • Part by part	When something is new to the audience, it is helpful to orient them by comparing what's new to something that's familiar *Whole by whole*: The current process takes three months, requires three reviews, and results in a 20 percent defect rate. The new automated process will take one month, require only one review, and will reduce the defect rate to less than 2 percent. *Part by part*: Let's compare the new process to one we've used in another division, the XYZ process. You will notice the first three steps, establishing our baseline, are the same. We deviate at step 4, where we have the user perform X instead of Y. Steps 5 through 7, the approval process, are again the same as the established process. Then we deviate again by compressing steps 8 through 10 them into one simple, automated step with the new process.
Teaching something new	General to specific	Start with a high-level overview that orients the audience and then provide the specifics *Example*: We have created a simple application for our clients to obtain account information, reducing the need for calls to our customer service area. Let's examine what that looks like from the customer's perspective, then consider how that will change the types of calls customer service will receive and how that will impact their training needs.
Convincing a skeptical audience	Specific to general	Articulate the specific recommendation and then expand to provide information about how you arrived at that recommendation *Example*: While there are a number of possible solutions to our high error rates, we've determined the most effective solution is to increase staffing by 20 percent. Let's look at how we arrived at this conclusion. . . .
Presenting an opinion or targeting a diverse audience	Order of importance • Decreasing • Increasing	Either present your case by starting with the most important point and continuing with subordinate points or build your case by starting with the least important point and continue with points that are of increasing importance, finishing with the most important *Decreasing*: I identified three key drivers of profitability. The most crucial is . . . and this is why we chose to focus our efforts here. The other two are . . . *Increasing*: I identified three key drivers of profitability. The first is . . . The second, which has a bigger impact, is . . . The third, and most crucial, is . . . , which is why we chose to focus our efforts here.
Explaining a process or providing instructions	Sequential	Similar to a step-by-step checklist, this walks through the information in the order the user will experience or use it *Example*: Let's start at the beginning. Once you log into the system, you will see X. Select either A or B and then submit your selection. Then, you will be presented with . . .

Still, some team members, like the CFO, will require greater detail. In addition, a new management team member might need to know the background about a particular project. Rather than presenting the nuances of every budget line and the detailed timeline of the project, you can anticipate these needs and either provide the information in advance or prepare a takeaway packet to meet the needs of all audience members.

Audience Analysis
Roles and responsibilities
Perspectives
Motivations

Selecting Your Audience

At a high level, there are three possible scenarios related to your audience: you select the attendees, someone else selects the attendees, an organizational requirement selects the attendees (like all of the members of a specific committee), or a combination of these (where some are selected by others, but you have the opportunity to select others to supplement the audience).

You Select the Audience

If you will choose the audience members, use your identified purpose to influence your decision making. Who will need to be present to accomplish your purpose? Here, you will use your knowledge of the potential audience members to select the most appropriate participants.

If your purpose is to confirm the user requirements you've gathered for a potential new system purchase, your audience should include users or individuals who represent users' interests and can speak to them, not just the programmers who will be building the system. If the users are not represented, gaps in their needs or misunderstandings about the priority of their needs can derail the system's rollout and approval, which come much later. This could require an expensive reworking of the solution, downtime while the issues are addressed, or an imperfect solution that does not meet user needs. Of course, this could lead to additional problems such as with morale, operational challenges, or client loyalty, depending on who your users are.

If your purpose is to facilitate internal agreement about the best course to propose to senior management from among two identified options, your audience will need to include stakeholders from all potentially affected areas, along with other important influencers. In this case, if you do not include all affected areas, objections identified later could impede your resulting proposal's approval or even its later implementation.

These are just a few examples to provide light on what to consider when deciding who to invite. Just as important, though, can be deciding who *not* to invite. There's no simple rule here. Instead, identify the role each audience member will play and resist including those who don't advance the achievement of your purpose. Don't include people just in case. The likely scenario is that they will be disengaged and feel the time was not well spent. The worst-case scenario is that they will be disruptive for the other audience members.

Keep in mind that potential objectors or others who might be difficult participants to manage should not be excluded for only those reasons. If they are crucial stakeholders to the conversation, you need them there. Excluding them will only delay their involvement, which could create turmoil later. To address anticipated objections, it can be helpful to plan conversations with them in advance of your presentation to identify and address their concerns or to create agreement about the role they will play during the presentation.

A benefit statement details the value of your presentation in terms that are meaningful for the *audience*.

- Your participation will ensure we collect meaningful information and perspective from your group so the solution we design will meet your team's needs.
- This sweeping initiative will require commitment from all areas of the firm to ensure we are efficient and cost conscious. Your involvement at this early stage will be crucial to your team's understanding of the new requirements and their ability to achieve the goals on which they will be measured.
- This project update will ensure you are informed about when and how the project will affect your customers. By participating in this meeting, you will be able to plan for future system outages and advise your clients, reducing customer complaints to your team.

Figure 3-2 Example benefit statements

Sending Invitations

To set the right tone from the outset, when sending the presentation invitations, be sure to include a clear benefit statement for the participants and for the organization (Figure 3-2). A benefit statement clearly identifies the value of attending from their perspective, not yours.

You also want to ensure that you set clear expectations for your audience about the presentation. In addition to obvious needs, like location and time, consider providing information that creates clarity about what they will experience and the presentation's format.

Almost everyone has been to a presentation where it's clear that one or more audience members are surprised that they were expected to know some baseline material or process that is unfamiliar to them. It is difficult for presenters to meet their objectives when some participants are processing unfamiliar information and others are ready to move on. Situations like this can be prevented by including expectations in the presentation invitation (Figure 3-3).

Details you might provide could answer questions about the presentation's purpose, its format, who else will be there, items the audience will need to learn or familiarize themselves with in advance, and materials or information they will need to have with them.

The more prepared your audience is, the more likely your presentation will be successful.

Invitation Tips

Identify the right people

Frame and articulate a clear audience benefit

Set clear expectations

Someone Else Will Select the Audience

In a wide array of situations, the selection of the audience members will not be under your control. Some examples are conference audiences, where participants register themselves; intact internal teams, such as when you're presenting to all management team members; and client audiences, where the participants are selected by another party.

Here, your best approach to understanding your audience, if they're unfamiliar to you, is to ask questions of the presentation

Subject: ABC Division Strategy Presentation
To: All ABC Area Managers

Join Anja Collazo and her team on October 2 from 1:00 to 4:00 P.M. for an interactive presentation about the ABC Division Strategy for FY202X. The goals for the presentation are to refine the strategy and establish clear goals for each area. Your thoughtful input into this process will be crucial to your area's success in the coming year.

Before the presentation:
Familiarize yourself with the attached strategy overview and the results of our recent market survey. Plan to spend at least an hour with these documents and consider how you will support the strategy in your area.

The agenda:
After a brief overview of the strategy, Anja and her team will answer questions about how we arrived at these decisions.

Then we will break into teams to explore how we will accomplish our goals over the next year. Be prepared to provide your thoughts about additional resources we will need to allocate for your team. *It will be helpful to have your most recent team scorecard and your current year budget allocations with you for this part of the conversation.*

Figure 3-3 Sample presentation invitation

sponsor to get a feel for the audience members' perspectives and potential contributions or reactions. Set aside time for this early in your preparation process.

You Can Alter or Supplement a Preselected Audience

During your analysis of a preselected audience, you might identify gaps or challenges you can suggest addressing.

Here's an example of how this can work in practice: You are presenting a new product to a potential client. Your purpose is to gain the client's agreement to authorize signing a contract for the new product. During your presentation planning conversations with the client, you discover the person with the authority to make a final recommendation has not been included in the audience. You can suggest to the client that this person be invited, so her questions can be answered before deciding on a recommendation. If this is not possible, you might need to alter your purpose, since it's not achievable without that key person in the room.

Here's another example: You are presenting to a current vendor about a new system you're implementing for processing vendor invoices. Your purpose is to convey high-level information about the new process and respond to questions about the implementation timeline and support you will provide, so the vendor can prepare for the change. During your presentation planning conversations with the vendor, you learn they have invited their entire accounting staff but not their managers or the account manager assigned to your firm. You note that the accounting staff is expecting that presentation will entail training on the new process. You can use this information to iterate your presentation's purpose to the vendor and suggest that the audience is not the right level for this initial presentation.

Questions about the Audience

Before you begin investigating your audience, it is helpful to identify what you want to know about them.

While the following is not an exhaustive list, answers to these questions will provide a solid baseline understanding and will focus your thinking on how to target the audience with your presentation.

- What are the audience's roles, responsibilities, tenures, and backgrounds?
- What is the depth of the audience's subject matter expertise on the topic?
- What are the audience's current greatest concerns in their organizations?
- What are the audience member's individual communication and decision-making styles?
- What are the audience's expectations for the presentation's purpose, depth, and interactivity?
- What does the audience know and think about you and your credibility with the subject?
- What organizational dynamics or internal political issues could affect the audience's ability to engage with the content?
- Did the audience members self-select into the presentation or were they assigned?
- How receptive will the audience be to what you're presenting?

If you work regularly with members of the audience, you might know the answers to these questions. Even so, it's useful to consider how the responses to each will influence their behavior and interactions during your presentation and how you can design and deliver in a way that addresses their needs, while also achieving your intended outcome.

How Can You Learn about Your Audience Members?

In circumstances in which you are not familiar with your audience, there are myriad techniques for gathering this information.

First, ask those who are familiar with the audience members. This could be an external contact, such as an event planner, a prospective client's project manager, or others with experience working with or presenting to them. Consider your network and who can provide these types of insights.

Use online resources, such as internet searches and professional profiles on social media. While this might not provide all the information you'd like, it's often enlightening to see someone's career progression and consider how it might affect his or her perspective. Of course, if audience members post about business topics on social media or follow others in their industry or technical field, you might be able to glean additional insights into their motivations by reading about what concerns or excites them.

Even if you have nothing else, consider what roles and responsibilities individuals with a particular title would have at their firm or in their industry. Risk managers, for example are primarily concerned about the risks of anything you propose. Customer service managers are more likely to focus on how the topic will affect their ability to address client issues. Plant managers for a manufacturer are likely concerned with how the topic affects the operations of the plant.

USING EMOTIONAL INTELLIGENCE TO ANTICIPATE AUDIENCE NEEDS

Now that you understand your audience and the invitations have been sent, use this information to anticipate possible questions and concerns that may arise during your presentation and prepare points of discussion to address them.

A good place to start is to mentally put yourself in your audience's shoes. Consider the information you've gathered about the depth of their baseline content understanding, their potential concerns, and their motivations.

Once you're there, consider the types of questions or issues they might raise. Often, questions will fall into one of three overarching categories:

- Content understanding or clarification
- Application to their roles or experiences
- Disagreement with your content or conclusions

When responding to questions, it's not enough to identify *what* is being asked; you must also anticipate the expressed or unexpressed emotion behind *why* it is being asked. This use of what is called emotional intelligence will help you prepare appropriate responses. For more information, see Chapter 2, Emotional Intelligence.

Content Understanding or Clarification

If you can anticipate the audience's questions in terms of understanding the content, you can build the information into your presentation. When your presentation is content rich or dense, consider ways you can segment the information to help the audience understand and then build on what has come before.

The audience may still mishear or misunderstood the information. Consider where you can add visual or other reinforcements that will help them understand. You can revise your outline after anticipating content understanding or clarification questions.

Alternately, there are times when the audience will want to go deeper into the content than you intended. To avoid derailing your presentation with these types of questions, identify how you will respond if someone wants to know more. One option is to offer to follow up with the individual after the presentation to answer any detailed questions. Another is to suggest a resource that will provide the level of detail the audience member is seeking. You could also plan a future presentation on this topic.

Some additional techniques for responding to different types of audience questions are included in the tip sheet at Table 3.3.

Planning how you will respond will ensure you feel confident to address various types of questions.

Myth: Questions from the audience always mean you didn't do your homework.

Audience questions serve many purposes. As a presenter, you want to encourage questions. They allow you to address concerns and signal that the audience is engaged in the conversation and with the content.

Application to Audience Members' Roles or Experiences

Your audience wants to understand how they can use the information you're presenting. This is particularly common when you are presenting new or revised information.

Think about how your audience is likely to use the content you're providing, considering their roles and responsibilities. Use this information to select examples or stories to help your audience connect with the content.

Table 3.3 Responding to Audience Questions

Question Type	Technique for Addressing
Off-topic issue	Acknowledge the question. Ask how this connects to the content or agenda (there may be a connection that isn't obvious). Offer to address this at another time.
Based on rumor	Acknowledge the rumor. Share information to debunk it or otherwise state that it is unknown. If the rumor's truth would alter some element of your presentation, indicate where this would apply and how.
Already covered in presentation	If it's simply missed or unheard information, answer the question matter-of-factly. If it's the result of confusion, elaborate until the content is clear. If confusion results from lack of familiarity for a small segment of the audience, offer to have a conversation or provide background information after the presentation or another set time.
Already asked and answered	Recap the answer. Ask if that addresses the issue; if not, offer to have a conversation or provide background information offline after the presentation or another set time.
Don't know the answer	If another present party knows, defer to that person, asking her to respond. Otherwise, state that you don't have the information and then offer to obtain it and follow up.
For strategic, competitive, or morale reasons, you cannot answer	Acknowledge the question and any emotional content underpinning it. State that you are not in a position to answer the question at this time.

Disagreement with Your Content or Conclusions

When your presentation challenges the audience's current content understanding or plans, you can expect disagreement. If they have deep knowledge that contradicts what you're presenting or if they interpret data differently, audience members will ask challenging questions.

When you anticipate that your audience will question the validity of what you're saying, you can preempt their objections by building a careful case with your content and being prepared to respond their questions. A good approach is to acknowledge their perspective and then provide details that support your position or content (Figure 3-4).

Sometimes, the audience will simply resist trying to understand, as with an audience member who is being told to learn a new process but who doesn't agree with the need to change the current process. These kind of resisters may pepper the presenter with questions, because they aren't able to understand the new system without first accepting that they actually do need to know it.

If the audience perceives the presenter as a threat, they might use questions to assert their dominance, trying to trip the presenter up on the details. Unnecessarily detailed questions can be a flag in these instances.

Question: Did you say that A comes before B? According to what I know, B comes before A. It's possible you misunderstand our process.

Response: I can understand the confusion. You're right. In the old process, B came before A. This was because it was more efficient in the previous system. When we considered the new information, we found that by reversing these two steps we were able to shorten the completion timeline and reduce errors. This will mean fewer late nights for your team and fewer customer complaints for your team to address.

Figure 3-4 Acknowledging others' perspectives

In rare cases, a senior audience member or subject matter expert will challenge or rebuke your content or conclusions in the form of a veiled question. Other participants might perceive this as a signal to be more aggressive with their own challenges.

If you are presenting to skeptical audience, recognize that you might receive more content-related questions than seem necessary. Plan how you will respond in a way that acknowledges any underlying emotion while addressing their questions.

Your credibility rests on your ability to address both the expressed and unexpressed messages in the questions. Additional insights into techniques for influencing others can be found in Chapter 7, Influence.

Myth: Good presentations are about controlling the conversation.

While you don't want a free-for-all, you do want audience participation. If you seek to control the conversation, your approach may limit audience input. For example, asking the audience to hold all questions until the end is a control tactic. This often means that audience questions do not get answered. As an alternative, invite questions or ask questions that check for understanding at key points during the presentation if it's a large group. To reduce the probability of losing control of your presentation, establish ground rules and set expectations for managing questions. A useful technique is to establish a "parking lot," where you capture questions that will be addressed later in the presentation or as a follow-up to the presentation.

DEVELOP YOUR PRESENTATION

You now have a clear purpose; data or other content to support that purpose; and a clear understanding of your audience's perspective, needs, and potential questions. Your next step is to develop the presentation itself. The following sections discuss the items to consider during this process.

Presentation Modality

Thanks to technology, your options for how to present your material have expanded beyond the in-person presentation. If your audience is geographically distributed, an in-person presentation might not even be an option.

Spend some time identifying or selecting the presentation modality you will use and understanding what's possible in that format. Will you project presentation slides, online demonstrations, or video? Will you be able to share content digitally in real time or will you need to provide paper copies of visual aids? Will you record the presentation video or audio and distribute that, instead, such as through a video or podcast channel?

The capabilities of the presentation modality should reinforce your purpose.

Support Materials

What support materials will you need to create, considering your purpose, the modality, and the audience's needs? Support materials can include handouts of data, process flows, product guides, job aids, or other items your audience will find useful to refer to during or after the presentation.

At this point in your preparation process, refer back to your outline. Will your audience members need more information to fully understand any of your planned content? Note this on your outline. What form could that information take? Is a simple resource list adequate or do you need to create specific content?

In cases when you'll present others' research or ideas, confirm that you have the correct permission from the authors and present citations providing credit in the form that the authors require.

If you plan to provide paper or digital support materials, determine when to do so. If you distribute detailed information at the start of or during your presentation, audience members may become distracted by focusing on the supplemental content.

Pro Tip

When presenting to an audience with different levels of experience, consider providing background information *before* the presentation. Alternately, you can provide additional information in a takeaway handout or digital download after the program.

If your presentation includes a demonstration or an example, consider its form and at what point it should be integrated into the program.

If you're soliciting input or other engagement from the audience, consider the need to incorporate digital software, a whiteboard, or a paper flipchart to capture their ideas. Your outline should include the questions you plan to ask to generate input.

Once you're satisfied with the placement and content of your support materials, identify the best format in which to craft them and spend the time to create them. Make them visually appealing and consistent with the brand you want to convey. If you embed hyperlinks within digital documents, use a URL shortener (like bitly or tinyURL) and test that all of the links are working.

To protect your formatting, it is a good practice to convert the support materials into PDFs before printing or digitally distributing them.

Presentation Visuals

In the case of a presentation, the adage about a picture being worth a thousand words is true. Visual materials include graphs or other representations of data, photos that emphasize key points or examples, screen shots, and graphics or icons that capture or reinforce process flows or ideas.

Referring to your outline, identify where visual elements could support your audience's understanding of key points or content. Then determine which you will need to create or locate and follow through.

Caution

Not all information, photos, and graphics that reside on the internet are available for distribution without permission, credit, or a fee. Review the site's terms of use and be certain to comply with them to avoid potential copyright law infractions.

Presentation Deck

You have your support materials and your visual elements in hand. Now, it's time to craft your presentation deck, if you plan to use one.

Many in-person and online presentations make use of software, such as PowerPoint and Prezi, to display visuals and key ideas.

Effective presentation decks can take many forms. The best are created to allow for flexibility during delivery and are primarily visual in nature. They become less useful when they can be used only in a linear way, progressing slide by slide through the deck, or when the slides are filled with text.

Myth: You should plan to present more content than you have time for.

Truly engaging presentations will never have extra time. Plan for exactly what you need to achieve your purpose, no more.

Myth: More slides are better.

Don't overdo the number of slides. Use the presentation deck to enhance your presentation not as a substitute for your role as presenter. You should be the center of the presentation, not your slides. In addition, the slides should not serve as a takeaway for the audience.

Emphasize Visual Elements

Text-heavy slides are boring, at best, and distracting, at worst. If you are presenting screen after screen of bullet points, for example, you will be tempted to simply read what's on the slide, leading to a dull presentation that lacks audience interaction. It also suggests that you don't know your content.

Note too that text slides can be distracting for your audience. They are more likely to read what's on the screen than to listen to what you're saying.

You should present only one major idea, point, or premise per slide, emphasizing a visual representation, rather than straight text. Compare the two slides in Figure 3-5. The first relies on text to present the details of the business problem, whereas the second presents a compelling image to show the drag the problem has on meeting targets and includes only two key phrases.

A

Our Business Problem
Analysis of our recent missed targets revealed:

- Slow response times
- Took three times longer than our targeted response time
- High error rate
- Significantly higher than last year: 20% higher
- 31% higher than our goal of < 6%

B

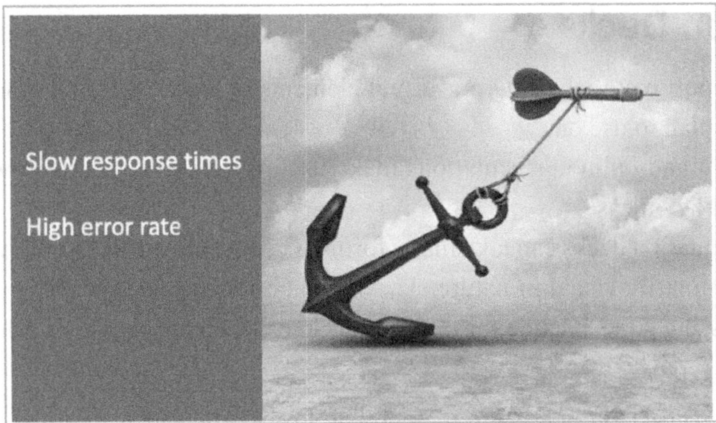

Figure 3-5 Text versus visual representation

Most presentation deck software includes the ability to capture details and notes that will be seen by only the presenter, like the percentages in Figure 3-5A, to make it easy for the presenter to reference.

In addition to the graphics you created earlier or other visual content you plan to embed, photographs can be used to reinforce your points, as in Figure 3-5B. Subscriptions to stock photography services are relatively inexpensive and will ensure you comply with copyright laws.

Many resources provide guidance about integrating compelling imagery into your presentation slides.

Pro tip
Within the presentation content, use hyperlinked icons or images to make it easy to jump to examples targeted to different audiences. The supplementary slides can be included in the presentation deck's appendix.

Building Flexibility into Your Presentation Deck

A flexible presentation deck makes it easy to adapt your presentation to different audiences. In addition, during an interactive presentation that's responsive to audience needs, such as during a sales presentation to a prospective client, you may find you need to adjust the order in which you present information.

Most presentation software doesn't lend itself to flexibility, but by using hyperlinks, you can build a responsive presentation that allows you to made adjustments easily during your delivery.

Figure 3-6 shows the first slide of a sales presentation. The thumbnail images depict the categories of information the presenter plans to address. Each of those images includes a hyperlink to the section of the deck that contains the relevant content, and each content slide includes a hyperlink back to this first slide. Essentially, the presentation is designed to operate as if it were a website, allowing the presenter to move freely throughout the presentation without being restricted by a linear format. The presenter can thus use the same deck to cater to diverse audiences.

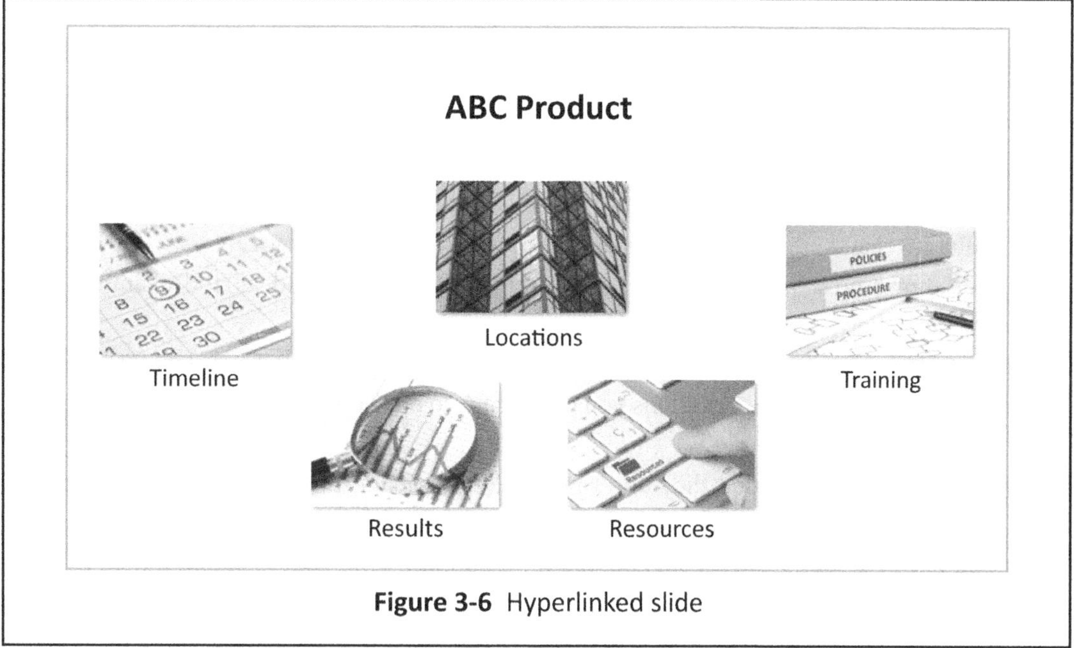

Figure 3-6 Hyperlinked slide

Talking Points

Once you've created the presentation slides, craft or refine your talking points. Working from your outline, align your key points with your visuals. Experienced presenters embed their thoughts into the notes function of the presentation software.

Regardless of the method you choose, start by planning a clear statement of your presentation's purpose. Why are you presenting this information, and why should your audience care? Remember to put this in terms that are meaningful from your audience's perspective.

Two frequently used methods for capturing talking points are scripting the presentation and creating bullet points of key content or ideas to cover. Each method has its pros and cons.

Scripting

Scripting is valuable for formalizing how you will articulate key ideas and transition from one to the other. For some people, capturing all of the nuances of the presentation in writing can help imprint important elements in their minds. It can also provide a sense of timing. By reading the script and timing yourself, you'll learn how long you need for the presenter-driven portion of the presentation.

The downside of scripting is that it can be restrictive. When a presentation is scripted, there's a temptation to read the script, which will sound exactly that way, as if you were simply reading to the audience. The script becomes a crutch for the presenter and locks the presenter to the presentation platform, leading to a less engaging delivery.

Last, with a script, there's little flexibility if an audience member asks a question or if the presenter wants to jump ahead.

Bullet Points

Bullet points are an alternative to scripting. They can provide support for key content points and transitions, while allowing the presenter to engage more fully with the audience.

Bullet points capture key ideas, quotes, statistics, references, and even questions to ask the audience. Crafting your talking points using bullets can help you plan the flow of the presentation, while allowing for easier editing than a script.

Rather than driving the presentation during delivery, the bullet points serve as prompts, providing reminders of content and transitions. They also allow you to prioritize your points, capturing key points at the first bullet level and supporting points at the secondary and tertiary levels.

Figure 3-7 shows how you could use bullet points for your main ideas and examples. Note the prompt for the next slide's topic.

Your bullet points could also contain page numbers or document titles of supplemental materials for the audience's reference and even questions you plan to ask to check audience understanding or to solicit their input.

The limitation of bullets is that they don't provide an indication of how long you will spend on a point. A single bullet in Figure 3-7 could take anywhere from thirty seconds to fifteen minutes to share. While you don't need to include all details in your notes, adding time notations throughout can help you refine your planning and will keep you on track during your delivery.

CUSTOMIZE AND PREPARE FOR DELIVERY

As you prepare to deliver your presentation, it's important to tailor and adapt your message and delivery to the specific audience's characteristics and to the circumstances surrounding the presentation. This includes making adjustments for the selected modality. For example, your delivery will be different if you'll be on a stage in front of a large auditorium, sitting at a conference room table with a few other people, or presenting virtually using a webcasting platform.

Practicing and updating your presentation and managing you own stress will set you up for success.

Our Business Problem

- Missed targets
- Analysis
  - Response times: 3× longer than targeted
  - Error rates
    - 20% higher than 2010
    - 31% higher than goal
      - Goal < 6%
- Client example—Susan's client missed her mortgage deadline because of our mistake and slow resolution
- Firm impact—reputation; social media complaints affecting sales
- *Transition*—exploring options to improve

Figure 3-7 Capturing key ideas using bullet points in the presenter notes

Practice Your Presentation

Practicing is the most frequently overlooked part of presentation preparation. After spending time with the content and customizing the presentation flow to the audience's needs, many presenters expect to show up and simply deliver what they've spent so much time planning.

Pro tip
While your intention will be to deliver all of your content, identify how you will handle real-life timing challenges that put you off schedule. Identify where and how you will abbreviate content or alter your delivery plans to finish on time while still achieving your presentation's purpose and intended outcomes.

Presentation practice serves several purposes. During your practice, you can identify gaps in your content, unnecessary details, or the need for additional audience interaction or even storytelling. It will validate your anticipated timing of your presentation. Practice also will help you identify style adjustments you can make to increase your credibility and ability to interact with the specific audience. Of course, practice increases your confidence in your ability to articulate what you had planned, which will help you manage any nervousness.

When practicing what you plan to say, be certain to include practicing with the technology you plan to use. This will help eliminate potential hiccups that can distract you during your presentation. If you don't have access to the actual presentation technology, work to replicate it for your practice sessions.

It can be helpful to record your practice sessions. Modern technology has made it possible to do this using your smartphone. These recordings will provide you with some good insight into how you sound and look as well as how well you articulate the content.

In addition to focusing on content during your practice, plan stylistic elements that can reinforce or detract from your presentation. Here are some suggestions:

- Tailor your presentation style to meet the audience's expectations.
- Speak in an energetic manner, using appropriate voice inflection.
- Maintain proper posture and use appropriate hand gestures.
- Manage your energy with movement and good body language.
- Use appropriate eye contact.
- Fully enunciate words.
- Avoid filler words, like *um*, *ah*, and *like*.

Pro tip
When presenting content with others, spend time practicing the handoffs and how you will interact with each other during the presentation. Define clearly how you will manage the nuances of co-presenting, like adding to or amending the other presenter's statements and addressing audience questions. Remember, your intention is to complement each other's delivery, not distract from the content or diminish the other's credibility.

If you are able to practice in front of a colleague or friend, have that person replicate audience behaviors to which you want to practice responding appropriately. For example the other person could bring up tangential issues or questions the audience could raise or engage in distracting behaviors, like side conversations or tapping a pen.

Augmented and virtual reality programs can help you practice. Some simulate an audience and its responses to your presentation, often indicating where you will need to adjust your presentation style to continue to engage the audience.

How much practice time is enough? A good general guideline is to set aside three hours to practice a one-hour presentation. If you are new to presenting this content or if the stakes for the presentation are high, you might want to spend additional time. In cases where you've presented this content before and have presented to this audience, you might spend less time. Still, don't let familiarity convince you to forgo practice.

The late Steve Jobs, CEO of Apple, famously practiced his keynote presentations for days before going on stage. Expert TED talk presenters share that they have practiced their eighteen-minute presentations up to two hundred times before going live. Your twenty-minute presentation to prepare your team for the new product rollout probably doesn't require that level of practice, but it does require practice to achieve your purpose.

Practice Stress Management

Regardless of how much we've practiced, many of us experience prepresentation jitters. These are our body's physiological responses to a perceived threat. Although these responses are ingrained, they can be managed through techniques such as deep breathing exercises, meditation, and mindfulness exercises. These techniques work for all kinds of stress.

Often, presentation stress is prompted by our worries that we will not be well received, either because we will make a mistake or because our audience will be unfriendly. Here are some additional techniques to help allay these concerns:

Pro tip

If technology is an important part of your presentation, have a contingency plan. Capture screen shots of an important website, download videos to your computer, create a portable backup file of your presentation, print your presentation slides, and/or arrange for a conference bridge as a backup to a video call.

- Memorize the first two minutes of your presentation. Fear responses are most prevalent during the first two minutes. If you can confidently recite your presentation introduction, your nerves will typically subside after that.
- Visualize a positive outcome. Imagine that, as you're presenting, your audience responds well, asking good questions and demonstrating welcoming body language.
- Recognize that the audience typically is more focused on the content than on you. You are simply a conduit for the information.
- Meet your audience members before you start your presentation. If they're unfamiliar to you, welcome some of them individually as they enter the room.
- Engage your audience early in the presentation with a simple question that requires a response.

Pro tip

We insert filler words when we need time to think. To eliminate these:

Slow down your rate of speech.

Pause instead of inserting a filler word.

Practice with someone who notes each time you use a filler word.

ENGAGE YOUR AUDIENCE

Earlier in your preparation process, you designed elements of your presentation for interacting with your audience. These included questions to prompt understanding and engagement. In addition to these, include questions that allow your audience to summarize key points. This can be an effective way to check their understanding.

For example, you can pause in your presentation and ask questions like these:

- Which of the three issues we've discussed are most important to the industry right now?
- What do you think is most important for customers to know about this change? Is this different from what employees need to know?

With a large audience, you can simplify the process by presenting a question and asking for a show of hands for agreement or disagreement. A show of hands can also signal their response to a multiple choice question.

Watch a sampling of TED talks to see how different presenters engage large audiences (www.TED.com).

One of the simplest ways to judge audience response and engagement is to observe them during your presentation. What does their body language signal? What are their facial expressions? If they seem disengaged, consider what you could do to involve them, like asking them a question.

Using good eye contact techniques can help with this. While you are presenting, select people at different places in the audience and speak directly to them, varying the person you're connecting with every minute or with each new idea or topic. Avoid settling on only one person for a long duration. Instead of seeming like a comfortable conversation, it can begin to feel awkward, and it reduces your opportunity to connect with other audience members.

Avoid the visual sweep, where you flit your eyes over the audience without connecting directly with any one person. With this tactic, you lose the ability to connect directly to different audience members.

In virtual settings, where the audience is in different locations, consider the need to incorporate additional audience interaction, so that participants stay engaged. If you are using technology that allows you to see the other participants, remember to look directly into your camera regularly, rather than only at the screen. This will create the impression that you are looking directly at the participants. It can be helpful to position the camera at the top of your screen and place key content nearby.

If you will not see your audience, make sure you welcome them by name as they log in and integrate many opportunities to ask ques-

Use technology to check the audience's understanding

Use mobile texting apps to have participants respond to multiple choice questions and project their answers on the screen.

Incorporate a simple tech-driven competition using an online learning game that allows you to customize questions. You can either select a few competitors or divide the audience into teams.

tions and to respond to questions via a chat function. Depending on the technology platform, you might also be able to ask the audience to contribute to whiteboards or to respond to polling questions on the screen.

When presenting virtually while seated, maintaining and projecting energy can be a challenge. You will often need to use only your voice to convey and generate interest and excitement, rather than your body language. Practice your voice inflection and volume to ensure you are projecting the right level of energy and using the correct tone to support your messages.

PRESENTATION PREPARATION WORKSHEET

The worksheet at the end of the chapter captures key questions to guide you during your planning and preparation process. Responding to the questions posed in the left column will help you systematically address key preparation elements and highlight where you need more information.

In situations when you will be co-presenting, completing the worksheet with your co-presenter(s) will ensure you are aligned about key presentation components. You can also share your responses to these questions with your manager, coach, or mentor to obtain feedback and suggestions and enhance your professional development.

• Conclusion •

The presentation preparation process enables you to design and deliver presentations with a clear purpose and flow of information, an appropriate amount of detail for your targeted audience, and a clear conclusion and next steps.

A well-designed and delivered presentation will engage your audience, promoting relevant questions, and fostering active participation in discussions, whether in person or virtually.

All of these elements will ensure you are credible, confident, and achieve your presentation's purpose.

Presentation Skills Worksheet

Presentation Purpose	
What do you want/need to accomplish with your presentation?	
What key elements do you want to include in your presentation development to help you achieve your purpose?	
What data or information do you need to obtain or gather, and what are reliable sources for this information?	
Are there specific examples you can include to help your audience connect with the data?	
What method(s) of development will best serve your purpose?	
Audience Profile	
Who will select the audience?	
Who must be there to accomplish your purpose?	
Who should *not* be there?	
What do you want to know about the audience? How will you find this information?	
What is the benefit of the presentation from your audience's perspective?	
What will you say in the invitation to set clear expectations for your audience?	
What questions do you anticipate? How do you plan to address these?	
Presentation Development	
What modality will you use and what capabilities are available?	

Presentation Skills Worksheet

Presentation Purpose	
What do you want/need to accomplish with your presentation?	
What key elements do you want to include in your presentation development to help you achieve your purpose?	
What data or information do you need to obtain or gather, and what are reliable sources for this information?	
Are there specific examples you can include to help your audience connect with the data?	
What method(s) of development will best serve your purpose?	
Audience Profile	
Who will select the audience?	
Who must be there to accomplish your purpose?	
Who should *not* be there?	
What do you want to know about the audience? How will you find this information?	
What is the benefit of the presentation from your audience's perspective?	
What will you say in the invitation to set clear expectations for your audience?	
What questions do you anticipate? How do you plan to address these?	

Presentation Development	
What modality will you use and what capabilities are available?	
How will you use these to enhance your presentation?	
What support materials do you need to integrate and prepare?	
Will you need permission to use some content?	
What visual aids or graphics will support key points? Will they be inserted into the presentation deck or into support materials?	
How will you build flexibility into your presentation deck, if applicable?	
How will you develop your talking points?	
Delivery Customization	
How and when will you practice and obtain feedback on your presentation delivery?	
How will you respond to distracting audience behavior?	
What technology do you need to familiarize yourself with and use during your practice?	
For items you identify as needing improvement, what is your plan for improving your skills?	
What stress management techniques will you use to manage nervousness during your delivery?	
Audience Engagement	
What questions will you use to engage the audience or check for understanding? How and when will you present these?	
How will you manage engagement if your session is virtual, considering tools available?	

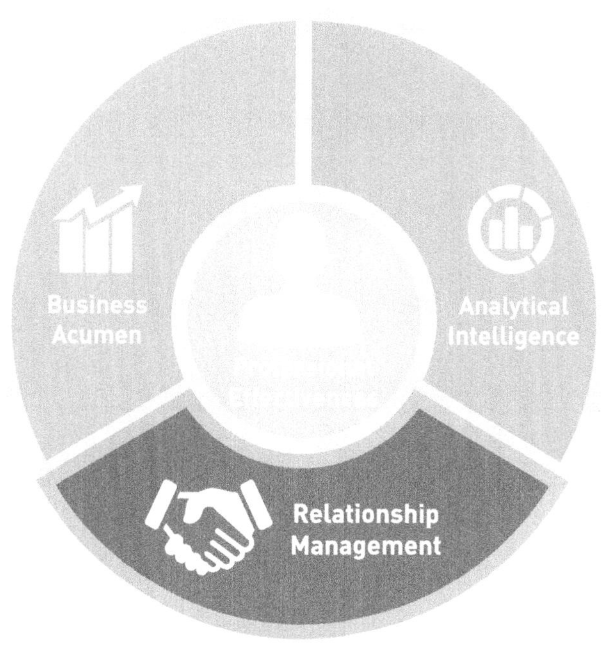

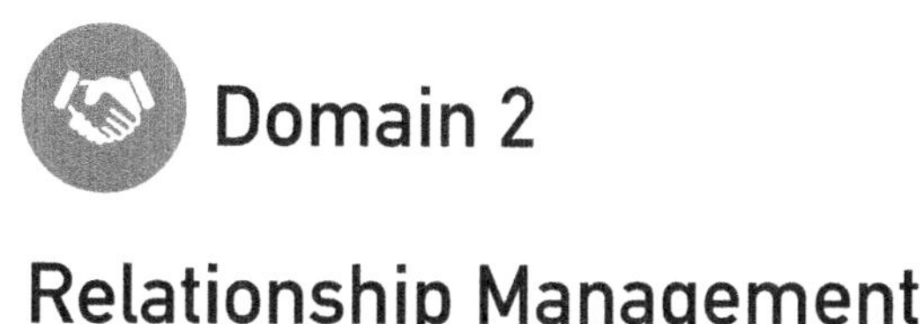

Domain 2

Relationship Management

Conflict Management

LEARNING OBJECTIVES

By the end of this chapter, you will be better equipped to:

- Understand the nature and root causes of conflict.
- Recognize how a manager's behaviors influence productive (or nonproductive) outcomes for conflict.
- Use best practices for managing workplace conflict.
- Understand why conflicts can escalate and how to put an escalation policy in place.
- Encourage others to manage conflict at the right level depending on the situation.
- Judge when a manager should reach out for assistance with managing conflict.
- Understand when having a conflict can be healthy.
- Choose which conflict resolution style to use in which situations.

INTRODUCTION

Take a moment to think about conflict. It's all around us. We see conflict in nature and in human nature. Conflict is what makes some of our favorite activities interesting. It's at the heart of movies, novels, television dramas, and plays; it's the essence of games and sports. On the other hand, most of us have had conflicts with co-workers, managers, vendor customers, or other stakeholders. As you know, conflict can escalate and do harm to a relationship. But it can also strengthen relationships, teams, and organizations. Conflict often leads to a resolution and consequently to a new state of affairs that's an improvement over the situation before the conflict began. Like it or not, conflict is a part of life. At times, we may wish to live in a world without it. But if you really think about it, you're likely to agree that the world is better off for it. The trick is to manage conflict, not to eliminate it.

Effective conflict management is the successful handling of conflict between individuals or groups. It helps foster creativity; improve relationships; and drive positive outcomes for you, your team, and the entire organization. Successful conflict management involves collecting information from all parties, identifying the root cause of the conflict, facilitating discussions and understanding, and developing possible solutions, ultimately obtaining buy-in from the affected parties.

Most workplace conflicts arise from one of two sources: escalating tensions between two individuals and group disagreements. In the former, typically two people are in a dispute over something they're unable to resolve through discussion. In the latter, two teams may see an issue from two vastly different perspectives and be unable to agree on a way forward, which threatens the organization's productivity. Either way, conflict management is a critical skill for managers because a successful resolution can make the difference between a functional and a dysfunctional work environment. Of course, not every disagreement becomes a conflict and not all conflicts require an intervention.

This chapter explores the common causes of conflict in the workplace, the different types of workplace conflict, whether a manager should step in, and how to manage conflicts effectively.

Workplace conflict is often viewed in a negative light. But when properly managed it can be beneficial for an organization and for the individuals who work there. Of course, some conflict is negative and unproductive. No one appreciates being called names, treated rudely, or disrespected. But there are plenty of healthy conflicts as well. Successful resolution requires openness and an ability to listen to ideas that seem counter to your own. That degree of openness requires team members to set aside their egos and avoid becoming defensive. The benefits of healthy conflict include learning about the diversity of thoughts, ideas, and opinions while creating team cohesion through creative problem solving.

Most workplaces include people from diverse backgrounds, with different needs and divergent ways of contributing to both the conflict and its resolution. Already, you can begin to see how conflict is unavoidable.

Many conflicts begin when one person feels there is a need for something and another person disagrees, saying either that there is no need at all or there is another need that must be met. Think about a time when you were in conflict with another individual and complete the developing conflict awareness chart shown in Figure 4-1. What were some of your needs? What were some of your contributions to the conflict? In other words, what did you do (or not do) and what did you say (or not say) that contributed to the conflict? For example, talking over someone so he can't express his point of view is a way to contribute to the conflict. Dismissing the other person's argument without questioning it or even listening to it is another way. Sometimes reacting sarcastically or mocking the other person's position contributes to the conflict because it insults the other person and may shut him down without offering anything constructive toward a resolution.

Myth: Whenever possible, conflict should be avoided.

Conflict can be healthy and productive, leading to increased understanding and a better workplace, but it must be managed properly.

My Needs	My Contributions to the Conflict

Figure 4-1 Developing conflict awareness

Of course, not all workplace conflict is productive. Unproductive conflict can negatively impact interactions among individual team members, and it can go beyond that, souring relationships across the organization, even among people who weren't involved in the original dispute. Productive conflict, on the other hand, can result in better communications, better relationships, improved work processes, and increased understanding.

Sometimes, the difference between an unproductive conflict and a productive one lies in how the manager handles it. Before we get into the specifics of conflict management, let's take a brief look at conflict in the historical context.

A HISTORICAL APPROACH TO CONFLICT MANAGEMENT IN THE WORKPLACE

The history of managing conflict in organizations revolves around the growth of industry, where the focus of conflict management was on identifying ways to mediate disagreements between organizations and their employees. Disputes were typically oriented around labor practices, workplace safety, pay, work hours, and benefits. Therefore, conflict management theories were targeted at negotiating compromises that allowed work to continue for the benefit of the organization.

Beyond strikes, walkouts, and other organized labor actions, we now recognize that conflicts derailing productivity take many forms, including interpersonal conflicts among employees, intrateam disagreements, and interteam disputes. Successful resolution is oriented as much toward understanding and collaborating on resolutions as on basic productivity measures.

American author and organizational psychologist Louis Pondy's 1967 model of organizational conflict describes latent conflict, which he defined as the "drive for autonomy," as forming the basis of a conflict "when one party either seeks to exercise control over some activity that another party regards as his own province or seeks to insulate itself from such control."[1]

If you think about workplace conflicts you have observed or participated in, this model may ring true. The tension arises out of a need for an individual or a group to seek autonomy around a project, a task, or the environment while another individual or group also seeks autonomy. Put simply, it sounds like a variation of:

"We do things this way."

"No, we do things *this* way."

MANAGING CONFLICTS: A STEP-BY-STEP PROCESS

Depending on the situation and who the conflicted parties are, a manager should be able to help resolve the conflict through a step-by-step process, as presented in Figure 4-2.

Each workplace conflict involves different personalities, situations, and risks to the organization. While there is no boilerplate for conflict management, managers should make a series of decisions and follow a set of steps. Depending on the degree of severity, you may need to act immediately by intervening and/or by escalating the situation, you may decide to wait a while before intervening, or you may conclude that the parties in conflict can and should work it out for themselves.

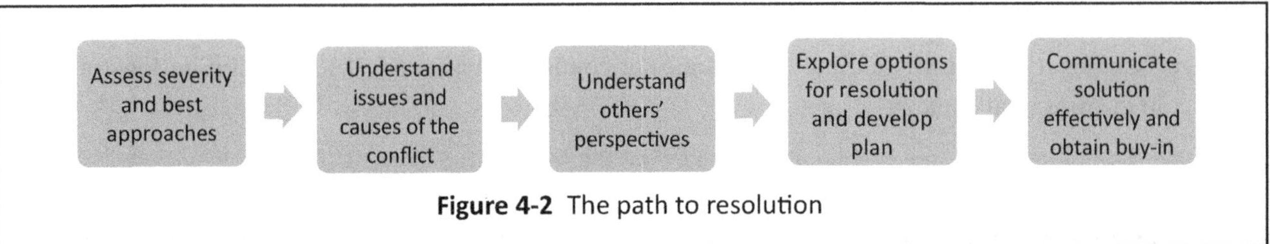

Figure 4-2 The path to resolution

Whatever the case, managers should take the following five steps to help determine the best way to manage a conflict.

Step 1: Assess the Severity and Best Approaches

As a manager, your role isn't to side immediately with either party, but to ask questions, to listen, and to get a sense of the situation. Asking questions is a constant throughout the process of conflict management.

Disagreement Versus Conflict

First, you'll need to determine whether you have a disagreement or a conflict on your hands. A typical disagreement involves a difference of opinion. A conflict usually involves action. For example, say an employee thinks a task should be performed a certain way, while her co-worker believes it should be performed another way. That's a disagreement. But when the first employee refuses to perform the task because her co-worker refuses to listen to her idea about how it should be done, that's a conflict.

If it's a disagreement, you'll need to decide whether to intervene or to let the parties work it out among themselves. The best way to tell a conflict from a disagreement is to listen. "I think the Yankees can win the World Series, and he thinks they're headed for the cellar" is a disagreement. "He praised the Yankees, so I threw his computer out the window," is a conflict (and certainly not a productive one). "Derek thinks we can handle a bigger workload, but I'm not so sure he's correct, so we're going to talk about it" is a disagreement. "Derek's a fool. He won't listen to anyone and I refuse to follow any of his instructions" is a conflict.

Productive Versus Unproductive

As previously described, there are two kinds of conflicts: productive and unproductive. If you are facing a conflict, which kind is it? In general, a well-managed productive conflict leads to a beneficial outcome; an unproductive conflict wastes time, resources, and energy and leads to more conflict if it's not resolved. An example of a productive conflict could be a dispute over how to achieve a goal. Say you're a manager for a leading website that offers information and education about automobiles. The head of technology wants to publish articles that are based on SEO research, targeting keywords that people use in their Internet searches. She argues that if people aren't searching for certain information about cars, then it's not worth publishing articles and blog posts containing that information. On the other hand, the head of editorial believes that by publishing such articles, the website is doing a public service. "Our job," he explains, "is to get relevant information out there. If we feel it's important to communicate, then readers will trust our authoritative voice."

The head of technology disagrees. "If no one is searching online for these keywords, then no one will even land on this article. It's not a good use of our resources."

Although neither party may feel it at the time, this is a healthy conflict that, if managed right, may lead to a solution that satisfies both individuals and helps the organization in achieving its mission of educating and informing the public.

An unproductive conflict, on the other hand, could be when two employees frequently bicker about minor issues that don't have much bearing on the organization's strategy or the team's direction. The issues over which they argue may seem petty to observers, but to the individuals in conflict, they're anything but petty. These squabbles can be stressful, distracting, alienating, and ultimately nonproductive. They tend to be more about personalities than organizational goals, more about personal attacks than professional differences. For example, say the head of technology and the head of editorial from the previous example just don't like each other. They say mean things behind the other's back, and sometimes their disagreements descend into name calling, which causes stress to everyone on both their teams. They don't cooperate, and it seems that they may even be trying to undermine each other's work. Here the issue isn't about the best way to deliver content to website visitors. In situations like this, no one may even know what the actual issue is. All they know is that these two don't like each other, and it's getting on everyone's nerves.

Pro tip
Successful conflict management begins with asking questions to help you understand the causes, issues, and the potential risks.

A manager should determine whether the conflict is productive or unproductive before taking steps to manage it. This determination also requires asking questions and listening to the answers. You'll need to assess the immediate and long-term risks associated with the conflict. In the automobile website example, the cause is evident: there's an honest disagreement between two professionals regarding the best way forward. If left unresolved, it could result in a perceived lack of direction; it may cause visitors to the website to be confused and dissatisfied with the content; it could even affect the organization's reputation. So, the productive conflict over content strategy needs to be resolved. Doing so will require a manager to take a series of steps. In the second example, where the root of the conflict is in a personal dispute, the immediate and long-term risks are also pretty obvious: The unproductive conflict could escalate to verbal abuse (or worse), low morale, and negativity, and not just between the two individuals but among all the members of their team.

When asking questions, don't stop after asking about the cause. Probe to learn about other forces that may be contributing to the conflict. Have the parties who are in conflict been in conflict before? If so, what was the earlier conflict about? Was it resolved? If so, how? If there was an earlier conflict that was not resolved, has it carried over into the current issue? What were the events that led to the conflict? Do either or both of the parties have a history of conflict with others in the organization? If so, don't judge, but do be aware.

Ask each party the same questions separately, so you can listen to each one's answers without the other party present. Think of each party's answers as his or her own story. Listen to each story and try to see where the conflict lies. Do they agree on what the actual issue is? If you think about past personal conflicts in your own life, you may recall that you and the other person have wildly different perspectives on the cause. Remember, you're still in listening mode. If you hear two different versions of the source of the conflict, don't correct one party or the other. Just listen and take notes so you can be sure that your memory is accurate after having heard both versions.

Here's a good rule of thumb for analyzing the situation: Once you have asked questions and elicited each party's perspective, you should be able to tell yourself two stories, each with a beginning, a middle, and an end. Since there's a conflict involved, each story should be different in one or more places. When you have a good grasp on each story, you're ready to begin managing the conflict.

By now, you should have a realistic understanding of how severe the conflict is. The answers to your questions may also have led you to know whether other things contributed to the conflict. In the example of productive conflict, the tech director and the editorial director are at loggerheads; try to determine if there any other factors may be at play. For example, each party could have a different incentive. The tech director may be driven toward the goal of producing evidence-based search engine optimization reports, while the editorial director is hoping that the website will win an award for producing quality content. If that's the case, you can see why there's a conflict. From the tech director's perspective, even if the site is winning prestigious awards, it might not be getting all the traffic it would be if its content strategy were driven by SEO results. And from the editorial director's perspective, every time he pitches an article, his nemesis over in tech shoots down the idea with the same old refrain: "We'll have to see what the SEO research says."

Scenario 1: Handling an Unproductive Conflict

No one in the office liked Pete, the new vice president of marketing and account services. He was a friend of Andrea's, the CEO of Phillips Industries a light manufacturing operation. Andrea had recruited Pete without telling her staff much about him. In the past, Andrea hadn't exactly sought her team's permission when she hired executives, but she usually introduced them to prospective hires and asked for their candid feedback. With Pete, it was different. He just showed up one day and began implementing a new marketing strategy that no one understood. Phillips is a conservative company in a small town. So, when Pete took out several billboards with unusual, flashy space age designs, employees grew nervous. Did Pete know the market? Did he understand the organization's clients and products? Previously, he had been marketing director at an e-commerce startup where his edgy ideas and colorful character were appreciated. He'd won a few awards for his original marketing campaigns. But now he was in a new town, working for a different kind of organization. There were whispers that the CEO had recruited Pete for personal reasons, not because he was the best fit.

One day at a team meeting, Robert, an account manager working under Pete challenged Pete on the elements of a marketing campaign. "Pete, do I understand this correctly? You want each account manager to handwrite and personalize seventy-five letters to prospects? This is cold calling. The list hasn't been vetted. You're asking us to do a whole lot of work for what historically promises minimal returns. Writing these letters will take a lot of hours. I don't think this is a good idea. It's not a good use of our time." The marketing team, which was gathered around the table, nodded and murmured in agreement.

Pete blew up. He stormed out of the conference room, pulling his phone from his pocket and calling Andrea, the CEO. "Fire Robert!" he demanded. "He disrespected me in front of the entire department. I can't work with him. Either he goes, or I go!"

Meanwhile, back in the conference room, Pete's team, feeling demoralized, talked among themselves about what they'd just witnessed.

"Pete won't listen to reason," said Steve, another account manager.

"What a thin skin," said Jill, a long-time marketing assistant. "All Robert tried to do was talk sense to him. He may be our boss, but he doesn't really know our business. You'd think he'd pay attention to us."

Robert had been working for Phillips for nearly twenty years. It was a close-knit organization. Andrea respected Robert and wasn't about to fire him. But she liked Pete too. He was creative and accomplished, though not very knowledgeable about the organization, its customers, or the team he oversaw.

Before Andrea even had a chance to respond, Pete made another call, this time to one of the company's major accounts, a parts supplier that had been working with Robert for over a decade. Pete maligned Robert to the director of the customer's purchasing department and promised that he personally would assume account management duties. If he didn't have the authority to fire Robert, he decided, he would demote him in the hope that Robert would leave Phillips on his own.

But Robert wasn't about to leave. He loved the company. And the rest of the team rallied around him.

After hearing Pete's complaint about Robert and Robert's complaint about Pete, Andrea knew she had to intervene.

Solution

If you were Andrea, what would you do?

First, she determined that the situation was a conflict, not a disagreement. It may have been a disagreement in the moments leading up to Pete's outburst in the conference room. But once he demanded Robert's head, and especially once he criticized Robert to a customer, Andrea knew she had a conflict on her hands.

It was easy for Andrea to determine that this was not only an unproductive conflict but a conflict in which she would have to intervene immediately. If not, the organization would lose people and its reputation would suffer. Andrea had to act fast.

Andrea invited Pete to her office. He arrived looking angry, still complaining about having been disrespected. Andrea was put off by his display of emotion, but she did her best to listen to Pete. Once she got his story, she sent Pete out and invited Robert to her office to give his version of events. The two stories had plenty of overlap. Pete had ordered his team to handwrite hundreds of cold call letters, which no one except for Pete believed was a good use of time. Both Pete and Robert agreed that Robert had questioned Pete's judgment. Pete insisted Robert had been trying to undermine him; Robert said he just wanted to register his displeasure at Pete's time-consuming, unproductive campaign. Andrea spoke to everyone else on the marketing team to get the full picture of what had just occurred.

After hearing everyone's story, Andrea arrived at an unavoidable conclusion: Pete's emotional outburst had been unwarranted and inappropriate. She thought about firing Pete, but he had just moved from another city to take this job, and he had shown great promise in his previous positions. So she put him on an action plan: He would enroll in an anger management program, join the local Chamber of Commerce, and spend an hour a day learning about the history of Phillips from long-time employees who knew more than he did about the company's background and culture. The anger management workshop, if successful, would help Pete work with his team without bullying individual team members. Joining the Chamber of Commerce would give him a healthy perspective of how business got done in the community. Learning about Phillips from veteran employees would show Pete how the company conducted business and, she hoped, smooth relations between Pete and his team.

Pete's action plan also included specific goals for learning to work with his team, how he would go after new business, and how he would communicate with customers. Finally, Andrea called the president of the client company that Pete had contacted. She apologized for the misunderstanding and assured him that it wouldn't happen again.

After which, she took Pete aside and explained, "The conflict was unproductive and hurtful. You made it personal. I appreciate your willingness to participate in an action plan, but I need you to know that if anything like this happens again, your job here will be in serious jeopardy."

Once you have completed your analysis and determined the severity of the conflict, you should begin to think about the best approach to manage it. Start by reviewing your notes and your memory of the discussions you had with the conflicted parties and with any others who may be affected by the conflict, such as team members and office mates. You'll find that by asking everyone involved similar questions, inconsistencies in one or more versions may appear. That doesn't necessarily mean that people are lying; it may simply mean that in an organization, as in day-to-day life, people see things from different perspectives and sometimes they remember events differently. Listening to everyone's perspective will always give you a better picture of what actually occurred and what the real issues are. If you interview six individuals separately, and each one provides a similar account, there's a high likelihood that their accounts are reliable. Look for holes and look for patterns. That's how you can get closer to the truth. Now that you have heard everyone's story, make every effort to verify. Are there any physical records to help you check out the different account? Is there a written document, a time sheet, a voice mail, or any other evidence? Even if other people's accounts verify what one person says, it's a good idea to seek out evidence if you can.

Use your best judgment to determine the level of severity. It may help to draw a 1 to 10 scale, with 1 being a low degree of severity, and 10 being a near emergency. How severe is the conflict? Could it affect the company's reputation? Could it lead to lawsuits? Might it escalate into violence? Could it result in people quitting? Is it bad for morale?

Step 2: Understanding the Issues and Causes of the Conflict

In Scenario 1, we saw the CEO needed to act fast because of the conflict's severity. But she still took time to understand the issue and its causes. As you can tell, the conflict began with a disagreement over a marketing strategy. It's helpful to understand that most people react to a conflict in one of three ways: fight, flight, or respond.

You've probably observed it in personal or workplace conflicts you have witnessed or been a part of. Some people tend to avoid conflicts altogether. That's a strategy that may or may not work, depending on the nature of the conflict and the other party. Some people, when thrust into a conflict, are inclined to fight. Perhaps they don't like being challenged or maybe they enjoy a good fight. Again, depending on the severity of the conflict, the potential risk to the organization, and the nature of the other parties involved, fighting it out can lead to a resolution. Obviously, not in a case like the preceding scenario. Fighting would likely have done damage to the organization. Finally, some people respond to a conflict without escalating it. If you're a parent, or you have observed parents with their children, you may be aware that sometimes when kids have a conflict, they are capable of resolving it themselves. That may be the best outcome because it leads naturally to increased understanding and improved relationships. The point is, the parent, the boss, or whoever is assigned to manage the conflict needs to understand these three reactions to conflict and make an appropriate decision about whether to intervene, and if so, how.

We can expand fight, flight, or respond into the Thomas-Kilmann conflict mode instrument:[2]

- Competing
- Collaborating
- Compromising
- Avoiding
- Accommodating

Think about times when you have observed each of these modes. In a business environment it's critical for a manager to use his or her business acumen to identify the mode of conflict as well as the root causes. What is being threatened by the conflict: workflow dependencies, organizational processes, or something else? And what is at risk and what are the stakes: the company's or department's reputation, people's jobs, or profitability? All of this must be considered. In addition, the corporate culture needs to be taken into account. What's the culture like in terms how conflicts are handled? Some firms encourage robust back and forth. Others discourage it. Some firms have a concrete set of accountabilities. In other words, if there is a conflict, everyone knows whose job it is to manage it; while other firms are less rigid. A manager usually has a good sense of the company's culture.

Another key point to consider: the relationship of the parties in conflict. Have they had conflicts before? If so, who managed it and what was the outcome? Have there been similar conflicts in the organization involving other parties? If so, how were those conflicts managed? If they were managed successfully, perhaps a similar approach in a new conflict would also lead to a successful result.

Pro tip

Set aside more time than you think you will need for your conversations. This will allow you to listen thoroughly and digest what's being said.

By now you should have a good sense of the conflict's scope so you can determine a time frame for resolution. Assuming that the situation is not a candidate for "knock it off" or "work it out among yourselves," you will need to intervene. As discussed, if it's an unproductive conflict that bears risk to the organization, act immediately. You should have enough information to make a plan. The plan should detail steps that will be taken toward a clearly articulated goal. The plan should also include a timeline.

In Scenario 2, Grant determined that the conflict between Noah and Juliet was productive. The two were friends, and they both wanted the same thing: for the company to grow and prosper. Their conflict was over how to make that happen. Grant determined that in the short run, the conflict would not lead to higher-than-usual turnover, low morale, a tarnished reputation, or lawsuits. But long-term, if unresolved it could lead to turnover, low morale, and dissatisfied clients. With the end of the quarter approaching, there was no reason to intervene immediately. Both Noah and Juliet were extra busy, the current workload was around fulfillment, and Noah wasn't presently signing new accounts or overpromising to anyone. Therefore, Grant decided to wait a few weeks until the new quarter.

Grant's proposed solution was to authorize overtime for reps and analysts who wanted it, which would enable the call center and the data group to turn reports around faster than before, although not fast enough so that Noah could continue to overpromise. As for Noah, Grant determined that he would explain the conditions and ask for a compromise. This way, Noah could still differentiate the organization when making his sales presentations, but he would promise only what he knew the teams could deliver. If Noah was unwilling to make that compromise, then Grant suspected he would need to escalate the conflict to the organization's finance department, which led the quota-setting process. But in conducting his research, Grant learned that Noah routinely surpassed his sales quota. So, the quota wasn't the problem. Noah would need to agree to a compromise. Now it was up to Grant to communicate to Noah exactly what each rep and what each analyst was responsible for and how, working at their capacity, they could not achieve what Noah had been promising. Also, Grant would need to communicate to Juliet how the sales team was motivated and compensated so that she could better understand Noah's position.

Scenario 2: Analyzing a Conflict

Noah is a sales representative for a company that conducts market research for a wide range of products and services. His role is to sign new clients, mostly manufacturers and service providers, who want to gauge customer satisfaction, gain insights into their marketing practices, and improve the quality of their offerings. The company employs market researchers who call consumers from a call center, marketing professionals who develop the surveys, and data analysts who produce reports.

Juliet is the company's call center supervisor. In that capacity, she oversees the reps who call consumers and conduct market research calls.

Noah is known as a super salesperson. Persuasive, gregarious, and ambitious, he puts in long hours working leads, making appointments, and selling the company's market research services. While Juliet appreciates Noah's drive and likes him as a person, she is becoming increasingly concerned about the expectations he is setting for prospective clients. Typically, it takes the data analysts three months to crunch the numbers and another few weeks to develop a report. Noah, she realizes, has been overpromising clients. Consequently, Juliet has received complaints from clients who obviously had unrealistic expectations about when the reports would be available to them.

One morning Juliet popped into Noah's office to inquire about the situation. "Noah," she began, "I really appreciate your efforts. You bring in more business than anyone else on the sales team. But I'm concerned that you're setting expectations we can't meet. We don't have the bandwidth, and we don't have the resources to complete all the surveys and produce the reports in six weeks. It's a twelve-week process. I'm wondering if you can take that into consideration when you talk with clients about timelines."

Noah listened. He seemed to get what Juliet was saying. But instead of agreeing, he pushed back. "We have more competition in the market than we did last year, I'm trying to make my number. Isn't there a way we can speed up the process on your end?"

Juliet shook her head. "Not without compromising quality, and no one wants that."

"True," said Noah. "But I've got to believe we can speed up with the resources that are on hand."

Unable to agree on the timeline for projects, Noah and Juliet approached Grant, the director of market research. Each presented their case to Grant. Noah wanted to differentiate the organization by turning around work faster than its competitors without sacrificing quality, and Juliet was not only cautious about overpromising clients but also concerned about morale among the call center representatives. "If they feel too much pressure, they'll seek employment elsewhere," she said.

"And if we can't produce those reports faster," said Noah, "they could be seeking work elsewhere for another reason!"

After the two left his office, Grant knew that this was a productive conflict. Neither Juliet nor Noah had said anything inappropriate, they weren't hurling insults at each other, and it was obvious that they both cared about the organization. They were friendly toward each other. But they disagreed vehemently.

Solution

If you were Grant, what would you do?

First, he called each party into his office for a one-on-one. He listened carefully to Juliet's complaint, stopping only to probe. He didn't judge. He listened. He got the whole story from her perspective. Her reps were feelings stressed, she said, because Noah had made promises to clients that the company couldn't deliver, not without hiring more reps and analysts, which wasn't in the budget.

Next, Grant spoke individually with Noah, who shared most of Juliet's opinions about the company. It was a great place to work, and everyone shared pride in their quality product. Listening to Noah, Grant understood his perspective as well as he'd understood Juliet's.

Grant knew that the two parties shared plenty of common ground. Neither was being unreasonable, but they were at an impasse. Noah was feeling pressure to make his annual sales quota, while Juliet was feeling pressure to produce work faster than she thought possible.

Because the conflict was productive, Grant didn't think he would need to escalate it to human resources, though he didn't rule out the possibility down the road of asking the organization's CFO to review the sales group's quota-setting methods. For now, he did his own study of the sales team's goals and of the research team's processes. Once he had all that laid out before him, he saw an opportunity for a compromise. He had the authority to grant overtime so that Juliet could add more resources without hiring new reps and analysts, which would still enable Noah to differentiate the organization to prospects. Juliet's team wouldn't be able to meet the expectations that Noah had set, but they could still out-deliver the competition.

But it was almost the end of the quarter, not an ideal time to effect changes. So, Grant scheduled another meeting with Juliet and Noah for three weeks later, when each would be feeling less pressure. In the meantime, he spoke with a couple of the market research representatives, an analyst, and a long-time member of the sales team so that he could hear their sides of the story.

With the issue analyzed, Grant's plan was to explore options for resolution, and he was confident that he could successfully manage this conflict.

Step 3: Understand Others' Perspectives

As you can see, regardless of whether a conflict is productive on unproductive, regardless of the degree of risk or the time frame in which the conflict should be resolved, there are a number of common elements involved in analyzing the situation and determining the best way to manage the conflict. Asking the right questions and listening to answers are key. This is a skill at which nearly anyone can gain competence. To be objective and nonjudgmental, be sure you ask all the parties to tell you the story from their own perspectives. You should interrupt their stories only to ask for clarification or to probe

Myth: When someone claims there's no need to talk about a conflict, you do not need to intervene.

Not everyone involved in a conflict wants to talk about it, and not every conflict requires intervention. But when an unresolved issue could affect an individual's emotional state, a team's morale, or the organization's mission, a manager will need to step in.

deeper into an element that you feel is important. Simply ask, "What happened?" And then listen. Probe by asking questions such as, "And then what happened?" or "Can you tell me more about that?"

For each conversation, establish and articulate a clear goal. "The purpose of this talk is for me to find out what actually happened. Once I have a good understanding, then we can talk about possible solutions." Also, be sure to set the terms of the conversation. "We're here to talk about what happened yesterday and what led up to it." With the scope clear, you can pull back if the individual's story gets too broad or too far away from the incident that you are there to discuss. "Okay, I understand that there is some dissatisfaction with the way the department runs, and we can discuss that at a later time. Now, however, I just want to hear about what happened yesterday." This will help you keep the conversation on track.

Pro tip

Communicate the source of the conflict, the solution and its benefits, the timeframe for resolution, and the consequences of the conflict not being resolved.

Questioning skills can be developed with a bit of practice. Typically, when asking about what led to a conflict, it's better to ask open-ended questions than close-ended questions. "Do you like Janet?" is a closed-ended question. A simple yes or no will suffice, but that doesn't give you a lot to work with. "What are your feelings about Janet?" is an open-ended question that is more likely to reveal important points.

Ask questions that enable you to gather information, and take notes. For information gathering, you should use a combination of open- and closed-ended questions. "What time did this occur?" is a closed-ended question that may provide important information. "Tell me how the process was supposed to work" is an open-ended question that could lead to vital information as well. Bear in mind that you are listening to stories. So ask questions that help you gain a better idea of the story. Look for consistencies (and inconsistencies) among the different versions of the story.

Ask diagnostic questions that help you to determine the root cause of a conflict. Think about when you visit your physician. You may say, "Doc, I think I need a knee replacement." After all, your knee hurts and you know that your uncle had a knee replacement after complaining about knee pain. But your doctor will want to ask you a few questions and run some diagnostic tests before ordering an invasive procedure. "When did the pain start?" "Have you been doing any strenuous activities lately?" "Have you experienced this kind of pain before?" "On a scale of one to ten, what level of pain are you feeling?" Similarly, when analyzing a conflict, ask diagnostic questions to help you see the big picture.

Ask about both facts and feelings. "Can you give me a few examples of when Steve ignored your ideas?" "You say that Steve brushed you off during a team meeting. How did that make you feel?" And don't forget: People are entitled to their feelings, and different people will express different feelings about the very same things, but facts are facts. Listen for both.

Always take notes. In some cases, you will have a number of stories to bear in mind, and it may be weeks or even months before a plan to resolve the conflict is implemented. Taking notes is the best way to ensure you are keeping everyone's story straight. And even when you aren't listening to a lot of stories and there is a short time frame for the resolution, it's still imperative to take notes in case your recollection of events is challenged later or, in a worst-case scenario, the conflict escalates into a lawsuit. If you wind up getting deposed or required to provide courtroom testimony, you will definitely want to rely on written documentation.

Maintain an open mind and an objective stance. Watch your body language. Remember, you are there to listen, not to judge. Even if the story you are hearing sounds farfetched, now is not the time to express your doubts. You are gathering information, not making a determination about who's right and who's wrong. Be open, appear open, and listen.

Use the AEIOU model for managing and defusing tense situations:

- Acknowledge the other person/people.
- Express your concerns.
- Identify a proposal or plan to move forward.
- Outline the outcome you anticipate.
- Reach an understanding.

You may begin to see already that AEIOU is a good model for addressing other people's conflicts as well as your own.

Pro tip

Set ground rules for meetings with more than one person. These can help you maintain control of the conversation and ensure everyone is heard. Helpful ground rules include allowing others to finish speaking before responding, limiting distractions such as cell phones, and committing to the conversation.

Step 4: Explore Options and Develop a Plan

So far in this chapter we have looked at a number of workplace conflicts that are typical of situations that may exist between individuals and among groups. You've seen the importance of listening to others, understanding different perspectives, and working to achieve a desirable outcome. But there are times when a conflict reveals broader issues within the organization. Sometimes interdepartmental processes or a lack of accountability (or a perceived lack of it) may generate a conflict. While conflicts are at their root about one party wanting something and another party wanting something else, they don't always present that way. When conflicts arise because of an organizational deficiency, it may be time to sit down with a working group—top management, human resources, and all the relevant stakeholders—to manage conflict by establishing new policies, procedures, or symptoms. Say you observe the same conflict occurring among different parties at different times. This may be a good time to take a deep dive into the policies or conditions in the organization that are at the root.

In such a case, once you have identified the right people to be in the room, be sure to state the conflict clearly, describe how it has occurred repeatedly among different groups or individuals, and then invite the group to discuss the nature of these recurring conflicts, the potential causes, and the possible solutions. Encourage brainstorming. And just as you do when you manage a conflict, be sure to ask both open-ended and closed-ended questions, and then listen to the answers as the group brainstorms solutions.

Now you can begin to develop a plan to resolve issues that have led to conflicts, involving all parties in identifying causes and solutions to ensure buy-in to proposed resolutions. Again, just as when you are managing a conflict, it's most important to get buy-in from everyone involved. Be sure to begin these sessions by stating a clear goal. For example, "Our purpose is to develop a set of decision-making procedures that minimize conflict by ensuring that everyone has a voice, that those who are responsible for making decisions get buy-in from everyone who will be affected by those decisions, and that the new procedures are communicated throughout the organization."

Analysis in hand, you're ready to manage the conflict. If you have determined that the conflict is unproductive, you may want to consult with the organization's human resources department. Specifically, it's time to bring them in if:

- One or more of the parties has made a threat.
- One or more of the parties expresses fear of the other.
- The disagreement has escalated to hostility.
- Other members of the team have complained that the conflict is making them feel uncomfortable.
- One or more of the parties involved is talking about bringing a legal action against the other or against the organization.

There are plenty of unproductive conflicts that managers can and should attempt to manage on their own, but if you encounter any of the conditions that were just described, it's time to call human resources.

Many productive conflicts can be resolved by the manager. Depending on the severity and the potential risk, it may need to be escalated to a higher level of management. If the editorial director is threatening to quit over his disagreement with the head of tech, and neither of them report directly to you, you may want to bring their managers into the discussion. Be sure to present your analysis to their managers, so that they won't need to start at square one. Whether to escalate a conflict will depend on several factors, including:

- Your scope of responsibility
- The degree of intractability among the parties
- What's at stake for the organization

This is where you need to apply your best judgment. Assuming that this conflict is something you feel you can manage, then your next step is to determine the optimal timing for a resolution as well as the optimal approach. As we'll soon see, not every conflict needs to be handled immediately. A manager's job is to assess risk to the company in terms of legal exposure, turnover, and damaged reputation. If it's evident that there is an immediate risk, immediate action should be taken.

Let's say you become aware of a conflict between two individuals that's personal. It began with a disagreement, then it escalated to taunts, name calling, and insults. An issue like this shouldn't fester. You'll need to deal with it immediately. The first thing to do is get as much information as possible. Next, determine whether the situation can be handled by a gentle but direct request to knock it off or if it needs to be escalated to human resources. Do you know the individuals? Have you worked with them before? Will they be responsive to your message? Is it possible they may be able to resolve this on their own? If so, then give them the opportunity to do just that. If not, but you feel there isn't a significant risk to the organization, then consider the "knock it off" approach.

The key concern, whether the conflict is productive or unproductive, is to analyze it before taking action.

Step 5: Communicate the Solution Effectively and Obtain Buy-In

When your plan for resolution is complete, you'll need to get all the parties to sign on. This requires clear and constant communication so all parties involved know what the plan is, what is required of them, and the timetable for rolling out the resolution. Getting buy-in and communicating the plan is pretty much the same whether you're facing a productive or an unproductive conflict and regardless of how detailed and complex the plan. Whether it's "knock it off" or "we're going to make a compromise," all parties need to understand what the solution looks like, how they will arrive at it, how long it will take, and—most important—how you arrived at it. What was your thinking? What's the rationale? People will be more likely to buy in to the solution if you have explained it clearly. They also need to know the consequences for failing to resolve the conflict and how a successful resolution will benefit all parties. In Scenario 2, the manager, Grant, would need to explain to Juliet, Noah, and the reps and analysts why his proposal makes sense, how he arrived at it, and why it's good for everyone. Remember, Grant's proposal of overtime for reps and analysts who want it calls for Noah to compromise and stop overpromising prospects. Grant may need to get down in the weeds with Noah and Juliet so that they can agree on a reasonable timetable for research and analysis.

In discussions with all involved parties, be sure to talk about the findings from your analysis. Describe the cause of the conflict as you see it. Then ask to make sure that everyone involved agrees on the cause. If not, hear out the dissenters. They may have a good point. The important thing is for everyone to agree on how the conflict got started.

Next, describe the solution. Talk about it in terms of how it addresses the root cause. For example, "The conflict we're facing comes from sales overpromising to clients, which places unrealistic expectations on the call center and the data analysts. The solution is twofold: I'm authorizing overtime for reps and analysts so we can deliver faster, and moving forward, sales and the call center will discuss reasonable expectations, which the sales team will use to project delivery dates for clients."

Discuss the benefits of this solution. "We should be able to differentiate ourselves among our competitors by delivering high-quality reports somewhat faster than the industry average because we'll have more resources to apply.

Ask for and get commitment to the solution. "Noah, let's hear your elevator pitch; tell me how you will talk about delivery time with clients and prospects. And Juliet, Let's hear how you'll talk about overtime opportunities with your team. Are you both committed to this plan? Will it work for you?"

Obviously, when two people are involved in a productive conflict, this process is likely to be smoother than when emotions are frayed, jobs and reputations are on the line, or the organization is exposed to possible legal action. But the steps are the same: Articulate the problem, explain your findings, describe the solution and how it addresses the root causes, talk about the benefits of the resolution, and get commitment from each party.

Last, consider the ways you will communicate your findings and your proposed solution. A Friday afternoon email may pass under too many people's radar. Not everyone reads their emails thoroughly. It's best to use multiple modalities of communication if you can. Send more than one email, discuss it in team meetings and in one-on-ones. Ask for feedback from everyone involved. Listen to their feedback because they may have good ideas and also because it will show you that your communication got through.

• Conclusion •

While some people believe that conflicts should be avoided at all costs, history has shown us that a conflict-free world is not feasible. What's more, conflict can be productive. It can lead to collaboration, understanding, motivation, and healthy competition. While some conflicts are unproductive, others are highly productive. And while each conflict is different because it involves different personalities, different situations, and different cultures, they also share many similarities.

Whatever the conflict, the manager can navigate a path to a solution by assessing the severity, understanding the issues and the perspectives of those involved, exploring options for resolution, communicating the solution, and getting buy-in. Some disputes can be resolved by the parties in conflict and might not need an intervention. Others will require intervention. Whether to intervene immediately or to wait for an optimum time depends on the degree of severity and the risk to the organization.

• Endnote •

1. Louis R. Pondy, "Organizational Conflict: Concepts and Models" *Administrative Science Quarterly* 12, no. 2 (1967): 296–320.
2. Kenneth Wayne Thomas and Ralph H. Kilmann, *Thomas-Kilmann Conflict Mode Instrument* (Mountain View, CA: CPP, Inc., 2007).

Motivation

LEARNING OBJECTIVES

By the end of this chapter, you will be better equipped to:

- Understand theories of motivation in modern psychology.
- Identify practices leading to motivation and demotivation in the workplace.
- Discuss why managers must understand what drives people to excel.
- Recognize the similarities and differences among employee motivators.
- Enhance employee motivation.
- Understand why other people might not be motivated by the same things that motivate you.
- Engage employees and understand what motivates them through conversation and regular feedback.
- Identify the myths and misunderstandings associated with employee motivation.

DEFINITION OF MOTIVATION

Motivation is made up of the internal and external factors that stimulate people's desire and energy to be continually interested in and committed to an activity, a job, a role, or a subject or to make an effort to attain a goal. When you're motivated, you know it. But knowing how to motivate others might not be as obvious.

As a successful manager who demonstrates proficiency in this competency, one crucial component of your role is to motivate people to perform well and to improve their performance (Figure 5-1).

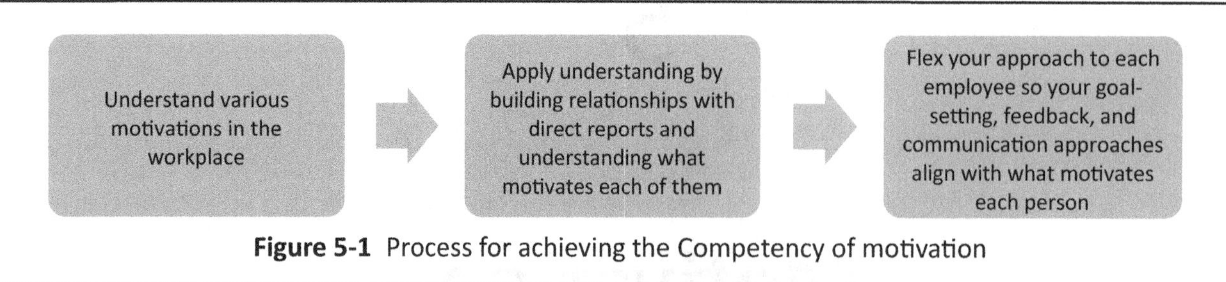

Figure 5-1 Process for achieving the Competency of motivation

To accomplish that, you will need to identify internal and external motivators based on *each* employee's personality, history, and preferences. Different things motivate different people. A manager's job involves knowing what, specifically, will motivate each of his or her reports. To motivate a team, a manager must align roles and developmental goals to create an individual strategy for each employee.

HOW OUR UNDERSTANDING OF MOTIVATION HAS EVOLVED THROUGH HISTORY

Psychologists have identified five types of theories for motivation. As you read about each type of theory, think about how it could apply to you and to your friends, colleagues, family, or employees. Don't look for a perfect fit, but look for tendencies, behaviors, and character traits that will help you understand how these theories could apply to people you know and to yourself.

Instinct Theories

Instincts are innate, unlearned behaviors. No one taught you how to scratch an itch. No one trains newborns how to suck. These are natural instincts. Theories in this category assume people are motivated to behave in particular ways because of human evolution. Behaviors that are likely to help us better adapt to our environment—to survive—are programmed in our species. In the early 1900s, American philosopher William James suggested one of the earliest instinct theories: that humans are characterized by instincts for attachment, play, shame, fear, anger, and love. Today, geneticists and neuroscientists continue to research and develop instinct theories such as the amygdala hijack theory,[1] which says, when people perceive a threat, they are motivated by an instinct for fighting, fleeing, or freezing. The theory suggests that when an individual perceives a threat, the amygdala (the part of the brain related to emotion) releases chemicals that fuel the fight, flee, or freeze impulse.

Incentive Theories

Incentive theories assert that individuals are motivated by the desire for an external reward as well as by the drive to avoid an external punishment. Psychologists such as Clark Hull initiated research in this area during the 1940s and 1950s. Incentive theories explore the significance for motivation of factors in an individual's external environment.

Most of us are familiar with Pavlov's dogs. Russian physiologist Ivan Pavlov became interested in dog behavior when he heard that dogs in the lab began to drool when they saw people wearing lab coats. The dogs, it turned out, associated the lab coats with being fed. This led to research in classical conditioning of instinctive behavior, such as salivating. (We should bear in mind, however, that while Pavlov's research has been critical for understanding incentive theories of motivation, no one is suggesting that employees are like dogs or that they should be trained through classical conditioning.) Later, psychologist B. F. Skinner introduced the term *operant conditioning* to describe the use of reward or punishment *after* an individual engages in a particular behavior to either encourage or discourage that behavior. The goal of operant conditioning is to trigger positive behavior from individuals by rewarding them every time they perform the behavior (positive reinforcement) or by removing a negative activity every time they perform the behavior (negative reinforcement). For example, if a child receives a hug for cleaning his or her bedroom, that's positive reinforcement. But say the child cleans his or her bedroom and is rewarded by not having to take out the trash. That's a negative reinforcement.

Myth: Employees respond consistently to Pavlovian training. Reward good behavior, and they'll always do it as long as you promise to reward them for it; punish bad behavior and they'll stop doing it as long as you threaten to punish them for it.

While Pavlov's experiments led to valuable insights about motivation, employees can't be effectively trained through classical conditioning alone.

Drive Theories

Drive theories assert that people are motivated, or *driven*, to undertake or avoid certain actions in order to resolve unmet physiological, emotional, or psychological needs. A simple example of a drive would be drinking a glass of water to quench your thirst. We all have physical needs (water, air, food, shelter) that we are internally driven to satisfy. We also have more complex needs, such as a need for human interaction and reassurance. Here's an example of a drive you may have observed in the workplace or in your day-to-day life: An individual attempts to resolve his or her unmet need for human interaction and reassurance by withholding information from another person in order to engage that other person in a conversation. That conversation isn't only a transfer of information but an opportunity for the first person to satisfy a drive to feel connected to and approved. Sigmund Freud posited that the two major drives for humans are sex and aggression. Subsequently, psychologists identified other human drives, such as the need for companionship, for approval, and for physical comfort. In each example, there is an internal tension that we are driven to resolve.

Arousal Theories

According to arousal theories, people are motivated to undertake or to avoid certain actions in order to increase or decrease levels of arousal—that is, the degree to which we are awake or attentive to what's happening around us. Most of us know someone we could describe as an adrenaline junkie. This cliché reflects arousal theories, which suggest that the person in question is constantly creating unnecessarily complicated and dramatic situations to receive a certain level of emotional excitement (often associated with the body's release of adrenaline in specific circumstances, such as riding a roller-coaster, skydiving, or narrowly escaping a mishap). Likewise, in a more sophisticated way, arousal theories explore the degree to which people create or avoid situations that increase or decrease their experience of intense emotions such as excitement, outrage, and fear. Early-twentieth-century psychologists Robert Yerkes and John Dodson sought to articulate a law of arousal, postulating that arousal, up to a certain point, enhanced performance of specific mental tasks, but past that point, arousal actually undermined cognitive performance. Think about when an athlete chokes under pressure, for example. That may be because he or she is overaroused. Or say you are given a repetitive, time-consuming, not personally rewarding, and not particularly stimulating task. Your attention may drift; you could feel yourself dosing off. That's an example of being underaroused. In that context, it's easy to see how motivation requires an appropriate level of arousal.

Humanistic Theories

Humanistic theories maintain that motivations are primarily cognitive, not instinctual or emotional. Motivations form in the brain's frontal cortex, not in the amygdala. According to these theories, motivation is not a matter of drive satisfaction, of instinctive pursuit of arousal, or of the avoidance of pain but of deliberation—sometimes conscious and intentional, other times intuitive, if not subconscious.

For example, say a scientist is doing important cancer research at a university or government center. One day, the scientist gets a call from a recruiter: a large pharmaceutical company is interested in employing her in its lab. The job would be more lucrative than the scientist's current position, but the work would involve developing drugs that would sell, not drugs that could one day treat rare forms of cancer. The researcher's spouse is advocating for the job while the rest of the family and friends are split. The researcher can't decide. But in a situation like this, it is evident that whatever decision she makes will be *cognitive*. It will be a binary choice: either A or B. This is neither fight-or-flight nor an automatic need to satisfy a drive.

Though perhaps tempered by intuition, unconscious inclinations, or personal feelings, motivation here is driven by thoughtful deliberation.

Pro tip

To motivate employees, collaborate with them. The simplistic carrot-and-stick approach disregards the fact that people are complex and motivated by different factors at different points in their lives. Reductive approaches to motivation can be offensive to employees, giving them the impression that managers are trying to manipulate them.

THREE CATEGORIES OF THEORIES IN ORGANIZATIONAL PSYCHOLOGY

Now that we've outlined the five types of theories of human motivation, let's narrow our focus and look at motivation through the lens of organizational psychology, sometimes known as industrial or occupational psychology. In this context, motivation is a dynamic process of the way an organization allocates its resources.[2] To better understand this concept, it helps to think of motivation as cyclical, not linear. Different things motivate us at different times in our lives. When your occupation is being a student, different things motivate you than later in life when your occupation is being a manager. Early in our careers, we are driven to achieve different goals than we are at mid-career or toward the end of our work lives. It would be unusual for a motivated individual to achieve what he or she set out for and then sit back and say: "Okay, well that was terrific. Now I am no longer motivated to do anything. So, I'll just sit here." Instead, once a goal is achieved, another goal arises, often quite different from the first goal and requiring different intellectual and emotional resources. In that context, indeed, motivation may be viewed as an allocation of resources. When you retire from the workforce, you are (we hope) still motivated, but the goals and the ways to achieve those goals are different. For instance, you may be motivated to get the most out of your retirement, which will probably require different resources than those that drove you in the workplace.

In organizational psychology, there are three major categories of theories around how we choose to allocate those resources.

Needs-Based Theories

Needs-based theories are generally of the incentive, drive, or arousal types. They assert that people's choices and behaviors reflect efforts to meet material and psychological needs. A theory of this type, well known in both popular culture and organizational psychology, is the *hierarchy of needs*, proposed by American psychologist Abraham Maslow. Maslow's theory may also be described as humanistic because of its focus on self-actualization—that is, our internal drive to fulfill our potential.

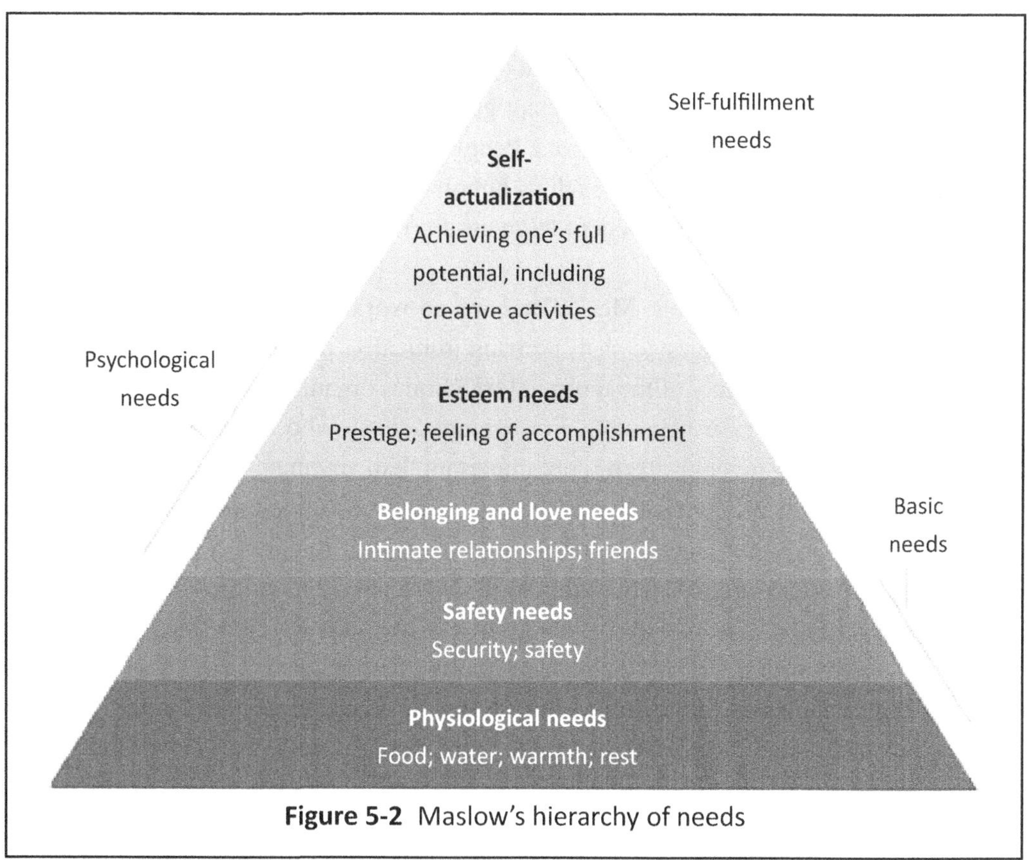

Figure 5-2 Maslow's hierarchy of needs

According to Maslow, all of us have needs, and our needs resemble a pyramid. At the lowest level are physiological needs for food, shelter, and clothing; at the highest level are cognitive needs for a coherent set of values by which to live, along with a theory of life's purpose and meaning (Figure 5-2).[3] In between are needs for security, love, belonging, and esteem. If an individual cannot meet the lower-level needs, he or she will not be able to meet the higher-lever needs. In other words, if you are worried about not having enough food to eat, you will likely not be able to reflect on the ultimate meaning of your life. According to Maslow's theory, people are driven first to meet subsistence-level needs for water, food, shelter, and clothing, and once these needs are met, they are driven to meet their more existential needs.[4] The theories of American management expert Ken Blanchard also incorporate a needs-based theory of motivation. His model of situational leadership assumes that individuals all have a need to develop in some aspect of their lives.[5]

Cognitive Choice Theories

Cognitive choice theories describe the mental processes involved in decision making and seek to account for the reasons an individual chooses one course of action over another. They parallel rational choice theory in classical economics, which assumes that individuals who are presented with enough information about costs, benefits, and the potential for risks and rewards will make a rational decision.

An influential cognitive choice theory, well known in organizational psychology, is the achievement motive theory, proposed by American psychologist Henry Murray and popularized by another American psychologist, David C. McClelland. According to Murray, the achievement motive is evident in individuals who undertake "intense, prolonged and repeated efforts to accomplish something difficult. To work with singleness of purpose toward a high and distant goal."[6] In other words, some individuals have a need to accomplish large, inherently valuable goals. People motivated by achievement, on this account, are not necessarily seeking personal success such as honors, awards, and promotions. Rather, they are seeking significant accomplishments that benefit large groups of people, such as their department, their organization, or their community.

In the book *The Achievement Motive*, McClelland and co-workers described the theory's relevance to organizational behavior.[7] He suggested that, perhaps ironically, people acting on the achievement motive may appear oblivious to many of the tools and techniques organizations have historically used to encourage and discourage particular behaviors. For example, those who are motivated by the need to achieve may feel that reaching a goal is itself more important than any material or financial reward they will receive for the achievement. They may not respond to praise or recognition because the personal satisfaction of having achieved the goal was all they were after. They might not even be concerned about their job security or their status with the organization. They are not driven to please their managers, but they are constantly seeking new, more effective and efficient methods for achieving goals. McClelland suggested that individuals with a strong achievement motive tended to make the best leaders because they subordinate their self-interest to the group interest. But this conclusion is debatable.

McClelland also postulated the affiliation motive, which is sort of the opposite of the achievement motive. People with a strong affiliation motive seek interpersonal relationships more than they seek goal achievement. Practically speaking, the two motivations are not quite opposites: Every individual may be motivated both by a desire for reaching goals and a desire for building interpersonal connections. But in work contexts, an individual may be driven more by one of these motivators than the other. People with a strong affiliation motive, for instance, may come to work mainly because they enjoy the interpersonal relationships they have there. For such individuals, the goal of the work is not as important as the opportunity to bond with colleagues while performing the work. Individuals with the affiliation motive can be diligent in their work, provided their desire to relate to others is fulfilled in the process. However, a strong affiliation motive does not necessarily express itself in behaviors such as doing more socializing than working. The affiliation motive expresses itself in behaviors of bonding with other people while getting the work done.

Self-Regulation: Metacognition Theories

Metacognition theories define motivation as "a self-governing cognitive mechanism that transforms motivational force into behavior *and* performance."[8] In other words, these theories attempt to identify the sources of phenomena such as determination. What makes an individual continue to work on a project or task when the goal becomes vague and the deliverable ambiguous? American psychologist E. Tory Higgins offers an answer in his theory of self-regulation: the promotion and prevention motives.[9]

Scenario 1: Strong Achievement Motive

Sam, a director at a consumer products company, has a strong achievement motive. He loves coming to work every morning; he is driven by the goal to protect consumers from counterfeit versions of his company's product. Sam's staff has a strong affiliation motive. They also love their work; they especially enjoy the relationships they have with one another as colleagues.

Initially, Sam didn't recognize that his reports had a strong affiliation motive. Indifferent to the positive, collegial ways they related to one another, he tried to rally them by appealing to department's goal of protecting consumers from counterfeit products. Continually articulating this goal didn't increase the employees' engagement or job satisfaction because they were not motivated by achieving abstract, overarching goals. Rather, relating to one another while doing their work is what motivated them.

Sam was frustrated that his team, while happy at work and quite productive, didn't seem to share his singular goal. They struck him as more loyal to one another than they were to the public.

If you were Sam, what would you do?

During routine feedback conversations, Sam kept an open mind. As he listened, he learned that what motivated him did not motivate his direct reports. He realized that his employees had a strong affiliation motive, while he had a strong achievement motive. With that realization, he took a different approach with his staff. He planned fellowship events—community service projects and recreational activities outside of work. This increased the opportunity for employees to connect with one another. He also started every workday by having a brief, socially oriented conversation with each employee. This relationship-building effort was a direct appeal to the employees' desire to affiliate with him. Once Sam began to appeal to their desire for affiliation, their engagement and satisfaction increased.

Myth: Everyone appreciates public accolades.

An individual who is introverted may prefer a private conversation to public accolades. Moreover, the need for appreciation is only one of many intrinsic motivators, and it may not be a primary motivator for every employee.

Promotion in this context does not refer to an individual's desire to be promoted within an organization. Rather, it refers to the degree to which an individual is willing to take risks to test a new idea, innovate, or accomplish a goal. An individual with a strong promotion motive might say, "One good new idea is worth a hundred mistakes." Individuals with a strong promotion motive may be described as tolerant of risk. On the other hand, people with a strong prevention motive may be described as intolerant of risk or averse to mistakes. An individual with a strong prevention motive might say, "It is better to do the same thing the same way, rather than risk making a mistake trying something new." While these motives appear to counteract each other, having employees possessed of both motivations is important for organizations, which must balance change with stability.

Recognizing the difference between the two motivators, and identifying which employees have a strong promotion motive and which have a strong prevention motive, can be useful for managers in keeping a diverse population of employees engaged in their work.

The Role of Self-Efficacy

American psychologist Alfred Bandura developed the concept of self-efficacy.[10] It refers to an individual's sense of being capable of performing a task and reaching a goal. It is related to confidence. Individuals who doubt their self-efficacy to perform a particular task lack confidence in their ability and thus might not even try to do the task.

The sense of self-efficacy is not a motivator per se, but it nonetheless bears on people's behavior, sometimes mitigating their motivation. For example, say you have a drive or a need to improve a particular process in your organization. But unfortunately, you also sense that you lack the capacity to design or implement the improvement. That is, you doubt your own efficacy, which could undermine your motivation. Practically speaking, managers need not only to understand what motivates different employees but also to create circumstances in which employees have the self-confidence to act on their motivations.

Pro tip

Apply your cultural awareness to help understand motivation. For example, in certain cultures, public recognition is viewed as disrespectful. In that context, a monthly group birthday celebration could be embarrassing, not affirming.

Intrinsic Motivators, Extrinsic Motivators, Discretionary Effort, and Engagement

While human resources professionals and management trainers may know of the theories just outlined, they often refer to them differently, using the terms such as *intrinsic motivators*, *extrinsic motivators*, and *discretionary effort*.

Many of these theories may be referred to as "theories of intrinsic motivation." They describe nonmaterial things that motivate individuals, such as achievement, the need for a coherent system of

Scenario 2: Innovation versus Prevention

Catherine is a manager who left an R&D department to work for a public agency. Possessing a strong promotion motive, Catherine loves to experiment. In a work environment, she is comfortable making mistakes and being wrong, as long as a good idea or innovation results.

When she arrived at the public agency, she was surprised by her new reports. They struck her as overly cautious—even complacent and lazy. It seemed to her that they just wanted to do the same things over and over again, never taking any risks and never even making any changes to increase efficiency.

Concerned about what she was observing, Catherine diplomatically discussed her perceptions with her employees during their quarterly goal-alignment meetings. To her relief, she learned that her new reports were neither complacent nor lazy. Rather, they had a strong prevention motive: Given that they were stewards of public funds, they believed that they needed to be cautious in their work. Catherine was pleased to know that her reports were committed, ethical, and professional. But she also believed that they were capable of making some changes without risking the public's trust.

If you were Catherine, what would you do?

Once she became aware of this difference in motivation, she should try to strike a balance between the two: encourage her employees to risk trying some new things by assuring them that they would not be penalized for errors committed while trying to improve a process, reduce costs, or enhance services and that none of the changes would be putting the public trust in serious jeopardy.

values, self-improvement, responsibility, curiosity, and a desire to avoid risks. By contrast, extrinsic motivators are material things, such as salary, benefits, bonuses, and promotions. Most employees are motivated by both intrinsic and extrinsic motivators, although some research suggests that intrinsic motivators may be most effective in getting employees to give discretionary effort,[11] which may be described as an employee's willingness to go above and beyond what is specifically required by his or her role. Related to the concept of discretionary effort is the popular concept of employee engagement. Engagement may be defined as an employee's willingness to expend effort (diligence).

A good example of engagement is when you are working on a project you care about and you don't notice time passing. You look up at the clock, see that it's already four o'clock, and you wonder where the time went. Engaged employees give their discretionary effort. They don't need to be told to get to work because they're already invested emotionally, physically, and intellectually.

In some fields and industries, such as code writing and other creative endeavors, appealing to intrinsic motivators, such as needs for autonomy, mastery, and purpose, may be the most effective way to sustain employee engagement and elicit discretionary effort.[12]

Emerging Area of Research: Prosocial Motivation

Prosocial motivators are impulses of concern for the well-being of others. A desire to minimize deleterious environmental impacts, eradicate testing on animals, and end child labor are expressions of prosocial motivation. Psychologists debate the question of whether prosocial motivation is altruistic. Is concern for others

Myth: Behavior can be predicted, provided you have a sophisticated enough formula for statistical analysis and you use the right stimuli to promote certain actions and discourage other actions.

Data and analysis can help us understand behavior and may help us predict it as well, but human beings are complex and don't always behave rationally. Observation and regular two-way conversations can help reduce your margin of error.

purely selfless or is it actually egoistic? Do people who want to protect animals do so purely for the animals' benefit, or do they actually derive some personal pleasure from this pursuit? Researchers also debate the nature of prosocial motives: Are they cognitive choices, drives, or incentives?

Resolving these questions is not, however, essential for understanding the ways prosocial motivators may inform employee choices and behaviors. In recent decades, organizational psychologists have researched and demonstrated the reality that prosocial or other-regarding motivators are at play in work situations.[13] Employees are often motivated in their professional lives to benefit something besides themselves and their organizations; they are also interested in the environment, underserved communities, consumers, and so forth. Understanding the degree to which an employee is affected by prosocial motivators is as useful for a manager as understanding the degree to which an employee is affected by the achievement motive or the promotion motive.

MOTIVATION AND PERFORMANCE MANAGEMENT

Most of the performance management mechanisms that organizations use today—starting the evaluation period with goal setting, ending the period by reviewing progress toward goals, and ideally, having a number of goal-alignment conversations in between—are based on management by objectives (MBO), a theory developed in the 1950s and 1960s by American academic and researcher George S. Odiorne.

Odiorne describes MBO as:

> A continual process whereby superior and subordinate periodically identify common goals, define each individual's major areas of responsibility in terms of results expected of him, and use the agreed upon measures as guides for operating each department and for assessing the contribution of each.[14]

According to Odiorne, Peter Drucker, and other proponents of this theory, MBO is the opposite of managing by controlling and directing.[15]

In principle, MBO gives people the autonomy to work toward goals in ways they identify as best for their own areas of responsibility. All members of an organization share in planning and therefore are ultimately committed to actualizing the plan. MBO incorporates motivation into the performance planning process by maintaining that employees who help set their own goals are more motivated to achieve them—more so than are employees who are told what to do and how to do it.

American organizational psychologist Harry Levinson explains:

> to motivate people successfully, management must focus on the question, "How do we meet both individual and organizational requirements?" When we make assumptions about individual motivations and increase pressure based on them, we ignore the fact that people work to meet their own psychological needs. Commitment must derive from the individual's wishes to support the organization's goals. Self-motivation occurs when individual needs and organizational requirements converge. Successful management systems begin with the employee's objectives. The manager's task is to understand the employee's needs and then, with the employee, assess how well the organization can meet them.[16]

Pro tip
Develop a clear understanding of exactly what intrinsic and extrinsic motivators appeal to specific individuals, and then tailor your relationships with each individual accordingly.

A manager's understanding of what motivates each employee is crucial to the performance management process. Effective performance management requires a manager to articulate not only organizational goals but also the means by which progress toward those goals will be measured, in ways that appeal to an individual's personal motivators.

MANAGER BEHAVIORS TO ENHANCE MOTIVATIONAL CLIMATE

Managers use a number of techniques to recognize the types of work to which specific motivators are relevant. Keep in mind that individuals have different motivators; what motivates a twenty-year-old is likely different from what motivates a forty-year-old, not to mention that culture (both the individual's and the organization's) plays a role as do personal history, individual preferences, and a range of social dynamics. And yet, people still have plenty in common. Don't think of the following motivators as rules but as guidelines to help you better understand your team, tailor the motivational messages you deliver to the group and to individuals, and think about rewards.

Pro tip
Know your employees. They are sophisticated and perceptive and may have several types of motivation operating at once. (See Chapter 9, Coaching for Performance, and Chapter 14, Talent Management.)

Extrinsic and Intrinsic Motivators: Generational Differences

People in sales roles or routinized work, such as manufacturing or construction, may respond well to extrinsic motivators, such as raises or bonuses. People in roles that require creative problem solving, such as biomedical research or software engineering, may respond best to intrinsic motivators, such as the opportunity to acquire new skills or the intellectual satisfaction of solving a challenging puzzle. In-

Scenario 3: Laissez-Faire Management

Hannah is a new manager who, earlier in her career, was micromanaged by her first manager. Back then she promised herself that if and when she became a manager, she would never do this to her own direct reports. Consequently, when Hannah became a manager, she adopted a hands-off policy with her employees. She would delegate tasks and projects, but did not provide timelines, standards for success, background information related to the work, or instructions regarding any special techniques or knowledge needed to complete the assignments. Hannah felt that she was respecting her employees by allowing them to figure out these things for themselves. She viewed them as intelligent and self-confident, and she assumed they would respond best to being left alone, learning from their own successes and mistakes. She assumed they would resent her for providing additional information and instruction, perceiving such behavior as micromanaging.

After she completed her first quarterly alignment conversations with each employee, Hannah realized she was doing something wrong. Four of her seven direct reports were behind on their projects. In conversations they indicated that they were not sure what to do. It occurred to Hannah that she might be giving too little direction. Ironically, the employees who were lagging did not feel respected by her hands-off approach. They felt frustrated and let down. They wanted to give their best efforts, but they didn't have the know-how, skills, and resources they needed to complete their work.

If you were Hannah, what would you do?

To remedy the situation, Hannah recognized that she had to balance employees' need for autonomy with their need for clarity. Providing direction to a team member who needs additional knowledge or skill development is not micromanaging or disrespecting that employee's autonomy. It is providing a sense of purpose that is itself motivational.

dividuals in these roles may be more driven to attend a conference or to take on a new challenge than they are to get a raise or a bonus.

We can break down intrinsic and extrinsic motivations and look at them in the context of generational motivation. The Defense Technical Information Center examined motivational factors such as responsibilities, compensation, work environment, advancement potential, and free time. The results suggested that advancement potential and free time were rated the highest factors among Millennials compared to Generation Xers and baby boomers.[17] One implication of the study is that to motivate Millennials, managers should consider emphasizing the possibility for advancement and opportunities for free time more than stressing money. You can test this theory by having a few conversations with friends, family members, or acquaintances from each of these generations. Ask what motivates them. What do they tell you? While you shouldn't expect uniform responses, you may begin to see trends that validate these research findings. Again, we're not suggesting a cookie-cutter approach, but a way to think broadly about which motivators may apply to which of your reports. Although the inferences drawn from these recent studies require further research, managers should bear the suggestions in mind.

Similarly, results from two other studies suggest that Millennials, like Generation Xers, are motivated by basic needs, such as the desire for belonging, and that they seek self-actualization through challenging and meaningful work.[18]

Extrinsic and Intrinsic Motivators: Phases of Life

Someone in midlife, who is raising a family and anticipating many expenses, may respond more to extrinsic motivators, such as the possibility of promotion and pay raises.[19] On the other hand, an employee nearing retirement may respond more to intrinsic motivators, such as the opportunity to leave a lasting mark on an organization by taking a leading role in a strategically important initiative, serving in a mentoring role to younger employees, speaking at a conference, or using paid time off for community service.[20]

Scenario 4: From Individual Contributor to Manager

Barry, a new manager, found his first year in the role challenging. His company based his performance evaluation in part on the way his direct reports evaluated him. Unfortunately, Barry's direct reports universally said that he created an atmosphere of distrust, in which he insisted they do things exactly as he would do them and discouraged them from showing any initiative. They complained that they always had to wait for his directions before doing anything. They felt that his distrust created an atmosphere in which being idle was better than being mistaken.

Barry was surprised and saddened by his team's estimation of him. He knew he had struggled to transition from an individual contributor to a manager. And he understood that for him, getting results with and through others, rather than through his own completion of tasks, was stressful. But he hadn't anticipated that his stress would result in demotivated, distrustful employees.

If you were Barry, what would you do?

Barry worked with his director to remedy the situation. He soon realized that not only had he focused on his employees reaching their SMART goals but he also insisted that they complete their tasks exactly the way he would have.

Through conversations with his manager, Barry recognized he hadn't allowed his direct reports any autonomy or sense of mastery over their work. This, in turn, demotivated them, leading them to be passive and reactive, awaiting his instructions, rather than resilient and proactive, seeking to solve problems quickly, using their own reasoning and skills.

After his year-end review, Barry became alert to the difference between tracking task completion and goal achievement and directing employees with their specific work styles and habits in mind. When he learned to focus on the former, the engagement and satisfaction of the team increased dramatically during his second year as a manager.

UNDERSTANDING WHAT MOTIVATES EACH INDIVIDUAL

Now that we have covered the top theories of motivation and looked at them in the context of self-actualization in the workplace, let's look at ways that managers can decide on which motivators to use (individually or in combination) with individual employees.

Myth: Most people have one primary motivator; if you know what it is, then you can control their behavior.

Multiple factors lead a person to choose one course of action over another in a given situation; it can't be reduced to a simple set of variables.

Begin by developing a set of questions to provide insight on the needs and desires of the individual. Then conduct one-on-one meetings to gather information and confirm understanding. Questions should include:

- What part of your work do you find most meaningful and why?
- What are your personal goals at this point in your life?
- What is a professional accomplishment of which you are proud and why?
- How do you take in and process information (visual, aural, or written communication)?
- How do you like to be recognized for achievements?
- How do you like to receive difficult news and information?

By listening to employees' answers and thinking about the various kinds of motivators discussed in this chapter, you should begin to recognize that what motivates you may not motivate those who report to you. And you may also begin to see the best ways to motivate these individuals.

There is a truism in clinical counseling: We give other people the type of help we would want to receive ourselves (this is a version of the golden rule). While this point of view may be helpful in preventing us from actively harming others, it obscures the reality that what we want for ourselves might not be helpful or even desired by the people around us and that our efforts to help others may consequently be misdirected. This is true for motivation as well: We tend to assume that what motivates us must motivate the people around us. But, as we've discussed, that is not always the case. Even if one of your reports is close to your age and from a similar cultural and socioeconomic background, he or she may be driven by forces you have never even thought about. The best way to find out is to ask.

Be self-aware: Reflect on the ways your life experiences, phase of life, and generation inform what motivates you. But also be aware of the differences between you and others who come from similar backgrounds and are in similar points in their lives and careers. Assess the degree to which you are moved to achieve or affiliate, to promote or prevent. Consider what level of needs you are trying to meet for yourself (a need for security or a need for self-actualization). Analyze the degree to which prosocial motivators affect you. With this self-awareness, look at yourself in relation to your employees. Do the same things that motivate you motivate them? Most managers will find that they and their employees have some common motivators but also some significant differences. Pay attention to the differences, think about the different theories described in this chapter, and try to discern how to appeal to the motivators that work for others, even if you don't share them.

PRACTICING THE PRINCIPLES OF MANAGEMENT BY OBJECTIVES

Once you gain a solid understanding of what motivates each employee (both intrinsically and extrinsically), determine how to align the individual's motivators to her role and the goals the organization needs that person to accomplish. Next, write and review a clear role description. You can use the roles and responsibilities chart shown in Figure 5-3 as a tool to help clarify roles, which—in conjunction with the employee's answers to your questions about what motivates her—will help you align her daily work to her intrinsic and extrinsic motivators. Start by asking whether employees know what is expected of them.

- For an individual employee: "Do people know what they can expect from you?"
- For your team in general: "Do people know what is expected of each other?"

After the employee completes the form, review each individual's goals and performance outcomes; then you can begin to align them with the motivators you know will appeal to each person.

DETERMINING COMMUNICATION STRATEGY BASED ON WHAT MOTIVATES YOUR REPORTS

At this point, you should have a fairly good idea of the factors that are likely to motivate each member of your team. Now it's time to tailor your approach to communication. After all, not everyone prefers to communicate in the same way. Some like oral communication. Others prefer written communications that they can reread and integrate at their own pace. Some people are more visual and may prefer a graphic image. Not everyone will process a message the same way. There are people who need to hear or read a message more than once for it to get through. Others don't appreciate repetition and feel their intelligence isn't being respected. You can learn these individuals' tendencies through regular and ongoing observation, by asking them directly, or perhaps by consulting with other managers who have worked with members of your team. Once you have some understanding of each employee's intrinsic and extrinsic motivators, you can determine the best way to communicate (orally, in writing, publicly, privately) positive and corrective feedback, recognition, changes in goals, and so forth to each person.

Then, as you implement these individualized communication plans, ask each person for feedback on your approach—and adjust your approach as needed.

Myth: Motivating employees is mainly a matter of expressing appreciation through social events, such as monthly group birthday parties, and small gestures, such as surprise thank-you notes and holiday gifts.

While parties, thank-you notes, and gifts may be appreciated, there's little evidence to suggest they will motivate an unmotivated employee.

Your Job Responsibilities	Rank in terms of importance to your job (1 = most important)	The percentage of work time you *actually* devote to the responsibility	The percentage of time you feel you *should* devote to the responsibility	Does the responsibility fit your skill set? (1 = no, 2 = somewhat, 3 = yes)	Do you like doing this responsibility? (1 = no, 2 = somewhat, 3 = yes)
1.		%	%		
2.		%	%		
3.		%	%		
4.		%	%		
5.		%	%		
6.		%	%		
7.		%	%		

Figure 5-3 Role and Responsibilities

• Conclusion •

Motivation is what drives people to stay engaged, to perform well, and to strive to improve their performance. Different things motivate different people; what motivates you when you're at the beginning of your career is likely not the same thing that motivates you in midcareer, as you approach retirement, or after you retire from the workforce. What's more, the things that motivate one individual might not be the same things that motivate another. Never assume that bonus pay, a raise, or accolades will motivate a specific employee. Some people are motivated by money and some by public attention; others are motivated by flexible work schedules, autonomy, or the opportunity to learn. While cultural and generational factors play a role and may broadly indicate what tends to motivate people in one age group or from a particular culture, managers should take individual differences into account. The best way to learn what motivates employees is simply to ask them. Identifying the intrinsic and extrinsic motivators of an employee or a team is only part of the solution. Once a manager understands the team's motivators, the next step is to align those motivators with each employee's responsibilities and goals.

Psychologists have long been interested in understanding motivation. Over the years, many theories have emerged. While it's essential to learn about the fundamentals of these theories, realize there is no a one-size-fits-all solution to the challenge of how to motivate people. Instead of relying on one single theory of motivation, managers should keep multiple theories in mind, with the understanding that some parts of each will be valuable in gaining a general understanding of what drives people.

• Endnotes •

1. The phrase was originally coined by Daniel Goleman. See Daniel Goleman, *Emotional Intelligence: Why It Can Matter More than IQ* (New York: Bantam Books, 1995).
2. Ruth Kanfer, "Motivational Theory and Industrial and Organizational Psychology," in *Handbook of Organizational and Industrial Psychology*, ed. Marvin D. Dunnette and Leaetta M. Hough (Palo Alto, CA: Consulting Psychologist Press, 1990), p. 81.
3. Abraham H. Maslow, "A Theory of Human Motivation," *Psychological Review* 50, no. 4 (1943): 370–396.
4. cf. Abraham Maslow, *Motivation and Personality*, 3rd ed. (New York: Harper, 1987).
5. Paul Hersey and Kenneth H. Blanchard, *Management of Organizational Behavior: Utilizing Human Resources* (New Jersey: Prentice Hall, 1969); and Paul Hersey and Kenneth H. Blanchard, "Life Cycle Theory of Leadership," *Training and Development Journal* 23, no. 5 (1969): 26–34.
6. Henry A. Murray, *Explorations in Personality* (New York: Oxford University Press, 1938), p. 164.
7. David C. McClelland, John W. Atkinson, Russell A. Clark, and Edgar L. Lowell, *The Achievement Motive* (New York, Apple-ton-Century-Crofts, 1953).
8. Kanfer, "Motivational Theory," p. 82.
9. E. Tory Higgins, "How Self-Regulation Creates Distinct Values: The Case of Promotion and Prevention Decision Making," *Journal of Consumer Psychology* 12, no. 3 (2002): 177–191.
10. Alfred Bandura, "Self-Efficacy Mechanisms in Human Agency," *American Psychologist* 37, no. 2 (1982): 122–137.
11. Kenneth A. Kovach, "Employee Motivation: Addressing a Crucial Factor in Your Organization's Performance," *Employee Relations Today* 22, no. 2 (1995): 1–42.
12. See Daniel H. Pink, *Drive: The Surprising Truth About What Motivates Us* (New York: Riverhead Books, 2009).
13. See, for example, Adam M. Grant, "Putting Self-Interest out of Business? Contributions and Unanswered Questions from Use-Inspired Research on Prosocial Motivation," *Industrial and Organizational Psychology* 2 (2009): 94–98.
14. George S. Odiorne, *Management Decisions by Objectives* (Englewood Cliffs, NJ: Prentice-Hall, 1969).
15. See Mary Parker Follet, "The Giving of Orders," in *Scientific Foundations of Business Administration*, ed. Henry C. Metcalf and H. A. Overstreet (Baltimore: Williams & Wilkins, 1926), pp. 29–37. Follet asserts that effective management "is to depersonalize the giving of orders, to unite all concerned in a study of the situation, to discover the law of the situation, and obey that."
16. Harry Levinson, "Management by Whose Objectives?," *Harvard Business Review* 81, no. 1 (2003): 107–116, hbr.org/2003/01/management-by-whose-objectives.
17. Ian N. Barford and Patrick Thomas Hester, "Analysis of Generation Y Workforce Motivation Using Multiattribute Utility Theory," Defense Acquisition University, Fort Belvoir, VA, January 2011, apps.dtic.mil/dtic/tr/fulltext/u2/a535500.pdf.
18. Russell Calk and Angela Patrick, "Millennials through the Looking Glass: Workplace Motivating Factors," *Journal of Business Enquiry* 16, no. 2 (2017): 131–139; and Wendy A. Campione, "Corporate Offerings: Why Aren't Millennials Staying," *Journal of Applied Business and Economics* 17, no. 4 (2015): 60–75.
19. Ruth Kanfer and Philip L. Akerman, "Aging, Adult Development and Work Motivation," *Academy of Management Review* 29, no. 3 (2004): 440–458.
20. Kanfer and Akerman, "Aging."

6

Collaboration

LEARNING OBJECTIVES

By the end of this chapter, you will be better equipped to:

- Use the collaboration process in your everyday work.
- Identify roles and responsibilities that guide collaboration and recognize areas of ambiguity or conflict.
- Create the foundation of collaboration, which includes accountability and trust.
- Find the balance between assertion and cooperation and know when to use them.
- Seek feedback from employees and work teams as a key collaboration point.

When people connect and work together in an interactive, interdependent, unified, cooperative, and synergistic way to achieve a common goal, we call it collaboration. It's critical to the survival of any business. In fact, as organizations grow flatter, they rely less on traditional hierarchal structures and more on teams. And teamwork, by its nature, requires collaboration.

Collaboration competency rests on six foundations:

1. Techniques to develop a culture of accountability
2. Team agreement to guide everyone's commitment to collaboration
3. Ability to assess communication and behavioral strengths and weaknesses of team members
4. Communication with others in a way that keeps them focused on collaboration
5. Conflict management techniques to deal with disruptions in collaboration
6. Trust and relationship builders that encourage collaboration

You may have noticed that many people use the word *collaboration* to refer to getting along, compromising on use of resources, or not bringing up challenging issues. These references dilute the key concepts of collaboration. So far in this book, we have looked at communication, emotional intelligence, presentation skills, conflict management, and motivation. These disciplines are critical components of the collaborative process.

Effective collaboration is founded on principles of accountability, assertion and cooperation, honest feedback, and team dynamics. For example, consider a project team in your organization. What do you see? If that team is effective, people involved in that project understand the goal, have clarity around the role that each will take, and agree on a process rooted in quality and a commitment to use the team's diversity to make decisions. With so many variables, you may need to see some form of an agreement to keep the collaboration process on track.

As with any organizational process, there is a natural tension between collaboration and competition. This is normal and, in fact, you may have struggled with the balance between the two. However, this balance is achieved not by talking about it but by emphasizing collaboration, not competition. Your challenge in business today is not to yield to the short-term gains from competition but rather to concentrate on the long-term value of collaboration. That requires a methodology, a lens through which you can begin to look at your team, gain a deep understanding of its dynamics, and optimize its potential. It's especially important today, because many companies are beginning to evaluate managers based on their teams' collaborations.

EVOLUTION OF BUSINESS COLLABORATION

While collaboration is a skill increasingly needed at every level in an organization, a new definition is evolving: As organizations restructure themselves from hierarchical to matrix to various hybrid forms, collaboration no longer follows organizational boundaries or even logic. In the past, managers could restrict efforts and outcomes based on people's job descriptions. Now, however, they are being asked to move away from the limitations of the job description into undefined areas, meaning these areas are not defined in the job description but are based on the needs of the business.

Several factors contributed to this evolution. Downsizing provided the force to move competition into the background and collaboration into the forefront of organizational practices. The metric was no longer how many managerial functions you had, but rather how much value your functions added to the organization. This meant a switch to a development mind-set in which functions needed to grow organically together rather than in isolation.

Globalization

Globalization provides additional opportunities for collaboration. Diversity in culture, language, and relationships means more mindfulness about those elements that redefine collaboration. You are no longer working with a person in the next cubicle or office. You are now working with someone in a completely different time zone, with different cultural drivers. You might start conducting conference calls at odd hours at night. You follow leadership directives from owners of the business in different countries. You

Scenario 1: Collaborating in a Communication Company

A well-known communications company became a classic study in the transition to collaboration. After divestiture, it drove defined functions down into management layers, exceeding stated job descriptions and, by default, causing the combination of those defined functions to evolve into a new set of largely undefined functions. This caused ambiguity and confusion. Collaboration was the critical technique for dealing with these undefined functions. If you were an employee who understood collaboration and applied its principles, you could work with this new phenomenon and add value to the organization. But if you insisted on keeping your functions as defined in your job description, you most likely would have heard that your functions were no longer needed by the organization. For example, say your job description was to monitor the IT operations. But nothing in your job description described how to implement the constant changes to the IT operations or how to be on a team that needed your expertise for a four-month project. As you can see in Figure 6-1, your undefined activities zone would have interacted with other people's undefined activities zone. Without principles of collaboration in effect, things got done but at a questionable cost–benefit ratio. This issue was exacerbated when the organization said you would be asked to do even more activities in the undefined zone without additional compensation.

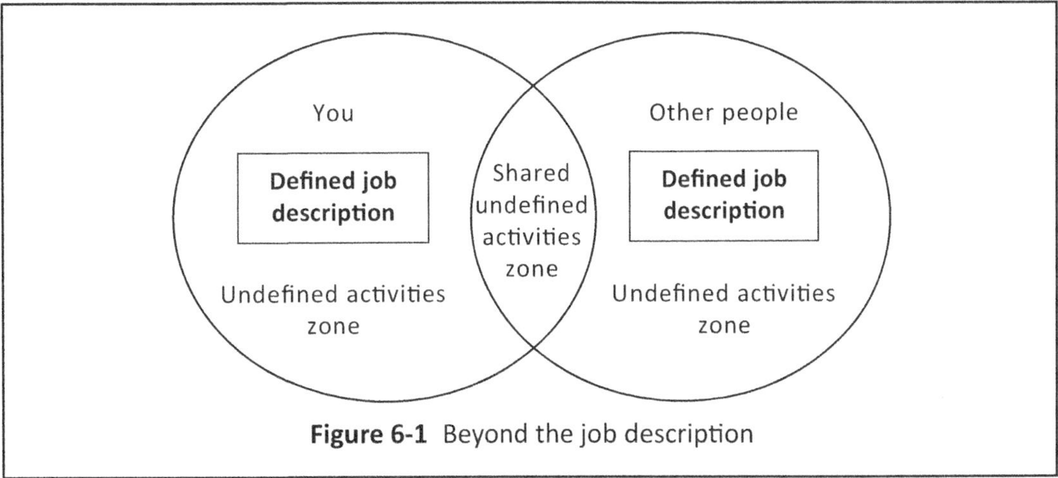

Figure 6-1 Beyond the job description

The company's downsizing added another pressure point that fostered collaboration and the need for efficiency gains. Your prescribed volume of outputs still counted, but the more important metric became your efficiency in producing those outputs. The norm became less budget, less head count, and more output. Under this directive, the length of your workday or strict adherence to scheduled work hours no longer counted. The new metric shifted the focus from what you did to how you did it. Collaboration provided the how. Even at the peer level within the organization, where competing goals often become a way of life, collaboration was needed to provide the agreement on a common goal and vision.

Pro tip
Technology without collaboration is just gathering and processing data. However, interpreting those data is a direct result of collaboration.

find yourself video conferencing or traveling to Milan, Paris, London, and Singapore for project meetings. You no longer follow a traditional way of doing things. Amid ambiguity and seemingly chaotic situations, you had to redefine *collaboration*.

The sharing of technical information and processes provides a baseline of reliance on each other rather than on one person. As technology evolves, you face significant increases in information sharing, in the complexity of problem solving and decision making, and in the need for teamwork. Today, technology pushes you to collaborate and work as a team. Without collaboration, you can easily become overwhelmed with data and be seen as ineffective when performing your functions. Collaboration helps prioritize information, use the strengths of each team member, and create significant value for the organization.

Work–Life Balance

In addition to the evolution of organizations, change in the work–life balance puts pressure on being collaborative. In the past, you understood the formula that success at work provided the ability to enjoy personal life. This was the work ethic for decades. But today, many of us want work and personal lives to be more in balance. Collaboration affords that balance by:

- Providing you and others with a voice on how to do the job
- Satisfying your personal goals during the execution of organizational goals
- Sharing roles and responsibilities
- Creating a platform of shared values with others

Today's framework of collaboration looks a lot like yesterday's. However, today's organizations are far more matrixed, and employees have far more fluidity in their roles, as shown in Table 6-1.

GOALS AND OUTCOMES FOR COLLABORATION

Achieving goals for collaboration starts with defining and understanding accountability. *Accountability* is your willingness to answer for the results you produce. It is an active process that requires behavior according to the five C's:

- Clear goals
- Choices
- Communication
- Commitment
- Connection

Table 6-1 Yesterday's Framework of Collaboration in Today's Translation	
Yesterday's Framework	**Today's Translation**
Challenging work	Creating new insights and ways of doing things provides for sustainability of effort
Development of skills and expertise	Working together helps leverage and grow the talents and skills of everyone involved
Proactive career management	Working well in the undefined areas shows the organization one's value when dealing with ambiguity and change
Equitable compensation	Equity is more than just extrinsic rewards
Work–life balance	Working with each other creates the base for finding ways for everyone to have the balance
Involvement in decision making	Inclusion in decisions is motivating
Critical questions: • Can I trust you? • Are you treating me with respect? • Is what I am doing making a difference?	Questions are part of the psychological agreement of working with others; a no to any of them provides the rationale for disengagement

The five C's encourage initiating discussions and contributing ideas that add value to the results. They mean seeking information and opinions to keep communication at the highest level, giving honest feedback, adjusting your communication and personal style to match the other person, and constantly evaluating how the collaboration is going (see also Chapter 9, Coaching for Performance, and Chapter 17, Style and Fit). The Five C's include knowing how to summarize what's being said and what's being decided, encouraging others to commit and participate, and working to solve problems using a diversity of ideas and views.

How can clear objectives and goals sustain a useful collaboration? The collaboration guide in Figure 6-2 is based on a partnership mind-set: treating and working with others as if they were your partners in getting results.

Although you may view this as tedious and time-consuming, it is important to realize that collaboration is not just a "let's work together" suggestion. It is a clearly laid out process to make certain that collaboration is achieved and, more important, sustained.

Defining Your Role in Collaboration

Key to your collaborative success is defining the role you need to take. In organizational dynamics, roles become the focal point of success or failure. After the goals are agreed to, if each person goes after them in an uncoordinated manner, chaos follows. So your next structural step should be to consider the logic of collaborating in the first place. To do that, think through the following five steps:

1. Explain the purpose of working together. Position it as a partnership in which all are committed to each other's success. Invite others to summarize their understanding of what has been agreed to.
2. Define how you and the others need and want to work together. Define the roles that each will need to take so the partnership can succeed.
3. Agree on how each item in the workflow needs to be done so your output can be a useful input into another person's workflow.
4. Clarify what success in the partnership will look like.
5. Keep checking with each other to make certain things are going in the right direction.

Figure 6-2 Guide for collaborating with others

Pro tip
Make certain your team understands what success looks like and that you acknowledge success when it occurs.

1. Show a clear reason for collaborating: "Here's why I think this should be a collaborative effort. Tell me what you think."
2. Describe how you see what collaboration will look like: "If we collaborate, the following will occur."
3. List possible negative consequences if collaboration doesn't work: "If we don't collaborate, this is what might happen."
4. Acknowledge and address possible objections: "I realize there are some things that can work against us."
5. Repeat your recommendation for an agreement and ask for feedback: "I strongly recommend that we follow this agreement."

When dealing with others in a collaborative effort, there are challenging roles that need to be exercised. These roles are defined through labels that have specific functions connected to them. They are:

- **Leader:** Assesses tasks and skills needed, creates the agreement, ensures that workflows are working and outputs are useful
- **Facilitator:** Ensures the effective functioning between the leader and others, keeps everyone talking
- **Recorder:** Manages the information needs of everyone, makes sure no one is out of the loop
- **Timekeeper:** Keeps everyone aware of priorities and deadlines, conducts crisp meetings
- **Opposition advocate:** Challenges positions, decisions, and reasons for doing things the usual way; keeps everyone out of group think
- **Observer/evaluator:** Provides honest feedback when needed
- **Coach:** Mentors others to be better than they are, finds strengths to build on
- **Logistician:** Handles the administrative tasks to keep the agreement alive

There are so many pressure points, because the manager often takes on several roles simultaneously, that we can easily lose sight of the value of collaboration. So make a deliberate effort to remember its value. Sometimes it's simply a matter of giving positive feedback or saying, "Thanks for helping out." It's essential to let others know that what they are doing is making a difference.

Scenario 2 illustrates communication, commitment, and connection from the five C's.

You may have worked with people who take energy away from others. Obstacles do occur, particularly when there are weak collaborators who take on counterproductive goals and roles. They tend to exhibit aggressive, emotional, and personalized disruptions. Often, they ignore others and will use off-putting body language. They will remain complacent; insisting on their high comfort zone while blaming everyone for mistakes and inefficiencies. They look for points of disagreement, not agreement. And they put self-interest above team interest.

How you handle these people is a test of your collaboration competency. Here are a few techniques to help you navigate the terrain:

Scenario 2: The Dysfunctional Team

Bob was the leader of a group of twelve salespeople responsible for selling sophisticated telecommunications equipment. His group, known for hitting their numbers, was from all outward appearances a well-oiled machine. But, in reality, it was not. The group had three factions: those close to Bob who supported him on everything, those who questioned Bob's decisions, and those who said little and went along with his decisions. The additional problem was that each of these three groups had their own informal leader to argue their positions at staff meetings.

Bob's competency was evident from his expertise but not his character. Everyone agreed that he knew more about the product line than even those in upper management. But he would belittle those who weren't producing or would make them a public example of what not to do. He would argue with those who didn't agree with him and would take exceptional time to question sales results and why people on his staff made their decisions. Even with his expertise, there was little trust between Bob and the majority of his staff. And there was even less trust among the three factions.

We'll get more into coaching in Chapter 9, Coaching for Performance, but for now imagine that you are brought in to coach Bob to become a more collaborative leader. You are tasked with creating a new process by which Bob respected his staff, the communications were adjusted, and integrity would take hold on his team.

What should you do?

Two key steps for coaching Bob are:

1. Schedule one-on-one sessions to unravel the intricacies of communication, particularly the negative impacts of Bob's style.
2. Coach employees on how to work with good results (using success as a teaching opportunity) and with setbacks (using delays as a learning opportunity).

Notice the areas of adjustment and improvement: communication, commitment, and connection.

- Look at disagreements not as conflicts, but just different positions.
- Don't take it personally; keep your emotions in check.
- Show empathy; acknowledge that you understand others' positions.
- Stay assertive and cooperative; this combination tends to help manage disagreements.

COLLABORATION STRUCTURE: THE WHAT, WHO, AND HOW OF WORKING TOGETHER

If you decide to take a collaborative approach to what you do day in and day out, consider certain structural issues. First, think about the *what*:

- Following a structured process to execute and achieve common goals and making no assumptions
- Finding ways to persuade others to get involved in your collaborative efforts
- Setting the example
- Teaching it, coaching it, asking partners to live it

Next, consider the *who*:

- Everyone and anyone working in an organization
- No distinction based on one's power base
- Various viewpoints from diverse people, willing to believe others may have a better perspective and understanding

Finally, think about the *how*:

- Outlining specific goals and results that add value to the organization
- Understanding each person's contribution and valuing it
- Looking for commonality in the organizational building blocks: goals, roles, processes, relationships
- Working the process of assertion and cooperation on each issue and knowing which to use and when
- Showing empathy and questioning and listening to see where others are coming from

This structural approach provides you with a number of advantages, such as getting more done in less time at a higher quality. You'll have more time to be proactive, and you'll likely face less stress and enjoy a better work–life balance. This approach provides an opportunity to expand your expertise bandwidth but can also bring a number of challenges: You may find yourself relying on others for results. It can also lead to group think, by which everyone feels like they have to play nice.

When you are faced with the challenges, sometimes the best starting point for reaching a collaboration agreement is by looking at what has not worked up to this point:

- What went wrong?
- What did I learn along the way?
- How did I add to the current reality?
- What could/should I have done?
- What can I do differently?

You may have noticed that that all of these questions tie into accountability. It takes a conscious effort to choose your level of accountability. That effort can be superficial or it can get to the core of accountability.

The next structural step builds on the bandwidth of your skills and abilities. If you intend to make collaboration work, you must have a set of skills like these, which, when woven together, create a significant platform from which a collaborative mind-set can be formed:

- **Communication:** Reaching an understanding not just transferring information
- **Emotional intelligence:** Balancing self-knowledge and social mastery
- **Conflict management:** Using the appropriate approach for the situation and balancing everyone's needs so they are addressed
- **Influence:** Persuading others to become engaged by laying out the logic and benefits of specific behaviors
- **Delegation:** Making delegation a development process
- **Coaching:** Finding ways to bring out the potential of others
- **Customer focus:** Viewing others in the organization as the end-users of one's outputs

COLLABORATORS' STANDARDS

The final structural step looks more deeply into the collaboration guide and to the dynamics of partnering when collaborators attempt to carry out the agreement. Some call it a code of conduct between collaborators.

In collaboration, there are two guidelines or principles that dictate the climate between collaborators: personal standards and organizational standards.

Personal Standards

Personal standards include your values and ask why you are motivated to partner with the other person. Is it a matter of claiming success or of *creating value*? The former is short term and sustains the accomplishment of your result. The latter is long term and positions you to sustain your results again and again. And isn't that what you need to do? It's not just accomplishing *your* goal, but everyone's goals. Value is created between parties, not claimed by either party.

Figure 6-3 is a worksheet to help you develop of a personal standard code of conduct or document of agreement to make this shift happen.

Organizational Standards

Organizational standards are more difficult to leverage. Often, they are mere talking points, not guides to behaviors. For example, many organizations promote core values but reward behaviors that run the opposite. Perhaps the best calibration of organization standards is to lock in on behaviors and decisions that add value to the organization and not to one's compensation package. This creates the need to consider your organization's culture.

	You	Collaborator(s)
What are our goals?	________	________
What do we need to do to get these deliverables?	________	________
When do we need the deliverables?	________	________
Which stakeholders do we need to work with to get them?	________	________
How will we measure whether the deliverables are what we expected?	________	________

Figure 6-3 Code of conduct or template for agreement

DIMENSIONS OF CULTURE

Organizational culture can have a profound impact on you whether you achieve collaboration or not. Culture has two layers, as demonstrated in Figure 6-4. Organizational cultures can vary from closed to strategic, entrepreneurial, dogmatic and open. If you take the impacts of any combinations of these cultures and add the need for accountability to them, you can get a sense of how hard it is to develop accountability in your personal sphere of influence.

If there are radical differences in the consistency of your thinking about accountability, it may be because the culture of your organization doesn't support accountability. If accountability were present, you and those you work with would see your joint reality, agree that everyone contributed to it, and together make choices to correct it. Unless you are willing to model these "reality" behaviors, then accountability will not evolve. Often collaborators need to move to a "subculture" mentality in their interactions. This doesn't mean going against the organizational culture—you have to work within that framework—but it does mean looking for opportunities to insert accountability into the way you deal with others and, if applicable, with your staff. What you put on the table is how people see your results, how people talk about you, and how people approach you. When a company is not strong on accountability, it is up to the project leaders or program leaders to take the initiative on their own and insert as much accountability as possible. It is about creating accountability steps in an organization that shows little interest in developing accountability.

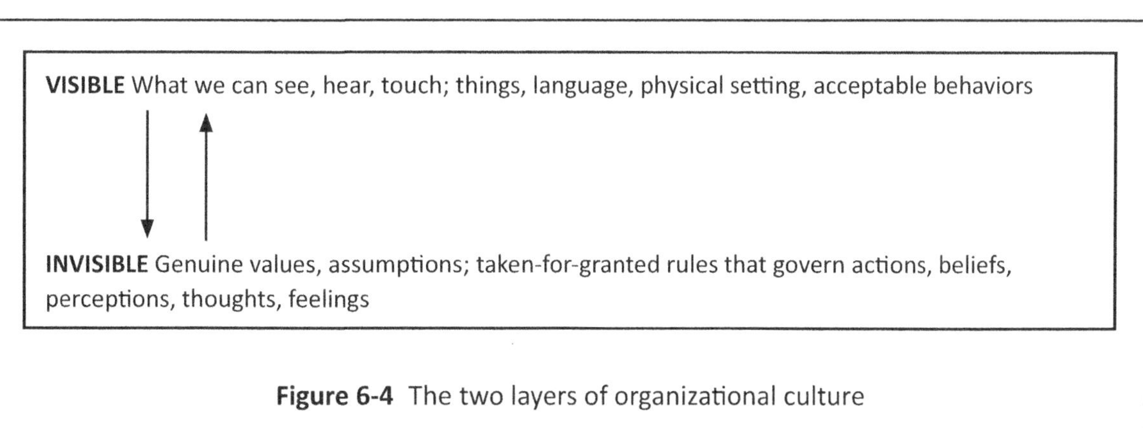

Figure 6-4 The two layers of organizational culture

One technique you may want to consider: Begin to view working with others or with your team in the ideal state. The concept of working toward an ideal organization is more than just a vision; it's a call to look at the reality of the human capital that you are working with or responsible for and looking for ways to grow and develop its core—that is, the talents and skills of each person. It means that you empower yourself to take advantage of these growth and development opportunities.

One simple way to gauge your abilities in this area is to conduct a brief strengths, weaknesses, opportunities, threats (SWOT) analysis of yourself in your current organization.

Think of yourself in your current position and organization. If you choose to take on collaboration and accountability, what is contributing to (or holding back) your success?

ACCOUNTABILITY FRAMEWORK

Any combination of collaboration and accountability starts with your mind-set and ends with behaviors.

SWOT Analysis

Internal		External	
Strengths	Weaknesses	Opportunities	Threats

Webster's defines *mind-set* as: "(1) a mental attitude; (2) a fixed state of mind." Both of these definitions are important when it comes to developing an accountability mind-set. Mental attitude reflects your emotional perspective on how your results are or will be accomplished. It is your reality calibration and produces either a closed or an open state of mind. A closed state of mind reflects your conclusion that things will not change or that you must continue doing things in a certain fashion, even if it doesn't make sense. In an open state of mind, you ask yourself, What if? Your answer will change the entire equation.

In addition to this defined mind-set, you have another that organically develops out of deep natural laws you and others have. It is a growth mind-set, which you might ignore but is essential for accountability and eventually collaboration. This one does not surface easily, particularly if your organization's culture is closed or dogmatic. In this mind-set, you look for ways to grow and develop your talents, not only to satisfy your needs but to develop your ability to add value to your organization and to people you work with. This mind-set lends itself to creating partnerships in all your projects.

This abundance mind-set says, "You and I are partners in running our part of the business. I will do whatever I can to help you be successful and I expect the same from you." It may sound utopian. But, so far, the fact is that the scarcity mind-set produces good companies but not great ones. Companies that have reached a level of greatness have done so through an abundance mind-set.

Myth: If someone refuses to partner in a project that requires collaboration, it's probably not worth the effort to recruit that person.

This is a scarcity mind-set. The principle you need to follow isn't about what you get back, but what you do to make the partnership work. It's a shift in mind-set that doesn't measure the value of collaboration in terms of what you receive from others but rather what you provide to make the partnership work.

As you saw in Figure 6-2, working together is not easy. It requires your commitment, but it also requires your accountability to keep that commitment. Workflows tend to be filled with tension, stress, and unrealistic deadlines that can easily affect the people flows. But work flows can be achieved when you do people flows well. People flow is treating others with respect, displaying a commitment to have them succeed, and letting them know they are making a difference. It is the interaction with others. Use the words *people flows* instead of *workflows*.

In the past, success in workflows got you raises and promotions. Today, success in people flows has become the measurement of success. Without your accountability to work collaboratively you will, by default, move toward a complete focus on workflows. This fosters a closed mind-set, which eventually dictates self-centered behaviors.

The guide to collaboration includes the words *explain, define, agree, clarify,* and *keep checking*. This vocabulary signals a proactive process in which specifics are defined while leaving room to work out details with each person. When partners are working together, each sees what will help the other and that becomes the principle. But partners tend not to limit themselves to assigned functions. Partners work with each other in mixing and matching their strengths and weaknesses in real time so all the dynamics of the partnership work.

STRENGTHS AND WEAKNESSES OF TEAM MEMBERS

You may have noticed that some people talk and behave more assertively than others. You may also have noticed that some people talk more about themselves and their reality or about how others are processing reality. On the other hand, you may notice others focusing only on the work that needs to get done. For some people, reality is connecting with those around them. For others it means producing and getting results.

You are constantly collecting data to do your job. Part of this data collection needs to include your perception of where you are in your approach and where others are in theirs. Understand that *assertiveness* and *focus* are dimensional and, most of the time, exist in combination. *Dimension* is another word for "style differences." It is used to reflect the fact that people have tendencies to use one or more styles, likely in combination. The word *tendencies* would work, but it short changes the intent behind defining styles. Each of us prefers our own dimensional combination based on our role and our personality, but we can flex them if and when needed. Sometimes the situation calls for a greater degree of assertiveness, for example, and other times it's best to step back. The key is to match your style with that of the other person to establish a partnership.

Pro tip

Often the biggest challenges to collaboration are the different styles that come into play. Be aware of the individual strengths and weaknesses that either help or hinder your collaborative efforts.

In general, the approach we take toward our jobs and in dealing with others suggests the dimensions in which we are likely to operate:

- Directors use a direct approach and focus on the job.
- Thinkers use an indirect approach by asking questions and focusing on the job.
- Talkers use a direct approach and primarily focus on their view of reality.
- Peacemakers use an indirect approach and focus on how others are dealing with their reality.

SITUATIONAL APPLICATIONS

No single dimensional approach is ideal. Each approach is important in certain situations. If you are going to collaborate effectively, you will need to become aware of dimensions and how to flex your approach to match that of the other person.

Use Table 6-2 to help organize your observations of people and their strengths and weaknesses.

Table 6-2 Four Dimensions of Behavior

Thinker	**Director**
Strengths • Ability to focus on high amounts of data • Ability to produce quality results • Ability to connect the dots	Strengths • Ability to get things done • Ability to keep everyone focused • Ability to accept risk
Weaknesses • Tendency to stay too long on data analysis • Tendency to ignore subtle people issues • Tendency to hold off on decision making	Weaknesses • Tendency to get impatient if results are not generated • Tendency to get uptight when time is being wasted • Tendency to control people and process
Peacemaker	**Talker**
Strengths • Ability to manage relationships better than most • Ability to downplay conflicts • Ability to read the nonverbal behaviors	Strengths • Ability to persuade and inspire • Ability to create • Ability to deal with change
Weaknesses • Tendency to be overly concerned about avoiding conflict • Tendency to be sensitive to feedback • Tendency to focus on relationships instead of on tasks	Weaknesses • Tendency to exaggerate • Tendency to go on gut feeling rather than logic and reason • Tendency to get impatient with data collection and analysis

Knowing how to listen and question is key. Managers who respond properly to a variety of styles have learned how to listen to and understand the perspective of the other person. Be mindful that the other person may have insight and a dimensional approach that are just as valuable as yours. The tension of asking effective questions and actively listening to the responses is proportional to the value you place on the information. High value means high questioning and close listening. Low value means marginal effort with these skills. In a partnership or collaborative effort, high value must be placed on all information that affects the process. It is imperative that all parties are on the same page.

The ability to give feedback is the capstone to the skills of observing, questioning, and listening. Effective feedback is specific, it's targeted on behavior, and it adds value to the other person. It builds on people's strengths, even in negative situations. Positive and corrective feedback is essential for collaboration and the execution of any agreement. Feedback must be delivered with respect, integrity, and empathy. It should add value to the other person and not come off as self-serving. Simply liking (or not) something the other person does is not justification for giving feedback. Justification occurs if you believe your feedback can build on a person's strengths or provide ways to minimize a weakness. You're adding value, not punishing.

Finally, the catalyst that starts the cycle of observing, listening, questioning, and giving feedback is your credibility, the combination of your expertise and character. Expertise refers to your knowledge base and your willingness to share that with others. Character refers to your principles of letting people know your intentions and working from a premise that your words and actions do and will match. Without credibility, the four skills have little impact. In fact, without credibility, others will interpret your collaborative efforts as self-serving.

GUIDING COLLABORATION THROUGH DISRUPTIVE TEAM DYNAMICS

The word *team* refers to two or more people working together. The principles of team dynamics are the DNA of every organization and collaborative team. The four elements of a working team are:

- Goals
- Roles
- Processes
- Relationships

These are the building blocks of collaboration, which you can fit together by following four steps. While collaboration should be the ultimate result of this process, there are often disruptions and concerns around each of the building blocks.

For example, if goals are not understood and agreed to, people gravitate toward achieving their own goals. If roles are not understood and agreed to, then turf battles ensue. If processes don't make sense, people create workarounds to get things done. And if relationships fall apart, people play the blame game or act like victims. All of these situations are real and can seriously undercut your ability to collaborate.

The steps to achieving collaboration involve turning the building blocks into actions:

1. **Set goals:** Be and stay inclusive; think in terms of possibilities; show interest and support for new ideas.
2. **Establish roles:** Identify how to work with others; conduct honest discussions on what each person needs to do so everyone is successful.
3. **Set processes:** Assert what you need; find out what the other person needs; be accountable; admit mistakes.
4. **Manage relationships:** Balance available strengths; respond to feedback.

All teams will face issues and concerns that can become obstacles to collaboration. Scenario 3 describes a situation in which obstacles have grown into disruption.

Once the organizational building blocks are in place, they need to be structured into collaboration. You will need to strategize your thinking. First get a clear understanding of why collaboration makes sense. Then find points where your skills and those of others can complement each other. Collaboration takes time. Allocate the time and make the effort to make collaboration work. Depending on the task, the organization and personalities involved, you may want to use the guide (Figure 6.2) to create a more formal collaboration agreement that each team member agrees to. You could distribute it via email.

Even with all the building blocks in place, you may face people who insist on a noncollaborative effort. Knowingly or not, they have a clear goal of disrupting and being obstacles to collaboration. Without assigning motive, non-collaborators behave in a number of ways:

- Skeptics or cynics don't trust anyone but themselves; they tear down anything that doesn't match with their view of the world.
- Hoarders keep all the information to themselves; they use information as a tool to maneuver themselves into the organizational spotlight.
- Solo artists prefer to do things by themselves and take all the positive recognition that comes with it while refusing to take responsibility for negative reactions.
- Narcissists are constantly justifying why they are better than others; they need applause and fear loss of image.
- Doormats give in quickly to go along; they never challenge or express what is really going on with them.
- Message killers feel like they have to top whatever is said; they control the interpretation of organizational and personal information.
- Pontificators think they know more than anyone else; they want others to believe that they have the highest level of expertise, and they take up all discussion time.

These disrupters tend to create "silo" thinking, cliques, group think, and hostile or aggressive battles. Much of these behaviors are verbalized and can be dealt with in a reasonable fashion. It's when they are not verbalized and become subtle behavioral patterns that they have significant negative impacts on you and your efforts to collaborate.

More than ever, fostering collaboration in these circumstances requires your best one-on-one communication skills. This means establishing a rapport, establishing a relationship platform on which communications can occur, finding common ground, and showing respect for the other person.

For example, skeptics or cynics may tear things down, but they do show passion for their beliefs; by respecting this slice of their behavior, you can begin the rapport-building process. Part of your preliminary discussion can include asking for the other person's help on a work issue or just expressing your appreciation for his or her involvement, even if, at this point, it still is somewhat negative. The key is to recognize the positive slice of behavior in neutral and nonjudgmental terms.

Above all, in these circumstances, collaboration means you will need a strong mental framework:

- Be an ally rather than an adversary.
- Focus on facts, not on assumptions.
- Be willing to ask how the other person sees things.
- Be able to restate the benefits of working collaboratively.
- Offer choices, not demands.

Myth: Disruptive people generally stick with just one disruptive behavior.

Unfortunately, they usually learn to combine disruptive behaviors and become a formidable obstacle to collaboration.

What if you have urgent deliverables and no time to build rapport and a long-term solution? Use one of the five approaches outlined in Figure 6-5. In this model, which is the combination of assertion and cooperation at both high and low scales, there is emphasis on assertion of what you need and cooperation with the other person so that he or she gets a need satisfied.

The context of this collaboration is not based on anything warm and fuzzy but on what you and others get paid to do: produce the deliverables. Clearly, the deciding factor on whether assertion and cooperation are high or low depends on what you believe needs to be accomplished.

THE KEY TO COLLABORATION

The essence of collaboration is agreeing that you have immediate deliverables and you will work with others to get what is needed. There will be times, however, when you have immediate deliverables and you will have to deal with cooperation at a later date. There are also times when you will need to put your issues aside and cooperate so that others get what they need to deliver. This is situational; be aware of which approach provides the most value. But no matter what situation, your mind-set is to achieve collaboration as much as possible. In this model, win–win is accomplished through strong assertion and cooperation on the part of everyone. Win–win is not limited to the "we work on ways so each of us have many deliverables." A win–win mind-set sees collaboration as the ultimate goal in all the quadrants, except for "Neither of us gets what we want." This is a more abundant interpretation of collaboration.

Scenario 3: Switching from a Work Group Structure to a Cross-Functional Team-Based Structure

About eight months ago, a company switched from a work group structure to a cross-functional team-based structure. A lot of people were moved into new working relationships. The entire process dictated that team members needed to work with one another more closely. In fact, many new relationships needed to be formed.

Jake, who has been with the company a long time, was recently reassigned to a large team from a small group in which he was an individual contributor. Because of his long tenure, he knew more than anyone else and often bragged about his knowledge and took advantage of it. In fact, he created his own shortcuts and avoided process requirements that interfered with how he thought things should be done. He usually kept the shortcuts to himself and became defensive if anyone challenged his methodology.

On three occasions over the past month, Paulina, one of Jake's team members, complained about Jake to Kerry, the team lead. According to Paulina, Jake wouldn't cooperate with her attempts to follow the processes as written. She also said that he never came to her with his process, which made difficult to coordinate results. Paulina, who has an MBA, is a recent hire and is concerned that people like Jake can be disruptive and prevent her from doing her job the way she believes it should be done.

This morning, Kerry asked Jake to talk about the situation. Before going to see Kerry, Jake catches Paulina in the hall and says, "Look. I know what this is all about. I know what's going on! You went to Kerry and complained about me. You should understand that I have been here a long time and I am the best in what I do. I was not hired to socialize with people, which you seem to like doing. And I am not about to coddle you and do your work for you. I don't appreciate you going behind my back and going to Kerry."

If you were in Kerry's position, what would you do?

Although there are many issues in this case, what stands out immediately is that both Jake and Paulina need to:

- Understand the goals of the team and why it was put together
- Appreciate that each takes on a different role and those differences add value to the team
- Get clarification on the process and why that process is important and in place
- Listen to feedback from each other

Kerry is aware that she may have to facilitate the sharing of feedback.

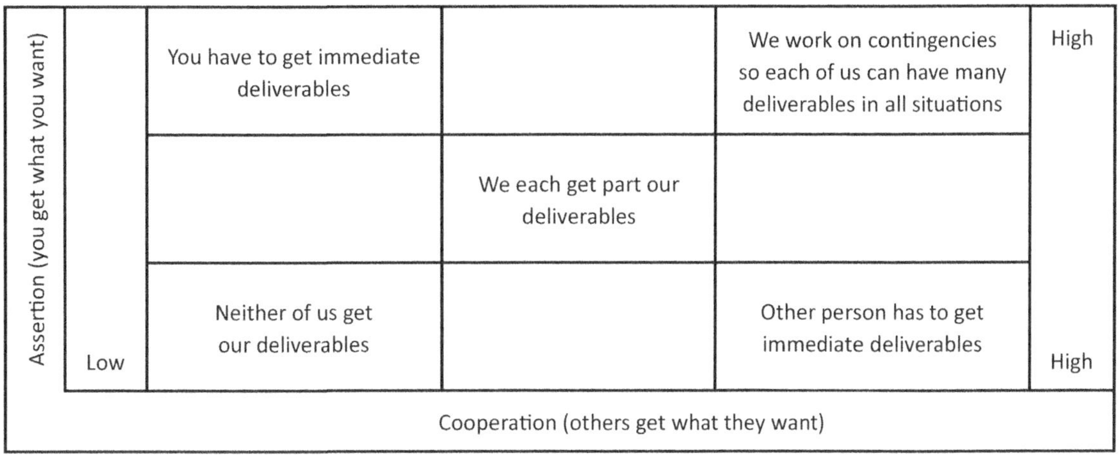

Assertion (you get what you want)					
		You have to get immediate deliverables		We work on contingencies so each of us can have many deliverables in all situations	High
			We each get part our deliverables		
	Low	Neither of us get our deliverables		Other person has to get immediate deliverables	High
	Cooperation (others get what they want)				

Figure 6-5 Five approaches for urgent collaboration

COLLABORATIVE TEAM COMMUNICATION

In a one-on-one situation, communication tends to reflect basic attributes of honesty, active listening, open-ended questioning, and disagreeing respectfully. However, in a group or team setting, things get more complicated.

First there is need for you to make certain the group or team communicates effectively. This means establishing rules ensuring everyone is involved; managing everyone's information needs; keeping track of priorities; and making certain that diverse viewpoints are encouraged, respected, presented, and understood.

Second, the challenge is to keep the group or team focused. There are several techniques you can use.

- **Brainstorming:** Freewheeling discussion; all ideas are valid; allowing a building of collective ideas and opinions that represent the group or team
- **Team huddle:** Allowing each person to speak, one at a time; round-robin discussion
- **Sticky notes:** Written notes posted on a flip chart; taking all the notes and organizing them under similarities or general categories
- **Brainwriting:** Written ideas created ahead of time, passed around the group or team members for positive/negative comments; discussion on comments
- **Mind mapping:** Visual brainstorm; key thoughts are placed on a flip chart and branches of ideas are added around each; collection of similar ideas that surface around each key thought
- **Group voting:** Several ideas prepared and presented; team members have a set number of points to assign to each idea; ideas with the most points become the basis for decisions

In all of these techniques, your focus is on getting everyone to express his or her ideas and perspectives. Collaboration at a group or team level means all members need to see their own ideas on the flip chart or included in the discussion. This means talking in "we" terms, finding places to build on ideas, appreciating the diversity, acknowledging what was said and felt, and encouraging candor and honesty.

Finally, you, as the manager, must engage in self-reflection:

- Have my thoughts and opinions been heard and understood? How do I know?
- Do I have to adjust my thinking toward what the group or team believes is the situation?
- What did I see or hear in the group that suggests we are on the same page?
- What is the impact of all this on how we do things going forward?
- How would I like to see the situation get resolved?

For a real-world example of what can happen when these techniques are applied, consider scenario 4.

CHARACTERISTICS OF SUCCESSFUL COLLABORATION

Although Table 6-3 is not a complete scorecard, it provides the metrics for knowing when collaboration characteristics are working effectively and when they are not.

As you become a better observer, you will begin to see more characteristics that typically lead to either good or bad performances: Some people value disagreements, for example. They like a hearty exchange, and they're open to other points of view; others see all disagreements as unwanted conflicts. Some people see obstructions to collaboration as learning opportunities, and they work through the obstruction. Others conclude that nothing will change and so why even try? They're not getting enough back, so they leave the collaboration because of the obstruction. Some people use inclusive language and adjust their communication style to that of the other person, while others come off as hard to read and off-putting. And, of course, some people use their networking opportunities to build bridges, while others use accusation and manipulation to build walls.

You will also notice that the effects good and poor collaboration have on performance levels, both yours and others. Imagine working in an organization of poor performance versus working in an organization of good performance. In a poor performance organization, your efforts will be limited to the letter of your job description. In a good performance organization, collaboration gets traction, and you are willing to release effort that is at your discretion. Collaboration becomes more reasonable. At that point, people are willing to use it more frequently.

COMMON COLLABORATION CHALLENGES

As we wrap up this chapter, let's take a look at a number of challenges managers face when it comes to collaboration along with sound, actionable advice for rising above those challenges.

Scenario 4: Creating a Functional Team

Jeff is a manager who was tasked with a thirty-person team that, at best, would be called dysfunctional. Work was being done but not at an acceptable level. In fact, Jeff had to expend an inordinate amount of time and effort fixing what people handed in so it could go up the line with some semblance of quality. He did this for a while and then decided to work on getting collaboration into this team.

At first, the team just looked at him during the staff meeting and had no response to any questions about collaboration. Then he asked, "Can anyone define what they think collaboration is?"

One person responded: "Is that where we play nice in the sandbox?" Not what Jeff was looking for, but it was a start. He turned his PowerPoint presentation to the first slide.

> Collaboration is a process whereby people connect and work together in an interactive, interdependent, unified, cooperative, and synergistic way to achieve a common goal.

Everyone looked at Jeff as if he was speaking a foreign language. Because he anticipated this reaction, he opened up the discussion by suggesting that they talk about only two things in the definition: "people connect" and "work together." He decided to use the brainstorming process for *people connect* and sticky notes for *work together*.

Using the brainstorming process, six groups of five people each generated a number of ideas. Jeff saw that he had to narrow down the choices because too many ideas generated in a brainstorming session can be overwhelming; with the team's approval he selected the five top items. As the process went on, it became apparent that two items from the brainstorm got the most votes: more honest communication and more patience with one another.

For the second issue (work together), Jeff had prepared a flip chart that had one word on it: accountability. He asked each person to generate as many attributes of it as possible, to write them on sticky notes, and put the notes on a flip chart. The volume of notes was so high that Jeff had to create another flip chart. When it was finished, he assigned three people to examine the flip charts, find the themes in the attributes, and organize the sticky notes into theme categories. While this was going on, Jeff asked each table to discuss why accountability is important in today's business.

When the sticky notes were organized, Jeff asked the three people to read out which issues came to the surface.

As it turned out, the key issue was that no one saw the benefit of working with one another. This became the basis for deeper discussions over several staff meetings until the team was able to dig into the root causes and come up with solutions. These were routinely reinforced until they became part of the team's culture. The process eventually yielded collaboration and excellent results.

Table 6-3 Collaboration and Performance Quality

Characteristics	Good Performance	Poor Performance
"We" versus "silo" thinking	• Inclusive communications • Collaboration begins to make sense	• "Us versus them" mentality • You and others constantly using defensive behaviors
Goals, roles, process, and relationships versus victim thinking	• Using goals, roles, processes, relationships as building blocks to get results • Having a proactive view of problems and issues	• No ownership taken by you and others on any issues • Blaming or telling good stories why collaboration is not possible
Focus on needs of others rather than on what you need	• Ability to find common ground • Understanding ways to get better results through working with others	• Satisfaction of all *your* needs but loss of credibility with others • No reciprocity with others; isolation from others
Equality versus following one's opinions	• Looking for and understanding other viewpoints • Understanding the limitations of your perceptions	• Getting stuck on seeing things only your way • Difficulty in adjusting to changes
Seeking input from others versus going in own direction	• Keeping conversation lines open • Finding reality calibration points	• Making decisions based on incomplete data • Ignoring changes in organization's strategy
Seeking inclusive decision making versus gut reaction	• Making decisions that are accurate, quick, and practical • Making decisions that make sense	• Making decisions in a vacuum • Making decisions based only on your emotions
Valuing diverse opinions versus dismissing other people's opinions	• Encouraging the expression of differences • Using dialogue to reach common understanding of difference	• Ignoring other people's opinions • Belittling those who are different from you
Finding places of agreement versus places of disagreement	• Avoiding judgment of other people and their views • Looking for something positive to build mutuality	• Seeing and dealing with disagreement negatively • "My way or the highway" attitude

- **Challenge:** I find it impossible to manage a group of people when many of them prefer to work by themselves and not get involved in being part of a team.
    - You need to have significant discussion on the goals, roles, processes, and relationships; group needs to be developed.
    - Avoid team-building efforts; they will only increase people's frustration.
    - Use directive behaviors to challenge the group to be more than they currently are.
- **Challenge:** As a manager, I get people to conceptually understand collaboration, but they are not motivated because they don't think it will benefit them.
    - Most likely, the group views collaboration as just another organizational message; it makes no sense to them because they can't see how it will affect their results.
    - Don't get disillusioned into thinking that people are merely paying lip service to collaboration, but not really buying in. Chances are they haven't yet seen the value; you need to explain the value to the organization and to the collaborators.
    - Show how collaboration impacts workflows, and show that collaboration can improve individual results and improve how the group is perceived in the organization.
- **Challenge:** I can't hold people accountable when the organizational dynamics pushes people to just react and get results.
    - Don't let people hide behind "that's the way we do things around here"; this is a poor excuse for not taking responsibility and it won't lead to innovation.
    - Have the group members define their desired work environment; pick one or two things to work on; celebrate even the smallest successes.
    - Look for situations when accountability did work; make these your teaching points.
- **Challenge:** As a manager, I have tried collaborative efforts, but they produced little outcomes for all the efforts I had to make.
    - Understand that collaboration takes time to move from conceptual to behavioral.
    - A constant in your process is to grow and develop the people around you; collaboration is just one tool to make that happen.
    - Think and teach: communicate, collaborate, and commit.
- **Challenge:** People get paid for only what is on their job description. Why should they leave that description to work collaboratively with people if there is no additional compensation for doing so?
    - Teach others that performance measurement is not about doing what's on the job description; it is based on how well you can operate beyond the parameters of the job description.
    - Collaboration is a key approach to dealing with the complexities of today's workflows.
    - You have to believe that people can no longer work in isolation and count on expertise to generate results. Work is now done with and through others; collaboration is the framework for this level of working relationships.

- **Challenge:** Collaboration is nice on paper. But the reality is I don't get any collaboration from my supervisor or from the organization. Why do it?
  - As a manager, you need to be a person of principle and someone who measures your value not based on getting what you get done but on how you get things done.
  - Collaboration is a matter of choice and not based on the whims of upper management.
  - You will have to accept that today's business world has gotten so complex that it needs collaboration as a foundation.

COLLABORATION COMPETENCY WORKSHEETS

The following guidelines will help you through the key points of making your collaboration efforts successful. Answer the following questions, being as honest and specific as you can.

1. Based on reality, what is your definition of collaboration? Does it target and achieve a common goal between yourself and others?
2. What do you want to achieve through collaboration? Why?
3. What are direct reports, peers, and leadership saying about your results, about your management style, and about how they want to work with you?
4. Are you developing your skills and talents to add value to your organization's collaborative efforts and to those you work with?
5. Describe the type of collaboration guide you use to keep collaboration on track.
6. Explain how you use various roles so that collaboration remains effective.
7. In your current capacity, how do you use the what, the who, and the how of collaboration?
8. If you have one, describe your personal code of conduct when working with others.
9. How accountable are you to the principles of communication, commitment, and connection with others? Explain.
10. Outline your professional SWOT.
11. What are you doing to work with the dimensional approaches of others?
12. What are your teaching points around goals, roles, processes, and relationships?
13. How do you balance your assertion and cooperation factors?
14. What are you doing to communicate more effectively in a team setting?
15. What are your success factors on collaboration?
16. When it comes to collaboration, how are you being more proactive rather than reactive?

The worksheet shown below will help hone your observational skills. Check to see how your observations of others frame out your perception of the people and behaviors presented. Place a checkmark under the dimension you believe is being used.

Determining Employees' Dimensional Approaches

Dimensional Approaches	Director	Thinker	Talker	Peace-maker
Jack likes to tell you what he did over the entire weekend				
Lin likes to stop at the doughnut store to get breakfast for the staff meeting				
Jayden likes to know when a project needs to get done and milestones to calibrate progress				
Miguel likes to be the center of attention when a project kicks off				
Alex tells everyone that things will work out and just to trust him				
Betty doesn't want to attend staff meetings and just wants to be left alone to work on the project				
Dev just wants everyone to get along				
Lucca wants things done his way and no other way				

• Conclusion •

In today's business environment, there are so many ways not to collaborate that it takes a complete focus on the benefits to make it happen. It takes constant awareness and commitment. There are several things you can do.

Consider a collaborative process in everything you do. In this mode, view your time as an investment in getting results that make sense in today's business environment. That environment needs more other-centeredness rather than self-centeredness.

Pay close attention to the roles you need to exercise in collaboration. Find places where you can foster trust and accountability. Understand you are balancing assertion and cooperation. Achieving that balance is based on the value you can add to others and yourself. Finding that balance is often more an art than a science.

Constantly ask for feedback on your collaborative efforts. And make collaboration an inclusive effort with others. Find points of synergy and leverage them.

These approaches take time. But the results from your efforts will make it inviting to work with you.

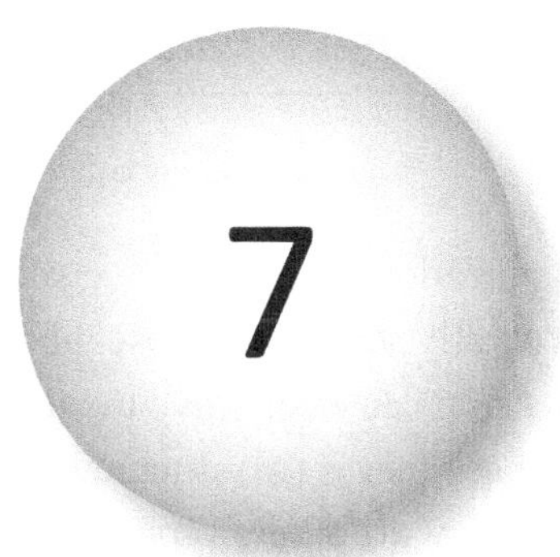

Influence

LEARNING OBJECTIVES

By the end of this chapter, you will be better equipped to:

- Identify and articulate a successful outcome and identify the needs of others in order to create a shared vision and develop buy-in.
- Understand what can be accomplished with the cooperation and support of stakeholders.
- Recognize the credibility and trust required to leverage personal power and negotiate for desired outcomes.
- Gain commitment from stakeholders and demonstrate willingness to incorporate input from others.
- Influence strategies created by gathering data, identifying the people involved, and positioning your rationale effectively.
- Build relationships and partnerships that result in mutual cooperation through trust, credibility, and communication.

The ability to influence or persuade others is one of the most significant attributes a leader or manager can have. It is, in practice, how organizations succeed internally. Sounds simple, right? But when we begin to look at the intricacies of this competency, we may find that it's a bit more complicated than we thought.

First, you need a power base, which is defined by the *Oxford* dictionary as "a source of authority, influence, or support." Human nature dictates that to function and accomplish things in social settings, a power base is essential. Power sources are found beyond what typically comes from your position in the organization. You may have power from charisma, power from deep subject knowledge, or power drawn from the politics of your organization. You may have seen these power bases in play. Typically, they are unilateral, meaning they generally serve only those who are in power instead of adding value to you and others. This unilateral dimension can easily give the use of power a negative connotation.

But there is also another power base that is two-dimensional and is formed by the combination of your knowledge and your relationship with others: your own power base. To gain a deeper understanding of it, you will need to acquire and agree with the following mind-set:

- Persuasion requires knowledge of the other person's perspectives, motivation, needs, and so on.
- Managing stakeholders' expectations is the test of your relationship building.
- Collaborative negotiation is the path for reaching your desired outcomes.
- Your ability to build professional relationships is almost entirely based on your credibility in the organization.

Putting this mind-set in organizational terms, your ability to influence effectively hinges on three factors:

1. Your behaviors and dispositions that invite trustworthiness and inclusion.
2. Your argumentation:
   - Your thought process for arriving at a logical conclusion based on understanding the points of agreement
   - Your critical thinking when creating value among the stakeholders, rather than allowing any single individual to claim value for himself or herself
   - Your conviction that the end result from the persuasion is best for all
3. Your ability to identify and deliver the benefits for each party.

More than anything, even more than perfect argumentation, is your ability to communicate and behave in ways that open the other person's willingness to be influenced by you. Subtle use of verbal and non-verbal expressions can significantly impact how you and others react to each other. These are the human calibrations we all tend to use to allow ourselves to be influenced.

Think about the last time you were influenced by someone. Did you pay attention to the calibrations defined in Table 7-1? These may seem like small factors, but when combined , they frame out the process of your ability to likewise influence others.

THE EVOLUTION OF INFLUENCE

Influence has been part of the business process ever since people began providing products or services for a fee. At first, influence centered on finding the sweet spot where an exchange made sense to both parties. As the business processes became more complex, a command and control approach to achieve the desired

Table 7-1 Influencing Calibrations	
Human Nature Calibration	**Translation**
Clarity of intention	Why is this person trying to influence me? Is there something in it for me?
Body language	Is there an honest and reliable connection that is making this influencing process worth my time?
Questions and listening	Is this other person interested in knowing where I am coming from and what's important to me?
Constant encouragement to talk	Do I feel like keeping this conversation going?
Personality connection	Do I sense a connection between myself and the other person? Are we talking the same language?

results became the norm. In fact, organizations structure themselves to keep the lines of command and control clear and active. One of the difficulties with this approach is the need to continue the organizational structure with more layers of management to ensure every issue is properly addressed. Positional power bases were created at each level to provide the authority needed to make decisions and act.

Organization structures grew to the point at which they became a hindrance to productivity. At some organizations, leadership assumed functions. These organizations required additional head count to carry out the new functions. They developed layer upon layer of management. In fact, some organizations required time-consuming committees just to study a particular project. The problem with all of this was that organizations could no longer sustain themselves in a rapidly changing marketplace. By the time decisions reached the stages where production or operations could occur, market windows closed and business was lost.

The initial response was movement toward flattening the organization. But did that work? Flattening the organization's structure looked good on the surface, but the mechanics of command and control remained the same. Instead of going through fourteen layers of management, one only had to go through seven. The command and control process became quicker, but it didn't go away.

As the structure changed, the workforce was changing too. Soon, command and control didn't make sense to the new workforce. Persuasion became the norm based on the benefit and logic of what is being asked. Managers with a power base in the shrinking organizational middle were now faced with questions from people they managed: "Why are we doing this? Why are we taking this approach? This doesn't make sense and therefore I am not doing it." In effect, command and control methods were receiving significant push back, particularly from those who were at the bottom of the organizational structure and who were experiencing impacts from the flattened structure. The use of authority to persuade was no longer as viable as an option. Pushing responsibility further down into the organization created the need for a new approach, the influencing approach or *teamwork.*

With the challenge to authority, most organizations went through a period of evolution during which they needed to develop teamwork. Team building sessions were conducted to help create these working relationships. In fact, employees would get evaluated on their team membership. In this subtle form of command and control, being labeled a non–team player could cost you your job. Team building became so popular that companies were formed just to provide this service. In some instances, millions were spent to get relationship structures in place. The problem with all of this was that, when people came back from team building training, influence hadn't changed much. A refined, more acceptable command and control approach encouraged employees to learn how to work with others or suggested the need for more training.

As organizations flattened, a loss of respect for authority began to emerge. This was most evident when the flattening led to layoffs and terminations. Some functions were no longer needed and neither were the people who carried out those functions. Authority now included the decision to downsize the organization, which broke the psychological contract of employment based on performance. No matter how hard you worked or how dedicated you were, your employment was at risk. In most cases this reaction to authority took the form of decreased effort and protection of one's functions and job, even if it harmed the organization.

Some form of command and control will likely survive. Current organizational structures allow it to exist. But many organizations are reaching new levels of excellence by giving the workforce a significant voice in the organizational building blocks: goals, roles, processes, and relationships. Influence over these four factors is at the core of keeping a successful, modern organization alive and growing.

Organizational restructuring ignored the real issue: the new marketplace demanded quick decisions and flexible action. Influence should have decentralized some of the command and control points. Under these conditions, influence itself was being redefined. It became more a matter of internal negotiation. This led to two questions:

1. What is your perspective on what we are facing?
2. What are we willing to exchange to get what we both want?

Negotiation needed to be collaborative and evolved into a mutual problem solving, not a distributive "I get what I want" process. Negotiation needed to be done in a manner that provided the basis for future negotiation. For example, if you provide me some of your time and expertise to finish my current pressing project, I can work on streamlining the process between your team and my team. The result of this collaborative negotiation establishes value for both rather than just one party claiming the value for itself and contributes to the strategic goals and mission of the organization as a whole. This requires a major shift in mind-set and approach.

The evolution of influence continues in your challenging and ever-changing business environment. Scenario 1 demonstrates that power bases can easily clash and no resolution or result can be accomplished without understanding each other's world.

GOALS AND OUTCOMES OF INFLUENCE

The influencing process allows you to achieve several results. The following factors are not in sequential order so you can combine them in a manner that makes sense to your operations.

One of the critical points with influencing is your ability to leverage the benefit and logic of your result for both parties. The benefit factor involves the value-added to the result by how each person con-

Scenario 1: Jack and Susan's Negotiation

Jack is the director of national sales at a large sports device company specializing in orthopedic hardware. Due to advances in technology, Jack is pressured to keep up with the demand, specifically for the Galaxy Series, which uses a new approach for reducing knee injuries. In early research, American football knee injuries were reduced by 25 percent, a significant number that has the National Football League (NFL) teams contacting Jack at all hours. The new device not only has the typical side bars that keep the knee from hyperextension but also has a new flexible plate to provide stability to the front and back of the knee. Jack is getting frustrated with the research division, which insists that more testing is needed before full production of the Galaxy Series can go forward. From Jack's perspective, Susan, the company's director of research, just wants to be certain that her division will not be blamed if something goes wrong. Jack understands all of this, but the market wants the product, and he needs to get it out there with the NFL teams before competitors pick up on this time-sensitive opportunity.

Susan believes that a product with a company label needs to be top quality. She has been known to delay launches of new products simply because she thought not enough research had been done to ensure public safety. The one thing that irritates Susan the most is pushy behaviors from her peers. She has the most difficulty with Jack who has a reputation of being arrogant.

Jack is frustrated with Susan's inability to get the new product out the door. Jack believes he has gone out of his way to work with Susan and expects Susan to respond to his efforts. She hasn't, and now Jack is getting quite upset with her. In fact, their last exchange was negative and ended up in a shouting match at the director's general meeting.

Jack is trying to figure out how he can work around Susan. He thought about escalating the issue to the CEO or even getting some of the other directors to rally around his position. He is not sure of the best options, but in his frustration, he sees no point in working with Susan any longer. From his viewpoint, Susan has to go, and for the sake of the bottom line in the company, he may have to start that process.

If you were Jack, what would you do?

You might wonder: How do professional, well-intentioned people reach this point? Primarily by insisting on one-dimensional positional power rather than on a two-dimensional relationship based on mutual expertise. If both parties were to reveal their true but hidden intentions and goals (Jack wants to increase market share and his own status; Susan is concerned about risk management), they would have a starting point. If you were sitting in this meeting, you would have seen their body language cues as both defensive and threatening. You would have observed that neither asked questions or listened to each other. You would have concluded that neither of the parties was concerned about communicating effectively.

Jack's tendencies were more assertive. Susan's tendencies were more analytical. It would be clear to you that they would need to adjust their communication patterns so that they could look for points of agreement rather than of disagreement.

You may find yourself in a situation similar to Jack and Susan. You can see that you will need to gain the other party's perspective if you are going to influence. It is difficult to negotiate anything with another person if you do not know how that person views the world and what issues are important. Otherwise, any attempt at influence will gain little result simply because your result will be one sided. Influence means that the result will benefit both parties.

ducts his or her portion of the business flow. It is a factor that reflects the emotional perspective. The logic factor stresses that it makes sense for each to go along with the other. It reflects the rational perspective.

Depending on the strength of each of these factors, the behavioral patterns will shift. The model shown in Figure 7-1 reflects this personal activity.

Pro tip
Benefit, or what the person you're influencing gains, contains a significant emotional element. Logic, the reasoning behind the influence, contains a significant cognitive element. The cement that holds these two together is credibility.

In psychological terms, influence is a process in which one person or group attempts to change the attitudes and thus the behaviors of another person or group for a specific purpose. In the past decade, as organizations have become flatter and as single employees have become responsible for multiple functions (such as individual contributor *and* manager), influence has become increasingly important. Today, more people than ever have to *manage across*, meaning they have to get results from peers and colleagues with whom they have limited formal power. While influence remains an important tool for those who have formal authority, it is crucial for employees, such as those in matrixed organizations, who must collaborate laterally, across departments and divisions. Figure 7-2 illustrates how influence is determined by several elements.

Credibility and Character

Credibility is the trust you gain because of your expertise and relationship. It is more than just believability. Credibility underlines the formula that each person has when dealing with another. The formula is this: Can I trust this person's expertise and motives? Am I being treated with respect? Is what I am doing significant to this organization?

The credibility/trust model brings out this formula (see Figure 7-3). Trust is created when both the competency and character factors merge.

Credibility exists in the minds of those you influence and persuade. If others don't see you as credible, you will have difficulty influencing them. Perhaps you got burned by someone trying to influence you without both competency and character working simultaneously. In fact, you may have experienced serious flaws in either of those factors before, during, and after that person's attempt to influence you.

In addition to knowing how your efforts fit into the big picture, your reliability lies in how well you execute your technical knowledge of operational issues, your social skills for interacting with different viewpoints, and your analytical ability to organize data for decision making. Character flaws also create questions in others. Your words and intentions need to match and be clearly expressed through your actions.

Stakeholder Management

Influence also requires stakeholder management, which is discussed in more detail later in this chapter.

Typical stakeholder management assumes that anyone who can impact or benefit from deliverables needs to be managed. In this view, stakeholders can be mapped either as allies or adversaries.

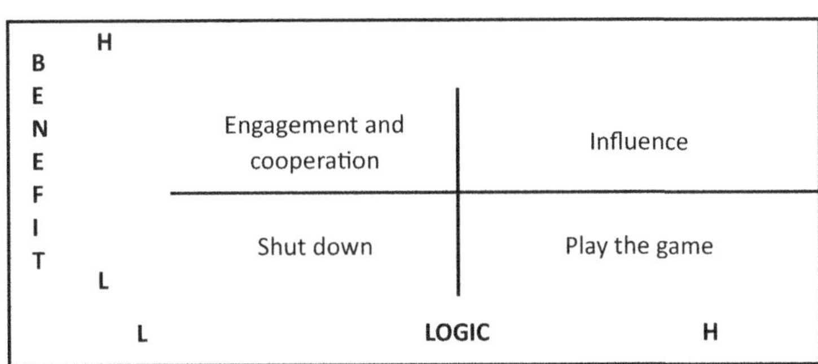

Benefit	Logic	Outcomes
High	High	• Positive behaviors • Communications make sense • Both see the value of working with each other • Would like to work with each other in the future
High	Low	• Test to gauge the value of working with each other • Guarded behaviors • Constant monitoring of benefits to self • Cautious about working with each other
Low	High	• Give the impression of being a team player • Provide little effort to work with the other person • Focus on keeping job • Do not want to work with each other unless forced to do so
Low	Low	• Focus on survival • Negative "whatever" behaviors become a weapon to send subtle messages • No interest in adding value to the organization • Complain and blame

Figure 7-1 The benefits and logic factors

In the influence process, all stakeholders are viewed as essential partners for obtaining deliverables. They are divided into three groups: core, secondary, and tertiary. This suggests that your core stakeholders need constant relationship attention and significant information about your plans. Give attention to and share information with secondary stakeholders, those who support your core stakeholder group. The tertiary group is made up of those with whom you don't personally interact but who interact with the

Myth: Influence is mostly a question of power.

It is impossible to influence using your power base (expertise and relationship) without a firm foundation of credibility (competency and character).

Understand Team Dynamics

Communication & Organizational Awareness

- Trust
- Credibility
- Expertise
- Style

Critical Thinking

Personal Currency

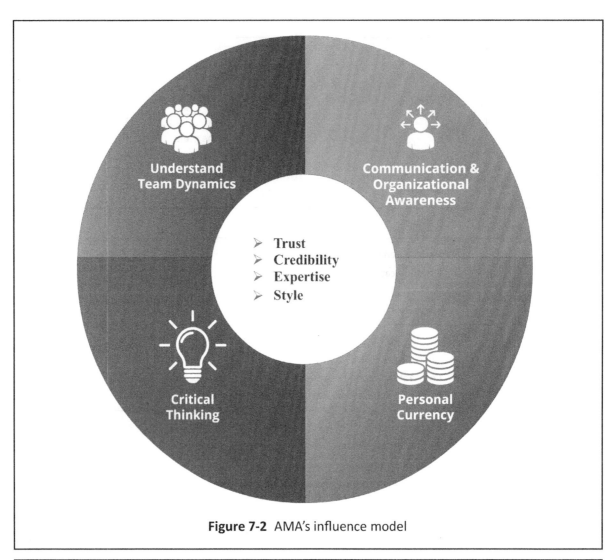

Figure 7-2 AMA's influence model

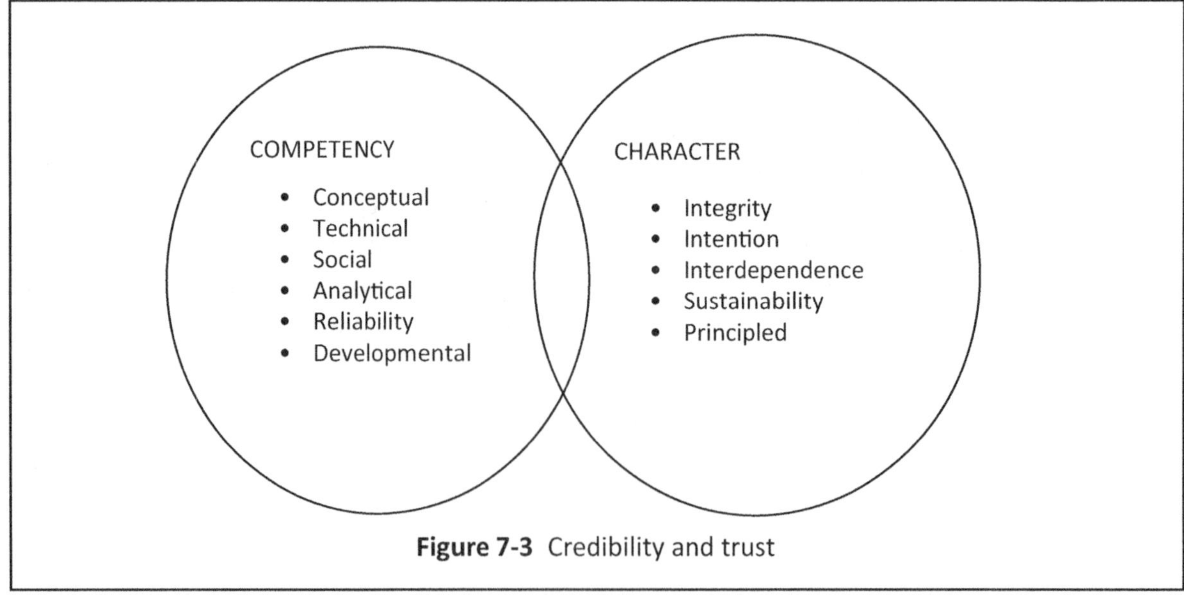

Figure 7-3 Credibility and trust

secondary stakeholders. Notice that your involvement in managing stakeholders decreases as you move from your core group. However, as detailed in Table 7-2, you should have a relationship with everyone on your stakeholder map.

A key element of your stakeholder management is to make certain that all the people in your stakeholder map understand what is happening and what they can expect because of their stakeholder status.

This is when the benefit and logic model is most needed. Stakeholders can and will impact your deliverables, and you want a positive impact. This doesn't happen by itself. You need to manage the information flow to all stakeholders and let them know why you are doing the project and how it will benefit them. Although it takes time, once you begin to manage your stakeholder map, you will notice significant improvements in your influence process.

Understanding Others

Besides stakeholder management, the most difficult part of influencing is probably attempting to understand the perspectives of the other person. How does he or she see the reality of the needed work and corresponding issues? You must understand where the other person is coming from. Understanding means more than appreciating another's perspective. It means learning about the drivers in his or her work world and putting aside biases to open up thinking about the current reality. Influencing without understanding takes less time but produces more short-term results. Remember, *influence* means more long-term results and outcomes; *convincing* means more short-term results.

In scenario 2, put yourself in the role of Morgan. Note that Morgan and Jim spent time in unproductive and remedial activities because they failed to understand each other's perspectives (also see Chapter 4, Conflict Management; Chapter 5, Motivation; and Chapter 9, Coaching for Performance).

You will face some people who are unwilling to partner with you. These people present a unique challenge. This situation puts your goals and the goals of the other person in the spotlight as well as the use of strategies so both goals are achieved.

Table 7-2 Stakeholder Map

Stakeholder	Level of Stakeholder	Stakeholder Process/Needs
Lin	**Core** (Your counterpart in a different division)	• Show value of your proposal • Constantly pay attention to the relationship; ask for feedback • Provide commitment to help with her goals
Alex	**Secondary** (Provides quality assurance for Lynn)	• Debrief him on your proposal and how it fits into Lin's goals • Inform him of your methodology
Suri	**Secondary** (Provides data to Alex)	• Establish a relationship • Learn the division's process from her
Miguel	**Tertiary** (Different division providing data to Suri)	• Provide an awareness of your project

STRATEGIES FOR ACHIEVING OUTCOMES

The strategies presented in Table 7-3 are useful and practical in most influence situations, particularly when things aren't going well. These strategies focus on goal achievement: yours, the other person's, and the organization's.

Influence is measured not just on whether you achieved your goal but also on whether the other person was able to achieve his or hers. This balance is difficult to maintain. However, aligning the other person's goals with your own and then with the organization's helps alleviate some of the balancing issues.

The Willingness Factor

Table 7-4 looks at balancing the willingness factor between you as manager and the other party so you can help achieve each other's goals. This delicate balance between your willingness and the other person's willingness is central to influencing.

You may wonder why you sometimes get no response from others. Most likely, you are not using the correct strategy. If you are always emphasizing your goals and having little discussion on satisfying the goals of the other person, then others will hesitate to work with you. The red flag in this situation is when neither of you is willing to work with the other. It's at this point that emotional maturity is required more than ever. In its absence, emotions will push the issues into a conflict mode, where little gets accomplished.

Obtaining the requisite willingness or commitment requires a few strategic steps. First, make certain that you view all the people you interact with as your stakeholders. Everyone in the influence process needs to know one another's perspectives. When this groundwork is in place, people will be more willing to be persuaded and influenced by you. Why? Because people tend to respond more positively when they see you creating value for others rather than claiming value just for yourself.

The Exchange Phase

Balancing the willingness factor uncovers the exchange phase, an important process that creates value between all parties. The exchange phase of influence requires your ability to negotiate.

For some, the word *negotiation* has a negative connotation. In most cases, it's seen as a measure of what you give and what you get back. But remember, in the influencing process, *exchange* means you and the other person are open to finding what will benefit you both. In influence, negotiation is measured not on what you get, but on what you give. In her negotiation textbook *The Mind and Heart of the Negotiator*, Leigh Thompson refers to negotiation as an "interpersonal decision-making process" that is "necessary whenever we cannot achieve our objectives single-handedly." Based on your previous experiences, this may not make any sense; yet influence requires this adjustment. Perhaps this is why there are not that many influential people in business outside of those who wield positional power.

Myth: If you communicate well, most people will overlook a flaw in your competency.
A flaw in competency creates questions in others.

Some people view a lack of reciprocity as a game changer or a reasonable red flag. Some may even see it as being taken advantage of. These are legitimate reactions, but here is where choice comes in. Partnership thinking is an investment in the relationship, one that is built on the logic that you want the other person to be successful just as much as you want to be successful in what you do.

Exchange is matching what you have to offer and what the other person needs. It can be tangible (time, resource) or intangible (encouragement, support). In influence, exchange is something to keep the relationship going. It is based on creating value rather than on claiming value.

Scenario 3 demonstrates that the exchange framework is dynamic and needs constant attention to find the perfect spot when reciprocity can work as well. In this case, Dave quickly found the exchange spot. But in other situations, it may not be that visible. You would need to work the issues to find it. In

Scenario 2: Morgan and Jim's Difficult Conversation

Morgan was excited when his boss asked him to chair the Omega Project team eighteen months ago. He had never chaired a team before and felt that this could have a positive effect on his career. The project involves the implementation of a new software program that could have a real bottom-line impact.

Jim is one of Morgan's team members and is responsible for the data coordination component. Over the years, Morgan generally has found Jim to be responsive and easy to work with. However, lately he seems to have lost interest in working on the team. This is not typical. Morgan is concerned with Jim's level of participation and his apparent disengagement from the project.

- Jim has missed three meetings and hasn't sent anyone to cover for him; before this, he was at every meeting.
- Jim's unavailability for meetings has resulted in the team being late with its monthly status reports on two separate occasions.
- Several weeks ago, Morgan had to make a major revision in Jim's section of the quarterly report because the piece he turned in was inadequate. If he had only submitted a draft of the report to Morgan like everyone else did, the problem could have been easily avoided. Again, this is not typical of Jim.
- Several times in the past three months, when Morgan had to call ad-hoc meetings he wasn't able to reach Jim. It would have been helpful if he had been available since these were issues in Jim's knowledge base.

Jim's performance (or lack thereof) could have a significant negative impact on the team. What makes the problem worse is that several team members have commented to Morgan about Jim's performance

Myth: If you reach out to someone who does not reciprocate, he or she will not make a good partner.
You have to choose to behave and think as a partner with others, even if they don't reciprocate.

and the effect it's having on the team. As one member said: "We need his input, and if he can't do the job, then we need someone who can."

Wanting to influence Jim, Morgan sits him down to discuss this matter. Initially, Jim responded defensively, as he had in previous discussions. But this time Morgan wants to understand Jim's perspectives. It took more than an hour but finally the truth came out.

It turns out that Jim has an emotional block and is not happy. He feels that Morgan made several major changes in his section of the quarterly report without asking for his approval. He was away for personal reasons, but thought Morgan could have easily contacted him.

For some reason, Jim did not get the invites to several meetings. Some people were having technical problems with email, and he was one of them. He had no confirmation about the meetings. In several meetings, Jim thought he was put on the spot when Morgan asked him to respond to questions about issues that Jim considers outside his expertise.

Further, Jim believes Morgan acts as if the data coordination people had nothing else to do but be dedicated to the Omega Project.

During the discussion, Morgan emphasized that the department is short staffed, with several retirements and no replacements. As a result, he revealed he had no choice but to involve Jim in several other projects. Looking back, Morgan admitted that what he's said to Jim didn't come out the way it was intended: "We need you to cover at least two other teams because they need our team's input. Do what you have to do to keep on top of the Omega Project, but don't let these other projects slip." Morgan took responsibility for putting Jim in an unfavorable spot. At last saw why the whole thing bothered Jim.

For his part, Jim admitted that he doesn't like the concept of the whole project. He wants Morgan and the team to succeed, but he sees failure as a real possibility. Morgan is willing to be open to Jim's view of the project and is convinced that this conversation can produce some valuable insights and decisions for adjusting work process parameters. On the other hand, Jim is glad that Morgan is willing to have a discussion on what seemed to him to be a "waste of time" project.

If you were Morgan, what would you do?

For starters, Morgan would need to understand Jim's perspectives, and vice versa. Without that element, both Morgan and Jim would have talked past each other, and influence would not have had a chance to occur. As the leader, Morgan has to be open to be influenced. With that step, he is in a position to influence Jim. This promises to be a difficult conversation because at this point in the project neither Morgan nor Jim has much credibility in other's eyes. Even though steps will be taken to resolve this matter, Jim needs to see Morgan differently and to acknowledge the partnership approach in Morgan's actions before he will allow himself to be influenced by Morgan. This is a long-term effort to repair the relationship and to establish a way they can both work together on the Omega Project and produce the type of deliverables expected by the organization.

Table 7-3 Influencing Strategies

- Including everyone into the influence process
- Looking for possibilities and different options to get results
- Bringing out the value of the benefits of your proposal for others and you
- Clarifying how the organizational goals, roles, and processes sequence guide influence
- Increasing your credibility by doing something that benefits without reciprocity
- Finding the common ground or points of agreement
- Remaining confident about the partnership approach, even during setbacks
- Challenging others to recognize your credibility
- Managing conflict when the other party disagrees
- Engaging in collaborative efforts
- Employing critical thinking to know what is important and driving value

Table 7-4 The Willingness Factor

Outlook	Manager	The Other Person	Strategy
High chance of success	Willing to achieve your goal and the goal of the other person	Willing to achieve his or her goal and your goal	Continue building the influence process through collaboration and targeted communication
Moderate chance of success	Willing to achieve your goal and the goal of the other person	Willing to achieve his or her goal but unwilling to achieve your goal	Work on building a better relationship; determine the emotional block in working with you
Low chance of success	Willing to achieve your goal but not the goal of the other person	Willing to achieve his or her goal but unwilling to achieve your goal	Look for the point at which you both want to achieve your own goals but not of those of the other; determine where a partnership can be established to achieve both your goals in collaboration
No chance of success	Unwilling to achieve your goal by working with the other person and unwilling to help the other person achieve his or her goal	Unwilling to achieve his or her goal by working with you and unwilling to help you achieve your goal	Review why you are unwilling to work with the other person; determine your emotional block; consider obtaining organizational support if either goal adds value

such cases, focused strategies of inclusion, clarification, finding common ground, and having a shared vision can all help find that point of mutual benefit (see Chapter 2, Emotional Intelligence, for additional support). At times, you may have difficulty finding the exchange spot. In these situations the influencer must provide something of value and be patient for the expected reciprocity.

Scenario 3: Dave's Recruiting Dilemma

Dave is responsible for creating the Knowledge Sharing and Information Management System for High-Top Corporation. He has put together a project plan and a group of experts from IT, marketing, finance, procurement, production, and distribution to act as a steering committee and support team for the initiative.

The goal of this new system is to create a way of preserving proprietary information. This is a significant concern because so many employees are coming into and also leaving the organization. The system is scheduled to go on line in twelve months, and the CEO is counting on Dave.

Dave has recruited experts from each part of the organization except for sales, probably the most affected unit in the company. He approached Odette, the vice president of sales to recruit Anne Smith, one of the sales unit's more successful people. Anne has been with the company for five years and is well respected throughout the organization. She has mentored many new sales reps, has extensive knowledge of the company's inner workings, and would be a great asset for the team.

The only problem is Odette is reluctant to let Anne become part of Dave's team. Odette is a cynical person, interested only in how she looks to the CEO. The sales division has beaten its quota every year for the last four years, mostly because of Anne. There's a rumor going around that Odette is suspicious about the knowledge sharing project. She believes it's just another "flavor of the month" effort and a waste of Anne's selling time.

Dave's initial conversation with the Odette was a challenge. Dave outlined that he would need Anne for six to ten hours per month for twelve months. As part of the exchange, Dave said he would be happy to acknowledge her efforts to the CEO during the kick-off meeting. Odette suggested that Dave take one of the new, less-experienced sales reps for the project, but Dave thought that would be counterproductive. He argued that Anne had so much depth and credibility that, without her, the project could easily fail.

If you were Dave, how would you handle this?

After going back and forth and getting nowhere, Dave thought of a better exchange. He was willing to limit Anne's time to six hours per month and to adjust one of the outputs from the new system to support the sales efforts. In effect, with the slight adjustment in both the time and the output, Odette would have the ability to increase sales even more, not only through Anne but via the rest of the sales team. Any loss of Anne's time in sales due to working on the project would be more than covered by the additional output Dave was willing to put into the system. Both agreed that this would work.

INFLUENCE AND COMMUNICATION PATTERNS

As we've seen, learning the perspective of the other party is key. This depends on your ability to match your communication pattern with that of the other person, including nonverbal body language cues. It also involves listening and questioning, which takes time and practice (also see Chapter 1, Communication).

One reason Dave could influence Odette in scenario 3 was because he adjusted his communication style to hers. He realized that while he was task driven, Odette was more people driven. Dave had to get creative to match up with Odette's interest in sales possibilities. He needed to be more aware of her concerns and provide her with solutions rather than with additional explanations of the problem. Eventually, by focusing on the people issues, and not just the process, Dave and Odette agreed to an exchange that would be in everyone's interest.

Pro tip
Learn to adapt your communication style to match the framework of the other person. It's a valuable aspect of influence that can be challenging to master.

As illustrated in Figure 7-4, each of us prefers a certain approach or dimension when dealing with others. One defining line is the *focus line*: job or people. The second defining line is the *assertion line*: direct (telling) or indirect (asking). When these lines intersect you have the makings of understanding the four fundamental preferences or dimensions.

People Issues

If you're like most people, you have a preference for one of the four quadrants shown in Figure 7-4, although you may use all the dimensions. Each situation presents you with a choice. Typically, you have a preference, but that's all it is.

As an influencer, you have to make a conscious choice as to which dimension matches up with the other person. If you are a style A person trying to influence a style D person, you must adjust your words and nonverbal behaviors so you don't turn off the other person. Your best intentions can never materialize into a result. If you want to be an influencer, you have to make the first adjustment. In this example, you, a style A person, must make two adjustments: become less direct and pay more attention to people issues. The reverse would occur if a style D person wants to influence a style A person.

These adjustments cannot be made unless one is ready (has the competency) and willing (has the motivation) to make them. Readiness means expanding one's bandwidth on understanding others and paying close attention to the primarily focus of the issue (job or people) and even closer attention to the communication pattern (direct or indirect).

Observation skills play an important role in the bandwidth expansion, which requires daily self-education in how others communicate. It means being aware that not everyone sees and talks the way you

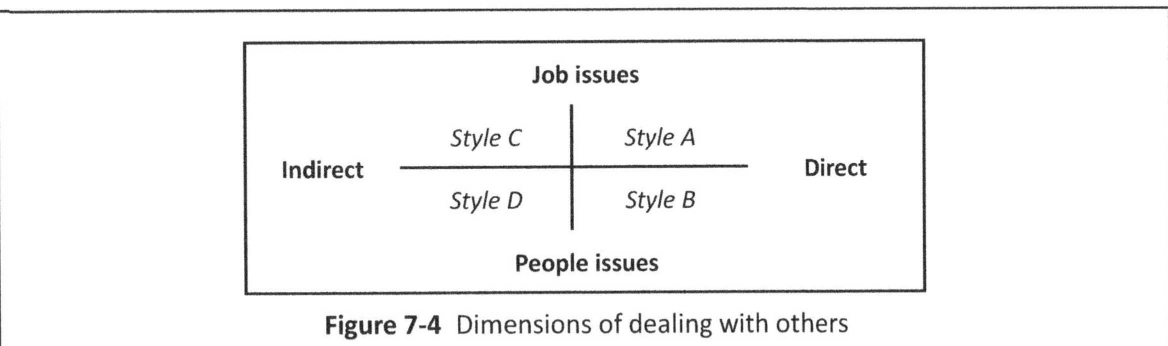

Figure 7-4 Dimensions of dealing with others

do. People will say: "I don't see it that way" or "I don't feel too sure about this" or "I think this will not work" or "I got it and let's move on."

Each of these differing viewpoints adds to your understanding. Without increasing your understanding, you may be looking at only 50 percent of the situation. But in fact, you need to look for 100 percent.

IMPORTANCE OF DEVELOPING CREDIBILITY

Although the credibility model makes sense, it's important to realize that both components—competency and character—need to be in constant development.

Technological advances and a higher-educated workforce may be challenging your competency. There is constant competition to gain knowledge to create power in the organization based on expertise. The first problem is that unless you increase your knowledge base, it quickly becomes obsolete and is dismissed by others as irrelevant or useless. You may have seen some peers reach the point where they are basically being ignored. Knowledge is power but so is the ability to apply new layers of knowledge in a constantly changing environment. This requires not just IQ but also emotional quotient (EQ), a measure of emotional intelligence (discussed in Chapter 2, Emotional Intelligence).

Character is something that you gain through an assembly of values and ethics known as your moral compass. Since everyone has a different set of values and ethics, it is more of a challenge for you to use EQ to remain credible. Differences can become obstacles to working together.

The starting point for this portion of the personal power base is when you begin to understand that all employees want to grow and develop their skills, abilities, and place in life. The term *value added* means that a person or event continues to add value to the outcomes. There's nothing new about people working together. But in today's business world, working together means that you have to add value to others' objectives so their goals, and yours, can be achieved in the best possible manner.

Trust is created when competency and character are working in the terms described. Any flaw in either component will negate trust and, in turn, credibility. Flaws can be avoided through your behavior, which range from honestly communicating one's thoughts to listening intently to what others are say, to being willing to try another person's approach. Behaviors are the vehicles signaling the sincerity and reliability of your competency and character.

Integrity

In almost all cases, integrity—matching your words and actions—gets center stage. Perhaps the biggest problem with integrity is not following through on your words even though you want to. It's often a question of not having enough time. Your intention may be good, but the execution gets sidetracked because your boss needs something immediately or the organization's goal moves in a different direction or you can hardly keep up with all the functions you have to do.

Myth: You don't have to show integrity about everything.
Either you demonstrate integrity or you will be perceived as duplicitous. It's a serious choice.

But the fact is that if you are going to influence you have to realize that character is more than just wanting to show integrity. It also includes making time to execute what you said you were going to do. This means acting with integrity must be a top priority, something urgent and important. This could mean considering moving some of your functions, at least temporarily, into a less-urgent category. And if there is any slippage on the execution, then you need to revisit that situation and inform people of your circumstances.

NEGOTIATE FOR DESIRED OUTCOMES

Influence is a combination of credibility (personal power), proper communication style, and negotiation. Assuming you have credibility and can flex your communication approach, the last remaining component of influence is negotiation.

As mentioned earlier, negotiation tends to have a negative connotation. You may use negotiation to buy a new car, but in the end, your focus is how much car can you get for the least amount of money; meanwhile, the dealer is seeing how much money he can get for the dealership without giving up too much on the car. This is a win–lose operation. In most cases neither you nor the car dealer gets everything you want.

In all negotiation, there is a settlement range: It goes from high (you are delighted) to middle (pretty much what you wanted) to low (you can live with it).

For example, look at the three levels of commitment outlined in Table 7-5. At the low end, you don't understand the purpose of the project or whether you need to deliver any inputs. In most cases like this, nothing is delivered; if it is, it might be done reluctantly. In the middle range, you both have some understanding and provide inputs when and if needed. In the high range, you have a clear understanding of the other person's perspective, the deliverables are more freely provided and often they're enriched.

The high range of agreement means a more concise understanding of why you and the other person need to work together. This means partnership. This means an assertion of what you will need or can provide and what the other person needs or can provide. This is the most productive use of exchange.

Not every effort results in a productive partnership. In some cases, neither of you gets what you want. When that occurs, typically, you and the other person will gravitate back to the low range of agreement and remain content. But if you want to be an effective influencer, you should focus on the high end as much as possible. This is collaborative negotiation.

Collaborative Negotiations

Collaborative negotiations provide the base for future negotiations. If both you and the other person are getting as much value as you need from your deliverables, then you both should be open to more nego-

Table 7-5 Inputs from a Project

Low Range of Agreement	Middle Range of Agreement	High Range of Agreement
I am not sure what you are doing with this project, but I will review it and add my inputs where they can help. We will need to talk some more.	Based on what you said, I can see the project will need some of my inputs. I will have them ready when you need them. I also want you to know I will need some of your inputs. Are we in agreement?	I have a good understanding of what you are trying to do with this project. It makes sense for me to work with you and provide whatever you need, when you need it. I think we also agree it makes sense for you to work with me on my project.

tiations. Both of you are more apt to provide deliverables that are mutually beneficial. It makes sense under these conditions. The challenge is to monitor the conditions.

Often, organizational issues that come into play change the collaborative calibrations. You may say you can deliver something, but then your priorities are changed for you, and you don't deliver as you said you would. This jeopardizes the agreements and, in turn, can unravel the collaborative effort. If this happens, you need to constantly check that what is going on, even with all the changes, is still perceived as collaboration. The old standard of "under promise, over deliver" still has some value in the organization (see also Chapter 11, Managing Projects).

If there is a sense that things are not working, in addition to the assertion, you will need to introduce the *cooperation feature*: "This is what I need and I understand what you need. Let me put my things on hold for a little while so we can make certain your issues are handled first."

Collaborative negotiation is a challenge. Try to see it as a problem-solving effort rather than a negotiation. This mind-set better frames the negotiation: You have a mutual problem that you both need to resolve. Use the following questions as a guide to this approach and to keep discussion on track:

- Why is this an issue for us?
- How is it a problem for both of us?
- What is the impact of this problem?
- What is the cause of this issue?
- What options do we have?
- What is the best option for us?
- Can we do it?

The problem-solving mind-set makes sense if you want to negotiate collaboratively.

Stakeholder Management

It is clear that as you enter into the world of stakeholder management, you enter into understanding the business drivers of each stakeholder and how to work within those worlds.

Scenario 4: XYZ Unit Manufacturing

Your company manufactures XYZ units, which an end user has incorporated into a new open space arrangement to creatively connect people. The end user of the XYZ units did not indicate exactly how many units would be needed.

Based on your proven past experiences, you believe this end user will need 1,000 XYZ units. Since each XYZ unit is made up of several components, you ordered 2,000 components (at $100 per component) from your supplier to complete the production run. The end user just called and said that he will need components for a run of only 500 XYZ units. This means that you have 1,500 components left on your shelf. Your end user price of $125 per unit leaves you in a financial hole.

The problem is that you signed a contract with the component supplier that stipulates "all sales are final upon delivery; no returns allowed."

You are now responsible for paying your supplier for all the components ($200,000) and working with the end user to resolve the issue of the unneeded 1,500 components. The end user accounts for 15 percent of your annual revenue. In addition, the components were customized for this end user and cannot be used for any other application.

What can you do?

You have several options:

- Talk with the supplier to negotiate a tiered payment approach to pay for the components.
- Talk with the end user to see if there are other opportunities to use the XYZ units in a different office space arrangement.
- Find out why the end user didn't need the other 500 XYZ units; perhaps he knows of another end user who might benefit from the units.
- Offer to work with the end user to achieve more accurate estimates and not rely on previous orders.
- Work with the supplier to see if the components can be more generalized, allowing them to be used in other applications.
- Absorb the loss and keep the client.

Stakeholder management is not easy. As an influencer, you will be challenged to navigate among the many variables and find the common ground between all parties. Just like in scenario 4, you have options for resolving the issue, all with the aim of keeping your current stakeholders as your future stakeholders.

Clearly, flexibility with your position and with your approach to others becomes paramount. As you move toward common ground among all, you begin to understand the benefits for all. Common ground is nothing more than pulling all the benefits together. It is at this spot where your value as an influencer becomes clear.

Deep within this process is the constant of your logic. Logic occurs on two levels: organizational and personal. Organizational logic reflects the goal and its execution. Personal logic reflects how doing something will help you and the other person do the job optimally. Both goals need to be addressed for the influence to be effective. Think of it this way: Organizational logic provides the framework for *what* needs to be done, while personal logic explains *why* it needs to be done.

This stakeholder mind-set becomes even more challenging once you apply it to the people you work with directly. You need to take stakeholder management to a level of partnership with your colleagues. This means that you both must have mutual agreement on the goals, roles, processes, and type of relationship needed.

At this point, you need a clear vision of why working together makes sense. This will require your understanding of what each receives from the partnership. Here you target the long- term value rather than the short-term one. Organizationally, the mantra is short term: Get it done and get it done right now. But this short-term focus establishes a scarcity mind-set in that there are limited resources and each has to get what benefits him or her. Your influence should embrace an abundance mind-set, which suggests that, if we can work together, we will find more resources and create new options. This scarcity versus abundance approach is a key to an effective influence.

It is interesting that expertise and intelligence (IQ) are practically givens in today's business. Training or increasing your expertise bandwidth can maintain the trust or credibility you already have. Building relationships or EQ, however, requires significant commitment on your part. The relationship factor is constantly under scrutiny and observation. The reality is that a flaw in the relationship can easily break the value of that relationship. For example, someone can destroy a relationship by saying one thing and doing something different, even just once, or by promising to deliver on something and then failing to do so. Effective influence requires the right balance between IQ and EQ.

BUILD RELATIONSHIPS AND PARTNERSHIPS TO SUSTAIN INFLUENCE

Within the influence process, relationship management is critical. In addition to learning the perspectives of your stakeholders and keeping the exchange lines open for value added actions, the ability to keep working with someone is essential.

Organizational living means adapting not only to stakeholders but also to peer groups, which are in a constant state of flux, being established, altered, and terminated. Under these conditions, your tendency may be to concentrate on a few co-workers rather than on expanding your relationship network. This is the challenge when you influence today.

Relationship networking means keeping your immediate network alive while expanding it by sharing it with others. You've probably seen it in the context of a job search. One person says, "Here is the name and email of a contact from my network who might help you get a lead." The other person responds, "Thanks. By the way I think my friend has a cousin who works in the same company that you are interested in. Here's the name and email of my friend." Most likely you have experienced such conversations. As an influencer, you need to use the same dynamic leveraging when building your organizational relationships.

INTENTION

Character includes an often overlooked element: intention. When you try to influence another person, your intention becomes top of mind for the receiver. The person being influenced wants to know why you are doing or saying something. What are you trying to accomplish? If you aren't clear in this, others either try to guess your intention or simply conclude you have a hidden agenda.

The process of influence has little chance of success if others don't know your reason. Are you doing it to make yourself look good or are you doing it to improve product value? If people don't know why you are trying to influence them, trust will not occur, and without trust there is no foundation for an influence process. Organizational living keeps everyone somewhat competitive; thus the other person may conclude that because you have no stated intention, you must be out from yourself.

There is one subtle item that makes intention somewhat iffy. It's the other person's perception of you. This perception is most impacted by your reputation. This is something that occurs fairly quickly when you first enter an organization, and it may be extremely hard to change. If you have a negative reputation, it is almost a certain formula for failure when you try to influence others in your organization.

Whether or not you know what your reputation is in the organization, good or bad, you are stuck with it. However, you should consider shaping another's perception of you, using the suggestions in the textbox entitled: Let Your Intentions Show.

INFLUENCING UP

Perhaps the biggest challenge to influence is when you have to influence upward into the organization. Clearly at this point you have no positional power to back up your recommendations. All you have is your personal power or credibility, and even they may be questionable if senior management doesn't know you that well.

So what's the solution? There are three steps.

1. **Partner with stakeholders who can support your credibility:** This involves talking with senior managers with whom you have a relationship in some form or another. It means getting information to establish your credibility with the other senior managers rather than hope it will somehow evolve. For example, ask about the senior managers' hot buttons. Ask about the organizational drivers. Prepare yourself to take on these issues and use your knowledge of them to establish your credibility. At this level in the organization you need at least rudimentary credibility for anything to work.
2. **Ask yourself what you would do if you were in the senior managers' position:** Try to see it through their eyes. What would be important to you? In effect, try to understand their

Let Your Intentions Show

- Reveal clearly and concisely what your intention is.
- Let people know the what and why of your actions.
- Provide people with new inputs about you.
- Ask for honest feedback about how others see you.

perspective, which means moving your reference frame from operations to strategy and strategic intent.

3. **Establish your credibility:** Let senior management know your level of expertise and some of your key results. Practice what you will say and how you will say it. Determine where your credibility is vulnerable. What issues would stump you and would you handle them if they come up. Practice being assertive and show confidence that your proposal or recommendation will benefit senior management and the organization.

These are not easy steps. But if done correctly, even if you don't get what you are asking for, at least you will have positioned yourself to be more credible the next time you address senior management.

Table 7-6 lists success factors and characteristics and describes them in terms of effective and ineffective influence.

COMMON MISUNDERSTANDINGS ABOUT INFLUENCE

Let's look at six of the most common misunderstandings about the influence competency and some suggestions for becoming better at it.

1. **Misunderstanding:** Only positional power works in an organization. It's the only way to get things done.
   - Although the initial assessment may seem correct, other power bases are just as strong. Your personal power base formed through credibility (expertise and relationships) can be even more powerful when it touches the key fabric of an organization.
   - Your personal power base is available throughout your career. It is a matter of recognizing that you do have it and that it can be grown and developed.
   - Check to see how others view your results, what people are saying about you, and how willing people are to work with you. Do others approach you for input or involvement in their projects? It's the litmus test of your power base.

Table 7-6 Effective Versus Ineffective Influence		
Factors or Characteristics	**Effective Influence**	**Ineffective Influence**
Proactive versus defensive	• Position the value or benefit of your proposal • Make choices about how and why you influence	• Allow the influence process to evolve on its own • Try to influence only through logic
Powerful versus powerless	• Leverage your expertise and relationship • Keeping the exchange open with the other person	• Conclude that only positional power works • Judge influence as a one-shot deal
Measuring reciprocity: what you get versus what you give	• Understand that reciprocity is an evolving process and may not be immediate • Measuring your value in what you provide first and then what you get back	• Wait to get something back immediately • Judge how much value you got in comparison to how much value you provided
Finding strategies verus giving up	• Use a multiple strategy approach to foster influence • Look for all options when you are in an exchange with the other person	• Stop influencing after one attempt and nothing happened • Stick with only one approach to influence the other person
Cultivating relationships versus hoping they happen	• Conduct a thorough stakeholder management • Understand the value of relationship in the influence process	• Let relationships fall apart • See relationship building as a low priority activity
Everyone is influenced differently versus all are influenced the same way	• Flex your communication style to match the other person's preference • Understand the drivers in the other person's world	• Not paying attention to the four quadrants of communication style • Use the same argumentation and approach for everyone
Stating one's position: assertive versus aggressive	• State what you need and a willingness to cooperate with what the other person needs • Be confident in your behaviors	• Intimidate the other person to go along with your proposal • Assert but don't cooperate
Create value versus claim value	• Look for options that give all parties as much as possible • Translate value as both tangible and intangible	• Be self-centered • Fight to look better than the other person
Other person's perspective: acknowledge versus dismiss	• Listen; discipline self to see the value of the other person's perspective • Realize your perspective is, at most, only 50 percent of reality	• Ignore the other person by not building on what he or she said • Find points of disagreement rather than points of agreement

2. **Misunderstanding:** It takes too much time to learn the perspectives of others. I get paid for getting results and relationship building doesn't buy me anything.
   - The truth is you do get paid for results. But the real question is, Are your results at the optimal or at the acceptable level?
   - Taking the time to learn the perspectives of others and to build relationships provides you the information you need to get to the optimal levels. It's an investment of your time, with a positive return.
   - In today's business world, it's not just a matter of getting results but of whether you can sustain the results. This is where relationships come into the equation.
3. **Misunderstanding:** I have tried to provide some value to others as the foundation of influence, but then I never got anything back in return to help me.
   - Because organizational living invites you to be more reactive than proactive, you may measure everything in terms of what you get back rather than what you provide.
   - Good influencers are more proactive; they measure things based on the value they provide more than on what they get back. This is a radical change in thinking.
   - To view your influence world differently, you must have a partnership mind-set. Treat others as your partners. and you will stay on track with this adjustment
4. **Misunderstanding:** Finding a common vision is easy to discuss but nearly impossible to implement.
   - It is challenging to find a common point where all parties can agree. It takes time to discuss and can be such a precious commodity that you end up with a scarcity mind-set that says, "there is only so much time and I have to use it as efficiently as possible." If you agree that the time investment has a positive return on investment, then you are on the right track.
   - Concentrate on finding points of agreement rather than points of disagreement. This is a key operation for you.
5. **Misunderstanding:** Influence strategies can come across as manipulative, and I don't want to take that chance. It could ruin my reputation.
   - Influence requires leadership skills. Those who don't want to influence colleagues won't have the ability to develop those leadership competencies. Managers won't tap them for leadership positions. There is nothing manipulative if your effort is to add value to the other party. It's manipulative if you try to add value only to yourself.
   - Influence carries the risk that it won't work. Many managers might not want to take that risk. The problem is that if they don't take the risk, they may end up in a more negative situation than they imagined.
6. **Misunderstanding:** I am too introverted to influence others. It's just better to keep quiet.
   - Being an influencer has nothing to do with introversion or extraversion. It comes down to your ability to flex your style to match the other person's. Introverts can be just as powerful as extraverts.

- Keeping quiet may work against you rather than help you. Remember, your reputation is rests on how others see you and your credibility.
- Saying that "this is the way I am" suggests you are locked into a position that others need to deal with. But the actual issue is how *you* deal with *them*.

Figure 7-5 provides a worksheet that will guide you through the key points of making your influence efforts successful.

• Conclusion •

Influence is the power to sway or affect a person or set of events. It needs a power base to be effective. If you don't have power provided by the organization, then you need to grow, develop, and leverage another power base. This is called your personal power base.

The first part of this personal power base is the combination of your expertise and relationship abilities. Some people try to bypass this combination and use either charisma, knowledge, or organizational politics as their power base. But these are one-dimensional and short-term.

The second part of this power base is your credibility. Credibility is when others you work with trust your expertise and relationship efforts. It is formed through the combination of your competency and character. These are the public and organizational displays of your expertise and relationships.

When using your personal power base, you should have a partnership mind-set. This mind-set moves you to combine both the logic and the benefits of your proposals. As simple as this seems, the benefit factor is critical. True influence doesn't occur unless all parties see the benefit to each party. This means your argumentation needs not only your reasoning but also the value you are trying to add. You will find when your proposal is not connecting, the strongest feedback you will receive will be some form of disengagement. This suggests that the benefit factor is missing.

During an influence process, inclusion is a key strategy to achieve your results. One of the best ways to activate this strategy is through flexing your communication style to match that of the other person. This will open up the process of questioning and listening. Your attention should be on understanding the perspectives of the other person so you can connect at the cognitive and emotional levels.

Personal power needs to grow continuously. You can develop your expertise through various methods. But relationships can be challenging. Relationships thrive on the giving and getting of value, however you and the other person define the word *value*. It can be something that helps you do your job more efficiently or provides a sense of making a difference. Each person defines value differently.

Exchange is the term used to reflect the giving and getting of precise value for you and the person you are influencing. The challenge will be to continue to provide value to the other person when he or she is not reciprocating. The key metric is value given rather than value received. This metric ties in closely with growing your credibility.

Finally, influence is a process, not a one-time event. When your influence efforts fail, ask yourself, Did my proposal get a fair hearing? Did others listen to me? If your answer is yes, then you have a platform on which to continue the influence process. If your answer is no, then you need to assess your credibility.

Key Points	Your Action Step
How is your credibility? Where is it vulnerable?	
How are your competency and character factors working?	
How is your personal power base (expertise plus relationship)? What are you doing to keep it growing?	
How are you balancing the benefit and logic factors when you are trying to influence?	
What are the points of agreement between you and the person you are trying to influence?	
Are you aware of your communication dimension? How flexible are you with it?	
How's your stakeholder management process? What are you doing to keep all three tiers (core, secondary, tertiary) informed?	
How inclusive are you?	
What's your strategy to activate your influence?	
Do you know your ranges of agreement?	
Do you look at negotiation as a problem-solving sequence and follow it?	
What are you doing to sustain relationships and partnerships?	
How confident are you about your recommendation?	
Are you aware of the value of your exchange? What is that value?	
Do you understand the other person's perspective?	
What is the consequence if you don't get what you want in your proposal?	

Figure 7.5 Your action steps worksheet

8

Delegation

LEARNING OBJECTIVES

By the end of this chapter, you will be better equipped to:

- Understand the function and purpose of delegation.
- Realize the potential benefits of effective delegation.
- Recognize the barriers to effective delegation.
- Create a culture that supports delegation.
- Determine what can and can't be delegated.
- Determine what to delegate.
- Conduct a delegation discussion.
- Tailor your methods and style to meet the needs of the delegate.
- Monitor to maintain control and support without micromanaging.
- Debrief and close out a completed assignment.
- Manage the challenges of delegating with a virtual workforce.

One of the most challenging transitions to make as a manager is to move from being an individual contributor—doing it yourself—to getting things done through others. Delegation is the process of assigning some degree of authority and responsibility for specific work to another person.

It is an important management competency that can serve to:

- Distribute work
- Provide employees with an opportunity to develop new skills or knowledge
- Create a more motivating work climate

The goals of this chapter are to provide you with an understanding of the process of delegation and to outline the steps and skills required to perform it effectively.

HISTORY AND CONTEXT OF DELEGATION

As long as people have worked within organizations, the person with the formal responsibility and authority for a process, or for the performance of others, has had to assign tasks and activities to employees to try to balance the workload and obtain an efficient use of human resources. However, as economies have evolved from primarily production and manufacturing based to being more service and information driven, so too have managerial responsibilities.

The nature of work is often different today than it was in the past. For many employees, daily activities have shifted from routine and standardized to unique and specialized. That shift in the nature of work along with social and cultural changes have led to changes in employee perspectives and expectations. A command-and-control leadership approach may have worked well in the past with standardized work processes designed to create operational efficiencies, but in many work cultures today, knowledge workers require a more collaborative approach.

Today when delegating, managers must not only distribute work but do it in a way that aligns employees' skill sets with often complex and specialized activities. In addition, managers are concerned with developing employees' skill sets and creating an engaging and motivating work climate.

Delegation has evolved from a relatively simple process of assigning work to a competency that requires the ability to:

- Diagnose and align the needs of both the organization and individual employees
- Provide varying amounts of guidance and support based on a delegatee's needs
- Monitor the employee's performance on delegated work to ensure both the success of the project and the development of the employee

Globalization and technology have added to the challenge of delegation. Increasingly, organizations operate within a global marketplace, which requires the interaction and integration of employees who may not be located in the same physical space, don't speak the same language, and have different cultural backgrounds.

Even managers working in organizations operating locally face the distance challenge, as many of their direct reports spend significant amounts of their time working from home or using flexible work schedules.

FUNCTION AND PURPOSE OF DELEGATION

Managers who delegate effectively have team members who are more capable and engaged, in part because of their delegation experience. Employees are able to take on increasing amounts of autonomy in managing their own work, which in turn frees up more of the managers' time, adding value to management and allowing them to work on higher-level activities that can't be delegated.

POTENTIAL BENEFITS OF DELEGATION

Effective delegation can benefit multiple stakeholders: the delegatee, other team members, the organization, and the manager.

Delegation for the employee:

- *Improves Motivation*: The nature of the work employees do and the practices of their manager go a long way in creating a motivational climate. Effective delegation can expand on the scope of work and add skill variety, task identity, challenge, meaningfulness, and autonomy to the job. All of these factors are associated with a more motivating work climate.
- *Builds Confidence*: Successfully completing an assignment builds a delegatee's self-confidence not only for the completion of a similar task in the future but also for taking on wholly new tasks and activities. Such confidence can lead to a pattern of success, which leads to greater recognition, opportunity, and compensation.
- *Develops Abilities*: To move from lower to higher levels of knowledge and skill requires experience. Effective delegation provides that experience; appropriate amounts of guidance and encouragement makes the journey smoother and faster.

Delegation for the manager:

- *Improves the Relationship with the Team Member*: Successful delegation builds two-way trust. By working with a team member to successfully complete an assignment, the manager learns to better trust the capabilities and the judgments of the employee. Because the manager provides the employee with what is needed to successfully accomplish the assignment, the delegatee perceives the manager as more competent, helpful, and concerned with others' success. That enhances the relationship.
- *Allows the Manager to Provide More Value*: When a manager contributes expertise and effort to the work group by directly performing a task, his or her effort is added to the performance of the team. The manager is providing additive value. When managers effectively delegate, they are free from the individual activity, which allows them to add value in a higher way by

helping the team develop more competence, creating a more motivational climate, removing barriers, and building employees confidence.

- *Improves the Manager's Overall Performance*: The right people, working on the right tasks with high levels of motivation leads to higher levels of performance. If managers are judged by the quality of the work performed by their team, then effective delegation is a necessity.

Delegation for the organization:

- *Increases the Pool of Competent Employees to Fill Vacancies and Capacity*: Effective and wide use of delegation leads to higher levels of competence for more members of the work team.
- *Can Improve the Morale and Effectiveness of Other Team Members*: Effective delegation allows other members of the team to recognize the opportunities and pathways available to them for developing new skills and operating more autonomously. In addition, team members benefit by having better bench strength within the work group.
- *Generates Data for Succession Planning*: As employees take on new and increasingly greater levels of authority and responsibility, delegation provides information about their capacity to move into higher or different roles within the organization.
- *Improves Retention*: People leave organizations for a variety of reasons, including feeling stagnant in their role, feeling their contribution lacks meaning or importance, and not seeing a pathway to developing new skills. Effective delegation can reduce those perceptions and help the organization retain its talent.
- *Optimizes the Organization's Resources*: Delegating the right assignments to the right people at the right level at the right time allows the organization to make the best use of its human resources. That increases productivity.

BARRIERS TO EFFECTIVE DELEGATION

Even with all of the potential benefits, delegation can be challenging. The challenges fall into three main categories. Barriers that reside within the manager, the employee, and the context of the situation itself.

The Manager

Barriers within the manager include:

- *Dysfunctional Beliefs*: Our beliefs often affect our actions. A manager's implicit beliefs about delegation can support or derail the delegation process. Dysfunctional beliefs can cause a manager to avoid delegation or to do it in a less effective way. Common beliefs that often (but not always) fall into that category include:

- No one can do it as well as I can—this may be true at the moment but delegating with the right level of guidance and support can help build competence within the delegatee and throughout the work team.
- If I delegate this task, I'm going to lose control over how it's done and what's produced—effective delegation practices allow the manager to stay in touch with the delegatee to ensure a successful final product.
- If I delegate, it will decrease my value within organization—successful delegation leads to higher performance within the team. Managers who build high-performing teams have value.

◆ *Comfort*: Managers who are technically skilled at a specific activity often find it more comfortable to continue performing the activity themselves rather than to delegate it. They know how to do it. They are good at it. It provides an intrinsic sense of reward and satisfaction when they perform it.

- Fear and need to control—managers may be concerned about the consequences of unsuccessful delegation. If the delegatee goes off track or fails to deliver a successful outcome, it may affect the team's or the organization's overall results. Ultimately the manager will be held accountable. That fear may lead to a practice of overmanaging, whereby the manager feels the need to retain control. By using the correct delegation practices, the manager can stay in touch and ensure a successful outcome without overcontrolling or micromanaging.
- Lack of skill—effective delegation has a defined methodology and requires specific behavioral skills. It's a learned process. A lack of delegation skill can lead to underdelegation, dumping work at the last minute when feeling overwhelmed, or overdelegating.

The Employee

Effective delegation involves two people: the manager and the delegatee. The beliefs and behaviors of the employee can create an obstacle to successful delegation. Those beliefs can lead to an unwillingness on the employee's part to commit to the delegation process.

Barriers within the employee include:

◆ *Fear of Taking on New Responsibilities*: Employees may fear committing to new responsibilities for a variety of reasons.

- They may worry that they won't be given the resources or support that they need from the manager.
- They may feel that they already have a heavy workload and that new responsibilities will detract from their overall ability to get things done.
- They may be concerned about failure and the consequences that they will suffer.
- They may have worked in past jobs where taking on additional responsibilities was viewed negatively by their co-workers.

  - They may hold a fixed mind-set, by which they have an implicit belief that their talents and abilities are fixed traits that can't be built on or added to. As a result, they may doubt their own abilities to learn or improve, so they avoid situations where that's required.

- *Lack of Motivation*: Motivation is unique to the individual and can differ from one task to another. When an employee does not see the personal value in taking on additional or new responsibilities, she may lack interest in the assignment. This, of course, raises other problems beyond just delegation.

The Context

National culture can have an impact on how delegation is viewed by both the manager and the employee. With globalization, managers may be required to delegate across cultures to employees who are guided by a different set of societal norms than their own. For more detailed discussions, see Chapter 18, Organizational Culture.

Power Distance Differences

The extent to which the members of a society accept the unequal distribution of power can have an impact on how employees view and accept the delegation of responsibility and authority. In national cultures where hierarchy is seen as essential and even beneficial (as in India), members higher up are often expected to take care of those lower in the hierarchy. Delegation could be seen as abdicating responsibility.

Managers from cultures with high uncertainty avoidance (as in Germany) may choose to delegate less in order to satisfy control needs. Likewise, in a culture that emphases high individualism (as in the United States) managers may try to do it all on their own rather than looking to get things done through delegation.

Physical Proximity

Managers are often responsible for the performance of team members with whom they are not co-located. When face-to-face contact is limited, this physical separation can be a challenge for effective delegation in several ways:

- Communication can be more challenging.
- Trust can be more difficult to develop.
- Oversight and monitoring can be more challenging.

Organizational Culture

The shared values, beliefs, and perceptions held by the members of the organization will have an impact on how delegation is viewed. Organizational culture can affect a manager's willingness to delegate. If power is centralized, if top-down expectations are such that it's the manager's personal responsibility to get it done, or if top leadership relies on an authoritarian, directive leadership approach, then managers will likely delegate less. Likewise, if the culture fails to reward initiative or those who seek greater responsibility, if it requires decisions to be made at upper levels of the organization, or if growth and development are not emphasized, employees may lack commitment to accept additional responsibilities and authority.

CREATING A CULTURE FOR EFFECTIVE DELEGATION

Culture is the shared values, beliefs, and behaviors of an organization or a unit within that organization. Those beliefs and values can be implicit and develop on their own or they can be more formalized. The inculcated values and beliefs essentially create the paradigm for "the way we do things here" and help establish norms for an individual's behavior. Those norms can affect both the perceptions and process of delegation within the organization or team.

An organizational culture that supports delegation is one in which:

- Delegation is an opportunity for growth and development.
- Members recognize there are stages or degrees of delegation and their level of authority may differ from one assignment to the next.
- There is a climate of high mutual trust between managers and direct reports.
- Communication is open, candid, clear, and timely.
- Employees expect to be held accountable.

Culture can develop over time through the interaction of a number of factors, including:

- *A Manager's Behaviors and Explicit Statements*: Team members often take their cues from the manager. Make sure you speak positively about and demonstrate behaviors that support the importance and value of delegation.
- *Repeated Behaviors by Group Members*: Pay close attention to team member behavior. Behavior that gets reinforced is more likely to continue. Recognize and reinforce behaviors that contribute to norms that support delegation.
- *Critical Incidents*: Recognize that high-impact behaviors can establish a precedent. Don't ignore negative responses to delegation. Seek to understand by asking questions and listening when those negative responses occur and offer guidance and support as needed to influence a more positive dynamic.
- *Conscious Choices by Group Members to Do Things in a Certain Way*: Discuss and agree on the benefits of delegation and how it will work within the team.

To build a delegation-friendly culture, managers can:

- Hold regular performance planning meetings in which the expectation of delegation is discussed
- Discuss and use a transparent process for delegation conversations
- Reach agreement with the delegatee for how the two of you will work together to ensure the delegatee's success
- Inform vested stakeholders about who is leading the project and that employee's level of authority
- Reinforce and recognize team members for their delegation performance

THE TASKS EFFECTIVE DELEGATORS PERFORM

Effective delegation requires that a manager master and engage in the following steps:

1. Determine the tasks to be delegated and align skills to available resources.
2. Give clear instructions and ensure team members have all necessary information, requirements, and resources and that they understand the timelines needed to complete delegated responsibilities.
3. Collaborate with the delegatee to determine the most effective plan to accomplish the desired goals in a way that will be mutually beneficial.
4. Adapt delegation based on the individual and his motivational and behavioral style.
5. Provide ongoing coaching and support without micromanaging delegated assignments (see Chapter 9, Coaching for Performance).
6. Debrief delegated tasks and projects to identify key learnings and provide both positive and constructive feedback.

WHAT CAN AND CAN'T BE DELEGATED

Many of the activities that managers normally perform have the potential for delegation. It's important to keep your purpose in mind. Why are you considering delegating? The two major types of reasons are work distribution and employee development.

Managers delegate for work distribution to:

- Move a task or project from their plate so they can focus on a higher-value activity
- Even out the distribution of work within the team
- Match skills to a needed task

Managers delegate for of employee development to:

- Help an employee develop new skills
- Foster self-confidence and self-reliant thinking within a team member
- Enrich an employee's motivational climate by increasing factors like job challenge, skill variety, task identity, meaningfulness, and autonomy

At times, your workload will drive what and when you delegate, but whenever possible delegation should be a proactive process to serve a specific purpose. When delegating to distribute and balance the workload or to free yourself up for more strategic activities consider the following:

- Tasks closely related to the work employees are already doing
- Tasks with clearly defined procedures and end results
- Repetitive tasks that naturally fit into the normal work flow
- Activities for which an employee already possesses the necessary knowledge skill and experience to perform successfully

When delegating to help a team member develop or enhance a skill or when working to build a more motivational climate, consider the following:

- The employee's career and professional needs and interests
- The employee's willingness and confidence in taking on new tasks
- Your time and ability to work more closely with the employee to provide resources, guidance, and support to ensure a successful outcome

Some types of activities, as a rule, should not be delegated, such as:

- Tasks of a highly sensitive nature, including salary reviews, discipline, and performance reviews
- Tasks that the manager has not thought through carefully
- Ambiguous tasks for which the desired outcomes are unclear
- Really important tasks that upper management expects the manager to handle personally
- Projects that could put the employee or the organization at unnecessary risk
- Assignments that could overwhelm the employee
- Mission critical tasks for which the risk of failure outweighs the benefits of delegating
- Core strategic functions, such as mission, vision, and performance management activities; team building; and building a motivational climate

DECIDING WHAT TO DELEGATE

It's useful to start the process of deciding what to delegate by identifying the tasks and activities you typically spend your time performing. Start by:

- Reviewing your calendar
- Examining your master task list
- Reviewing any and all to-do lists
- Looking at your work goals and key result areas for the current year and the previous year
- Create a delegation template (see Table 8-1 for an example)

As you consider your current responsibilities and activities one at a time, ask yourself, "Is this something someone else can do or learn to do?" As you begin to identify specific tasks to delegate, keep in mind that activities with a high task identity (beginning-to-end work with concrete outcomes) are generally more motivating than pieces of a job. Likewise, while delegation will involve the assignment of routine tasks and activities to distribute work evenly, it shouldn't involve only those types of assignments. Try to balance more basic assignments with more interesting or developmental projects.

After completing your list, review it, paying particular attention to the activities you identified as unsuitable for delegation. Are you holding on to a task or an activity simply because you feel comfortable with it? Is there a valid reason for retaining it for yourself?

Evaluate tasks in terms of distributing the workload as well as suitability for employee development.

THE PROCESS OF DELEGATION

As shown in Figure 8-1, delegation is a three-step process.

Step 1: Preparing to Delegate

Just as a good point guard in basketball is always thinking about distributing the ball to a teammate, a good manager is always thinking about distributing the workload. A manager bases delegation decisions on identified needs for distributing work, developing an employee's capabilities, or improving the motivational climate.

Identify What to Delegate

Once you've identified the purpose you hope to accomplish, identify what you can potentially delegate to achieve it. Delegation can involve the assignment of authority and responsibility for different scopes

Table 8-1 A Completed Delegation Template				
My Tasks and Activities	**Approximate Time Spent**	**One Time or Recurring**	**Visibility and Importance**	**Suitable to Delegate (Can someone else do it or learn to do it?)**
Reviewing and responding to email	10 hours/week	Recurring	Low / high	No
Weekly staff meeting agenda preparation	2 hours/week	Recurring	Medium / medium	Yes
Weekly staff meeting facilitation	1 hour/week	Recurring	Medium / high	Maybe
Communicating upward with my boss	2 hours/week	Recurring	High / high	No
Annual budget preparation	20 hours/year	Recurring	Medium / high	No, but others could be involved
Budget review and tracking	5 hours/month	Recurring	Low / high	Yes
Responding to an escalated concern	2 hours/issue	One-time issues	High / high	No

of work, including tasks, work packages, projects, and functions. For whatever scope, clearly identify the outcomes required for successful completion, for example:

- At the task level: "Obtain customer complaint records for the past twelve months by Friday."
- At the work package level: "Research, analyze, and prepare a report with a Pareto analysis of the underlying causes of shipping complaints by October 1."
- At the project level: "Reduce customer complaints about damaged shipments from 6 percent to 2 percent by April 1."
- At the function level: "Develop and manage the annual team budget."

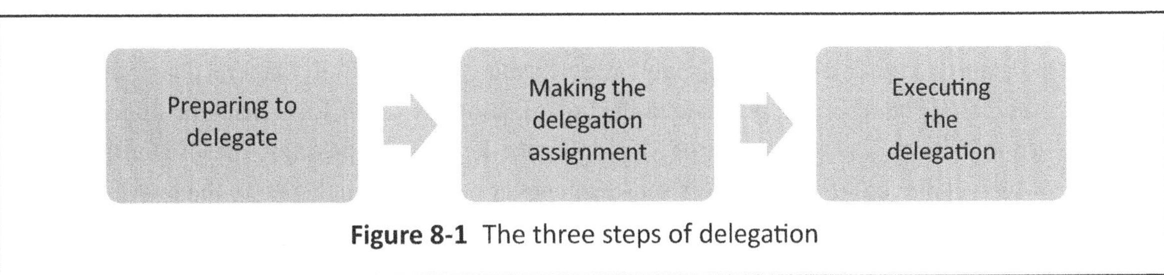

Figure 8-1 The three steps of delegation

Analyze the Work

Before you identify whom to delegate to, you need to have a clear idea of the work itself and the skills required to accomplish it. Review the goals or final outcomes of the assignment by answering the following questions:

- What tasks have to be accomplished to achieve those goals?
- How much time is required for an experienced employee to perform each of the tasks?
- What type of knowledge and skills are required to perform each of the tasks?
- How much time is required for an inexperienced employee to perform each of the tasks with my guidance and support?
- Is there a critical path or steps that must be taken or issues that must be addressed?
- What about the scope of the assignment? Will I delegate the entire scope of work or select pieces?

Identify Whom to Delegate To

Depending on your original need and purpose for delegating, you may already have a delegatee in mind. You may, for example, intentionally look for an assignment to help a specific employee develop new skills. At other times, when your purpose is to reduce your personal workload, distribute work, or align skills with an organizational assignment, the work may have to come first, and you will need to identify the right employee to delegate it to.

In those situations, it may be helpful to compare possible delegatees on several different criteria.

- *Skills and Experience for the Assignment*: Competence is task specific. Has the employee performed this type of work before? How was her performance? High results on other types of tasks do not necessarily make her a good candidate for this type of assignment.
- *Current Workload*: Consider the employee's current workload when making a delegation assignment. If your intent is to evenly distribute the work within the team to improve productivity, you won't want to overload any one individual. A high current workload doesn't automatically disqualify a candidate, but it does raise the issue of whether you might have to redistribute that employee's current work to make room for the new assignment.
- *Job Level*: Generally, you should attempt to delegate to the lowest job level of employee capable of performing the work. If the assignment is one that can be successfully completed by either of two employees, one of whom is a Level 1 machine operator responsible for running a single machine and the other is a technical lead responsible for providing ongoing assistance to other employees as well as performing her own individual responsibilities, all other things being equal, delegate to the organizationally lower level machine operator. While it may not always hold true, the higher the level of the position, the greater the value of that employee's time. It makes sense whenever possible to delegate to the lowest level to maximize the return on time invested.

Table 8-2 Delegation Analysis Based on Employee Attributes				
Name	**Skill and Experience for This Assignment**	**Current Workload**	**Job Level**	**Level of Guidance, Support, and Time Needed**
Susan	Low	Medium	Analyst	High
Min	Medium to high	Medium	Analyst	Low
Derrick	High	High	Senior analyst	Low

In the examples shown in Table 8-2, Min might be the best choice as a delegatee for an assignment intended to distribute work within the team. On the other hand, if you were looking at the delegation as a developmental opportunity, then Susan might be the better choice.

Level of Delegated Authority

As part of your preparation, give some thought to the appropriate level of responsibility and authority to delegate. Although the final decision about those issues may not occur until you discuss them with your identified delegatee, it's important think about these issues and plan ahead of that conversation.

Responsibility and authority are not the same. *Authority* refers to the level of power or decision-making rights that have been granted to an individual. *Responsibility* refers to accountability for an outcome.

The old axiom of "You can delegate authority, but you can't abdicate responsibility" is an important principle for managers to keep in mind. You can delegate the authority to take certain types of actions and to make certain types of decisions; however, you, the manager, are ultimately responsible for the results of those actions and decisions. Delegatees have accountability for their own performance, but the final responsibility is *yours.*

With that in mind, as in other situations, the level of authority that you delegate is important and needs to be aligned with:

- The complexity and needs of the assignment
- The delegatee's experience and skill for the assignment
- Your availability to provide guidance, support, resources, and oversight

Authority can be delegated at different levels. Table 8-3 shows one way to parse those levels.

By way of example, Level 5 delegation occurs when the manager completely trusts the employee's abilities to accomplish the assignment. The delegatee has complete authority for the process and the outcomes that it generates. At this level, the responsibility for those outcomes, while still ultimately the manager's, is now shared with the delegatee.

Step 2: Making the Delegation Assignment

Once you have decided exactly what to delegate and to whom, the next step is to conduct a delegation discussion with the prospective delegatee. This is where the assignment of authority and the agreement

Table 8-3 Levels of Authority	
Level 1	Follow my instructions to complete a task.
Level 2	Let's discuss it. We'll decide together about the best way for you to approach it. You implement the plan. If you think that you need to deviate from our plan let's reconnect before you act.
Level 3	Let's discuss it. You make the final decision about the best way to proceed. You implement the plan. Keep me informed.
Level 4	Let's agree on the goal. Take whatever action you believe is most appropriate. Keep me informed of what you've done.
Level 5	Decide and act on your own.

on outcomes take place. The delegation discussion should be a collaborative, two-way dialogue, not a one-way information dump.

The intent of the discussion is to:

- Create mutual understanding
- Ensure clarity of expectations
- Develop a delegation plan that is mutually beneficial

Ideally, the discussion will be conducted face to face, but in situations where the manager and employee are not co-located that may not be possible. At a minimum, the discussion should be held over the phone or video conferencing. Because of the greater potential for misunderstanding, avoid communication that does not take place in real time.

What to Discuss

During the discussion, provide the delegatee with the necessary information, requirements, and resources needed to complete the assignment. The way you approach the conversation and the level of detail you provide may differ from one discussion to the next based on factors like:

- The employee's level of experience and knowledge for the assignment
- The employee's level of interest and engagement in the potential work
- The level of authority you choose to delegate

A conversation with a delegatee who is experienced and motivated for the delegated work should be less detailed than a delegation conversation with an employee who's never performed the type of work being delegated and who may lack confidence in his or her ability to successfully complete it.

In general, consider the six steps listed in Figure 8-2 when planning for the delegation conversation. What's discussed within each step is specific to the assignment and experience and capabilities of the potential delegatee. Think of each step in the conversation as being scalable. It can expand and address more information or it can contract and address less, depending on the needs of the delegatee. Each step is described in more detail in the following paragraphs.

1. Describe the assignment. Within this step the following topics should be discussed, depending on the experience, skills, and engagement level of the delegatee:

- Identify the purpose of the conversation
- Describe the assignment and outline the work you are delegating
- Explain the value of the work to the team or organization
- Discuss why you are delegating the task to the employee and the potential benefits.
- Specify the desired results, including the specific deliverables or outcomes for which she will be accountable
- Describe the level of authority you are delegating
- Discuss the timeline and desired deadlines
- When delegating for development, describe how you will ensure employee receives any needed guidance and coaching to accomplish the assignment

The manager is often doing most of the talking in this step, but it shouldn't be one-way communication. As you describe the assignment, engage the employee by asking questions and using active listening. Use the employee's answers to test her understanding.

2. Check understanding and confirm alignment. A lack of understanding and alignment of expectations will likely lead to unsuccessful delegation. Managers ask, "Do you have any questions?" or "Do

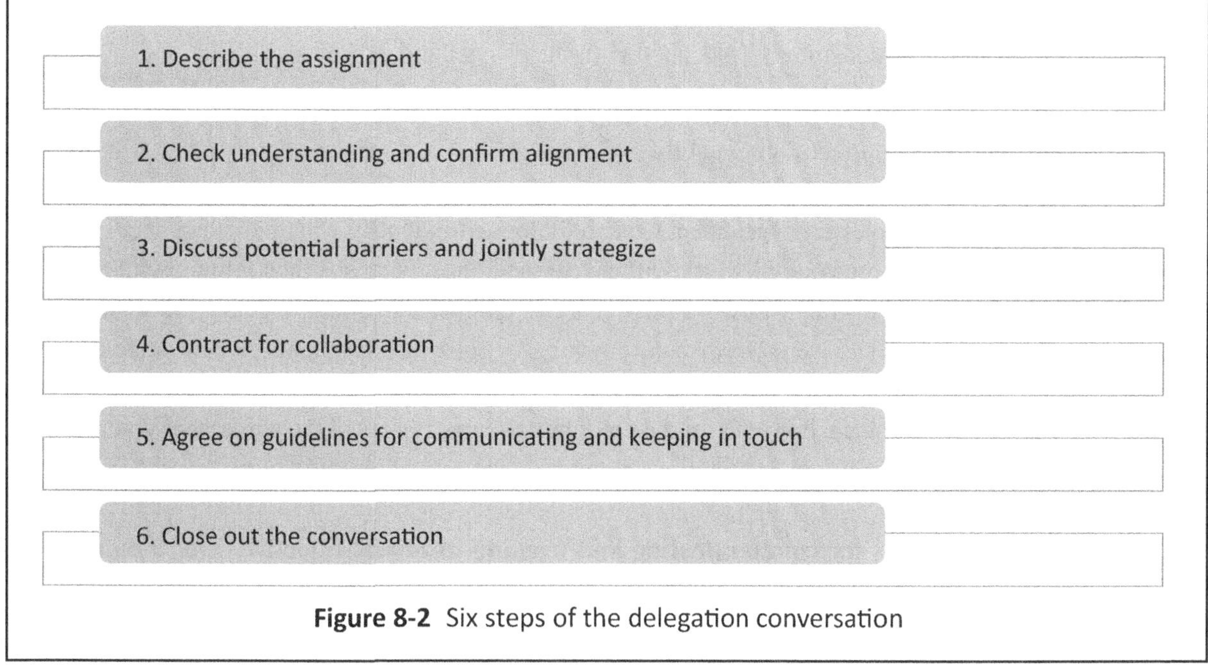

Figure 8-2 Six steps of the delegation conversation

you understand?" to attempt to check alignment. There's nothing inherently bad about those types of questions but they may not generate accurate information about the employee's understanding of the assignment. It's a better strategy to ask the employee to summarize the assignment in her own words. As she does, you can once again use questions and active listening to test expectation alignment.

3. Discuss potential barriers and jointly strategize. This step is always important, but even more essential when delegating for development to an employee who does not have direct experience and the skills for the work being assigned. Begin by soliciting potential problems from the employee. Ask the delegatee, "What problems or barriers do you see in accomplishing this assignment?" As she identifies potential roadblocks and challenges, engage her in a collaborative problem-solving discussion about what she could do to prevent or respond to the issue if it occurred. Try to facilitate her self-reliant thinking; she is likely to have more ownership in strategies and solutions she thought of herself than in your prescriptions. If she doesn't or can't identify potential issues that you are aware of or if she can't identify useful strategies for preventing or responding to challenges, provide guidance and direction that's tied to her level of authority to help her proactively develop a plan. One potential roadblock that often arises is the employee's current workload. She may feel she has too many other responsibilities or tasks that will interfere with the accomplishment of the new assignment. If that's the case, engage the employee in a conversation to explore those potential conflicts and work with her to reprioritize the existing workload. If necessary, consider redistributing responsibilities or tasks to other team members.

4. Contract for collaboration. Effective delegation requires style flexibility. Managers need to be able to adapt their approach based on the needs of the delegatee. Those needs may differ based on factors such as these:

- Employee's knowledge, skills, and experience for the task
- Employee's interest in the assignment
- Employee's self-confidence to perform the work
- Employee's time constraints associated with the project and current workload
- Employee's preferred work style
- Assignment's importance and visibility

In this step, you need to engage the delegatee in a dialogue to identify what her exact needs are and to reach agreement about how you will work with her to meet those needs. When talking with an experienced delegatee assigned a straightforward project she is enthusiastic about, this may be as simple as agreeing to be available if she wants to discuss anything or runs into problems. When delegating for development to an employee who's never performed the type of work required, you may need to agree to provide much more guidance, how-to's, and oversight. It's important that the agreement you reach be explicit and concrete. Ambiguity in expectations about how the two of you will work together can damage your relationship.

5. Agree on guidelines for communicating and keeping in touch. Effective delegation requires ongoing communication and monitoring. Without clear guidelines, the manager may fail to provide adequate guidance, support, or oversight and the delegatee may underperform or outright fail, which means the manager has failed. Sometimes managers end up overmanaging, with a constant stream of emails, phone calls, or drop-in visits to check on the status of the assignment. The two primary methods for staying in touch and providing oversight are:

- *Scheduling Regular Checkpoints (Daily, Weekly, Monthly)*: A preset schedule allows the manager to review progress and provide any needed guidance. The number and frequency of checkpoints depend on the level of authority being delegated. One consideration is the potential to recover from a setback. If you discover the assignment is behind schedule or off-track at the checkpoint, you need sufficient time to recover and get back on schedule to meet the assignment's goals.
- *Breaking the Assignment into Milestones*: Once the assignment has been deconstructed, the manager and the employee can collaborate on a schedule for completion of the milestones and schedule times to reconnect to review and discuss progress. Such meetings will usually coincide with the scheduled completion date of each or selected milestones.

In addition to formalized checkpoints and milestones, it's often useful to discuss the types of circumstances in which the delegatee should reach out to the manager between scheduled meetings. It's good practice to not only emphasize that the employee has the option of contacting you at any time should questions or concerns arise but also to identify any specific situations when, if they were to occur, you would want the employee to contact you directly as soon as possible. This is increasingly important as the amount of authority being delegated increases. When the authority reaches Level 5 (decide and act on your own) this procedure can be an essential tool for avoiding delegation disasters. This places conditional limits on the delegatee's authority if specific circumstances occur, while allowing her relative autonomy for the assignment overall.

6. Close Out the Conversations. Bring the discussion to a positive, natural conclusion by:

- Summarizing any points you believe need reinforcing
- Confirming the employee's level of commitment for the assignment
- Expressing confidence in the employee's ability to accomplish the assignment

Step 3: Executing the Delegation

Once the assignment has been delegated, the manager's role becomes primarily one of monitoring and providing any needed guidance and support. Here some considerations:

- *Notify Stakeholders*: One support action you may need to take is to notify stakeholders of the involvement of the delegatee and the authority that you have delegated to that employee. This will help establish the power and credibility the delegatee needs to work with those stakeholders.

- *Follow the Plan*: You'll have an agreed-to communication plan from the delegation conversation. Stick to it. Avoid the temptation to overmanage and supervise more closely than the level of authority that you've delegated requires.
- *Manage at Checkpoints*: Use the regularly scheduled checkpoints to track the progress of the assignment and to ensure that it is being completed correctly and on time. Within those regularly scheduled meetings, continue to provide any organizational or contextual information that may have a bearing on the successful completion of the assignment.
- *Coach*: The scheduled checkpoints can also serve as opportunities to provide coaching to help the delegatee accomplish the assignment and to enhance his or her skills.
    - Engage the employee in a discussion about the progress of the assignment
    - Review any milestones or metrics
    - Review the ongoing resource needs and ensure that the delegatee has what is needed
    - Ask questions to get the delegatee to talk about the aspects of the assignment that are going well as well as about any difficulties or challenges
- *Difficulties and Roadblocks*: Problematic issues are more than obstacles to the completion of the assignment; they are also developmental opportunities. If and when problems occur, skilled managers facilitate a conversation in which delegatees identify their own strategies and solutions for overcoming them. That self-generated problem solving will improve the employees' competence as well as their self-confidence for solving future challenges. If there are problems employees' can't identify the solution for, provide guidance or additional resources to help keep the assignment on track. If necessary, you may need to:
    - Renegotiate with the employee to reassume selected parts of the assignment to help lighten the workload on the employee
    - Run interference with another department or function
    - Manage upward to obtain resources or decisions from people senior to you within the organization
- *Close Out the Assignment*: At the conclusion of one-time tasks or projects, you should meet with the delegatee to close out the assignment. Bringing the assignment to a natural conclusion means:
    - Reviewing the deliverables to gauge alignment with the original goal
    - Discussing lessons learned
    - Providing coaching to help the employee anchor key learnings
    - Reinforcing the delegatee's performance and accomplishments
    - Sharing credit for the role of the delegatee with other team members and stakeholders within the organization
    - Thanking the employee for his or her efforts and achievement

DELEGATING WITHIN VIRTUAL TEAMS

Increasingly, managers are responsible for the performance of individuals with whom they are not co-located. Global markets have led to global presence. The international production and exchange of goods and services have led many organizations to move to more dispersed, geographically based structures. A software company, for example, may be based in one country and locate its development operation in another country where there's a readily available pool of talent. It may have its production facility in a third country where labor costs are more advantageous and resources are more available. Even in locally based organizations, managers must expect to manage people whom they may not see on a regular basis. Flexible scheduling is a given in many organizations. Working from home is more and more commonplace. It can save the organization the cost of setting up infrastructure and additional facilities, and it's an attractive feature for both recruiting and retaining quality talent. Technology has accelerated the trend. Web-based services for participating in meetings, sharing information, collaborating, and working more synergistically on projects continue to evolve. Remote delegation is a reality.

The trend of delegating to remote team members, despite its potential benefits, has challenges.

- The lack of face-to-face interaction, both formal and informal, can have a negative impact on trust.
- Misunderstandings can occur more frequently because of cultural differences.
- Time zone differences make communication even more challenging.
- Mission, vision, and context are often diluted or lost in translation across geographic distance.
- Priorities often become blurred and misaligned.
- Oversight is more difficult.

Virtual Delegation

There's no single strategy to eliminate the inherent challenges of remote delegation. However, there are practices that can make virtual delegation a more effective process.

Work to Create Alignment of Expectations

Similar to face-to-face delegation, remote delegation requires a clear description of the assignment and level of authority being delegated. When delegating to remote team members, managers often rely on the efficiency of email to communicate the assignment. While email can be useful as a pre-read or follow-up, the actual delegation conversation should be a real-time, synchronous, two-way discussion. Use the six-step process shown in Figure 8-2 to help manage that conversation.

Overcommunicate the Why

Remote team members are often less aware of what's happening within the organization than are local employees. That lack of information and understanding can lead to the employee feeling disconnected or isolated, which can affect how he or she goes about the assignment. When delegating to remote employees, provide them with the contextual and background information available. Why is assignment important? Help them to understand the value of the assignment by relating it back to the organization's mission and the work team's goals.

Be Transparent about Your Intentions

A manager's credibility, and the trust that accompanies that credibility, is partly related to how his or her intentions are perceived. Trust is somewhat more challenging with remote delegation because of the lack of face-to-face interaction and the ambiguity in really understanding one another. Be concrete and transparent in explaining your positive intentions. Don't assume that the delegatee will understand why you are doing what you're doing or why you are suggesting what you are suggesting. Explain it.

Cultural Competency

Become more culturally competent and adjust your style and practices. Oftentimes, in geographically dispersed teams, culture differences can lead to misunderstandings. National culture can affect a variety of aspects of organizational life, including gender roles, strict adherence to time and schedules, and manager–employee relationships. These affect how people respond to delegation and empowerment. Learn about any cultural differences that may exist. Become more culturally competent. Demonstrate your respect and responsiveness by adapting your style and practices to the employee's cultural dynamics as much as possible. For more on these these issues, see also Chapter 17, Style and Fit.

Use Technology to Support

Make mindful, collaborative choices about how to best use technology to communicate and track performance. Discuss and agree on the best platforms and circumstances for:

- Document collaboration
- Real-time phone calls
- Email
- Instant messaging
- Text
- Voicemail
- Video conferences
- In-person site visits

Use screen-sharing apps or meeting management apps when conducting delegation conversations to visually anchor key expectations. Agree on and use file-sharing or project management programs, which can be updated by the employee to track progress.

Plan for Oversight

One of the biggest challenges in delegating to a remote employee is the manager's inability to physically observe the performance of the employee. Recognize this inherent limitation and plan how you will overcome it. Give careful consideration to how you will monitor and track the employee's performance and progress on the assignment. The specifics of that tracking and monitoring should be discussed and agreed to in the original delegation conversation when you make the delegation assignment. The regularly scheduled checkpoints that you develop in that meeting will serve as an important piece in providing effective oversight. For some assignments you may want to use additional methods. Project management software can provide a web-based mechanism for task assignment and management, time tracking, file sharing, and collaboration. In assignments that require close oversight, end-of-day reports can be used to track how remote employees have spent their time each day and to create a record of progress between regularly scheduled checkpoints.

Work to Build the Relationship

Trust is often more difficult to establish when you aren't physically co-located. Trust is built naturally over time, as we interact with people and get to know them. When we are co-located we see them regularly, we run into them in the hallway, we talk informally, and we begin to expand our understanding of who they are, including their competencies and their intentions. Without that regular contact, our understanding of who an employee is grows much more slowly. When we don't have that knowledge, it's difficult to trust. Take steps to get to know remote employees and actively work to help them to better know you as well. Site visits are invaluable. If it's not possible to physically visit remote employees, build time into your regular conversations and scheduled checkpoints to share appropriate non-task-related information. Ask them about their interests and the events happening in their lives, without crossing any boundaries about their noncompany activities. Share appropriate details from your own life to help employees better understand you as a person.

VARYING YOUR DELEGATIVE STYLE

Delegation involves assigning varying levels of authority, thus managers must adapt their delegative style to best meet the needs of the delegatee. Simply put, a manager's delegative style is the way to make the assignment and work with the employee.

Your delegative style rests on two primary factors. The amount of guidance that you provide about how the activity should be approached and the engagement you attempt to create by soliciting input and involving the employee. As mentioned earlier, the lower the employee's direct experience and skill with the tasks in the assignment, the greater the need for guidance from the manager. The lower the employee's confidence or enthusiasm for the assignment, the greater the need for the manager to engage the employee in the process. When guiding, the manager generally takes the lead and tells the employee; when engaging, the manager generally solicits the employee's input (Table 8-4). Guidance behaviors are primarily focused on the task itself, while engagement behaviors are more focused on the employee's attitudes about the assignment and his or her relationship with the manager.

Some examples of guidance and engagement behaviors follow.

The delegation of authority within Levels 1 to 4 always requires some amount of guidance and engagement. Even the delegation of Level 5 authority requires that you provide at least low levels of guidance and engagement to ensure that both you and the employee are in alignment on the goals of the assignment and that you are clear about any expectations the delegatee may have of you.

In addition to considering the employee's direct experience and ability and his level of engagement for the specific assignment, you may need to adapt your approach based on the employee's personality and preferred work style. People differ in myriad ways, and those individual differences can affect:

- How employees process information
- What type of information employees seek
- How employees make decisions
- How employees prefer to communicate
- How employees learn best
- The degree of variety and challenge employees like in their jobs

Table 8-4 Guidance Versus Engagement in the Delegation

Examples of Guidance Behavior	Examples of Engagement Behaviors
During the Delegation Conversation	
• Unilaterally specify the direct outcomes and deliverables • Define the steps and process to be followed • Point out potential obstacles and prescribe the strategies to be employed to overcome them • Specify the amount of time that selected pieces of work should take	• Collaboratively discuss and agree on the specific goals of the assignment • Solicit the employee's ideas for how to go about accomplishing the assignment • Facilitate a discussion about when the employee can take the lead in identifying potential problems and plan strategies to overcome them
While the Assignment Is Being Executed	
• As the assignment progresses, demonstrate and teach the employee how to perform certain activities • Be specific, providing direction about what should be accomplished or how it should be done • Monitor and evaluate the employee's performance • Provide corrective feedback about what the employee could do differently to be more effective • Provide oversight	• Solicit the employee's opinions about how the assignment is going • Emphasize the organizational whys for the overall assignment or for specific milestones or activities • Act as a sounding board for employee concerns • Help the employee develop self-confidence by facilitating discussions that allow the employee to diagnosis problems and to determine solutions • Provide reinforcing feedback that focuses on what the employee has successfully accomplished • Offer encouragement

- Employees' comfort with planning and personal organization
- Employees' relationship with time

These differences, and others, combine to develop each employee's preferred work style. Oftentimes when there are significant differences in work styles, people are prone to look at the other party as being wrong or as having a weakness. We all have strengths and weaknesses, but we should avoid automatically viewing a different work style as having inherent problems. Such differences are simply individual preferences that lead to different ways, not necessarily bad ways, of going about an assignment. Effective delegation requires that managers adapt their style to best meet the needs of delegatees. Meet people where they are, not where you'd like them to be. To do that:

- Understand your own style preferences because effectiveness begins with self-awareness. How can you understand others if you don't understand yourself?
- Become more skilled at reading people and sizing up their preferences. Learn more about personality and work style. Become a student of the people you interact with, especially your direct reports.
- Value differences, and look at individual differences as a source of strength or a potential asset.

In addition, adapt your approach to best meet the needs of the other person. Delegation is a partnership that you have a major stake in. The employee's performance on the assignment affects the overall productivity within your work team. Recognize that the only person you have complete control of within that relationship is you. Develop behavioral flexibility so you can shift from what feels most natural to what is most needed for a given situation. We all have innate preferences and habits, which combine to influence how we typically interact and communicate with others. Behavioral flexibility involves our willingness and ability to move beyond our default habits and natural tendencies to effectively use a greater range of communication and interaction behaviors.

DELEGATION EFFECTIVENESS INDICATORS

When managers practice effective delegation, they:

- Demonstrate a willingness to delegate routine as well as more complex and important assignments to others.
- View delegation as a collaborative process.
- Communicate the context, goal, and desired outcomes clearly.
- Work to ensure the employee has the appropriate level of authority and required resources to successfully complete the assignment.
- Reprioritize the employee's existing workload, if needed.
- Build in checkpoints and step approvals as required to monitor and coach performance.

- Work to ensure the delegatee really understands the goal and importance of the assignment and is in alignment about to collaborate.
- Vary their approach from one delegation assignment to the next based on the needs of the delegatee.
- Use agreed-on checkpoints to monitor progress and provide coaching.
- Hold people accountable for accomplishing agreed-to assignments.

When managers practice ineffective delegation, they:

- Do not delegate.
- Do not trust the process of delegation or prefer to perform task themselves.
- Dump assignments on employees without consideration for their workload.
- Delegate responsibility but don't provide adequate authority or resources.
- Delegate only low-value activities.
- Delegate only small pieces of activities to accomplish a goal.
- Do not adequately explain the goal, context, or desired results.
- Delegate without monitoring.
- Do not hold people accountable for results.
- Do not vary their delegation approach based on the needs of the employee.
- Do not get agreement with the employee about how they will work together.
- Delegate inappropriate activities.

See also Table 8-5.

Table 8-5 Manager's Misunderstandings and Facts

Misunderstanding	Fact
• Delegation means giving the employee complete control and autonomy for an assignment • Delegation is simply a way for a manager to distribute work • After delegating an assignment, it's best for a manager to stay out of the delegatee's way to let him accomplish it on his own • The delegatee is solely responsible for the success or failure of the assignment • I don't have time to delegate	• Effective delegation involves giving the employee the right amount of authority based on his level of experience and engagement for the tasks he will be required to perform • Distribution of work is only one reason to delegate; effective delegation is also a tool for developing employees and for creating a more motivational work climate • Managers are responsible for staying in touch with the delegatee during the assignment to monitor progress and provide ongoing coaching and support • When delegating, a manager can't abdicate responsibility; while the delegatee is accountable for his own actions and performance, the manager is ultimately responsible • Delegation is an investment; over time effective delegation will free up a manager's time to work on higher value activities

Scenario 1: Delegation for Work Distribution

John is the store manager of a national retailer offering plumbing supplies to contractors and construction firms. He opened his branch from scratch in a new market two years ago. At that time, he was able to bring on Kelly, an experienced assistant manager from another branch.

The first thing John did after hiring the staff was to make a list of all the tasks and activities that he needed to accomplish. From that list he identified activities that he felt would be appropriate to delegate to Kelly. He considered Kelly's experience at the previous branch, the complexity and importance of the tasks, and his time and ability to provide ongoing supervision and monitoring. From that list of potential assignments, he selected one recurring activity—inventory control and reporting—that he thought matched Kelly's demonstrated experience and knowledge. On a piece of paper, he:

- Identified the tasks that had to be completed each week for Inventory control and reporting
- Estimated how much time would be required to perform each of the tasks
- Identified how much time he would need to spend working with Kelly to ensure the successful accomplishment of the assignment

He concluded that since the inventory system was standard across all of the branches and Kelly had worked with it in the previous store, he probably had the experience required to assume the authority for inventory control and reporting in this store without a great deal of additional training. Once John was clear about what he wanted to delegate to distribute the work, he sat down with Kelly to conduct a delegation discussion. During that conversation John:

- Explained what he was interested in delegating, its importance, and why he wanted Kelly to take on the assignment
- Engaged Kelly in a dialogue to gauge his interest and motivation for the assignment
- Discussed the specific tasks and outcomes required for weekly inventory control and reporting
- Described the level of authority that he wanted to delegate

Before going any further John asked Kelly to summarize his understanding of the assignment. As Kelly talked, John asked clarifying questions and actively listened to ensure alignment of expectations

From there, John and Kelly discussed and identified potential problems that might occur and agreed on strategies to implement if they did occur. They talked specifically about what Kelly needed from John to successfully take on the assignment, and they agreed to regular weekly meetings to review progress. Before concluding the conversation, John expressed confidence in Kelly's ability to take on the new assignment.

Scenario 2: Delegation to Develop New Skills

In addition to the eight full-time employees at John's store, management trainees are rotated by corporate through select stores as part of a two-year onboarding leadership training program. John is responsible for developing the two management trainees currently assigned to his store. He uses developmental delegation as a key tool. A week ago, John sat down with Erica, one of the trainees, to discuss a developmental assignment to learn the payroll system. In that initial delegation discussion, John began by describing the purpose of the conversation, the developmental assignment that he wanted to make, and why it was important for Erica to learn the payroll system. They agreed on its importance as well as on Erica's need for specific guidance. After discussing the specifics of the assignment and how they would work together, John and Erica agreed to an initial meeting scheduled for the next day to provide her with training on the system. They also agreed to a regular checkpoint, every Tuesday at 10 A.M. to review her progress. At the first checkpoint meeting, John engaged Erica in a discussion to determine her progress and comfort with mastering the system. By asking good questions and actively listening he discovered that she was unclear about a specific aspect of the process. He provided additional guidance about how to perform the activity. They followed the planned meeting every Tuesday until Erica mastered the payroll system.

Scenario 3: Delegation to Improve the Motivational Climate

Tamika, a counter clerk, was one of John's first hires when he opened the store. Over the last two years she's been a steady performer. She's mastered all of the tasks required of her and has demonstrated initiative by taking it on herself to begin to learn and assist with the product displays. John wants to delegate additional authority to Tamika to help improve her motivational climate by increasing her autonomy and by adding more skill variety to her daily work. In looking at possible assignments, John decided to see if Tamika was interested in taking on a bigger role with the product displays. When they sat down to meet John began by reinforcing Tamika's positive performance and initiative and told her that he was interested in speaking with her about taking on some additional activities. After briefly explaining the possible assignment he asked Tamika if it was something that she would be interested in getting more involved in. When she affirmed that she would, John then used the six steps of the delegation conversation to reach agreements and clear expectations about how they would work together to ensure that she was successful with her new responsibilities.

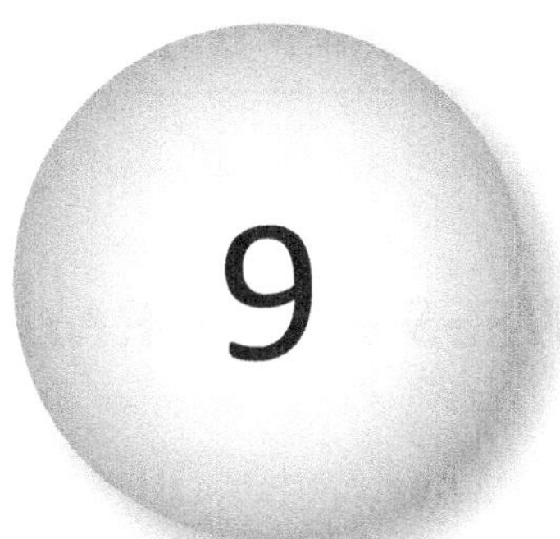

Coaching for Performance

LEARNING OBJECTIVES

By the end of this chapter, you will be better equipped to:

- Assess employee performance and work with employees to develop clear criteria so they can objectively assess their own performance.
- Work with employees to help them identify and commit to specific measurable and realistic goals.
- Present feedback on behaviors and performance to employees and empower employees to collect and analyze feedback from their colleagues and stakeholders. Use active listening techniques to empathize with and demonstrate understanding of employees' point of view.
- Guide employees to develop a plan for their development and growth, aligning performance goals to organizational goals.
- Manage your own and employees' emotions by keeping a calm tone and engaging in open discussion. Support employees in tolerating their own emotions even when challenging and unpleasant.
- Hold employees accountable for achieving their performance goals and address performance problems in a timely and fair fashion. Encourage employees to hold themselves accountable and proactively seek help when at risk of falling short.

This chapter is not meant for professional coaches but is intended for managers who are tasked with both getting things done and building an independently capable team at the same time.

COACHING FOR BUSINESS PERFORMANCE

Coaching for performance is an ongoing, collaborative process of evaluating employee performance, setting goals, providing feedback, identifying development opportunities, and brainstorming plans of action to achieve personal goals in alignment with organizational needs.

Our job as managers and leaders is to build independently capable people and teams. Before we get into the strategies, tactics, and tools of coaching, let's examine where they come from and why they were developed.

A Brief History of Coaching

Coaching entered the business world on the heels of three innovations: Peter Drucker's management by objectives (MBO), the human potential movement of the 1960s, and the world of athletics.

MBO gave a human aspect to the scientific management movement of the early twentieth century. Scientific management, in which workers were studied to determine the most efficient actions and motions to achieve some outcome, was based on the notion of humans as cogs in a machine. While it may have had some relevance for simple, repetitive assembly-line tasks (although even there it ignored the potential for insight and innovation among these workers), it simply wasn't suited to an organization made up of "knowledge workers" who needed to think on their feet and coordinate with others.

In the mid-twentieth century, modern organization, accountability and assessment according to an objective, and an agreed-on standard had to mesh with the art of motivation and the growing understanding of human nature. Managerial talent was now seen as a corporate asset, and industrial scientists set about studying and documenting best practices in leading, motivating, assessing, and rewarding performance.

While much of the DNA of coaching was contained in Drucker's extensive writing and teaching about management, it was the human potential movement that began to explore and innovate techniques for humans to better themselves. Thinkers like Abraham Maslow (remember his famous pyramid) and Viktor Frankl elevated self-actualization to a serious place in the discussion of human needs. In places like the Esalen Institute in California, the wide-open spirit of the 1960s was channeled into encounter groups, Erhard seminars training (EST), Gestalt therapy, and other modalities for promoting the growth of authentic, self-actualized human beings.

Two influential bestsellers published within a year of each other in the mid-1950s—William H. Whyte's management tome *The Organization Man* and Sloan Wilson's novel *The Man in the Gray Flannel Suit*—savaged the notion of corporation as a conformist entity that drained employees of their personality, ideas, and souls in pursuit of the dollar. The human potential movement turned its sights to this world, as companies began hiring psychologists, counselors, and therapists to maximize the potential of their human capital.

As this new movement searched for a name and a model, some athletic coaches began articulating principles of human development and growth that crossed from sports into business. Great athletes, after all, had coaches who helped them identify weaknesses, practice deliberately (with careful attention to process and outcome) to overcome them, and improve based on feedback they could collect and process themselves. And since athletic performance is far more observable and objective than business performance, coaching principles and techniques that didn't work in sports were jettisoned quickly in favor of those that did.

In the last two decades, business coaching has proliferated, with hundreds of schools, certification programs, and approaches training coaches and with thousands of organizations, large and small, embracing coaching principles and techniques. These days, just about every large organization hires outside coaches to work with their executives and high potential contributors.

At the same time, coaching is woefully underused as a managerial approach. Few companies have cracked the code of becoming a coaching organization by applying the principles and practice of coaching internally, as part of the DNA of the management style and philosophy. A coaching organization works with their C-suite leaders to help them become, among other things, better coaches to their direct reports and those direct reports become better coaches to their employees, and so on down the line.

Key Concepts of Coaching for Business Performance

Coaching for performance overlaps with many other skill sets, including those related to communication, management, goal setting, teaching, and listening. What differentiates coaching from other ways of managing employees is the focus on empowering employees to improve their own performance and capability. How these other skill sets get deployed within a coaching context are explored next.

COACHING SKILLS AND COMPETENCIES

Asking Questions

All managers must ask questions to figure out what's going on. MBO consists of setting goals and constantly comparing current reality to those goals. While progress reports, presentations, and spreadsheets may contain the top-line details on how things are going, they don't provide nuanced understandings of why things are the way they are.

Let's say that only 17 percent of employees have filed their personal goals and objectives (PGO) report by the due date. What's behind that number? Are there systematic obstacles employees must overcome? Was the memo buried and so failed to come to their attention? Did the memo clearly lay out the expectations? Are they busy with other work and perceive this as not important?

The MBO manager must answer these kinds of questions to solve the 17 percent problem and elevate it to 80 or 90 percent or whatever meets their stated objective. Such questions aim to satisfy the manager's own curiosity and serve as means of achieving objectives.

The coaching manager also asks questions, but with an additional goal: to help employees increase their own understanding. If an employee is guided, through genuinely curious questioning, to recognize that his or her own advancement depends on setting and meeting objectives, that employee may spontaneously discover time to complete and turn in the PGO report.

Deep Listening

Asking questions is a pointless formality if the manager is unwilling or unable to listen to the answers. MBO managers listen for the answers they need and expect. Coaching managers listen deeply for subtle clues and unexpected directions. The key trait necessary for deep listening is curiosity. Here's the five-step process:

1. Listen closely to what is being said and how it's being said.
2. Ask open-ended questions to understand the context and the employee's thoughts, feelings, and actions in that context.
3. Repeat back what you've heard.
4. Check with your employee to make sure he or she feels understood; if not, find out what you missed or got wrong.
5. Repeat Steps 1–4 as many times as necessary.

If an employee seems to be dismissing the importance of the report, deep listening may reveal that the same report last year was met with indifference, ignored, or criticized for lack of ambition. Thus the employee simply doesn't believe the organization will offer support or return a sense of value and trust.

Teaching

When we have knowledge and skills that can assist our employees in carrying out their jobs, we have both reason and responsibility to teach them what we know.

Coaching managers teach when appropriate: when they have the needed information and when their employees are receptive to that information. Receptive employees have the time to attend to what's being taught and aren't distracted by putting out other fires. They are also aware of gaps in their capabilities that could affect their performance and are open to growing.

One mistake managers often make in teaching is to use a pseudo-Socratic questioning style that translates into "Guess the answer I'm thinking of." When a manager has domain expertise, they should simply share it.

In addition, coaching managers don't overteach; instead they provide just enough content to allow employees to implement the new idea in the real world. This way they gain confidence, experience, and relevant feedback so theory becomes practice.

Performance Management: Goal Setting, Assessment, and Feedback

Performance management is made up of a diverse set of skills, including the ability to set clear and objective standards, assess employee performance based on those standards, and provide actionable feedback to correct any discrepancies between desired and actual behavior and outcomes.

Coaching managers include their employees in every step of this process; again, the goal is not just to get employees to independently and collaboratively do their jobs, but to help them become independently capable of improving and growing and developing themselves.

Rather than impose standards and hand out objectives, a coaching manager will collaborate with individual employees to identify standards and objectives that make sense in the context of their organizational contribution. That way each employee owns the goals and is internally motivated to achieve or exceed them.

Coaching managers also assess performance collaboratively, helping their employees gather their own feedback on an ongoing basis, rather than waiting for an evaluation from on high.

In addition to providing actionable feedback, the coaching manager encourages their employees to proactively gather their own feedback and use it to correct their course rapidly.

Collaborative Exploration

By *collaborative exploration*, we simply mean "being curious together about what's going on and why." This orientation is really at the heart of coaching. It's about working together, which requires effort and commitment from the employee as well as from the manager. It's about curiosity, which is the fuel for insight and novel thinking. And it's about profound respect for the employee, which is the growth medium for honesty, self-reflection, and vulnerability (see Chapter 6, Collaboration).

Promoting Accountability

Managers are ultimately responsible for the performance of their employees and units. It's easy to hold employees accountable (although, in our experience, that approach doesn't work well). It's much more complex to build a culture and individual relationships in which employees feel safe to hold *themselves* accountable for their own performance and the solutions to their own problems.

In many ways, self-accountability is the goal of all coaching: developing employees to take responsibility for their words and actions and for improving their performance through feedback and innovation. Self-accountability allows employees to accomplish their job tasks and functions.

Coaching managers, through curiosity, collaboration, and respect, create a safe space for honest self-assessment and vigorous problem solving. By focusing on the behaviors and the outcomes, rather than the individual person, the coaching manager makes it okay for employees to admit mistakes, seek help, and self-correct early and often.

And this kind of supervision conveys trust that the manager believes in the employees enough to let them make mistakes, learn from those mistakes, and continue developing their capabilities.

While promoting accountability is highlighted in the coaching process (discussed later in this chapter), it is deeply embedded into the entire process, at every step and during every interaction with employees.

Skillful Communication

Coaching requires two superpowers that will determine the effectiveness of all the coaching tools and methods at your disposal: the ability to communicate skillfully and the capacity to tolerate powerful emotions (discussed in the next section), both your own and those of your employees.

These come together in your capacity to handle difficult conversations with professionalism. After all, it's easy to be a great coach when everybody's happy and when things are going well. The challenge comes when you have to deliver negative feedback to a team or an employee who may be unprepared for that feedback or when an employee's behavioral blind spots are threatening the success of an important initiative. It's human nature to avoid confrontation whenever possible and to prefer to comfort rather than get honest with a problem employee.

Skillful communication begins with assuming positive intent on the part of your employee. Before providing feedback on unacceptable or problematic behavior, you must look for and communicate your appreciation for the positive values the employee is upholding, at least in his own mind. For example, if your employee is destroying morale by constantly criticizing his own direct reports, you can acknowledge his loyalty to the value of high standards or fairness, while providing feedback on the undesirable consequences of the way he's promoting those values. This is different from the sandwich technique of sticking criticism between two pieces of positive feedback. Rather than hiding or softening the criticism, empathizing with employees allows them to be more open to the constructive feedback about the gaps between actual and ideal performance. When you acknowledge positive intent, you are able to set clear standards without causing employees to get defensive or lose face.

Emotional Courage

When conversations become uncomfortable, we often lose control of our own emotions and expressions. It's critical to maintain a calm and steady tone during sessions in which your employee may become angry or upset or withdrawn. By so doing, you're communicating that you can handle the employee's emotions and will not get drawn into a shouting match or other form of dysfunctional behavior.

Staying calm allows you focus on behaviors and objective facts, rather than getting distracted by personalities and emotions. We're not saying that the emotions themselves are distractions, not fit for consideration. Quite the opposite. Emotions are usually the drivers of behaviors that we don't understand, and helping employees surface, express, and resolve these emotions can be critical to helping them improve. That's not the same thing as getting hijacked by our own emotions, unable to move the conversation in productive directions.

Emotional courage requires coaching managers to be able to tolerate their own unpleasant and often uncomfortable emotions and physical sensations, which may be triggered by the words and actions of others. It's different from ignoring or repressing such emotions and sensations, in that managers are aware of such feelings but keep them from leaking into their words and actions.

When the coaching takes place in person or via a video platform, it's important to maintain an open and engaging disposition. Let your posture be undefended—that is, with arms and legs uncrossed and leaning forward or mirroring the body language of your employee, which builds rapport. Demonstrate your interest by holding eye contact and nodding and offering "uh-huh" and "okay" interjections at appropriate moments.

Acknowledge the employee's perspective by paraphrasing what she just said and asking if you summarized her view correctly.

Even though there is a power and rank dynamic, you will be most effective as a coaching manager if you seize the conversation as an opportunity to learn and grow as well. So don't worry if you have some work to do in developing these superpowers. As long as you enter each coaching relationship and session with a sincere intention to be of service, your employee will be more likely to respond generously to your requests for feedback on becoming a more effective manager and coach.

COACHING AS A MANAGERIAL STYLE

The easiest way to explain the coaching manager style is to contrast it with the other two predominant styles: directive manager and delegating manager.

The Directive Manager

The directive manager issues orders, and expects them to be followed to the letter. While this style has its place (where no independent judgment is required of the employee), it has several significant drawbacks. First, the manager may give wrong directions, and won't realize it since there's no effective feedback mechanism. Employees are often closer than managers to key issues, like disgruntled customers or a tepid market. When managers impose their solutions without input from employees, they are likely to be suboptimal. Second, the directions won't apply to all circumstances, so the employees' outcomes will be suboptimal, and they won't have the ability to adapt. Third, and most damaging, the directed employee will not grow and become more capable, wise, engaged, proactive, or effective over time.

In the top–down world of directive management, the manager sets the goals and informs the employee. In complex knowledge-based organizations, this approach suffers from three shortcomings. First, it jettisons the powerful motivation generated by autonomy, which allows the employee to choose and commit to outcomes, rather than just being told what to achieve. Second, it squanders the employee's own experience, judgment, and wisdom in identifying worthy goals and objectives. Third, it fails to develop employees' goal-setting muscles, so that they are not prepared to manage others should the opportunity for advancement arise.

The Delegating Manager

The delegating manager either doesn't care how it is done, as long as it is done, or cares but provides no input, guidance, or support. This manager tells employees, "Get it done" and provides no guidance, education, or discernment along with the mandate. While employees enjoy wide latitude for individual preferences, styles, and creativity, this approach too is costly. Employees who lack the experience of the manager are apt to perform poorly and are unlikely to gain skill or wisdom without a manager to help them process the experience and gain insights for next time.

The Coaching Manager by Comparison

The coaching manager's style combines direction, accountability, and—crucially—the building of independent capability in employees. Rather than setting goals *for* employees, the coaching manager sets goals *with* employees. Rather than solely providing performance review feedback, the coaching manager guides employees to gather their own feedback so they can self-correct in real-time, rather than quarterly or annually. And rather than imposing a development plan, this type of manager collaborates with employees to help them identify their own areas of growth and concrete tactics for achieving that growth.

Benefits of Coaching as a Managerial Style

Employees who are coached, rather than directed or delegated to, are far more invested in the success of their efforts. With responsibility comes ownership, and when we own our outcomes, we are much more likely to do everything possible to get the ones we want.

When we coach employees, we help them become proactive. Because they know we will ask them questions such as "So what did you learn from that experience?" and "How did you solve that problem?" they will prepare their answers before the conversation. Which means they will get in the habit of assessment, of self-reflection, and of "postmorteming" their successes, failures, and everything in between to inform their future efforts.

Because coaching fosters curiosity and trust rather than judgment and defensiveness, issues come to the surface much more quickly and can be resolved sooner. When employees discover they won't always get punished or shamed for mistakes, they are much faster to acknowledge problems to themselves, admit them to others, ask for help, and roll up their sleeves to make things right.

In addition, organizations that embrace coaching as a managerial default display much higher morale. Coaching includes the entire person, and not just the rational mind. Coaching involves the mind, the emotions, and the body, for both the coach and the coachee.

THE GUIDE MODEL OF MANAGERIAL COACHING

The AMA has developed the GUIDE model to help managers navigate the coaching process with their employees. The model consists of five stages:

G: Gather data on performance

U: Understand the impact

I: Interview to discuss recent performance

D: Develop an action plan

E: Execute plan; examine progress

The following sections delve into each of these stages (Figure 9-1).

Gather Data on Performance

The purpose of the first stage, gathering data, is to understand the present state: how the project is going, where it might be at risk, what the likely outcomes are. Now is also the time to learn what prior actions and decisions contributed to the current conditions.

The conversation would include questions like these:

- Where are we with identifying potential new marketing use cases?
- What's the essence of the issue as you see it?
- How do the results you've been getting match what you were expecting or hoping for?
- How do you account for these results?
- How do you know this? On what basis do you draw this conclusion?

During this stage, coaching managers can also offer their own direct observations:

- Here's what I'm seeing . . .
- Here's what others are saying . . .
- Here are the results and outcomes achieved so far . . .

Understand the Impact

The purpose of the second stage, understand the impact, is to discover the implications and consequences of current conditions, why these outcomes matter, and what's at stake. Managers can ask questions like these:

- What is the impact on you?
- What concerns do you have about the current situation?
- What are the consequences of not addressing this situation?
- Whom does this situation affect?
- How are these results important to you? To the organization? To others?
- How could you find out?

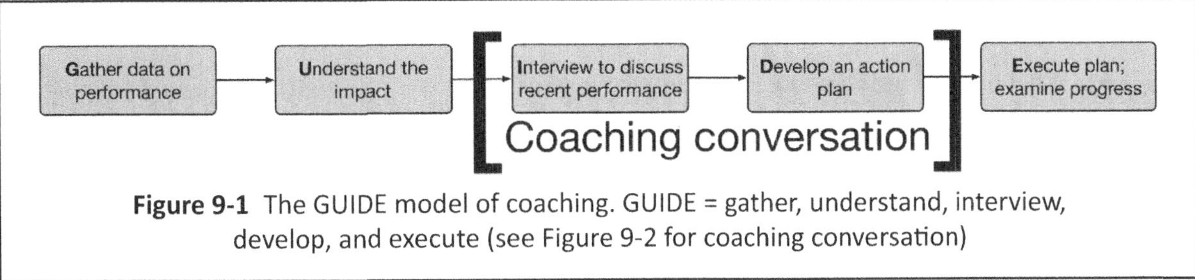

Figure 9-1 The GUIDE model of coaching. GUIDE = gather, understand, interview, develop, and execute (see Figure 9-2 for coaching conversation)

Interview to Discuss Recent Performance

The purpose of the interview stage is to explore the employee's contribution to the current conditions, whether positive, negative, or indifferent. By the end of this stage, both manager and employee should be clear on what the employee did that worked well and what missed the mark in some way.

The goal here is to move from generalities to specifics and to discover patterns of behavior that can be altered for the better. Managers can ask questions like these:

- What precisely did you do at that moment?
- What were you thinking when that happened?
- What exactly did you say in response?

Develop an Action Plan

The purpose of the action plan stage is to help the employee prepare future behaviors that will be aligned with your mutually agreed-on goals. Once you both understand the impact of the employee's earlier decisions and actions, you can brainstorm future actions and create implementation intentions based on expected future cues. Questions at this stage include the following:

- When do expect to be in a similar situation in the near future?
- What can you do in that situation that will give you the results you want?
- Can we role-play that conversation?
- How will you know if it's working or not?

Execute Plan; Examine Progress

The purpose of the final stage in the GUIDE model—execute plan; examine progress—is to move from coaching into meaningful action and build accountability into the process. Once the employee has a clear action plan, he or she tests it in the real world and notices the results. Questions at this stage include the following:

- How did it go?
- What happened when you tried . . .
- What did you discover when you tried . . .
- What parts of the plan did not get implemented?
- What got in the way?
- What will you try next time?

Putting the Components Together

The G and U stages are generally taken by the manager before the coaching session, although employees should be encouraged and given tools and skills to gather their own data and attempt to make sense of it on their own. This is one of the key meta-goals of managerial coaching: to build employees' capacities to self-develop on their own initiative.

The time and location of coaching sessions can contribute to, or undermine, their effectiveness. While drive-by coaching can be useful, the power of coaching comes from predictability and accountability. When people know what is expected of them, when those expectations are communicated regularly, and when the feedback they receive is tied to those expectations, their performance will be on target. When coaching is inconsistent and haphazard, employees will regard it as an unreliable gauge for behavior, and the manager will come to the conclusion that coaching doesn't work.

Therefore, managers should treat coaching sessions with as much gravity as any other meeting. Employees need to feel respected and protected before they will be honest and vulnerable with their managers. Coaching sessions must be private and have a minimum of distraction.

The physical location is one part of the coaching session setup. The other part is preparing for a productive session by identifying your desired goals for each session in advance. Is there an issue that needs attention? Do you have questions? Are you trying to foster accountability? Is there a status report that needs to be communicated? Entering the session with a clear objective will ensure that you and your employee don't waste time or miss the opportunity to achieve an important individual, team, or organizational goal.

The I and D stages involve the coaching conversation between the manager and the employee. Based on the data and an understanding of the impact of that data, the manager and employee (1) set future goals, (2) use the past to identify strengths and gaps, (c) explore and fill in blind spots about employee performance and impact on others, and (d) collaborate on an action plan going forward. The results of these repeated interactions is to foster not just top–down accountability, but proactive self-accountability by employees for their own performance and impact on the organization.

The E stage takes place outside of the coaching session and provides the input for the G and U stages of the next round of coaching.

THE COACHING CONVERSATION

The coaching conversation includes five steps, as presented in Figure 9-2. It requires competency in a set of tasks and behaviors related to each step.

Step 1: Set Goals and Communicate Expectations

Because managerial coaching is concerned, ultimately, with achievement of organizational objectives, the coaching conversations must be focused on the outcomes of the employee's words and actions.

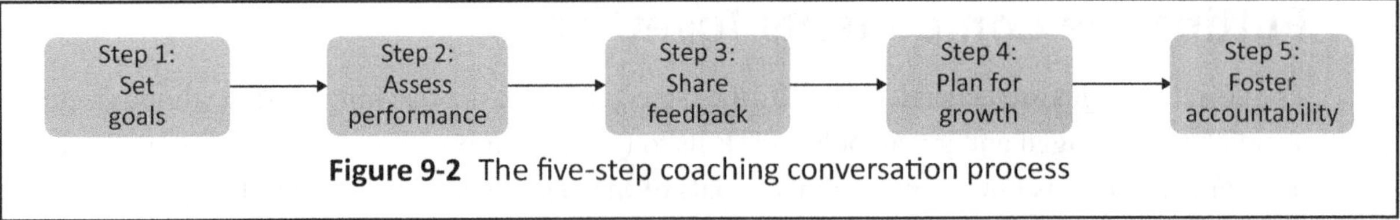

Figure 9-2 The five-step coaching conversation process

The first step in the coaching conversation process is to set and document clear, specific, and measurable goals for the employee. This includes determining what and by when—key results and timelines—so progress can be measured objectively and gaps addressed proactively.

It's almost always a good investment of time to collaborate with your employee to set goals. Your team expects you, as manager, to have a better view of organizational goals and a more objective impression of their individual strengths and weaknesses. The employee brings self-knowledge, hands-on experience, and career development preferences to the conversation. The coaching conversation combines these elements to align individual performance goals to organizational goals.

Engage the employee with questions such as the following:

- How do you want things to be?
- What are you trying to achieve?
- What new results to you want?
- What improvements are you looking to make?
- What possibilities do you see?
- How will you know if you've achieved your plan?

Once goals are established and agreed on, manager and employee have something to talk about in the rest of the coaching conversation process. Now performance can be assessed against those clear, agreed-on, and objective measures of success.

Step 2: Assess Performance

The second step in managerial coaching is to objectively assess employee performance based on the goals and timelines agreed on in step 1. Directive managers hold top–down performance reviews. Managers who embrace coaching, on the other hand, encourage their employees to gather, analyze, and interpret relevant data so they can assess their own performance (step 5) relative to standards and goals.

At the start of the coaching relationship, simply ask the employee to share any evidence she's already collected or noticed about how she's doing and how others view her work and workplace demeanor. Then share your assessment of her progress and/or challenges (based on answers to your questions in the gathering data and understanding the impact stages of the GUIDE model), reviewing agreed-on goals and comparing them to the current status.

You can help your employee connect her own behavior and actions to the outcomes with questions such as the following:

- What actions did you take that led to these performance results?
- What was your role in producing these results?
- How would you assess your performance so far?

Step 3: Share Feedback and Listen Actively

Sharing perspectives to assess employee performance is the start, not the end, of managerial coaching. In step 3, there are several topics to explore, depending on what was established in step 2.

If the employee's self-assessment differs significantly from your assessment based on objective and subjective data, don't simply correct the employee. Your conversation will be much more useful and more supportive of growth if you seek to understand the employee's perspective and then demonstrate that understanding *to the employee's satisfaction*. At that point, she will be more open to hearing your perspective, and accepting and acting on feedback from you and other colleagues.

If there is a gap between expectations and performance, you may need to clarify the expectations; it's possible that the employee doesn't actually know what her goals are.

Even if there is a significant performance gap, resist the urge to speak about only problems. Acknowledge behavior that is in line with organizational goals, not so much to boost the employee's morale but to point to a positive outcome that can be emulated in other settings.

Again, try to understand the employee's perspective around any performance issues. Explore what's missing for her and what's getting in the way of her success. Does she lack resources, such as time, money, and support? Does she need additional skills training to accomplish the goals?

Always move the conversation from the general to the specific. Often, we speak in generalities. The employee may report, "I always find out about the spec changes too late to do anything about them." Probe for details about when this happened recently, by asking specific questions: "At what time did you get the email about the last batch of changes? What changes were requested? How much time would you have needed to get them completed? How did you respond to the email?"

Here you can ask questions that engage your employee to become more aware of the thoughts that motivated her decisions and actions:

- How did you see this situation?
- What did you see or hear that caused you to act?
- What interpretation did you make of that circumstance?
- What crossed your mind when you . . .

Active listening is an important part of this phase of coaching. By *active listening*, we mean not just a set of techniques (concentrate, understand, respond, remember) but the spirit or intention behind the techniques: sincere curiosity about your employee's perspective and experience.

If you're curious and fascinated by a subject, you don't have to remind yourself to pay attention; you just do. If you're really interested in what someone has to say, you don't have to sit with a cheat sheet of techniques that demonstrate interest; you just hang on that person's every word.

You don't check email or spreadsheets. You put your phone away. You lean in. You ask questions whenever you're unclear about something. You check your understanding with your counterpart: "Is that how it was?"

Few of us have the experience of being deeply listened to on a regular basis. If you are lucky enough to have a deep listener in your life, you know how affirming that kind of interaction can be. You understand that active, curious listening is a gift that can bring out your best thinking. That's the kind of impact you can have as a coach to your employees.

Once you and your employee are confident you understand the situation from her perspective, you can offer specific and actionable feedback. Is she exhibiting unproductive or alienating behavior? Is she missing opportunities to be more efficient or effective? Could she be proactive and prevent small issues from growing into big problems? Give actual examples, so the employee can picture a new way of doing things in future.

Often, your employee will engage in the same behaviors with you that are getting her into trouble elsewhere in the workplace. Perhaps she's interrupting too often or talking too much or showing up late. Because it's human nature to avoid conflict, no one else in the organization may have ever brought these behaviors to the employee's attention. One of the gifts of coaching (although it may not feel like a gift at the time) is honest and brave feedback. You have an opportunity to point out these behaviors and how they affect you, so the employee can discover the impact of her behavior on others and begin to make different choices. Here's where developing your own emotional courage muscle pays off: with intention and practice, you become willing and able to have these uncomfortable conversations.

As part of this step of the coaching conversation, you can also request feedback on your managerial behaviors and how you can improve in your role. By doing so, and listening attentively and asking clarifying questions, you're accomplishing three important things:

1. You are modeling a growth mind-set and a hunger for feedback; traits that are necessary for personal and professional development.
2. You are building rapport and trust by establishing coaching as a reciprocal, two-way sharing of impressions and assessments.
3. You are gaining valuable insights into your own blind spots and limitations, insights that are unlikely to come from formal performance reviews conducted by your own supervisor.

Step 4: Plan for Growth and Improvement

The next step in the coaching process is to help your employee operationalize the feedback and insights into future action to close any performance gaps and generate professional growth.

If this step is conducted skillfully, your employee will take concrete action to address the issues identified in the previous step. If not, the employee may miss opportunities for development and make little or no progress in her development.

The first coaching skill to be deployed in this stage is to help your employee identify the obstacles to growth. Most of the feedback and advice she receives isn't shocking or even surprising: listen better, focus on the important stuff, be more proactive. If telling someone what to do were sufficient, that person would have addressed all the issues already. It's the obstacles to growth that are holding your employees back, and these roadblocks need to be identified and addressed.

For example, take an employee who has trouble focusing on her most important work and constantly gets pulled in a dozen different directions. As the manager and coach, you want to help her uncover the forces, internal and external, that support the behaviors she's asked to change.

Ask the employee to tell you about a recent time when she found herself multitasking instead of focusing. Ask clarifying questions until you can see the movie and hear her internal narration of that moment. Collaborate to explore the environmental factors that support or undermine deep and focused work. Too many open browser tabs? A desk situated next to the open door of the kitchen? Loud and persistent new message notifications?

Find out what the employee was thinking and feeling as she checked her email a dozen times and started working on an unrelated expense report and took a walk to chat with a colleague about a booth display for a conference the team hasn't even committed to yet. Does the employee have a fear of missing out on another opportunity? Is she procrastinating the important work because she's afraid of the stakes involved or the scrutiny it will receive? Is she missing a key skill, such as slide deck design? Is the employee too hungry or tired to focus properly?

You can help your employee address her thinking with questions such as these:

- What options did you consider?
- What did you hope to gain?
- What were you thinking and feeling at the time?

Next, brainstorm how to address the obstacles. This is a great time to ask your employee for her thoughts, rather than issuing directions and suggestions. It's crucial that the employee own the solutions, rather than having them imposed on her by a higher authority. You can offer options as well; ideally, these are presented as a scaffolding on which the employee builds her own creative solutions.

Encourage open and honest communication here, so your employee doesn't feel pressured to agree to some plan of action because her manager told her to do it. If the employee doesn't think something is going to work, she needs to say so without fear of disapproval, so you both end up with a plan you believe in enough to actually implement.

Finally, tie the plan of action to times and places and situations, so it gets done. Identify the next time the employee has an opportunity to try the new behavior, and help the employee visualize her actions in that scenario. "When I return to my desk, I will set my computer and phone to do not disturb for the next ninety minutes and close all browser tabs. I will open PowerPoint and Excel, and produce ten slides before getting up to taking a five-minute walk-and-stretch break."

If the scenario in which the new behavior will be inserted isn't predictable, like the next time that employee has a conversation with a particular co-worker, then help her craft an "when–then" plan: "When I next sit down with Sharon, I will take two deep breaths and then ask her to share her goals for the conversation."

The key here is to set up triggers for the desired behaviors, so that the employee doesn't continue to go through the days and weeks without making progress.

Often, the new behavior will require emotional courage: a willingness to tolerate an unpleasant feeling like fear or shame and the strength to take action while still experiencing that feeling. You can ask the employee to visualize that moment and imagine what it will feel like to not check email for an hour and a half or to sit and listen to feedback from a colleague without interrupting. Help her see that the feeling is tolerable, even if it isn't pleasant. Allow the employee to build emotional courage during the coaching session by giving her the opportunity to experience that feeling and be okay at the same time.

Make sure both you and the employee understand the direct linkage between the habit or behavior and the performance goals or standards at issue. In other words, we want to enhance the employee's ability to focus or to remain engaged in difficult conversations because it will lead to a specific and measurable outcome. And the employee will be held accountable—and hold herself accountable—for both the key behaviors and the outcomes.

Step 5: Foster Accountability and Engage in Performance Management

The ultimate goal of coaching as a manager is to teach your employees to hold themselves accountable. You accomplish this by reinforcing the habit of personal accountability in each coaching session and by giving them ever-increasing autonomy as they earn it by proactive self-accountability.

You and your employee ended the last coaching session with a clear and specific development plan tied to specific outcomes relevant to the organization. As a result of the coaching session, your direct report is going to do something different, new, unfamiliar, not her default. A key agenda item of the next coaching session must be to ask, "How did it go?"

Begin each coaching session by referring back to your agreed-on goals and expectations for the employee. You can ask her to remind you both: "Let's start with your goals and key results. What are you trying to accomplish specifically, and by when?"

Next, ask for a progress report, along with any gaps that need addressing. Here's where you inquire about her homework: implementing the new habits and behaviors to become more effective. Ask her to tell you about the opportunities to practice these behaviors. Did opportunities arise? Did the employee try? How did it go? Did she ask for feedback in the moment? Does she have any evidence as to how she performed?

Here are some more questions to prompt accountability:

- How's it going?
- What progress have you made? How do you know?
- What's working?
- How would you assess your progress so far?
- How is what you're doing accomplishing your goal?

- What are some open loops or unfinished business?
- What are you learning in all of this?
- What's different from what you expected?
- Where do you go from here?
- What's next?

At this point, we're back to step 2, performance assessment. Armed with new experiences and new information, we can collaboratively identify relevant performance gaps, both at the input (behavioral) and output (results) levels.

As a manager and coach, you're always balancing two goals: to solve the problem at hand and to develop your employee's ability to problem solve in the future. With rare exceptions, we recommend erring toward building future problem-solving capability in the employee. While the presenting problem may be urgent and important, representing a crisis or at-risk deadline, much greater long-term value resides in addressing issues that are important and not urgent. This is where you build skills and relationships and make plans that allow you to prevent crises from occurring in the first place.

Coaching at its best does not come with a sense of urgency. Therefore you want to ask for the employee's suggestions before you share yours, and ask questions to help the employee evaluate potential solutions instead of telling her the right answer.

Building accountability also means encouraging proactivity. Rather than waiting for the next scheduled coaching session or project review, teach your employee to proactively turn to you for support and assistance whenever a milestone is at risk.

COACHING SCENARIOS

What follows are two common types of coaching challenges managers face.

Scenario 1: Pushy and Dismissive Team Leader

A common use of coaching is to fix an employee with a bad habit. Often, the employee has considerable strengths and skills and contributes significantly to the organization's success but also exhibits problematic behaviors that demotivate or even alienate the team or colleagues. The employee may be unaware of the problem, because he hasn't received clear and direct feedback about it or he may rationalize it as not a big deal. The employee may even feel that this behavior is effective and so dismiss any concerns as "HR covering their ass."

Let's go through a session in which Donald, a team lead, is being coached by his manager, Maxime. The complaints about Donald were raised by his team. Maxime values Donald's work ethic, his demonstrated commitment to the company, and his analytical rigor.

Maxime begins by saying, "Donald, good to see you. I wanted to talk with you today about feedback I've received from several members of your team. That you are pushy with your ideas, and you don't listen to them. I want to make sure you're bringing your team along with you in this new initiative, and I know how important that is to you. Are you willing to be coached on this?"

Maxime has done three important things here. First, she leads with the punch line: "You're pushy and you don't listen to your team." In our effort to make our employee feel comfortable, we often bury the lede in chitchat or praise. This usually backfires. The employee is thinking, "Where is this going? Am I in trouble here?" Leading with the punch line both gets the employee's attention, and treats him like a partner in problem solving rather than a problem to be solved.

Her second move is to place the problematic behavior in the context of positive intentions: "I know how important that is to you." She has separated Donald's behavior from his intrinsic worth and acknowledges their shared values and mission.

Third, Maxime doesn't force coaching on Donald. Doing so would, ironically, make her guilty of the same pushiness that Donald displays. Instead, she invites him to participate: "Are you willing to be coached on this?"

She's done all these things with confidence, modeling the kind of strong leadership Donald seeks to embody without being pushy and showing a willingness to listen.

If Donald says yes, he is willing to be coached, then Maxime can proceed with his buy-in, and ownership of the process and outcome. Her next move is to ask lots of questions to assess Donald's awareness of the problem and to discover Donald's perspective and thoughts. Does he see his behavior as pushy and dismissive? What is he aware of? What feedback has he gotten from this team, either directly or covertly? What are some things he's been seeing or hearing that might be evidence or clues or suggestions that his team perceives him this way?

Maxime asks with genuine curiosity, listens intently, and follows up with clarifying questions, both to make sure she hears and truly understands Donald's perspective and to check whether Donald feels heard and understood. Once a picture emerges of his awareness and his blind spots, she can share specific behavioral feedback that she received from his team. "At Tuesday's planning meeting, Ramesh expressed concern over whether the timeline was realistic, and you interrupted him and told the group that it was nonnegotiable and they should work harder instead of complaining."

At this point, Maxime may need to go into teaching mode, explaining to Donald the principle of blind spots: that all of us inevitably do things that we're not aware of and that all of us produce outcomes in others and in the world that we're not aware of. This does two important things: it empowers Donald to change, since the first step in addressing a blind spot is to discover it. And by normalizing the issue, it reduces any sting or stigma that Donald may feel. This isn't Donald being bad or broken, but Donald being human.

During the conversation about blind spots, Maxime keeps checking in with Donald. Does this make sense? Can he think of examples of blind spots in others? Is he okay with the idea that he may have a few himself? Maxime can further reduce the stigma by sharing a story of when she was made aware of a blind spot and what happened when she had the opportunity to address it.

Next, Maxime and Donald assess the obstacles to his embodying good listening. Is it a knowledge gap? She asks him to describe good listening, to see if he knows it when he sees it. Is it a skills gap? She notices whether he can demonstrate good listening in the coaching conversation. Does Donald lose the ability to listen well when stressed? Through questioning and observation, she forms a preliminary diagnosis.

In this case, let's assume that Donald is simply unfamiliar with the practice of good listening and up until now has been unaware of the effects of his communication style on his team members.

Next, Maxime shares best practices for good listening with Donald: listening with curiosity, repeating back, summarizing, checking for understanding, and so on. Maxime consciously models these behaviors in the coaching session and occasionally points out that she's doing so. This helps Donald see that good listening isn't a trick or hack but a natural mode of human communication and that it feels good to be listened to and acknowledged deeply. As well, he discovers that listening and empathizing doesn't make him into a pushover.

Maxime turns to the task of showing Donald how to read teammates' reactions to his communications. In other words, how to collect his own, firsthand, real-time feedback about how he is doing. What will he see that will indicate that he is listening well or that he is operating out of command and control mode and not listening at all? She guides him to visualize an upcoming conversation in which he listens well and notes the words, actions, facial expressions, tonality, and energy of his counterpart. She also helps him become sensitive to the words, actions, and impact of people when they don't feel heard and appreciated.

At this point, Donald has new insights and may have practiced a new set of skills, but he doesn't yet have a plan to integrate his knowledge and preliminary practice in the real world. Maxime coaches Donald to look forward and identify opportunities over the next week to put good listening into practice. Who will he be speaking with? How will he initiate good listening?

Maxime takes the part of one of the conversational counterparts, and she and Donald role-play the exchange. During the role-play, she coaches him on things he can do better, and they repeat that part of the conversation until he consistently demonstrates good listening behaviors. This way, Maxime communicates clear expectations for Donald's behavior.

Finally, Maxime seeks to empower Donald to learn and grow on his own, by teaching him how to look for, notice, and interpret the behavior of others as evidence of his ability to listen well. She encourages him to actually ask the person he's in conversation with, "How's my listening?" By requesting direct feedback from his team members, Donald accelerates his learning and doesn't have to rely on chance or delayed feedback to inform him on his progress.

In addition, humans suffer from confirmation bias: the tendency to see only the evidence that supports their preconceptions. This means that if Donald becomes a better listener, and even grows to listen well 95 percent of the time, his team members will notice only the 5 percent when he is impatient, imperious, or distracted. By asking for direct feedback, Donald orients their attention toward the changes he is making and allows them to stop reinforcing his old, dysfunctional behaviors through their expectations.

Suppose Donald said he was *not* willing to be coached? Did Maxime's move backfire? Not at all. If he's really not willing to receive coaching to resolve this issue, then any attempt would simply be a waste of time. As you'll see, Maxime's initial response to a no may seem counterintuitive: appreciation and gratitude. It would be much easier for Donald to lie and pretend to want coaching; the fact that he can be honest with her means that they have a genuine relationship.

Maxime responds by saying, "Thank you so much for letting me know. I'm really curious about your reasons for not being open to coaching on this. Can you share them?"

Exploring Donald's resistance may dissolve it, in which case the coaching conversation can continue. If Donald continues to refuse coaching, Maxime puts the ball in Donald's court: "How would you like to inform your colleagues that this coaching relationship won't be happening?"

The big mistake here would be to insist that Donald accept the coaching. First, he would resent and ignore any advice. Second, and more serious, it would undermine the entire basis of coaching, which seeks to increase individual capability and accountability. All Maxime can do is ask questions and point Donald to the natural consequences of his decisions and actions.

Scenario 2: Employee Gets Promoted and Needs to Manage Former Colleagues

An effective use of coaching is to help an employee take on new capabilities and expand her capacity to act in new situations. In this scenario, Zephyr has just been promoted to a supervisory position over several of her co-workers. Her manager, Idris, opens the coaching session by leading with the punch line.

Idris, says, "Congratulations, Zephyr. You've earned a bigger role in the organization, based on your past contributions and your potential. And from my perspective, the skills that have gotten you to this point aren't going to be sufficient going forward. So while I expect you to leverage the considerable strengths that got you this promotion, I hope you recognize that you'll have to do some things differently as well. Are you open to some coaching as to what that might look like?"

Again, for the sake of this discussion, we'll assume Zephyr agrees to coaching. Idris goes right into curiosity, asking about Zephyr's goals in this new role. Specifically, he wonders, "How do you want to show up as the boss?"

Zephyr responds, "I need to show my team that I'm a strong and decisive leader, so I'll come in and tell them exactly what they need to do." Idris is tempted to jump in and correct her, but as a good coach, he realizes that he needs to understand Zephyr's thinking in order to address any shortcomings in her reasoning. He asks, "What do you think might happen if you don't tell them exactly what to do?"

If Zephyr's response indicates that she feels insecure about her new position of authority and wants to make sure that she shows up as a strong leader from the get-go, Idris can address her concern directly, without making her feel wrong or dismissing her worries. Always looking for opportunities to develop his employees' capacity to gather and learn from feedback, he asks, "You could try that. How will you know if it's working or not?"

This question allows Zephyr to imagine herself in her new role and consider what specific responses from her employees would indicate a successful transition. Idris is balancing two objectives: letting Zephyr learn from her own experiences (that is, mistakes) and preventing a catastrophic error that Zephyr may have a hard time recovering from. Idris walks the line by going back and forth between questions designed to help Zephyr think clearly and strategically about her approach and advice based on his own experience and expertise around this challenge.

This is also an opportunity to help Zephyr increase her empathy skills and habits. Idris might ask her to imagine that she is an employee of a new manager. How would she want that manager to act in her first few months?

Suppose Zephyr gives a more suitable answer, one that doesn't set off alarm bells in Idris's mind: "I want to support and grow their capabilities while not setting myself up as arrogant or superior to them. And I want to stay friends."

Idris then coaches her to identify some potential strategies for achieving these objectives: "In that case, what should you continue doing? And what do you think needs to change in how you relate to them?"

Based on Zephyr's responses, Idris may engage in some teaching about how to be the boss of your colleagues. He may share stories of how his own friendships changed when he rose to supervisory authority over colleagues and how he learned to deploy positional, rather than personal, power to hold them accountable.

Idris challenges Zephyr to anticipate her coming challenges and develop new insights to deal with them. He asks, "What things do you have to think about differently now?" They might discuss the difference in significance of her behavior as an individual contributor and as a leader of a team. They might consider different scenarios for which she can prepare strategically.

Once they both feel comfortable that Zephyr has chosen worthy objectives and identified strategies likely to achieve those objectives, Idris shifts the conversation to self-accountability. How will Zephyr know if her behaviors are getting her the outcomes she wants? What are the observable and measurable criteria for success?

These key results, once identified and agreed on, serve as the foundation for their ongoing coaching sessions. The key results are the standards against which Zephyr and Idris will together evaluate her performance, based on the observations they both will make. Because Zephyr has co-created these key results and knows what they are, she is much more likely to succeed in her transition because she can quickly self-correct if she doesn't see the outcomes she wants. And because Idris can also see any gaps between the standards and the observable results, he can intervene proactively to help Zephyr make the most of her new opportunity.

SKILLS FOR SUCCESSFUL COACHING

Active Listening versus Being Distracted or Rushed

Coaching, like all forms of real-time communication, requires that both parties are fully present for each other. You as the manager must set the tone by putting away distractions and giving your employee your full attention during the conversation.

Not only do you pick up on subtle linguistic and behavioral clues that can help you be more effective but you also communicate that your employee and his or her growth is important to you. You build trust, connection, and goodwill by listening to your employees more fully than they've ever been listened to before.

Humble Self-confidence versus Arrogance or Timidity

Humble self-confidence is not thinking poorly of yourself but letting go of ego and pride as you regard and assess your performance. As a coach, humility about what you don't know is crucial; acknowledging your imperfect knowledge leads you to ask questions. And self-confidence allows you to trust the coaching process as long as you bring your full attention and intention to it.

If you act arrogantly as a coach, bestowing pearls of wisdom on your employees, they will at best follow your advice without developing their own capabilities and at worst disengage and become passive. And if you are timid, afraid of sharing your ideas and experience, then your employees fail to benefit from your contributions to the shared exploration and problem solving.

Curiosity versus Knowing: Asking Probing Questions versus Relying on Assumptions

Closely related to arrogance versus humility is the distinction between being curious and thinking that you know. When you believe that you know something, definitely and fully, you cease being curious about it. The minute you say to yourself, "Oh, I get it" during a coaching conversation, consider that a red flag and pivot back to asking questions.

Growth versus Fixed Mind-Set

According to psychology professor Carol Dweck, people with a growth mind-set believe they can improve their performance through diligence and effort. Those with a fixed mind-set, on the other hand, assume that all their abilities and potential are set and cannot be improved. Coaching is all about growth and change. As a coach and manager, you must embody and communicate a growth mind-set to your employees if you want them to model it and take control of their own development.

Collaborating versus Grandstanding and Taking All the Credit

As a coaching manager, you have to be willing to let your employees shine without needing to take the credit for your team's accomplishments. Nothing deflates morale as much as a superior taking credit for the employees' hard work.

Emotional Strength versus Emotional Fragility

As we've seen, one of the most common and debilitating obstacles to powerful action is our fear of how we will feel. As a coach, you will be able to help employees take action in spite of their negative and unpleasant feelings and to the extent that you can tolerate your own.

Brainstorming and Creative Thinking versus Latching on to the First and Most Obvious Solution

A good coaching conversation generates new insights, which become the springboard for innovative approaches and solutions. Unlike guesses on standardized tests, the first solution that comes to mind is rarely the best one. Generally, it's an obvious answer that the employee has already thought of. Be willing to brainstorm and offer unusual and even silly options to move beyond the obvious.

Exploring Specifics versus Staying in Generalities

One of the most common ways people stay confused is by thinking in generalities. If your employee tells you, "I always get nervous when I'm asked to speak at meetings," there's nothing useful you can offer based on that information. Whenever you hear a generality, inquire about a specific example: "Tell me about the last time that happened. What were you thinking and feeling as you were being introduced? What did you do before the meeting to relax? How did you prepare for your presentation?" The answers to these questions can offer opportunities to try new things and resolve or mitigate the problem.

FAQS AND COMMON MISUNDERSTANDINGS

How Can I Coach and Be Someone's Boss at the Same Time?

This question of how to both lead and coach stems from an assumption that coaching undermines the natural power relationship between boss and employee: the boss gives orders and the employee obeys. While there may be contexts and industries where this management style still has merit, it doesn't work well in knowledge industries where autonomy, initiative, and teamwork are critical for success.

If your goal as a boss is to support the performance of your team, rather than to tell them what to do and how to do it, then coaching is a perfect fit. As a coach, you build trust and rapport so they come to you proactively when they need help. They don't try to hide their weaknesses out of fear of punishment but instead focus on getting the support they need to get the job done well.

Some managers worry about the risk of being held accountable for outcomes that result from employee mistakes. It can be a challenge to loosen the reins in the short term, but the longer-term benefits of coaching—the creation of a self-accountable and proactive employee—generally outweigh the risks of mistakes along the way. And delegation without coaching is definitely riskier than delegation with coaching.

Coaching Is the Same as Advising or Instructing

Traditionally, coaches were taught never to advise or instruct but instead to guide clients to discover their own inner answers. Whether this policy works in a pure coach–client relationship, we have our doubts, but in the context of a coaching manager, it's totally appropriate for an experienced manager to share insights and impart his or her expertise to employees.

Instructing, however, is only one part of the coaching process. The heart of coaching, as is clear by now, is to empower employees to improve their own performance and capability. Simply passing on knowledge is insufficient to grow self-accountability; employees must practice brainstorming options, choose and commit to a plan of action, and actively seek feedback for continuous improvement. In addition to sharing information, the coach must facilitate the process by which employees take the reins of their own development.

How Can I Coach an Employees to Improve if They Don't Recognize the Problem?

Often, getting an employee to recognize a problem is the first step in coaching him to solve it. That's why teaching about blind spots is such a useful move, when coupled with objective evidence that a problem exists. As long as the coaching manager has access to data that show a gap between desired and actual outcomes (whether for an individual employee, a team, or an entire division or organization), there's a problem somewhere. The goal of the first stage of coaching is often to move the employee from unconscious incompetence (he doesn't realize he has a problem) to conscious incompetence he acknowledges he has a problem). If an employee simply refuses to see, acknowledge, and take responsibility for problematic behaviors, he may not be coachable.

Coaching Is Only for Problem Employees

Coaching, in most successful organizations, is generally reserved for the most valuable and highest potential employees. Just as all top athletes have coaches and absolutely rely on them to keep them at the top of their game, top employees and those groomed for leadership are typically the ones on whom development resources are lavished. Just because a manager with a harsh or remedial style calls what they do coaching, doesn't make it so. Coaching is for anyone with room to improve. Usually, it's the A-level talent whose improvement moves the needle the most for the organization.

Coaching Takes too Much Time; Employees Should Just Do What I Tell Them to Do

If your team simply does what you tell them to do, then you don't need to coach them. If all your employees do what you tell them, *and* your instructions are superior to their ability to improvise in the moment *and* the employees are willing to work under those conditions are at least as driven and competent as those employed by your competitors, then there's no need to change your management style.

If any of those hypotheticals comes up short, and you aren't getting the results you want by working with the best people, then you might consider coaching as a smart time investment.

It's true that being directive is sometimes appropriate. When the task is straightforward and you've done it successfully in the past and there's little to be gained by employees struggling to figure it out for themselves, then a directive management style can save time and unnecessary agony.

Most of the time in a knowledge organization, however, teams are solving complex problems that haven't been solved before, and employees must develop problem-solving muscles and not just the habit of obedience.

Coaching Feels Like Doing Therapy

If you mean that coaching can bring up strong emotions, especially negative ones that typically aren't seen as appropriate in the workplace, then yes, coaching can do that. Unlike therapy, however, coaching isn't trying to figure out the past or even heal it. Instead, coaching focuses on future performance, on helping employees get traction and achieve great things. One of the biggest obstacles to doing the right thing is fear of feeling an unpleasant emotion or sensation. We avoid confrontations because we don't like the feeling we get in a conflict or are afraid the other person won't like us anymore. And so crucial things go unsaid.

One of the most important parts of coaching is to help employees follow through on their commitments to act, even while experiencing the negative emotions that stopped them in the past. If you as a coach are able to handle your employees' negative emotions without needing to shut them down or wallow in them or explore their origins, then coaching doesn't feel anything like therapy. Instead, it's an opportunity to help them practice feeling the feeling and taking action anyway.

If I Coach My Employees, They'll See Me as Weak and Won't Respect Me

Actually, you'll garner more respect if you show your employees that you care about them, you believe in them, and you are brave enough to show them your own weaknesses and vulnerabilities.

I Don't Want to Know about My Employees' Personal Problems

What's worse than knowing about your employees' personal problems is when those individual problems become your professional problems because they interfere with employees' ability to perform in the workplace. Since you can't make those problems magically disappear by not knowing about them, you might as well make room for them in your coaching conversations. You don't need to pry for details; simply acknowledging that a tense marriage or increased responsibility for an aging parent or a child's diagnosis will inevitably affect the employee's work life can make the employee feel heard and understood and valued and supported. Often that's enough to mitigate the problem. When more help is required, you're in a position to do so.

How Can I Coach an Employee Who Has a Skill Set That I Don't Have?

The basic principles of coaching don't require technical expertise in the domain at issue. While you may not be able to give specific instruction or advice about how to solve a C++ coding issue or the structural dynamics of flow as a nonexpert, you can help your employee identify roadblocks, brainstorm options, take actions, seek feedback, compare results to goals, and iterate the process.

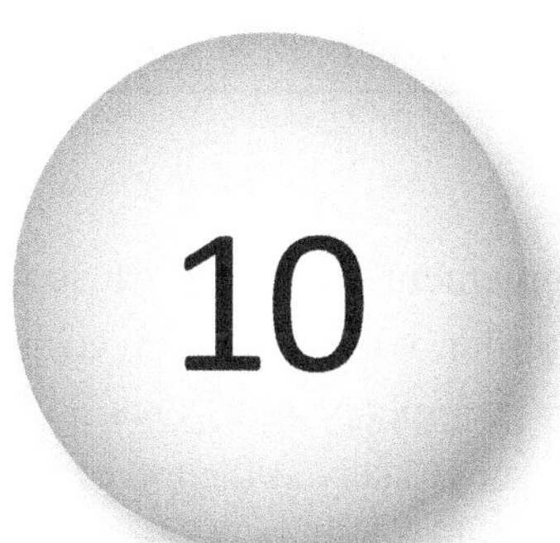

Managing Change

LEARNING OBJECTIVES

By the end of this chapter, you will be better equipped to:

- Collect information about the drivers and anticipated value of a change.
- Identify the ways in which a change will affect your team, including benefits and technical and emotional barriers.
- Share information about a change, including its impacts.
- Express confidence and support in individuals' and the team's ability to be successful with a change.
- Establish ongoing two-way communication, seeking and listening to team members' concerns and potential solutions and sharing new information and results.
- Apply communication, emotional intelligence, conflict management, motivation, collaboration, and influencing skills to manage resistance and promote a successful change implementation.

The ancient Greek philosopher Heraclitus observed that life is flux, meaning that all things change. Nowhere is this more evident than in the world of work today. Organizations are continuously adjusting their strategies, processes, and talent to stay competitive or to anticipate and keep up with economic, demographic, or technologic shifts.

As managers, we are charged with implementing these changes and ensuring their outcomes are successful. Yet, what might seem simple on paper is often confounded by the complexities of managing the people tasked with executing the work.

Why is change so difficult to implement? In part, because when you change something, you create ambiguity for people. What was familiar, whether perceived as good or bad, will change to something unfamiliar. This ambiguity naturally prompts people to resist change. The effects of this resistance can be disastrous for an organization striving to stay at the top of its field.

Successful managers are adept at achieving targeted outcomes in this environment. They lead their teams through change by communicating the change's value and impact and providing support. They anticipate concerns and resistance and identify strategies to address them. They also include others in decision making to gain buy-in and commitment.

It's the combination of these intentional actions that makes them effective.

In this chapter, we explore how approaches to managing change have evolved and present techniques for preparing, communicating with, and supporting the individuals in your organization to successfully adopt change. In practice, the development of the managing change competency involves the activities depicted in Figure 10-1. We provide tactical guidance and examples to bring these to life and enable you to realize effective change outcomes for your team and your organization.

WHAT WE KNOW ABOUT MANAGING CHANGE HAS EVOLVED

Historically, managers took a directive approach to managing change. They made decisions about what changes to implement and how to implement them with the least disruption. They then instructed their teams on the best ways to proceed and closely monitored their progress.

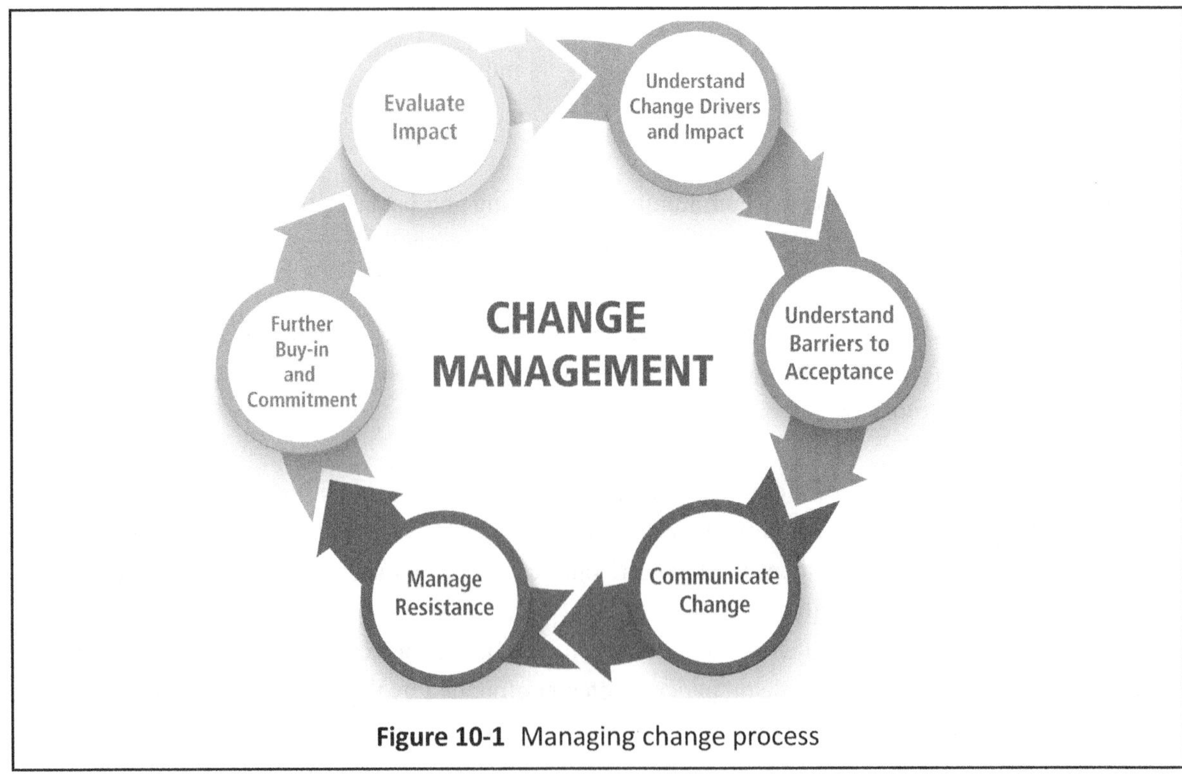

Figure 10-1 Managing change process

This directive approach focused on addressing technical needs, such as providing instruction on new processes or roles, but did not address psychological factors, like internal resistance to change that could derail the change efforts.

In this environment, managers shared information on a need to know basis, communicating only when necessary and, in many cases, keeping imperfect or ambiguous information to themselves. The expectation was that employees would intuitively know and understand the strategy and reasons for the change or that they didn't need or care to know.

Managers' failure to invite or address employees' concerns or suggestions sent clear signals that their input was not important or welcome. This often led to poor morale among team members and lost opportunities to include employee input that could improve outcomes.

In analyzing poorly executed change efforts, experts have identified the lack of attention to the emotional impacts of change as a critical factor in change initiative failures.

We process change as a loss of the familiar and of perceived control. Thus managing change requires us to address both emotional and technical transitions in order to be successful and achieve our intended goals.

Modern, integrated change management techniques address both emotional and technical needs of employees and of the managers themselves. Employing these techniques requires managers to recognize and prioritize the importance of obtaining employees' buy-in to changes and engaging them collaboratively in the solutions. In addition to the skills discussed in this chapter, skills addressed in Chapter 2, Emotional Intelligence, and Chapter 7, Influence, are crucial to a successful change effort.

By focusing on tactics that prompt open communication and transparency around decision making, addressing feelings of loss, inviting employee involvement in solutions, and celebrating interim successes, managers reduce transition times from the old to the new.

The results are change efforts that are more likely to achieve their goals.

ASSESS CHANGE READINESS

Implementing a change effort is complex. As we've noted, managers must plan to address both technical and emotional issues that might impact the initiative. Because each initiative is different and every organization or group that will be affected by the change is different, it's crucial that managers consider their organization's or team's culture and readiness for change during the planning stages.

What's New?

- Address technical and emotional needs.
- Foster open communication.
- Engage employees in solutions.
- Celebrate interim successes.

Myth: Those who object to change are just being difficult. It's a conscious choice.

Fear of failure, fear of success, and low tolerance for ambiguity are just some of the instinctive responses we have to change. Often, those who object to change are working to overcome their instinctive responses but need help getting there.

Fear of failure is driven by a general concern about being inadequate in a new role or with a process and, with or without validity, job insecurity. Fear of success, while almost counterintuitive, comes from a desire to maintain the status quo: If employees are successful with the new requirements, they will be asked to continue on the new path, thrusting those employees into an undesirable role or responsibility. Low tolerance for ambiguity is a discomfort working in an environment in which the end goal or the path to get there has not been clearly defined.

Fear of success and fear of failure often appear the same; employees may articulate reasons they think the new course of action won't work or they may actively advocate for the old way. Minor hiccups and obstacles are not perceived as opportunities to make improvements. Instead, they are viewed as evidence the decision to change is inherently flawed. Those who have a low tolerance for ambiguity ask for direction, for clear steps to follow, and for validation of their activities and decisions; they struggle in situations where they are required to be creative.

All three can lead to low morale and slow the change implementation.

Understanding the current state allows the manager to identify potential conflicts and plan tactics to acknowledge and address them.

Items to consider when analyzing the organization's current status include:

- The organization's current structure and its culture
- The current pace of change and responses to change
- Potential conflicts prompted by the new change

Let's look at each in turn, using an example of a relatively simple potential change to demonstrate the possibilities.

Current Structure and Culture

As an example, suppose you currently manage the regional sales force for a business technology sales organization. To address financial pressure to cut overhead costs, you are planning to eliminate administrative support roles and have sales representatives manage their own order troubleshooting and reporting.

Technical Workflow

While assessing your organization's readiness for the projected change, it's important to evaluate the current workflow, including what's working and what's not and how the current state came to be. This will lay the foundation for how people in the organization will perceive the change.

Example 1: Technical Work Flow

In our sales organization, sales representatives work in the field, traveling within a geographic region to secure new and follow-on orders. They have always had administrative support to manage their order processing and generate required customer and firm reports. Until two years ago, orders were filed on paper, so sales representatives called their orders in to staff in a central location to expedite them.

Two years ago, the firm implemented technology that enabled electronic order and report creation from any location. This eliminated the need for many administrative roles, and over time the number of support people dwindled; as support people left the firm or were promoted, the workflow was consolidated. Now, each administrative support person, whose primary role is to troubleshoot order problems and file reports, handles three sales representatives. The current workflow allows the sales reps to stay focused on sales, where they are under increasing pressure to perform, rather than getting bogged down in liaising with order fulfillment and technical support groups. Generally, this works well, although during busy times, the administrative people have been overwhelmed, leading to delays and unhappy customers.

Team Roles and Dynamics

As you've noted, the administrative support team has been compressed over time. The remaining sales support personnel are overworked, which has led to friction with the sales team. Sales reps resent having to share a support person, and all have complained that their customers' needs aren't being prioritized. In some cases, reps have begun managing their own order troubleshooting to expedite the process and maintain customer goodwill, although they recognize it's a trade-off: Time spent salvaging a relationship means time away from securing new customers. In response, the sales support personnel resent being circumvented, because it sends a clear signal that they are not trusted to follow through. It also leads to duplicated efforts when reps do not communicate their involvement. General cross-team morale is low, and everyone feels that the firm should hire more administrative support.

Existing Communication Patterns and Standards

Since sales reps are in the field, there is little regular interaction with the team, as a group. Weekly team calls, which include sales reps and support staff, focus on providing data about the team's performance against its goals and sharing how senior management views their performance. If there are changes in strategy or new product rollouts, these are described, and training is assigned to ensure everyone is well versed. There is no discussion of what processes could be improved, and when team members have made suggestions in the past, there has been no follow-through by management. This pattern echoes the communication patterns among management levels: information is handed down, but there's little opportunity to provide feedback or to influence decision making.

As a result, employees have taken to complaining among themselves about management's tone deafness, lack of vision, and unreasonable demands.

Team Roles and Dynamics

Team dynamics are a crucial consideration. Take stock of current team members' roles and their tenure. The stability of the current team, its typical interactions, and trust among team members can influence how welcoming they will be of change and how supportive they will be of each other during the process.

Communication Patterns and Standards

In addition to team communication patterns—how team members communicate among themselves—assess how communication flows up and down the organizational structure. How are messages about challenges, successes, and changes typically transferred within the organization and how are they received? Are there regular opportunities for employees to provide ideas and input or is the typical information flow from the top down? When employees do make suggestions, how are these suggestions processed within the organization?

If the organization doesn't foster open communication and provide opportunities to influence decision making, employees often feel powerless. Alternately, when the organization communicates goals clearly and invites collaborative problem solving, employees feel empowered; they have an ownership stake in the resulting solutions.

Current Pace of Change and Responses

Changes do not happen in isolation. They occur and are received in the broader context of other changes happening in the organization. If the environment is one of constant change, it can be difficult for employees to assimilate all the changes or to see the bigger picture of how the continuous flow of changes are interrelated and connected to a bigger vision for the organization.

Other Changes: Past or Concurrent

Consider what other changes have occurred recently or are currently happening. Who did they impact and how? Are employees still struggling to understand and integrate other changes, or have they taken them in stride and implemented them without much disruption?

Results of Past Changes

Have past changes been successful or failed? More important, why? Looking objectively at the results of past change efforts and their influencers may provide a window into what's working or not in the organization. Such information can act as a crystal ball, providing a view of how future change efforts that are managed in the same ways are likely to play out.

Dialogues around Change

Do people within the organization welcome change as a way to improve themselves and the organization's results or do they resent change and view it as a type of punishment? Listen to the dialogues of people within the company and how they talk about change. Do they perceive positive outcomes, even if there are bumps along the way, or is change generally something to withstand? Or worse, do they believe that, if they refuse or resist change, things will stay the same?

Potential Conflicts

Once you have a sense of how change has been managed in the past and how it is perceived, turn your attention to the specific change you are planning. What conflicts could be prompted by the change? If you can anticipate these, you can create a plan for addressing or mitigating them. Any conflicts not identified and addressed early on could derail your change initiative.

Potential conflicts generally fall into one of two main categories: technical/structural and interactional. Alternately, you can think of this as what and who will be impacted.

What Will Be Impacted

Most changes have a technical or structural component. They will affect one or more of these items:

- Workflow
- Roles and responsibilities
- Skill requirements
- Reporting and communication paths

Whenever any of these items change, there's a high likelihood for conflict to surface during implementation. Mapping the technical changes can help identify where those conflicts will occur (see Example 2).

Who Will Be Impacted

While it's often evident who will be directly impacted by a change, there are many others who will be indirectly impacted, on both structural and interpersonal levels. You should account for all those affected and their interactions during planning.

It can be helpful to map the impacts captured during your technical/structural assessment and extrapolate out the ripple effects to those who will be affected indirectly. Who will this affect and how? Be sure to include formal and informal leadership in your mapping exercise.

Pro tip

Include all who will be directly and indirectly affected by a change when assessing the organization's readiness for change.

Making a Change Readiness Determination

No one right answer can be found for whether an organization is ready for a change. Instead, you must use the information you've gathered during your assessment process to guide your decision about whether to implement the change and, if so, when and how.

In the example we've been working with, you are the manager deciding on what changes to make and when to implement them. If, based on your assessment, you determine the change would cause more disruption than the value it would bring, you can reconsider your plan or alter the timing. If you determine the change is the right course of action, you can use the information you've gathered to plan your change communication strategy and to develop a plan to manage anticipated resistance.

Example 2: Technical and Structural Impacts

Even the relatively simple planned change in our sales organization will affect workflow, roles and responsibilities, skill requirements, and reporting and communication paths, as seen in the chart, which captures only direct impacts on the sales reps and the sales support staff. If we were to extend this out more broadly to everyone in the organization whose work will be affected, we would see a much longer list of affected processes.

Direct Effects of the Change	
Technical/Structural Area	**Effects**
Workflow	Sales reps will interact directly with order fulfillment and technical support groups to address order problems and report filing. Sales reps need to reorganize their own work to accommodate these additional requirements.
Roles and responsibilities	Sales reps will take on additional responsibilities for troubleshooting and report filing. Job descriptions need to be updated. Compensation will not change. Sales support staff will be eliminated.
Skill requirements	Sales reps need training on efficient troubleshooting and the technical requirements of report filing.
Reporting and communication paths	Information flow among back-office groups and sales reps need to be established. The feedback loop from sales reps to management for problem escalation needs to be created.

In many instances, you will not be the person who is mandating the change. Regulatory bodies or even senior leadership may require you to implement a change they have already approved. In these situations, it's still important to perform a readiness assessment, including your own readiness to change, so you can plan for success.

PLAN YOUR CHANGE COMMUNICATION STRATEGY

The cornerstone of the success or failure of many organizational changes is communication, discussed more fully in Chapter 1, Communication. As a manager, your role is to facilitate understanding and adoption of the change by articulating the vision and the plan and by carefully crafting your responses to any resistance you receive.

Example 3: How Interactions Are Affected

The graphic below shows both direct and indirect interactions and how they will be affected by the change. Here, you can see that, although the direct impact will be on only the sales reps, the sales associates, and you as manager, there are many others in the organization who will be indirectly affected, as will customers. It's at the intersections that conflicts can occur.

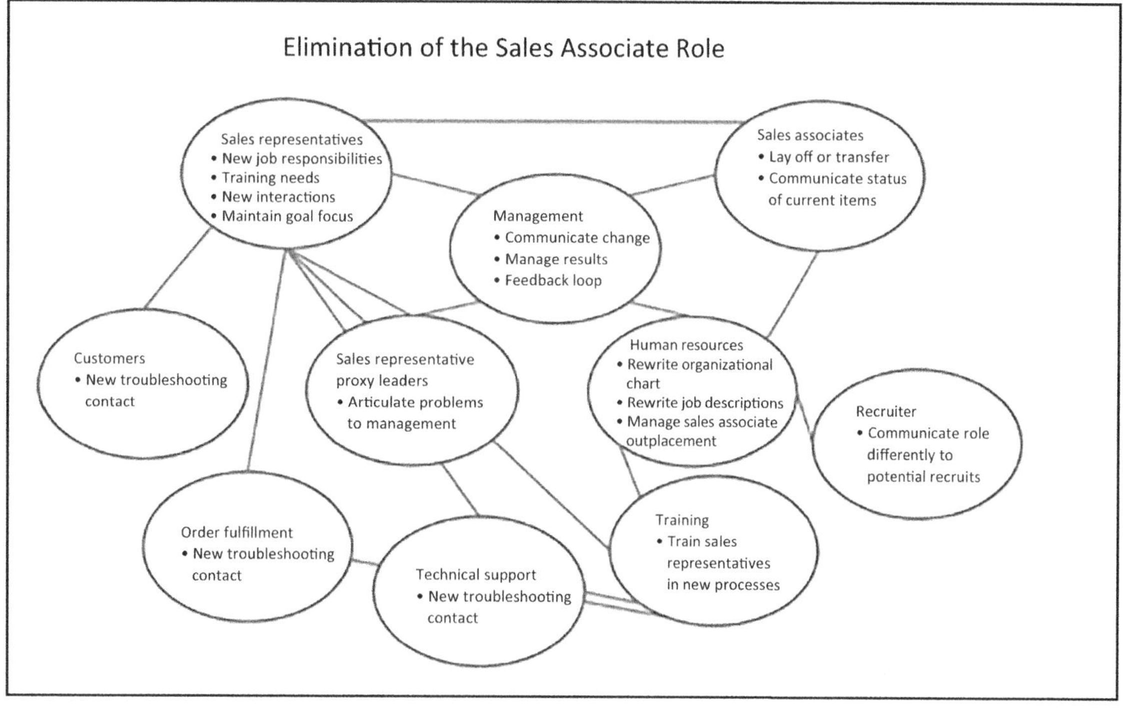

When designing your communication strategy, it's important to plan for success. To do this, start by identifying the need for the change, then ensure you understand the strategy underpinning the change. Once you've established the need and strategy, outline your action plan for implementing and communicating the change. Last, consider questions you think your team will ask and prepare your responses.

In situations in which a change has been mandated and you are not personally committed to it, working through this process helps you consider how to articulate your own position about the change to your team and others.

Identify the Need

Behind every change effort is a perceived need. To plan your communication strategy, first identify and understand that need. What is prompting the change?

Example 4: Using the Underlying Need to Drive Change Decisions

If the need for cost cutting at our business technology sales company is driven by lower revenue because a new entrant into the market is poaching our clients, this understanding can prompt different thinking about how to spur profitability. Alternate courses of action are shown in the chart below.

While the list given in the chart is not exhaustive, several actions offer the possibility of the desired impact. They would also be significant change efforts in themselves; still, any proposed action should be weighed against the current plan's pros and cons.

Last, the impact of doing nothing should be considered. Is this a short-term financial blip that will resolve itself? What is the hazard of changing nothing? Knowing the answers to all of these questions will provide you with information you need to plan your communications with your team and others.

Some Alternate Courses of Action	
Alternate Action	**Likely Outcome**
Increase sales targets to improve revenue	Failure to increase sales; decrease sales rep retention
Lower sales commission rates	Decrease sales rep recruitment and retention
Reduce the number of salespeople	Decrease sales revenue
Reduce investment in new software development	Decrease future revenue opportunities
Reduce travel expenses	Decrease sales revenue
Cut management salaries	Decrease manager recruitment and retention (management is already lean)
Reduce facilities overhead by having sales support work from home	Increase employee satisfaction without loss of service; lease commitments would reduce immediate impact (possibility to explore long term)
Hire more sales associates	Increase client satisfaction and retention; allow sales reps to focus on new client acquisition; increase revenue; decrease bottom line
Revamp installation process	Near-term expense; in long term, reduce customer complaints, increase retention and revenue; reduce sales associate workload

In the example we've been using, it would be easy to point to the need to cut costs as the primary driver. However, this would be only part of the story. Cost cutting is being pushed down from the top of the organization. Why is this? What internal and external forces are influencing this?

Have revenues declined and the organization is losing money? Are benchmark competitors more cost-efficient? Are vendor prices increasing? Are shareholders or other owners applying pressure? Does the organization have an anticipated future expenditure it needs to plan for now? Are there structural changes in the industry or economy that mean the organization will have to be leaner to survive? Is there a different reason?

All needs are valid and important to understand in order to consider alternate courses of action: What else could be done, and what are the likely results of those actions? Will they address the need?

Understand the Strategy

What if you are not selecting the change strategy? For example, let's consider a situation in which the organization has decided to purchase and implement a new, integrated software solution to manage projects and client contacts throughout the organization.

Just as we did earlier, we need to assess the history of what's changing and the current impacts of the status quo. Who will be affected by the change, both directly and indirectly? We also need to understand the underlying need driving the change and why this strategy is being pursued instead of other possibilities.

Often, we will select a strategy that's worked in the past. If that's the case here, identify what contributed to the earlier positive outcomes. Are those the same circumstances now?

Next, develop clarity about the intended outcomes. In the case of our new software, what metrics or other dynamics does the organization hope to change? How and why do they expect that this solution will realize these outcomes? It's also important to understand the timeline for when they expect to achieve the desired outcomes.

By developing a thorough understanding of the strategy, you will equip yourself with the information you need to develop a plan for communicating and implementing the change.

Outline the Action Plan

Taking the information you've gathered, create your action plan for the change initiative's tactical implementation. Then overlay your plan for communicating the change initiative.

Your communication plan should incorporate each of these elements:

- Ensure all team members and other affected parties receive consistent information.
- Share the vision for the change strategy: why this, why now?
- Share tactical considerations, such as effects and timelines.
- Answer questions from team members.

Communication Planning Considerations

- Who will be affected?
- How will they be affected?
- What is the timeline for implementation?
- What support is available?

Well-handled communications begin the mental transition process from the old way to the new way. This does not mean that everyone will be on board, but that they will have enough information to begin processing the loss of the current way and to begin envisioning the new way.

The key elements to consider in your communication planning are:

Pro tip

It's generally better to communicate with the entire team at once, at least initially, to ensure message consistency and reduce the likelihood that your messages will be misconstrued when shared at the water cooler.

- *Communicate to All Who Will Be Affected Directly and Indirectly*: Select the right vehicle for communicating to everyone affected. Is this a face-to-face meeting? If some team members are remote, plan for how you will include them. Are there follow-on messages or instructions that need to be delivered to only a segment of the audience? Plan your approach for these messages and build them into your communication strategy.
- *Include Information About How Team Members Will Be Affected by the Change*: It's important to acknowledge that the change will not be business as usual. Include information about role and responsibility changes, process changes, and potential obstacles the team or individuals will face. While you may not have perfect information about some details of the change, share what you know and set expectations for when you will have more information to share. If you anticipate specific emotional responses from team members, plan to acknowledge their disappointment, frustration, anxiety, or excitement.

Myth: Communicate only when you have "perfect" information

Sharing what you know now rather than waiting for perfect clarity will promote an environment of open, transparent communication and provide an opportunity for team members to provide input early or begin preparing themselves for changes. This does not mean you should pass along rumors. Instead, share organizational decisions as they're made and you're authorized to share them.

> **Myth:** Communication should be on a need to know basis only
>
> *"Need to know" in a changing environment is anyone who is directly or indirectly affected by the change.*

- *Share the Timeline for Implementation*: This can be high-level in initial meetings, but specifics about when tactical pieces of the plan are scheduled should be shared as quickly as they are available. Be certain to include interim points at which certain milestones or results are expected to be achieved.
- *Share Resources Available for Support during the Implementation*: If the organization will provide training, consultant support, or other assistance during implementation, make this clear to team members and let them know how and when they can access these tools. Understanding that there has been thought put into supporting their efforts can help allay anxiety.

Prepare Responses to Questions

As part of your planning for the initial communications, consider the questions your team may pose and prepare how you will respond. When gathering your list of potential questions, organize them into categories: strategic, tactical, emotional/personal, and other. Put yourself in your team members' shoes: What would you want to know? In fact, some of questions they pose will be the same as those you had when you first considered or heard about the change.

Common questions include:

- Why change?
- Why this strategy, why not some other strategy?
- Why now?
- What does this mean for another initiative, department, or customer?
- How will this affect process?
- How will this affect my work?

The more complete your list of anticipated questions, the more likely you will be prepared to present or respond with information that will address your team's concerns.

MANAGING CHANGE RESISTANCE

As noted earlier, resistance to change is normal. Whether articulated by team members or not, there is likely to be reticence to change. Your management of communications throughout the change process will help mitigate resistance and provide team members with confidence that their concerns are being heard and addressed. During changes, keep the following communication guidelines in mind and design processes during your planning to help foster open communication:

- *Maintain Transparency and Authenticity*: In most cases, it's helpful to share information when you have it, even if it is incomplete. If you are unclear on something or don't know the answer to a question, tell your employees you don't know. If someone suggests there's a better way to proceed than what you had previously envisioned, acknowledge this. It's important to be a conduit for information and ideas but don't pretend or imagine you know all the answers.
- *Invite Responses*: Encourage team members to share their feelings and suggestions. If a suggestion is unrealistic, recognize the contribution, facilitate an open discussion of the suggestion's possibilities, and suggest or invite alternatives.
- *Listen and Observe Reactions*: Not all team members will vocalize their concerns. Listen to tone and observe body language during interactions and ask questions to draw out concerns when you sense team members are not being forthcoming. Don't make assumptions about your employees' positions, though. Your goal is to hear them and identify ways to assuage their anxiety or anger.
- *Address Obstacles*: Even the most successful change efforts will hit speed bumps along the way. Note current or anticipated obstacles and share how you or the team can address them.
- *Focus on Benefits and a Common Vision*: Keep the intended benefits of the change effort front and center during your communications with individuals and the team. While it's good practice to acknowledge obstacles, it's equally important to remind team members of the value of their efforts. To this end, don't forget to celebrate interim successes along the way.
- *Communicate Continuously and Frequently*: Plan to stay visible and communicate regularly with the team, sharing information and gathering their insights and feedback on how things are proceeding. This will serve two distinct purposes: It will help you stay abreast of their feelings and technical progress, and it will reassure them that new information and feedback will be shared as it's available, so they can adjust their activities or expectations.

Pro tip

With remote team members, use visual virtual technology during one-on-one and team meetings to help improve communications with you and the rest of the team. Also, plan regular one-on-one conversations to keep communication channels open, so geographically remote employees don't feel overlooked or out of the loop.

If you have remote team members, it's especially important to plan your efforts to keep them involved and connected to the larger team's efforts.

Managing Team Resistance

Team resistance can take many forms. While sometimes team resistance is overt and clearly stated, generally, evidence of team resistance is more subtle. One indicator of team resistance is a communication shutdown, when team members refuse to engage in discussions about the change. Others are similar to what you might see with individual resistance, except they're more widespread among team members: carelessness with new processes or other attempts to sabotage the change effort, bonding among team members over what's not working, complaining to other groups or in small subgroups, or general malaise among the team, usually evidenced by high absenteeism.

To address team resistance, it's important to engage employees in positive team activities that focus on solving problems, rather than complaining about them. Identify key obstacles that team members could help solve and create a task force to design solutions. Promote the task force's work and celebrate its wins.

It's also important to get people talking about their objections without fear of retaliation. Plan ways to encourage this, whether in team meetings or in smaller groups. To start the conversation, you can share your own concerns about the change and how these have evolved.

Pro tip

While people need to vent and be heard, it's also important to facilitate an exchange that focuses on positive outcomes from the change and a collective effort to achieve these. To manage this conversation transition, collect concerns and then refocus on the goal: "How can we overcome these issues, so that we can accomplish what we've set out to do?" If responses are slow in coming, suggest something you could do to address an issue. This can nudge the conversation in the right direction. Reassure team members that, together, you're capable of solving whatever issues arise.

Managing Individual Resistance

Individual resistance, like team resistance, is sometimes overt, but is often more subtle. It becomes evident when the rest of the team is working to implement the change and solve problems, but one individual does not engage with the rest of the team's efforts. The individual can either withdraw or lash out at team members who are on board. Of course, other negative behaviors, such as absenteeism or despondency, can also be indicators that an individual has not made a transition to accepting the change.

In these instances, it's important to engage the individual in a one-on-one conversation about his or her concerns. As in a team meeting, keep an open mind and do not judge the person's feelings. Share your own concerns and how you overcame (or are overcoming) them and focus on the positive outcomes the team has experienced so far. When possible, tie intended outcomes of the

Myth: People who complain about something that's not working will be happy to hear it's changing.

Just because people complain about something doesn't mean they will welcome changes. Many other factors are involved, including how much control they feel over the changes and whether they perceive the changes as addressing their complaints.

change to something that the individual cares about. For example, a more efficient process that will reduce the number of unexpected late work nights to make deadlines.

Reassure the individual that you have every confidence he or she will be successful with the new process, and be sure to recognize that person's individual progress as it occurs. In some cases, when a lack of control is driving the employee's concerns, asking for suggestions and empowering the employee to implement them can help as well.

DEFINE AND COMMUNICATE THE CHANGE'S IMPACT AND GAIN COMMITMENT

Your planning process's focus is on successfully achieving the change initiative's intended impact. To accomplish this, clearly define the targets and milestones for the change efforts and obtain others' commitments to them.

Define and Communicate Change's Intended Impact

Consider the overarching goal for the change. Is it to create efficiency, to mitigate risk, or to generate revenue? Next determine how the organization will measure its success. If metrics exist or are being designed to measure the change efforts, gather information about the inputs to those metrics and confirm the levers your team can affect. By when should your team's efforts be seen in the data and by how much should it change?

Creating Milestones

Also consider the milestones for the implementation itself. By when should you complete each phase, what is involved in each, and how will you know it's been done successfully? What is acceptable prog-

Example 5: Metrics for New Software Implementation

The overall organizational metric that is being targeted is a 10 percent increase in revenue as a result of faster launches of new products and product enhancements. Your group manages one piece of the product development cycle. Among the metrics tracked for your team is its ability to meet assigned deadlines, which the organization expects to compress once the new software rollout is complete. While the company will be tracking revenue, your team's impact will be felt most fully at the operational level: How quickly can it execute the piece of the product development cycle for which it is responsible without decreasing quality? If the expectation is that the team will save two weeks on its part of the development process, what are reasonable interim deadlines and milestones for tracking the success of your team's efforts?

ress versus good progress versus exceptional progress? The more clearly you define these in advance, the easier it will be to set expectations during your communications with the team.

Capture information about the organization and team goals, and plan how you will communicate these in a compelling way. It will be important for team members to understand how the changes they are making locally will contribute to the organization goal.

Team members will also want to know how you'll track their progress. How will you keep their goals and progress visible? At what points will you celebrate their achievements, and how will you celebrate them?

Pro tip

Create a simple, easily understood graphic that represents key milestones and targets and post this in a visible location. Update it regularly, as information becomes available, and use the process of adding updates as an opportunity for team huddles to discuss what's working and what could be improved. To keep the focus positive, cheer small wins early in the process, when results might not yet show in the data.

Gain Commitment to the Change

During your initial communications with the team, your intention is to share information but also to gain commitment to the change. Although commitment doesn't require complete agreement on all aspects of the implementation, it does require that team members agree that the change, if implemented successfully, will have a positive impact on the achievement of goals that they care about.

Commitment is typically gained in phases:

1. Agreement that the end goal is worthy
2. Acknowledgment that this change will help achieve the end goal
3. Willingness to engage in the activities required to execute the change or to improve the planned activities

Depending on the scope of the change, team members and individuals might need time to process your initial communications before committing to the phases. Plan a reasonable timeline for check-ins or followup meetings, as a team and with individuals, to discuss the change and answer questions.

At an individual level, each employee will want to understand what he or she needs to do as part of the change. Be prepared to share this information in individual meetings. If details still need to be defined, share what you know and consider asking the employee to be involved in creating necessary definition.

Myth: Team members will engage with change in order to keep their jobs.

Heel-dragging compliance is, obviously, not the same as true engagement and commitment. To maintain their employment, some individuals will participate but will not truly engage. This is not your goal.

Myth: Those who don't object to change are committed.

Silence does not necessarily equal commitment. Commitment should require an oral or written assertion of agreement on the goal and engagement in the work to achieve it. When you observe this is not happening, have a follow-up conversation to identify an employee's position and address concerns.

If you witness evidence of staff or individual apathy about engaging with the changes, consider why this could be occurring. Return to your assessment about the organization's readiness for change and do some further analysis. Are people already overwhelmed? Are they being asked to process too many changes too quickly? Have past change efforts been unsuccessful or was there a penalty for their success, such as an increased workload or a layoff? What is their general engagement level with the organization or with you? Do they trust the organization or you? Do they care about the organization or the team? What other factors could be influencing their lack of commitment?

Objectively evaluate your communications to date. Did you make a compelling connection between the change effort and a benefit to them that they care about? Were your communications clear and were the timelines you presented perceived as manageable?

Depending on the issues identified, you might need to revisit your plan or your communications. Don't hesitate to consult with others who may have useful suggestions.

PREPARE AND SUPPORT TEAM MEMBERS TO PROMOTE CHANGE ADOPTION

To promote adoption of the change, plan ways you can support team members and individuals to enable their success. Earlier in your planning, you identified resources and training required for the team or individuals. In addition to communicating these plans, be certain to follow through and check in to ensure team members have received what they needed.

Also consider whether you need to provide additional support, such as individual or team coaching. A coach could be someone involved in delivering the training, someone from another part of the organization, someone from your own team, or even you, depending on the coaching topics. The techniques addressed in Chapter 9, Coaching for Performance, will prepare you to be effective with your coaching efforts.

While it's tempting to hover over team members as they're beginning to implement changes, most people do not respond well to being micromanaged. While your intention might be to signal your involvement and availability, there's a delicate balance between being perceived as an accessible resource and being perceived as a micromanager. The former signals support, while the latter signals distrust in their abilities.

Instead of hovering, provide clear expectations for the work; provide necessary resources, including guidance about when to escalate problems and what they are able to decide themselves; and express confidence in the team's and individuals' abilities to be successful with the change. When you do check in, be sure to acknowledge their efforts and celebrate their successes.

ENGAGE YOUR TEAM IN IMPLEMENTING THE CHANGE

Two tactical ways to engage your team in implementing change are to involve them in regular communications with stakeholders and to involve them in decision making.

Manage Ongoing Communication during the Change Process

Effective management of ongoing communication during the change process can help maintain momentum and ensure the team receives the feedback and resources they need to remain nimble and make course corrections.

Identify the best communication channels for sharing their successes, frustrations, and feedback during the change and involve other stakeholders when it's appropriate. Some examples are:

- Weekly reports that share activity highlights, results to date, and plans for the following week
- Regular, scheduled meetings with stakeholders from other groups to gather input and share information about plans
- Client focus groups or surveys to collect information about how their experience has changed
- Regular, scheduled team meetings to share progress reports and feedback received as well as coordinate team efforts and make plan adjustments
- Start-of-day or end-of-day meetings with all team members to coordinate daily efforts and ask for assistance
- Regular, scheduled vendor meetings to coordinate implementation plans and ask questions

Assigning management of any of these communication processes to specific team members will expand their perspectives and prompt their engagement in problem solving.

Include Team Members in Decision Making

An effective strategy for gaining buy-in and support for the change is to include team members in decision making. While not all decisions are open for debate, most change efforts provide opportunities for

> **Myth:** It's appropriate to isolate or exclude naysayers.
>
> *Naysayers can be toxic to team engagement. Excluding or isolating them from team discussions and decision making with only exacerbate their feelings of being excluded. Instead, work to engage them and encourage others on the team to do the same.*

Myth: Every team member needs to be committed.

While it would be ideal to have all team members' commitments, this isn't always realistic. It's most important to have commitments from informal and formal leaders on the team and from those in "mission-critical" roles. Focus your efforts here.

input and discussion about the best ways to proceed with key implementation elements. In addition, some decisions can be owned by the team, rather than prescribed by management. Identify these during your action planning and articulate them early in your change communications.

Pro tip

It can be helpful to assign the most vocal critics of the current process to a change implementation task force for the team. They will have insight into hazards the team should avoid with the new process, and their engagement will involve them in the solution, rather than leaving the solution open to their general criticism.

Engaging team members in decision making helps them feel empowered to contribute to the change effort. In addition, it will prompt ownership and accountability among team members.

It's important to create an environment in which your team feels like they are partners in the change's success. To this end, continuously invite feedback from the team about what's working and what's not and ask for suggestions or solutions that are identified by the team or other stakeholders.

Solicit Team Feedback on the Process

Every change implementation is a continuous learning opportunity for the team, for individuals, and for you, as a manager. To ensure that all concerned maximize this opportunity, set aside time at regular intervals to ask those involved for feedback.

The focus of this feedback should be on the change process itself, not the decision to change. It will be important to make this distinction clear to the team before gathering their input. Key questions to ask include:

- How effective were decision-making processes when planning and implementing the change?
  - Did all team members have a voice and feel heard?
  - Were decisions made at the right levels?
  - What should we change about implementation decision making?
- How smoothly were implementation decisions communicated and executed?
  - How should we amend communication of implementation decisions and processes?
  - Was there a clear process for addressing challenges or obstacles?
  - What suggestions do you have for improving coordination and communication?

Example 6: New Software Implementation

The decision about the software selection has already been made by the organization, but your team members' input is useful for many other decisions about the implementation. Among these are timing and sequencing of the training, suggestions for resources to make a smooth transition, and ideas for how to port current information into the new system seamlessly. Depending on the size of your team, you can select or ask for volunteers to make recommendations for each of these and use the suggestions to guide your decision making.

Although you can facilitate this conversation, you can also engage a third party to gather and share the responses so team members feel comfortable being forthright. A third party's role can also help you maintain some objectivity when reviewing the collected responses and minimize the possibility that you will appear defensive.

Regardless of who collects the feedback, acknowledge all suggestions and follow up by sharing how you plan to incorporate the input for the future. If a suggestion is not feasible, acknowledge the suggestion, explain the challenges, and provide an explanation of what can be done instead.

• Conclusion •

Managing change is a challenge for all organizations and managers. To increase the probability that a pending change effort will be successful, dedicate yourself to planning thoughtfully for both tactical and interpersonal elements related to the change. By following through with clear, continuous, and open communication, you will mitigate change resistance and build genuine team commitment and engagement around problem solving.

This resulting collaborative approach will strengthen your team's capabilities and improve the likelihood that your team and the organization will realize the change's intended benefits.

Managing Change Process Worksheet

Table 10-1 summarizes key questions to guide you during your change implementation.

Table 10-1 Worksheet for Managing Change	
Understand Change Drivers and Impact	
What is the need driving the change?	
What are the intended outcomes of the change? How will they be measured?	
What is the current structure and culture of the organization? • Technical workflow • Team roles and dynamics • Communication patterns	
What other changes are occurring or have recently occurred? What have been the results of and responses to these changes?	
Understand Barriers to Acceptance	
What technical/structural conflicts could be prompted by the change? Consider: • Workflow • Roles and responsibilities • Skill requirements • Reporting and communication paths	
What interactional conflicts could be prompted by the change? Consider all who could be impacted and their current interaction dynamics.	
How are individuals and teams likely to respond to the change? Why?	
Communicate Change	
Who will you include in change communications? • Who will be directly affected? • Who will be indirectly affected?	
What formats will you use to communicate with affected parties and how often? • Local stakeholders • Remote stakeholders	
How will you articulate the vision for the change strategy? • Why this? • Why now?	

What tactical information will you share relating to changes, potential obstacles, timelines, milestones, and success measurements? Will this differ by audience?	
What resources will you make available to support the change, and how will you communicate these?	
How will you keep progress visible during the change implementation?	
What questions do you need to prepare to answer or respond to? • Strategic • Tactical • Emotional	
Manage Resistance	
How will you establish an environment of transparency and authenticity?	
What methods will you use to invite responses and feedback from those affected?	
What behaviors will you watch for to identify resistance?	
How will you address obstacles during the change process?	
What benefits and/or common vision will you communicate that will resonate with each audience?	
How will you ensure communication channels remain open throughout the change process?	
Further Buy-in and Commitment	
How will you gain commitment to the change at each phase? • Agreement that end goal is worthy • Acknowledgment that change will help achieve end goal • Willingness to engage in activities to execute change or to improve activities	
What tactics will you use to engage team members in decision making?	
How and when will you solicit team member feedback on the change process?	

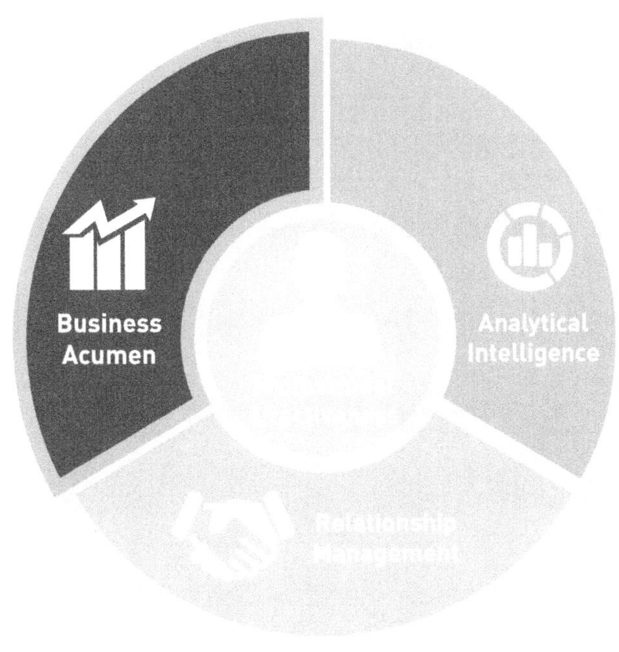
Business
Acumen
Analytical
Intelligence
Relationship
Management

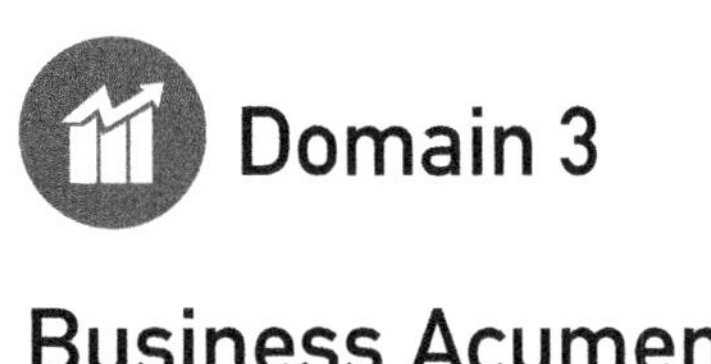
Domain 3
Business Acumen

Managing Projects

LEARNING OBJECTIVES

By the end of this chapter, you will be better equipped to:

- Understand the basic project management skills business managers need.
- Plan the work required to complete a project.
- Document many project artifacts to enable success, including project plans, budgets, risks, and assumptions.
- Identify, analyze, and manage stakeholder expectations.

Myth: Operational and support efforts do not need project management skills.

Project management is needed in an operational environment to allow for items with defined goals, such as process improvement, development and introduction of new processes, and meeting internal needs. A single figure of accountability and requisite skill set who maintains a bird's-eye view of these types of activities and their dependencies will help ensure everything runs to plan.

PROJECT MANAGEMENT SKILLS

While we are performing our day-to-day operational activities as business managers, we observe the activities and frustrations of our staff. Managers work on several tasks that simply require an ad hoc, daily operational approach to the work. This routine work is generally in support of other operational functions and can be managed on that basis, ensuring that the already-defined tasks are completed as planned and meet the desired outcomes.

However, if we are excellent at doing our jobs as managers, we often see within these activities and frustrations various opportunities to improve our work and the work of those who rely on us to foster an environment that enables operational success. Such opportunities for improvement often benefit from being managed as projects, driving results that allow the realization of benefits. To be successful in these endeavors, a manager must understand and use basic project management skills, including the following concepts:

- Operational project management
- Stakeholder relationships management
- Requirements development
- Project communication
- Project planning
- Project execution

A BRIEF HISTORY OF PROJECT MANAGEMENT

Before we undertake an examination of the nature and role of project management, let's consider its origins. Project management, as a practice, has been around for a long time and has evolved to a disciplined approach over several hundred, even thousands, of years. In its earliest evolution, project management was defined as the act of assembling people to systematically achieve a shared goal.

Evidence of project management essentials were apparent in the building of the Great Pyramids of Giza, circa 2550 This project took twenty years to complete. There is evidence that the project had a timeline (which included an ambiguous deadline; it had to be completed before the pharaoh's death) and staffing plans. There is evidence that prototypes were built in a design-and-test approach.

The Great Wall of China, circa 206 , had evidence of labor planning, essential to project management today. Emperor Qin Shi Huang demanded the project's labor force be organized into three groups—soldiers, civilians, and criminals—and work was planned according to their availability and cost.

In the United States, project management started to formalize during the Industrial Revolution (1750–1850). During this era, consideration had to be made not just for manual labor but for mechanized manufacturing as well. One of America's early great technological feats, the transcontinental railroad (completed 1869), was one of the first government-funded projects to require large-scale project management, even though it was not called *project management* until much later.

More modern project management tools and techniques began gaining strength in the early 1900s with the development of the Gantt chart in 1912, which was an improvement on the earlier harmonogram developed by a Polish economist in 1896. The term *project management* was not coined until 1954, by a U.S. Air Force general named Bernard Schriever. Program evaluation and review technique (PERT) came along shortly thereafter, in 1958. The following decade saw a focus on the discipline of project management, the growth of career opportunities, and the creation of several groups promoting its standardization, such as the American Association for the Advancement of Cost Engineers (AACE) in 1956 and the Project Management Institute in 1969. Project management software tools were developed as early as 1977.

OPERATIONAL PROJECT MANAGEMENT

Many efforts that business managers and their teams must complete require cross-team communication and collaboration and are generally unable to be adequately performed solely within the team itself due to various factors. These tasks are better managed as projects. Collaboration from other teams may include the following:

- Approval
- Information
- Physical completion of work toward the goal
- Expertise and guidance
- Additional resources
- Compliance requirements (and ensuring they are met)

Operational project management entails managing operational or support functions as if they were projects.

Examples of Operational Project Management

The level and formality of operational project management required for typical operational activities strongly depend on such factors as:

- Effort complexity
- Collaboration needs
- Costs associated to achieve the task
- Timeline for implementation

Operational project management skills are used, for example, to manage the establishment or improvement of a process or the creation of a new template.

Process Establishment or Improvement

If we wish to create a new process or improve an existing process, we must be certain we are doing so in a manner that actually achieves the intended benefit. The intended benefit of a newly established process may be to enable the performer to achieve the objective. The intended benefit of improving an already existing process may be simply expressed as an *improved process*. The nuance comes in discerning what is to be improved. For example, is it the documentation that needs improvement or the process itself? What about the process needs to be improved? How much time does it take to complete the documented process? How many and what types of resources are (or should be) involved in it? These facts are identified via requirements documentation, discussed later in the chapter.

At the heart of a project is the individual or collaborative effort that is planned and executed to attain some kind of intended benefit(s), which ends on completion of that effort. We need to be certain that we have clearly identified the process issue. A *process issue* is an item that causes a given process to not perform in the way it is intended. The project of establishing and documenting the process itself may help participants figure out *why* it had not been performing well. The project of improving the existing process may enable them to break it down and make judgments about *how* it can be improved.

For example, let's look at an established process we might need to follow to enable the approval of an expense report and eventual reimbursement to the employee.

The current process steps are as follows:

1. Employee creates the expense report.
2. Employee provides receipts and documentation.
3. Manager ensures the expenses are reimbursable.
4. Manager approves expense report.
5. Accounts payable reconciles and checks the expense report.
6. Accounts payable issues a check or direct deposit to the requesting employee.

Let's assume this process has already been defined and documented but there are now concerns that employees feel it takes too long to get reimbursed for expenses We now know that a process issue has been identified: reimbursement for expenses takes too long.

We then determine what we earnestly need and wish to achieve. In this case, we want to reduce the amount of time it takes to obtain reimbursement once an expense report is submitted by an employee. The concern must be properly captured, documented, and agreed to. This may include determining (if not already known) the average amount of time it takes an expense report to get reimbursed so that a baseline measure is identified (the *current state*). The analysis can then be broken down by each of the steps taken in the expense reimbursement process—in this case, the times related to the steps taken once the employee completes a expense report, as shown in Table 11-1.

The manager must also identify the root causes of the current timeline. In this case, we can see that it takes the manager five days to ensure the expenses are reimbursable and to approve the expense report. Is it possible that someone more familiar with reimbursable expenses should be responsible for that

Table 11-1 Sample Expense Report Processing	
Process Step	**Average Duration (Days)**
Employee creates expense report	N/A
Employee provides receipts and documentation	N/A
Manager ensures expenses are reimbursable	5
Manager approves expense report	
Accounts payable reconciles and checks expense report	4
Accounts payable issues a check or direct deposit to the employee	3

step? Or perhaps managers need more training so they can perform that step more quickly. Or does the system need to remind managers more frequently to review employees' expense reports?

Much of this information is gained through stakeholder engagement (discussed later in the chapter). It's also important to make sure that any plan to reduce the time needed for these steps is in line with company policies and requirements.

Once the requirements are fully understood, plan the work it will take to improve the process. The project manager will need to determine the budget (depending on the work environment), evaluate other factors (such as communication and technology, see Chapter 1, Communication, and Chapter 21, Development and Innovation), consider risks (what could go wrong), and oversee the implementation of the work required to complete the project. When it is all over, a post-project assessment must be conducted to ensure the effort completed actually did reduce the time it takes for employees to receive their reimbursement—the intended goal of the project—which is part of closing a project. All of these steps are explained in this chapter.

Myth: Project process is more crucial than implementers.

A smooth, well-planned project process is key. Without people making intelligent decisions around process, however, projects fail. There are many anecdotes in the project management world about how insufficient expert engagement or inadequate skills development led to failed projects, even though process had been worked out to the letter.

Creating a New Template

Another task typically performed in an operational capacity is creating a new template. This may appear to be simple to do but, when looked at holistically, may actually be complex.

For this discussion, we play the role of manager of the purchasing and subcontracts department for a medium-size government contractor. It has been determined that the organization needs to create a standard subcontract template. Heretofore, the subcontracts have been created on an ad hoc basis, leading to errors in the documents, such as missing important requirements (for example, scope and insurance) and including unnecessary requirements. Missing items can lead to significant risk for the organization—for example, missing or unclear scope documentation could incur additional costs when the team later integrates the omitted scope into the subcontract. Inclusion of unnecessary requirements can prolong the negotiation process, costing the company time and money. Forgetting to include insurance requirements can lead to unrecoverable losses for the company if the subcontractor causes a work-site accident. The goal of the new subcontract template is to make the job more efficient for purchasers and subcontract administrators and to lower risk. It should also simplify the negotiations with subcontractors.

It would be easy for the manager to assume the template could be created solely within the team. It is likely, however, that the team will discover they must consider constraints, requirements, and other deliverables only after engagement with various stakeholders. For instance, a template may have to include consideration of several laws, rules, regulations, or even formatting requirements about which the team may not have been aware.

If the knowledge possessed by other teams is not used, the new template may contain inaccuracies. But by using a project management approach to complete this seemingly simple task, the manager avoided significant negative execution, legal, financial, and compliance ramifications for the organization.

Engaging Operational Staff in Projects

Chapter 9, Coaching for Performance, discusses factors related to developing a plan for improvement and growth, including aligning staff performance goals to the organizational goals through management by objectives (MBO). Ongoing process improvement and its relationship to project management can be a factor that leads to excellent performance. A staff who plays an instrumental role in the successful and useful development and implementation of processes, procedures, and templates—and gets it right the first time—provides excellent fodder for performance goals. When we use project management techniques to achieve operational objectives, we can significantly improve the chances that the created solutions will have long-term positive impact. These are skills that a good manager would want their team to learn and utilize.

Prioritizing Operational Project Management Efforts

Managers may find themselves working in a business environment that requires several improvements that could benefit from the use of project management skills. The need for significant improvement could be due to a variety of positive and negative factors:

- Prior poor leadership
- Poor interrelation of tasks
- Poor understanding of values of tasks
- Staff resistance to change

- Newly imposed governmental or other regulatory requirements
- Introduction of new technologies
- Failure to seek new markets
- Employees with high institutional knowledge who no longer document processes
- Newly formed team unaware of shortcomings

Regardless of how or why, several items will likely require the use of project management skills and need to be prioritized to ensure success. Prioritization of projects in an operational environment can be achieved in a number of ways, a few of which are described in the following sections.

Table 11-2 Determining Complexity versus Simplicity

Complex (Requires Advanced Project Management Skills)	Simple (Requires Elevated Project Management Skills)
Many stakeholders	Few stakeholders
Difficult personalities	Easygoing personalities
Anticipated resistance	Anticipated acceptance
Long timeline to completion	Short timeline to completion
No champion	Backing from senior leadership
Vague scope	Clear scope
Senior leadership micromanages	Senior leadership stands back

Prioritize by Simplicity or Complexity

By focusing on the structure of tasks, the business manager prioritizes projects by discerning and choosing those that may be the least complicated to complete. Complexity and simplicity can be determined by a number of factors (see Table 11-2).

Prioritize by Importance

Sometimes it may be necessary to prioritize projects by importance. Some factors that can relate to project importance are:

- *Legal/Regulatory Requirements*: Is the project required to meet some new law or regulatory requirement (local, state, or federal) that will, in turn, keep the organization out of trouble?
- *Corporate Compliance Requirements*: Has the organization's internal compliance group determined a current process does not meet corporate compliance-related needs?

- *Senior Leadership Visibility*: Does senior leadership really care about the project, and are they counting on its success to reach some kind of business or other strategic goal?
- *Employee Satisfaction*: Does the project represent something that will improve employee morale and retention?
- *Budgeting Needs*: Will funds be forfeited if not used in the current fiscal quarter or year?
- *Resource Needs*: Will the resources needed to complete the project be unavailable later due to other commitments?
- *Deadline Driven*: Has a deadline for completion of the project been imposed?

Prioritization by Urgency

Managers, if they are able to, may choose to prioritize projects by picking the items that must be completed first. If something is urgent, this means that it must be completed in accordance with some kind of deadline. Determine whether the potential projects are deadline driven; sorting them by the deadline may be one way the operational project manager determines priority.

Prioritization by Urgency and Importance

Prioritization that considers both urgency and importance may be needed, rather than assessing merely one or the other. The operational project manager must be clear about the difference between importance and urgency. An important project does not always have to be completed right away, but an urgent project must be completed as soon as practical. Project managers must spend time not only on items that are urgent but also on items that are important. This can help alleviate stress that comes from having too many tight deadlines as well as aid in the management of stakeholder expectations regarding where their pet project may fall in the order of priority.

When we understand how to identify, communicate, and document urgency versus importance, we can overcome both our own and our stakeholders' natural instincts so we can focus on unimportant but urgent activities. In this way we can clear enough time to do what is essential for our success.

This approach can move good operational project managers from always being in firefighting mode into a position of preventing the fire. It also helps grow their career as well as the skills of their team.

The Urgency × Importance Prioritization Matrix

In August 1954, President Dwight D. Eisenhower stated in a speech: "I have two kinds of problems: the urgent and the important. The urgent are not important, and the important are never urgent." This be-

> **Myth:** Project success depends entirely on execution.
>
> *Believing this can lead to going short on the project planning process because you are not giving enough weight to planning, an equally important project development phase. If execution is put before effective planning, expect expensive reworking, decreased team morale, and scope creep or failed objectives.*

came known as the Eisenhower principle and is said to be how the president organized his workload and priorities. If we take this concept to another level and quantify the level of importance and the level of urgency, we can develop a model, or matrix, by which more objective prioritization can be achieved. This matrix may be valuable in helping you determine which potential project, among many, should be tackled first, last, and in between, in order of their appearance on the Urgency × Importance Prioritization Matrix (Table 11-3).

The matrix is based on a scale of 1–10, with 1 being the least urgent or important and 10 being the most urgent or important. Once you have scaled each project for urgency (U) and importance (I), multiply the two ratings to calculate the $U \times I$ score. Then sort the projects in descending order by the $U \times I$ score; the higher the score, the higher the priority of the project. The result is a list of your current projects in descending priority.

An additional matrix provides the rationale for each of the urgency and importance ratings and serves as a secondary tool, enabling conversation to ensure key stakeholders agree with your assessments and, ultimately the project prioritization. The Rationale Matrix looks similar to the Urgency × Importance Prioritization Matrix, but each cell of the matrix includes an explanation for the given urgency and importance rankings.

Being objective when determining the urgency and importance rankings is one key to success. Creating an explanation of the ratings aids in this. Table 11-4 is an example of an objective urgency scale based on a project's completion date.

A quantification scale for importance is also of value. Quantification considers the stakeholders and the overall effect the project has on the organization. For example, a project championed by the president or CEO has a greater importance than a project that pertains to only a few employees. Likewise, a project that has an impact on a major corporate objective is more important than one that does not. The quantification scale helps ensure consistency in the scoring of projects by stating clearly what types of rationale should be rated higher than others.

Table 11-3 Urgency × Importance Priority Matrix

Project Description	Urgency (U)	Importance (I)	$U \times I$ Score
Project 1 description	10	10	100
Project 2 description	8	10	80
Project 3 description	9	7	63
Project 4 description	10	5	50
Project 5 description	4	10	40
Project 6 description	8	4	32

© Lisa Mathews, MBA, PMP, 2017.

Table 11-4 Sample Urgency Quantification Table	
Urgency Score	**Description** **(The project must be completed within . . .)**
10	1 week
9	1–4 weeks
8	1–2 months
7	2–3 months
8	3–4 months
6	4–5 months
5	5–6 months
4	6–7 months
3	7–8 months
2	8–9 months
1	Over 9 months, undefined

Other factors related to project prioritization include the following:

- *Personal Passion*: Within reason, be certain that projects are not picked as a priority simply because they are a personal pet project.
- *Business Impacts*: Take into consideration how the projects will affect organization. How will the project outcome benefit the business manager, the team, the company, and all of the internal and external customers?
- *Agility*: The ability to quickly and effectively respond to changing situations and needs. Priorities can shift and change due to factors that may be beyond the manager's control, which means prioritization of the projects selected may also change. Success may depend on one's ability to recognize these shifts and adjust project priorities (or the prioritization of projects) accordingly.
- *Emotional Intelligence*: When a business manager needs to manage efforts as a project, the interpersonal considerations and relationships are different from business as usual. Consider the skill sets discussed in Chapter 2, Emotional Intelligence, and Chapter 7, Influence.

STAKEHOLDER RELATIONSHIPS MANAGEMENT

Project stakeholders include anyone involved in or who has an interest in a project, its plan and execution, and its intended benefit(s). For business managers, this can mean understanding the downstream impact of actions their team takes. In this section we discuss the various types of stakeholders to consider, how a business manager can ensure the right people have been identified as stakeholders, the needs of stakeholders, and how a business manager can get what is needed from the stakeholders.

Types of Stakeholders

Before we introduce the many different types of stakeholders, we need to discuss the various ways stakeholders can be viewed.

Internal and External Stakeholders

Some stakeholders we need to work with are internal to our team, our project, and to our organization. Others are external and include some who are outside of our organization's control but nonetheless may need to be considered in operational project management decision making (Table 11-5).

Table 11-5 Potential Internal and External Stakeholders

Internal	External
Sponsor	External customer or client
Project team	End users of project's outcome (if external persons affected or believe they are affected)
Program manager	Supplier
Portfolio manager	Subcontractors
Internal customer or client	Government
End users of project's outcome	Local communities
Other operational manager	Media
Other functional manager	
Other administrative manager	

Primary and Secondary Stakeholders

Primary stakeholders have a major interest in the success of the project and/or are directly affected by the outcome. Secondary stakeholders also help complete the project but serve in roles that may be of a secondary concern. One should not equate *secondary* with *less important* (Table 11-6).

Direct, Indirect, and External Stakeholders

Direct internal stakeholders are internal to our organization and are directly involved in the project or are directly affected by the project and one or more of its outcomes. These individuals are concerned with the day-to-day activities of the project, such as the project manager and the project management team.

Table 11-6 Sample Primary and Secondary Stakeholders

Primary	Secondary
Customers	Administrative process owners
End users	Financial process owners
Sponsors	Legal expertise
Project manager	Purchasing/subcontracting (if needed)
Project team	

Indirect internal stakeholders are internal to the organization but are not directly involved in the project or directly impacted by it. They are generally not involved in the day-to-day activities of the project but rather are concerned with the finished product, such as internal customers, end users, and regulators.

External stakeholders are not within the organization but may be affected by it or may have influence over it (think in terms of government regulators, external end users and customers, contractors, vendors, and so on).

Key Stakeholders

Stakeholders can make or break the project success. They can help the operational project manager obtain the right people, equipment, supplies, and other resources for the project. They can answer questions or get the operational project manager in touch with the right people with the right answers. Stakeholders can provide much-needed expertise for areas outside of the business manager's and team's area of knowledge. Some individuals may fall into more than one stakeholder category. For purposes of operational project management, the following types of stakeholders may be most appropriate for consideration.

Project Sponsor

The project sponsor is the person who can ensure resources (funding, people, materials) are available to complete the project. This person is the highest-level champion of the project. Chapter 9, Coaching for Performance, discusses the many different roles a sponsor may have within an organization.

What should a manager involved with project management expect from the sponsor?

- Defining decision channels clearly
- Taking action on requests and recommendations
- Providing assistance during conflict resolution
- Providing constructive feedback
- Enabling the interface between the operational project manager and other departments
- Offering protection from political infighting

What should a sponsor expect from a project manager?

- Providing complete and accurate information
- Minimizing organizational disruption during project execution
- Providing not just alternatives but also recommendations
- Managing most interpersonal problems at the project team level
- Accepting accountability for success or failure of the deliverables
- Projecting a self-start attitude and demonstrating capability

The sponsor's involvement is largely related to the project size and importance. However, other factors may come into play, such as the sponsor's level of trust in the project manager and the project team, the sponsor's own project management experience, competing priorities, and the culture of the organization. The level of involvement may essentially fall into three categories, as presented in Table 11-7.

Myth: A set project resource plan means no new projects.

A set project resource plan and allocation should not preclude pursuing other project requests that demonstrate high potential value or solve more immediate operational needs. The plus side of putting new projects on hold once a project plan is set is that continued focus may yield faster project completion. However, a negative to this is that the manager could miss major opportunities.

Other Stakeholders

- *Project Manager*: The operational manager who is now responsible for ensuring completion of the project and its primary goals and objectives.
- *Project Team Member*: Someone who is working to complete the project as defined in the project plan. Team members provide status to the project manager and may also rely on the project manager to remove barriers to success.
- *Users or End Users*: Those who will use the output or deliverable of the project.
- *Beneficiaries*: Those who will benefit from the result of the project. Along with the sponsor, they can help ensure the right level of support.
- *Resistors*: Those who are against the project itself. They may be found in any category of stakeholders, including key stakeholders.
- *Regulator*: Someone who may be needed to ensure the output of a project meets certain legal or regulatory compliance requirements.

Identifying and Analyzing Stakeholders

It is important to identify the project stakeholders as early as possible because their influence on the project execution and outcomes may be significant. They will likely be significantly involved in gather-

Table 11-7 Sponsor Involvement Levels

Micromanagement	Invisibility	Effectiveness
Sponsor is excessively involved in the day-to-day project activities May occur when the sponsor does not yet know or trust the project manager and team or the project manager has not clearly communicated plan, goals, and so on	Sponsor is not seen or heard from for long periods of time and may refuse to make decisions or delay making decisions Happens when the sponsor lacks interest in the project or is driven by self-interest of fear of bad decisions	Sponsor is involved as needed Requires the project manager to know when to reach to the sponsor for help, assistance, guidance, or resources

ing the project requirements (discussed later in the chapter). Therefore, be sure to take the time from the onset of the project to identify the stakeholders and ensure you understand their needs.

Identifying Stakeholders

Be certain that all stakeholders have been identified. But how do we know we have identified all of the stakeholders we need to? And when is enough, well, enough? This is a bit of an art and a science. The following discussing presents a few ideas that can be used to ensure we've identified all of the stakeholders.

Review the project planning documents that have been developed along the way. For example, the project's requirements may give several hints as to who the project stakeholders are and should be. Review the existing organizational processes to be certain the right people are involved and engaged at the right times.

Begin to ask about stakeholders early in the process. This can be done through the use of basic information-gathering techniques, such as individual brainstorming. In the beginning, this may involve just sitting down and pondering the answers to a series of questions, such as "Who [what person or organization] could be impacted by this?" "Who may have interest in this project?" "Who may think they are impacted by this project?" "Who may have the expertise we need for this project?"

Then, as the effort naturally progresses to the point at which you begin to engage with some of the key stakeholders, be diligent in asking them the same types of questions: "Who else do you believe should be involved in this project?" "Who else may be impacted by this project"? "Who else may have an interest in this project?" In this way, the operational project manager is performing due diligence in attempting to ascertain who all the stakeholders may be. Other key questions that should be asked are:

- Who gains or loses from the project's success?
- Is any local community impacted by the project or its outcome?
- Who are the competitors?
- Who are the suppliers?
- Who wants to complete the project successfully and who does not?
- Who is the user of the end result of the project?

- Who has the authority to influence the project or its outcome?
- Who has the authority to make the project succeed or fail?

Next, the manager needs to ensure that sufficient time is allowed to perform stakeholder analysis and mapping. The manager who fails to do this risks overlooking some of the stakeholders.

Be certain that the appropriate methodology is being used. Learn from past mistakes and from the lessons of others. This can serve as a starting point to ensure comprehensive stakeholder identification.

Analyzing Stakeholders

Key to successful stakeholder management is discerning and documenting each stakeholder's needs, attitudes, and influence on the project itself. How to do this can vary significantly depending on the type and breadth of the project being undertaken. See the box at Figure 11-1 for some of the methodologies.

Stakeholder Challenges

The need to work effectively with stakeholders can be important for success. Essential management skills can ensure stakeholder challenges are being addressed properly.

- Maintaining a positive and optimistic attitude in all relationships, no matter how difficult
- Addressing all concerns and applying empathy to stakeholder needs
- Asking open-ended questions and being constructive when both providing and receiving feedback
- Identifying the challenges and their causes and understanding the impacts of those challenges to the project success
- Responding in a timely and consistent fashion after learning of challenges or difficulties
- Showing appreciation and formally recognizing the stakeholders' contributions to the project and its goals

The project manager's ability to influence and persuade can be key skills for addressing stakeholder challenges.

Influencing Stakeholders

Consider the skills required for the influencing competency (see Chapter 7, Influence) and their application to stakeholder management in project management. Never underestimate the value of the project stakeholders. They can provide the project manager and the project team with essential support, materials, money, and other types of resources. They can provide reputational support by simply expressing that they believe in the project and its project manager. Stakeholders also can be important for gathering requirements, understanding what tasks must be performed to complete those requirements, knowing how long those tasks can take (in terms of effort and duration), and being aware how much they could cost.

Power/Interest Grid

The Power/Interest Grid (or Matrix) is a simple tool that helps a team categorize project stakeholders. This tool helps the project manager focus on the key stakeholders and how much power they have to assist (or harm) the project, combined with how much interest each stakeholder actually has in doing so. As a result, this tool can help the operational project manager determine stakeholder prioritization and whether there are other stakeholders that may need to be considered to counter the potential negative effects of a particularly powerful and influential stakeholder who is unsupportive of the project. A permutation of this grid would assess the stakeholders in terms of attitude and influence (Figure 11-1).

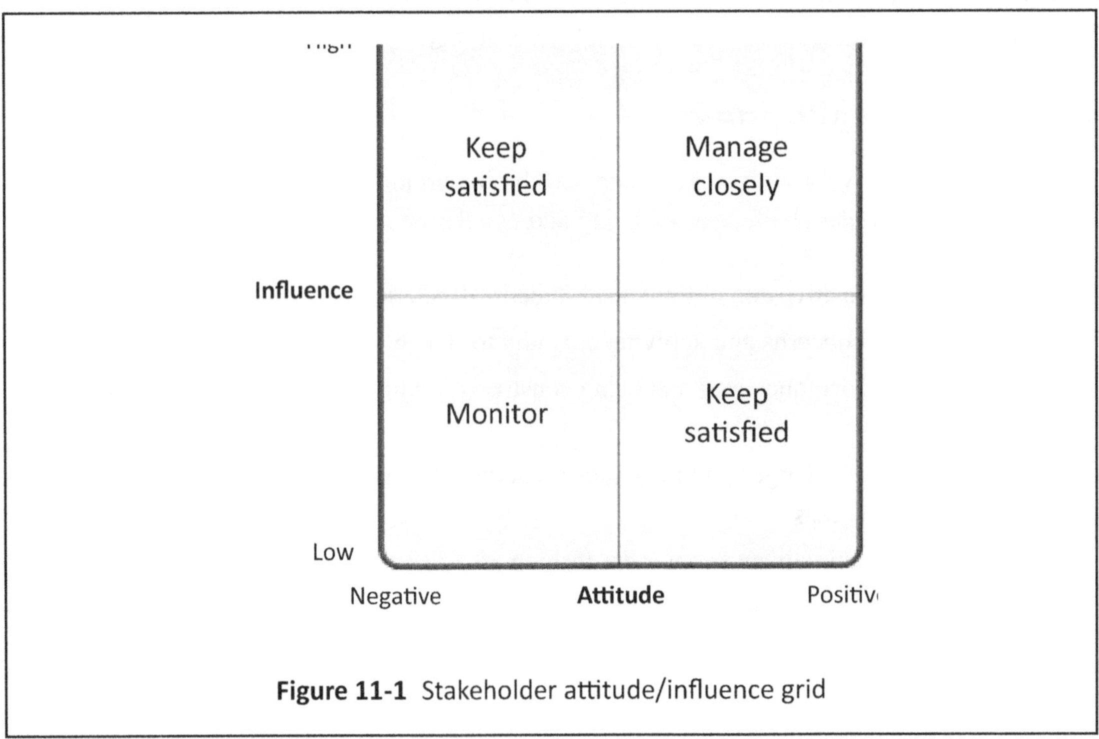

Figure 11-1 Stakeholder attitude/influence grid

Engagement Assessment Matrix

Another way to analyze stakeholders is to determine their *current* level of engagement and decide what the *desired* level of engagement is. This is captured in the Engagement Assessment Matrix (Table 11-8). There are five levels of engagement.

1. *Unaware*: Stakeholders who are presently unaware of the project and its potential impacts to them or their teams
2. *Resistant*: Stakeholders who know the project is going on but are resistant to it.

3. *Neutral*: Stakeholders who are aware of the project but neither support nor resist it.
4. *Supportive*: Stakeholders who are aware of and supportive of the changes the project represents.
5. *Leading*: Stakeholders who are aware of the project and are actively engaged in ensuring its success. Ideally, the sponsor key stakeholder is in this category.

Table 11-8 Engagement Assessment Matrix

Stakeholder	Unaware	Resistant	Neutral	Supportive	Leading
Sponsor					C
Customer				C	
End user		C		C, D	
Vendor			C		
Functional manager			C		
Regulatory agency			C		

The grid is created with the stakeholders identified along the left-most column. Along the top of the grid are the five categories. A "C" denotes each particular stakeholder's *current* engagement level. A "D" indicates the *desired* engagement level.

Threat/Asset Assessment

A quicker analysis of stakeholders is to simply categorize them as (or perceived as) being a threat or an asset. In this way, the project manager can keep a simple list of those stakeholders he or she will need to spend time with to keep their support and seek their advocacy or gain their support or, at the very least, prevent their sabotaging the project.

When performing operational project management tasks, particularly when needing to influence and engage with various and sundry stakeholders, business managers are truly tasked with using and demonstrating a culmination of several of the other business management competency areas. Figure 11-2 shows the interconnectivity among all these skill sets and the practice of stakeholder engagement.

Persuading Stakeholders

At times, it may be necessary to engage stakeholders in proactively offering suggestions and ideas to reach workable solutions for the project. This will require using influencing skills, along with skills in

Myth: Data are more valuable than feelings and perceptions.

When project teams rely too heavily on data and metrics they may misinterpret data or misunderstand how a project supports their organizational goals. It is better to make sure the entire team has shared feelings and perceptions that support core project objectives, which in turn enables more appropriate and accurate analysis of the data.

persuasion and negotiation. Since managers who work on projects that impact multiple departments often do not have formal authority over many of the stakeholders, they must be able to convince others to take action on their behalf.

Direct attempts to persuade others may incite colleagues to resist and polarize. Because persuasion is a learning and negotiating process, it must include the following three *phases*.

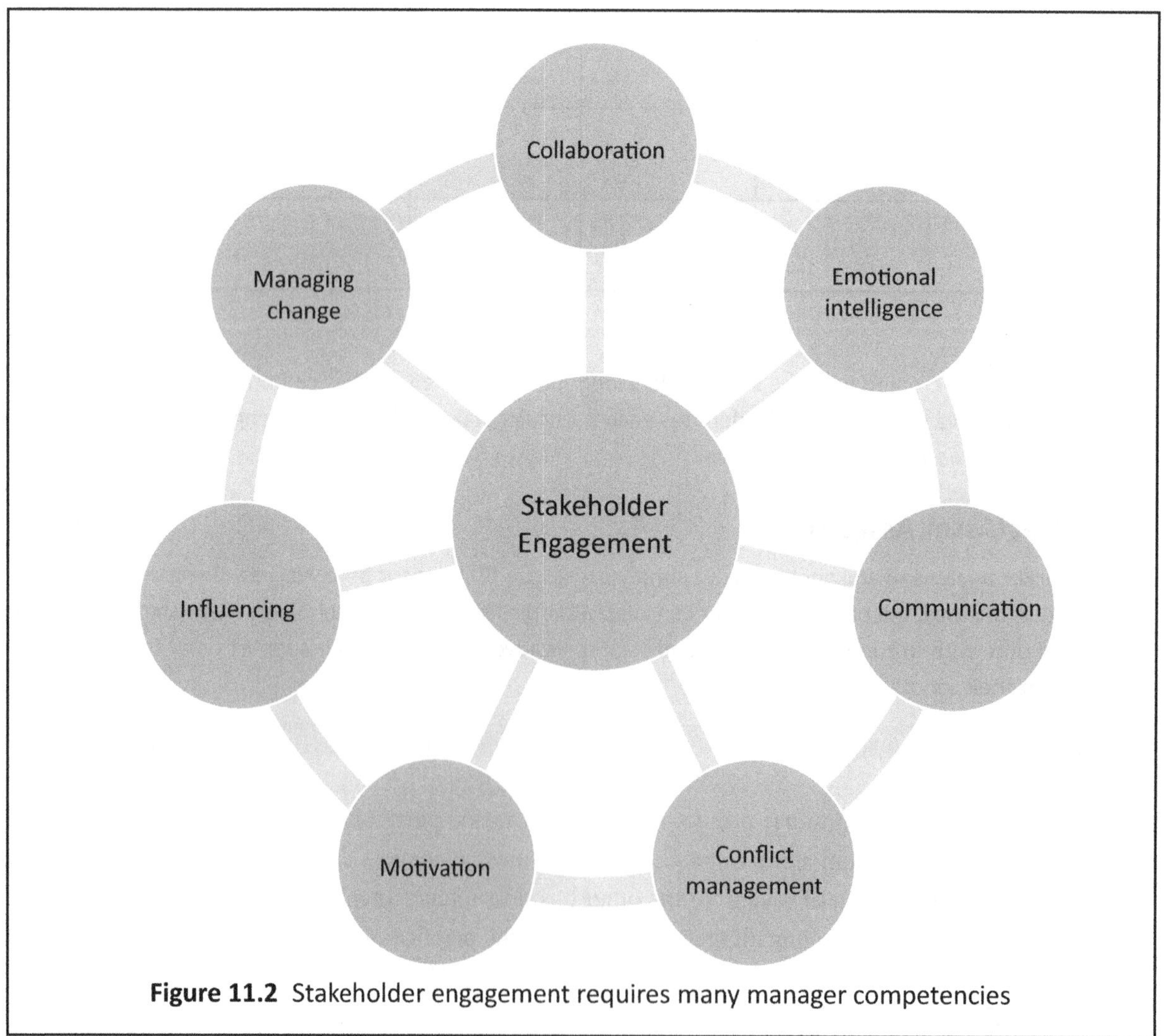

Figure 11.2 Stakeholder engagement requires many manager competencies

1. *Discovery*: Before attempting negotiation, consider the issue or concern from every angle. Attempt to remove any personal bias during this process so the concern may be viewed as objectively as possible, thereby allowing the discovery of varying perspectives.
2. *Planning*: Before presenting ideas, plan ahead by learning about the audience and preparing arguments. Discussion occurs both before and during the persuasion process.
3. *Discussion*: Affected stakeholders must be invited to discuss solutions, debate the merits of each position, offer honest feedback, and suggest alternatives. Test and revise ideas to reflect the stakeholders' concerns and needs. Success depends on being open-minded and willing to incorpo l rate compromises.

The three primary *components* of persuasion are:

1. *The Message*: Arguments that are logical, coherent, and cogent/convincing are the most persuasive. This is the content of the persuasion, including the data, reasons, and analysis. Several techniques enhance message preparation.
   - Tell the other party what they are going to be told, actually tell them, then tell them what was just told to them. This helps reinforce the idea presented.
   - Use the rule of three. Ensure there are only one to three key arguments in support of the ideas. Up to three items is probably all that the audience will be able to grasp and retain. It is a common belief that listeners most easily remember items when they are actually structured in sets of three (think of the three blind mice or the three musketeers). Thus be sure to narrow your ideas down to now more than key points, and remember that having three points may help make the ideas more memorable.
   - Present a solid metaphor or analogy to make your point and influence the audience. The effective use of storytelling can help make the idea more relatable to the audience. Drawing from past business experience, you may be able to share a "lesson learned" from a prior effort and relate it to the current situation to increase impact.
   - Identify clearly the key takeaways the audience needs to remember in one day, one week, and one month, depending on the project and its requirements.
2. *The Messenger*: This component relates strongly to the actual and perceived character and credibility of those who are attempting to persuade others. We are more likely to be persuaded (even without inclination to be) by someone who is perceived to be an authority. The use of personal powers, as discussed in Chapter 7, Influence, may be key. Even when business managers do not have legitimate power, they may be able to use their personal powers to establish authority. The relevant personal powers are trust and credibility. Moreover, we are more likely to persuade others if we have given them something. This kind of reciprocity may not be tangible, but can include:
   - How well you listen to others and their concerns
   - How respectful you are of others' views

- How well you acknowledge the views of others
- How empathetic you appear to the comments/concerns of others

3. *The Audience*: This component involves not just who the audience is but how the audience will experience the message being provided and how well the audience is managed. The differences in people's preferences when preparing the materials and the delivery may enhance audience management. Consider the following:
   - *Inductive versus Deductive*: Some people prefer inductive reasoning (moving from fact to conclusion), whereas others prefer deductive reasoning (deducing fact from given set of information).
   - *Wants versus Needs*: Identifying and understanding the differences between wants and needs can ensure stronger relatability.
   - *Content versus Process*: One's personal orientation to content or process likely needs to be accounted for in both preparation of the materials and how questions will be responded to.
   - *Fact versus Feeling*: When attempting to persuade others, a good manager understands that both facts and feelings are important and need to be responded to appropriately in communication with stakeholders.

Once agreement is reached, document the impacts to all potentially related project artifacts, such as the project baseline plan and risks. Last, be certain to receive sign-offs from all appropriate stakeholders, ensuring joint understanding of all potential project impacts.

REQUIREMENTS DEVELOPMENT

A requirement is any item that is needed in order to meet one or more project benefit(s). At their highest level, requirements are broken down into product requirements and project requirements.

Product requirements are the tangible and measurable qualities of the intended output of the project. In subcontract template example we used earlier in this chapter, the product requirements include a description of how that template would look (is it in an electronic format? paper format?) and what it would contain (signature lines, various fields, yes/no options, and so on). Product requirements are needed to ensure the intended output of the project meets the need for which the project is undertaken. These items tend to more tangible; one can physically see the result of the requirement. They are gen-

Myth: Project management best practices must always be followed.

Best practices may not always be the best plan of action for all specific projects. The best practice should be used as a helpful guide, but the monitoring of results and findings will best shape a manager's own, niche-specific practices.

erally formulated in terms of size, shape, appearance, or functional capability. Simply put, they are *what* the project is creating.

Project requirements need to be in place to ensure the project team can be successful in its execution. They may include things such as meetings, project artifacts, and senior leadership support. Project requirements are often intangible, as one cannot generally physically see them, but we know whether they are present (such as the example of senior leadership buy-in). In some cases, they are tangible, such as a series of approvals or draft documents. Simply put, they are the "*how*" the project and the project team behaves.

It is the operational project manager's role to resolve any conflicting requirements. If such occur, the operational project manager must meet with the interested parties and resolve the conflict to reach a mutually agreeable solution, which often requires the skills noted in the Chapter 4, Conflict Management, and Chapter 7, Influence, as well as the persuasion and negotiation skills noted earlier.

Capturing Requirements

Several methods may be used to capture requirements.

Stakeholder Input

When all of the stakeholders have been identified and task areas have been created, assigning responsibility to the person(s) responsible for completing the tasks (usually members of the project team and other stakeholders; sometimes referred to as *task owners*) can be one way to guarantee requirements are gathered. Those who will be responsible for performing the work or ensuring needs are meet by the project are often the best source of information regarding what is required for success.

Brainstorming

Creative thinking is required to solve problems and is an excellent qualification of effective operational project managers. The proper use of brainstorming techniques may enable creative problem solving and lead to effective requirements gathering. The operational project manager would function as the facilitator of the brainstorming session, engaging the right stakeholders, or the people who are knowledgeable about the needs of the project and its intended outcomes and benefits. The facilitator must know brainstorming best practices:

- *Planning the Session*: Be certain the right information is in place so the brainstorming session can go well. This includes identifying participants to enable diversity of thought.
- *Conducting the Session*: Capture the ideas presented. Combine similar ideas where possible. Break complex ideas into smaller, simpler problems and examine each independently. Allow time for each member to brainstorm independently. Rank the ideas in terms of viability, applicability, financial considerations, and customer reactions and then attempt to reach agreement on the requirement. Assign responsibility for requirements and confirm they are properly captured, documented, expressed, and later, completed.

- *Golden Rule*: It is often stated that the golden rule of brainstorming is "there is no bad idea." This is a misstatement, as bad ideas are often presented in a brainstorming session. In practical application, the golden rule is that all ideas are to be heard and documented. One does not take the time to assess the quality of the idea, lest the natural flow of those ideas be stifled. A good facilitator fosters an environment free from the fear of judgment.
- *After the Brainstorming Session*: Be sure to thank and recognize the participants. This will help encourage their ongoing participation and attendance in future sessions. Be certain that the requirements have been captured in a way everyone understands, even to those who did not attend the session.

Document Analysis

Document analysis involves evaluating the documentation of a present condition to perform an as-is analysis to help drive the gap analysis for discovering the needed requirements of the "to-be" condition. Updates to those same documents may wind up being a requirement on its own as a way to capture the project's process.

Focus Groups

Pro tip

The ideal size for a focus group in this context is five to eight participants.

A focus group is a gathering of the intended end users for the output of the project so the team can gain feedback about the current process, opportunities, needs, and so on. This method is different from brainstorming in that it is not as managed of a process and is not as closely or thoughtfully facilitated. One weakness of focus groups is that the "loudest voices in the room" can lead and distract the conversation, leading to "crowd following" and lowering the productivity of the session. Thus the information gained on end-users' requirements may be only the least common denominator of the desired features.

Interviews

Interview stakeholders to find out their expectations and goals in order to best manage them. Formulate questions that will enable the conversation to reveal the stakeholders' differing perspectives and properly address and weigh their inputs. Active and empathetic listening skills are valuable here (see Chapter 1, Communication, and Chapter 2, Emotional Intelligence).

Observation

Observation can be either passive or active. Managers acquire new knowledge through passive observation and interpret it in terms of their current knowledge. Through active observation, managers use experimentation to verify new knowledge and may add new knowledge as well. Managers can use either of these approaches to uncover implicit requirements, which are often overlooked.

Surveying

Surveys are best used to gather information from many people. Surveys can be designed to ask the participants to choose from given options, express agreement or disagreement, or rate statements. For example, in the case of improving the expense report processing time, a survey could be used to obtain users' expectations of how long the process should take compared to the current time frame. A well-designed survey provides qualitative guidance to ensure accurate responses, but surveys should not be used for prioritizing requirements or features.

Documenting the Requirements

All requirements must be documented in a manner that is understood not just by the parties who created them but by anyone who may need to understand them later to enable verification. One of the techniques used is the SMART model.

- *Specific*: Ensure the requirement is concrete, detailed, and well defined.
- *Measurable*: When possible, use numbers, quantity, and comparison points.
- *Agreed To*: Ensure all applicable stakeholders are in agreement.
- *Realistic*: Confirm the requirement is possible given the available resources.
- *Time Bound*: Describe a defined timeline.

A SMART requirement for the expense reimbursement project may be as follows: Reduce total processing time from the initial employee submission through repayment by two business days within the next three months.

No matter what tool is used to document the requirements, ensure that such documentation describes how the identified requirements help meet the needs of the project. Know that the requirements may be adjusted based on new information. This concept is called *progressive elaboration* and is a natural occurrence during a project lifecycle; as we learn new things (make progress in establishing our project), we adjust (elaborate) our prior information to be certain there no discrepancies and improve the project's artifacts. Requirements must be as unambiguous as possible as well as measurable and testable. One must be able to determine whether the requirements were attained as documented, thus consistency of language is key.

Preventing Scope Creep

Scope creep is uncontrolled changes or continuous growth in a project's scope and intent. As hinted by the word *creep*, it is a subtle process that starts with small adjustments and ends up in projects that take far longer to complete or lose focus on its intent. Scope creep differs from *progressive elaboration* in that the latter is intentional. Scope creep occurs *after* those requirements have been documented and agreed to and includes items that were not previously agreed to and that are performed absent appropriate change control.

Table 11-9 provides some reasons scope creep occurs on projects and offers some preventative solutions.

Table 11-9 Potential Reasons and Preventions for Scope Creep

Reason for Scope Creep	Preventative Technique
Lack of clarity and depth in original requirements documents	Solid requirements documentation, using SMART or other documentation techniques
Unmanaged contact between various team participants/ stakeholders, resulting in decisions absent project manager control	Regularly scheduled meetings; solid and communicated change management procedures
Starting project execution before documentation of requirements	Sponsor/senior leadership support, mature communication and stakeholder engagement techniques
Do-it-yourself (DIY) participants because of lack of foresight, engagement, and planning	Sponsor/senior leadership support
Overstated promises	Manage stakeholder expectations

PROJECT COMMUNICATION

The effective operational project manager analyzes and documents communication requirements and continuously monitors those communications to ensure the frequency and techniques used are appropriate and effective.

Myth: A project manager should never prematurely end a project.
There are cases for which it might be a better idea to kill a project than to proceed:

- *The end goal becomes obsolete*
- *Costs or time balloon unmanageably due to oversights, becoming irrecoverable*
- *Another team resolves the concern before completion*

Methods of Communication

Managers may find it difficult to choose a method for conveying information to and among stakeholders. The best method for any given situation is affected by various factors, including technology. For example, if there is an urgent need to communicate information to one person, a phone call may be faster than email. If the information is confidential, establishing a consistent rhythm for meeting in secured spaces may be the best way to share information.

The methods may also be adjusted based on how formal or informal the communication needs to be. If formal communication is required, the best method may be to ensure it is in writing, either through the postal service, email, or memo posted to a shared location. If informal, the manager may choose a phone call, video conference, or face-to-face conversation.

Before engaging in a method of communication, the operational project manager should carefully consider the communication's objectives.

Communication Frequency

The frequency of project communication by and between the stakeholders depends strongly on the preferences of the stakeholders, the type of communication occurring, and the project needs. Communication frequency can also vary based on at what point in the project cycle the communication needs to occur. For example, while gathering requirements, communication needs may be quite frequent, but during project execution, they may lessen. When a project is winding down and nearing closure, some escalation of communication frequency may be needed to ensure all affected stakeholders agree that requirements were met to enable closing procedures to commence.

Ensuring Communication Efficacy

During project execution, operational project managers should make sure communications are working, checking that the communication plan accurately and adequately reflects what is actually going on. If it does not, managers need to determine whether to adjust the actions or the plan.

Project managers should also periodically check in with their stakeholders, asking if they feel well informed or whether communication is too frequent. If complaints are received or overheard that indicate an issue, the manager may need to consider adjusting the communication strategies and, therefore, the plan. This monitoring should go on periodically throughout the life of the project.

Documenting the Communication Plan

Document the communication needs into a communication plan. The plan is often best captured in the form of a matrix, including explanations for the various methods and reporting needs, to ensure common understanding (Table 11-10). The matrix should be updated through the life of the project, based on results of communication monitoring, as described earlier.

PROJECT PLANNING

A key factor to operational project management success is ensuring that the key stakeholders agree the proposed plan is reasonable and achievable. The contents of the project plan may vary greatly based on the type of environment in which the project is taking place and the expected rigor. Some key factors to include in the project plan are a timeline, a budget, incorporation of communication and other requirements, and consideration of risk.

Project Timeline

A project timeline is created in cooperation with key stakeholders. It should provide an explanation of how long the project will take, and for longer efforts, it should detail points of progress, or *milestones*, that can be measured along the way. Milestones mark specific points along a project timeline, such as anchors (project start and end dates), or indicate specific items or issues that need to be tracked for solid project management purposes. They have no duration and no resources assigned to them.

Business managers and operational project managers are not expected to be experts in the creation of a project timeline or baseline; those are for career project managers, who are managing very large-scale and complex projects. However, operational project managers should be aware of important development points, including creating a basic project timeline, understanding relationships between tasks, communicating the timeline (the schedule the operational project manager conveys to leadership), and relating the timeline to a budget (when necessary).

Table 11-10 Sample Communication Matrix

Project Name: ____________________

A **Communication Matrix** is used to capture the salient points to be communicated across the management of the project. These include:

Description	Audience	Owner	Medium	Frequency

Creating the Project Timeline

The following ten steps ensure a timeline is achievable and realistic.

1. *Review the Requirements*: Be certain that all the requirements have been agreed to by the key stakeholders and that they are clearly understood.
2. *Identify Task Areas*: If the project is quite large, identify task areas that can be completed by one person or team, breaking the work down into manageable pieces. In formal project management, this is referred to as a *work breakdown structure* (WBS); here we use the term *task areas*, a less formal approach. By identifying task areas, the project manager can begin to better understand and communicate the full scope of the work. Task areas can be broken down into lower-level tasks to obtain even greater understanding and provide further definition and detail.
   - The top task area represents the final deliverable or project in its entirety.
   - Sublevels contain lower-level task areas that can be assigned to an organizational department or unit.
   - Sublevels may be further broken down into specific tasks (see step 3).
   - Sublevels must be unique and not duplicated across the project.

   Task areas offer an efficient way of splitting up work among functional managers, whose teams are responsible for specific work that contributes to the project (Figure 11-3).
3. *Create a Task List*: When looking at the requirements, develop a list of the tasks needed to complete the requirements. If task areas have been defined, have the team member responsible for performing each area create the task list. This step may be completed concurrently with step 2, which could reveal missing requirements and lead to further iterations. This is an example of progressive elaboration; as we learn more about the work we intend complete, we discover factors that may affect other artifacts we created along the way.
4. *Put the Tasks in Chronological Order*: When the tasks are put in chronological order, managers may realize additional tasks are needed. This step helps enable and encourage conversation by and between the various task area leads (if applicable), so that communication points can be discerned and established. Each team should be aware of the expectations of other teams. When expectations differ, managers may need to negotiate and control conflict (see Chapter 4, Conflict Management). Often the operational project manager may serve as the facilitator of such conversations.
5. *Establish Relationships between the Tasks*: For larger projects, establishing connections among tasks may be far too complex for simple handwritten planning or basic suite software tools. Thus project scheduling software may be needed. If the operational project manager discovers the work is exceedingly complex, he or she may consider, at this point, the need for a career project manager, from within or outside of the organization. It is strongly recommended that this step in the project planning process be performed in collaboration with the project team and key stake-

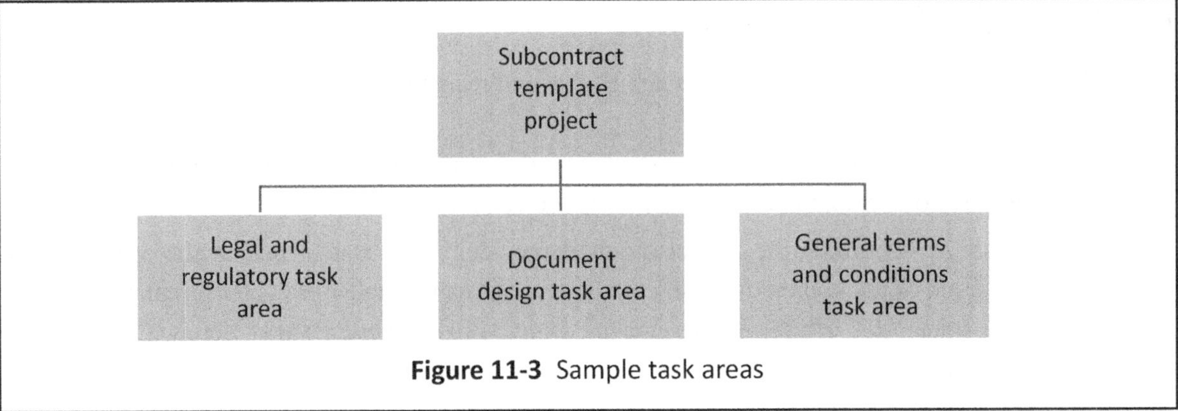

Figure 11-3 Sample task areas

holders so that all relevant interdependencies can be identified, considered, and communicated. There are four basic types of task relationships: finish to start, start to start, finish to finish, and start to finish.

6. *Determine Task Durations*: The team needs to determine how long each task will take to complete, taking into account the resources needed to complete the task, the complexity of the task, timing, and other factors. The project manager considers the duration of the tasks and their relationships when determining how long the entire project will take. It is one of the key practices in solid project management, as this enables management of stakeholder expectations.
7. *Determine Resource Needs*: Resource needs are determined by estimating the amount of resources it will take to complete each task; in other words, how many hours employees will work on the given task. In addition, the project manager will need to estimate needed non-personnel resources, such as material, travel, money, and time.
8. *Determine Costs*: If required by the organization, the manager must estimate the costs associated with the required resources. For example, the manager would calculate costs by multiplying the hours required for each resource by the employees' hourly salary. If other costs are identified in step 7, the costs are calculated in this step. In these cases, it may be a good idea to employ the support of the organization's internal purchasing department, which may be best equipped to obtain quotes from any outside experts, consultants, material suppliers, and so on.
9. *Finalize the Project Plan*: When finalizing the project plan, the project manager is ensuring that all applicable stakeholders have agreed that the plan (including the requirements, tasks,

Myth: Expert project management skills are needed to manage any project.

All business managers must have some level of project management skill to define, execute, and implement initiatives within their operational environment. However, expert project management skills are not necessary to achieve success for most internal projects.

timeline, and resource needs) is sufficient. This finalized project plan is often referred to as a *project baseline plan*.

10. *Initiate Change Control*: Before reaching this final step, the operational project manager should have considered all the other artifacts that were created during steps 1 to 9. This includes stakeholder planning and analysis, the communication plan, and risk response plans. From this point forward, any changes made to the project plan must go through a formal change control process. The level of formality may change based on the size and complexity of the project. Change control involves ensuring that the project plan remains unchanged, except in limited circumstances (as discussed in the next section), so that status may be properly captured and reported in comparison to it. In some organizations, this step may be referred to as *freeze the baseline*.

Change Control

A project baseline plan should change only when the desire to change the plan is due to factors generally outside the control of the project team and, even then, only after the team has determined the impact the change will have on the project and has communicated such to the key stakeholders.

An example of an appropriate change is when senior leadership demands that resources assigned to the project work on other, higher-priority efforts within the organization. When this happens, the project manager and/or the project team must decide whether to find others to perform the planned efforts (affecting the resource analysis) or to wait for those resources to again become available (likely affecting the timeline). In either case, a change to the baseline would be necessary so stakeholders' expectations for the timeline and resources are managed appropriately.

The project manager is the gatekeeper of change control and is responsible for determining if the project baseline plan must be updated or if leadership can simply be informed of the new execution plan and how it now compares to (and potentially varies from) the project baseline plan.

Finish to Start

The finish to start relationship tells the team that a task must finish before the subsequent task can start. The first task is called a *predecessor*, the subsequent task is called a *successor*. With this relationship, the successor task can start *immediately* after the predecessor task finishes. Finish to start is generally the most commonly used task relationship. In some cases, we may not want the successor to start immediately, but the finish to start relationship still makes the most sense of all the available options. In these cases, we may build in some wait time after the predecessor finishes, which we refer to as a *lag*. The resulting relationship is that we know the predecessor task must finish before the successor task can start, but we want the successor task to start after a particular amount of time has passed. An example of a finish to start relationship for the subcontract template development project, introduced earlier, is as follows: The predecessor task is "Create first draft template" and the successor task is

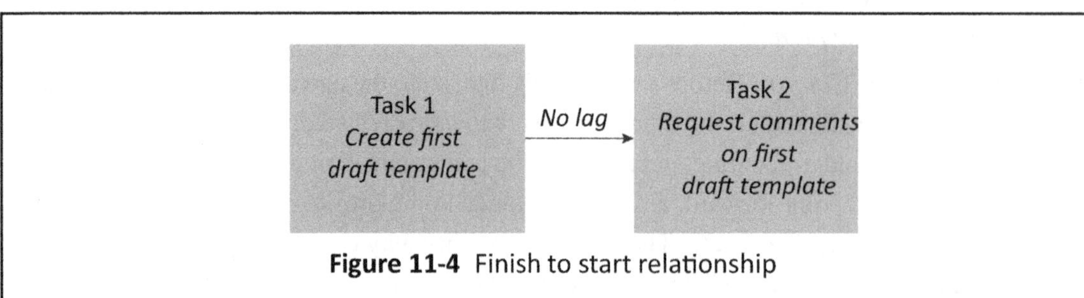

Figure 11-4 Finish to start relationship

"Request comments on first draft template." Thus we clarify that we will not request comments on the draft template until it has been completed. This relationship, with no lag, is presented in Figure 11-4.

Start to Start

The start to start relationship indicates that the predecessor task must start before the successor task can start. Some project managers use the start to start relationship to signal that two tasks can start together; however, this is not accurate. Rather, the best way to indicate that two tasks can start at exactly the same time is to make them both a successor to the same predecessor, using the finish to start relationship (in this way, they both can start *immediately* after their mutual processor finishes, rather than after a predecessor starts). With a start to start relationship, the successor relationship starts *after* the predecessor starts (not at the exact same time). Use this relationship if the two tasks can start in short succession. If one task must start before another and the second cannot start immediately after use the lag to indicate the wait time between the start of the predecessor and the start of the successor. A start to start relationship for the subcontract template development project would be, for example, the task "Research content requirements" (let's call this task 1) and the task "Create first draft template" (task 2). We do not want to wait until all the content requirements have been researched before starting work on the first draft; instead we want to incorporate requirements into the draft as we find them. In addition, before working on task 2, we need the information that comes from task 1—for example, at least a week's worth. However, task 1 does not need to be finished before we can start creating the first draft of the template (we may feel differently about a second draft, a third draft, or the final product). Therefore, the best and most proper relationship would be the start to start, as shown in Figure 11-5.

Finish to Finish

The finish to finish relationship is used to indicate that a predecessor task must finish before a successor task can finish. For the subcontract template project, we do not want to finish the final template until after we have finished researching the content requirements. For example, we may want to allow a week to incorporate the final results of task 1 into the final first draft template (task 2). This relationship is shown in Figure 11-6.

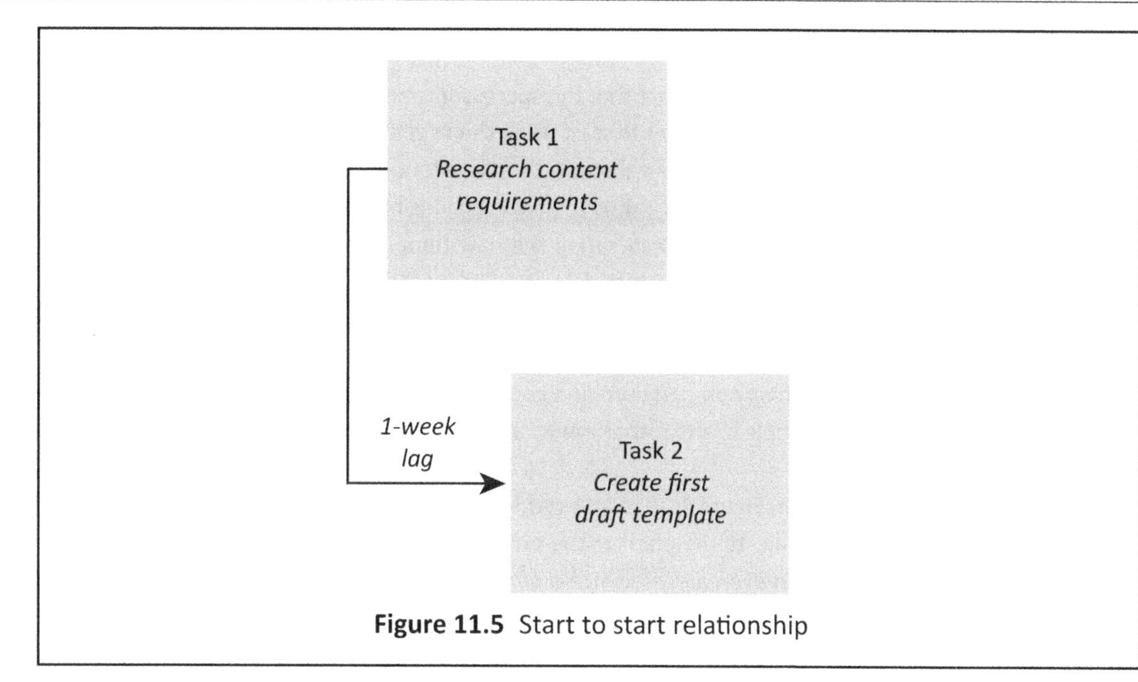

Figure 11.5 Start to start relationship

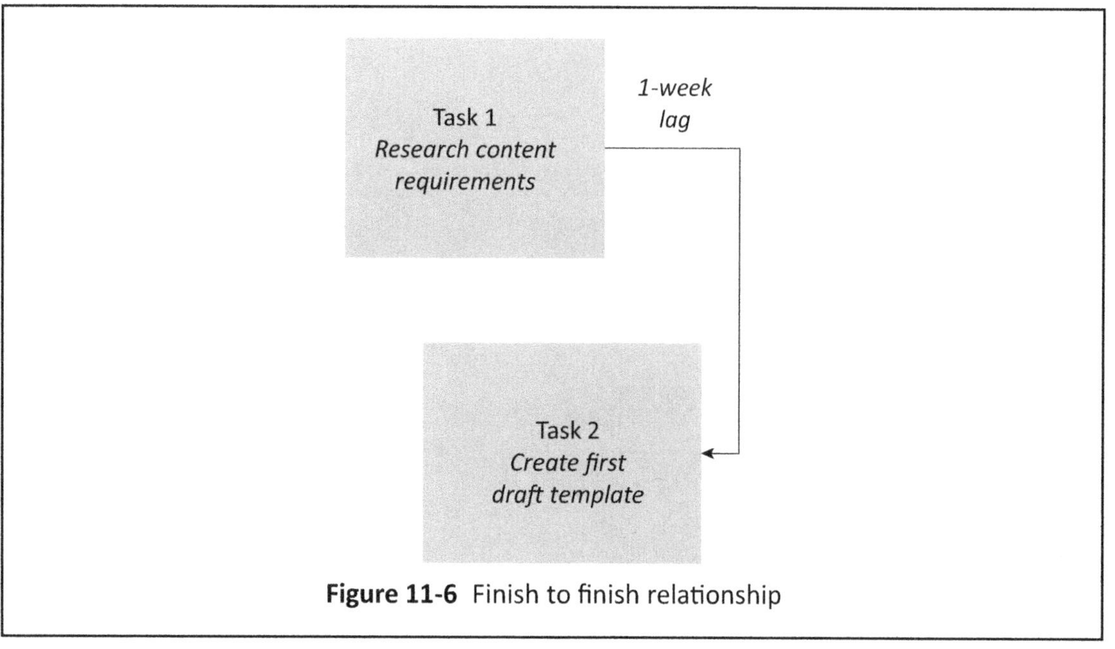

Figure 11-6 Finish to finish relationship

Start to Finish

The start to finish relationship is used to indicate that the successor cannot finish until the predecessor has started. For the template project, we may want to start using the new template before we finish using the old one. In fact, we may want to want to roll out the new template for use on subcontracts under a certain dollar value so that we can work out any kinks; thus the two versions be used concurrently for a little bit. The organization will stop using the old template when the new template is available to all relevant end users and it has been determined that the new template satisfies most of the requirements. The new template task continues until such time as the new template is determined to meet all requirements, which may require several iterations and updates. This relationship is presented in Figure 11-7.

If we look at all the relationships outlined here and consider other tasks that may need to take place to create the new template (multiple drafts, other input, and so on), the project can be summarized by Figure 11-8.

The graphical display shown in Figure 11-8 is referred to as a *precedence diagram* and can be a valuable and effective tool to communicate the plan for the project. When a precedence diagram represents an entire project, it is known as an *overall precedence diagram*. It is also possible to create partial precedence diagrams, which show only a part of the project and are connected with at least one other precedence diagram. Not all project participants are interested in a heavily detailed presentation. A manager at the highest level, for example, may want to see only the precedence diagram with milestones of the project and not the precedence diagram of the individual milestones.

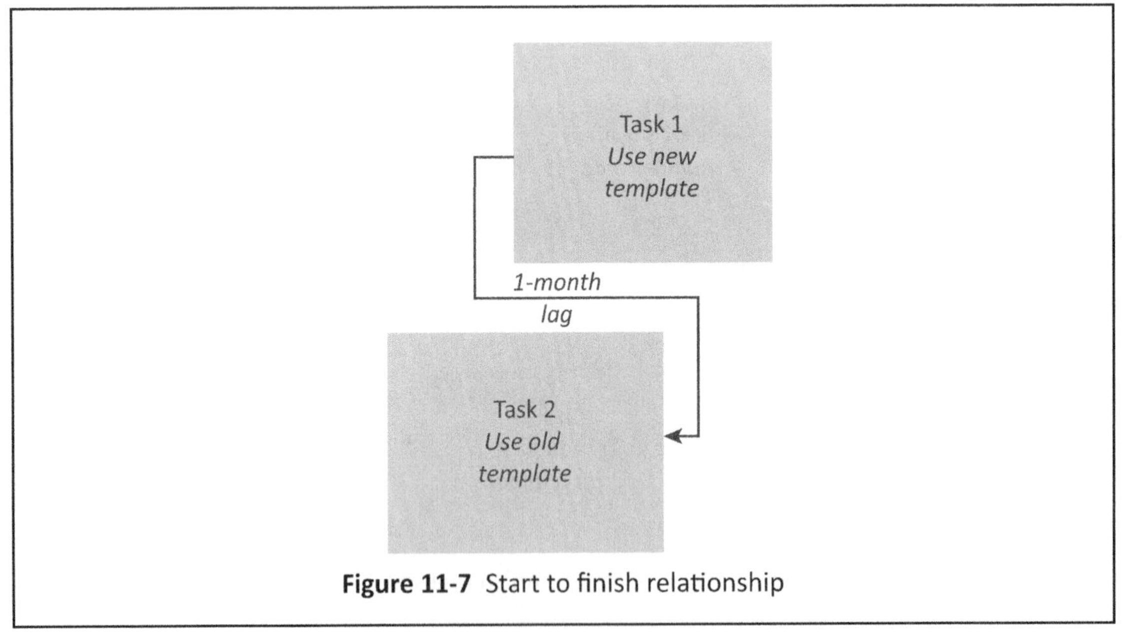

Figure 11-7 Start to finish relationship

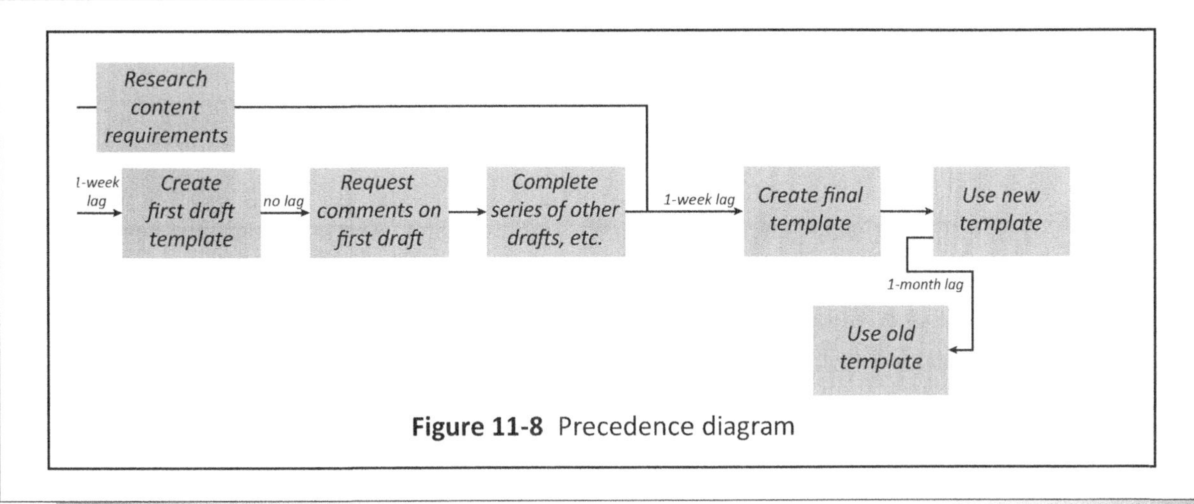

Figure 11-8 Precedence diagram

Any collateral documentation that is affected must also be updated. For example, during project planning, if the team decides to respond to a risk by bringing on additional personnel, the task durations and resource needs may need to be adjusted. If a new resource is needed during project execution, the resource plan, the task duration, and the stakeholder analysis may need to change.

Estimating Techniques

When developing the project plan (steps 6 and 7), the manager must estimate task durations and resources. This requires having a sound estimating process to ensure accurate information is gathered, a thorough analysis is conducted, and informed decisions are made. While estimating is not an exact science, employing best practices and techniques will enhance the process. The following helps ensure successful project estimates:

- Start with a solid understanding of the project's scope (steps 1–5)
- Gain insights from historical data gathered from past similar projects
- Get the right people involved, including experts both within and outside the functional team

Estimates should be realistic and achievable. There are guidelines and considerations for developing good, solid estimates for time or resource.

- *Historical Information*: Historical information is the best source for making estimations (for example, if the organization did something similar last year, find out how long it took, how many resources were involved, how many hours it took, and so on).
- *Ownership of the Estimate*: Generally, the most accurate estimates come from those who are answerable and held accountable for them. This is supported by the concept of the designation of task areas.

- *Level of Detail*: The smaller the unit of work being estimated (brief tasks, for example), the more accurate the estimate is likely to be. However, too much detail and too many tasks can be counterproductive, causing unnecessary administrative effort.
- *Distribution of Estimates*: In any scenario, the best estimate has the same likelihood of being over as being under the actual time or cost (normal distribution). Using only the worst-case (pessimistic) estimate generates arbitrarily high estimates. And using only the best-case (optimistic) estimate generates desired, but probably not realistic, results.
- *Human Productivity*: Be mindful that people cannot be expected to be 100 percent productive over the course of a business day. It would not be unreasonable to suggest that up to 30 percent of the average day is wasted on unproductive activities. Also, be aware that individuals often over- or underestimate the time they believe tasks can be completed in. Consider the difference between duration and effort. For example, if someone states that a task will take her a week to complete, you may be tempted to capture that as forty hours. However, a more clear and accurate estimate of resources comes from understanding what percentage of the employee's time that week will be devoted to completing the task. Perhaps it is only 10 percent. That results in a much lower resource use (four hours versus forty hours) than may have originally been captured and calculated. Thus the *time* or *duration* of the task is still five days (assuming a week is five business days), but the needed *resource* is only four hours.
- *Time, Cost, and Resource Trade-Off*: The guideline for determining the time, cost, and resource trade-off has two parts. First, if a task is going to be shared by more than one person, additional communication, complexity, and perhaps conflict may reduce the team's efficiency in completing the task. Second, if an individual is working on multiple tasks within a single day, the inherent factors of stopping and starting create inefficiencies, thereby reducing that person's productivity.

Pro tip

Historical information is often available in an organization's project and business archives, and managers and stakeholders may have personal experience.

Three-Point Estimating

Three-point estimating is often used to improve the accuracy of estimates by taking the pessimistic, optimistic, and most likely perspectives into consideration. (It was first used by Booz Allen Hamilton and the U.S. Navy on the Polaris missile submarine program.)

The program evaluation and review technique (PERT) takes into consideration the time uncertainty associated with completing the task due to unknown and/or unrelated disturbances. PERT uses a weighted average to find project durations and is based on the beta distribution, a continuous probability distribution from statistical modeling.

$$\text{Estimate} = (O + 4ML + P)/6$$

O = optimistic estimate (everything goes great)

ML = most likely estimate (some things will go wrong and some will go great)

P = pessimistic estimate (everything goes wrong)

Myth: A project is a failure if it does not finish on time and within the required resource plan.

In most environments, success is measured more by the achievement of goals than by what it took to get there. Managing stakeholder expectations along the way can help ensure that everyone is engaged and understands how changing needs and wants may affect the timeline and resource requirements.

A standard three-point estimate can be used for other distributions:

Estimate = $(O + ML + P)/3$

Building in Tolerances in Estimates

From an estimating point of view, it is a good practice to build in some tolerance or confidence levels (also known as confidence intervals) when determining costs and duration of a project or even, in some cases, individual tasks.

Building tolerances into project schedules, resource needs, and budgets brings an element of reality into project management. Suppose the estimated cost of the project is $530,000, and when the financials are closed out at the end of the project, it is discovered that the actual cost was $530,500. Is the project a failure? It is not, *if* it falls within the range of tolerance established in the estimates. Examples of tolerances and confidence intervals follow.

Pro tip

Some organizations collect productivity information, and some managers must rely on personal observation and experience to determine productivity rates. The best source may be obtaining research materials related to your industry.

- Time
  - Interval 1: 24 weeks ± 4 weeks
  - Interval 2: 14 weeks + 2 weeks, − 1 week
  - Interval 3: June 22–June 28
- Resources/costs
  - $50,000 ± 10 percent
  - XX full-time equivalent (FTE) months + 2 months
  - $75,000–$100,000

Note that the confidence of the estimate should get better (tighter confidence interval) as the project progresses, because some tasks have been accomplished and there is less work left to complete.

For example, look at the examples of time estimates just listed. At the start of the project, the duration is estimated at twenty-four weeks plus or minus four weeks, which is a wide range. However, eleven weeks into the project, the estimate has been updated to fourteen weeks to completion plus two weeks or minus one week. Notice that while the project has lost one week off the original target schedule (of

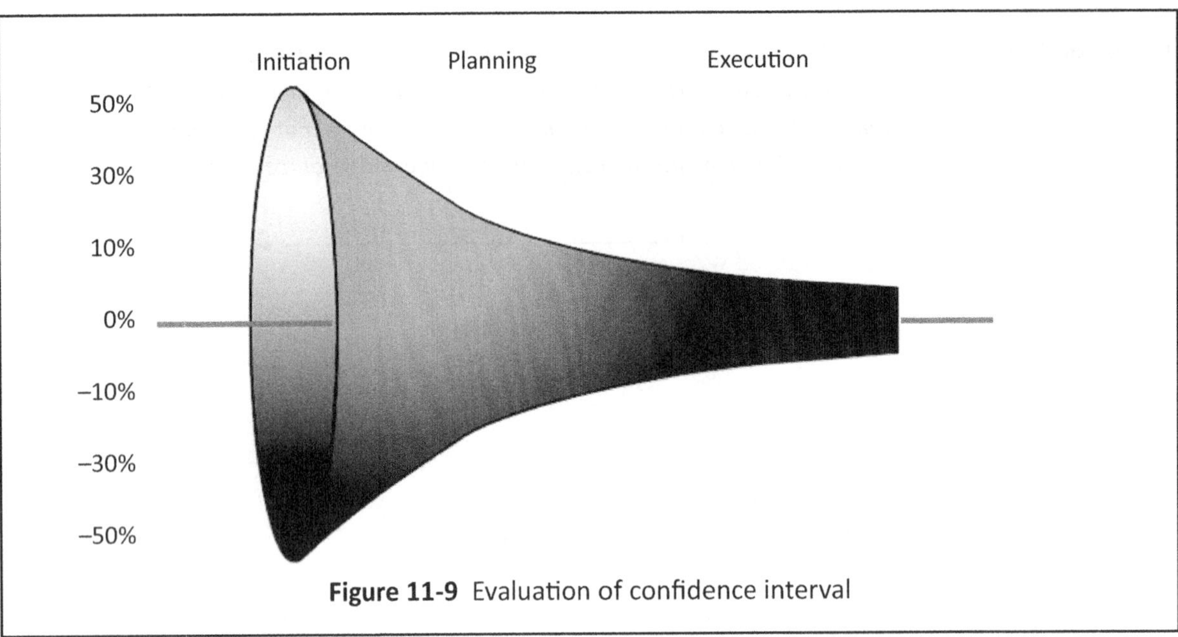

Figure 11-9 Evaluation of confidence interval

twenty-four weeks), the confidence interval has shrunk. Finally, when the project is within a month or so from completion, estimates are updated to specific dates, with a confidence interval of only six days. Again, the project may have slipped from the previous target, but the accuracy of the estimate has improved. At this point, the project manager and the stakeholders can see the light at the end of the tunnel, and the team can be more confident in the estimate (Figure 11-9).

Considering Risk

A risk is an unknown incident that is anticipated or expected to occur during the execution of a project plan. If the incident does occur, it could cause a negative impact on any one of the factors contained in the project plan.

Note that the terms *risk* and *issue* are commonly used synonymously, which is incorrect.

- Risks occur in the future; issues are problems occurring in the present.
- Issues are often more urgent than risks but not necessarily more important.
- It is the project manager's job to prevent risks from turning into issues.

In project management, there is an emphasis on preventing risks, also called *threats*, that will adversely affect the project. The topic of risk is quite elaborate; the operational project manager needs to have a solid understanding of how to identify and analyze risks and then develop plans to try to prevent them from derailing project progress.

Identifying Risks

As project managers develop the initial project artifacts (the stakeholder analysis, communication plan, and project baseline plan), they should be asking themselves and the team, "What could go wrong?" Risk identification should also occur throughout the life of the project. As the project progresses, new risks may present themselves, especially when changes are approved and implemented. As with other project management processes, the identification of risk should be iterative. The tools and techniques used to gather requirements can be adapted to identify risks. Once risks are identified, they should be captured in a spreadsheet, often referred to as a *risk register*. At first, this register will contain minimal information, such as:

- A description of the risk
- An explanation of what is at risk (time, cost, resources, and so on)
- A list of what task or tasks could be affected if the risk occurs

Analyzing Risk

Risk analysis is the process of evaluating risks with the goal of prioritizing them. Dozens of project risks are typically identified; however, the team will not have the time or resources to address them all. By arranging the risks into a prioritized order, the project manager can focus on the most critical for keeping the project out of trouble.

Project risks are most commonly evaluated along two dimensions: the *probability* that they will occur and the *impact* to the project plan if they do occur. They are often rated low, medium, or high in each dimension.

These assessments are normally conducted during meetings attended by those most familiar with the risks. Each risk identified on the risk register is evaluated and rated. A Risk Matrix is often used to help organizations score risks and guide the team during the development of risk responses (Figure 11-10).

Once the risks have been mapped onto the Risk Matrix, a rough prioritization can be determined: the highest priority risks are positioned toward the upper-right corner and lower priority ones toward the lower-left corner.

Pro tip

If you have identified a lot of risks for your project, it may be best to develop a risk response for the top 10 to 20 percent first, then consider the remaining risks as time permits.

Risk Response Planning

Risk response planning is performed after the analysis and prioritization have been completed. The responses should be appropriate and should consider:

- Priority of risk (using probability and impact or, in some cases, urgency and importance)
- Cost
- Timing

Risk responses can be categorized into strategies that will determine explicit actions to be taken to carry them out.

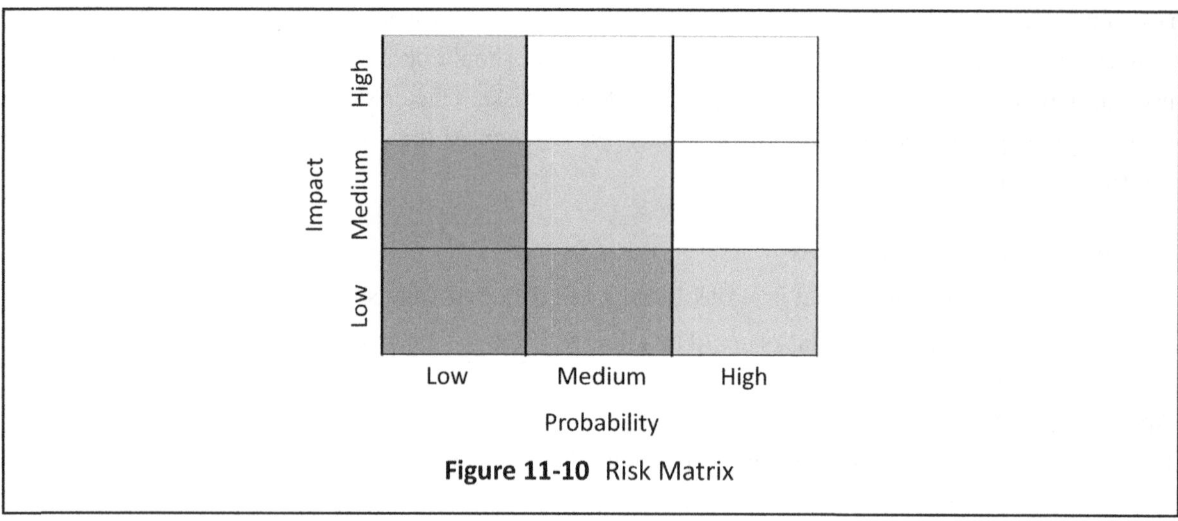

Figure 11-10 Risk Matrix

Potential Responses to Risks

- *Avoidance*: Eliminate the risk by removing its source. This usually means changing the project scope. For example, if the risk is that a resource will be unavailable because she is in high demand, select another resource to complete the task.
- *Transference*: Reduce the probability and/or impact of the risk by giving it to someone better able to handle it. Transference is usually done by outsourcing to an expert or another organization. For example, a lawyer can be hired to consider the compliance requirements related to the subcontract template rather than relying solely on internal resources—and contract with the lawyer to include defense for any related noncompliance penalty.
- *Mitigation*: Do something different or extra with the intent of reducing the probability and/or impact of the risk. Note that mitigations almost always add scope, schedule, and cost to projects and, therefore, are usually reserved for the highest priority risks. For example, hire three external consultants to help write the process documentation instead of asking the highly demanded recognized expert to do this.
- *Acceptance*:
  - Active (contingency/plan B)—don't do anything to avoid, transfer, or mitigate the risk now, but create an alternative plan that the team will execute if the risk event does occur; thus the team is be prepared.
  - Passive—do nothing. If the risk occurs, deal with it then. This is a common approach for low-priority risks.

Ongoing Risk Consideration

Throughout the execution of the project, it is important to review the risk register. Periodic review of the register includes:

- Determine whether risks are still valid (could they still occur or has the risk passed?)

Myth: Stakeholders know what they want.

While stakeholders often have a clear idea about what they want out of the project, they often do not have clear ideas about each and every step that it takes to get there.

Most are unaware of the dynamics within the framework of a project.

- Determine whether risks are closed (they occurred and were handled)
- Keep an eye out for new or emerging risks and capture them on the register
- Review risk response responsibility to ensure the responsible party is monitoring the risk
- Assess whether the probability and impact noted for each risk is still viable or needs adjusting

PROJECT EXECUTION

Essential to project success is implementing the project plan as it was created, based on a systematic approach to ensure that the right people, processes, and tools are in place to meet the project needs and achieve the desired benefits. During this phase, the operational project manager will focus on four key processes:

1. Communicating information to key stakeholders and other stakeholders as needed in accordance with the communication plan
2. Managing people according to the competencies of a qualified business manager, inasmuch is allowed by the organization's operational project management structure
3. Following the project management steps, such as reviewing for communication plan effectiveness, monitoring change management, gathering status, providing for the ongoing review and assessment of risk, and executing risk strategies as planned
4. Ensuring project benefits are considered throughout the project, and items are adjusted to meet the intended benefits

Project Status

During project execution, ongoing status must be captured to determine how the project is progressing compared to the initial plan. In project management, this is referred to as *statusing*, or understanding the status of the project at specific points in time. It is important to assess the status at regular intervals so issues or problems, such as timeline slips, can be determined as early as possible so they can be addressed to improve performance and minimize impact. The frequency of status updates varies: For long-term projects (greater than three months), biweekly or even monthly statuses may be sufficient. For

Project Name ______________________________

Date ______________ **Team Member Name** ______________________________

Team Name ______________________________ **Period** *(from/to)* ______________

Team Project Status *(1–5: 1 poor, 5 excellent):* ***Overall*** ______________

Schedule ______________ ***Budget*** ______________ ***Scope*** ______________

Accomplishments:

ID	Task Code	Task Description	Effort (Hours)	Actual Cost ($)

Issues:

ID	Task Code	Issue Description	Identified By	Issue Response Plan	Help Required? (Y/N)	Complete? (Y/N)

New Risks *(not previously identified):*

ID	Task Code	Risk Description	Identified By	Risk Response Plan	Risk Severity (1–10)

Miscellaneous Notes/Barriers to Success:

ID	Note

Figure 11-11 Individual project team member status report

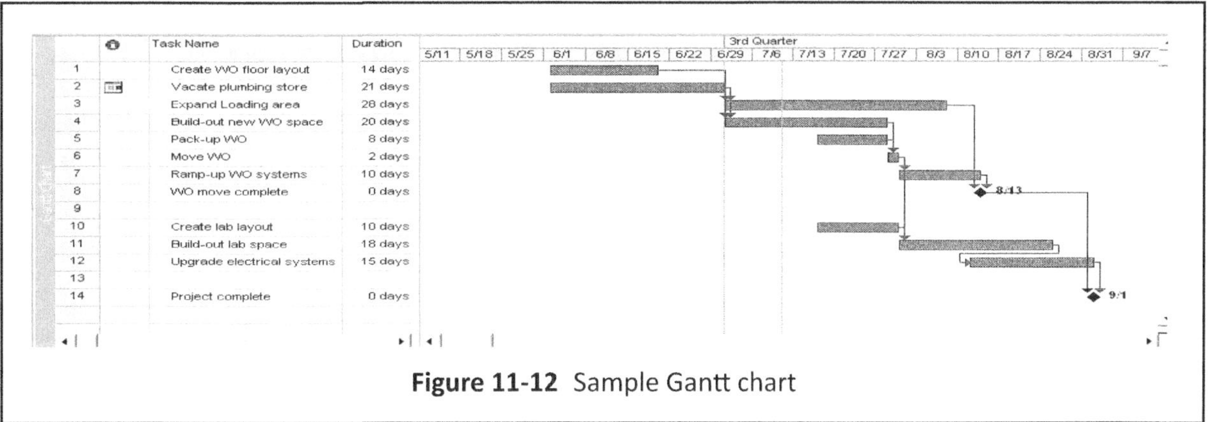

Figure 11-12 Sample Gantt chart

shorter-term projects, weekly or even semiweekly statuses may be necessary. If the project is high risk, fast paced, and has a lot of interdependent moving parts, daily statuses may be required.

Determining Status

Several methods are available to determine the status of the project. Key, of course, is the communication plan and ensuring the right people are engaged at the right time. Some techniques include:

- *Management by Walking Around (MBWA)*: Physically check on the status of the project by viewing the work product or talking to staff. This requires close contact and solid relationship building.
- *Meetings*: Conduct regular meetings, ensuring the purpose of the meeting is clear in the communication plan. The project status report template indicates topics to discuss in these meetings (Figure 11-11 provides a sample). The team member project status report (described below and in Figure 11-11), can provide fodder for the team meetings, allowing the opportunity to ask questions and obtain clarification for information the status reports may contain.
- *Status Templates*: For larger projects, consider using a template to seek and receive statuses. For example, the template indicates what (according to the project plan) should have been completed in the past week, what should be completed in the current week, and what should be completed in the following week. The responsible team members note what actually was completed in the past week as well as what they expect to complete during the week and the following week.
- *Deliverable Reviews*: Review tangible outputs of the project as it progresses, such as draft documentation.
- *Team Member Status Reports*: In more formal environments, the project manager can request a status report from team members. This report includes the name of the person/team reporting, the period being reported, accomplishments, risks, and issues, as shown in the individual project team member status report template (Figure 11-11).

Myth: Project managers must have direct technical knowledge of what they are managing

Project managers often come from different backgrounds from the work they are handling and managing but can still perform well. Project managers do not necessarily need the technical skills of the work they are managing, but they do need an essential understanding of what work it will take to get the project done.

Reporting Status

Operational project managers should also be providing periodic status reports to their leadership and/or sponsor. Reporting requirements, formats, and templates vary by organization, but as a best practice, the project status report should contain the following:

- An executive summary, no more than a page long, providing the current state of the project and highlighting any significant matters that the sponsor needs to be aware of. The sponsor should enable success of the project and thus needs to be kept abreast of areas in which he or she can help remove barriers.
- A description of challenges the project manager is facing, providing more detail than is given in the executive summary.
- A brief description of accomplishments the project team has made since the last report. While it may be easy and tempting to focus only on challenges, it is always good to be certain to communicate what is going well.
- An action plan for the next period so the sponsor knows what decisions have already been made and how the project manager and team plan to proceed.
- A Gantt chart or similar graphic representation of the project's initial baseline compared to its current execution plan (Figure 11-12).

Project Management Software

Based on the size and complexity of the project, the operational project manager may need to use project management software, which is more advanced than traditional office tools such as word processors and spreadsheets. Project managers can choose from a variety of software tools. Depending on the organization, the types of projects being managed, and individual skill levels, the project manager may opt to purchase add-ons to increase software functionality.

COMPETENCY PROGRESSION

All business managers need various levels of project management skills, depending on the type of work being managed. To be effective, the operational project manager needs, at minimum, an elevated level of project management competency (Figure 11-13).

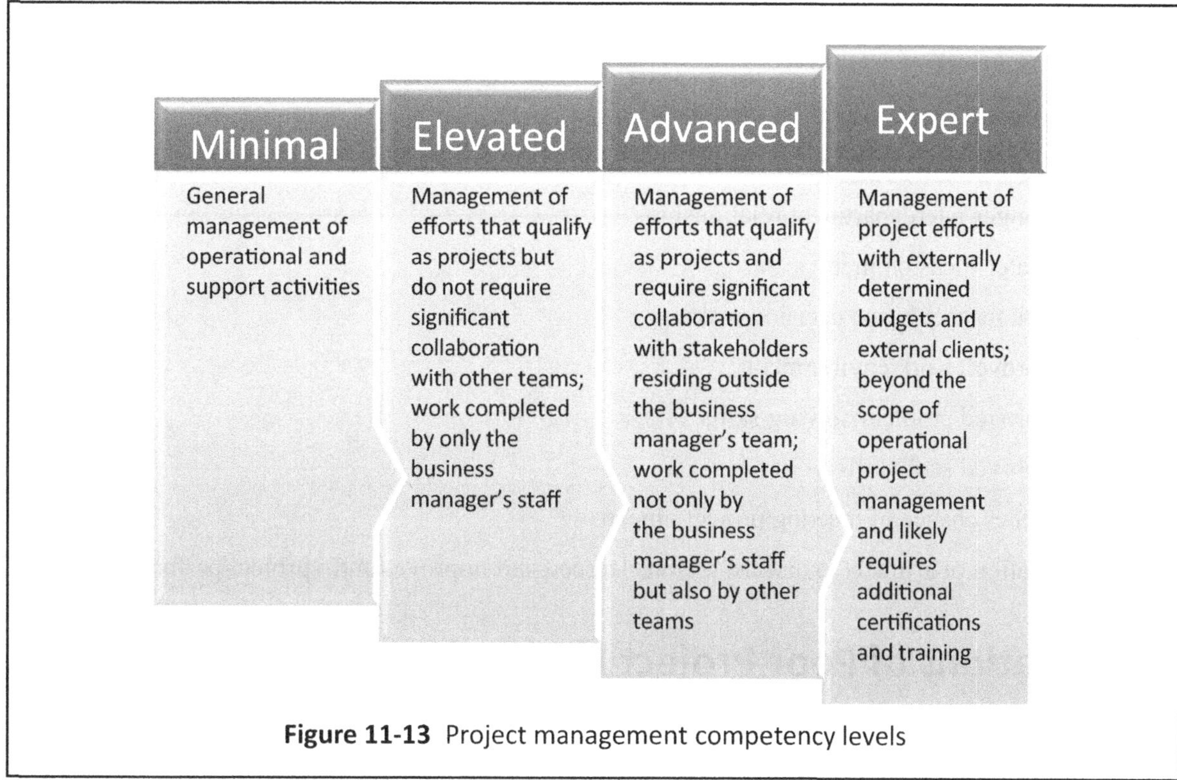

Figure 11-13 Project management competency levels

Benefits of Project Management Skills to a Business Manager

- Clear identification of task objectives
- Effective engagement of stakeholders
- Opportunity for growing staff skills
- Improved relationship with internal customers
- Improved change management
- Optimal decision making
- Improved resource management
- Identification of time limits
- Earlier identification of execution concerns
- Increased predictability

Ramifications of Good Project Management Performance

- Increased chance of achieving benefits
- Resolving problems more quickly

- Better solution fit the first time through better planning
- Less rework
- Team viewed as a solution provider
- Organizational stability
- Stronger interdepartment relationships
- Greater focus on metrics
- Stronger fact-based decision making
- Improved work environment
- Improved problem-solving skills
- Improved staff skills
- Greater chance of meeting project objectives
- Creation of artifacts to discern lessons learned and improve future project performance

Ramifications of Poor Project Management Performance

- Extensive rework
- Poor interdepartment relationships
- Overworked, unhappy staff
- Unrealistic stakeholder expectations
- Failure to meet objectives
- Work does not progress per plan
- Needs and goals improperly communicated
- Decisions made without appropriate stakeholder involvement

• Conclusion •

The successful business manager needs solid project management competencies to effectively and efficiently drive change and process improvements in the organization. The examples provided in this chapter, such as the improvement of an existing process for expense report reimbursement and the creation of a new template, represent the types of factors that business managers may need to make sure take place to enable their team's success. Project management competencies can help ensure team members consider all the necessary collaboration points, and efficient project management also involves the practical application of many of the other core competencies.

12

Financial Acumen

LEARNING OBJECTIVES

By the end of this chapter, you will be better equipped to:

- Identify the key financial drivers of the business as well as the manager's contributions to the overall success of the business.
- Identify financial conditions that impact the team's budget, operations, and functions to create processes for budgeting and forecasting.
- Analyze financial data to identify trends and issues that are important to the business and interpret the results to make decisions and/or recommendations.
- Summarize financial data and present in a clear and comprehensible format.
- Plan and develop budget strategy to support organizational goals based on financial data, previous performance, and forecasting.

Accounting and finance are said to be the universal languages of business. If this is true, then why do so many managers struggle in this area? To be an effective manager you must possess a working knowledge of this universal business language.

If accounting and finance together make up the universal language of business, then developing a working knowledge of this discipline will help ensure the manager possesses the acumen for understanding the financial impacts of daily decisions and has the ability to communicate effectively with peers and leadership. First we discuss the mechanics of accounting and then how these mechanics are applied and analyzed.

Accounting, at its basic level, includes recording all business transactions and events and then reporting them in the form of financial statements. Along with footnotes explaining details of accounting methodology, the statements tell the story of the business's financial condition and results of operations.

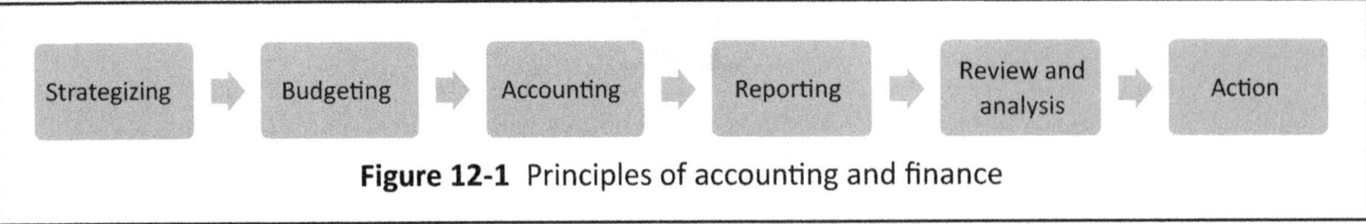

Figure 12-1 Principles of accounting and finance

Finance is the analysis of these statements to understand how well the business is performing, where problems may be present, and whether continuing investment in the business is advisable.

Figure 12-1, unlocks the principles of accounting and finance. Your understanding of these principles affects your ability to interact with leadership, develop effective plans for the future for your area of responsibility, and reduce risks. Such knowledge enables you to successfully propose, implement, and monitor tactical options to improve operations and grow the business.

ACCOUNTING ACUMEN

The Background of Accounting

Luca Pacioli is the first known author of the concepts of double-entry accounting (Figure 12-2). He wrote the treatise *The Rules of Double-Entry Bookkeeping: Particularis de Computis et Scripturis* in 1494. It is based on the relationships of debtors and creditors in business transactions. He is quoted as saying, "All the creditors must appear in the ledger at the right-hand side, and all the debtors at the left. All entries made in the ledger have to be double entries—that is, if you make one creditor, you must make someone debtor."

The Axiom

From Pacioli's writings, we derive the accounting rules applied worldwide. The universe of transaction reporting (accounting) is broken down into these five major categories:

1. Assets
2. Liabilities
3. Equity
4. Revenue
5. Expense

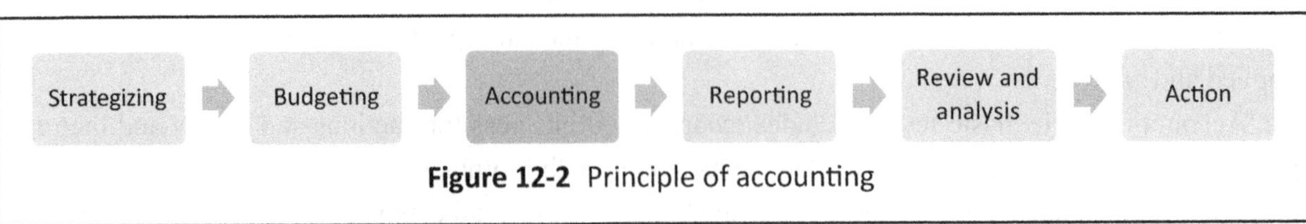

Figure 12-2 Principle of accounting

Myth: When I deposit a check at the bank, the teller says to credit my account.

Shouldn't they be debiting my account, since that deposited check is increasing the value of my bank account?

From Pacioli's teachings, *all* transactions are recorded within these five categories, coupled with the concept of double-entry accounting using debits and credits under the following rules. Debits are positive numbers and credits are negative numbers. In this two-column system, debits are always shown in the left column and credits in the right column. Each transaction must include debits and credits of equal amounts. As a result, every transaction will sum to zero.

Debits and credits are applied to each category, as seen in Table 12-1.

While as a manager outside of accounting you will probably not be involved in many of these details, it is important for you to be aware of the basics so you know what the accountants are talking about when you ask them questions about your performance reports and they ask you about various business decisions.

Putting It All Together

As the accounting for business transactions is completed for a reporting period, the balances in the various accounts are summarized from the general ledger into a trial balance. The trial balance is simply a listing of the balance in each account from the general ledger into two columns, debits and credits. The trial balance is then used to:

- Adjust for errors in the recording processes
- Insert noncash entries, such as depreciation deductions and intercompany entries
- Introduce accruals, such as
    - Entries for which no invoice is available but for which the organization has earned revenue

Table 12-1 Impact of Debits and Credits on Financial Statements

Financial Statement	Category	Debit	(Credit)
Balance sheet	Assets	Increase	(Decrease)
	(Liabilities)	Decrease	(Increase)
	(Equity)	Decrease	(Increase)
Income statement	(Revenue)	Decrease	(Increase)
	Expense	Increase	(Decrease)

Source: Table ©2006, Miles Hutchinson, CGMA, reprinted with permission.

Table 12-2 Trial Balance						
Account	**Preliminary**		**Adjustments**		**Final Results**	
	Debit	Credit	Debit	Credit	Debit	Credit

- Benefits the organization has received from products or services, including labor for which the related payroll has not yet been processed

Once the adjustments are recorded, the trial balance is updated (finalized) and used to produce the financial statements. The trial balance generally takes the form shown in Table 12-2.

The Financial Statements

The body of financial reporting is made up of the following financial statements:

- Income statement
- Statement of shareholders' equity
- Balance sheet
- Statement of cash flow
- Other comprehensive income or loss

Pro tip
The income statement is commonly referred to as the P&L, or profit and loss statement. The common phrase, "What's the bottom line?" comes from this statement, as the bottom line, the net income, is the clearest measure of success for a company.

As Table 12-1 demonstrates, all transactions are recorded in either the balance sheet, the income statement, or both. The other statements provide additional insights by summarizing specific activities derived from those two (Figure 12-3).

Each statement has a specific purpose.

Income Statement or Statement of Profit and Loss

The income statement presents the results of operations by matching revenues earned with expenses related to those revenues (cost of

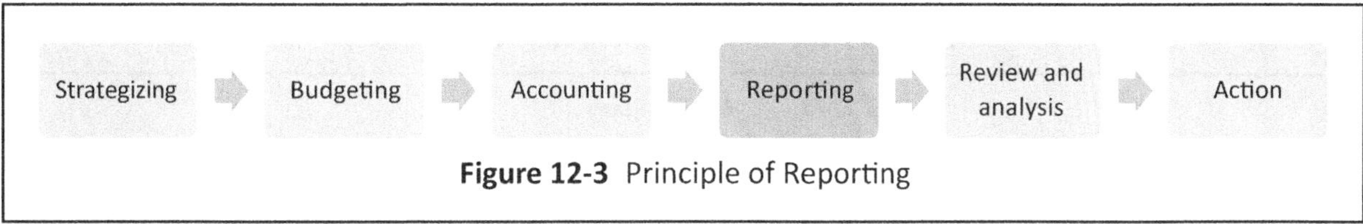

Figure 12-3 Principle of Reporting

goods and services sold) and expenses incurred to run the business (operating expenses). It is presented for a specific *period* of time (such as a month, quarter, or year).

A typical format for the income statement is shown in Table 12-3.

The manager will be more focused on income from operations than on the net income or bottom line because the items following income from operations are not controlled by the manager. In addition, businesses tend to incentivize managers to manage their income statement results down to the income from operations line.

Statement of Shareholders' Equity (Including Retained Earnings)

The shareholders' equity statement presents activity related to the various accounts within the equity section of the balance sheet (discussed later in the chapter)—for example, common stock, paid-in capital, retained earnings, other comprehensive income or loss, and treasury stock. It is presented for a specific *period* of time.

The section of the statement covering retained earnings is key to understanding how the income statement information (discussed earlier) transfers into the balance sheet (Figure 12-4). Retained earnings is an accumulator bucket of the company's entire history of profits, losses, and dividend payouts to shareholders. Each reporting period, the company summarizes its operating performance into one number, the net income or loss. This number is then transferred into retained earnings. Next, the company determines (at the board of directors level) whether to pay a dividend to shareholders. If it pays a dividend, is the total is deducted from retained earnings (as this amount of earnings is no longer retained).

Balance Sheet

The balance sheet presents assets (things owned), liabilities (things owed), and shareholders' equity (owners' net worth). The balance sheet will tell the reader what the enterprise owns, its debts and obligations, and the shareholders' investment in the company. Looking at this information over multiple periods can identify significant changes, both good and bad. The balance sheet can be used to measure the enterprises' liquidity and financial leverage. It can also be used in conjunction with the income statement to determine profit as a percent of total assets, the level of profit compared to shareholder's equity, and return on capital.

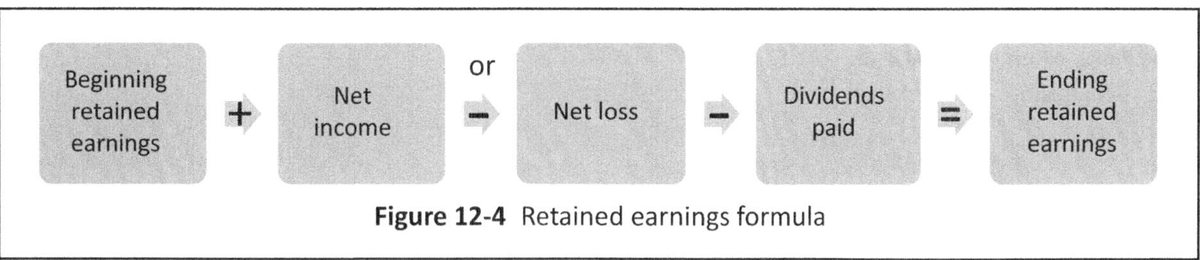

Figure 12-4 Retained earnings formula

Table 12-3 Income Statement for XYZ Company		
XYZ Company **Income Statement** **For the Period Ended 12/31/2000**		
	Current Year	**Prior Year**
Revenue		
– Cost of goods or services sold		
= Gross profit		
– Selling, general, and administrative (SG&A) expenses		
– Research and development expenses		
= Income from operations		
+ Interest income		
– Interest expense		
± Other nonrecurring items (e.g., gain or loss on disposition of assets)		
= Pre-tax income		
– Income tax expense		
= Net income		

The balance sheet is presented at a point in time by summarizing the balances in various accounts. It must balance, meaning the balances in the asset accounts must equal the sum of the balances in the liabilities and equity accounts. The formula is given in Figure 12-5.

The same period of time is used for the balance sheet as was used for the income statement, except that it presents a status report at a specific *point* in time (a freeze frame). To reiterate, the income statement reports the activity of the enterprise for a *period* of time, whereas the balance sheet provides a snapshot of the enterprises' financial condition at a *point* in time.

A typical format for the balance sheet is given in Table 12-4.

Pro tip

The income statement and balance sheets are two of the most well-known financial statements. What's the difference? The income statement covers a period of time (usually one year), whereas the balance sheet is a snapshot at a particular moment.

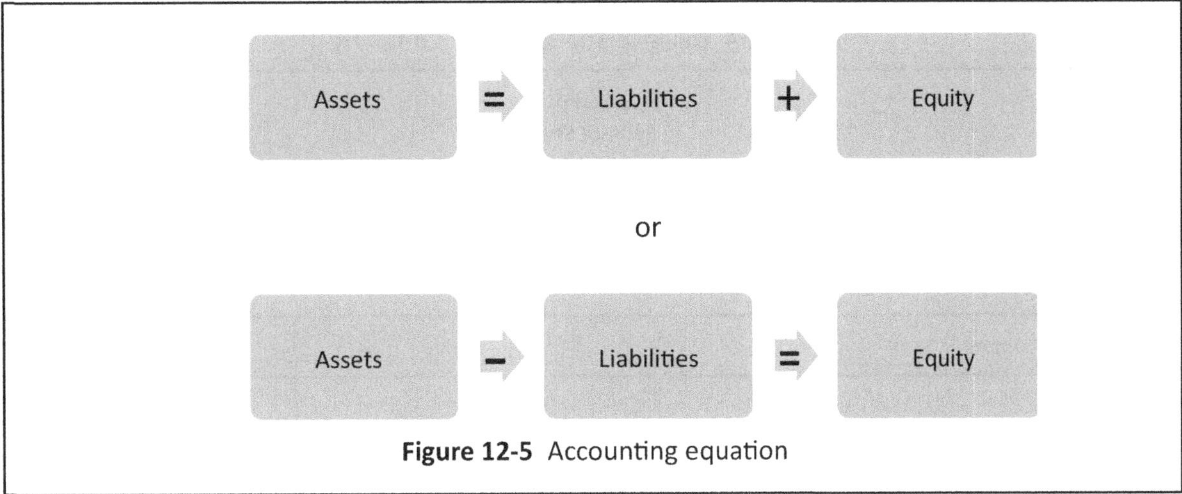

Figure 12-5 Accounting equation

Statement of Cash Flow

The statement of cash flow summarizes all transactions affecting cash for the same period of time in three categories:

1. *Cash Flow from Operations (CFO)*: Converts the income statement to a cash basis
2. *Cash Flow from Investing Activities (CFI)*: Summarizes changes in the balances in the long-term asset accounts
3. *Cash Flow from Financing Activities (CFF)*: Summarizes changes in the balances in the long-term liability accounts and the equity accounts

A typical format for the cash flow statement is given in Table 12-5.

The main purpose of the cash flow statement is to show all of the movements of cash for the period covered by the income statement. It is structured in three distinct sections to (a) convert the income statement back to a cash basis, (b) to show how cash was used or provided from the long-term asset section of the balance sheet, and (c) to show how cash was used or provided from the long-term liabilities and the equity section of the balance sheet. This statement will show whether the enterprise is funding growth in long-term assets (part b) through operational cash flows (part a) or from borrowing and equity capital (part c) or both.

Other Comprehensive Income or Loss

The statement of other comprehensive income or loss presents foreign currency translation and related risk containment by management (hedging contracts). Managers who are not part of this hedging activity will not be involved with this statement or the decisions leading to its results.

Table 12-4 Balance Sheet for XYZ Company		
XYZ Company **Balance Sheet** **As of 12/31/2000**		
	Current Year	**Prior Year**
Assets		
Current assets		
Cash		
Marketable securities		
Accounts receivable		
Inventory		
Prepaid expenses		
Other current assets		
Total current assets		
Long-term assets		
Land		
Buildings		
Furniture fixtures and equipment		
Less: accumulated depreciation		
Fixed assets, net of accumulated depreciation		
Intangible assets		
Less: accumulated amortization		
Long-term investments		
Other long-term assets		
Total long-term assets		
Total assets		

continued

	Current Year	Prior Year
Liabilities and Equity		
Liabilities		
Current liabilities		
Accounts payable		
Accrued liabilities		
Short-term debt		
Current portion of long-term debt		
Other current liabilities		
Total current liabilities		
Long-term liabilities		
Long-term debt		
Unfunded pension costs		
Other long-term liabilities		
Total long-term liabilities		
Shareholders' equity		
Preferred stock		
Common stock		
Paid in capital		
Retained earnings		
Treasury stock		
Other comprehensive income or loss		
Total shareholders' equity		
Total liabilities and equity		

ACCOUNTING GUIDELINES

Frequently, alternative accounting treatments are available for specific transactions. Rules have been established in the United States and abroad to address these alternatives and prescribe acceptable treatments.

While most managers will not be involved in determining the proper accounting treatment of most transactions, they will be affected by these decisions. The effects will appear in their financial reports and discussions surrounding major business decisions. Managers should therefore be aware of the rule-setting bodies and how they interact with one another.

United States: AICPA, FASB, FAS, and Principles Based

Only certified public accountants (CPAs) can join the American Institute of Certified Public Accountants (AICPA). Under the AICPA, the Financial Accounting Standards Board (FASB) sets the standards, known as generally Accepted Accounting Principles (GAAP), for accounting and reporting for U.S.-based companies. U.S.-based publicly traded companies must adhere to these principles. Non-U.S.-based publicly traded companies must follow similar principles established by the International Financial Accounting Standards Board. These rules are collectively known as financial accounting standards (FAS). They are principles (rather than rule or formula) based. Examples of U.S. GAAP include:

- *Historical Basis of Reporting*: Account balances reflect the original cost of items rather than their fair market values at the time of reporting. This rule is consistent with the conservatism.
- *Conservatism*: The reports will follow a conservative approach to presenting the financial condition and results of operations.
- *Relevancy*: The financial report with provide the user with relevant information at the time of the report; when in conflict, the rules of historical cost and conservatism will overrule relevancy. The notes to the financial statements describe the accounting principles followed in the financial statement presentation.
- *Matching*: The financial statements must be presented using the accrual method of accounting to most accurately reflect the true earnings performance of the organization.
- *Materiality*: The financial statements will present all transactions accurately and in the time period in which they actually relate. Errors will occur, but at what point must the financial statements be restated to fairly present the financial information? The answer requires judgments by the accounting leadership and their financial auditors; in essence, if the error (or group of uncorrected errors) is so significant to the interpretation of the financial condition or results of operations that, without the corrections, readers could be misled, then the error (or group of errors) is material and correction must be made.

Table 12-5 Statement of Cash Flow for XYZ Company		
XYZ Company **Statement of Cash Flow** **For the period ended 12/31/2000**		
	Current Year	**Prior Year**
Cash flow from operations		
Net income		
Add back non-cash expenses (depreciation and amortization)		
(Increase) decrease in account receivable		
(Increase) decrease in inventory		
(Increase) decrease in prepaid expenses		
(Increase) decrease in other current assets		
Increase (decrease) in accounts payable		
Increase (decrease) in accrued expenses		
Increase (decrease) in short-term notes payable		
Increase (decrease) in other current liabilities		
Cash flow from operations		
Cash flow from investing activities		
Purchases of fixed assets		
(Sales) of fixed assets		
Changes in intangible assets		
Changes in other long-term assets		
Cash flow from investing activities		
Cash flow from financing activities		
New borrowings		
Repayments of long-term debt		
Repurchase of treasury stock		

Dividend payments		
Sales of treasury stock		
Sale of preferred or common stock		
Cash flow from financing activities		
Net increase (decrease) in cash		
Change in cash due to foreign currency translation gains or losses		
Cash: beginning of the period		
Cash: end of the period		

- *Single Entity*: An entity is separate from its owners in the eyes of the law and must be reported upon separately from its owners.
- *Specific Currency*: U.S.-based organizations must use the U.S. dollar as the reporting currency. Foreign affairs of the business must be converted to U.S. dollars using the prevalent exchange rate and be included in the financial statements.
- *Fiscal Period*: The organization must report its financial condition and results of operations for each fiscal year. The fiscal year may be a calendar year or end on another specific date within the year; each period presented in the financial reports must be for the same length of time.
- *Full Disclosure*: The organization must explain the information presented in the financial statements in sufficient detail for the reader to understand the specific accounting principles on which the information is based. In addition, the organization must provide specific disclosures about the makeup and nature of significant account balances as well as any pertinent information that is not present in the financial statements but would influence an informed reader's interpretation of the statements.

Note, that while not required by law or regulations, private companies may also be compelled by creditors, lenders, or equity holders to comply with these principles.

With a principle-based framework there is the potential for different interpretations of similar transactions, which could lead to extensive disclosures in the financial statements to explain positions taken.

In addition to rules promulgated by the FASB, the Securities and Exchange Commission (SEC) requires additional disclosures by publicly traded companies. These include a more detailed discussion of certain expenses, like officer and director compensation and the addition of management's discussion and analysis of financial condition and results of operations (MD&A) to the financial report. The primary SEC reports include the 10-Q (quarterly report) and the 10-K (annual report).

Securities and Exchange Commission

Additional guidelines in the form of governmental regulations are required of publicly traded companies owned by a U.S.-based parent company. The primary components of these requirements are described later in this chapter.

International Accounting Standards Board and International Financial Reporting System

The International Accounting Standards Board (IASB) oversees the administration of the accounting guidelines for most other countries. The guidelines are collectively referred to as international financial reporting standards (IFRS) (formerly the international accounting standards). These standards are rules based, meaning they set specific mechanical requirements for accounting for each type of transaction. They result in consistent accounting methodology for similar transactions across diverse business types and tend to require fewer disclosures to explain accounting methods used to produce the financial statements.

The FASB and the IASB are collaborating to eliminate differences in accounting and reporting standards between the two organizations. Examples include:

- *Revenue Recognition*: Regulators of GAAP and IFRS have agreed on how to account for earned revenue in a vast array of businesses (construction, mining, consignment, warehousing, retailing, and so on)
- *Accounting for Research and Development Costs*: GAAP requires these costs to be expensed immediately, whereas IFRS records them on the balance sheet as long-term assets and then evaluates them for substantial impairment (translation: write-off to expense) annually

Once the project is completed, the two groups intend to maintain a continuity of new standards.

Governmental Accounting Standards Board

Governmental entities follow governmental accounting standards (GAS), which are established by the Governmental Accounting Standards Board (GASB), which is also under the guidance of the AICPA. In addition, U.S. government agencies must comply with regulations established by the federal government.

Non-Profits, Not-for-Profits (nongovernmental organizations)

Non-profits, not-for-profits (including nongovernmental organizations or NGOs) follow standards prescribed by the FASB written to address issues peculiar to their business model.

Alternative Accounting Methods

There are two basic accounting methods: cash and accrual. The cash method is based on the checkbook—that is, what came in and what when out of cash. The accrual method is more complicated, more precise, and paints a more accurate picture of the enterprise (Table 12-6).

Cash Method

Known as checkbook accounting, the cash method is permitted for tax purposes for smaller companies (under $25 million in revenues) and when inventory is not a significant component of the business activity. Since it is easier to apply this method, small businesses may choose to use it, even though it does not provide a true picture of profitability and completely ignores accounts receivable due from customers, accounts payable due to vendors and other accruals.

Consider bicycle hacks in New York City. They do not have inventory. They only have one fixed asset: their bicycle. With the cash basis of accounting they will get a reasonable picture of profit for the day, week, or month, and their balance sheet is also very simple.

Next consider food vendors, who have a cart full of inventory. The inventory not sold at the end of the day is not a cost of sale for the day. These vendors need to consider using the accrual method of accounting and track their inventory on hand on the balance sheet rather than expensing it when purchased to get a true picture of profitability at the end of the day, week, or month.

Accrual Method

The accrual method is required by GAAP and IFRS. All publicly traded companies must use this accounting method. Many private companies, governmental entities, and NGOs also adopt the accrual method because of its more fair and accurate presentation of operational results.

Table 12-6 Recording Revenue and Expense Using the Cash and Accrual Accounting Methods

	Cash	Accrual
Revenue	Recorded in the time period when the cash is received	Recorded in the time period where it is earned
Expense	Recorded in the time period when the item or service is paid for	Matched to the revenue that it helped earn (cost of goods and service sold) and in the time period where the item is benefited from (operating expenses)

Other Required Documentation under GAAP and/or the SEC

In order for the financial statements to be usable by readers outside the company, certain other disclosures are required. Managers may be involved in their preparation or perhaps will need to provide information to accounting to enable them to craft these required disclosures.

Footnotes to the Financial Statements

GAAP requires financial reports to contain a description of the business, key accounting policies, and details explaining significant account balances in the financial statements. Any liabilities of the company not specifically disclosed in the balance sheet (known as off-balance sheet financing, primarily including lease obligations) must be summarized. Stock options granted and not yet exercised and legal proceedings must also be summarized along with the opinions of management and legal counsel of the likelihood that any of the proceedings could adversely affect the financial statements as presented in a material respect—that is, in any way that would affect the readers' assessment of the financial report in a significant way.

MD&A

Management must compute the changes in all account categories presented in the financial statements from one reporting period to the next and explain the main reason(s) for the changes. This is intended to provide the reader of the financial report with a deeper understanding of the direction the company, for better or for worse. Management must also present all key risk factors it is exposed to and its access to the capital markets to continue to finance its operations going forward.

Pro tip

Financial reports are only as good as the level of integrity and accuracy allow. Certified auditing firms and management's report of review of internal controls over reporting and disclosure can lend credibility to the validity of financial information.

Report of Certified Public Accounting, Auditing Firm

Both GAAP and SEC regulations require the financial statements be presented under an opinion letter from the filer's CPA firm. This opinion should be read carefully to determine whether the CPA firm rendered an unqualified opinion, qualified opinion stating reasons for the qualification or a disclaimer of opinion, and the reason why they could not render an opinion as a result of their audit. In addition, all publicly traded companies must be reviewed by the CPA firm regarding their internal control environment. This review is finalized with a formal report from the CPA firm regarding their findings.

Management's Report of Review of Internal Controls over Reporting and Disclosure

Management is required to perform an annual review of its internal controls over financial statement reporting and disclosure. Both the CEO and the CFO must sign a letter stating the nature of their review, as they are ultimately responsible for the financial report being in compliance and the results of their review. Look at this letter and note whether the company identified any significant control deficiencies or material weaknesses that were not remediated and retested for compliance by the end of the fiscal year for the report being published. As a manager, your focus on this information should be to assist financial leadership in the identification of problems and subsequent modification of processes, documentation, systems, and so on and to remediate them so the report will not contain "significant control deficiencies" or "material weakness" statements.

BUDGETING

As you develop your understanding of the accounting model, you become equipped to use it for planning purposes. The budget process is led by the accounting function but developed from each manager's statements of purpose and plans for execution (Figure 12-6). Managers congeal their purpose and tactics for execution of the strategic plan and then inject the results into the accounting system of the business.

Each department, location, and business unit manager identifies the amount by which each account under their control is expected to be affected, usually over the following twelve months. The time horizon may be longer if prescribed by leadership or if the manager's projects have longer expected lives.

The Budget Process

The budgeting process includes the following major activities:

- Sales plan to determine realistic sales volumes, pricing, and distribution costs
- Production, operating and financing expense budgets to support the sales plan
- Pro forma P&L
- Capital budgets, developed simultaneously with the operational budget
- Financing plans, which consider available capital, growth goals, and capital budget needs beyond available free cash flow and cash reserves, feeding back into the pro forma P&L as interest expense
- Cash flow projections from operations, investing, and financing activities
- Pro forma balance sheet, which recognizes changes in various categories based on strategic initiatives, cash flows from operations, capital expenditures, divestitures, tax planning, and financing requirements

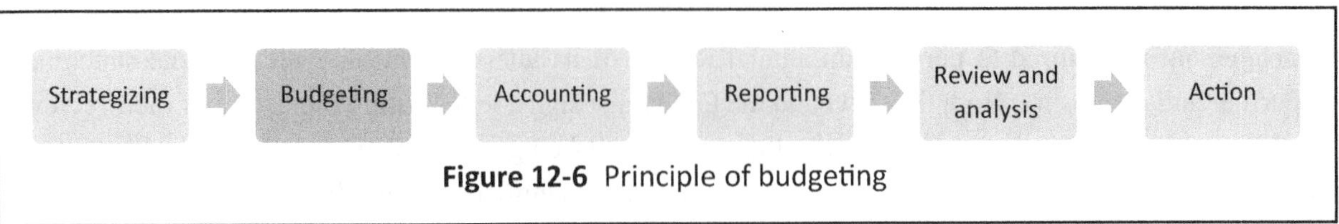

Figure 12-6 Principle of budgeting

Table 12-7 Operational Budgeting Tools		
Budgeting Tool	**How It Works**	**Best Used For**
Incremental	Learn about price changes from suppliers, human resources, and so on and adjust prior year numbers with anticipated price and volume shifts	Raw materials, labor, distribution costs, leases, utilities, real estate and personal property taxes, advertising contracts
Flexible	Prepare the budget using the separation of fixed and variable costs and adjust the budget to actual volume of activity before comparing it to actual results	Breaking down variances into volume price and efficiency variance components to better manage each aspect of a variance
Zero based	Assume a zero start point with no building and no staff, and map out what it would take to operate and achieve stated goals as efficiently as possible	Compare resulting analysis to the current situation, analyze gaps, and use for setting goals for eliminating gaps over several years
Responsibility or activity based	Analyze process flows for non-value-added steps and other inefficiencies	Improve processes during the budgeting campaign

No single symbiotic operational budgeting tool is best, and the tools are not mutually exclusive (Table 12-7). The planner must choose the best tool for each account or category being budgeted.

Once developed and refined, budgets from the lowest level of departmentalization are rolled up into location budgets, then into division budgets, and finally, consolidated into a projected corporate income statement, balance sheet, and statement of cash flows. This information is then used by leadership to determine the cash and financing plans needed to supplement the organization's operating cash flows. Debt or equity (or both) financing may be required to supplement operating cash flows to accelerate growth beyond what the company can support through current operations.

Reporting Using Budget Data

Once the budgets are approved, they are incorporated into the business reporting system in order to produce comparative reports. These reports are intended to provide managers with a monthly gauge of performance against plan. This budget versus the actual results report is usually presented in a format like that shown in Table 12-8.

Managers are responsible for developing and then managing by their budgets. Thus they are responsible for alignment between their budgets and their actual activities and results. Managers are also responsible for addressing any resulting variances and must analyze their results (often with assistance from accounting) and prepare a report to explain significant variances. They often use support from the accounting department coupled with their own understanding of the impacts of decisions they have made to identify things to continue doing and things to change.

Table 12-8 Budget Versus Actual Results Report

Department, Business Unit or Division:						
Budget versus actual report for the period ended [Month] 2000						
	Month			Year-to-Date		
Account	**Budget**	**Actual**	**Variance**	**Budget**	**Actual**	**Variance**
Sales						
Cost of goods sold						
Gross profit						
Selling, general, and administrative						
Operating profit						

Addressing Budget Variances

When confronted with either positive or negative variances, the manager should work with accounting to perform the following analyses to determine appropriate actions going forward:

- Is the information in the report accurate?
- What are the significant variances?
- What are the key issues with each variance: Why and how did they occur? Can they be managed or must they simply be accepted as outside the company's control?
- What which variances are due to timing, are temporary, and are permanent?
- How can positive variances be leveraged to perpetuate the benefits?
- How can the adverse impacts of negative variances be minimized?

These reports are usually reviewed with the next level of leadership to determine their support of the manager's plan as well as longer-term impacts and other adjustments that may need to be made to the corporate plan.

FINANCIAL ACUMEN

As we move from how accounting is performed to how to use the resulting financial statements, we find ourselves crossing over from the mechanics of how accounting works to how to analyze the results of

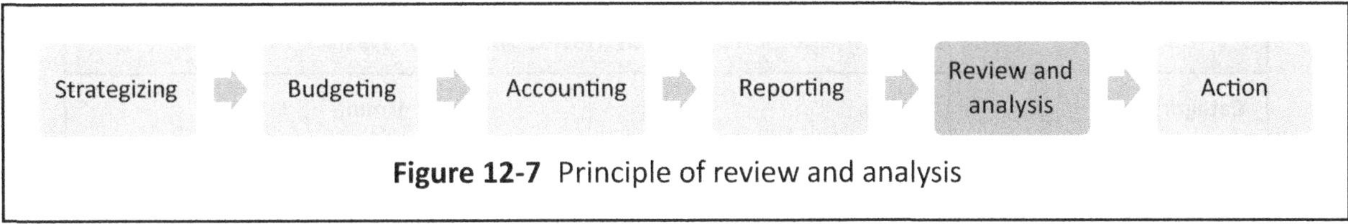

Figure 12-7 Principle of review and analysis

the accounting process. The components to this analysis include the performance of ratio analysis and horizontal or trend analysis coupled with a study of the footnotes and MD&A (Figure 12-7).

Fundamental Versus Technical Analysis

Fundamental analysis consists of reading through the financial statements, footnotes, and—for publicly traded companies—the MD&A for information about the health, performance, and strengths and weaknesses of the company.

Technical analysis helps investors determine when to purchase or sell a security. Fundamental analysis should be undertaken by the investor before applying technical analysis techniques. To do otherwise may indicate the investor is simply following the crowd when making investment decisions.

Types of Fundamental Analysis (Horizontal and Vertical)

Horizontal or trend analysis is the comparison of financial data over multiple reporting periods (see Chapter 16, Managing and Mastering Data). Differences in dollar amounts of a single account or category are computed and then the percent change is computed. Next, comparisons between related accounts are analyzed.

Vertical analysis is the review of related accounts or categories within a reporting period. This analysis pivots primarily on computing financial ratios and comparing them to prior periods to develop trends or to benchmarks—for example, industry standards, peer groups, and broader indexes.

Ratio Analysis

Financial ratios are part of the tool kit that makes up the key financial drivers of the business. They are referred to as lagging indicators because they are measures of things that have already occurred. Other drivers include customer service statistics, activity or volume tracking, and scrap rates. Collectively, these drivers are known as key performance indicators. Financial ratios are divided into subcategories, depending on the message they deliver (Table 12-9).

Managers of the business are responsible for identifying and managing key components of the income statement and the assets deployed in their business unit. Accordingly, they are tasked with managing the results of operations (income statement impacts) and the impacts their decisions have on the balance sheet.

For example, if your operating margin (income from operations divided by sales) was 10 percent last month but this month it dropped to 9 percent, you should understand how and why this happened. You

Table 12-9 Financial Key Performance Indicator Ratios		
Category	**Ratios**	**Formula**
Liquidity: identify the ability to meet short obligations as they mature	Current Ratio	current assets ÷ current liabilities
	Acid (or quick) ratio	$\frac{\text{cash + marketable securities + accounts receivable}}{\text{current liabilities}}$
Activity: determine the operating cycle and where and for how long the company ties up its working capital	Days sales (cost of goods sold) in inventory (DSI)	$\frac{\text{average inventory}}{\text{cost of goods sold} \times \text{days in reporting period}}$
	Inventory turnover	days in reporting period ÷ DSI
	Days sales in accounts receivable (DSO)	$\frac{\text{average receivables}}{\text{sales on credit} \times \text{days in reporting period}}$
	Receivable turnover	days in reporting period ÷ DSO
	Days in accounts payable (DAP)	$\frac{\text{average payables}}{\text{cost of goods sold} \times \text{days in reporting period}}$
	Operating cycle	DSI + DSO − DAP
Leverage: measure degree of financial risk related to liability versus equity capital	Total liabilities to total stockholders' equity	total liabilities ÷ total stockholders' equity
	Long-term debt to stockholders' equity	total long-term debt ÷ total stockholders' equity
	Long-term debt to total invested capital	$\frac{\text{total long-term debt}}{\text{long-term debt + stockholders' equity}}$
	Interest coverage	earnings before interest expense ÷ interest expense
	Debt coverage	$\frac{\text{current maturities of long-term debt}}{\text{cash flow from operations}}$

continued

Profitability: understand the operating performance of the company compared to benchmarks of competitors, other companies in general, and itself over time	Gross profit percentage	gross profit ÷ sales
	Operating profit percentage	income from operations ÷ sales
	Net profit percentage	net income ÷ sales
	Return on equity	net income ÷ stockholders' equity
	Return on invested capital (ROIC)	$\frac{\text{net operating profit after tax}}{\text{total invested capital}}$
	Return on assets	net income ÷ total assets
	Economic value added (EVA)	ROIC – weighted average cost of capital
Cash flow: gauge overall operating performance on a cash basis; understand ability to meet short-term debt obligations from operating cash flows	Cash flow return on investment	cash flow from operations ÷ total invested capital
	Cash flow coverage of long-term debt	$\frac{\text{cash flow from operations}}{\text{current portion of long-term debt}}$

analyze the changes in each line of the income statement, from sales to income from operations and identify:

- The key reasons for the decrease
- What cannot be controlled
- What can be controlled and by whom

Then you would produce your report for leadership and prepare to take all reasonable remedial actions.

The Operating Cycle

Start preparing your report by evaluating the operating cycle, which is made up of the activity ratios described in Figure 12-8.

The fundamental question is, What can be done to shorten the cycle in total days without jeopardizing relationships (with customers and vendors) and profitability (via sales volume, cost as a percent of sales, and avoiding back orders on inventory)? This is a basic analysis required of all enterprises to maintain efficiency and the highest profitability with the limited resources available (such as cash, inventory, receivables, and payables, otherwise known as *working capital*). The longer the cycle, the fewer times the enterprise can complete the cycle in a reporting period (for example, a year). The shorter the cycle, the more times it can be completed, thus yielding more sales and profits from the same amount of working capital.

- When your receivables rise without a requisite increase in sales, find out why. Who is paying slower than normal and why?
- When your inventory rises without a requisite increase in sales, find out why.
- When your payables cycle shrinks, determine if it is a managed change and the company is benefiting from early pay discounts or if your volume of activity has declined requiring a requisite decrease in accounts payable.

Continue by managing significant variances between budgeted and actual activities. Apply a rigorous review process to identify any unusual or unrecognized activity in your accounts. Consult with the accounting department to drill down as far as necessary, including a review of source documents supporting specific transactions and interviews with the people involved in initiating and authorizing said transactions to understand why things happened. Next determine whether any corrective action is needed and your best course of action.

Then evaluate key ratios and trend them over time within your business unit to identify anything unusual that may require further investigation. You may experience positive variances and will want to understand how they occurred and whether they can be leveraged in the future. For example, you learn that sales rose 5 percent over last month. What caused this and how can it be leveraged for a repeat this month and the next?

If information is available to permit benchmarking against the competition, perform a comparative analysis of your ratios with theirs to determine where you might be ahead of or behind the pack. In either situation, determine what you can do to leverage this information and adjust your tactics accordingly. Benchmarking information for public companies is available from their published quarterly and annual financial reports on their websites (required by the Sarbanes-Oxley Act) or the SEC website (www.sec.gov/edgar.shtml). Private company information is reported in summary by NAICS code (small groups of similar companies) by Robert Morris and Associates (www.RMAHQ.org) and Hoovers (www.Hoovers.com). Non-profits are required to report to the IRS on Form 990, and this information is available to the public upon request to the non-profit organization. Many such businesses post reports on their websites.

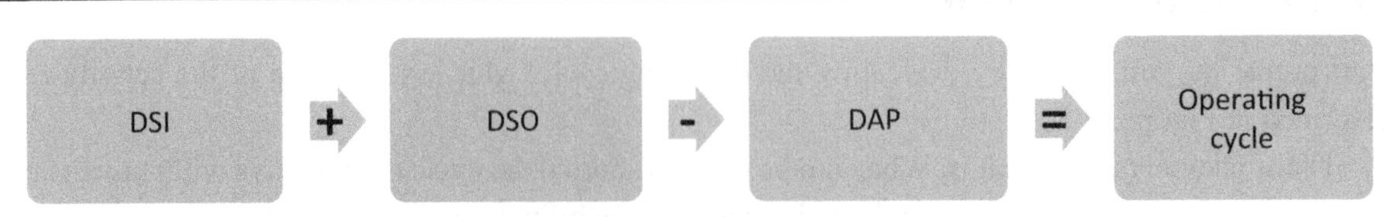

Figure 12-8 Operating cycle. *DSI*, days sales in inventory; *DSO*, days sales outstanding; *DAP*, days in accounts payable.

Myth: Finding the break-even point is as simple as figuring out when you make back the money you invested from the profits that the investment generates.

There are a number of variables that factor into measuring the profitability and break-even point, such as fixed and variable costs, volume, time, and methods of financing.

Profitability Analysis Using Price, Volume, and Variable and Fixed Costs

The basic profitability model applies a break-even point analysis. It is used by for-profit enterprises to determine the point at which it will stop losing money (the break-even point) and begin producing a profit. This model will provide managers with insights into the volume, pricing, costs, and overhead of a product, product line, or business unit. It will help establish the optimum sales price and provide a yardstick to determine when a product is likely to produce profits.

This type of analysis requires an understanding of cost and cost behavior. Here we apply the terms *variable costs* and *fixed costs*. Variable costs relate to production and are fixed per unit of production. They vary with changes in volume of production. Fixed costs do not vary with changes in volume. Some examples provided in Table 12-10 may help clarify these definitions. The basic model for performing this type of analysis calls for an assumed price and cost structure and a target operating profit (Table 12-11).

Assume the price of your product is $100, the variable costs to produce and sell it is $50, and the total fixed costs of the physical plant and overheads is $5,000,000. In order to break even (show neither a profit nor a loss), how many units must be sold? Table 12-12 provides the solution.

The variable costs are deducted from the sales price to determine the contribution margin per unit. Next, the target profit and the fixed costs are added together to determine the needed total contribution margin. Finally, the target total contribution margin is divided by the available contribution margin per unit to determine the total needed units of sales to reach the goal of zero profit.

If the desired profit is changed to $1,000,000. Now how many units must be sold to reach the target profit? See Table 12-13 for this solution.

Table 12-10 Variable Costs Versus Fixed Costs

Variable Costs	Fixed Costs
Total cost varies with changes in volume	Total cost does not change with changes in volume
Raw materials	Manufacturing overheads (machine costs, plant costs, and so on)
Direct labor	General and administrative costs (salaried personnel, human resources, IT, accounting, the C-suite, and so on)
Sales commissions	

Table 12-11 Cost Volume Profit Analysis

	Variable Costs Per Unit	Required Volume	Fixed, in Total Costs
Sales			
Variable costs			
Contribution margin			
Fixed costs			
Target profit			

Table 12-12 Cost Volume Profit Analysis: Break Even

	Variable Costs Per Unit	Required Volume	Fixed, in Total Costs
Sales	$100		
Variable costs	50		
Contribution margin	$50	100,000	$5,000,000
Fixed costs			5,000,000
Target profit			$0

This model may be applied to any business whether focused on manufacturing or services. Use the knowledge gained to raise awareness in cross-functional teams and to adjust your plans and tactics to improve profitability. For example, consider your sales representative who consistently lobbies for a decrease in sales price. She is convinced that this would lead to increased volume and higher profits. So, as her manager, you tested her assertions with this profitability analysis model and discovered that the suggested decreases would rarely translate into improvement in the bottom line (target profit). The model demonstrates that discounting price by, say, 10 percent will not improve results unless the volume rises by a larger factor. This is because the model is not linear. Using the model, you see a decrease in sales price of 10 percent requires an increase in sales volume of 11.6 percent just to sustain the target profit of $1,000,000. When you increase the sales price by the same percentage, the volume can drop 9.39 percent without profit erosion. Your conclusion is to work smarter not harder. Producing and selling less at a higher price may be a better tactic to improve bottom line performance.

Capital Expenditure Planning

Capital expenditure (CAPEX) planning covers a broad range of acquisitions, including asset purchases, leasing alternatives, make versus buy alternatives, outsourcing alternatives, and business mergers and acquisitions. It can be used by any enterprise.

Table 12-13 Cost Volume Profit Analysis: Target Profit			
	Variable Costs per Unit	Required Volume	Fixed, in Total Costs
Sales	$100		
Variable costs	50		
Contribution margin	$50	120,000	$6,000,000
Fixed costs			5,000,000
Target profit			$1,000,000

There are several phases or steps to planning for a capital expenditure:

1. Initial cash outlay requirements
2. Ongoing operational impacts of the acquisition (such as changes in sales, changes in variable costs, and changes in fixed costs as a result of the acquisition)
3. Financing requirements
4. Setting a benchmark or required rate of return for the project

Setting an appropriate benchmark rate of return for a project requires a knowledge of the company's weighted average cost of capital (WACC) and its current return on invested capital (ROIC). Both of these metrics require definition to help understand their relationship to one another and why they both help determine an enterprise's required rate of return on major asset additions.

Weighted Average Cost of Capital

WACC examines the enterprise's long-term debt and shareholders' equity. It then combines the after-tax cost of debt with the shareholders' demand for return on their investment in a weighted summary to determine the enterprise's cost of doing business. The math is shown in the chart above.

ROIC

ROIC measures the enterprise's operating performance compared to its long-term invested capital. The numerator is the net operating profit after tax (NOPAT) and the denominator is the sum of the enterprise's long-term debt and its equity. The equity is not drawn from the balance sheet, as this is the book value of the equity. Rather, it is measured at market value. Market value is equal to the average number of shares outstanding times the price of the equity at the measurement date. The measurement date should be correlated to the other data used in the computation, such as by the date of the financial statements.

ROIC = NOPAT ÷ total capital at market value

Capital Component	Formula		Weight Factor		WACC Factor
Long-term debt	$i \times (1 - t)$	×	debt / total capital	=	
Equity at market capital	$R_f + (R_{mp} \times \beta)$	×	equity / total capital	=	

i = weighted average interest rate on the long-term debt portfolio
t = effective tax rate of the enterprise
R_f = risk free rate of return (U.S. Treasury Bonds are a proxy for R_f)
R_{mp} = market premium, the amount of additional yield an investor expects when moving from risk free investments into equity investments. Use the market index the target equity trades under and subtract R_f to arrive at R_{mp}
β = volatility measure comparing the movement in the price of the equity security versus the index it trades under over a period of three to five years

EVA

ROIC and WACC are subtracted from one another to arrive at the company's Economic Value Added® (EVA). The formula is:

$$EVA = ROIC - WACC$$

When EVA is positive, the company and its investors enjoy a premium yield on invested capital. The minimum required rate of return for CAPEX candidates is the company's ROIC. Conversely, when EVA is negative, the company must take action to move the EVA in a positive direction or risk failure. The minimum required rate of return for CAPEX candidates is the company's WACC.

In addition, some projects may suggest more risk than others due to their extended time lines, volatile cash flows, delayed cash flows, and so on. In these situations, project-specific risk premiums should be added to the generally established hurdle rate for each candidate (explained later in the chapter).

Time Value of Money

Measuring the rate of return of a CAPEX candidate requires the use of time value of money principles, such as net present value, internal rate of return, and discounted payback.

Pro tip

A dollar tomorrow isn't as valuable as a dollar today. The value of future dollars are discounted due to the risk of never receiving tomorrow's dollar as well as a sort of penalty for not having access to it to use today.

Net present value (NPV) requires the evaluation of the expected cash flow impacts of a project over its entire estimated useful life, discounted back to the time period when the project was brought on line using the required rate of return as the discount rate (also known as the *project hurdle rate*). The concept of discounting assumes the longer one waits for the cash flow from the investment, the less it will be worth.

Discounting is the inverse of compounding. For example, suppose you have $1,000 to invest in a project (your present value). An opportunity comes up where you can make 10 percent on your money but you must keep it invested for three years. How much will your investment be worth at the end of the three years (your future value)? To answer, begin with the formula for future value of a single deposit:

$$FV = PV \times (1 + i)^n$$

In this formula, *PV* is the initial investment (present value), *i* is the estimated rate of return, *n* is the number of compounding periods to maturity of the investment, and *FV* is the future value to be obtained from the investment. In the example, we would multiply 1.1 times itself three times ($1.1 \times 1.1 \times 1.1 = 1.331$) to arrive at the future value of $1 in three years or 1.331. Next, multiply this future value factor by the present value (of $1,000) to arrive at our resulting payout (future value) of $1,331.

Using a CAPEX analysis model (shown later in this chapter), we will estimate the future cash flows for each year of the project. Our concern is to fairly match the *future* cash flows to the *initial* cash outlay for the investment to determine whether we meet our required rate of return (hurdle rate). Since the future cash flows are not received in the same time period as the initial cash outlay, they are not worth the same as the initial cash outlay. In order to be fair in the comparison of future dollars to today's dollars, we must adjust the future cash flows to what their value would be as if we received all of them today. To do this we turn to the formula for present value theory.

$$PV = 1/FV \text{ or } PV = 1/(1 + i)^n$$

So, we compute the present value of each future year of cash flow of the investment by first computing the future value factor for each year of the project using the hurdle rate. Next, invert the *FV* factor to arrive at the *PV* factor for each future year. Next, multiply each year's expected cash flow by the *PV* factor for the respective year of the cash flow. Then add all the discounted cash flows together to arrive at the PV of the cash flows (today's value of the future cash flows).

Table 12-14 Capital Budgeting Process: Investment Return Versus Cost of Capital

Hurdle Rate = ?	T0	Y1	Y2	Y3	Y4	Y5
Initial cash outlay						
Change in sales						
Decrease in expenses						
Increases in expenses						
Depreciation						
Operating income						
Tax expense						
Net income						
Add back depreciation						
Cash flow						

Scenario 1: Determining the Financial Viability of a New Project

Assume your department wants to purchase a new machine costing $50,000. The machine will permit an increase in output from an existing production line. Customer demand exists for the higher resulting volume (sales should increase by $8,000 annually). In addition, productivity and efficiency are expected to improve, saving operating costs of an estimated $20,000 annually. New operating expenses for the machine are estimated at $4,000 per year. The equipment has a life of five years and the company's income tax rate is 25 percent (combined federal and state). The company's ROIC is 10 percent, and its WACC is 8 percent. Should the project be undertaken on a financial level? These assumptions are presented in Table 12-15.

Table 12-15 Capital Budgeting Process: Determining Annual Cash Flows

Hurdle = **10%**	T0	Y1	Y2	Y3	Y4	Y5
Initial cash outlay	-50,000					
Change in sales		8,000	8,000	8,000	8,000	8,000
Decrease in expenses		20,000	20,000	20,000	20,000	20,000
Increases in expenses		-4,000	-4,000	-4,000	-4,000	-4,000
Depreciation		-10,000	-10,000	-10,000	-10,000	=10,000
Operating income		14,000	14,000	14,000	14,000	14,000
Tax expense	25%	-3,500	-3,500	-3,500	-3,500	=3,500
Net income		10,500	10,500	10,500	10,500	10,500
Add back depreciation		10,000	10,000	10,000	10,000	10,000
Cash flow	-50,000	20,500	20,500	20,500	20,500	20,500
Discount factor		0.909	0.826	0.751	0.683	0.621
Discounted cash flows	-50,000	18,636	16,942	15,402	14,002	12,729
NPV	$27,711					
IRR	29.9%					

Next, we selected a hurdle rate based on the company's trailing ROIC and WACC. Then we discounted the cash flows at this hurdle rate for years one through five years. Using the present value concepts—$PV = 1/FV$ or $1/(1 + i)^n$—we computed those present value factors at the hurdle rate or required rate of return (10 percent in this case) for each year of the project—for example, the year one discount factor is computed as $1/(1 + 0.10)^1$, or 0.909; the year two discount factor is computed as $1/(1 + 0.10)^2$, or 0.826; and so on through year five.

$1/(1 + 0.10)^1$, or 0.909; the year two discount factor is computed as $1/(1 + 0.10)^2$, or 0.826; and so on through year five.

Finally, we compare the sum of the discounted cash flows to the initial cash outlay, which is already stated in today's dollars and does not get discounted. The result is a positive NPV. Thus we can conclude the project generally makes financial sense.

As an added measure of profitability, we solved for the discount rate that would yield a zero NPV. This yields the internal rate of return (IRR) for the project. In this analysis, the IRR is 29.9 percent. The project is projected to produce a return of 29.9 percent, which is well above the company's required rate of return of 10 percent.

Other factors to consider include the discounted payback period, which is 2.94 years, and whether there are any additional risks not quantified by the model. A reminder on payback: To compute the time it takes to receive a payback of your initial investment, identify when the sum of the discounted future cash flows equals the initial cash outlay.

Projects competing for limited funding can be prioritized based on their internal rates of return. If competing projects have different lives or different initial cash outlays, the IRR ranking is the only method that will consistently provide an accurate comparison. Avoid applying the following ranking tools to your projects:

- Profitability index (which fails to account for differing project time lines)
- Equivalent annual annuity method (which fails to account for differing initial project cash outlays)

Finally, subtract the initial cash outlay from the PV of the future cash flows to arrive at the net present value (NPV) of the project. We analyze the result to determine whether the project has financial viability. If the NPV is positive, we have met and exceeded the required rate of return (hurdle rate). Conversely, if the NPV is negative, we failed to meet the required rate of return.

To this analysis we add the computation of the discounted payback. Here we determine the point in the future at which we are projected to receive our initial investment back from the discounted cash flows. The benchmark for this computation is industry and company specific. It depends on a number of factors, such as considering the estimated productive time horizon of the project, whether the cash flows are distributed evenly over the life of the project, seasonality and shut down, and cleanup costs at the end of the project's life. The shorter the estimated time line of the project, the faster we need a return of our initial investment (Table 12-14).

Operational Planning

The operational budget is a primary planning tool used to express strategy in monetary terms. Other planning tools include the capital budget. Together these budgets are used to determine the financing budget, the working capital budget, the resulting cash plan, and possibly, a short- and long-term financing plan.

• Conclusion •

Many companies suffer from failures at fundamental levels of management:

- Not developing refined strategic planes (failing to plan is planning to fail)
- Not communicating, or poorly communicating, corporate strategy
- Not translating strategy and goals into effective tactics and actions
- Not developing, communicating, and using effective key performance indicators
- Not releasing financial reports in a timely manner (within two days of month's end for managerial reports), rendering them relatively ineffective
- Not requiring managers to negotiate with each other to spread demands for decreased operating or production costs among themselves in the most effective manner, pulling back ownership of budget proposals to top leadership
- Not holding managers accountable for missing targets, goals, and budgets
- Not proactively training managers to manage and grow into higher levels of leadership
- Not giving managers room to maneuver, make mistakes, and learn from doing (micromanaging)

FAQs

Question 1: Where did the double entry system of accounting originate?

Answer 1: It originated in Italy in the late 1400s and was created by Luca Pacioli, deemed to be the father of current day accounting.

Question 2: I still don't understand the terms *debit* and *credit.*

Answer 2: Luca is referring to any ledger or journal of record of financial transactions in a business system, whether it be the general ledger, a supporting ledger or journal, and every entry in the ledgers and journals. Table 12-2 indicates that the debit entries are merely left side or left column entries while credit entries are right side or right column entries. Study the table and the surrounding guidance to solidify your understanding. For example, assume your paycheck of $1,000 is deposited into your bank. How does the bank record this event? See Table 12-16 for the solution. Next, write a check for Girl Scout cookies. How does the bank record the transaction? See Table 12-17 for the answer. How would these two transactions appear in your personal general ledger? See Table 12-18 for the answer.

Table 12-16 Debits and Credits: Paycheck Deposit			
Date	**Account Description**	**Debit**	**(Credit)**
1/31/2001	DDA payable: Ralph Pleasant		(1,000.00)
	Cash in bank	1,000.00	

Table 12-17 Debits and Credits: Girl Scout Cookie Purchase			
Date	**Account Description**	**Debit**	**(Credit)**
2/5/2001	DDA payable: Ralph Pleasant	$25.00	
	Cash in bank		(25.00)

Table 12-18 Debits and Credits: Bank Balance			
Date	**Account description**	**Debit**	**(Credit)**
1/31/2001	Cash in bank	1,000.00	
	Salary revenue		(1,000.00)
2/5/2001	Cash in bank		(25.00)
	Food expense	25.00	

What is your bank balance after these two transactions? Answer: $975.00 debit balance. Your perspective of your bank account is as an asset. How does the bank report your bank balance to you on your bank statement? Answer $975.00 credit balance. You see, the bank is looking at your account from their point of view. When you make deposits, they owe you more money, an increase in their liability to you. When you make payments from your account, they owe you less money. They are looking at the events in your account from their liability point of view and they are reporting them to you from their perspective. So you should view the bank reporting as backwards from your perspective, because it is.

Question 3: Are there other ratios besides those identified in this chapter?

Answer 3: There are several ratios related to specialized industries, such as banking. In addition, ratios can be computed using the statement of cash flow to provide an analysis of performance and financial strength from the standpoint of the cash generated from operations and then used to grow the business (cash flow from investing activities) or provided from financing activities (cash flow from financing activities). Also, remember that the story derived from a static (single time period) ratio analysis will reveal much more information when those results are trended over multiple time periods of equal length.

Question 4: Where can I find additional resources to extend my learning of this topic?

Answer 4: The internet is a very rich resource. Just Google your question. In addition, search your favorite bookstore for titles like Finance and Accounting for Nonfinancial Managers. There are several books with similar titles available to help you.

Question 5: My company wants to acquire additional operating capacity. As the manager, how should I go about evaluating the options?

Answer 5: Use discounted cash flow techniques described in the "Capital Expenditure Planning" section of this chapter. Apply these techniques whether you acquire another business with the desired capacity or you build the capacity yourself.

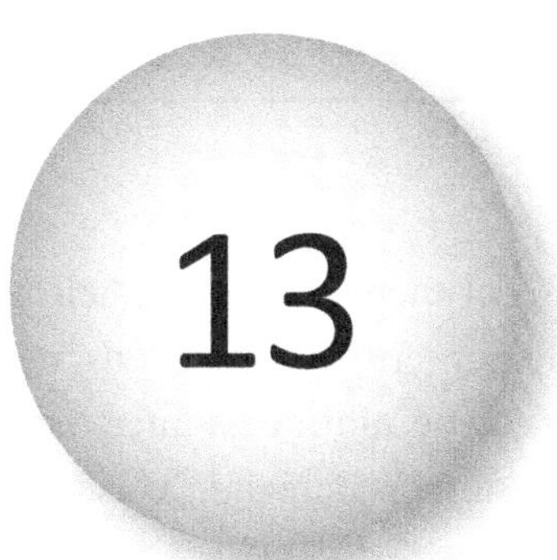

Customer Focus

LEARNING OBJECTIVES

By the end of this chapter, you will be better equipped to:

- Understand the purpose and practice of customer-focused decision making.
- Identify methods to listen to customers' needs and feedback.
- Recognize methods to design customer-centric experiences and reduce customer hassle.
- Develop methods to address customer exceptions and personalization.
- Develop ideas to inspire, coach, and empower employees to own customer experiences and deliver superior experience in every interaction.
- Recognize the importance and role of the internal customer as part of the external customer experience delivery.

Achieving these goals will allow you to manage your team more effectively and with greater sense of purpose, to be aligned with the organizational strategy, and to work more collaboratively with other parts of the organization.

CUSTOMER FOCUS: THE DEFINITION

In the last two decades, the era of the customer emerged as the most powerful disruptor to organizations worldwide. Equipped with online access to knowledge, price comparisons, customer opinions, and social media tools, customers redrew the relationships with their vendors. They are now in a position of power to demand higher quality products and fair pricing and with a customer experience that will re-

Pro tip

If we connect the dots, customer centric organizations deliver exceptional customer experiences by managing and optimizing the customer journey, which results in higher customer satisfaction.

spect them and solve their problems. To address the emerging customer era, organizations needed to recalibrate their operation to become more customer focused and respond faster to the evolving customer demand. Customer focus became the theme of those efforts.

Customer focus is the practice of proactively designing the organization's value around the customer's expectations and unmet needs and addressing internal and external customer needs to support business goals. Becoming customer centric creates a distinct alignment between all stakeholders in the organization and ensures that together they pursue the same goal, which is creating and retaining profitable customer relationships. To achieve this level of alignment, a manager needs to go beyond the superficial declarations of intentions, "we all love our customers" and create a nurturing environment in which every employee, and the team as a whole, are aware, trained, empowered, and measured on delivering value through the lenses of customer focus.

As such, being customer focused requires a mind-set that places the customer at the center of every decision, product design, new process deployment, and communication campaign. It starts with solicitation of customer feedback and active listening, with the intention of creating business value through customer-focused decisions and actions. This level of customer focus is applicable at every level of the organization, it is not relevant only to customer service functions or to product design departments. Everyone in the organization contributes in a direct or indirect way to the value created for customers; therefore, it's important to align their thinking, decisions, and actions to support the objectives of the customer-focused organization. While a human resource (HR) director may feel that his or department does not require customer-focused thinking, a deeper look into that role will unveil a significant responsibility. If The HR director recruits and hires people who are strong on the technical skill set and low on empathy or communication, for example, that director will be affecting the quality of experience delivered by the organization. The sales team or servicepeople who act on behalf of the organization will be lacking core skills required in a customer-focused organization.

Achieving it at a manager level, will require assessing team members' skills and readiness, coaching, and empowering employees at all levels to take action, resolving customer issues and delivering customer-centric value.

CUSTOMER FOCUS: THE OUTCOME

Customer focus, when delivered correctly, should result with impact on your business metrics and key performance indicators (KPIs). First and foremost, every organization needs to capture and retain its customers. Their metrics are directly linked to the customer behaviors and decisions to purchase more. A study comparing the S&P companies' stock return over a ten-year period, compares them to the stock return of the leading firms in customer experience. Forrester Research, a global research and advisory firm, discovered that leading customer experience companies were outperforming the S&P companies by a three-times factor. While the S&P firms' stock return was 75 percent over the ten-year period, the leading customer experience firms achieved a 213 percent return.[1] A study conducted by Strativity Group, a global experience design firm, in the automotive industry discovered that car dealerships who earned top of the customer satisfaction score were 59 percent more profitable than their counterparts who earned low satisfaction scores. When considering your customer-focused decision, link it to a business outcome and ensure that is equally beneficial for customers and the organization. The financial impact that a customer-focused behavior creates are measured in three key areas:

- *Increase Customer Loyalty*: Customer-focused decisions should lead to selling more products, finding new customers, increasing cross-selling and upselling opportunities for existing customers, and creating value that will increase customer retention.
- *Increase in Customer Advocacy*: Customers using social media and other tools create a greater circle of products fans through their personal recommendations.
- *Decrease in Cost to Serve*: Responding to customer's needs in a customer-focused manner often shortens the service time and the number of people engaged, driving down the cost to serve.

Research has shown that in addition to the customer impact, customer-focused organizations enjoy an additional benefit: increased employee retention. According to the Temkin Group, a customer experience firm, exceptional customer experience directly correlates to customer loyalty. The study of ten thousand customers demonstrates that 79 percent of customers who rank their experience as "very good," are likely to recommend the product or service to a friend, and 87 percent of those customers are likely to purchase again. Those numbers shrink as customer experience satisfaction decreases. On the other hand, 41 percent of customers who experienced a bad interaction with the organizations are likely to either stop purchasing or spend less with the brand.

Additional impact of customer focus is found among employees' engagement and retention. Employees who operate based on customer-focused principles feel a greater sense of purpose and accomplishment and as such tend to stay longer, hence reducing the costs of attrition.

It is imperative to recognize that customer focus is not just an additional competency required of you as a manager. It is a competency that will allow your organization to keep its promises to its customers and therefore achieve its business goals.

THE EVOLUTION FROM CUSTOMER CARE TO CUSTOMER EXPERIENCE

Since the evolution of scientific management, led by Frederick Winslow Taylor in the early twentieth century, companies were developed and evolved around products and efficient production. The prevailing thinking was that as long as products were good quality and available to customers, they would sell. Generations of entrepreneurs followed that model and focused their efforts on development of products that they could sell to the public.

As the art of product selling evolved in the 1960s, a new framework was developed to further establish it. The famous four Ps evolved from the term *marketing mix*, coined by Neil Borden, and were developed as a strategic framework for product success. Product, pricing, placement, and promotion were the pillars of strategic thinking. This product-centric approach has always assumed and taken the customer for granted. Products were mostly developed based on the ingenuity of entrepreneurs and were ready to surprise customers who didn't even know they needed those products. Many of those products were faced with rejections by customers who failed to understand how the product fits in their lifestyle. A case in point is the car radio, an innovation that took over thirty years to get widely accepted because customers saw more threat and risk in it (such as causing customers to fall asleep during driving) than value worth capturing.

During those years of product centricity, the way to handle customers was delegated to a department. Customer service departments were emerging as a way to calm down upset customers who didn't receive the promise value or who were tricked by overaggressive salespeople. The customer service department was often treated as an afterthought and was there merely to prevent upset customers from storming into headquarters with their complaints and issues.

As long as product quality and availability were not consistent, product centricity allowed companies to differentiate based on products and win in the marketplace. Simply put, customers didn't have much of a choice. The selection of quality products was not diverse, and product availability was widely inconsistent among regions.

The Shift to Six Sigma

As the Six Sigma and the total quality management (TQM) movements took off in the 1980s, many producers of inferior products were able to close the quality gap and produce better quality products at competitive prices. A case in point was the emergence of Japanese products, which moved to the top of customer considerations in electronics and automobiles after decades of being considered inferior to Western products.

These new competitors forced establishments to reconsider their competitive advantage. The core of value proposition started to shift from products to processes. Making products available, reliable, consistent, and fast were the cornerstones of the new value proposition. Companies started to differentiate based on their ability to deliver products reliably, and standards such as ISO 9000 (a set of guidelines for quality management systems) and business process reengineering helped organizations optimize their processes and operation. FedEx and UPS, with their regional logistics centers and overnight delivery service revolutionized the new value proposition and supported the shift toward the reliable availability of products. But eventually, product reliability became merely table stakes and was easily copied by all competing players. Organizations were again facing the challenge of how to differentiate in the marketplace.

This time, however, the search for value met new customer trends that forced companies to rethink their approach altogether. In the last century of product centricity, organizations had a significant advantage over customers. They controlled the information and distributed it at their own pace and quantity.

They often knew more about their products than their customers and shared only what they deemed necessary to make the sales. The power of information was on the organization's side.

The Internet

The Internet, however, ushered in a new era of customer power. Information became more readily available by both institutions and individuals. Customers gained free access to product knowledge and could easily compare prices, qualities, and customer views. The information advantage, which was traditionally held by organizations, shifted quickly to customers. They now had the upper hand and started to demand a different, more reciprocal relationship with their vendors. A great example is the consumer pressure on Nike and other fashion companies who manufacture in Asia. The difficult conditions of employees in Asian factories resulted in consumer revolt, and forced Nike and others to reevaluate those conditions and demand better treatment of employees, even though those employees all worked for outsourced companies and were not directly employed by Nike. Growing customer awareness, due to the widespread knowledge provided by the Internet, combined with social media, which provided greater voice to all, ushered in the age of the empowered customers who require organizations to redefine their relationships and the value they deliver to highly informed and empowered customers. Customers now demand and expect a more personal experience. Welcome to the customer-focused organization.

Newly empowered customers discovered they had a greater voice and impact than before. Equipped with online tools and like-minded people, customers started to assert their rights and demand a better experience across the whole customer journey they experienced with their vendors. As such, the practice of customer experience and the need to become customer focused evolved from a department and into an organization-wide practice. Thinking about customers was now core to the future of the organization and required dedicated efforts by *everyone* at the organization. Thinking about customers became the new competitive advantage. The customer was brought to the center stage and is now sitting at the executive conference table.

The expansion of customer thinking and focus from a department to everyone and the elevation of customer focus from managing customer interactions to a strategic discipline gave rise to the new practice of customer centricity. This discipline required a new management framework and new tools and techniques to enable organizations to make decisions and deploy products and programs that are relevant to customers and place the customer at the center of them all. Being customer focused became the new competitive advantage. While all organizations have pursued this focus, the rate of success of shifting from product centricity to customer centricity has differed widely. Those who made the shift faster had a greater chance of succeeding in the marketplace.

CUSTOMER FOCUS: THE COMPETENCY MODEL

As demonstrated in Figure 13-1, the customer focus competence consists of five key elements.

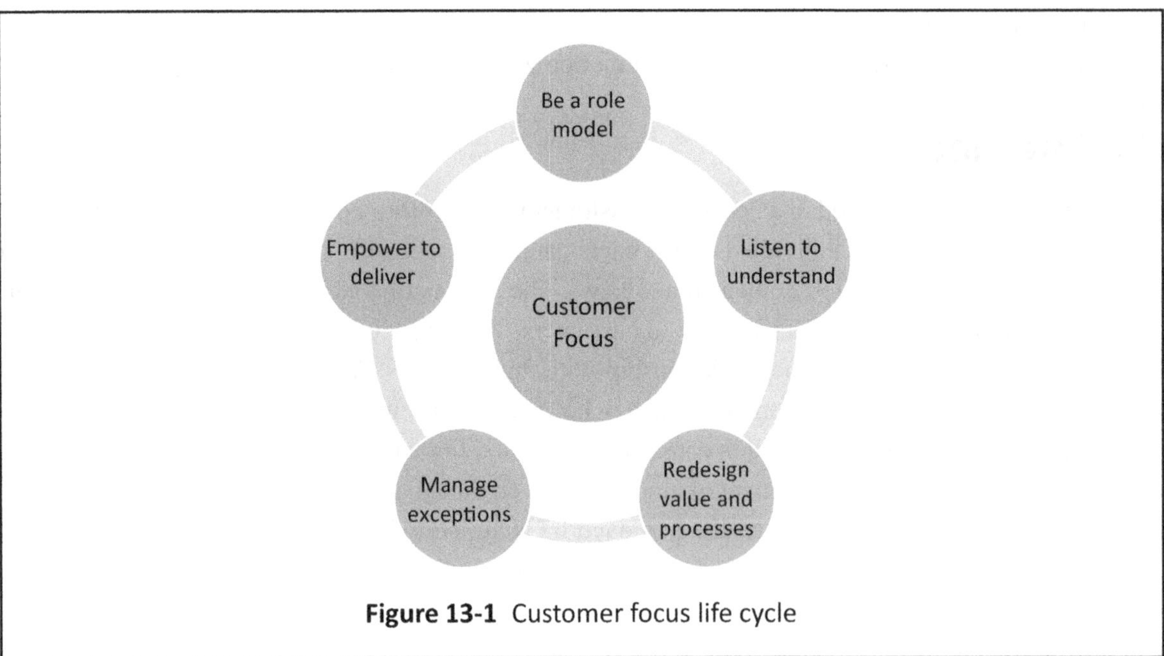

Figure 13-1 Customer focus life cycle

Be a Role Model

Ultimately being customer focused starts with you. If you demonstrate the thinking, decision making, and behaviors you seek from your employees through your everyday performance, they will be more likely to follow you (see Chapter 2, Emotional Intelligence).

Take a quick look at your everyday routines and the way you conduct team meetings. Those two examples illustrate opportunities to weave in customer-focused thinking and behavior and to model the behavior you seek from your employees. As a manager, you should be asking yourself:

- How much time do I dedicate to the customer during a team meeting?
- Is the customer a central theme of our meeting and discussion?
- Do we apply the customer viewpoint to the way we consider alternatives and make our decisions?
- How often do we speak about the customer during our ongoing communication, both oral and written?
- How much time do we dedicate to listen to the voice of the customer?
- How do we respond to customers' requests related to us directly or indirectly through other departments in the organization?
- What is our attitude toward customer complaints? Do we treat them as a burden or as an opportunity to create loyalty?

By reflecting on these questions, you will be able to start painting the picture that your employees see. They do follow your actions and approach. If you model a customer-focused approach, they will follow.

Here are some quick ideas you can start incorporating into the way you lead and so become the champion of customer centricity.

- When possible, start your day by contacting a customer and thanking that person for his or her the business.
- Review regular customer surveys to identify opportunities.
- Start every meeting with a customer story describing the customer's challenges, emotions, and opportunities.
- Volunteer to meet customers face to face, if this is not part of your current responsibility.
- If appropriate, and agreed to by the salespeople, go with them to see customer.
- If possible and deemed worthwhile, spend time at the contact center to get a true appreciation of customers' needs.
- Remind your employees that customers are the reason we are employees and that customers pay our bills.
- Connect employees to the organization's mission.
- Speak about customers as human beings not budgets or quotas.
- Share personal examples of your experience as a customer, encouraging others to share their experiences.
- Demonstrate empathy when customer problems arise.

Being a role model is critical to creating a customer-focused environment among your employees. If you want them to understand that the customer is everyone's job, you need to start by demonstrating that it is *your* number one job too.

Listen to Understand

Being customer focused is more about listening than about telling. Oftentimes we think we know what the customer wants based on our previous interactions with other customers. This is a common mistake we ought to avoid. Treat each customer as a unique human being, make no assumptions, and listen in order to deeply understand the customer's viewpoint and needs.

Product-centric companies are often listening to customers in a biased way. They have a solution, and they are looking for the problem that will cause customers to buy that solution. It is like the "law of the hammer." The salesperson who sells hammers sees everything as a nail. After all, she has the solution for nails. The listening that product-centric companies conduct is with predefined intentions of selling not of creating new value for customers. In a customer-focused organization, the listening is equated to a blank piece of paper. We are listening in the purest way with the goal of learning new things and then going back to design a customer centric experience that customers will desire and ultimately purchase. Such listening requires a different approach.

While traditional customer listening is done in the form of interviews and surveys, those are often biased by the type of questions we ask, and they often lead to the answers we expect. In customer-focused listening, we try to elevate listening to a pure and unbiased level so we can learn new insights. The following list provides several methods we can use to ensure we are truly listening to the customers and gaining meaningful insights. For more about listening, see Chapter 1, Communication, and Chapter 2, Emotional Intelligence

- Design questions that are exploring possibilities not validating assumptions.
- Use third-party vendors to ensure objectivity of your research.
- Use natural sources to understand your customers (such as social media discussions instead of relying on deliberate surveys that may not fully expose the customer's view) so you can observe them in their natural ecosystem rather than intervening with targeted questions.
- Conduct ethnography exercises in which customers share their emotions more freely.
- Seek to understand clues, pain points, and situations not solutions; you are in charge of developing solutions, but customers can provide clues for new ideas.
- Refrain from providing solutions, just allow for the listening to happen.
- Ask probing questions to fully understand customers' intentions, then expand your questions to understand the impact of issues on customers' lives, emotions, and pain points.
- Focus on emotions and seek to understand each customer's emotional state when he or she interacts with your organization
- Use images, personal journals, observations, and other methods to solicit customer insights.

The tendency to focus on quantitative data gathering and customer listening often prevents the organization from identifying new opportunities and deeper customer issues and aspirations. Getting comfortable with qualitative insights and the emotional state of the customer may take time, but it will provide greater, more meaningful insights to guide you on the journey to become customer focused.

Redesign Value and Processes

Based on the insight you gather from customers, you should align your products, programs, processes, and overall value proposition to fit customer needs and expectations. This requires developing new skill sets that allow you to apply human-centric design (HCD) and customer-focused thinking to your programs and processes design. HCD is a design and management framework that places the human perspective at the center of the design process. For example, when designing a new cancer treatment center, a hospital focused on efficiency and trying to serve as many patients as possible every day. That design assumption resulted in a plan to minimize patients' wait time. However, after consulting with patients, the hospital discovered that many wanted to stay and engage with other patients because they were seeking a support group of like-minded people. The efficiency design principle was in conflict with a human-centric design and ignored the emotional needs of the customers. From the initial definition of needs through the actual design of features, user interface and any other aspect of the final product is filtered through the human experience. For product-centric organizations, HCD does not come naturally. Oftentimes research and development people see their knowledge as superior to the customer's knowledge. In the past, they used the customer to validate but not to innovate. With HCD, the customer is integral to the whole design and development process, and the human voice is expressed and seen in the final outcome.

Manage Exceptions

The product-centric company treats all customer issues as part of a process. They design processes and policies that are supposed to address customer issues in the same exact way. This approach ignores the unique customer situation that no two customers are the same. In a customer-focused approach, organizations approach each customer as a unique individual and seek to find a creative solution for each customer's needs or exceptions. The flexibility to manage exceptions separately and address certain situations uniquely is critical but requires a new approach to processes and policies. Companies can no longer hide behind their processes and try to force the customer to accept them. They need to use the processes smartly when they are applicable. However, recognize that when those processes do not apply, you need to provide a creative solution that addresses the customer's wants and within the customer's context. As a manager, you will need to develop this new skill set of managing exceptions. If your organization is compliance focused and ridden with policies and processes, most likely your employees will not be ready to embrace exception management and will prefer to hide behind the well-defined policies. Evaluate your policies and talk to your supervisor about the most appropriate course of action. (For more on this, see Chapter 14, Talent Management.)

Your approach to preparing your team for handling exceptions should include:

- Defining examples of exceptions and how to address each one of them
- Illustrating how different customers who seek the same product may be using it in a different way
- Providing emotional context for exceptions, such as a passenger who missed her flight (rational pain point) but is in distress because she is missing her best friend's fortieth birthday and is sorry to disappointer her (emotional context)
- Allowing exceptions to be managed outside the typical KPIs and measurements so employees will feel confident applying a solution (remembering such solutions support the organization's goals of creating lasting and profitable customer relationships)
- Creating an exception tracking KPI to acknowledge that it is an integral part of your customer-focused approach
- Reviewing and tracking how exceptions are managed by employees
- Providing coaching and recognition to increase the commitment to exceptions management

Often employees are frustrated when they are implementing a policy they know does not fit the customer's expectations. With exception management, we can do the right thing by the customer but also by the employees. Developed and implemented correctly, exception management becomes another way your organization fulfills its brand promise and becomes truly customer focused.

Empower to Deliver

Empowering your employees to be able to respond to customer needs as they interact with them is key to success. Customers prefer to work with individuals who are in a position to solve their problem(s) and not automatically escalate it to managers. Empowerment is key to giving your employees the tools and authority to manage the responsibilities you gave them.

Do not assume, however, that all employees are seeking empowerment right away. For many, empowerment may represent learning a new skill set. For others, it might be a reminder of the last employee who took initiative and then was let go. They will approach empowerment with caution. Your goal in empowerment is not just to provide it, but to inspire people to actually use it. Here are some guidelines to launch your empowerment program:

- Develop case studies that illustrate the uniqueness of each customer and how a simple request may mean something different to different customers.
- Conduct training to clarify what empowerment is and how to use it.
- Conduct role-plays to develop employee confidence in the empowerment you provide them.
- Provide tools so employees are able to manage exceptions in a responsible way.
- Support your employees even if they solved a problem differently from the way you would have.
- Celebrate employees who take advantage of empowerment, especially during the early stages of the journey to being customer focused.

For employees who were trained to enforce policies, exceptions management and the concept of empowerment can be scary and counterintuitive. Implemented correctly, managing exceptions can be liberating and inspiring as the employees discover the trust you have in them to do the right thing by the customer. It is important, both by example and via written guidelines, to be clear about where and how exceptions can be made and what lines cannot be crossed.

One last word of advice: Many managers also find empowerment to be a scary concept. They are concerned employees will make mistakes, but they, as managers, will have to bear the consequences. Other managers fear empowerment will render them redundant. Empowerment is a sign of leadership strength. Strong leaders know empowerment does not take away from their power but rather amplifies their influence. The more empowered their employees, the greater their impact. As for employees' mistakes, yes, they will happen. Just as you made mistakes when you started. Mistakes are part of the learning process, and trying to avoid them is stripping the organization and your employees from their ability to grow. More important, this deprives the customer from better solutions and a better experience from empowered employees. Rather than trying to avoid all mistakes, companies should focus on failing fast and making adjustments quickly after learning from those mistakes.

DELIVERING CUSTOMER FOCUS AS A MANAGER: THE BEHAVIORS

Several behavioral guidelines support managers' efforts to deliver a customer-focused message and increase their competence in this area. When these behaviors are mastered consistently across an organization or team, customer-focused competency is elevated and customer relevancy is ensured.

The Customer Is You

Think about yourself as the customer and how you would like to be treated in a specific situation. Lead employees by example when you interact with colleagues who will be your internal and external customers. Your actions should demonstrate a commitment to continuously deliver value to customers through ongoing listening, design, and actions. Reflect on the way you start your day and make up your daily schedule; then ask yourself what you could do to demonstrate your commitment to customers through small visible actions. As suggested earlier, one way is to contact a customer every day to thank him or her for doing business with you (without soliciting additional business). This sends a clear message to your team about your priorities.

Listen beyond Words

While customers know their pains or needs, they don't always know the solution. To get to the solution, we need to listen to the complete verbal and nonverbal story shared by the customer. Treat each customer as a unique individual and use active listening to capture each person's needs. Listening beyond words requires training for a new skill set (see Chapter 1, Communication, and Chapter 2, Emotional Intelligence). Employees are usually trained to listen with a corporate perspective and respond with predetermined corporate answers. To learn to listen beyond words, consider the following techniques you can deploy with your team:

- Discuss the role of emotions and how important it is to see the full picture of the customer, verbal and emotional as one.
- Strive always to show customers that you and the organization care about them and want them to feel good about their experience with you. You will be surprised how many of employees refrain from doing so because they think there is no room for emotions in the workplace.
- Focus on words that evoke the right listening and avoid those that create barriers. Choose emotional-evoking, authentic language, and customers will feel freer to share.
- Choose your questions carefully, avoiding yes and no questions and focusing on open-ended questions that solicit real answers.

- Practice open-ended conversations with your employees; use language and express emotions that are authentic to the situation. Help your employees feel comfortable conducting such conversations with customers.

Optimize Processes

In a customer-focused organization, employees at all levels understand and appreciate that customers' needs drive the process, program, product, and service design. There is a clear recognition that doing the right thing by the customer should result with the right thing for the organization.

THE MANAGERIAL COMPETENCE OF CUSTOMER FOCUS

Being customer focused is not just a matter of declarations, as some think. This is not about posting some pictures with inspirational statements to think about customers in everything you do. It is a diligent way of placing the customer at the center of every decision and ensuring that every aspect of the organization's performance is designed to attract, add value, and retain customers. In short, being customer focused goes beyond a mind-set and into a set of seven tasks and activities. In the following sections, we highlight those tasks and the actions required to deliver on them.

Task 1. Establish the Role of Customer Focus to Achieve Business Results

To establish the role of customer focus, you need to create clear alignment between being customer focused and achieving the metrics and KPIs of your department(s). Every employee needs to see customer focus as the way to achieve his or her objectives. To do this, review the objectives and tasks of your employees and make sure they have a line of sight as to how they impact customers. In addition, review employees' performance metrics and ensure they are held accountable to customer-related metrics, such as satisfaction scores, customer lifetime value, and complaint reductions. From cost reduction and improving profitability, customer-focused decisions and programs deliver exceptional results to organizations. You need to analyze the impact of customer focus on your team's objectives and performance and inform all employees so they see customer focus as the North Star of the organization's performance.

Task 2. Actively Solicit Customer Feedback to Understand Customer Needs, Aspirations, and Issues

We often think we know what customers want, we assume and then miss the target. This misconception occurs because, after serving millions of customers, you assume customers are all the same and their preferences never change. Both assumptions are incorrect. Design a method for constantly engaging with a fresh customer perspective that challenges assumptions and provides fertile ground for new ideas to improve the customer experience. Your organization already has multiple tools for customer feedback, from a voice-of-customer system to custom market research, tap into those and share your insights with your employees. Some simple ways to get started include:

- Visit the company's contact center and listen to calls.
- Ask operations to share the most common customer complaints, especially complaints that point out existing workflow problems or recurring mistakes.
- Ask the market research department to share customer studies.
- Conduct phone-based interviews with new customers who selected your brand.
- When appropriate, conduct interviews with departing customers who left your brand.
- Ask sales for the most common customer objections to buying the products.

Each of these sources of knowledge will enrich your understanding of the customer and provide new insights to reflect on and potentially solve.

Task 3. Insights without Actions Are Wishful Thinking

You need to take actions on the insights you have received from the customer feedback. And you need to do it fast before your competitors take actions. To do so, you need to treat customer-focused innovation as a discipline and not as an ad hoc activity. Develop a systematic design process to create processes and programs that deliver customer value. Such systematic design process should include a checklist to ensure your design is always customer centric.

Here's an example of a checklist for a customer-focused approach:

- Review and map all relevant customer data.
- Conduct a customer journey map to identify all customer touchpoints associated with the relevant episode or process to be designed.
- Validate any proposed change or design with customer feedback.
- Align your team members to the different aspects of the customer journey so they can gain a line of sight as to the impact each has.
- Gather insights from each team member regarding the areas each can impact and ways to do it.
- Apply the proposed design to a customer persona to ensure fit.
- Include emotional context in your design.
- Validate with customers before launch.
- Consider including customers during the design process.

Note that customer focus is often about behaviors and not just process design. When behaviors are coupled with process design, the best outcome is achieved. When reaching deep understanding and connection with the customer's viewpoint and challenges, your employees will be better suited to assume the right behaviors. As a manager, you can make the most impact by helping your team see the customer as a unique individual and as a person in need, whom employees have the responsibility to help within the confines of their personal power.

Ensure that your innovation and design mechanisms consider the complete customer journey and not just the phase in the journey that your team is responsible for. It is easy to have a myopic view and focus on just your part of the process. For example, if you lead a sales team, you will focus on the process of closing the deal. You will likely neglect the invoicing process, which you consider to be the finance department's responsibility. However, the invoicing process is an integral part of the sales process, from the customer's perspective. The customer expects it to be as pleasant as the sales process. Your team members need to see the whole picture from the customers' perspective as they approach the process design. The customer sees the complete journey, and you need to make sure that your innovation provides a holistic solution for the customer. Doing so may require collaboration across different departments and sharing the innovation and design process. Such collaboration is further evidence for customer-focused thinking (see Chapter 6, Collaboration).

The innovation process can be a simple ideation workshop in which you use creative tools to reimagine the customer experience or immersive sessions of living in the customer's lifestyle and conditions to better appreciate the customer's physical and emotional needs. The main purpose in whatever path you take is to propose and create solutions and processes that address customer needs and create a pleasant experience.

Following the innovation, is execution. Ideas are powerful only when they are deployed in real life. Make sure the innovative design you initiated passes the plot stage and is implemented on a large-scale process or program (see Chapter 11, Managing Projects). It will require some change management skills (see Chapter 10, Managing Change) and negotiations (see Chapter 7, Influence) across the organization.

Task 4. Complementing the Customer Focus through Innovation and Process/Culture Redesign

Your employees need to own their part of the experience and deliver a performance that demonstrates the organization's commitment to customer-focused performance. They need to care for each customer as if he or she were the only one who mattered at that moment and deliver empowered solutions to reduce hassle and increase customer satisfaction. To achieve that level of commitment, you ought to create a culture of customer-focused accountability by engaging all employees to own every experience.

Culture redesign consists of inspiration as well as clear performance guidelines. Create mind-sets and develop culture frameworks and principles to guide employees through the desired behaviors. Make sure to role-play the desired performance and ensure all employees understand the scope of empowerment in their hands to solve customer issues without escalating to a manager.

While most managers want to believe that they are empowering, it is important to ensure that employees see it that way. Empowerment goes beyond a promise to have an employee's back. It requires creating a tool kit for success, empowering every employee to own customer issues. This tool kit should document the scope of empowerment and should provide examples, visuals, and online and onsite training to ensure every employee is willing, capable, and ready to deliver customer-focused performance. At a leading U.S. airline, the tool kit for success includes a mobile device with all the relevant passenger information and the authority to compensate an upset customer on the spot with either cash or air miles. The tool kit includes guidelines that support the flight attendant's decisions, so the employee can feel safe when using the tool kit. By providing relevant customer information (such as name, status of loyalty, and mileage account number) and the authority and guidelines to compensate, the airline empowers employees to do the right thing at the right moment without exacerbating customer complaints and allowing for negative emotions to fester.

Such a tool kit for success should include the following:

- Clear, documented empowerment guidelines
- Examples of the right and wrong way to use the empowerment
- Authority and funds to compensate or do the right thing
- Training on how to use the empowerment correctly
- Review of successful usage of the empowerment
- Access to customer data in order to make the right decision
- Support of employees who use the tool kit incorrectly to ensure other employees that is safe to use the empowerment

Task 5. Success Is Achieved When Measured

Measuring success is applicable to customer-focused performance. As a manager, you ought to establish clear metrics and track them across your organization. The selected metrics should be clear and achievable, so every employee can understand how he or she contributes to the completion of the metric. Customer satisfaction, reduction of customer complaints, and increase in customer referrals are some of the metrics associated with tracking customer-focused performance. If your team is responsible for account receivables, creating a target around sales growth may be irrelevant for your team. But the ability to resolve customer complaints within one interaction is an excellent example of both customer focus and cost reduction.

Task 6. People Do What They Are Paid to Do

If you want your employees to assume a customer-focused approach, then give them the right incentives and rewards to do so—for example, allocating a portion of their annual bonus to achieving the customer-focused metrics or gifting a dinner for two to employees who demonstrate an "above and beyond" customer-focused initiative. Nonmonetary rewards can be effective as well, if financial conditions are difficult. If you select to use a nonmonetary reward, such as dinner with the CEO, a free day of volunteering, or a special certificate, ensure that the reward is in fact desirable and implementable.

Dedicate a budget to your reward and recognition program, and pay attention to early adapters who assumed a customer-focused mind-set before the majority of the team did. You need to quickly recognize these early adapters, to signal to the rest of the team that customer focus is not a fad and will not disappear in a matter of weeks.

Task 7. Failure As a Path to Success

Since customer focus is about understanding unique customer needs and addressing them individually, it is likely that failure will be an integral part of the path to success. Coach employees who fail to embrace the customer-centric culture (see Chapter 9, Coaching for Performance). Create an environment that analyzes failure and mistakes, allowing them to happen as long as they are part of a learning environment. Let your employees feel comfortable experimenting, knowing that you will be there to support and guide them.

CONTEXTUAL SCENARIOS FOR THE COMPETENCY

To further apply the customer-focused competency, examine the chapter's three scenarios and the manager's customer-focused responses.

Scenario 1: The Customer Feedback Is Here

Jeff is a team leader of the customer care team and is responsible for customer complaints and issues. The monthly customer feedback report, which is based on customer surveys, was released and this month it showed a sharp decrease in customer satisfaction. The primary reasons raised by customers included areas that are under your responsibility as a manager. Several customer comments point to specific issues and individuals who are working for you, the manager.

Initial Response

Jeff issues a detailed memo explaining why the decrease in customer satisfaction was caused by factors out of his control. Due to the flu, he was short of staff, and there was a spike in invoicing errors. The combination of the issues resulted in customers who didn't receive the responses they needed. He proposed to ignore that month's report and wait for a report that more accurately reflects typical conditions.

The Customer-Focused Response

Jeff's manager, Heather, initiated a conversation with Jeff to better understand the reasons behind his memo and lack of accountability. While recognizing his arguments, she focused the conversation on four key questions:

1. What did you do within your power and proactively during the period in question to alleviate customer issues and complaints?

2. Did you seek external help to cover for the shortage in staff?
3. Is there any followup we can do with upset customers and offer them some form of apology or compensation?
4. What's the plan to avoid or prepare for a similar situation in the future?

Together they developed a short- and long-term plan that will address customers' issues, attempt to rectify the damaged relationships, and develop a contingency plan for the future.

"After all," Heather said, "our internal issues are not the customers' fault or interest."

Scenario 2: Redesigning a Process

For customers to return or replace your software, they need to follow several steps before a refund will be issued. The customer needs to submit in writing the reason for the cancellation, provide proof that the software was removed from any computers, and be subject to a call to verify the reason for the departure. After further investigation, you discovered that the multistep process was established in the 1980s when software was sold on disks and later on CD-ROMs, when there was a risk of purchasing one license and then using it in multiple computers. Now, that programs are downloaded and activated electronically, customers were unhappy following the process, and it further aggravated their negative emotions toward the company. It's time to simplify the process. However, the legal department is refusing to change it, citing legal exposure and potential software theft.

The Customer-Focused Response

Work with your team to build the case for the proposed change. Illustrate how using the antiquated approach is likely to result in further damage to the company in the form of negative customer advocacy and social media exposure.

- Set up a workshop to assess and consider alternatives to the current process. Make sure that all relevant stakeholders are represented, including legal, finance, and sales.
- Map all the relevant stakeholders' concerns and issues.
- Develop an approach that addresses those issues.
- Isolate extreme cases from the mainstream design to ensure you are not penalizing most of the honest customers.
- Design a new process with stakeholders and propose a timeline to pilot the new process.
- Pilot the newly designed process.

- Assess success of the pilot and adapt when needed.
- Communicate effectively the rationale for the change and the way the change will take place.
- Celebrate your success and use it as fuel to tackle more non-customer-focused processes.

Throughout the process, refrain from being the master solution maker and empower your people to think differently. If needed, benchmark against other companies outside of your industry to get ideas and reaffirmation of what is the right way to simplify the process and make it more customer centric.

Scenario 3: The Upset Customer

The Smith family planned for their annual vacation since Christmas. Dave, Dianne, and their three children Donna, Derek, and Darlene were excited to board the plane to Hawaii. A traffic accident on the highway delayed their plans and they arrived twenty-five minutes after the plane left the gate. Amy, the airline gate agent, was staring at them blankly and instructed them to call the customer service helpline to be re-booked. "The next available flight is not until tomorrow afternoon" she declared with an attitude. "You should have left your home earlier and accounted for such unknowns."

The Smiths demanded to speak to a supervisor, and that is when Paul got involved. He listened to them intently and empathized with them. "Please allow me to speak with Amy, and we will get back to you shortly." Paul then excused Amy to a back room and conducted the following conversation.

He asked Amy: "If this had been your sister and her family, what would you have done?"

After acknowledging that she would have approached the problem differently, Paul coached Amy to follow these customer-focused principles:

1. Share empathy and acknowledge the hardship and disappointment.
2. Offer the family the use of a lounge where snacks and other amenities are available.
3. Provide them with the option of flying with a connecting flight.
4. Remind the family to call their hotel in Hawaii and notify them about their delay.
5. If relevant, offer a discount to a nearby hotel.
6. Thank them for choosing the airline for their vacation.

"Customers always have options, and they chose to fly with us," Paul said. "We should always be there to help them and show our gratitude."

CUSTOMER-FOCUSED SUCCESS FACTORS

Customer-focused behaviors and performance deliver financial results. It is the way to achieve your goals. The benefits of practicing a customer-focused behavior include:

- Better business results, such as sales growth, customer retention, and customer satisfaction
- Greater collaboration between employees who are operating on the same agenda, which reduces friction and increase speed of execution
- Increased sense of purpose and fulfillment among employees, which increases employee retention and lower costs of attrition
- Greater sense of self-satisfaction and personal achievement, which reduces personal stress
- More time to plan and manage when employees are empowered to address customer issues, which allows you to reach greater goals and gain a sense of growth and advancement

Lack of customer focus creates a culture of helplessness and low engagement among employees. A high dependency of the manager to solve all problems leads to lack of empowerment and creates an environment of firefighting and finger pointing. Such culture does not maximize employee productivity and makes many doubt the reason they work for the company. After all, employees want to feel empowered and that they make a difference. Being customer focused creates indispensable pride, which makes employees stay even during tough times. It sends employees home every day feeling like paper pushers not impact creators. The ultimate impact is more upset customers and highly demoralized employees.

FAQS AND COMMON MISUNDERSTANDINGS OFTEN SEEN WITHIN CUSTOMER FOCUS

The following are common misconceptions often associated with a customer-focused approach. In this section we provide you with messages and communications to address such misconceptions.

- *Customer Focus Is Part of the Customer Service Department*: Customer focus is not just the role of customer service; it is everyone's job. Every employee, every manager contributes to the value delivered to customers and, as such, is responsible to be customer focused.
- *Customer Surveys Are Chasing for a Score*: Customer surveys are not about a score; they are about learning how to improve. If deployed correctly, they will be a gold mine of ideas for the future and will serve as alerts of things that need to be improved before it is too late.

- *Customer Focus Is About Giving Away Stuff for Free*: Customer focus is not about giving customers everything they want; it is about being diligent and doing the right thing by the customer and the organization.
- *Empowerment Is Giving Away the Shop*: Empowerment does not mean free license to spend recklessly; it is about the responsibility and accountability to do the right thing in each situation.
- *Customer Focus Is Optimizing Processes*: Customer focus is not a process; it is about adapting to each customer's needs. It may include some process optimization. However, that is not the goal, it is merely a tool, if it is relevant. The goal is delivering customized personalized value that fits the customer's needs.
- *If I Empower People, I Lose Power*: Empowerment does not diminish the manager's role; an empowering manager is much stronger in influence.
- *Customer Focus Culture Is About Communication*: Culture is not what the memo says, it is what people are doing when the manager is not around. You need to design an ecosystem of tools, mind-set, and behaviors to lead people to do the right thing by the customer and the organization.
- *Customer Focus Is Just Saying the Customer Is Always Right*: The customer is not always right. Often the customer is misinformed and in some rare situations, the customer may try to take advantage of the situation. We need to listen intently to the customer's stated needs and then, if we find that the customer is not right, we need to educate the customer and provide the facts.
- *Customer Focus Is About Managing Complaints; No One Likes to Do It*: Complaints are not a burden; noncomplaining customers go to the competition. We should embrace complaints as a last chance to save the relationships and retain the customer's business. In rare situations when the customer's business is not profitable, we may then decide to let the customer go. But first we should try to solve their issues.
- *Customer Focus Will Increase My Costs*: Customer focus is not about increasing costs; it is about increasing revenues. Many organizations who became customer focused discovered that they actually lowered costs overall by listening to customers and adapting to their needs as opposed to trying to force their ways on the customers.

• Endnote •

1. Harley Manning, Kerry Bodine, and Josh Bernoff, *Outside In: The Power of Putting Customers at the Center of Your Business* (Eugene, OR, New Harvest 2012).

Talent Management

LEARNING OBJECTIVES

By the end of this chapter, you will be better equipped to:

- Identify and practice the steps involved in talent acquisition and the advantage of asking open-ended interview questions.
- Understand what the STAR method is and why it is important.
- Recognize the importance of talent alignment and how to go about aligning employees to their roles and responsibilities.
- Establish the most and least effective ways to share feedback with employees.
- Understand how to create and implement a successful succession plan.
- Recognize how to remain consistent when measuring talent and performance.
- Identify the different kinds of workplace harassment and what the manager's role is in intervening.

Talent is the number one asset at most organizations. Talent management (TM) is a set of integrated processes designed to attract, develop, motivate, and retain productive, engaged employees. The management and safekeeping of that asset is a top priority for managers on all levels. Companies lose tens of thousands of dollars every time an employee quits. Managers should do their best to create an environment that encourages employees to perform at their peak.

Myth: Business professionals may ignore talent management when they take on new roles as supervisors or managers because they feel human resources is more administrative than strategic.

The ideal scenario in the business world today is that managers and the human resources team collaborate to create a great place to work, where people are treated fairly, rewarded for their efforts, excited to come to work, and able to produce excellent results.

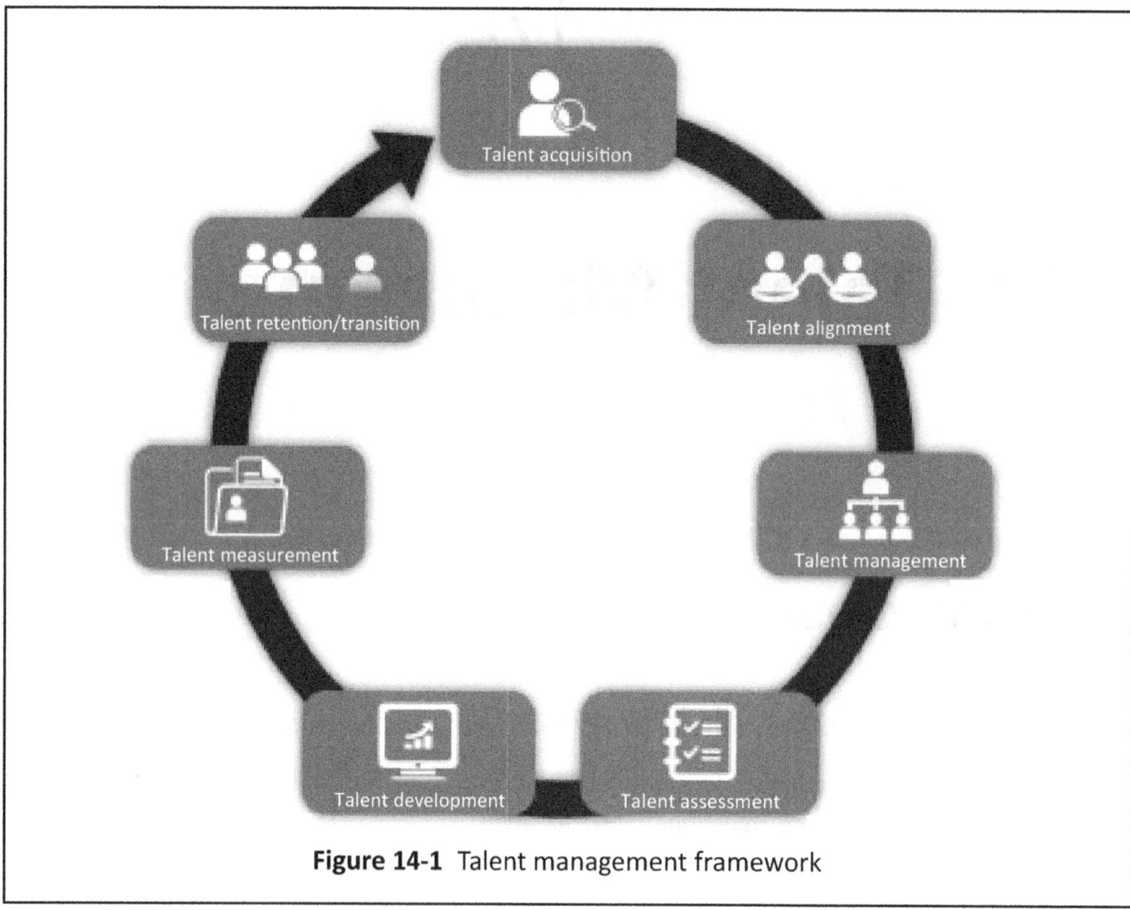

Figure 14-1 Talent management framework

Managers should demonstrate a deep understanding or comprehension of the TM cycle—in other words, the life cycle of an employee starting on the first day of employment. The consulting firm McKinsey & Company first coined the term *talent management* in a 1997 research paper and again in *The War for Talent* (2001). In recent years, TM has become a role in many big organizations. Companies benefit from treating talent as their top asset. They're more likely to retain those individuals and cultivate them to perform at an even higher level.

When managers know and embrace TM, they align potential or current goals through talent acquisition, talent development, and talent motivation (see Chapter 5, Motivation). They champion a culture of diversity and inclusion (see Chapter 21, Diversity and Inclusion), and a respect and reasonable understanding of employment law. Figure 14-1 shows a framework for the various aspects of TM.

TALENT ACQUISITION

Talent acquisition is the first step in the process to get talent into your organization. By following the steps described here, you'll be able to identify qualified talent and select the best possible candidates for the job. Manager responsibilities in talent acquisition include reading and updating the job description (JD). In our constantly evolving business world, responsibilities change. Use your own knowledge of the job to write its description, but also be sure to consult with others, such as your leader, your peers, and the person who is or was in the role most recently.

The JD should include, but not be limited to:

- Job requirements
- Specific behaviors that ensure successful performance
- Employee's expected level of responsibility
- Specialized skills, knowledge, formal education, and prior work experience necessary and relevant for successful performance

The description should also mention concrete and intangible competencies. A concrete competency could be the skills needed to operate equipment or machinery. An intangible competency could be the level of creativity needed for the job.

Work with the recruiter, either internal or external to your organization, to get candidates that are highly qualified for the position. Tell human resources (HR) anything else that's not in the job description, such as a preferred work style, skill sets that are most needed in your department right now, how soon you need the role to be filled, and any other information that might be helpful to the recruiter. Ideally, the recruiter will conduct phone screens and send only those candidates who possess the skills and qualifications that are needed.

The Interview

The most important aspect of an interview is to know what you can and cannot ask during it. Ask only job-related questions. This means questions about candidates' prior work experience and why they're looking for a new position at your company. Under no circumstances should you or anyone on your hiring team ask about the following:

- Age
- Gender
- Race
- Ethnicity
- Sexual orientation
- Gender identity
- Religion
- Family or parental status
- National origin
- Disabilities
- Criminal records

Pro tip
Before the interview, think about the questions you want to ask.

If other members of your team will be interviewing the same candidate(s), take time to coordinate beforehand who will focus on which areas, such as technical skills, people and leadership skills, and fit within the team.

Types of Questions

Open-ended questions typically are short, but they give the candidate an opportunity for a long, robust answer. They usually start with How or What. Here are some examples:

- What are the three main aspects of your leadership style?
- What are the primary parts of your background that would make you an excellent fit for this job?
- What do you do outside of your specific role to learn and grow as a professional?

Behavioral or competency-based questions are the other main type of interview questions. One of the main researchers in this area is Paul C. Green, who wrote the book *Actions Speak!: The Newest Ideas on Behavior-Based Interviewing* (2012). The main principle in the book is "Past actions are the best predictor of future performance." As you think about questions, keep this in mind. The way a candidate handled something relevant in the past is a good indicator of how that candidate will likely handle similar situations in the future. That's why it's a good idea to ask behavioral and competency-based questions that encourage candidates to share examples from their past. Some examples include:

- Tell me about a time when you had someone on your team who wasn't performing well.
- Describe a situation when you didn't get along with a colleague.
- Give me an example of a success story you've had as a leader.

After you ask a behavioral question, listen carefully and don't prompt any answers. Many candidates will ramble on about the situation but never get to the actions they took and the result of those actions. The best candidates, however, will provide a concise answer using the STAR method:

- Situation
- Task
- Action
- Result

Closed-ended questions are designed to help you get specific information.

- Asking candidates if they know specific software.
- Asking candidates if they would be able to put in time outside normal work hours.
- Asking candidates what their college major was.

As you prepare your open- and closed-ended questions and ask them at interviews, be ready to dig down by probing into the candidates' answers. Probing allows you to delve into the reasons for their behavior and their decisions.

- Why are you looking to come to our organization?
- Tell me more about why you handled the challenging situation that way.

You can also probe by asking follow-up questions such as:

- What is it about our values that attracted you to our organization?
- Can you elaborate on that?

While you may certainly ask spontaneous, follow-up questions during the interview, we recommend you prepare your questions in writing in advance. Asking all candidates the same series of questions is a technique known as a *structured interview,* and can be beneficial to help compare candidates more objectively. This practice can also be a useful defense against allegations of hiring discrimination. It can also be beneficial, however, to spend time reviewing each candidate's resume and the job description so you can tailor the questions to their experience and competencies. A good rule of thumb is that 50 percent of the questions should be the same and 50 percent different, based on each candidate's specific experience.

Pro tip

When you use probing, be sure not to overuse the word *why*. It may be interpreted as slightly judgmental.

Debriefing

As soon as the interviews are over, conduct a debrief meeting with the other interviewers. If the interviewer has three candidates in the morning, a good time to debrief is over lunch. The idea is to discuss each candidate while memories are fresh. You can start by having each person say yes, no, or maybe to the question of whether the candidate should be hired. Start with the most junior interviewer. This way your colleague won't feel obligated to agree with the senior person.

If your decision is unanimous, let the candidate know as soon as possible. If yes, now you shift into sell mode. Make sure the candidate knows you're interested in hiring him or her. Reach out and ensure other interviewers do the same. It's never too early to begin thinking about onboarding and assimilation. Who will train this person and when? What are the most important aspects of the organization's culture for the candidate to know?

Every organization has its own hiring practices. While protocols, timelines, and the details of decision making change across companies, one thing remains constant: the goal is to hire someone with not only the right skill set but also the best fit with the company moving forward. We talk more about fit in Chapter 17, Style and Fit, but right now, let's take a look at how to align employee skills with company needs.

TALENT ALIGNMENT

Now that you have acquired talent, you'll want to make sure that the new hires (and all employees for that matter) are aligned the right way to the right things. Of course, everyone has strengths and weaknesses. Talent alignment means assigning your team members the responsibilities that match their strengths as best as you can. Ideally, the employees continue to work in your department, but this is not always the case. Sometimes switching them to another group could be a better fit for the individual and for both teams involved. If someone has great potential elsewhere in the organization, you should encourage an internal move that matches talent with opportunity.

Strategic Vision and Goal Setting

Talent alignment requires vision and planning. As a manager, you know the organization's strategy and you also know what leadership expects everyone to accomplish. It's your job to make sure your team members know it too. The best way to achieve this is putting together a development plan with each of your direct reports. A development plan sets formal, annual goals, and it helps keep everyone on the same page. Each team member's plan will align his or her talent with the organization's goals.

In some cases, an individual's goals do not align with the team's, and this might be an opportunity for an employee to transition to another department. That could come to light while working on the development plan, or the development plan could reveal areas where a team member wants to grow and excel. Don't hoard your people. Is there a lateral move or a special project that will give this person the experience he or she seeks? Even if it's on another team, it's in everyone's best interest to match talent with opportunity.

Pro tip

Communication is critical. Employees want to know where they stand, especially new employees. Tell them. Be transparent. Share feedback constructively. Talk about changes in the department and the company. If you don't, beware: When people sense a change but there's no explanation for it, they tend to get nervous, and their performance is impacted by it (see Chapter 1, Communication).

TALENT MANAGEMENT

So far, we have focused on acquiring talent, and then once those people are in the organization, making sure they are aligned and stay aligned with the business strategy as the company evolves. Here, we take the next step—moving talent around (figuratively and literally) as needed to have employees in the roles and locations that create the best win/win scenarios for them and the employer.

Mobility

A critical component of TM is mobility. How much breadth of experience does an employee get as a member of a team, a department, and the entire organization? Let's look at three types of mobility: internal, domestic, and global.

Internal mobility is defined as people moving between groups as appropriate based on their own goals and business needs. As mentioned earlier, managers should be a conduit to people moving over or up so employees can develop professionally. Many high-performing organizations have formal rotational programs and employees who have worked in several departments during their tenure with the company.

Domestic mobility can be defined as people moving to other locations, whether for business needs or personal circumstances. For example, maybe your sales are up in the north and lagging in the south. Look for employees who are eager to relocate. If your organization is big enough, with locations in multiple cities, encouraging domestic mobility could be a win for employees and the company.

Assuming you're involved in the solution, work with leadership and human resources on this. Things to think about include:

- Ways to announce the openings or process to the current city's employees
- Application process for the transfer (including when to tell the current boss)
- Company's process for selecting which employees to transfer
- Moving expenses
- Raise and/or bonus
- Temporary living expenses in the new city
- Transportation (flight) for the entire family from current city to new city
- Assimilation into the new city for the employee's spouse (such as job search help)
- Home sale and home purchase support
- Tax assistance
- Repayment agreement (if relocated employees leave the company within a certain time frame, they would have to repay all or a portion of the moving and transfer costs)

Global mobility is defined as employees moving internationally to create win–win situations for the individual and the organization. If global mobility is possible at your organization, it can be a worthwhile development opportunity personally and professionally for employees. Some employees want international experience and choose an employer based on the company's ability to give it to them. Of course, global mobility entails a higher degree of difficulty and a longer time frame to execute than domestic mobility. Acquiring visas can be a lengthy process, for example. International rotations usually last eighteen to twenty-four months (sometimes shorter or longer, depending on the situation). An assignment like this is a big step that you will want to reserve for your best employees. Expatriate packages can be costly to an organization. While the employee is abroad, the manager must maintain regular contact and think early about re-assimilation. Employees who accept a long-term assignment should return in a higher-level domestic role, thanks to the international experience.

TALENT ASSESSMENT

Talent Assessment focuses on observing your employees' strengths and weaknesses and giving them real-time feedback (positive or constructive). Speak to them as soon as possible about whatever they did that deserves recognition. Take notes of these moments, which will make it easier to write the performance review at midyear or year's end.

The best way to share feedback (orally or written) is by giving employees plenty of specific examples of what they did. You can use this framework:

- *Situation*: Describe the situation and background.
- *Behavior*: Give specific examples of what the person did or didn't do.
- *Impact*: Share the impact that the behavior had on you, the team, and the organization.

Here's an example of positive feedback:

- *Situation*: Monday's project update meeting.
- *Behavior*: When the client asked questions about their database access, you said you didn't know but that you'd find out and get back to them as soon as possible.
- *Impact*: It set a great tone for our team and helped strengthen the credibility we have with the client. You showed that we are happy to go the extra mile. Well done! I'm grateful to have you on the team.

This is one way you can share constructive feedback:

- *Situation*: Monday's project update meeting.
- *Behavior*: When the client asked questions about their database access, you said we'd get back to that later in the meeting, but never did.
- *Impact*: This made it seem like you didn't care about their concerns. We want to make sure we are giving them exceptional client service, and in this situation, we fell short.

If the person is getting positive feedback, you can stop after the impact piece. If you're giving constructive feedback, continue the discussion.

If the situation is rather minor, brainstorm what the employee can do differently next time. Use coaching techniques (Chapter 9, Coaching for Performance) to ask the employee open-ended questions such as:

- What can you do differently/better next time?
- How do you want to address the situation with the client?
- What lessons did you learn from this experience?

Transfer ownership to the employee, who is the one who should be responsible for correcting the issue. If the performance issue is more severe or has happened repeatedly, more remedial action is needed:

- Remind the employee of the requirements of the job, what's in the job description, company policy, or whatever is appropriate given the situation.
- Ask questions to find a solution and the next steps.
- Assess if progressive discipline is necessary.

Progressive Discipline

Progressive discipline is a talent performance practice that refers to the steps an organization follows when an employee continues to underperform. The actions become increasingly more severe. The primary purpose is to help employees improve job-related performance. Typically, progressive discipline steps are:

- Counseling (the situation previously described)
- Oral warning
- Written warning
- Second written warning
- Suspension
- Termination

Your company may have all six of these or it may have fewer steps. Whenever a problem develops, consult with human resources and see what the policy is. Consistency is important. Or stated differently, inconsistency can cost your company tens of thousands, if not millions, of dollars in damages. In *Schreiner v. Nordstrom* (2006), a court allowed an employee's age discrimination case to proceed. This was because, even though the employee had been correctly fired for a wrongdoing, no other employee had ever been disciplined in any way for the same act of misconduct.

The steps given here are not an absolute right. You should follow them if it's a *performance* issue. However, if the person has committed a serious *conduct* infraction, you can move to termination more quickly. Your organization's written procedures likely stipulate that, depending on the severity of the infraction (such as theft, acts of physical violence, and insubordination), progressive steps can be bypassed, and the organization can proceed directly to termination.

For example, in *Timmerman v. U.S. Bank* (2007), a bank manager was terminated for refunding thirty-one overdraft fees to two employees' accounts in violation of company policy. After her termination, she filed a lawsuit claiming sex and age discrimination. As evidence, she said that the company failed to apply its progressive discipline policy. But the federal court of appeals dismissed her claims because, among other reasons, the bank's policy did not require it to follow a progressive discipline policy for this type of violation.

One final thought on what to do when you have an employee who has severe performance and/or conduct issues: Exhibit *managerial courage* to resolve the situation. Often, managers are too nice or afraid to act or unsure what to do, so they do nothing. It's important to act quickly, consult with human resources (who will consult with legal), and work on employee improvement or move to terminate if progress isn't made (discussed later in the chapter).

Proper Performance Management Will Inspire Your Team

Let's return to some positivity about performance management. Being proactive and sharing great, timely, and regular feedback will motivate your employees. The most beneficial part is that it boosts morale and doesn't cost the company a dime. When you have inspired team members, they will be more likely to go the extra mile for you, the department, and the organization. Everybody wins.

Performance management also:

- Improves employees' behavior
- Clarifies job requirements
- Develops a mutual understanding between managers and employees about performance expectations, goals, and measurement criteria
- Encourages employees to express themselves openly on performance-related issues
- Identifies an organization's strongest performers
- Identifies employees with the greatest potential
- Improves employee performance
- Improves morale
- Reinforces positive behavior
- Strengthens the working relationship between managers and employees

All of this can best be achieved if managers understand that performance management is an ongoing process, not just an annual event. When this happens, you and the employee have more interaction, which helps cultivate your relationship. Better relationships lead to more efficient work, more motivation, and an overall happier work environment.

The no surprises rule allows for more discussions about things other than performance. For example, the end-of-year conversation and other discussions throughout the year can focus more on long-term career development than simply evaluation.

Spend time developing your employees. You can help through training, mentoring, leadership development, coaching, and career development. Let's take a look at each of these disciplines.

Myth: Employees should be able to hit the ground running on day one and learn quickly on their own.

Even the most productive and best-trained employees need guidance. Managers are responsible for providing on-the-job training. This is the most common way people learn.

Training

Training is appropriate for your employees when you need skills that do not exist in your department or are not available in enough of your employees. Training is also appropriate when you need a specific standard of skill performance and workers are not performing up to that standard, or when there has been a change in technology, methods, or required behavior that renders current skills obsolete. If you are proactive about succession planning, you should think a lot about training. You may work in an industry that requires training, such as accounting or health care, or you may recognize that training demonstrates a commitment to your employees and functions as a recruiting and retention tool.

Successful training depends on a cooperative effort between managers, human resources, trainers, trainees, and leadership, all of whom play distinct and important roles in the training process.

When training employees, embody the platinum rule: treat them as *they* want to be treated. This differs from the golden rule, which is to treat others as *you* would want to be treated. The platinum rule is a better way to lead. When training, recognize that different people learn differently, and some individuals may need you to show them. Others may be more independent. People could be visual learners, or social learners. Whatever the case, matching the style of the learner produces the best results.

Typically, it's a manager's job to identify employees who are likely to benefit from training and to provide support and encouragement to employees participating in training programs. Let them fully immerse themselves in the training courses.

Be sure you allow employees to use their newly learned skills back on the job, that you encourage continued growth and development, and that you attend training yourself. This will show that you believe training is important.

Pro tip

Some organizations require the newly trained employee to share any new skill, insight, or process with colleagues so they too can get the benefit (and it helps further justify the cost of training).

Mentoring

It's important for employees to have a mentor. You may be that person for each of your team members, or they may prefer someone else who is impartial (for navigating any issues with you). Support them however they want to be supported, which goes back to the platinum rule.

Mentoring someone means sharing your own experience and giving advice *when asked.* That last piece is a key distinction. If you give advice when the person doesn't want it, that individual isn't likely to be receptive to what you say.

A structured mentorship program is formal and set up by the manager and human resources. An informal mentoring relationship, on the other hand, is often established naturally over time and can be mutually beneficial to both parties. It happens when colleagues develop connections with each other.

The less experienced person then feels comfortable going to the more experienced person for advice on how to resolve certain situations, such as:

- Career development questions
- Who to go to for answers to particular questions
- Finding out about new opportunities and openings at the company
- Sharing ideas about different ways of doing things.

You can establish yourself as a mentor by getting to know your employees, treating them with respect, running a fair department, giving them developmental opportunities, empowering them to do their work, being open to their ideas, and otherwise being an inspiring manager/leader.

Leadership Development

A lot of employees want to become managers. They aspire to have your role if you get promoted, transfer to another department, or leave the company. Support them by giving them opportunities to develop their leadership qualities. For example, you can have them supervise other less experienced members of the team. This is a win–win scenario because you can spend more time and energy on higher-level initiatives, and they can learn to lead by working with someone who is performing duties that they already know.

You can also delegate someone to lead a special project or initiative (see Chapter 8, Delegation). This gives the employee a chance to manage something from start to finish and to learn what works well and what doesn't. It sets the employee up for success when he or she achieves a formal manager position. If appropriate, you can also send employees to leadership-related conferences and training courses.

Coaching Versus Mentoring

If training is about transferring knowledge to an individual or a group, coaching is about developing the knowledge that they already possess (see also Chapter 9, Coaching for Performance). Coaching is asking employees questions to help them figure things out on their own; mentoring occurs when employees ask their mentor for advice, and the mentor gives it. A mentor might say, "Here's what I've done. . . ." A coach wouldn't say that.

Career Development

Career development supports employees' goals as they work on organizational goals. This allows for a motivated workforce, which results in greater productivity.

Carve out time to have career development discussions with the people you manage. This means talking to them about their long-term goals and aspirations and not just their to-do items. To best do this, you need to cultivate a relationship with your team. As noted earlier, get to know them, support them, trust them, and empower them. When these things happen, your team will feel comfortable sharing their goals with you in career development meetings.

Above all, encourage your employees to take responsibility for managing their own careers. No one should care about it more than they do.

Here are some additional steps you and employees can take to aid in their career development:

- If your company has a database of employee skills, interests, and knowledge, encourage your team members to regularly update it.
- Periodically review the content of each employee's database information to make sure you're aware of what each has done and what each wants to do. Search the database when looking for someone to fill a role permanently or on a project.
- Align employees' goals with those of the organization.
- Help employees establish a timeline and identify resources needed to achieve their career goals. Resources may include short-term training, mentoring, assigning responsibilities to help them accomplish their goals, and encouraging or providing further formal education (such as a pursuing a degree).
- Facilitate and/or encourage skip-level meetings. This means an employee meets with *your* manager periodically. Doing so ensures two-way dialogue between colleagues who may not usually interact one on one. This is a way for you to help your team members get more exposure to organizational leadership as well as to uncover any potential issues between you and the employee.

TALENT MEASUREMENT

Earlier in the chapter we discussed the mechanics of the performance management process. Talent measurement typically focuses on two areas: the end-of-the-year performance review process (filling out the final evaluation and giving the person a rating) and compensation. We'll address each separately.

If you are completing a human resources provided performance management form, be consistent with other raters and with the company's process. Some managers say they are hard graders as if this were a badge of honor. It's not. A performance management system or process is only as good as the people completing the evaluations. If managers aren't consistent with one another, then the process falls apart.

The myth of the feedback "sandwich method" has persisted for awhile. This tactic has the manager write something good, then something bad or constructive, and end with something good. This way of thinking is appropriate only if the person does a good job two-thirds of the time and has room for improvement a third of the time.

Don't eat the sandwich! Instead, evaluate as appropriate based on the year the employee had. If the person is a superstar, document all the excellent accomplishments and end with what's next: what to do to get promoted, how to lead cross-functional projects, and so on. Using the sandwich method could actually be insulting. On the other hand, if the person is having a poor year, start with the lead story:

Scenario 1: Career Development

Raheem works for you and you work for Amit. Raheem reveals in his skip-level meeting with Amit that he doesn't enjoy the work he is doing and would like to transfer to another group within the organization that is more aligned with his interests and long-term career ambitions.

What should you do? When someone brings up an issue like Raheem has, ask the following questions:

- What's his rating? Transferring to another group is likely dependent on that. If he's a poor performer, he should improve his current performance first, and then he would be eligible to transfer.
- Is it something personal between you and Raheem? If you don't get along well with him or maybe sense some friction, explore that with him and assure him that you're on his side and will help him succeed at the company.
- Does he simply want to do different work because that's what he's more interested in? If so, and he's a good or better performer, support his transfer and put in a good word for him with potential new groups. You would rather keep him in the organization (even if it's in another department) instead of losing him to another company.
- Is he talented but not a fit for his current role? Do you see potential in him? If that's the case, you and the organization could help him find something within the company that's a better match for his skills and experience.
- What's the job description (JD) for his position? Has he been performing those duties or has his role changed? That happens sometimes. If he does transfer out, edit the JD as appropriate.

there is significant room for improvement. That should be the focus of the evaluation. To do otherwise would not be showing managerial courage.

Once the forms are done, some companies have the manager give the year-end ratings to the employee. Other organizations use a committee to decide. Regardless of what the process is, the next step is to communicate it to your team members. Transparency is key.

If you are responsible for year-end performance ratings, here are some things to think about:

- Will you have a bell curve or forced ranking? This means that human resources or leadership gives you guidance on how many people should be in each performance category. There have been some controversial cases involving this in recent years.
- How will you handle special circumstances such as someone on medical or maternity leave? Someone shouldn't get a lower rating than usual just for being out for medical reasons. Some forward-thinking organizations even have a grandfathering policy that lets people who are out for more than six months keep their rating from the prior year. Regardless, make sure you don't discriminate against the person for medical-related reasons.

- Will you or someone in HR look at ratings results with a diversity lens, ensuring no group is receiving disproportionately low ratings? The answer to this must be yes. Someone should sort the ratings results by race and gender to make sure your organization is treating all groups fairly.
- How and when will you share the ratings results with each employee? It's important that everyone finds out around the same time. Otherwise it can lead to needless worry, bad feelings, gossip, and more.

The second important aspect of talent assessment is compensation. Although some managers are involved in setting salaries and determining raises and bonuses, many are not. The key here is the same as for year-end performance management: Be transparent. Discuss the process with your employees. Explain how the company figures out everyone's raises and bonuses, including the rationale. Help your team understand how much is in their control and how much is based on company or department results and what they can do differently to get a bigger raise or bonus going forward.

Your organization may be large enough that it has a formal compensation methodology. This is often done through salary surveys, which obtain information on what the pay range is for all positions and levels in your industry. Leadership will then determine a compensation strategy. For example, they may choose competitive salaries, which will be near the average, or highly competitive salaries, which are higher than average (perhaps because talent in your industry is hard to get and/or keep).

Pro tip

While pay raises across the board are important for morale, there are also times when an employee's performance really does merit different compensation. People are often motivated by money. If the employee does an exceptional job compared to her peers, she should get a bigger raise and bonus. If her performance is poor compared to her colleagues, she should get less.

Other factors on compensation include:

- Local and regional talent pools
- Talent strength at competition
- Specialized positions required highly skilled, certified or licensed individuals
- Collective bargaining agreements

The actual pay increases granted under a merit system largely depend on:

- Employee performance
- Ability to attract and retain employees through means other than salary
- Departmental and organizational budgets and performance
- Economic conditions
- Salaries paid by competitors

Scenario 2: Compensation

Trina is rated a 5 at the end of the performance year. This is the top rating category at ABC Company. She is a senior associate, making $60,000 a year.

Rob is also a senior associate and is rated a 3, which is the average or middle rating category. His current salary is $80,000, which is at the high end of the range for employees at that staff level.

You have $8,000 in salary raises to split between them. Raises can be anywhere from 0 to 10 percent. You also have $6,000 in bonus funds, which can be split as you see fit. How would you allocate raises and bonuses? What dollar amount and percentage would you give to these employees? Why? What should you do?

Judgment comes into play when deciding on raises and bonuses. Here are some potential suggestions:

- Give Trina the entire bonus amount; she earned it by outperforming Rob significantly this year.
- Give Trina 75 percent of the raise budget ($6,000), which is 10 percent of her salary (the maximum raise you can give someone).
- Give Rob 25 percent of the raise budget ($2,000), which is a low percentage of his salary. However, he's making a lot of money and didn't contribute at a high level given what he's making, especially compared to Trina. Rob probably won't be happy with his raise and bonus, but the reality is, you need him to up his game. If he decides leave, that's not the end of the world. Someone making top dollar should be a top performer.

Another essential aspect of compensation reviews is, like performance management, the importance of sorting the (preliminary) results by race and gender. Be aware if any group is paid less on average. You may know that a gender pay gap exists and many men are paid more than their female counterparts for the same work. Managers involved in setting salaries have an opportunity to reduce or even eliminate this gap.

TALENT RETENTION/TRANSITION

Now that we have covered interviewing, hiring, and aligning talent, let's take a look at the keys to retaining employees and why some leave the organizations that hire them.

The best way to retain all your high-potential and high-performing employees is to cultivate a relationship with them and find out what motivates them. This goes back to the platinum rule. Treat your employees as they want to be treated. For example, some may be most motivated by money. If that's the case, work with leadership and human resources to get them the maximum raise and bonus they deserve. For other team members, verbal recognition may matter most. In those instances, be sure to compliment them often on the great things they do.

There are countless ways to motivate employees, including opportunities for promotion, a fair and respectful working environment, and causes about which they are passionate. Lead and manage in the way that they want to be led and managed. How do you know how they want to be led and managed? Ask them.

Pro tip

Manager must learn that the answer is sometimes no. If decision making is as transparent as it can be, the rationale is explained, and employee input is encouraged and taken seriously, then employees may not like the rejection, but they can live with it.

Employees often leave one job for another. Unfortunately, it's not always because of what the new employer is offering, but because the old employer failed to meet certain needs. So long as they are not being offered higher compensation elsewhere, employees often leave their current role for one or more of the following reasons:

- Appropriate supervision
- Appreciation/gratitude
- Belief in organization's values
- Boss available as a resource
- Challenging work
- Commitment to work–life balance
- Enough guidance or instruction
- Enough training
- Feedback
- Feeling part of the company
- Flexible work schedules
- Fun
- Good fit with their boss
- Growth opportunities
- Ideas valued
- Interesting work
- Recognition as an individual
- Respect
- Strong company branding image
- Their suggestions taken seriously
- Technological capabilities
- Two-way communication between self and leader
- Their work taken seriously.

You can also think of this as a list of ways for you to be an excellent manager.

Talent Transition

The hardest thing to do as a manager is involuntary termination. However, this is sometimes unavoidable. When you know what to do and how to do it, letting someone go can be less painful and awkward for all involved. Key steps for performance-related terminations include:

- Progressive discipline (covered earlier in this chapter), *including documentation* of what was said to the person and when
- Assessing if you, human resources, and leadership did everything reasonably in your power to help the employee
- Make sure you or HR has contacted an employment attorney for legal advice on the situation, especially if the employee being terminated is in a protected class (more on this later)

Of course, layoffs or reductions in force are handled differently. There is no progressive discipline and no question of whether you and human resources tried to help the employee(s). There should still be a legally defensible methodology for how people were chosen for the layoff or reduction.

Assuming that you don't escort people out immediately after letting them go (a practice that is prevalent and appropriate in some industries, especially financial services) there are a few things to keep in mind for the termination meeting. First, some employees may be relieved by being let go. If they have been through an unsuccessful progressive discipline, they will likely know it's coming. Nonetheless, make sure three people are in the room (employee, human resources representative or a member of leadership, and you). You and the human resources/leadership member should be at the room ten to fifteen minutes early so you're ready when the person arrives. As stated earlier, different organizations have different protocols for hiring and different protocols for terminating too. At some companies human resources takes the lead, while at others, the manager may be the first to speak.

Regardless of how your company handles it, keep the meeting brief. Here is one way it could go:

> YOU: Thanks for coming down. We called you in here to let you know that today is going to be your last day with the company. I asked Scott from human resources to join us so that he can walk you through the next steps.
>
> SCOTT: I have forms here for you to look through and sign. They contain information on what to do about your benefits, laptop, company cell phone, and the like. I am here all day today so please feel free to come to me with any questions on any of the documents. You will then come to me with the completed exit checklist when you are finished.

A few more things to keep in mind for the termination meeting:

- Don't apologize
- Use a caring but decisive tone
- Human resources should know the number for security in case it's needed

- Under supervision give the employee time that day to get and personal files he or she needs off the company computer
- Make that day the employee's last day
- Tell the employee to behave professionally for the rest of the day (no scathing emails or making a scene)
- Don't engage in a debate or lengthy discussion about why this happened

You may want to consider the circumstances surrounding the termination, and if appropriate think about the calendar: Although it may seem callous, there is a reason termination is same day. Telling the employee the day before can cause a longer period of anxiety, especially if the employee suspects it may happen. The employee could also not come into work the next day if you say something the day before, which could cause a host of other issues.

Succession Planning

There are two sides to replacing people who are stepping out of their roles: the supply side and the demand side. Organizations with older workforces may have many employees eligible for retirement but not enough talent available and developed to fill existing roles. You'll should have a plan to identify the need and prepare existing talent to assume those vacant areas. On the other hand, companies that skew younger—tech firms and startups, for example—usually have flat organizational structures. Consequently, they have many employees who are ready for promotion, but not enough open spots. Again, in this situation, you should communicate in a transparent manner and let your employees know they're on your radar. Be creative. Tiger teams, special projects, lateral moves, and training opportunities may help you retain your talented team members who want to get promoted.

One common succession-planning tool is a talent review meeting that uses a nine-box grid, as shown in Figure 14-2. This tool measures a candidate's potential while keeping an eye on performance. First, decide where each employee belongs on the grid, then communicate that information and work it into the employee's individual development plan.

LEGAL FAQS

As a manager, it's important to know some legal terms and laws. You can always check with human resources or the legal counsel's office. Table 14-1 contains the issues and situations managers most frequently ask about.

The most important law for you to know is the Civil Rights Act of 1964, specifically Title VII. The relevant section of the legislation says:

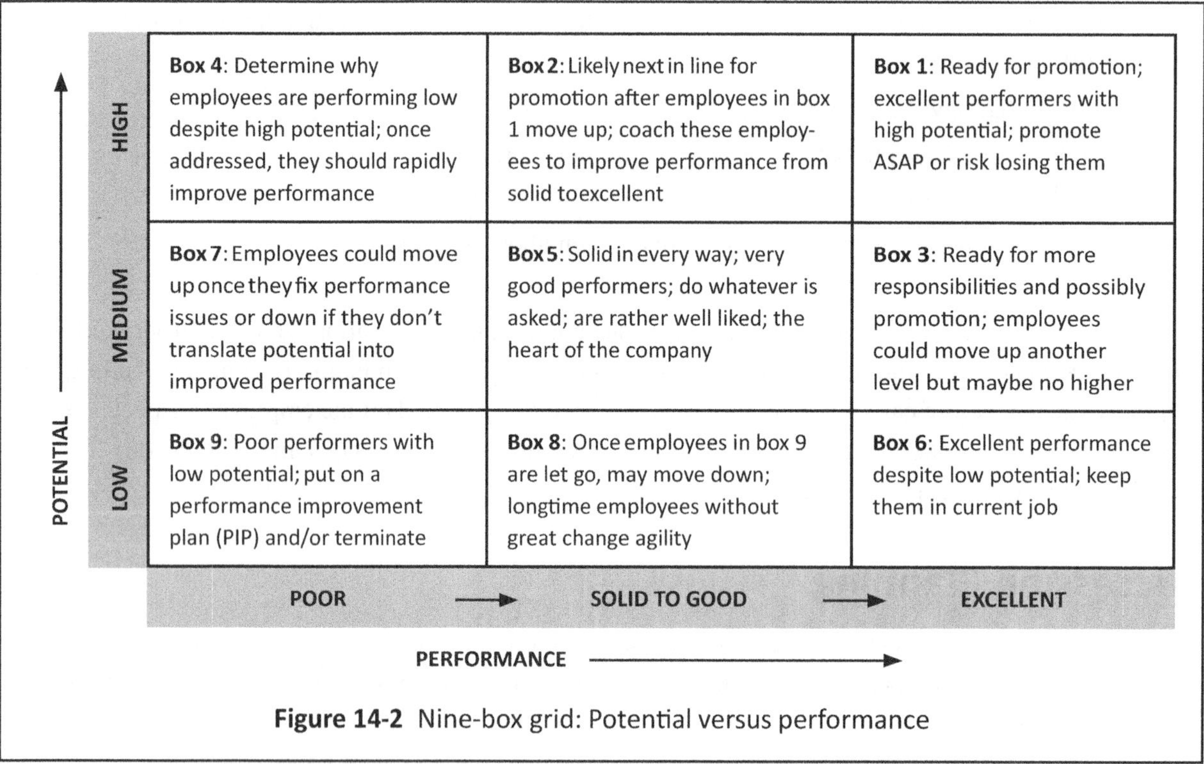

Figure 14-2 Nine-box grid: Potential versus performance

It shall be an unlawful employment practice for an employer—

(1) to fail or refuse to hire or to discharge any individual, or otherwise to discriminate against any individual with respect to his compensation, terms, conditions, or privileges of employment, because of such individual's race, color, religion, sex, or national origin; or

(2) to limit, segregate, or classify his employees in any way which would deprive or tend to deprive any individual of employment opportunities or otherwise adversely affect his status as an employee, because of such individual's race, color, religion, sex, or national origin.

The courts, many companies, and municipalities have expanded this law beyond the five categories of race, color, religion, sex, and national origin to protect people in some or all the following additional *protected classes,* which is another key term for you to know:

- disability: physical or mental
- age (forty and older)
- genetic information
- marital status
- sexual orientation
- gender identity and gender expression
- AIDS/HIV infection

- medical condition
- political activities or affiliations
- military or veteran status
- status as a victim of domestic violence, assault, or stalking

As a manager, if you're in doubt about anything legal, contact human resources immediately.

SEXUAL HARASSMENT

Know the laws around sexual harassment (also discussed in Chapter 18, Organizational Culture, and Chapter 19, Ethics). You're likely aware of all the sexual harassment charges in recent years. Some states have mandated sexual harassment training for all employees. As a manager, it's important for you to know specifics, plus how to create a harassment-free environment and what to do if someone comes to you to report a claim of sexual harassment.

Sexual harassment is defined by the U.S. Equal Employment Opportunity Commission (EEOC) as follows:

> Unwelcome sexual advances, requests for sexual favors, and other verbal or physical conduct of a sexual nature constitute sexual harassment when this conduct explicitly or implicitly affects an individual's employment, unreasonably interferes with an individual's work performance, or creates an intimidating, hostile, or offensive work environment.

Some key facts, as defined by the EEOC, include:

- The victim may be a woman or a man.
- The harasser may be a woman or a man.
- The victim need not be of the opposite sex.
- The harasser may be the victim's direct supervisor or manager, a supervisor in another department or geographic location, a member of senior management, an agent or representative of the employer, or a co-worker within the organization.
- The harasser may be a consultant or salesperson doing business with the organization or any other nonemployee, such as a vendor, client, customer, or workplace visitor.
- Sexual harassment can occur away from the workplace or during nonworking hours when it is related to the employee's work duties or relationships.
- Sexual harassment can occur without economic injury to the victim.
- Sexual harassment can occur without resulting in the transfer, demotion, or discharge of the victim.
- The victim does not have to be the person being harassed; the victim could be anyone adversely affected by the offensive conduct.

Table 14-1 Legal Terminology That Managers Should Understand	
Adverse impact	A considerably different rate of selection in hiring, promotion, or other employment decision that works to the disadvantage of a certain race, sex, or ethnic group. You don't intentionally discriminate, but that's the effect decisions have had. As a manager, consider the results of your decisions in these areas and be sure they don't have an adverse impact.
Defamation	Injury caused to an individual's character or reputation resulting from another individual issuing false or malicious statements either orally or in writing. This is relevant for you as a manager because a former employee may give you as a reference. Most companies will tell you to refer all inquiries to human resources, who will simply confirm title held and dates of employment. You wouldn't want to say anything bad about a former employee because that would make you susceptible to a defamation lawsuit.
Disparate treatment	Disparate treatment means rules and policies are purposely applied inconsistently, causing a negative impact on protected classes. This is different from adverse impact. In that, the employer didn't discriminate on purpose. With disparate treatment, the employer did. As a Manager, you should never discriminate, purposely or inadvertently.
Employment-at-will	A legal doctrine stating that an employment relationship may be terminated either by the employer or employee at any time, for any or no reason. While you can follow the letter of the law and terminate someone for no reason, you should follow the spirit of the law and fire someone only for just cause and with more than necessary documentation. In this era, with websites like Glassdoor, a company's reputation is important. You don't want potential candidates to think your organization treats its employees unfairly.
Harassment	Conduct or actions based on race, religion, sex, national origin, age, disability, military membership, or veteran status that are severe or pervasive enough to create a hostile, abusive, or intimidating work environment for a reasonable person. Treat your colleagues with respect and be sure your team members do the same. If anyone ever comes to you complaining of harassment, speak to human resources immediately so an investigation can begin. Also, thank the employee for coming forward and assure the employee that the company takes such matters seriously.
Just cause	The guiding principle used by employers when engaged in some form of corrective action or discipline for employees. You have just cause to terminate someone if that person has been in the full progressive discipline process and has not improved.
Negligent hiring	A claim made against an employer based on the premise of an employer's obligation to not hire an applicant the employer knew or should have known was unsuitable and was likely to behave inappropriately toward other employees. Occurs when the employer didn't bother to ask—for example, if a candidate has had four jobs in two years, ask during the interview why the candidate left each of those companies.
Systemic discrimination	A pattern of discrimination that on the surface appears neutral but is discriminatory through its application of policies and practices. For example, if your workforce is mostly white and you do most hiring through employee referrals, most of whom are also white, your company is guilty of systemic discrimination.

To determine whether an action constitutes sexual harassment, you must ask the question, How would a reasonable person respond or react? A *reasonable person* is a judicial construct of a hypothetical individual intended to represent an "average" or "ordinary" person. The reasonable person standard performs a critical role in determining whether an act is offensive or objectionable.

What Harassment Looks Like

Workplace harassment comes in many forms—some subtle, others obvious. Let's take a look at the three forms that seem to occur most often, leading to disputes, adverse actions, litigation, and ill will that undermine workplace satisfaction and productivity.

Quid Pro Quo

By definition quid pro quo (which means "this for that") harassment can be committed only by those in managerial or supervisory positions. Supervisors are defined as individuals with, or perceived as having, the authority to recommend tangible employment decisions affecting the employee and/or directing the employee's daily work activities. Quid pro quo harassment involves a significant change that impacts employment status, such as promotions, demotions, salary changes, career development, or termination as a result of either an inappropriate exchange or refusing to engage in such an exchange. Quid pro quo harassment often involves rewards or threats.

For example, a supervisor implies to or tells a subordinate that he or she must engage in sexual behavior or face termination. Upon refusing the demands of the supervisor, the subordinate is fired.

Hostile Work Environment

Hostile environment harassment occurs when an employee is routinely subjected to some aspect of a work environment that a reasonable person would find severely objectionable or offensive. The harassment may be sexual in nature or it may not be. Unlike quid pro quo harassment, which can be perpetrated only by someone in authority, a hostile work environment can be created by co-workers, representatives of the employer, or anyone doing business with the organization as well as senior management, supervisors, and managers.

Myth: One inappropriate joke constitutes a hostile work environment.

Hostile environment harassment involves regular and repeated action and must be severe or pervasive enough to interfere with a person's work. Examples include demeaning language, sabotaging the victim's work, indecent gestures, leering, and offensive jokes.

Third Party

In third party sexual harassment, the victim is not the one being harassed but is someone who nonetheless is affected by the offensive conduct.

An example of quid pro quo third party sexual harassment would be when a supervisor is having an affair with an employee and grants him or her a promotion, even though someone else is better qualified. Third party sexual harassment could occur when an employee witnesses constant displays of flirtatious behavior and physical exchanges between two co-workers, finding it increasingly difficult to concentrate and work.

Role of Manager

When an employee approaches you and reports harassment, let the employee know you and the organization take the matter seriously. Thank the employee for sharing such a sensitive matter and ask for permission to share with human resources and the legal counsel's office. While confidentiality is important, remind the employee that you cannot guarantee it. As part of the investigation, human resources will need to talk to the appropriate people but will certainly exercise discretion and tell people only on a strict need to know basis.

Remind the employee that the company has been put on notice and then inform the appropriate leaders. Human resources will then speak to legal counsel, investigate the matter by interviewing all relevant parties, and then resolve the investigation.

An employee may come to you and say, "Please don't tell anyone, but . . ." Tell that individual that you must say something and investigate the matter. To do otherwise is irresponsible and negligent.

Other Key Harassment Points

- **Open door policy:** An employee can report harassment to any level of management; this protects the employee in case his or her manager is the one harassing. Assuming you are an excellent manager, you may mentor or know people in other departments. They may feel comfortable coming to you. Regardless of who the person is or in what group that person works, follow the advice given here and report the claim to human resources.
- **Zero-tolerance policy:** Most companies have this policy, which means no harassment of any kind is tolerated. Any incident could result in serious ramifications, up to and including termination.
- **Retaliation:** A manager cannot treat the person who files a harassment complaint any differently once the investigation is under way or completed. Usually, human resources warns the person being accused that the company has a zero-tolerance policy for both sexual harassment *and* retaliation against someone who reported a claim of sexual or other harassment. In other words, someone can be fired for retaliating regardless of whether the initial claim was true.

Pro tip

Keep in mind that different people have different tolerances and different ways of responding to events. What is fine for one individual might not be acceptable for another.

CREATE A CULTURE OF TRUST AND LISTENING

It's important to create a respectful workplace where ideas are encouraged and listened to and colleagues treat each other well. Of course, there is no law mandating that, but respecting others is the best way to work and a good way to retain employees. Your organization likely has a section in its employee handbook and policies and procedures manual about respect. Familiarize yourself with how the company wants you and others to act.

At great places to work, people trust one another. Hire people you feel you can trust, and show your trust in them. Respect and empower them, be transparent with them, and they will be more likely to trust you. Seek out your employees for their ideas on how to make the department and company an even better place to work. Even if you don't implement every idea, be sure to acknowledge them all. Show that you're listening. Show that you care.

Keep in mind that trust can be cultivated. Do team-building and -bonding activities as appropriate so people can get to know each other better, trust each other more, and have some fun in the process (see also Chapter 6, Collaboration).

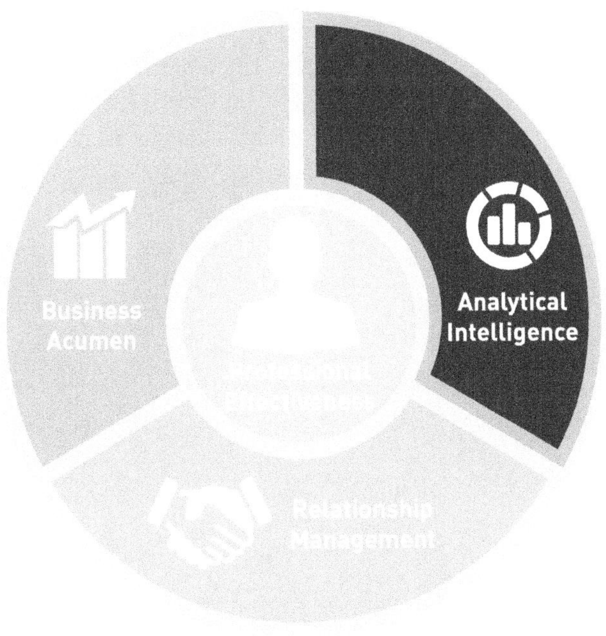

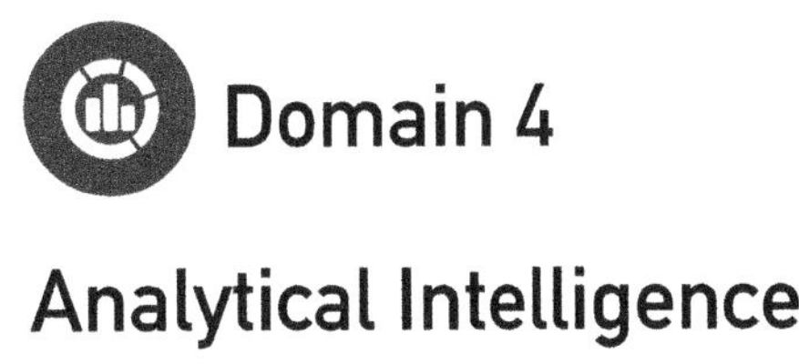

Domain 4

Analytical Intelligence

Critical Thinking

LEARNING OBJECTIVES

By the end of this chapter, you will be better equipped to:

- Employ the three bundles of critical thinking skills: being alert to cognitive biases, assessing persuasion techniques, and recognizing faulty reasoning when drawing conclusions.
- Recognize the importance of self-awareness for critical thinking.
- Be familiar with techniques useful for identifying specific biases.
- Identify specific patterns of weak arguments and persuasion techniques.
- Correct faulty reasoning that leads to mistaken or irrelevant conclusions.
- Craft scenarios to anticipate how critical thinking skills may inform specific work situations.

Critical thinking is the objective analysis and evaluation of an issue in order to form a judgment. Managers demonstrate strong critical thinking skills by assessing alternative viewpoints. They are aware of their own thought processes and are able to communicate their rationale. They translate abstract ideas into tangible results and make reasoned decisions. Psychologists often define critical thinking as any thinking that is goal oriented, which in professional settings means critical thinking is usually applied to problem solving and decision making. Critical thinking is distinct from other higher-brain functions, such as creative thinking (for example, brainstorming), memorizing and recalling information, and automatic thinking (or the brain's engagement with routinized processes, during which the brain can give attention to other matters at the same time).

Pro tip
Critical thinking is not necessarily a specific process, the way project management and market analysis have specific processes and distinct steps. Rather, critical thinking involves bundles of interrelated cognitive skills.

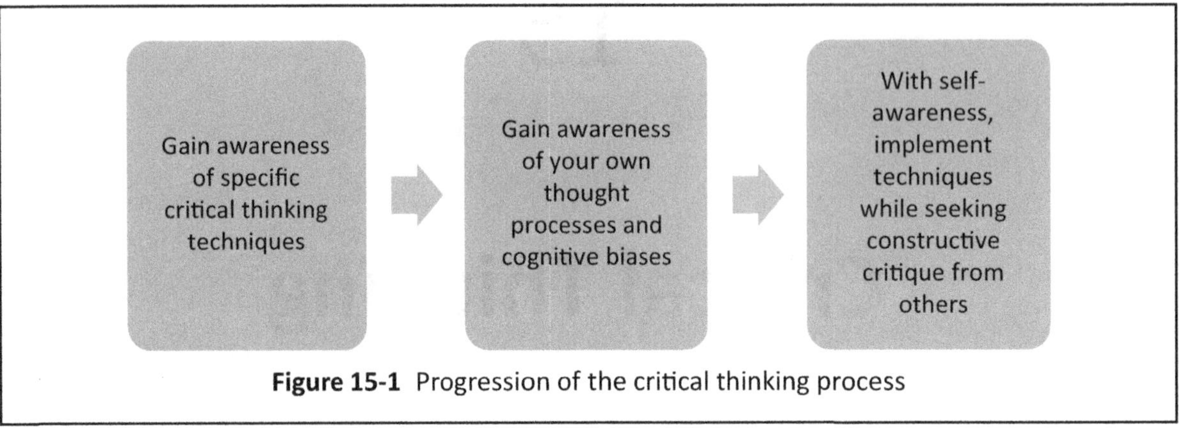

Figure 15-1 Progression of the critical thinking process

For managers, critical thinking entails being alert to cognitive biases that cause mistaken assumptions, assessing persuasion techniques and arguments that obscure facts and relevant information, and recognizing faulty reasoning that can lead to conclusions that do not actually solve the problem at hand. These are transferable skills, meaning they are relevant across many business domains, ranging from financial analysis to strategic planning.

This chapter explores each of these skills as well as foundational abilities that support critical thinking. It also explores the evolution of critical thinking in management, the relationship between emotion and critical thinking, and real-world situations that call for critical thinking. Finally, this chapter orients you to the progression of critical thinking practice, which is illustrated in Figure 15-1.

EVOLUTION OF CRITICAL THINKING IN MANAGEMENT

The historical foundation of critical thinking is the development of inductive and deductive logic, beginning in Western thought with Greek philosophers, such as Socrates. An essential critical thinking tool is the challenging, open-ended or Socratic question, designed to help clarify a particular idea or subject. *How do you know what you are saying is true?* exemplifies the Socratic question and captures the essence of critical thinking. Following Socrates, two schools of philosophers, the Cynics and the Skeptics, advanced the development of critical thinking. The Cynics emphasized questioning established civic conventions. They critiqued traditional social values such as family duties, property ownership, and the desirability of wealth and reputation.

The Skeptics asserted that humans are not able to maintain any reliable perception of objects. Thus it is not possible for anyone to make assertions beyond those that describe an individual's immediate experience. In the Skeptic's estimation, the assertion "This hot water is burning my hand" is reliable, an accurate representation of reality, and true. The assertion "History moves in cycles of building up and tearing down" is not reliable and must be viewed agnostically as possibly true or possibly false.

Myth: Critical thinking is a set of soft skills that enable one to please and soothe senior managers.

Critical thinking is a hard and set process that involves using both inductive and deductive reasoning to find flaws in plans, proposals, reports, and strategies. Conveying the results of one's critical thinking may require tact and diplomacy.

Between the ancient world and the Renaissance, critical thinking persisted in the form of philosophy of religion and ethics, such as proofs for God's existence, debates about the nature and origin of evil, speculation about the inherent moral status of specific actions, and questions about the roles reason and revelation play in knowledge.

During and after the Renaissance, critical thinking developed along with the emergence of experimental science. Debates about the origin of knowledge continued: Does knowledge come through rational reflection (Descartes's assertion, "I think therefore I am") or does knowledge come from experience and empirical observation? In addition, changes in traditional beliefs, such as a revision of the belief that the earth is the center of the universe, demonstrated critical thinking at work. The skeptical writings of empiricist David Hume and theories of truth and knowledge developed by German rationalist Immanuel Kant represent critical thinking in the eighteenth century. In the nineteenth century, Jeremy Bentham and John Stuart Mills's development of utilitarianism; the emergence of cultural anthropology, psychology, and other social sciences; and the development of methods of critique, starting with Karl Marx, informed what today constitutes critical thinking.

The current concept of critical thinking as a workplace set of cognitive skills started to cohere in early twentieth century philosophy of education. For example, John Dewey, often regarded as a founder the modern critical thinking tradition, developed ideas that are still current regarding the ways people learn and form consciousness and reasoning abilities. Dewey wrote that critical thinking is the "active, persistent, and careful consideration of a belief or supposed form of knowledge in the light of grounds which support it and further conclusions to which it tends."[1]

By the mid-twentieth century, psychiatrists and cognitive psychologists developed theories about the brain functions involved with critical thinking as well as about environmental factors, such as conditions of uncertainty, that can inhibit critical thinking. For instance, psychologist Edward Glaser, noted that critical thinking is not just a set of cognitive skills but also a psychological state in which the individual possesses an "attitude of being disposed to consider in a thoughtful way the problems and subjects that come within the range of one's experience."[2]

In the early twenty-first century, many organizational leaders began to recognize that a large proportion of the workforce lacks critical thinking skills just when the need for critical thinking, due to global-

Myth: Critical thinking is an innate skill that cannot be taught.

In reality, critical thinking is a set of learned skills that can be enhanced through practice. Critical thinking ability and its supporting analytical reasoning skills are not functions of intelligence.

ization and other economic changes, is increasing. The lack of facility with critical thinking may be due to shifts in higher education. Most traditional liberal arts areas of study, such as history, English, and biology have critical thinking skills embedded in their curricula. More recently developed areas of study, such as marketing, management, and finance tend to focus on gaining proficiency with specific processes and techniques and thus often do not have critical thinking skills embedded in their content. More traditional areas of study involve asking critical questions, such as: How do we know this process really works? Where did it come from? Is it relevant here? Consequently, there is increasing emphasis on critical thinking training in the workplace.

Insights from cognitive psychology regarding inductive and deductive reasoning as cognitive functions and the study of biases and heuristics have informed current ideas about critical thinking in the workplace. The ability to reason logically is often impaired by psychological factors such as cognitive biases, unexamined rules of thumb, and unanalyzed emotional responses to specific situations. Techniques to compensate for psychological impediments include thinking counterfactually, recognizing that some necessary information may be missing and is not obtainable in a particular situation, and seeking to eliminate ambiguity (unclear meaning of information) while recognizing that the uncertainty of "you don't know what you don't know" cannot be fully eliminated.

COGNITIVE SKILLS SUPPORTING CRITICAL THINKING

Critical thinking involves two types of thought processes: deductive reasoning and inductive reasoning.

Deductive Reasoning

Deductive reasoning is the process of considering a series of givens (data) and drawing a conclusion from them. In logic, deduction is represented in syllogisms, such as:

Premise 1: A boiled egg is solid inside its shell.

Premise 2: I am holding an egg that is solid inside its shell.

Conclusion: Therefore, the egg I am holding must be boiled.

The mental process of connecting premise 1 to premise 2, and drawing a conclusion from premise 2 is deduction. People use deductive reasoning to make sense out of their experiences. Deductive reasoning involves the brain's ability to draw inferences. Inferences are thoughts. The syllogism just given involves drawing a categorical inference, which is the brain's ability to remember or imagine a general category (boiled eggs), observe a specific thing and its characteristics (a particular egg), compare the specific to the general, and understand what the specific thing is. People also use deductive inferences when processing conditions. In logic, conditions are represented by if-then statements:

If we get funding, then we will launch a new product.

We are getting funding.

We will launch a new product.

If we get funding, then we will launch a new product.

We are not getting funding.

We will not launch a new product.

To draw either of these conclusions, the brain employs conditional deductive inferences. These examples show that drawing categorical and conditional deductive inferences can be simple. But it can also be difficult. We may jump to a conclusion without having considered enough givens, and we may have trouble processing the uncertainty represented by *if*. Difficulties with conditional reasoning are explored further later in this chapter.

Inductive Reasoning

In contrast to deductive reasoning, inductive reasoning is the brain's ability to examine a conclusion and determine whether it validly follows from the information presented with it. In other words, induction is the ability to assess one's own or another's reasoning itself; induction involves asking if the reasoning behind a conclusion is sound (logical and truthful) or unsound (flawed logic and/or untrue information). For example, suppose you need to review a proposal that your company hire a certified financial planner to be on call for employees to provide them with financial advice. The proposal sites a study of two hundred companies. According to the study, companies that hired an on-call certified financial planner also reported a reduction in the number of sick days taken by employees.

The report concludes that hiring certified financial planners leads to a reduction in the number of days employees miss work. The proposal you are reviewing sites this research as justification for your company hiring a certified financial planner.

You would use inductive reasoning to assess the validity of the proposal, including the validity of the research cited in the proposal. In this case, the research used to justify the proposal may be dubious. There are many reasons, besides access to a certified financial planner, that could cause a reduction in employee sick days. Does the research adequately rule out all these other reasons, and demonstrate that hiring certified financial planners actually causes a reduction in sick days?

Asking questions such as these is the process of inductive reasoning. Inductive reasoning could lead you to hold off on the proposal until you can get a clearer picture of the actual benefits that hiring a certified financial planner to advise employees could have for your company. And putting a hold on the proposal could save you from making a costly mistake in starting an employee program that is largely ineffectual.

The Physiology of Deduction and Inductive Reasoning

As brain functions, deduction and induction can be described both neurologically and psychologically. Neurologically, deduction and induction occur in the frontal cortex of the brain, which is the center of cognitive functions. Critical thinking is called a higher or executive brain function because it occurs in the frontal cortex. Emotion, balance, and motor skills are called lower brain functions because they occur in the amygdala and cerebellum, which are below the frontal cortex. Critical thinking is essential to other executive brain functions such as decision making.

Psychologically, deduction and induction can be represented as ongoing processes of making observations (taking in data), comparing the observations to mental models (conceptions of reality from previous experiences), making a prediction about the best action to take, and taking the action. The process starts again as you observe new data, based on the new situation created by the action you just took. Figure 15-2 represents this process, which some cognitive psychologists call the *hypothetico-predictive process*. This term refers to the idea that when we are critically thinking we are constantly making a theory or hypothesis about what to do in response to the information we encounter, as filtered through our current knowledge (which is at the same time our making a prediction about what will be the best thing to do). The arrows in Figure 15-2 refer to the inferences our brains draw (that is, our thoughts), which are the mechanism by which we make sense of our experiences and respond accordingly. Although deductive and inductive reasoning are distinct cognitive functions, we typically do not experience them as such. Rather, our brains shuttle constantly between the two (in a process sometimes called abduction). Figure 15-2 also shows this shuttling, or abduction. The right side of the figure (moving from observations, through mental models to prediction) involves deductive reasoning. The left side of the model, taking action and making a new set of observations, involves inductive reasoning.

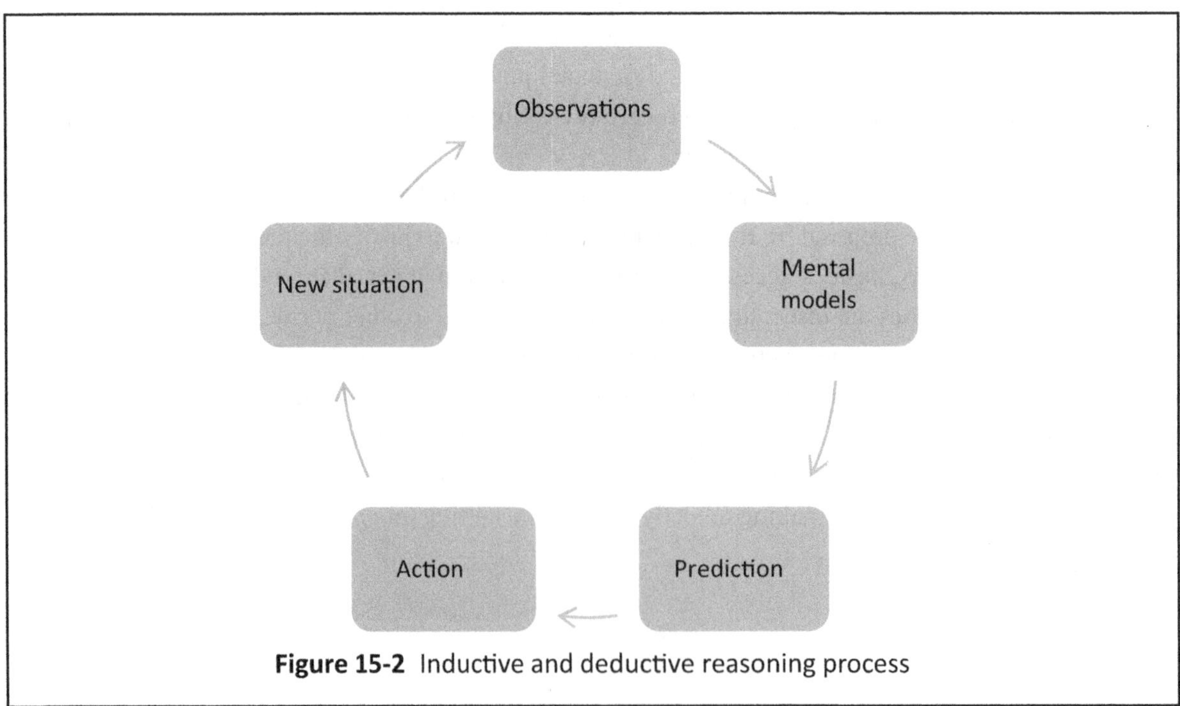

Figure 15-2 Inductive and deductive reasoning process

Most of the time, the hypothetico-predictive process occurs in seconds, and we are unaware of it. In some sense, critical thinking is the effort to slow down this process, so we reason about our actions more thoroughly. Assumptions—such as cognitive biases, which interfere with the ability to draw the correct inference from observations—are part of an individual's mental models. A discussion of specific biases that interfere with critical thinking is included in this chapter.

The process of reasoning deductively and inductively entails more fundamental analytical reasoning skills, such as the ability to recognize patterns and anomalies and the ability to abstract from the facts of a particular situation principles common to all similar situations.

ANALYTICAL SKILLS SUPPORTING CRITICAL THINKING

The following sections discuss the skills needed for critical thinking.

Identifying Patterns and Anomalies

The ability to identify patterns is foundational to critical thinking. In its simplest form, a pattern is a relationship among different things: people, data, situations. When identifying or framing a problem to be solved, look for patterns; if there is no pattern, then that particular situation is an anomaly, or a one-off. Often, an individual cannot identify a pattern because he or she is looking too closely at details. The expression "Can't see the forest for the trees" captures this predicament. This can happen when a problem solver is focused on individual pieces of information instead of looking at the way different pieces of information relate to each other. For example, when reviewing customer satisfaction surveys, a manager may focus on one particular negative customer comment and may not think to look for other similar comments. If there are no similar comments in the other customer reviews, the negative customer comment is not part of a pattern and, standing alone, may not give an accurate picture of all customers' experiences.

Abstracting from the Particular to the General

The ability to step back from the trees to see the forest involves another elementary cognitive skill, the ability to abstract or generalize. For example, if my keys get stuck in the ignition of my car, I might assume all cars of this same model will have the same problem. Recognizing the relationship of the specific to the general helps the problem solver identify a solution or try known remedies to a problem.

Recognizing Cause–Effect Relationships

The third elementary skill is the ability to recognize cause–effect relationships. There are two types of causes: necessary and sufficient. A necessary cause is something that is required for particular outcome to occur. For example, for there to be embers in a fireplace, there had to be a fire. Fire is a necessary cause of embers. A sufficient cause is something that could make a particular outcome possible. For example, a match is a sufficient cause for a fire; a match could be the cause of a fire. However, a match is not a *necessary* cause of a fire. A number of other things (for example, rubbing two sticks together) could also cause a fire. The ability to distinguish between necessary and sufficient causes is foundational to critical thinking. For instance, to accurately identify the cause of the fire, the problem solver would have to understand that matches are only one of a number of sufficient causes of fire and would have to identify all the other sufficient causes and then rule each sufficient cause out to arrive the actual cause of the specific fire in question.

Just as the brain finds it difficult to deal with conditions (if-then), the brain also often finds dealing with sufficient causes difficult (it is psychologically easier to assume that a sufficient cause is a necessary cause because this seems to reduce uncertainty and speed problem solving). But distinguishing between the necessary and the merely sufficient is important. Assuming something is necessary when it is only sufficient results in incomplete analysis of a problem and thus ineffective solutions.

Organizing Items in a Linear Order

The ability to put things in a linear order is the fourth cognitive skill foundational to critical thinking. Linear ordering is identifying relationships among items based on their characteristics and organizing them relative to each other. Psychological studies suggest that people rely, at least partly, on spatial imagery or some sort of spatial representation to achieve linear ordering. Linear ordering can involve organizing people, information, steps in a process, and physical objects. Basic forms of linear ordering involve establishing what must come first, second, third, fourth, and so on; what is smallest and biggest; what is most productive and least productive; what is most expensive and least expensive.

Recognizing Rates of Change

Recognizing rates of changes is another elementary analytical reasoning skill crucial for critical thinking. Is something—costs, customer service requests, returns, orders—increasing or decreasing? There are two types of rates of change. A rate of change (increase or decrease) that remains constant is linear (2, 4, 6, 8, 10 represents a linear rate of change; the initial amount increases by two each time). A rate of change (increase or decrease) that becomes more rapid as it continues through time is exponential (2, 8, 64, 1,024 represents an exponential increase; the initial amount first grows by four, then by eight, then by sixteen).

Myth: Lighting can't strike in the same place twice.

This cliché refers to the assumption that a particular problem will not repeat itself or that the occurrence of one type of problem ensures that additional problems are unlikely. This rule of thumb is mistaken and represents more magical thinking than sound reasoning. The occurrence of a problem in the immediate past is not a good predictor of what may happen in the future.

An exponential rate of change may not follow constant ratios, as does the example just sited. For example, two bacteria in a petri dish can multiply to 256 after eight hours and 16 million after twenty-four hours. (The example of bacteria, though unpleasant, also illustrates why recognizing a rate of exponential change, either of increase or decrease, can be crucial.) Exponential change can mean a problem is quickly becoming dramatically worse and needs immediate attention. Likewise, exponential growth can mean a company must be particularly attentive and agile to meet demand.

Making Sound Probability Judgments

The ability to make probability judgments is the sixth cognitive skill on which critical thinking rests. Probability judgments involve looking for the likelihood that something will or will not happen. Probability is technically, or statistically, defined as the number of ways a particular outcome can occur divided by the number of possible outcomes. More generally, it is a type of personal, predictive judgment about possible consequences of information and actions. Many work situations call for the latter type of probability judgments because there is often not enough available data or time to calculate statistical probability. A problem solver makes a probability judgment simply by asking a question such as, What are the odds—what is the likelihood—of *X* or *Y* happening? For example, deciding what to wear involves a probabilistic judgment about the weather. Similarly, taking a medicine involves a probabilistic judgment about the likelihood of side effects. Psychologists have identified a cognitive bias, the gambler's fallacy, which can make probability judgments difficult. The gambler's fallacy involves thinking that because an event hasn't occurred recently, it probably won't happen anytime soon, or that because an event has happened recently, it won't repeat any time soon. This pitfall involves misunderstanding the probability of specific events occurring or recurring.[3]

Pro tip

Avoid analysis paralysis by recognizing tasks that do not require critical thinking. Routine tasks, particularly those that are part of an established processes, such as checking time sheets and completing expense reports, rely on automatic thinking, not critical thinking. Another antidote to analysis paralysis is recognizing when new information simply conveys the same knowledge as existing information, only using a different format.

Thinking Hypothetically

Finally, the ability to think hypothetically is a building block of critical thinking. Thinking hypothetically is theorizing, or imagining possible situations and outcomes, based on the information available in the present. Like probability judgments, hypothetical thinking involves the ability to generate predictions and visualize what consequences are more or less likely to result from particular courses of action. Hypothetical thinking produces assumptions useful for problem solving, but they have to be tested against data and revised in light of new information. For instance, suppose you manage an order fulfillment process and orders to multiple addresses in a particular zip code are routinely late. An initial assumption might be that there is a problem with the employee(s) driving the delivery truck. This assumption provides a place to start solving the problem, but it has to be validated or disproven by looking at other variables in the fulfillment and delivery process, such as procedures in the warehouse and travel conditions in the zip code in question. The real cause of the problem might be ongoing road repairs in that region, not driver error.

CRITICAL THINKING SKILL 1: BE ALERT TO COGNITIVE BIASES THAT CAUSE MISTAKEN ASSUMPTIONS

Certain assumptions are necessary to formulate questions and gather information, even to *begin* solving a problem. However, assumptions can become problematic when they are not revised in light of additional information and when they are mistaken for facts.

Being alert to assumptions that involves applying insights from cognitive psychology. Many assumptions are based on cognitive biases, which lead to problematic assumptions. The four common types are belief bias, atmospheric effect, anchoring, and misinterpreting conditional information as absolute or certain.

Belief Bias

Belief bias occurs when the subject matter of a problem connects to an individual's experiences and opinions. Perceptions based on previous experiences and opinions interfere with the ability to think critically about the problem itself. Preexisting beliefs about certain subjects can become data that an individual imports into a situation, although those data are not relevant. Consider this prompt from a psychological assessment:

- Joe holds many status meetings for his department.
- Mary likes meetings.
- Mary has transferred into Joe's department.
- Mary has transferred into Joe's department because he holds many meetings.

Is the conclusion true or false? Based on the information given, it could be true or false. But some people want to say the conclusion is true, because they have a belief bias about a woman who likes meetings. They assume she must be looking for a boss who likes them too. This example illustrates how belief bias can function as an assumption that can lead to the wrong conclusion. There are not enough data in this case to draw any definite conclusions about why Mary transferred into Joe's department.

Atmospheric Effect

Atmospheric effect is a metaphorical term that describes the way in which certain words and grammatical constructions predispose individuals to accept as correct or valid conclusions that may not be so. Words such as *some, all, no*, and *not* make it more difficult to evaluate an argument or draw the right conclusion. Consider a prompt from another psychological assessment exploring cognitive bias:

- No advertising executives live in the suburbs.
- All people who live in suburbs shop at strip malls.
- Conclusion: no advertising executives shop at strip malls.[4]

Is the conclusion true or false? The conclusion is likely false. But many people think that the conclusion is true because a series of propositions starts with a negative proposition, e.g., 'No advertising executives,' creates the expectation that the conclusion following from the propositions will also be negative. (For the conclusion to be true, the second statement would have to say "*Only* people who live in suburbs shop at strip malls.")

Anchoring

Anchoring refers to a tendency to give precedence to the first piece of information encountered when researching a solution or decision. The first piece of information may not be the most accurate or relevant, but because it is first, it may become the scale by which the accuracy and relevance of all subsequent information is assessed.

Confusing the Conditional with the Certain

The fourth cognitive bias is misinterpreting data as certain when they are conditional. Psychological studies suggest that our brains want to convert ambiguity and uncertainty to certainty. Categories with uncertainty (some things, sometimes) or uncertain conditions (if-then) can be hard to process mentally. Consider the following statements:

- Viewright, Inc. produces microscopes.
- Some microscopes are shipped via ground.
- There are ten microscopes to be shipped today.

Myth: Critical thinking takes too much time. It would be faster if I just did it.

This myth may reflect a bias for action, meaning looking busy and doing something seem more important than researching and analyzing. In reality, thinking is essential for effective action. Critical thinking speed comes with practice. Just as practicing a sport or musical instrument increases proficiency, likewise persistently using critical thinking skills enhances their performance.

Should you choose:

1. Ship the ten microscopes via ground.
2. Find out which microscopes should be shipped via ground today.

If you answered 2, you are correct. However, when this item is part of a timed assessment, most participants answer 1. The reason is that the brain tends to convert or misinterpret the uncertainty represented by *some* microscopes, as an absolute, or certainty, *all* microscopes.[5]

To summarize, the critical thinking skill of recognizing assumptions is largely the task of being aware of the types of cognitive biases that lead problem solvers to import irrelevant information or misinterpret the information that is relevant. Recognizing assumptions entails understanding why the brain makes assumptions in the first place. As the brain goes through the process of making observations, comparing to mental models, making predictions, and taking actions, it, out of necessity, must make some assumption, even to know what additional observations to make and information to gather. Nonetheless, processing uncertainty is a challenging cognitive function. The brain consequently makes assumptions, not just to initiate problem solving but to compensate for uncertainty, often compensating for the cognitive challenge by providing itself a false certainty that undermines critical thinking.

CRITICAL THINKING SKILL 2: ASSESS PERSUASION TECHNIQUES AND ARGUMENTS THAT OBSCURE FACTS AND RELEVANT INFORMATION

Effective managers are able to maintain an objective viewpoint when evaluating arguments and information, which largely involves inductive logic and reasoning. To assess another person or group's reasoning, a critical thinker needs to be able to recognize patterns of weak arguments and persuasion techniques, which are often used to make flawed data and poorly reasoned conclusions appear to be relevant, comprehensive, valid, or cogent.

The following sections describe eight patterns of weak arguments that are particularly relevant to critical thinking and management.

Circular Reasoning

Circular reasoning is a pattern of weak argument in which the person or group making an assertion responds to requests for elaboration by restating the original assertion in different words. In other words, the argument restates the original position, rather than providing evidence for the original position. Here are some obvious examples: The earth is round because it is circular. The famous American newscaster Walter Cronkite was an effective communicator because he was good at communicating. An out-of-date air conditioner makes a lot of noise because out-of-date equipment is noisy.

Typically, critical thinkers encounter circular reasoning in forms that are more subtle than these examples. A common form is an appeal to authority: "We should do *X* because important person *Y* told us *X* is important to do." The reality of a situation is that an individual may have to do *X* because a more powerful person says to do it, but the force of the powerful person's authority does not in itself explain or even ensure that it is the right thing to do. Similarly, circular reasoning often takes the form of self-referential authority. For example, a researcher may refer to only her own previous research to indicate the validity of her current finding. Or a report claims to be credible because the person who produced the report asserts that he is trustworthy and produces only credible reports. Looking for additional sources and data to corroborate or verify claims and conclusions is the most effective way to overcome these sorts of circular arguments. But recognizing that a circular argument is being put forward is essential to recognizing the need to seek corroboration.

False Dichotomy

A false dichotomy is an attempt to create a binary choice—to suggest a black or white solution to a problem—when, in reality, there are a number of viable options and gray areas. A false dichotomy is meant to generate anxiety and promote one conclusion or option beyond any others by suggesting extreme consequences if any other course is pursued. An example of a false dichotomy is this: We can either stop using cars or destroy the earth. The person making this point wants to persuade others that the only possible action is to stop using cars. In reality, there are many other actions that could also save the earth.

Slippery Slope

Another pattern of weak argument meant to generate anxiety and coerce a particular choice or course of action is the slippery slope: If situation *A* happens, then, before you know it, *B, C*, and *D* will happen and then catastrophic situation *E* will result. This is a tactic for undermining ideas or plans by suggesting that a worst-case scenario will necessarily result if the idea or plan in question is implemented. An example is this: If we have stricter sanitation grades for restaurants, virtually every restaurant will go out of business due to the increased costs. There is no necessary, much less immediate, relationship between increased sanitation standards for restaurants and their going out of business. The goal of the slippery slope argument, in this example, is to invalidate the idea of increased standards by suggesting it will lead to a calamitous result.

Ad Hoc Reasoning

Another pattern of weak argument critical thinkers should recognize is ad hoc reasoning. *Ad hoc* is Latin for "to this." An ad hoc argument is an attempt to prove a point, at any cost, even by referring to purported data that are irrelevant and/or false. No matter what objection is brought up, the person making an ad hoc argument will find an explanation (perhaps not a legitimate one) to invalidate the objection. A critical thinker must recognize that in order for a conclusion to be true there must be some circumstance under which it could be false; otherwise, there is no way of telling the difference between true or false.

An ad hoc argument is designed to persuade others of an assertion's truth by suggesting that the assertion is non-falsifiable (never false). In reality, the non-falsifiability of the ad hoc argument only renders the assertion in question incoherent. A true assertion can be falsified. For example, a television show claims that extra sensory perception (ESP) works only when everyone present in a group believes in it. When the person with purported ESP fails to demonstrate the ability, the failure is because someone present didn't believe in ESP. In this case, the problem is never with ESP itself; ESP, in this situation, is non-falsifiable. The ad hoc reason in this example is the insistence that for ESP to work, everyone must believe in it.

Ad Hominem

Another pattern of weak argument with a Latin moniker is ad hominem, which may be translated as "to the person." An example of an ad hominin argument is:

> PERSON A: I can see you put a lot of time into this report, but you needed to review data from as far back as 2010, not just the past two years.
>
> PERSON B: You don't know what you are talking about. Your glasses are so thick I am surprised you can read anything at all.

Person B's response is ad hominem. Ad hominem is a weak or invalid form of argument because it responds to a legitimate observation with an attack on an irrelevant personal characteristic of the individual making the initial observation. An ad hominem attack can also be directed at a group. Like other forms of weak argument, ad hominem is an effort to divert attention away from a point that someone finds problematic while putting the person or group making the point on the defensive. Ad hominem arguments are also intended to generate strong emotional responses that can, neurologically, temporary shutdown the brain's ability to think critically.

Tu Quoque

A weak argument similar to ad hominem is tu quoque, a Latin phrase which may be translated as "you, too." An example of a tu quoque argument is:

> SUPERVISOR: You can see on your time card that you have been late three days in a row. We need to address this issue.
>
> EMPLOYEE: You are sometimes late too, so how can you criticize me.

The employee responds to the manager with a tu quoque. The goal of this type of argument is to discredit an individual or group's position by asserting that the individual or group is prey to the same issue that the individual or group seeks to address. Tu quoque is a weak or invalid argument pattern because the standing of an individual or group does not bear on the validity of assertions the individual or group may make. In the example, the employee is late, and the situation must be addressed, regardless of the status of the supervisor. Tu quoque responses are a way to divert attention from the salient point in an argument or to put another person on the defensive. An effective way to overcome a tu quoque argument is to reassert the facts under discussion.

Bandwagon

Another common pattern, the bandwagon argument, involves this kind of assertion: Everyone is doing *A*, so you need to get on the bandwagon (join the club, get with the program) and do it too. The bandwagon argument, like similar patterns, plays on a kind of fear, what is now colloquially called FOMO (fear of missing out). In other words, the bandwagon is an attempt to coerce a course of action by playing on the fear of being left out of a group and possibly made fun of. Others get on the bandwagon to protect their status or for other reasons.

An example of a bandwagon argument is: The most successful, powerful executives have a particular app on their smartphones. If you want to be viewed as successful and powerful, you better get the app. In reality, however, the app may not be right for every executive. Moreover, having the app on one's smartphone does not guarantee that an executive will be perceived of as successful and powerful.

Red Herring

The final pattern of weak argument relevant for critically thinking managers is the red herring. This is a diversionary tactic that is meant to distract from the key issue at hand. Typically, an individual or group will employ this when they cannot address, or simply want to avoid, the issue at hand. Here is an example of a red herring:

> INTERVIEWER: What is your company doing to reduce the amount of mercury in your fish, which seems to be poisoning your consumers?
>
> EXECUTIVE: I know people are getting sick because the level of mercury in seafood may be unsafe, but what will the fishermen and fisherwomen do to feed their families? Our company provides employment to hundreds of fishermen and fisherwomen, and we are committed to helping them sustain their livelihoods.

In this example, the executive may appear to be staying on the subject because the executive is talking about fish; moreover, the needs of anglers are legitimate concerns. In reality, bringing up the needs of the people who catch the fish, although their needs are real, diverts attention from the question of mercury in fish, which harms consumers.

* * *

To summarize, the ability to evaluate arguments and information involves the skill of identifying patterns of weak argument, which obscure facts and play on emotions. All of the patterns discussed have this in common: They should raise a red flag and lead a manager to ask, "Why is this person or group employing a weak argument rather than supplying relevant information and directly answering questions." Being able to say, diplomatically, "It sounds like you are using a persuasion technique, why are you falling back on one of those?" is a way to redirect a person or group deploying one of these patterns.

Reacting to a situation based on emotion is the opposite of a reasoned response. Critical thinking occurs in the brain's frontal cortex and emotional responses occur in the amygdala. When an individual perceives

Myth: Emotions get in the way of critical thinking.
While this is partially true, emotions can also provide useful data for critical thinking.

a threat, the amygdala may release chemicals that trigger a fight, flee, or freeze response in the individual, temporarily shutting down his or her critical thinking ability.

However, an analysis of one's emotions (as opposed to acting on them) can provide data that enhance critical thinking. In other words, emotions can be rationalized into self-awareness, which enhances recognition of cognitive biases and alertness to missing information. Assuming that critical thinking and the very experience of emotions are opposites may lead individuals to deny they have an emotional response to a situation. This can be a mistake. While managing outward emotional reactions to situations is important in organizational life, pretending that emotions do not exist at all ignores an important source of information. Moreover, psychologically, emotions do not go away. When they are ignored, they eventually express themselves in ways that may not be appropriate.

Managing emotions by identifying them and asking what is causing them is a more effective response. For example, if a manager is using inductive reasoning to assess a conclusion and begins to feel anxiety or alarm, asking, "What am I feeling right now and why am I feeling it?" can be instructive.

While the first impulse of many accomplished professionals might be to push such feelings away, such emotions, similar to intuitive or gut judgments, are triggered by some important aspect of the situation that is not immediately apparent through conscious deliberation. For instance, a feeling of anxiety can lead to recognition that important information is missing and that a conclusion needs to be revised in light of further investigation.

Ultimately, the critical thinking skill of identifying weak arguments and persuasion techniques is a way of ensuring you are objectively looking at all relevant data, unclouded by sentiment, in order to draw the right conclusion from those data. This skill sometimes involves dissecting conclusions other people have drawn and want you to accept as rationales for particular courses of action. Drawing the right conclusion from relevant data and vetting the conclusions other people present form the basis of sound decision making and problem solving.

CRITICAL THINKING SKILL 3: RECOGNIZE FAULTY REASONING THAT LEADS TO CONCLUSIONS THAT DO NOT SOLVE THE PROBLEM

An effective manager can draw conclusions to identify the appropriate tools, resources, and expertise to develop the best solutions and to translate abstract ideas into tangible results and actions that can be understood and viably considered. Several cognitive strategies help ensure that a critically thinking manager draws a conclusion that addresses the problem at hand and that logically follows from the information available.

Recognizing Confirmation Bias

First, drawing conclusions effectively involves recognizing a common psychological tendency to accept conclusions that conform to or reinforce what an individual or group expects or hopes to see. Looking only at evidence that supports an anticipated or hoped for conclusion is confirmation bias. To question assumptions and draw the right conclusion, a manager with a critical thinking competency will seek disconfirming or confounding evidence that undermines a proposed conclusion and will figure out how to address that evidence.

If the confounding evidence can be refuted, the conclusion is more likely right. For example, an individual has the opportunity to invest in the development of an app. The person thinks and reads more about how quickly people can make money from a successful app. Based on this research, the individual invests in the app development. Thinking only of the success stories, as in this example, is the confirmation bias. The success stories confirm what the investor already thinks. To compensate for confirmation bias, the investor would also need to consider the failure rate of apps and evaluate the likelihood of a return on investment as well as the potential for losing the investment.

Related to confirmation bias is the problem of non-falsifiability, alluded to briefly in the discussion of ad hoc arguments. To better understand non-falsifiability, consider the work of Benjamin Rush.

Rush (1745–1813) was a physician, scientist, reformer, signer of the Declaration of Independence, and professor of chemistry at the College of Philadelphia medical school. He believed bloodletting would cure most illnesses. He subjected all of his patients who had serious illnesses to bloodletting. If the patient recovered, Rush credited bloodletting. If the patient died, he claimed the disease was so bad, nothing would cure it.

Where was the flaw in Rush's reasoning? He dismissed or ignored all evidence that contradicted his theory about bloodletting. In other words, his theory was non-falsifiable or could not be disproven.

Logically, when a theory, or conclusion, cannot be disproven, it also cannot be proven. Consequently, to know that a conclusion is likely the best one in given situation, a critically thinking manager has to be able to identify under what circumstances the theory or conclusion would be wrong or invalid. To test the value of bloodletting, Rush would need to investigate all of the factors that lead to patient recovery (for instance, determining whether the patients had other variables in common besides bloodletting), and he would need to withhold bloodletting from a set of seriously ill patients to see if they also recovered or died without the treatment. These tactics would enable Rush to be more certain that bloodletting was, indeed, the variable that caused patient recovery.

Employing Counterfactual Thinking

Counterfactual thinking is an effective way to compensate for confirmation bias and to avoid conclusions that are non-falsifiable. Counterfactual thinking "is the ability to look at a situation from a variety of perspectives, especially from the point of view of others who are likely to have values and frames of reference that differ from one's own."[6] In addition, counterfactual thinking may also involve seeking contrary evidence or confounding variables, attending to rather than ignoring or suppressing disconfirming evidence. Specific counterfactual thinking techniques include having a colleague play the role of devil's advocate (this is distinct from someone who is just negative or nay-saying) and consciously distinguishing between correlation and causation. Correlations may be irrelevant or misleading, and managers often confuse correlation with causation. A correlation occurs when two things happen at the same time, such as the following statement: When the weather is hotter, more thefts occur.

Many people have an instinct to assume that a correlation indicates causation. In realty, a correlation may suggest causation or it may be nothing more than a coincidence. Managers may make poor decisions when they assume a correlation indicates causation. Therefore, analyzing correlations to determine whether they indicate causation is important.

Based on the statement about temperatures and thefts, many people assume that the parallel between higher temperatures and higher rates of theft means that higher temperatures actually cause more thefts. However, this is not true. There is a variable connecting temperatures and crime: opportunity. When it is warmer, more people leave doors and windows open, which permits more successful thefts.

Researchers arrived at this conclusion about the relationship between temperature and rates of theft by using counterfactual thinking. They reviewed and ruled out all of the variables, besides temperature, that might explain increased theft rates. Researchers thus identified the one variable—opportunity—that connects temperature and theft rate.

Anyone can use the technique employed by the researchers. When you are faced with a correlation and you need to determine if it indicates causation, identify contrary facts that would undermine the apparent relationship between the correlated variables. For example the following statement is a correlation many people assume indicates causation: When employee morale increases, productivity increases. To test the assumption of causation, identify contrary facts or confounding variables that would suggest there is not a causal relationship between the two variables. One confounding variable would be that people are more productive when they are worried about being laid off.

Understanding the Illusion of Validity

A different set of challenges related to drawing conclusions derives from a general tendency to use too small of a sample, or a nonrepresentative sample, as grounds for a particular conclusion. A specific expression of this tendency is a cognitive bias called the illusion of validity. Individuals and groups are prey to this cognitive bias when they assume that a set of information provides a solid foundation for making predictions, simply because those data present a consistent pattern. For example, suppose you have the results of a survey of customers from a particular geographic location and time frame. The survey may present patterns about customer preferences. But the survey results are relevant only for the participants in the survey. The survey results do not provide enough information to make predictions about how other groups of customers in other regions and time frames might behave. The illusion of validity would occur, in this example, if a manager assumed were to draw conclusions about the behavior of many or all customer groups from the behavior a particular group at a particular time.

Another specific instance of relying on too small of a sample is basing a conclusion on ideas or information that come immediately to mind rather than thoroughly looking for all relevant information. Said differently, relying too heavily on personal, often anecdotal knowledge can lead individuals and groups to make assumptions and discount or fail to seek relevant data. Consider this management example: Two employees complain to their manager about a third employee's attitude. The manager concludes that the entire department has a problem with the third employee. The manager may be drawing the wrong conclusions. Two complaints make up too small of a sample from which to draw a conclusion about an entire department. The manager could also be relying too heavily on interpretations that come easily to mind based on previous experiences. The manager would need to review the facts of the third employee's performance before drawing a conclusion about the employee.

Another way to compensate for the illusion of validity and related biases is to be alert to missing information. This usually requires deliberate questioning. Some psychological studies find that people tend to assume any set of information they receive is complete or sufficient to solve a problem in question. To offset the tendency to rely on too small or nonrepresentative samples, remember the largest category of knowledge is "you don't know what you don't know." Everyone is aware of subjects they know thoroughly; and, everyone is aware of subjects of which they have limited knowledge. For example, an accountant knows that she has a vast knowledge of accounting, and only a limited knowledge of medicine. Drawing the right conclusion involves recognizing that, in addition to being aware of the extent and limits of your personal knowledge (like the accountant in the example), there are some subjects or fields of whose existence you are completely unaware. This third category of knowledge is sometimes called "DKDK:" you-don't-know-what-you-don't-know. Drawing the right conclusion involves recognizing you are likely unaware of even the existence of some subjects. Seeking feedback from others, whose experience and expertise differ from yours, is an effective way to uncover missing information and overcome the challenge represented by not knowing what you don't know.

Avoiding Entrapment

Drawing conclusions often involves judgments about correcting a mistake or remedying a failure. In these situations, groups and individuals sometimes cannot draw the right conclusion because they are prey to a cognitive bias referred to as entrapment. Entrapment inhibits the ability to determine when to cut losses. This pitfall involves feeling that time and money should be invested in a failing project or program simply because a great deal of time and money has already been invested in the project. In other words, individuals and groups become entrapped by focusing on things that have already been invested. They are unable to recognize that the initial investment will not be recouped (initial investments of this sort are often referred to as sunk costs), and that they are only losing more money by allowing the failing thing to continue.

Recognizing the Relevance of Intuitive or Gut Judgments

A final critical thinking skill important for drawing conclusions is recognition and assessment of individual intuitive or gut judgments. A number of psychologists have found that critical thinking involves both intuitive and analytical mental components—that is, it is a dual cognitive process. Intuitive components are characterized by quick pattern recognition and rapid responses to information. They are so fast they seem instinctual, automatic, or gut. Through experience, what started out as a learned analytic process becomes intuitive. While intuitive judgments speed thinking, they sometimes lead people to misjudge the likelihood of events based on their recall of similar instances. Psychologists often describe these intuitive or gut judgments as composed of heuristics (rules of thumb).

Everyone develops rules of thumb through their professional lives. The more frequently an individual experiences a certain situation, the more rules of thumb the individual develops, which serve as instinctive guides in subsequent, similar situations. As illustrated in Figure 15-2, the brain automatically tries to find a parallel between a new situation and a situation already experienced (mental models). Sometimes, an individual's heuristics fit the new situation, and sometimes they do not. Because they do not always fit, critically thinking managers have to be self-aware and deliberate about using personal rules of thumb.

To summarize, the critical thinking skill of recognizing faulty reasoning is partly a matter of alertness to types of cognitive biases (such as confirmation bias and the illusion of validity) that can lead us to be overly credulous of predictions and results that *seem* to confirm our hopes and desires. Recognizing faulty reasoning is also a matter of remembering the limits of our knowledge (in any given situation, there is much we don't know, and we don't even realize we don't know it). Finally, it is employing a healthy skepticism regarding the data we encounter as well as the arguments other people make to us. Seeking to disprove data used to support conclusions (and thus possible solutions and decisions) is a skeptical endeavor with a good intent: to avoid mistakes and ensure success.

WHEN IS CRITICAL THINKING IMPORTANT?

Critical thinking is essential for managers in a number of circumstances.

Negotiating Purchases

Engage in critical thinking in any situation involving the possibility of up sell. Such situations particularly require the ability to sidestep persuasion techniques and recognize weak arguments. Suppose, for example, a roofing company suggests that while a property manager is renting the equipment to repair an office building's roof, the manager should go ahead and replace the entire roof to avoid incurring the cost of renting equipment again later. The manager should be cautious: The cost of renting equipment may be a small percentage of the cost of replacing the entire roof. In this case, the manager should actually analyze the costs and not be taken in by a persuasion technique. Or suppose a vendor offers your organization a purportedly good deal on a supply or a service, claiming they care only about the success of your organization. As the manager responsible for such a contract, you should ask the vendor critical thinking questions, such as, "How will *you* benefit if I take you up on this deal?" "What will *you* lose if I don't take you up on this deal?"

Vetting Proposals

As suggested by the last example, a second situation requiring critical thinking is reviewing and vetting any type of proposal, ranging from changing a program or process to changing business strategies, such as entering a new market or launching a new product. Consider this statement: Last year's program participants did not like the opening retreat, so this year's retreat must be changed. Is this the right conclusion? Not necessarily. This may be an occasion for which the illusion of validity comes into play. The opinion of last year's participants may not tell you anything about the expectations and preferences of this year's participants. Consider a similar example: A survey of existing customers tells us we should not change our warranty program; therefore, we should not change our warranty program. Is this the right conclusion to draw from the survey data? Not necessarily; the opinion of existing customers represents a kind of confirmation bias. Your organization would need to find a way of interviewing people who are no longer your customers, and base conclusions about the warranty program on feedback from both satisfied and dissatisfied users. Consider a third example: We should move into that geographical region because three of our competitors are entering that region. Is this sound reasoning? Not necessarily; your organization needs to do more research to establish whether it is actually protecting or gaining market share from competitors by entering that region or is, instead, simply getting on the bandwagon with competitors, without actually securing an advantage for itself. When reviewing any proposal, always ask, "Who benefits?" from acceptance of the proposal. Identify what unstated stakeholders would benefit from and may be driving the proposal.

Pro tip

Recognize that some data have limited predictive ability. For example, what a survey tells you about the particular people surveyed may not be relevant to the perceptions or behaviors of other people whose responses you want to anticipate.

Triaging, Prioritizing, Setting Timelines

Situations that call for organizing, ordering, triaging, and prioritizing form a third category of circumstances in which critical thinking is essential. Such situations include developing and launching something new (a product, program, or initiative) as well as responding to crises. Analytical skills are required for figuring out what data are relevant for determining the need for something new and then for establishing the steps for creating and implementing it. Linear ordering and pattern recognition, used together, make up the critical thinking skills of examining assumptions and assessing the validity of conclusions (see also Chapter 16, Managing and Mastering Data).

Deciding how best to respond to a crisis also requires examining assumptions and recognizing persuasion techniques. Consider a situation in which a company launches a new product. Research shows the product is safe and focus groups enjoyed using the product. Once the product is launched, complaints about the product spread across social media. An uncritical emotional response to such a public relations issue might be simply to pull the product. But a more reasoned response, employing critical thinking, would involve assessing the number and geographical location of the complaints, researching the veracity of the complaints, and developing a staged response, aligned with the collection of new information.

Performance Management

Finally, performance management often calls for critical thinking (see Chapter 14, Talent Management). Objectively evaluating an employee's work quality and interpersonal behaviors requires skills associated with the tendency to:

- Rely on assumptions, such as compensating for belief bias
- Draw conclusions, such as compensating for confirmation bias
- Draw conclusions from too little information
- Draw conclusions by reference to at-hand knowledge and rules of thumb

• Conclusion •

It is important to note that effective critical thinking involves dispositions or habits of mind. Chief among these are the willingness to ask questions, a sense of curiosity, a desire to find the truth in a given situation, and a willingness to be wrong or to be disproven without becoming defensive or feeling intellectually insecure. Critically thinking managers persevere in the face of obstacles and mistakes, perceive effort as a path to mastery, learn from others' critiques, and recognize lessons in others' successes. Another hallmark of critical thinking is to always ask questions (such as, "How would we know this is true?") and to seek constructive criticism from people with different, sometimes opposing points of view. The mind-set that supports critical thinking also includes a willingness to engage in constructive conflict to clarify ideas and close gaps in information or logical reasoning.

Maintaining the mind-set and mastering the critical thinking skills themselves are both essential to effective management. Critically thinking managers are able to make decisions and solve problems in a timely way because they are able to quickly identify which data are relevant and which are irrelevant for a particular situation. They are also able to assess the quality of data, determining which are trustworthy and which are not based on sound research or valid sources. Likewise, managers who master critical thinking achieve better outcomes because they act only on high-quality data and because they are able to recognize possible gaps in their own reasoning and compensate for gaps by asking others to critique their thoughts and conclusions.

• Endnotes •

1. John Dewey, *How We Think* (Boston, Massachusetts: D.H. Heath & Co., 1910).
2. Edward Glaser, *An Experiment in the Development of Critical Thinking* (New York: Columbia University Press, 1941).
3. Diane Halpern, *Thought and Knowledge: An Introduction to Critical Thinking* (New York: Psychology Press, 2017), p. 12.
4. Ibid.
5. Ibid.
6. Raymond S. Nickerson, *The Teaching of Thinking* (Hillsdale, New Jersey: Lawrence Erlbaum Associates, 1985).

Managing and Mastering Data

LEARNING OBJECTIVES

By the end of this chapter, you will be better equipped to:

- Provide an orientation to the practice of managing and mastering data.
- Gain a better understanding of why data have become much more integrated into the day-to-day responsibilities of the manager.
- Discuss how to ask good questions and collect relevant data.
- Discuss how to approach analyzing the data and communicating the results in a way to influence others to take action.

INTRODUCTION

Your ability to manage and master data is critical to your credibility and performance as a manager. For example, take a moment to think about all of the different tasks a manager is expected to complete: from setting work priorities and assigning staff, to monitoring the quality of products and services produced, to problem solving when something goes wrong, to keeping an eye on your employees' performance and looking for ways to develop them to the next level.

Now think of the data you routinely use to accomplish these tasks:

- When setting work priorities, you are leveraging data related to production goals (such as manufacturing so many engine parts per day)
- When assigning individuals, you are comparing their capabilities and their levels of experience (and productivity and ability to work with others on the team)

- When monitoring the quality of products and services, you are pouring through quality metrics and customer feedback, triangulating the information by leveraging both data sources together to identify potential issues and to see where things can be improved
- When problem solving, you are likely gathering whatever information you can to try to identify what the actual problem is as well as some potential solutions to implement
- When monitoring the performance of your people, you are continually capturing performance data from a variety of sources, including your own observations and the feedback from others who work with your team members
- When reviewing personal data, you must aggregate information into annual performance reviews, which provide a summary of performance trends throughout the year.

Each of these managerial tasks requires you to leverage data to do your part in planning, making accurate decisions, and identifying how to develop your people, both individually and as a team.

When we talk about managing and mastering data, we are referring to your ability to ask the most insightful, business-relevant questions, to know how to collect and analyze data, and then to interpret and communicate the results in a way that answers the questions and influences people to take action.

HOW THE ROLE OF MANAGER IS EVOLVING BECAUSE OF DATA AND ANALYTICS

To understand how the role of manager is evolving, we must first understand how our whole society is being transformed by data. Essentially, we are witnessing an amazing digital transformation that affects every aspect of our society (discussed in greater detail in Chapter 20, Technology). As David Reinsel and his colleagues at IDC note, this digital transformation "is about the integration of intelligent data into everything we do."[1] We now live in an age where everything we do, consisting of every behavior and every action, seems to be connected somehow to data.

Much of these data are gathered through our mobile devices. According to Radicati Group,[2] the total number of mobile devices connected to the Internet will top 13 billion in 2019 and are forecasted to exceed 16.8 billion by the end of 2023. And the growth in data created online by all devices, including emails and Facebook posts and Twitter, is staggering. For example, the Radicati Group estimates the total number of business and consumer emails sent and received *per day* will exceed 293 billion in 2019 and are forecasted to grow to over 347 billion by year end 2023.[3] Internet Live Stat estimates that Google processes about 40,000 searches per second (3.5 billion searches per day and 1.2 trillion searches per year), while Twitter users generate 6,000 tweets per second (500 million tweets are sent each day and 200 billion tweets per year).[4] As for Facebook, over 2.4 billion people are active users every month (nearly 1.6 billion daily) generating over 4 Petabytes of data every day.[5]

And as consumers, we are also buying more and more devices that create and consume data on their own. These Web-enabled devices are collectively called the Internet of Things (IoT). Examples of IoT devices are the Amazon Echo device, doorbell cams, and Wi-Fi-enabled thermostats that can be adjusted via a smartphone.

IDC predicts that in 2025, "75% of the world's population will interact with data every day," "each connected person will have at least one data interaction every 18 seconds," and "many of these interactions are because of the billions of IoT devices connected across the globe, which are expected to create over 90ZB of data in 2025."[6] Looking at all data sources in total, IDC predicts that the global datasphere will grow to 175 ZB by 2025.

Pro tip

ZB refers to Zettabytes, or a 1 followed by 21 zeroes. Based on an estimate by researchers at University of Hawaii, that may be more than the total number of sand grains on beaches and deserts in the world.[7]

That is *a lot* of data. And the trend is for this information to be accessible real-time to consumers, including managers like you. IDC predicts that in 2025, "49% of the world's stored data will reside in public cloud environments" and "that due to the infusion of data into our business workflows and personal streams of life, that nearly 30% of the Global Datasphere will be real-time by 2025."[8]

Taken together, this means our world is becoming more and more digitized and how we live and work will continue to adapt to the growing accessibility to data and information. The next section focuses on how the role of manager is evolving with this digital transformation.

The Role of Manager and the Digital Transformation

If we consider employees to be the most important asset of a company (and, *ahem*, we should), the manager is responsible for leveraging this asset to achieve the greatest value to the organization. The actual tasks managers are expected to complete can be quite varied, highlighting the practical nature of the job. As Sam Lewisohn so eloquently put it nearly a century ago, "Management is the art of getting things done."[9] In this regard, the goal of managing people hasn't really changed, though how we accomplish the goal has.

Managers today are being asked to do more than they ever have had to do. Generally, organizations are running flatter and leaner, which is putting more decision-making power into the hands of managers in the organization. This shift in decision-making responsibility has been accompanied with a cry from managers for more data to drive more informed decisions in real-time.

Table 16-1 illustrates how data have thoroughly infiltrated all aspects of the manager's role. Based on a list of thirty-one work activities associated with the manager role (as identified by O*Net[10]), the work activities are organized into two buckets:

- *Collecting and Analyzing Data*: contains ten work activities and entails finding, collecting, and organizing information into a format that can be analyzed as well as examining the data in ways to gain insights and understanding
- *Leveraging Data to Influence Action*: contains twenty-one work activities and entails interpretation of the results from the analyses and making decisions and influencing others to act

The takeaway from this analysis is that managers are leveraging data in pretty much every task assigned to them. If managers don't have mastery over the collection and analysis of data or the ability to report and influence action on results, they are going to fall behind.

Given that the proliferation of data is predicted to grow exponentially, the trend is also going to be that managers will need to become more adept at driving some of the research and data analytics on the "front lines." Essentially, the proliferation of data has led to a shortage of data scientists, forcing managers to take on more and more of the actual data collection, analysis, and reporting of results. Leong speaks of the lack of skills in the current workforce for conducting research, such as math, business, legal, and data architecture skills.[11] The shortage of data scientists simply means that the ability to manage and master data is becoming increasingly critical, and those managers who have the right skill sets will be highly sought after.

Working with data requires a baseline knowledge of the following terms:

- *Population*: the entire group of people or things you are interested in knowing something about. For example, the population of left-handed people consists of everyone in the world who is left-handed (Worldatlas.com estimates about 10 percent, or 770 million). The population of giraffes consists of every giraffe in the world (about 111,000, based on an estimate from the Giraffe Conservation Foundation).[12]
- *Sample*: a smaller group that is meant to be representative of the larger group. It is often impossible to capture information from every person or thing in a population, so we must focus on a smaller group that mirrors the larger group. There is no way we could capture data from every leftie or giraffe in the world, so we instead look at smaller groups that represent the larger groups. As a researcher, it is critical to evaluate if the sample is representative of the population.
- *Variable*: a characteristic of something that you measure. For example, if you are interested in studying the body temperature of adults, then you take a thermometer reading from a sample of adults and record the results. The variable in this case is "adult body temperature" and consists of all of the readings that were captured.
- *Outlier*: a data value outside the expected range. When we take a measurement of something, we expect the result to fall within a certain range. For example, if we take the temperature of a large group of adults, we would expect the range to be between 97°F and 99°F (per WebMD).[13] However, if we notice that one of the adults has a temperature measured at 104°F, this measurement would be an outlier because it falls outside of the normal range. In this particular case, the result may mean that the temperature reading was wrong (an error) or that the adult unfortunately has a very bad fever and should see a doctor.
- *Average*: a measure of the center of a distribution of scores for a variable. For example, if a class takes a test, the average grade reflects how well the whole class did on the test, even though individual students in the class each had a different score on the test.
- *Standard Deviation*: a measure of how different the scores are distributed within a group. For example, a small standard deviation on test grades within the class indicates all the students' scores are close to the class average, while a large standard deviation indicates test scores that were more spread out.

Table 16-1 Manager's Role Working with Data	
Collecting and Analyzing Data	**How Do Data Factor into the Role?**
Interacting with computers	Using computers to gather information from internal or external sources (doing online research to find data on consumer trends)
Performing administrative activities	Maintaining electronic records and files (keeping travel expenses updated)
Getting information	Gathering information from different sources (the act of actually collecting data)
Documenting and recording information	Storing information in a usable format (typing of data into a spreadsheet)
Processing information	Organizing information to be more accessible (sorting sales leads based on likelihood of sale)
Identifying objects, actions, and events	Defining the qualities of an event (determining criteria that define a heart attack)
Analyzing data or information	Capturing important context about data (documenting when the data were collected)
Judging the qualities of things, services, or people	Providing ratings on things based on experience (estimated value of a customer)
Estimating the quantifiable characteristics of products, events, or information	Making estimates about the qualities of things (the percent of boots that are red)
Evaluating information to determine compliance with standards	Comparing information against standards (percent error rate)
Leveraging Data to Influence Action	**How Do Data Factor into the Role?**
Monitoring and controlling resources	Reviewing a budget report
Monitor processes, materials, or surroundings	Reviewing a production dashboard
Making decisions and solving problems	Reviewing data supporting different possible decisions
Interpreting the meaning of information for others	Explaining what information means to a stakeholder
Provide consultation and advice to others	Providing some guidance to what someone should do based on the results of an analysis
Leveraging Data to Influence Action	**How Do Data Factor into the Role?**
Updating and using relevant knowledge	Continually improving your own knowledge and experience

Leveraging Data to Influence Action	How Do Data Factor into the Role?
Thinking creatively	Leveraging new results to come up with alternative solutions to problems
Establishing and maintaining interpersonal relationships	Using social media (like LinkedIn) to learn more about people
Communicating with supervisors, peers, or subordinates	Sharing presentation of analyses to alert management about production issues
Communicating with persons outside organization	Compiling a white paper of research and analysis for potential clients
Resolving conflicts and negotiating with others	Doing a benchmarking study to assess market rates for paying vendors
Selling or influencing others	Creating a pitch document that shares compelling data for someone to buy your product
Guiding, directing, and motivating subordinates	Sharing engagement survey results and steps the manager will take to improve things
Coordinating the work and activities of others	Looking at the availability of staff to engage on a new project
Developing and building teams	Reviewing results from a team-based survey on personalities of team members
Organizing, planning, and prioritizing work	Creating a Gantt chart based on similar projects done in the past
Coaching and developing others	Reviewing the annual performance review of individual employees compared to the norm
Developing objectives and strategies	Drafting a new strategic focused on industry analysis
Training and teaching others	Identifying employees who are stagnating in terms of growth and development
Scheduling work and activities	Examining the breadth of required projects and identifying individuals who are overcommitted
Staffing organizational units	Creating a battery of selection tests that can predict future success in the role

Given the degree to which managing and mastering data have infiltrated the role of manager, it is important to examine how different aspects of the role have evolved. The next sections present three distinct roles that managers must now play to be effective.

Role 1: Educated Consumer

So much of the work of managers now involves leveraging data and information that are gathered from others. It is not uncommon for managers to involve outside partners throughout the research process, the manager making requests for specific data reports or analyses to help with day-to-day planning and decision making. Being an educated consumer means knowing exactly what you need in terms of data or analysis, clearly articulating that to the people gathering the information, and then assessing the quality of the data and analysis when results are returned back to the manager.

Managers are also bombarded by analyses and white papers from outside researchers, focused on areas of importance to management. For example, it is not uncommon for potential new vendors to provide research to managers letting them know why their product or service is right for the job and better than their competitors. As an educated consumer, a manager needs to take a critical eye to this research to assess generally the credibility of the research findings, and specifically the quality of the data, analyses, and recommendations.

Davenport suggests that managers should never stop asking questions throughout the research process.[14] When working with research partners, always ask critical questions about the source of the data and the sample it was gathered from (and how representative it is of the population you are interested in). Also check to see how researchers dealt with data outliers (data values outside the expected range) and missing data and what assumptions were made in their research and why they chose the analytical approach they did. Finally, managers should ask about the likelihood that other variables might be causing their findings.

Role 2: Curious Researcher

A second role for managers to play is to become the curious researcher (the white lab coat is optional). To manage and master data, managers need to tinker. They need to explore the data and information to better understand what the results actually mean and how different findings are connected. It's not enough for a manager to do a simple analysis and move on. It is critical that the manager fully explores the results. Though time consuming, this curiosity is actually a critical step in building the credibility of the research. Not fully exploring the analyses and results often results in misinterpretation of results or spurious findings, both of which result in bad decision making and losses of credibility.

Being curious also tends to be the fun part of research, leading to unique insights that can positively affect business results. For example, Leong suggests the combination of creativity and flexible thinking can make a huge difference in producing actionable results, while reducing time, effort, and costs.[15] Leong cites an example of a data analyst who claimed to predict riots with a high level of accuracy in the wake of Ferguson. By thinking creatively and being curious about how to best predict riots, he looked at a number of different types of predictors. Surprisingly, the best predictors weren't what you would initially think (such as indicators of social discontent and anger). Rather, the best predictors were the spikes in sales at hardware stores of riot-related components such as crowbars and flammable fluids. In this case, curiosity led to new predictors of riots.

To be a curious researcher, managers need to invest time in exploring data from different angles. Try to surface new questions that need answers. Poke at findings to uncover new lines of thinking. Uncover the biases and assumptions that are often embedded in the research to see how they could affect the way you leverage the data for your own purposes. Finally, look critically at your own research in the same way that you look at others' research as an educated consumer.

Role 3: Trusted Adviser

A third role to play is as trusted adviser. With the proliferation of data into the workplace, coupled with the lack of data scientists, other managers and leaders in the organization struggle to make sense of the data and to make decisions. As a trusted adviser, you can gain influence in the organization by helping others understand what they need to do. As Chin and co-workers suggest, the talent challenge is not only to find data scientists but also to groom "translators."[16] Companies need managers who know the business and who are also experienced in analytics to partner with others to identify opportunities, suggest solutions, and influence change.

Critical to being a trusted adviser is the ability to present data and the results of research in a compelling manner that influences people to action. As Davenport laments, presenting and communicating results to other executives is one thing that many "quants" (data scientists) discount or overlook, which creates an opportunity for managers.[17]

To present data and results in a compelling manner, managers must become storytellers. Though the results from research can sometimes speak for themselves, they often lack context and a sense of "what next." Storytelling gives others a simple frame in which to understand the results and a sense of next steps. When telling stories, it is important to understand your audience. Managers adept at storytelling adjust the story to different groups. For example, when telling the story to the senior leadership team of a company, you may want to consider the results within the context of organization's strategic goals and what the CEO plans to present at the next board meeting. However, when telling the same story to lower-level managers, you may want to consider the results within the context of the day-to-day decisions and business challenges facing those managers. For a deeper dive into some of the underlying competencies for storytelling, refer to the three chapters in Domain 1, Professional Effectiveness. Focusing on these competencies will absolutely raise your game for storytelling.

Your Credibility As a Manager Is Tied to Data

In summary of the first part of this chapter, it is important to highlight how a manager's ability to manage and master data is tied to a manager's credibility. A manager's credibility is core to the power he or she has to influence people to act toward achieving a set of shared goals and objectives. As we've discussed, more and more of your credibility hinges on your ability to make evidence-based decisions that persuade others to act.

If we examine the five dimensions of leadership credibility identified by the Leadership Research Institute (Table 16-2),[18] it is clear that a manager's credibility is significantly affected by his or her ability to work with data. For example:

- Your *competence* is tied to your ability to ask good questions, collect data, analyze data, and report results in a compelling manner, and your ability to leverage the analyses of others while being mindful of how the analysis was done and having a sense of the quality of the data.
- Your *character* is tied to your ability to accurately portray results and to avoid situations in which you may be seen as masking issues or highlighting spurious results.
- Your *courage* is tied to the level of clarity of your messaging on issues that are difficult to raise and your ability to avoid the temptation to adjust your findings based on a concern that the person you are sharing results with will shoot the messenger.
- Your *composure* as a leader is affected by how you present information. If you present information in a way that is alarmist or in a way that puts things out of context, then people will attribute this to your disposition and how you process information (clouded by emotion; disorganized).

Table 16-2 Manager's Credibility and Managing and Mastering Data

Credibility	Managing and Mastering Data	Positive Example	Negative Example
Competence	Asking good questions, working with and analyzing data, reporting data in a compelling way	Posing a clear question answered by the right data with the appropriate issues highlighted up front	Completing an analysis in which data errors are apparent and the evidence presented doesn't match the question
Character	Dealing with data integrity issues (how you frame things)	Presenting work in a simple, clear way that is accurate	Presenting information in a way that masks issues or highlights something erroneous
Courage	Delivering a clear message (not hiding key findings, not burying the lede)	Framing a challenging issue in a way that is hard to deny	Hiding an important finding because you are afraid of what people will think
Composure	Presenting data and information in a professional manner (give people an impression of what you are thinking and your state of mind)	Presenting clean charts that accurately convey the message without embellishment	Presenting busy charts that are difficult to interpret, not putting things in the right context, being alarmist
Care for people	Taking the time to present information in a format that speaks to people	Producing a chart that matches the way people discuss the issue, increasing buy-in	Presenting results in a way that is inaccessible or uninterpretable by your audience

- Your *care for people* as a manager is affected by the way in which you consider the audience when communicating results. If people feel you didn't take the time to consider their perspective, your credibility will be affected.

In terms of a clear example of how intertwined one's credibility is with data and analytics, go no further than weather forecasters. Weather forecasters are some of the brightest, most analytical people out there and the statistical models they run and interpret are incredibly complex, mirroring the complexity of Mother Nature herself. As mentioned at a conference, the fact is that separating the credibility of the weather forecaster from the accuracy of the predictive weather models is nearly impossible.[19] Remember, the weather models don't get blamed when it rains and you don't have your umbrella; the weather forecaster does. And as Dennis Mersereau points out, "even though the accuracy of forecasts is better today than at any point in human history, people are enraged when one is even the slightest bit off the mark."[20] Elliott, a weather forecaster herself, has written about her reactions to the often vitriolic comments people make when they are affected by inaccurate forecasts.[21] She says people often associate the level of inaccuracy with an agenda to beef up interest in weather and to drive local consumer behavior for shovels and salt.

The point here is that your credibility as a manager is directly tied to the quality of the work you do with data. If you are able to effectively manage and master data, your credibility will be enhanced. If you do not, your credibility will suffer. For a deeper dive into the importance of credibility in driving your ability as a manager to get things done, see Chapter 7, Influence.

We move now to the second part of this chapter, which provides a grounding in how to analyze data to generate insights, make decisions, and influence people to action.

THE PROCESS OF ANALYZING DATA

To help organize the many details and considerations tied to analyzing data, the AMA has created a five-stage analysis framework (Figure 16-1). Each stage is critical and can affect the quality of the outcomes of the research (and, of course, your credibility as a manager). You will notice in the figure that the framework is broken into two streams, one for do-it-yourself managers and the other for managers who outsource the analysis. Each of these streams requires the same or similar tasks, but when outsourcing, managers must ensure they get what they need.

The five stages, each beginning with the letter *P*, are discussed in detail in the following sections.

Purpose Setting: Stage 1

Given that stage 1 is the foundation for the remaining four stages, Purpose Setting is the most critical to get right from the start and is worth investing time and effort. As Davenport warns, if you frame the problem incorrectly, no amount of data or sophisticated analysis will get you to the right place.[22] The goal of this stage is to articulate clearly what the purpose of the analysis is. The most important task to

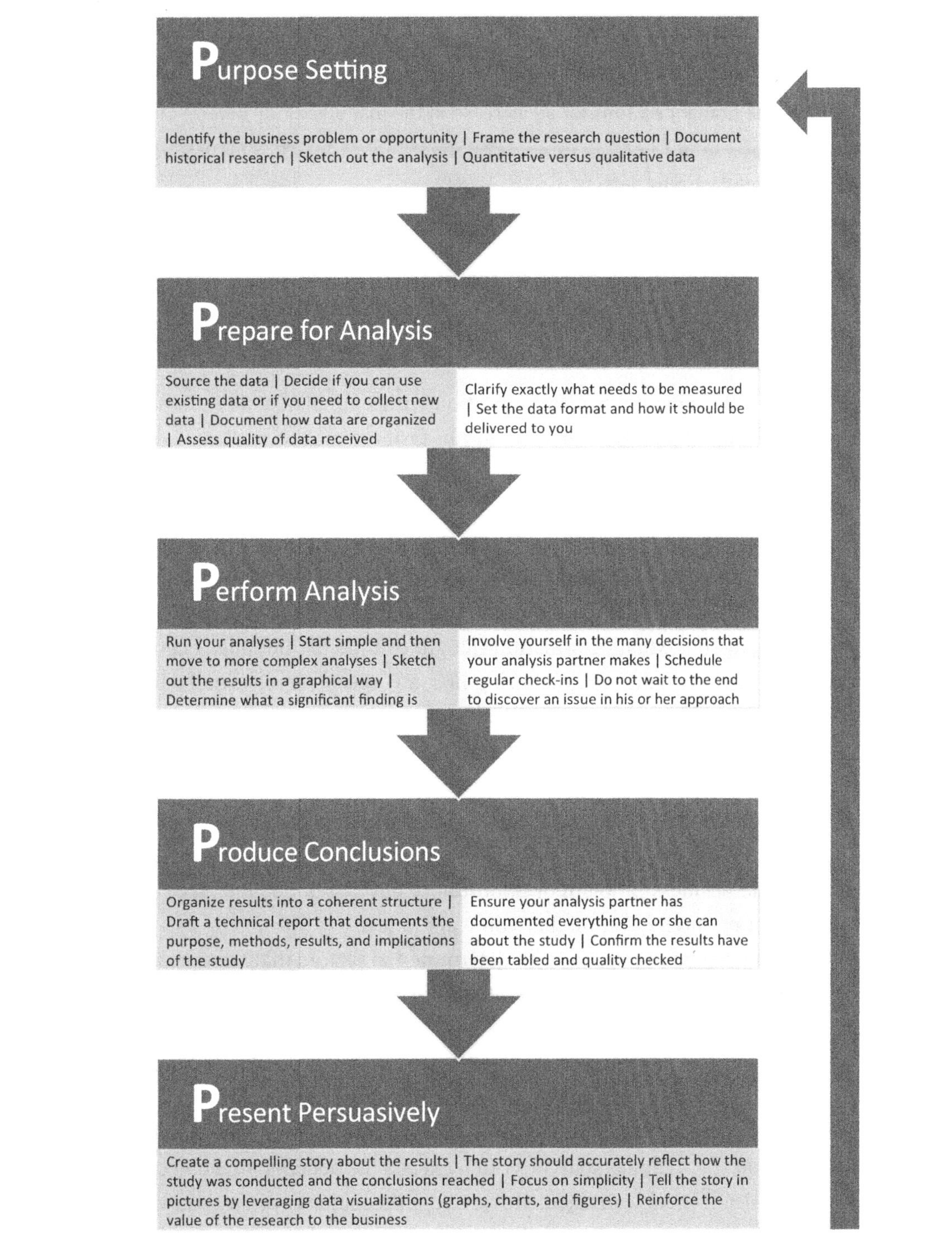

Figure 16-1 AMA's five-stage framework for analyzing data. Note: darker boxes are for solo projects; lighter boxes assume the manager is working with a partner.

Evolution of a Research Question

Bad: To see what is causing the manufacturing defects of a part.

Okay: To identify the primary reasons for an increase in the manufacturing defects of a part.

Better: To test if increases in employee turnover on the manufacturing line for Product A led to increases in manufacturing defects.

Best: To test if introducing quality incentives for employees on the manufacturing line for Product A will lead to decreases in manufacturing defects and increases in employee morale within the next six months.

accomplish at this stage is to frame the research question with such clarity there is no ambiguity as to what the research will be about. It also makes it incredibly easier to make decisions down the line as you prepare for and perform the analysis.

The first step in framing the research question is to document exactly what the business problem or opportunity is. For example, if the business problem is that you are finding significant increases in defective parts being manufactured at a particular plant, it is critical to document everything you can about the defects that are being discovered (frequency, severity, description of defect, likely causes) as well as any potentially important contextual information (length of time the item has been manufactured at the plant, turnover of employees on the manufacturing line, any recent changes in the use of materials or vendors of materials, and so on).

A common step missed in this process is documenting any historical research that was done on the issue or on an area that is related to the issue. Experts in research analytics see research as a cycle that builds on previous research. Having a clear summary of related research gives the current research project roots to grow from and increases the credibility of the research.

Once the details of the business problem or opportunity have been documented, the next step is to clearly articulate the exact research question that you want to test.

This research question can be *exploratory* (to determine the factors that are causing the defects) or *confirmatory* (to confirm that recent morale issues of employees is causing the defects). In addition, the research question can also be *predictive* (to test if the addition of an employee incentive for quality will decrease manufacturing defects in the future), suggesting a causal relationship.

Many critics of data analytics make the point that the cost of doing analytics often exceed the benefits. In many cases, this concern is warranted. However, in the majority of cases in which the value of analytics was limited, it is the case that there was a lack of investment in documenting the context of the business issue as well as a failure to articulate a clear research question.

Pro tip

Davenport suggests drawing a picture of the analysis you plan to run, including all of variables you are measuring.[23]

To do this effectively, it is important to document how each variable affects the others in the model. If done well, the picture should clearly depict the actual research question you are testing.

The final step of this stage is to think through the kind of analysis that is needed to answer the research question. Generally two types of analyses are conducted: analyses looking at the *relationships* between variables (for example, the correlation between engagement of employees and quality of service) and analyses looking at the *differences* between groups (employees incentivized to manufacture quality parts will have fewer defects than employees not incentivized).

Clarke makes the important point that if these analyses will be used to make decisions that significantly affect people or the business (or both), it is critical that there be "transparency and auditability of the decision process and the decision criteria."[24] You should assume that your methods for collecting and analyzing data will be scrutinized when you use the results to drive a decision that affects people.

One final consideration for researchers is the type of data collected. Data come in two forms: quantitative (numbers) and qualitative (words). Either type of data can be leveraged effectively to answer research questions, though quantitative data tend to be more typically used. However, it is highly recommended that when working with quantitative data, an effort is made to collect some qualitative data. In practice, this takes the form of interviewing customers or employees regarding issues tied to the research question. When quantitative data are combined with qualitative data, researchers can often present a more compelling argument. The data are seen as an objective frame for the results, while the qualitative are seen as the color commentary that is so critical to connect emotionally with certain audiences. As Shapiro shares, quantitative data are often given more weight, but data only go so far for describing why something is happening.[25] Qualitative data are critical for uncovering why people think what they think and do what they do.

Prepare for Analysis: Stage 2

Once there is clarity as to what you need to measure and what analyses will be run, it is time now to source that data. A decision needs to be made at this point as to whether the manager will collect the data or will have another party collect it, such as an internal data analyst or outside data source (such as a consulting firm or marketing firm).

When sourcing the data, managers will often have to evaluate the feasibility of using data that are not exactly aligned with how the variables were initially defined. For example, if the study is on defects in manufacturing and you want data on the percent of products showing a certain kind of defect, perhaps the only data you can get your hands is the percent of products that are error free. In this example, although the two measures are similar, they are not really measuring the same thing and might yield different research outcomes.

Pro tip

Regardless of whether the manager collects the data or outsources this task, the manager needs to remain engaged throughout the data-collection process because outside partners may make assumptions that can have a profound impact on the quality of the data and credibility of the outcomes.

This issue is quite common, and researchers in organizations are often in the ironic situation of being buried in data but not having the right data they need to feed into their analyses. In this situation you have three options: (1) keep your original research question and source the exact data you need (which may require you to create a new measure), (2) alter your research question and methodology and substitute out the old variable with a new variable (sometimes referred to as a proxy measure), or (3) scrap the research study altogether because the data you need don't exist or will cost too much to justify the study.

In the case that you need to develop a new measure because there isn't a good proxy, it's critical to gather and incorporate the thinking of different stakeholders. An example is when Qualcomm did research on the factors that drive their innovation pipeline.[26] Qualcomm conducted structured interviews and a literature review across various academic fields. This certainly helped researchers determine a set of potential factors that resonated with key stakeholders. Another source of useful information when creating new measures comes from open-ended comments from surveys. When clients ask for help developing new measures related to engagement of employees, managers often work with open-ended comments from previous surveys to get at the "flavor" of the measure being created.

Once a manager has sourced the data, it is critical now to document how the data need to be organized. This documentation is very important for three reasons. First, if you are sourcing the data from a partner inside or outside the organization, this documentation serves as a way to ensure the partner knows exactly what you want. Second, it gives you clarity as to what to expect so that you can start preparing your files for the analysis. Third, it helps with the data sniff tests you want to run before your run your analyses. This documentation could include a host of information about each variable being measured, including when the data were collected, the actual question text displayed (if a survey), the rating scale being used, what the potential rating options were, how outliers will be identified, and the plan for dealing with any missing data.

The final step of this stage is to receive the data and prepare it for analysis. This is an incredibly important step because any missed errors in the data could result in very time intensive rework or worse and the communication of error-prone results, which will affect the credibility of both the study and the manager (recall the what happens to weather forecasters who make inaccurate predictions).

Underscoring this point, Haug and Arlbjorn say the consequences of poor data quality affects decision quality, operating costs, employee performance, job satisfaction, and customer satisfaction.[27] Clarke also warns that any uncertainty in the quality of data in decision processes should be addressed because inferences from bad data will result in a misallocation of resources, which lowers profitability in private sector and policy outcomes in the public sector.[28] And when these inaccurate inferences are applied to people in the real world, the results could be really unfair, such as unjustified discrimination.

To assess the quality of the data received, it is critical to first examine the context of each variable to ensure it matches what was described when sourcing the data. This information would include how the data were sourced, the rating scale, any adjustments made to the numbers, and the precision in which data were stored (for example, to how many decimals are numbers rounded). It should also be clear how missing data were treated and how outliers were handled. Finally, Clarke implores that there should be little ambiguity about the date and time when the data were collected.[29] For example, there may be time-sensitive measures—such as annual rainfall, marital status, or tenure—that can become dated quickly or that can measure something different from what you intend.

Perform Analysis: Stage 3

Like cooking, research is all prep until you throw it on the stove. If you have successfully navigated through stage 1 (Purpose Setting) and stage 2 (Prepare for Analysis), stage 3 should be relatively straightforward. The goal of this stage is to do the actual analyses that will yield answers to your research questions.

As mentioned earlier, you will generally run two types of analyses, one looking at the relationships between variables and the other looking at differences between groups.

If you are looking at the relationships between variables, you are assessing the degree to which variables are correlated. An easy way to visualize a correlation is to plot two variables on a scatterplot (Figure 16-2). Each dot represents a particular person or group and represents two values, one for each of the variables you are studying. When you plot all of the pairs of values, you create a cloud of dots, which gives you a sense of the relationship between the two variables. When the dots form a tight cloud that extends a certain direction, it shows a relationship. However, if the dots form a loose cloud that doesn't have a particular trend, it shows the lack of a relationship.

If you are looking at the differences between two groups (or the same group over time), you are assessing the degree to which the groups' means on a particular variable are different. An easy way to visualize the differences between two groups is to plot the two groups on a bar graph (Figure 16-3). Each bar represents a group and should display two pieces of information, the average of each group for the variable (the bars on the bar chart) as well as the standard deviation of each group for the variable (typically a vertical line extending in two directions from the top of each bar). Both pieces of information are critical in examining if there is truly a difference between the groups.

The charts in Figure 16-3 show three possible outcomes from a hypothetical study of the kind of coffee offered in a company's breakrooms. The study focuses on the impact of introducing dark roast coffee into the coffee service. Specifically, satisfaction with the coffee service is being compared between two groups, those with the dark roast coffee service and those with the existing medium roast coffee service.

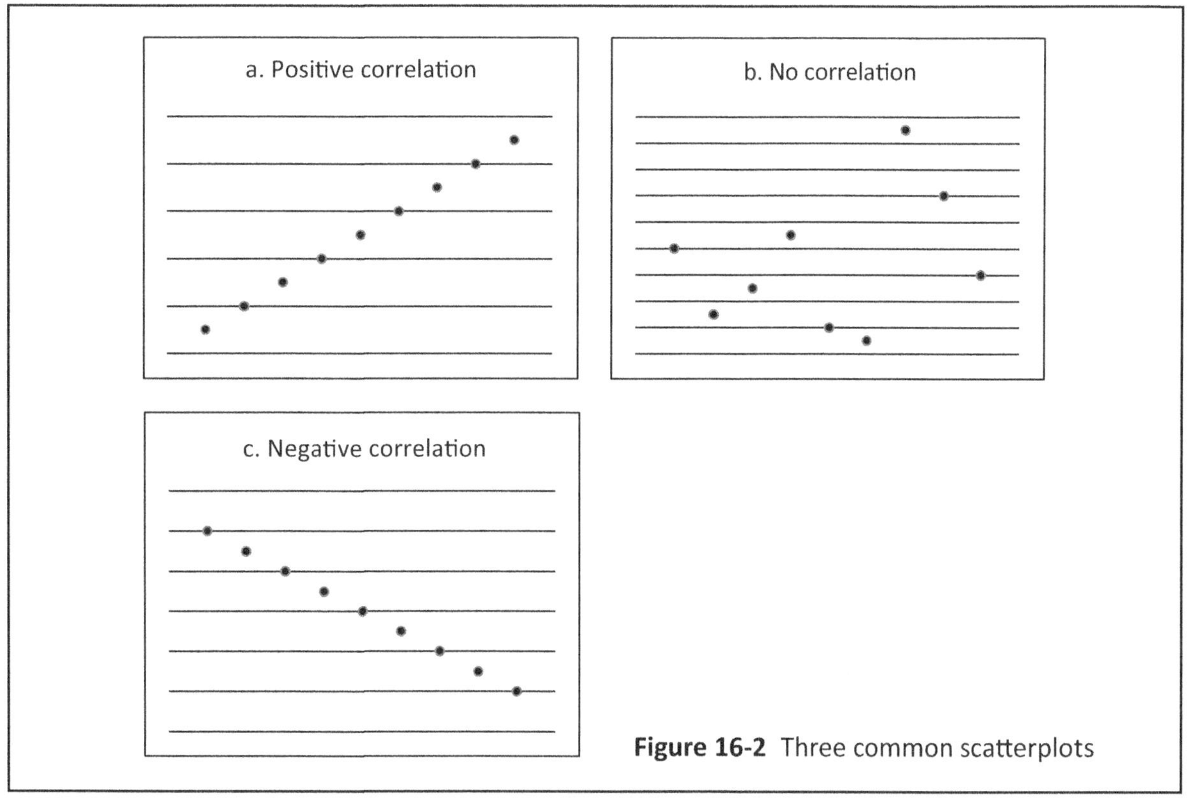

Figure 16-2 Three common scatterplots

In the case in which each group's bar is different and the standard deviation is low (Figure 16-3a), you can be confident that there really is a difference. If each group's bar is not different (Figure 16-3b), and regardless of the standard deviation, you can be confident there isn't a difference. Finally, in the case where there is a large difference between the bars but the standard deviations are high (Figure 16-3c), you can say there is a difference between the groups, but you are less certain about whether that difference is significant because the differences measured within the groups might be stronger than the differences between the groups.

Pro tip

When analyzing data, start with more basic analyses and then build on them to study more complex models. Try to avoid starting with the most complex, sophisticated analyses.

By starting with a basic analysis, the researcher is able to first understand how different variables are working, which helps build a strong foundation to support the more sophisticated analyses that will be run later. For example, if your study is to examine the degree to which the introduction of an incentive for quality work results in a reduction in manufacturing defects, your first analysis may be to examine if there was a change in the number of manufacturing defects in general, and then you might follow up with a sophisticated analysis to compare the differences in manufacturing defects between employees who receive the incentive and employees who don't.

If you are outsourcing the analysis stage to an internal or external partner, it is critical that you involve yourself in the analysis phase. There are many decisions that your analysis partner may need to make regarding how to do the analysis, decisions that you may make differently given your experience. One suggestion is to schedule regular check-ins with the analysis partner either before or after specific analyses are going to be run so the partner can walk you through the analysis and any decisions he or she needs to make, while giving you the opportunity to weigh in and suggest changes. These meetings also serve to keep the momentum going on your research and prevent any bottlenecks or delays (bad things happen when people rush through the analysis phase to get it done).

Produce Conclusions: Stage 4

Once the analyses have been run, and you have produced the appropriate number of pages of output (also likely greater than the number of sand grains in the world), it is time to start organizing the results into a coherent structure. Here is where having made a strong investment in stage 1 (Purpose Setting) really pays off. It is highly recommended that the researcher start building slides or a technical report to outline the detailed findings of the study. Critical sections of the technical report are outlined in the following list:

- *Purpose of the Study*: This section summarizes the key points from the Purpose Setting stage and provides the rationale for the study. It is a good place to review any historical research that is relevant to the question. It is also a good place to provide any initial context about the business issue or opportunity that will be important for interpreting the results. The section should end with a clear set of research questions that the current study is focused on answering.

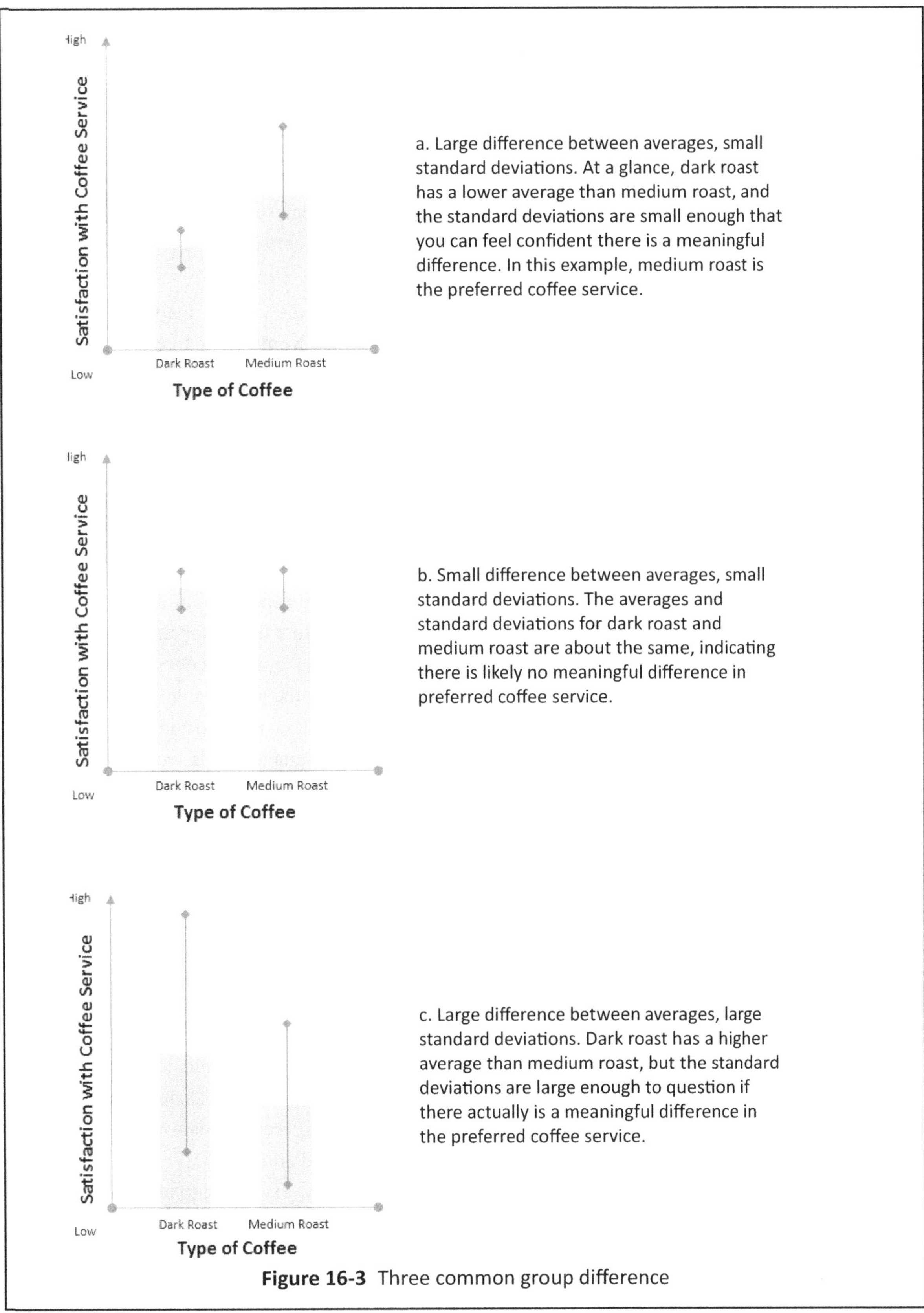
High
Satisfaction with Coffee Service
Low
Dark Roast
Medium Roast
Type of Coffee
a. Large difference between averages, small standard deviations. At a glance, dark roast has a lower average than medium roast, and the standard deviations are small enough that you can feel confident there is a meaningful difference. In this example, medium roast is the preferred coffee service.
High
Satisfaction with Coffee Service
Low
Dark Roast
Medium Roast
Type of Coffee
b. Small difference between averages, small standard deviations. The averages and standard deviations for dark roast and medium roast are about the same, indicating there is likely no meaningful difference in preferred coffee service.
High
Satisfaction with Coffee Service
Low
Dark Roast
Medium Roast
Type of Coffee
c. Large difference between averages, large standard deviations. Dark roast has a higher average than medium roast, but the standard deviations are large enough to question if there actually is a meaningful difference in the preferred coffee service.

Figure 16-3 Three common group difference

- *Methodology*: This section summarizes how the study was conducted and which analyses were done. It should begin with a clear indication of who was included in the study, whether it be people or teams or whatever you are collecting data on. Once the sample is identified, then the variables measured in the study should be identified and described in detail, including any notes provided by the sources of the data. Any fact that could affect the interpretation of the results needs to be included, so be sure to provide as much information as you can. Following the variables should be a section outlining the analyses that were run. The results don't need to be presented yet, but the rationale for using a certain test should be documented.
- *Results*: This section summarizes the results obtained from the various analyses conducted. As recommended in stage 3, results should be documented from simple to complex. Thus typically the first results displayed are simple statistics on each of the variables, such as average, standard deviation, and sample size (typically the number of people or teams that data were collected from). Then simple tables might be displayed to capture the relationships between variables and the differences between groups. Finally, more detailed results are displayed from the more sophisticated analyses that were run.
- *Implications or Conclusions*: This section is a summary of what the results tell us in relation to the initial research questions. The section usually starts with a clear indication of what the most important conclusions are, including what results were expected and what results were not expected. If there were follow-up analyses to further refine the initial results, they would be summarized here as well. In addition, this is a good place to document any issues with the study that may affect the interpretation of results, including the potential impact of data errors or missing data, outliers, and the use of proxy variables. It is also a good place to highlight areas for future research. Finally, note that the language in this section should be very similar to the language used in the first stage (Purpose Setting); thus there should be a story-like quality to the narrative.
- *Executive Summary*: This final section is a high-level overview of all of the most critical information and findings presented in the other sections. There should be a logical sequence to the information presented, and it should clearly articulate the most important conclusions from the research.

Present Persuasively: Stage 5

The final stage of the analysis framework is to effectively communicate the results to provide valuable insights to stakeholders, to help decision making, and to influence people to act. There are two key areas to focus on to present persuasively: creating a compelling story and creating data visualizations that translate complex results into simple pictures conveying meaning and emotion.

The secret to creating a compelling story is to focus on simplicity. Try thinking of the simplest way to tell the whole story with as few details as possible. Similar to the classic television game show *Name That Tune* in which contestants compete to identify a song in as few notes as possible. The same concept applies here, in that you want to give people a thorough understanding of the whole story (the "song") but in as few words as possible (the "notes").

Pro tip

When telling a story about the results, don't bury the lede by including lots of unnecessary detail and analysis. Be clear about what the most important findings are and use metaphor and analogy to make the findings accessible and relatable to your audience.

Burying the lede is a term from newspaper editors that underscores the importance of prioritizing which findings get the most attention (make sure your headline and first paragraph is the most important story). If a research finding is critical to your stakeholders, make sure it is the first thing you talk about. The second tip is to use literary devices like metaphor and analogy, which helps bring people into the story by making it more relatable. Remember, the people you are trying to influence with your study's findings are likely overwhelmed with information throughout their day. If you want them to make a decision or to take action, you need to cut through all of the noise by presenting a clear and compelling story.

One area that can trip up managers is how to best explain unanticipated results or results that run contrary to what was expected. To effectively address unanticipated results, it is best to be clear that results were inconclusive or contrary to what was expected. In addition, highlight to stakeholders what was gained by trying. For example, in the course of a research study you might discover bad data being recorded on a performance measure; these bad data may unfortunately ruin your analysis, but discovering and fixing the bad data could also be a real value to the business. Finally, learn to celebrate the failures and try to learn from them. Frankly, failure is inevitable, and how teams doing analyses deal with failure will determine the degree of success later.

Besides telling a clear story in a presentation, it's just as important to tell a clear story through thoughtful data visualizations. As Murray points out, a picture can convey rich data insights in a very efficient manner and can also communicate emotion.[30] Thoughtful data visualizations can help people find agreement on issues and opportunities.

The following are some notes on creating charts and figures that convey a clear message:

Tips for Presenting Study Results

- Be clear about your level of confidence in the results; do not oversell them. If you think the results of an analysis are shaky, note it. But also clarify why you think it's still valuable to report the results.
- Offer insights into how the confidence in results can be improved in the future with additional research; clarify the path.
- And when articulating the value of the research, emphasize not only the value of prediction but also the value of the process itself: what insights were gained through the process of doing the research, what data sets are cleaner and more useful now than before, what skill sets were learned and how might these skill sets be leveraged to tackle future research questions.

- Keep each chart's design simple and show only the most critical data. If you flood the chart with details, you bury the lede.
- Have a clear title on the chart that conveys what is being presented.
- Clearly label the axes of the chart so people know exactly what is being displayed.
- If you have multiple charts on the same page, arrange them in a way that adds to the storyline.
- Include footnotes to convey details critical for interpreting the chart, such as the meaning of the rating scales (for example, 1 = Strongly Disagree; 5 = Strongly Agree).
- Most important, socialize the charts and figures with different people to ensure they are conveying the messages you intend.

COMMON MYTHS AND TRAPS RELATED TO MANAGING AND MASTERING DATA

Correlation Is Not Causation: A common trap that researchers fall into is overinterpreting a relationship between two variables. For example, imagine you find a strong positive relationship between ice cream consumption and the number of calls to 911 to break up fistfights. If your conclusion is that the more ice cream people eat, the more likely people will come to blows, you have likely overinterpreted the relationship between these variables. It is much more reasonable that it is the weather that drives both ice cream consumption and fistfights; in other words, the hot and steamy weather of summer increases both ice cream consumption and fistfights, while cooler seasons decrease them both. Be very careful when making statements of causation, and if your intent is to show causation between two variables, you must design your study in a way that tests the causal relationship.

Confirmation Bias: Another common trap for researchers is to shape their research, intentionally or not, toward what they believe is true. Take, for example, a scenario in which a girl wants her family to get a cat. Her solution is to pull together and administer a survey to gauge everyone's interest. Essentially, she wants to collect evidence that everyone in the family wants a cat and, in true confirmation bias fashion, she ends up asking a bunch of questions related to the kind of cat to get (for example, she asks for preferences for fur color, size, and age), but she never actually asks the yes or no question, Do you want a cat? Clearly, there is a pretty large confirmation bias at play, and her credibility for doing the survey about getting a cat remains a little suspect. The lesson here is that researchers have to be very careful about introducing bias into the research based on what they believe to be true. In a business setting, it could cause a large hit on your credibility as a manager.

The Observer Effect: One final trap for researchers to avoid has to do with the fact that humans tend to act differently when they know they are being watched. Think of how you might act differently when you see a state trooper in your rearview mirror or when your coach is looking your way during practice. In both situations, you are likely doing whatever you can to impress these observers (slowing down to the speed limit and picking up your pace running around the track). This willingness to impress an observer can cause all sorts of problems with research, and so researchers need to be careful to control these kinds of responses. A classic example of this effect occurred nearly a century ago at a factory (the Hawthorne Works of Western Electric) that assembled parts for telephone networks. Researchers in industrial efficiency wanted to determine the optimal amount of light to boost productivity on the factory floor. Results showed clearly that when lighting levels were increased, worker productivity increased. But that's not the end of the story. Because results also indicated that when lighting levels decreased, productivity increased as well. In fact, productivity increased at all levels of lighting, even down to the point where workers were essentially working in moonlight. This effect, also called the Hawthorne effect, simply shows that people change their behavior when they know someone is paying attention to them.

• Some Final Thoughts •

In closing, the role of manager is evolving to be more data oriented, and your ability to manage and master data has become a major driver of your credibility as a manager. Your credibility and influence can be enhanced by effectively playing three roles: the educated consumer, the curious researcher, and the trusted adviser. Each of these roles is affected by your ability to conduct compelling research, and the AMA five-stage analysis framework is a helpful tool to plan for and execute data analysis. By following the stages, from Purpose Setting to Present Persuasively, the credibility of your research will be stronger and will ultimately enhance your ability to make better decisions and to influence people to take action.

• Endnotes •

1. D. Reinsel, J. Gantz, and J. Rydning, "The Digitization of the World: From Edge to Core," White Paper US44413318, IDC, Framingham, MA, November 2018, www.seagate.com/files/www-content/our-story/trends/files/idc-seagate-dataage-whitepaper.pdf.
2. "Mobile Statistics Report, 2019–2023, Executive Summary," Radicati Group, 2019, www.radicati.com/wp/wp-content/uploads/2018/12/Mobile-Statistics-Report-2019-2023-Executive-Summary.pdf.
3. "Email Statistics Report, 2019–2023: Executive Summary," Radicati Group, 2019, www. radicati.com/wp/wp-content/uploads/2018/12/Email-Statistics-Report-2019-2023-Executive-Summary.pdf.
4. Internet Live Statistics, data from August 30, 2019, www.internetlivestats.com.
5. "Stats," Facebook, data retrieved August 30, 2019, https://newsroom.fb.com/company-info; and J Weiner and N Bronson, "Facebook's Top Open Data Problems," Facebook Research, October 22, 2014, https://research.fb.com/blog/2014/10/facebook-s-top-open-data-problems.
6. D. Reinsel, J. Gantz, and J. Rydning, "The Digitization of the World: From Edge to Core," White Paper US44413318, IDC, Framingham, MA, November 2018, www.seagate.com/files/www-content/our-story/trends/files/idc-seagate-dataage-whitepaper.pdf.

7. Robert Krulwich, "Which Is Greater, the Number of Sand Grains on Earth or Stars in the Sky?" *Krulwich Wonders*, NPR, September 17, 2012, www.npr.org/sections/krulwich/2012/09/17/161096233/which-is-greater-the-number-of-sand-grains-on-earth-or-stars-in-the-sky.

8. D. Reinsel, J. Gantz, and J. Rydning, "The Digitization of the World: From Edge to Core," White Paper US44413318, IDC, Framingham, MA, November 2018, www.seagate.com/files/www-content/our-story/trends/files/idc-seagate-dataage-whitepaper.pdf.

9. S. A. Lewisohn, "Managerial Achievement through Human Organization," *American Management Review*, 12, no. 1 (1923): 7–10.

10. "Summary Report for . . . First-Line Supervisors of Non-Retail Sales Workers," O*Net, last updated August 6, 2019, www.onetonline.org/link/summary/41-1012.00. *O*Net* refers to the Occupational Information Network and is the nation's primary source of occupational information. The O*Net database profiles almost a thousand occupations based on hundreds of descriptors. It is a hugely valuable resource for researchers, human resource professionals and managers.

11. Kon Leong, "Your Team Doesn't Need a Data Scientist for Simple Analytics," *Harvard Business Review*, October 30, 2018, https://hbr.org/2018/10/your-team-doesnt-need-a-data-scientist-for-simple-analytics.

12. Mwaniki, Andrew. (2018, May 16). What Percentage Of The World Population Are Left Handed? Retrieved from https://www.worldatlas.com/articles/what-percentage-of-the-world-population-are-left-handed.html; How many giraffe are there and are they 'endangered'? Retrieved from https://giraffeconservation.org/facts/how-many-giraffe-are-there-and-are-they-endangered/

13. "What is normal body temperature WebMD?" (2019). Retrieved from https://www.webmd.com/first-aid/normal-body-temperature#1

14. T. H. Davenport, "Keep Up with Your Quants," *Harvard Business Review* 91, nos. 7–8 (2013): 120–123.

15. Kon Leong, "Your Team Doesn't Need a Data Scientist for Simple Analytics," *Harvard Business Review*, October 30, 2018, https://hbr.org/2018/10/your-team-doesnt-need-a-data-scientist-for -simple-analytics.

16. J. K. Chin, M. Hagstroem, A. Libarikian, and K. Rifai, "Advanced Analytics: Nine Insights from the C-suite," in *Analytics Comes of Age*, ed. McKinsey Analytics (New York: McKinsey & Co., 2018).

17. T. H. Davenport, "Keep Up with Your Quants," *Harvard Business Review* 91, nos. 7–8 (2013): 120–123.

18. S. M. Rumery (2019, October 14), "Assessing Your Leadership Credibility and Influence" (2019). Retrieved from https://www.linkedin.com/pulse/assessing-your-leadership-credibility-influence-rumery-aka-rum-.

19. S. M. Rumery, "Journey Ahead: Tighten Your Bootstraps and Hold On for the Ride," paper presented at the Psychic Powers Not Required: Advanced Predictive Modeling in Organizations Symposium, Twenty-Ninth Annual Conference of the Society for Industrial and Organizational Psychology, Honolulu, HI. May 15–17, 2014.

20. D. Mersereau, "Cloudy with a Chance of Online Rage: Why Meteorologists Have so Many Haters," *Observer*, June 4, 2018, https://observer.com/2018/06/why-do-meteorologists-and-weather-reporters-receive-so-much-hate-mail.

21. B. Elliott. (2016, January 21). Don't be mad at your meteorologist for a poor forecast. We're mad enough at ourselves. Retrieved from https://www.washingtonpost.com/posteverything/wp/2016/01/21/dont-be-mad-at-your-meteorologist-for-a-poor-forecast-were-mad-enough-at-ourselves/.

22. T. H. Davenport, *How Managers Should Use Data* [video], *Harvard Business Review*, June 11, 2013, hbr.org/2013/06/how-managers-should-use-data.

23. T. H. Davenport, "Keep Up with Your Quants," *Harvard Business Review* 91, nos. 7–8 (2013): 120–123.

24. R. Clark (2016). Big data, big risks. *Information Systems Journal,* 26, 77–90.

25. J. Shapiro (2018, October 12). Help your team understand what data is and isn't good for. Retrieved from https://hbr.org/2018/10/help-your-team-understand-what-data-is-and-isnt-good-for

26. B. G. Roberts and J. Tobey, "Advising Organizational Strategy through Employee-Based Predictive Analytics," paper presented at the Psychic Powers Not Required: Advanced Predictive Modeling in Organizations Symposium, Twenty-Ninth Annual Conference of the Society for Industrial and Organizational Psychology, Honolulu, HI. May 15–17, 2014.

27. A. Haug and S. Arlbjørn, J. (2011), "Barriers to master data quality," *Journal of Enterprise Information Management,* Vol. 24 No. 3, pp 288–303.

28. R. Clark (2016). Big data, big risks. *Information Systems Journal,* 26, 77–90.

29. Ibid.

30. E. Murray, "How Data Visualization Supports Communication," *Forbes*, January 28, 2019, www.forbes.com/sites/evamurray/2019/01/28/how-data-visualization-supports-communication/#54638d3b2cce.

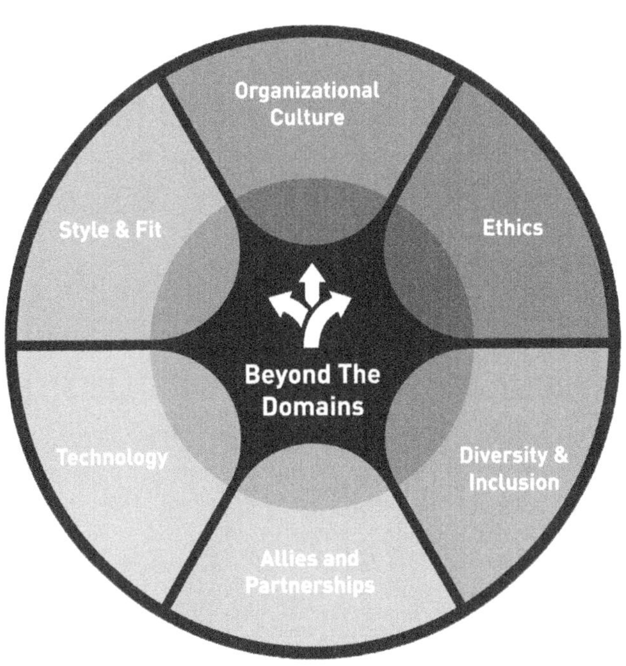

Beyond the Domains

17

Work Style and Work Fit

LEARNING OBJECTIVES

By the end of this chapter, you will be better equipped to:

- Identify components of work style.
- Assess your and your direct reports' work style preferences and fit.
- Use that knowledge to inform how you manage your team in an effort to enhance individual and team performance.
- Coach employees to support alignment with their work styles to the team and organizational goals.

Have you worked on a team and in an organization where you felt like you were in the right environment and were valued, respected, and appreciated, making it easy to accomplish goals? Have you felt like an outsider within a team or thought you didn't belong in the group? These feelings are your perceptions about whether your experience, style, and preferences are valued and supported. Feeling accepted for who you are and how you prefer to work has a large impact on your overall satisfaction with your manager, team, and organization. Many of the challenges you face as a manager are tangible and tactical. Managers are also faced with more intangible challenges and experiences within their organization, many of which are covered in this book, including communicating effectively (Chapter 1, Communication), handling conflict (Chapter 4, Conflict Management), dealing with changes (Chapter 10, Managing Change), and leveraging different styles and fit. As a manager, you are well aware of the multiple roles you play in your effort to get work done with and through others on a daily basis.

A HISTORY OF STYLE AND FIT

The concepts of style and fit are not new, but they have taken on new meaning and focus in the last several decades. In his 1909 book *Choosing a Vocation*, Frank Parsons introduced a vocational guidance approach that later evolved into trait and factor theory. The theory's main tenants are that workers need to assess their traits (aptitudes, achievements, interests, values, and personality) and align that understanding with the knowledge of different work roles (Sharf 2006). Parson's theory was revolutionary at the time, when vocations were chosen primarily based on availability.

In the 1960s, John Holland argued that career choice and adjustment reflect an individual worker's personality, and his theory of types has since been one of the most widely researched career development theories. Holland's theory identifies five categories of both people and work environments: realistic, investigative, artistic, social, enterprising, and conventional. Congruence, the relationship of a worker's personality and his or her environment, is one of the major tenets of Holland's theory (Sharf 2006), which underscores the importance of work style and fit.

Segregation and discrimination based on sex, race, religion, and ethnicity were outlawed by the Civil Rights Act of 1964, which offered unprecedented opportunities in employment and education for minority populations. Minorities no longer faced the same barriers to accessing quality education and finding decent employment opportunities. As a result, the workforce became more diverse, and co-workers were no longer segregated based on racial differences, which allowed opportunities for interaction, understanding, and appreciation between previously separated populations of workers.

Two decades after Holland's theory was created and the Civil Rights Act was passed, work adjustment theory was developed by Rene V. Dawis and Lloyd H. Lofquist to describe how workers interact with their work environments, including the concepts of satisfaction (how satisfied someone is with the work he or she does) and satisfactoriness (how satisfied the employer is with the worker's performance). Adjustment style, according to Dawis and Lofquist, describes how an individual interacts with the work environment and considers activeness (when a worker tries to change the work environment to fit personal preferences), reactiveness (when a worker tries to change himself or herself to adjust to a work environment), and perseverance (the length of time someone can tolerate negative working conditions) (Sharf, 2006).

Evolution of career development theories highlights changes in the global economy and the resulting impact on employees' perceptions of what they are seeking in work arrangements. One of the most profound changes in the way employees think about work has to do with the abolition of the traditional psychological contract that encouraged employee loyalty and performance in exchange for continued employment. Globalization and increased pressure on companies to perform in a competitive market have led to more corporate downsizing and outsourcing, leading to a decreased sense of security, loyalty, and corporate trust for employees. Although employers are unable to guarantee employee job security, they can provide a sense of meaning, purpose, and opportunities for growth and development.

In the late 1990s, Walter C. Borman, U. Christean Kubisiak, and Robert J. Schneider identified seven primary dimensions and seventeen secondary dimensions of work style:

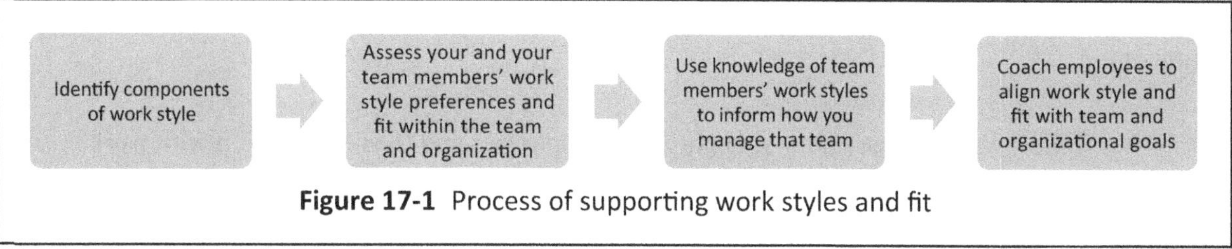

Figure 17-1 Process of supporting work styles and fit

1. Achievement orientation (effort, initiative, persistence)
2. Social influence (energy, leadership orientation)
3. Interpersonal orientation (cooperation, concern for others, social orientation)
4. Adjustment (self-control, stress tolerance, adaptability, flexibility)
5. Conscientiousness (dependability, attention to detail, integrity)
6. Independence
7. Practical intelligence (innovation, analytical thinking)

Elimination of the psychological contract along with technological changes and the diversification of the workforce that have occurred in the last few decades have led to workers to realize a lifelong career is neither a given nor necessarily a benefit of employment. Pursuing work that is meaningful in environments that fit with personal preferences is more important to employees than it was in the past. People seek an employer who allows them to express an authentic work style, who accepts and values them for that style, and who offers a work environment that fits their preferences. Being flexible and adaptable and thriving in completely different work teams and environments are keys to success for both managers and individual contributors. As workers and work environments continue to adapt and change, more variables and choices in organizations for broader populations of workers become available and more attention is being given to work style and fit. Therefore, assessing these elements in yourself and others is becoming an increasingly important skill for managers to possess. You can benefit from understanding the impact of work style and fit, not only as you carve out your own career path but with respect to how you support your direct reports with fit and flexing their work style preferences within your organization. This chapter addresses the areas illustrated in Figure 17-1 to assist you with supporting work styles and fit within your organization and team.

IDENTIFY COMPONENTS OF WORK STYLE AND WORK FIT

Researchers and experts vary on the definition of work style and its components. For the purpose of this chapter, *work style* is defined as an employee's preferred approach to work, including how that person thinks, organizes, and completes work. Work style includes the ability to express and adapt work preferences in areas including, but not limited to, personality, values, communication style, conflict resolution, and decision making. Experiences also contrubute greatly to style. Work fit is defined as the ability to effectively accomplish job responsibilities while expressing an authentic style, leveraging greatest strengths, and feeling like you're in the right environment.

Some of the many factors that contribute to creating and developing employees' work style are the following:

- *Values*: Aspects that are most important to employees and their satisfaction with work
- *Personality*: The summative way people interact with their world, including how they take in information, relate to others, structure their surroundings, and recharge
- *Motivation*: The internal and external factors that stimulate people's desire and energy to be continually interested and committed to an activity, a job, a role, or a subject
- *Management Style*: The approach leaders use to provide direction and support, offer feedback, motivate employees, and engage employees in goal accomplishment
- *Communication Style Preferences*: How people prefer to express themselves, orally and in writing, at work
- *Strengths*: Skills, knowledge, and abilities that support positive performance; may be identified by employee or blind spots
- *Development Opportunities*: Skills, knowledge, or abilities that need to be developed in order to be effective in current or future roles; may be identified by employee or blind spots
- *Conflict Management Approach*: How people typically navigate and deal with interpersonal challenges and differences of opinion
- *Decision-Making Approach*: The process people use to come to a decision and the factors that affect that process
- *Emotional Intelligence*: Awareness of one's own and others' emotions

IDENTIFY WHY WORK STYLE AND WORK FIT ARE IMPORTANT

Managers who are effective at assessing and leveraging diverse work styles have an appreciation for the positive impact that diversity has on work teams and organizations, and they have the ability to create and effectively develop diverse work and project teams to achieve the best outcomes. As discussed in Chapter 9, Coaching for Performance, managers can enhance their credibility by being able to flexibly alter their management style to accommodate various needs and situations. Managers who are effective in this area will also be seen as having strong coaching and communication skills. All of this results in more motivated and engaged teams who feel supported, heard, and valued.

On the other hand, when managers are not effective at assessing and leveraging different work styles, they often assume their personal work style is the "right" one and have little patience or appreciation for other approaches, leading to alienation of employees. Managers' lack of flexibility in style may result in poor working relationships and decreased effectiveness on goals. Lack of empathy, listening, and coaching skills for diverse styles will lead to decreased credibility (see Chapter 1, Communication;

Chapter 2, Emotional Intelligence; and Chapter 9, Coaching for Performance). The resulting impact of not being savvy in assessing and leveraging different work styles could lead to disengaged and unmotivated team members who feel disempowered, unsupported, and undervalued for their ideas and contributions.

Assess Your and Your Direct Reports' Work Style Preferences and Work Fit

You should assess the preferred styles of yourself and your team to develop and optimize your team's results. Understanding the many variables that impact work styles is a helpful first step, and assessing your own preferences in relation to your team and organization is important. You should encourage open dialogue with team members about their preferences and consider how you can support your team in being more effective. When employees share feedback with you on these areas and you adjust your style to address the feedback, a collaborative approach to appreciating and fostering different work styles will evolve.

Assessing Your Style and Fit

As a manager, it is important that you are aware your own work style, how it fits within the organization, what is serving you well, and what you should change to be most effective. Think about how your style fits (or doesn't fit) with your supervisor's, other superiors, peers, and direct reports' styles. Following are questions that will shed light on what's working well and where you could focus your energy:

- What are your top priorities and values? Are they being honored at work? How do they align with the organization's values and strategic goals?
- Are there certain relationships with people in your organization that could benefit from enhanced understanding and trust? If so, how does your work style compare to theirs?
- How does your management style and approach relate to your supervisors and other superiors? To your peers? To your direct report's preferences? What changes can you implement to work more effectively with your colleagues?
- What feelings do you have when going to work? Excitement? Happiness? Anxiety? Dread? What specifically causes those feelings? For the elements that cause negative feelings, what's within your control to change and adapt and what's not within your control?

Question: Why is fit so important to employees? Why not focus on doing the job well and find fit at home or in outside pursuits?
Answer: Feeling like you belong and fit is a basic human need. Employees who feel comfortable in their work teams and organizations and feel like they can express their authentic selves and preferences will experience higher levels of engagement, motivation, creativity, and productivity (all proven through research to impact the bottom line).

- Are you able to express your authentic personality and communication style preferences at work? If not, why?
- Are your strengths being identified and leveraged at work? Or are you spending time using skills that aren't your greatest strengths? What changes can you implement to more effectively leverage your strengths?
- How do you handle conflict, make decisions, and tolerate change in comparison to your colleagues?
- Are you able to structure your work in a way that works for you?
- Does the pace of your team and organization work for you? Where is there tension?

When you better understand your own work style and preferences and whether they fit with the team and organization, it will be easier for you to identify potential tweaks you can make to your style, the environment, or both.

Assessing Your Direct Reports' Work Style and Fit

Assessing employees' work styles should not require an advanced degree in psychology or certification in several assessment instruments. Simply asking questions about their work preferences, values, motivators, and demotivators and how they prefer to interact with managers and their peers can be an eye-opening experience. Observing their work behaviors will also enhance understanding of their work styles and preferences, including how they:

- Prefer to communicate
- Pace their work
- Structure their days
- Handle conflict
- Deal with change and ambiguity
- Respond to their own and others' emotions

Question: How do I accurately assess my own and someone else's work style? What are the best questions to ask? Do I need to use assessments?
Answer: Assessments are not required to gain an understanding of a team member's work style. Simply asking employees open-ended questions about their work preferences, communication, personality styles, and values and observing their behavior at work can be helpful and eye-opening. If you'd like to use assessments, discuss options with human resources, a consultant, or other trusted colleagues to determine which may be most helpful for your team.

Encourage regular, consistent communication about preferences among your team. The following discussion offers ways to better assess your direct reports' styles. You may want to spend time assessing your own style and preparing for development conversations with your supervisor as well.

Use Your Knowledge of Team Members' Work Styles to Better Manage Your Team

Diversity of thought, experience, work preferences, and perspective is essential for high functioning teams. Without that teams miss out on critical opportunities and creative problem solving. As you become attuned to your own work style, you can adapt your style in an effort to increase your team's productivity and engagement. Managers who understand the work styles of their employees can create optimally balanced and effective teams to decrease gaps in problem-solving and decision-making approaches. In addition, managers can better assess their direct reports' fit within the team and the organization and make suggestions to further enhance that fit. Managers who hire and retain diverse teams and encourage differing perspectives and approaches are more likely to gain disparate potential solutions to work challenges.

After gathering critical information about your direct reports' work styles and preferences, what do you do with that knowledge? How can you make the information actionable? Several ideas for leveraging knowledge of team members' work styles to help inform how you lead the team are discussed next.

Determine What Changes You Should Make to Your Management Style

Managers can, and should, adjust their management style and approach to support their direct reports' development levels and work preferences. Use the feedback employees share with you about their style preferences to make adjustments in how you are working with them.

If you learn that a team member prefers to first process information and ideas before sharing her thoughts, allow them the time and space to do that by including agenda items or things to consider before meetings or by encouraging her to think about particular challenges before offering her ideas and suggestions.

You'll work with people who like to structure and organize their days and plan ahead as well as those who prefer last-minute time pressures and spontaneity. Honor differences in the team's approach to work by clarifying the expected outcome and deadlines and allowing your direct reports flexibility in how they structure their time and resources to meet those goals.

How you offer both constructive and positive feedback is a critical component of management that should be altered based on employees' needs and preferences. Research-backed recommendations suggest offering 75 percent positive feedback to 25 percent constructive feedback in an effort to motivate, engage, and retain employees. Catching people doing things well and sharing the impact that

Myth: I shouldn't have to flex my management style to meet my direct reports' needs. I treat everyone the same.

There are many potential consequences to not flexing your style, including your employees perceiving you as being less credible than a manager who adapts and flexes style, decreased motivation, trust, productivity, creativity, and engagement among your team.

their behavior has on their and the team's performance is important. Employees will also be more open to hearing constructive feedback (instead of building up walls to protect themselves from the feedback) when they realize you're noticing what they're doing well. Some employees may appreciate recognition for accomplishments in public forums like an all-hands meetings and others may feel incredibly uncomfortable. Employ the approach that is most effective with each of your direct reports for the best results. For more information, review Chapter 9, Coaching for Performance.

Honor Individual Employees' Values

Once you have an understanding of your team members' values, you can make alterations to help honor those values. For example, if time autonomy is one of your employee's top values, determine if there are opportunities for you to give that person more authority over work deadlines. Someone who values career advancement should be encouraged to create short- and long-term career goals and identify, with your support, activities that will help him or her reach those goals.

Asking employees about what's most important to them and encouraging them to take the time to think about their values and whether or not they are being honored in their role will help them understand that you care about them as people. Encourage employees to consider realistic tweaks to their role, environment, schedule, and so on that will better support and honor their values. Through these efforts, employees will understand you are a caring, creative, and flexible leader who's willing to take the initiative to support the team.

Allow Employees to Express Their Authentic Personality, Communication, and Work Preferences

Encourage employees to express their unique personalities and encourage them to communicate in the way that is most comfortable for them, as long as it doesn't conflict with team or organizational expectations. Consistently reinforce that diverse ways of thinking about and tackling work assignments are important elements for high functioning teams by highlighting and celebrating different approaches. Encourage employees to identify and appreciate different work styles within the team and to address conflict or friction that arises from those differences in a timely manner.

Assign Projects and Stretch Assignments Based on Team Members' Preferences and Goals

When creating project teams, identify employees who have differing communication styles, personality, and decision-making preferences to ensure a balanced approach to the project. Consider employee strengths, including employees who can leverage their strengths when working on the project. Also consider any development or potential growth opportunities for your employees. Determine employees' level of commitment, interest, and motivation on the project; people who feel they have the opportunity to opt in or out will be more engaged and motivated. It's also important to consider each potential project team member's current workload and how this project will fit with their other assignments (see Chapter 8, Delegation).

When Hiring and Developing Your Team, Consider the Current Talent on the Team

When you have a vacancy on a team, assess the strengths of the current members and assess opportunities to fill in gaps in experience, knowledge, background, and perspective. Identify strengths and potential gaps within the team by considering the current team members' personality styles, communication

Question: What can I do as a manager to support employee fit?
Answer: Take the time to get to know each individual employee and his or her work, communication, and personality styles in addition to each one's motivators, values, and priorities. Learn about your employees' career goals and have ongoing discussions with them about their strengths and any opportunities where they'd like to grow and develop. Help them understand how their preferences align with the team and organization and where there are gaps or opportunities for more alignment. Offer coaching to support their success and growth and focus on catching them doing great work.

styles, decision-making approaches, and work preferences. Seek talent that offers diverse perspectives, approaches, and experiences (see Chapter 14, Talent Management). When diverse styles are appreciated, encouraged, and valued, retention and engagement are supported.

Coach Employees to Align Work Style with Team and Organizational Goals

One of the key ways you can support your direct reports is to help them adapt and thrive in their work environments and coach them on how to be more effective. If a direct report has a work style that is counter to the style that is encouraged and supported on the team or the organization as a whole, you need to address that difference and coach the employee on how to be effective while also expressing his or her authentic tendencies and styles. Sharing information about the senior management styles within the organization, about how work gets done, and about what behaviors are accepted and not accepted helps employees thrive and be successful (see also Chapter 18, Organizational Culture).

If collaboration is a must, and an employee is more comfortable working independently on projects, consider solutions to meet the needs of both the team and the individual employees. For example, you can encourage collaborative project meetings and assign various tasks to individual employees who can then determine how to complete those tasks.

Managers should ensure that behavioral expectations for successful fit within the team and the organization are clear to all employees If an employee's style does not support the team or organization goals, and coaching for performance is unsuccessful, managers should have transparent and timely conversations about what behavioral changes need to be made, how those changes will be measured, and the consequences of not implementing changes (see also Chapter 9, Coaching for Performance).

STYLE AND FIT SCENARIOS

Managers who assess and honor various work styles and pay attention to how they and their team members fit within the team and the organization are more effective than managers who do not pay attention to these important variables. The scenarios included in this chapter describe two actual managers and the impact their style had on their teams.

Question: What if one of my employees doesn't fit with the work culture?
Answer: Help your direct reports identify what exactly isn't a fit and brainstorm potential changes that can be made to assist with fit. Often relatively easy but powerful tweaks can be made to enhance fit. If efforts continue to fail to ensure a better fit between the employee and the team or organization, you should have a transparent conversation with the employee.

Scenario 1: High Emotional Intelligence Manager Jane

Jane has a high level of emotional intelligence and is aware of her preferred work style. She consistently assesses her values and her current work environment in addition to assessing her five direct reports' primary values and motivations to determine if there is a fit or if tweaks or major changes need to be made. After assessing her team's values and motivators, Jane determines what changes she can make that will honor those preferences. She provides the appropriate amount of support and direction to her direct reports when managing their work by assessing their styles, their development levels on projects they own, and gaining agreement from them on how she can best support them with their work.

Jane encourages different thought processes and approaches to work, and she creates project and work teams with individuals who have different ways of thinking, organizing, and approaching work, resulting in outcomes that are more complete and effective than seen for other teams. Project team assignments are made after taking into consideration the strengths, development needs, and career goals of members on her team. She consistently encourages and rewards employees for sharing their honest opinions, especially when they differ from her own. When there is an opening on a team, Jane assesses team strengths and areas of opportunity to assist with identifying candidates that can help fill gaps. She regularly asks her direct reports for open and honest feedback on her management style and what she can do differently, and she makes changes in her approach to better support individuals and the entire team. She is not afraid to have transparent, timely, and difficult conversations when the style of someone on her team has an adverse effect on either individual or team performance. Communicating and expressing work preferences is encouraged and Jane's team feels supported, valued, and engaged as a result of her strong and flexible management. Jane's team consistently receives very high levels of engagement and retention.

Scenario 2: Authoritarian Manager Lenny

Lenny is overly confident about his approach to work and management style, and he assumes his seven direct reports should alter their style to work with him, not the other way around. He does not take the time or energy to step back and assess his own style and how it impacts the team, and he has no interest in learning about the style or preferences of his direct reports. Fitting in for his team equates to carrying out assigned duties without pushing back or questioning his direction and goals.

Lenny talks more than he listens and does not ask for, or hear, feedback that differs from his own opinion. Project assignments are made based on Lenny's career advancement goals. He takes all of the highly visible projects for himself and delegates the more menial projects to his team, without taking into account the team members' strengths and goals. Communication about the work Lenny completes and the impact it has on the team is rarely shared, so the team feels as if they were operating in a vacuum.

Lenny manages by fear, using intimidation, threats, and yelling to get people to do what he wants them to do. He recruits and hires people who have a similar style and approach to work as he does, which decreases the diversity of thinking on his team. Because he discourages the sharing of ideas and opinions that differ from his own, the team doesn't share their thoughts. They follow his orders because they believe doing so enhances their job security, not because they align with his thinking and goals, which results in making decisions with limited information and less than ideal team outcomes.

Lenny's team members do not share work challenges or difficulties they experience because they are afraid he will blame them for any challenges they face. Lenny is seen by his team as an inexperienced, highly ego driven, and narcissistic manager. His team members do not trust him and avoid interactions with him as much as possible. As a result of Lenny's short-sighted command and control approach to managing, his team receives consistently low engagement scores and has high turnover.

• Conclusion •

Take the time to consider your own style and fit as well as your direct reports' styles and fit in an effort to enhance understanding, communication, and support on your team. Use the knowledge gained about yourself and your team to make adjustments in how you manage the team in an effort to fully leverage the team's strengths and styles. Address behaviors that are misaligned with the team or the organization

Myth: When a new person joins the team, they should adapt her style to match the manager's style and the team's in order to be successful.

Requiring your team members to mimic your style not only decreases their ability to express their authentic selves and approach to work but also decreases your ability to gain diverse perspectives and approaches when trying to tackle complex challenges. If you identify and leverage employees' strengths and allow them to express themselves and their preferences, you'll see better engagement, motivation, productivity, and creativity than if you demand that everyone adapt to your style and preferences.

in a timely manner, and coach employees on the most effective way to align their styles and fit. Managers have an inordinate amount of power and ability to shape their direct reports' work experiences, and they should exercise that power to achieve outcomes that are beneficial to both employees and the organization.

• Reference •

Shard, R. S. *Applying Career Development Theory to Counseling*. Belmont, CA: Thomson Brooks Cole.

Organizational Culture

LEARNING OBJECTIVES

By the end of this chapter, you will be better equipped to:

- Understand organizational culture and its effect and influence on a high-performance working environment.
- Discuss the six dimensions of organizational culture.
- Have an impact in developing and supporting organizational culture.
- Use a multistep process for shaping, molding, and sustaining a desired organizational culture.
- Define culture in a multicultural structure.
- Adapt personal values to fit with organizational culture.

INTRODUCTION

Is the structure of your organization about to change due to advances in technology? Has your CEO instructed management to adapt to a new way of working driven by global changes in the marketplace? Are you wondering how to adjust to younger, multitalented new hires who seem to be speaking a different language and introducing new behavior to the organization? Are you hearing the latest talk about flat hierarchies? Has human resources come up with new ideas on how to be a "fun culture" while you are trying to get your stressed-out team to keep up with the latest changes in processes? Are you expected to find time to be a mentor while managing your ever-increasing tasks and deadlines? And what about your management style? Have you been told that it needs an upgrade?

What's New?

- Organizations *are* cultures.
- Organizational culture is linked to high levels of productivity, quality, and efficiency.
- Culture change involves personal and organizational changes.

As managers, we need to constantly adjust to changing production cycles, new hires, and intercultural differences in how people work. We do this to create value, which, in return will lead the organization to have a competitive edge in the field.

To become effective, managers need to display a set of competencies that shape, create, and mold organizational culture.

Organizational culture refers to the shared beliefs, assumptions, and expectations held by the members of an organization; it's their distinctive way of perceiving context, norms, and values. In this chapter, we present techniques for understanding, supporting, and contributing to the organizational culture that accomplishes your goals and meets your company's needs.

In practice, the development and sustenance of organizational culture requires the activities outlined in this chapter and illustrated in Figure 18-1. We provide tactical guidance and examples that bring these to life and enable you to build a resilient culture where people work together toward the overarching goal of achieving organizational success.

THE EVOLUTION OF ORGANIZATIONAL CULTURE

We cannot begin to understand organizational culture without first recognizing its relationship with organizational behavior. Research into organizational behavior, and the related discipline of management science, began as early as the 1920s. One of the first studies to examine how organizational culture affected workplace behaviors was the Hawthorne Studies at Western Electric. According to the Hawthorne effect,[1] which was recorded during these studies, changes in culture improve employee productivity, but only for a period when the change is novel. Once employees are acclimated to the cultural shift, their productivity returns to its prior levels. In other words, culture is largely shaped by employee attitudes and behaviors. Organizational culture is fluid and must be sustained through adjustment while being promoted by the leaders of the organization.

In the 1960s, psychologists and sociologists began to recognize organizational culture. In 1965 MIT psychologist and management professor Edgar Schein conducted one of the first studies to reveal the importance of organizational culture and its effects on employee behavior. By the late 1970s and early 1980s, as international competition increased and more foreign companies were operating factories in the United States, understanding organizational culture became critical to business leaders.

The subject of culture has become a mainstay of organizational development since the early 1980s. What began as a desire to explore a better person–organization fit led to the practice of *work fit*, accord-

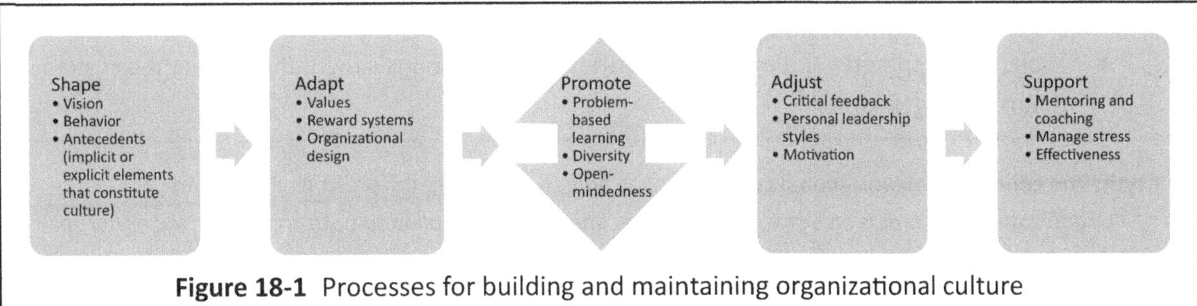

Figure 18-1 Processes for building and maintaining organizational culture

ing to which an individual's response to a given situation is derived from a combination of the individual and the circumstances in which that individual finds himself or herself (see Chapter 17, Style and Fit). But if person–organization fit is the main factor being considered during the hiring process, it can lead to hiring individuals who would fit only the current culture. In the late 1980s and early 1990s the concept of diversity shifted the way organizational culture was viewed. With the expansion of businesses into other countries and the absorption of other cultural working styles, the concept expanded to person–culture fit, meaning the employee fit into the national culture of the company. However, as attention shifted away from national cultures and back to the organization's culture, this practice did not last.

Following this shift, human resources management became interested in organizational culture and its potential to affect performance. Organizational culture is often perceived to offer a nonmechanistic, flexible, and imaginative approach to understanding how organizations work. Consequently, organizational culture is often considered to be the great cure-all for most organizational issues.

With the advent of intercultural communication, which studies the way people communicate across different cultures within an organization, and research into leadership, equality, and inclusion in the workplace, the exploration of organizational culture continues to impact the relationship among organizations, workers, and the workplace. As such, managers have moved beyond their traditional roles and become leaders who influence, inspire, and motivate, concentrating on the added advantage of internal innovation as a strategy to remain competitive.

DEFINING ORGANIZATIONAL CULTURE

An organization's norms, beliefs, and values can be associated with symbols, behaviors, stories, and myths that express the culture and help socialize people into the organization. These accumulated shared patterns, drivers, and motives—whether observed or perceived—may allow the group to adapt and adjust to new problems in the organizational context.

This definition highlights three key characteristics of organizational culture:

- It is passed on to new employees through a process of socialization and adaptation, which can stem from the founder's vision, the industry environment and attached cultural traits, and the national culture.

- It influences our behavior and social conduct at the workplace.
- It operates implicitly and explicitly at different levels and is salient throughout the system that is the organization.

Myth: The concept of organizational culture applies only to corporate, for-profit environments.

Organizational culture is inclusive and adaptive, and it can be applied to both corporate and nonprofit cultures. It is distinct from corporate culture due to its natural and organic occurrence and because it's less socially and consciously constructed by managers. Managers, however, do have a crucial role in shaping, creating, and molding workplace behaviors.

To better understand how organizational culture is formed and informed, and how employees and managers can gain a competitive advantage by using it, the following discussion explores its various traits, elements, and characteristics.

Dynamics of Organizational Culture

Organizational culture has different layers, as shown in Figure18-2 Some lie right on the surface, observable and explicit. Others are attributed to belief systems and assumptions, which are considered implicit layers.

At the visible level, organizational culture is about artifacts, such as manner of dress, the use of titles, myths and stories about the organization, observable rituals, special decorations, and so on. The

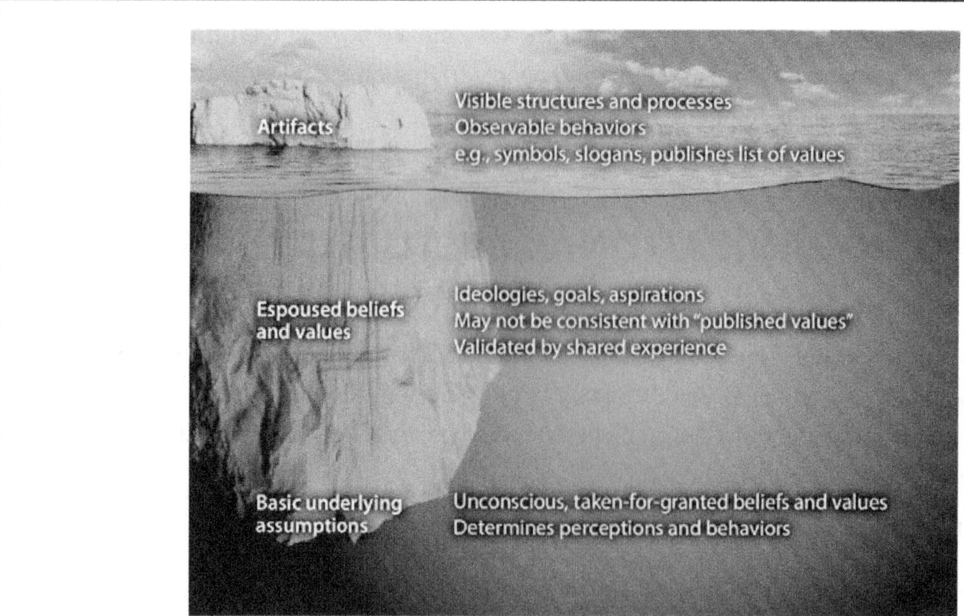

Figure 18-2 Schein's model of culture

visible layers of organizational culture are easier to access and change than the less visible aspects. For example, it's easy to change a dress code but not a deeply held value.

Values are concepts that pertain to enduring belief in a particular method or end state. There are two types of values:

- *Espoused*: The stated values and norms preferred by an organization. Usually, the expression of espoused values can be found in the vision and mission statement of an organization. The belief is that employees will adopt the aspirations communicated to the employees and that managers should walk the talk.
- *Enacted*: The values and norms exhibited by employees. On a daily basis, employees pick up routines, rituals, and other artifacts from their organizational context and ascribe these values to the organization. For example, in a fast-paced startup, one of the values may be *speed* so employees may walk, act, and even speak quickly.

As managers, we must learn to recognize gaps between espoused and enacted values as the mismatch can influence employee attitudes and organizational performance. Therefore, a proper induction process for new arrivals and a regular cultural-fit survey for existing employees allows the managers to see the signposts of adaptation or the indicators of a mismatch, allowing for a fast and appropriate response. Values are harder to change than artifacts, but they can be edited by drafting new espoused values and making sure they align with the enacted values. However, unlike values, basic assumptions are nearly impossible to change.

Less visible aspects, which are much harder to change, are worldviews, belief systems, deeply held assumptions, mission, and vision. These elements are more than just parts of the organization; they make the organization what it is at its core.

SIX DIMENSIONS OF ORGANIZATIONAL CULTURE

Between 1967 and 1973, IBM psychologist Geert Hofstede conducted a large-scale survey of national values differences across IBM's international subsidiaries. Hofstede's findings, which emerged from his team's analysis of survey responses from 117,000 employees, became one of the first quantifiable theories that could be used to explain observed differences between cultures. The theory outlines six dimensions of culture (see also Chapter 8, Delegation) Think of it as six different spectrums along which cultural differences can be looked at and better understood.

Power Distance Index

The power distance index is the degree to which the less powerful members of a society accept and expect power to be distributed unequally. A large degree of power distance points to the acceptance of a hierarchical order in which everybody has a place. A low power distance means people expect a more equal distribution of power and a good reason when there are inequalities.

Individualism Versus Collectivism

High degrees of individualism suggest a preference for a society in which people are expected to take care of only themselves and their families. On the other extreme is collectivism, a society in which people expect their needs to be met by others and in which individuals contribute to the betterment of all. Broadly, this dimension is about whether individuals in a society refer to *I* or *we*.

Masculinity Versus Femininity

A society's masculinity index shows preference for achievement, competition, and assertiveness. It expects material rewards in exchange for success. At the other end is femininity, with an emphasis on cooperation, consensus building, caring, and protection of the weaker members of society. Think of this index as tough versus gentle.

Uncertainty Avoidance Index

The uncertainty avoidance index defines people's degree of comfort with uncertainty and ambiguity. There is always an unknown. Some societies (just like some individuals) deal with that reality better than others. Nations with a strong uncertainty avoidance index tend to have rigid belief systems and a general intolerance for the unorthodox. Countries that are weak in this index tend to have a more relaxed attitude when it comes to facing the unknown.

Long-Term Orientation Versus Short-Term Normative Orientation

Societies that score low on the long-term versus short-term normative orientation dimension prefer time-honored practices and traditional norms; they are generally suspicious of change. Those with a high score on this index are less tied to tradition and more inclined to revamp education systems to prepare for change.

Indulgence Versus Restraint

Indulgent societies encourage gratification, the enjoyment of life, and the pursuit of pleasure. Restrained societies on the other hand, value the delay of gratification and stricter social norms.

***

Managers who want to build and contribute to a high-performance culture should learn the six dimensions and practice spotting them among members of different cultures who are working together. Hofstede's dimensions can be a good starting point for conversations that lead to deeper understanding of people's behavior, how they interpret other people's behavior, and how it all impacts the way work gets done.

DEVELOPING A HIGH-PERFORMANCE CULTURE

An organization's culture may exhibit varying degrees of strength or weakness, depending on variables such as leadership ability and experience, cohesiveness of member identity and organizational environment, value consensus, and individual commitment to adapt and to share collective goals. A strong culture is not necessarily a prerequisite for a successful organizational culture. Rather, it is the nature of the shared values that bears more weight than the strength itself. In this context and as detailed in Table 18-1, culture enhances organizational performance through strength, fit, and adaptive perspectives (see also Chapter 17, Style and Fit, and Chapter 21, Diversity and Inclusion).

Table 18-1 Strength, Fit, and Adaptive Perspectives

Strength Perspective	Fit Perspective	Adaptive Perspective
The strength of the organizational culture is directly related to the firm's capital performance. The assumption is that strong cultures create goal alignment, employee motivation, and the appropriate structures and channels of communication to enhance and to strengthen organizational performance.	The culture must align with its industry context. The assumption is that the correct fit will contribute to higher performance yields..	Risk taking, trusting, and embracing a proactive approach by the members of the organization will contribute to better performance

The adaptive perspective has found its way into the leadership canon, focusing on leaders who inspire, persuade, and influence to foster and to preserve the adaptive core of the culture.

What are the criteria of a high-performance culture? Results. The ability to achieve goals, outpace the competition, increase market share, and acquire premium levels of financial returns while attracting high-performing new talent, including high potentials. In this context, cohesion is a central element, with high levels of employee morale and satisfaction, human resource development, and teamwork. Employment, engagement, and proactive participation foster empowerment and commitment. In return, committed, satisfied employees produce effectiveness.

The Socialization Process

Organizational socialization means learning the values, norms, and behaviors that permit an employee to participate in the organization. This process can happen vertically—for example, through a dedicated top–down process, where the vision, mission, and purpose of the process or project are being communicated from senior leadership to lower level management. Yet, the process can also take place in a hori-

Pro tip
Organizational socialization turns newcomers (new employees, job candidates, consultants) into functioning members of the organization by promoting, reinforcing, and enhancing the organization's core values and belief systems.

zontal way, such as through peer-to-peer engagement, but also with direct reporting and frequent check-ins (instead of the regular performance reviews). It's a key mechanism used by organizations to embed their organizational cultures. Embedding a culture involves teaching about the organization's preferred values, expectations, and behaviors, including the assignment of desk/office space, explicit rewards and promotion criteria, training programs, coaching, leadership's reaction to crises, workflow structure, standard operating procedures (SOPs), town halls, and messages on sharing organizational leadership's processes.

Management and Mentoring to Embed Organizational Culture

It is crucial to understand the role of structure and leadership in organizational culture. They act as a conduit for mutually reinforcing positive loops of communication and shared learning about the group members, whether they are near or far, working online, or in remote locations. In the context of organizational culture, the manager is also tasked with providing an environment that enables the team to go in new directions while facilitating beneficial, innovative, shared learning opportunities.

One typical leadership task enacted by managers is mentoring, which can serve as a tactic for embedding organizational culture. At the same time, it also offers and promotes a sense of membership.

Managers can impact workplace culture through other activities such as:

- Facilitating effective interpersonal relationships through supportive feedback, active listening, and conflict resolution
- Fostering coordination within the organization and with external units and managers by sharing information across departmental boundaries
- Motivating and inspiring individuals to be proactive, make an extra effort, and work vigorously
- Cultivating diversity, equality, and inclusion
- Fostering an orientation toward serving customers, involving them, and exceeding their expectations
- Encouraging continuous improvement, flexibility, and productive change among individuals in their work life
- Facilitating effective, cohesive, smooth-functioning, high-performance teamwork

Shaping the Personal and Organizational Culture

Managers need to shape themselves and their teams by incorporating the vision statement into their daily work lives. Industry standards and other cultural patterns and foundational values (such as the founder's vision or the behavior of senior leaders) contribute to shaping the space.

Table 18-2 presents the nine steps (along with a series of explanatory substeps) for shaping organizational culture by incorporating aspects of vision, behavior, and historical precedent.

Table 18-2 Step-by-Step Approach to Developing and Strengthening Organizational Culture

Steps[a]	Action Plan
1. Reach consensus regarding the current organizational culture	• Identify individuals who have global perspectives on the organization • Establish a dialogue structure for conversations to take place and to flow • Ask probing questions (What is happening in the organization? Who are key contributors? What is not happening?) • Identify what created and creates organizational culture • Define the expected behaviors of the current and potentially new culture (norms)
2. Reach consensus on the preferred organizational culture by leading thorough and conclusive discussions	• Determine how to be highly successful in the future[b] • List the demands you could face internally and externally • Define the areas in which you should be leading edge, whether as a market leader or early influencer of the industry • Determine whether you are currently underdeveloped (assessed through risk, SWOT, or other analysis tool)[c] • Define the areas of special strength you can use to differentiate your organization • Identify the best you have ever been and how to duplicate it • Determine the type of culture that will support these changes
3. Establish new organizational character	• Probe for what norms, artifacts, and behaviors should shape the organization • Test for when the group will know the new cultural phase has been reached[d] • Establish a corporate character • Preserve some positive features and build in new elements
4. Create a vision through stories that illustrate the desired future culture	• Develop stories that exemplify and characterize the new key values, desired orientations, and behavioral principles • Tell the stories in the team meetings and get feedback • Articulate the lessons to be learned and the morals of the stories
5. Set a strategic action agenda	• Create readiness by identifying the advantages of the future state, identifying the changes and the impact of not changing, showing gaps between current team or department performance and required performance, and rewarding behaviors compatible with the desired change in relation to the market, industry, stakeholders, employees, and colleagues • Explain the *why*, not the *what*; communicate caring and esteem to those involved in the culture change process and include those who may have difficulties in adjusting to change • Focus on how decision-making and problem-solving processes are being designed and implemented and by whom • Generate social support by building coalitions of supporters for the change and empowering them by placing them at the center of decision-making processes and critical events that may have an impact on the organizational culture; involve those affected by the change by listening to them; identify champions and change agents who can serve as role models and positive energizers • Provide information and be as transparent as possible

continued

Steps[a]	Action Plan
6. Acknowledge immediate small wins	• Find something easy to change, change it, and publicize it • Recognize and highlight each change to create an opportunity for celebration
7. Recognize leadership involvement	• Reflect critically on personal leadership skills through awareness training and perspective taking • Ask what is needed for new leadership competencies • Develop facilitative leadership skills
8. Identify metrics, measures, and milestones to maintain accountability	• Establish criteria and key indicators of progress • Check for the collection of metrics (e.g., through feedback loops, informal discussions, and surveys) and test for employee referrals, internal transfers, employee assistance programs, attrition rate, and work–life balance • Establish a rhythm for monitoring and verification of progress
9. Create a communications strategy	• Identify the means of communicating change, the channels through which continuous communication can be supported, the type of information, the audience, and the stories to be shared • Use communication to generate enthusiasm and positive energy

[a] Stakeholders in the organizational hierarchy need to decide on a cycle, which has to be negotiated and agreed on. This ensures constant aligning with the vision, checking in with members of the collective, and critical feedback. The cycle has no blueprint because it depends on hierarchy, organizational structure, and industry.
[b] See, for example, Y. Tsai, "Relationship between Organizational Culture, Leadership Behavior and Job Satisfaction," *BMC Health Services Research* 11 (2011): 98.
[c] See for example, S. Nackerud, "Why Engage in (Social) Network Analysis?" University of Minnesota, https://dash.umn.edu/social-network-analysis, for more on engaging in social network analysis to measure and explore how individuals and groups relate to and interact with one another and how this interaction creates or changes organizational makeup.
[d] This can be done through regular check-ins, town halls, storytelling, and visioning.

Effective leadership is visionary, innovative, and risk oriented. It is the glue that holds together the organization, the team, and the department. It drives commitment and innovation.

Vision

Pro tip
The vision of the leader can become the vision of the team as members get a sense of unity, a sense of belonging, and personal identification with the organization.

An important aspect of shaping organizational culture is vision. A clear vision allows you to establish the narrative with which the organization or team will operate. And it allows for commitments to be declared and agreements to be made between mentor and mentees. This provides the mechanisms for individuals to thrive and for teams to adapt and learn.

See Scenario 1 for an example of how vision drove a significant culture change in one organization.

Scenario 1: Vision Driving Culture Change

In an effort to become more competitive, the top management team of a well-known company initiated significant organizational change. The organization is a large multinational business that manufactures circuit boards for the microelectronics industry. Its environment is fast paced, quick to change, and extremely competitive. The introduction of self-managing work teams was a key element that top managers identified for achieving desired organizational change. These managers were concerned, however, that initiating self-management might not survive the command-and-control work culture that had developed in the organization and had become institutionalized over the previous twenty years.

Senior leadership used a multistep methodology for diagnosing and initiating a culture change. Top management first convened a leadership team that consisted of about twenty-five representatives from management, employees, and the union. Their goal was to reach agreement on the type of organizational culture needed to meet the competitive demands of the future and sustain participative processes such as self-managing work teams. The next task was to reach consensus on the preferred culture. Team members were asked to share what they thought the future culture should look like. The various groups reached consensus on a preferred organizational culture profile. The crucial element that brought these groups forward was the vision shared by the leading managers that energized the team members to move forward.

Adapt to the Value System

Managers need to adapt their own organizational values to the espoused value system. They need to create a new reward structure, allowing for positive behavior to be shared and the creation of a new organizational culture that allows for employees to feel included and encouraged to participate and to contribute.

This can take place by:

- Enabling dialogue among team members and other groups
- Supporting buy-in from senior leadership
- Promoting behaviors conducive to problem solving

Pro tip
Culture doesn't mean buying pizza for your team or having table tennis tables. It's not a night out at the company's expense, nor is it a team retreat at a fancy hotel. These are rewards, recognition, or team building—not culture. Culture is the life and breath of a company.

Scenario 2 provides an example of how one organization adapted the values of its founder to build an excellent organizational culture.

Promote the New Culture

Managers need to continuously promote the new culture in order for socialization to take place, making it easier for newcomers and older generations alike to keep the dynamics of an innovative workplace. Research with best-practice, high-performance organizations shows us this is achieved by constantly encouraging learning, a diverse environment, and safeguarding open mindedness, so all voices are heard

Scenario 2: Southwest's Employee Focused Culture

Southwest Airlines began flying with just four planes in 1971. Understanding how important culture and customer service was becoming, Southwest implemented its vision early on. Based on the U.S. Department of Transportation's most recent data, Southwest Airlines is the nation's largest carrier in terms of originating domestic passengers boarded. The company has been profitable for over four decades, and its legendary culture is one of its greatest assets. The founder, Herb Kelleher, has been credited with instilling the idea that happy employees create happy customers, and profitability follows.

With core values of "Warrior Spirit," "Servant's Heart," and "Fun-LUVing Attitude," Southwest asks employees to embody hard work, perseverance, proactive customer service, and lighthearted fun in everything they do. Managers are encouraged to hire for attitude and train for skill. Southwest's culture of service thrives on appreciation, recognition, and celebration. The company works to appreciate every employee through local and companywide culture committees. Southwest employees take time to recognize one another formally and informally through internal awards and programs, such as the Winning Spirit Award. The company has several prestigious corporate awards that employees can be nominated to receive, like the President's Award. And it recognizes service through milestone anniversary celebrations.

Celebrating is something that Southwest is known for; the company history is full of fun and creative events, and employees enjoy annual companywide celebrations such as spirit parties, chili cookoffs, and Southwest rallies. On top of company-sponsored events, employees enjoy participating in locally hosted celebrations and recognitions for life events and milestones.

Because of this employee-focused culture, Southwest employees are often featured in the airline's commercials, ads, and *Southwest: The Magazine*.

Myth: Managers are generally stuck with the culture they inherit when they start with the organization.

Effective managers emphasize the role played by human relations, and they seek opportunities and platforms to share their knowledge and to communicate the changes in culture they would like to see. As the growth of Southwest Airlines has shown, this emphasis on a positive organizational culture positively impacts customer service, which positively impacts the customer experience and increases sales.

and each and every contribution counts. For example, McKinsey & Company found that organizations with higher performing cultures create a threefold return to shareholders.

Promoting a strong organizational culture allows strategic benefits that include:

- Continuous interweaving of individual cultural values into a shared team culture
- An increase of cultural understanding among all employees (for more, Chapter 21, Diversity and Inclusion)
- Stability of cultural values and meaning over time

With new forms of organizations (flatter hierarchies or matrixed organizations, for example), the concept of strength of culture is especially relevant. For example, we see many virtual organizations with social networking in which members of the same organization rarely interact face to face. They enact their culture in cyberspace. Even then, it's interesting to observe how strongly culture emerges and how—even in online interaction—groups go through the norming and forming stages or how some individual members develop power and status through the frequency of their interactions.

Sometimes, branch offices or product divisions of a large company may develop their own unique subcultures. Only strong communication channels can prevent a fragmentation of the culture as differentiated subcultures develop. This differentiation can cause a lack of trust and interdependence and, in severe cases, can hamper employees' professional growth. Constantly promoting core organizational values may help counter the threat of fragmentation and of subcultures. See Scenario 3 for an example.

Pro tip

To be effective, managers must be sure that cultural elements are consistent in conveying values.

Monitor and Assess Progress

Managers need to keep the process moving by constantly monitoring and reassessing progress. They can do so by learning how to give critical feedback, how different leadership styles can be acquired and shape their employees, and on how inspiring stories can motivate.

First, check and assess the following are in place:

- Members have an organizational identity.[2]
- Managers act as facilitators and bridge builders to enact collective commitment.
- The organization promotes and contributes to social system stability through rituals focusing on the human story and condition of the organization, including awards and a work–life balance philosophy.[3]
- The culture helps shape behavior by helping members make sense of their environment.
- The culture enables a creative and innovative environment, where members can constantly learn and adapt to new problems successfully.

Scenario 3: Salesforce and Volunteerism

Salesforce, a cloud-computing company, made volunteerism an integral part of its organizational culture. Salesforce has built a reputation as a business that values philanthropy, diversity, and responsible corporate citizenship. The customer relationship management (CRM) maker is one of the most highly valued cloud-computing companies in the nation and as of this writing employs 19,000 people.

Through its Integrated Corporate Philanthropy model, Salesforce has made volunteerism and community service pillars of its organizational culture. Starting with onboarding, new employees are urged to give back to communities, and every employee gets seven paid days off each year for volunteer activities.

When Salesforce launched, CEO Marc Benioff and co-founders worked to define and document the company's shared vision and align everyone on big goals. Jody Rennick Kohner, Salesforce senior vice president of employee marketing and engagement, says this top–down alignment on mission, values, and purpose is crucial to preserving the company's dynamic, and culture fit is a key hiring criteria from leadership to entry-level roles.

- The culture supports diversity in race, ethnicity, gender and gender identity, work styles, and work preferences allowing everyone to have a voice in sharing ideas, concerns, and feedback.

Second, adjust by providing critical feedback and by adapting your personal leadership style. Leaders' strategies, practices, values, styles, and examples influence culture by:

Pro tip

A truly positive working culture is reflected in every meeting, dictates every decision, embodies every result, and lives in every conversation you have with employees. It's an unequivocally authentic way of being, every day, and in every imaginable situation. You are a team and the outcome of providing a positive organizational culture is employees who are genuinely engaged to deliver results.

- *Prioritizing Transparency*: Employees who feel included and in the loop on important decisions are motivated to be more engaged and do their best work. One study found management transparency was the number one factor contributing to employee happiness.[4] Communicate with your workforce early and often to foster a culture of trust and inclusion.
- *Hiring for Cultural Fits*: A 2005 study showed strong culture fit can mean greater job satisfaction, stronger identification with a company, longer tenure, more commitment, and superior performance. Start by defining the key tenets of your organizational culture. Then integrate these criteria into your employer brand messaging, job content, and interview processes.
- *Making People Feel Like They Belong*: Feelings of safety and belonging in employees can improve communication, collaboration, and alignment, which will ultimately boost company revenue. Once you've defined your culture and hired people who align with your values, encourage them every day to be themselves, follow their instincts, and get involved with the rest of their group.

Organizational culture and meaning is an interactive process between managers and organizational members. Therefore, the manager can shape many types of meaning through:

- Personal modeling
- Telling inspirational stories
- Using rites and rituals
- Understanding the impact of history

At best, leaders make use of their communication skills to influence meaning, by using:

- Metaphors
- Jargon (the language that is peculiar to a particular profession, an organizational culture, or a well-developed vision or program)
- Contrast (the leader highlights an essential trait by placing one person, one object, or idea in opposition or contrast to another)
- Spin (seeing events in different perspectives. For example, is finishing third a good or a bad thing?)

The Importance of Support

As a manager, you can support individual contributors and teams by providing mentoring and coaching, sharing resources, learning how to manage stress, and measuring performance effectiveness. If you want to channel communication that alleviates resistance to change, keep these key criteria in mind:

- Frontload strategy and culture as a leadership priority, whether on the strategic or the operational level.
- Conduct joint and comprehensive analyses of current cultural patterns and practices.
- Appoint a focal team for organizational culture made up of your team members.
- Enable a learning environment.
- Set up an early-warning mechanism for crisis management purposes.[5]
- Allow for more independent and self-reliant teams to foster owned solutions that can grow organically along the lines of the standard operating procedures.
- Continuously monitor and evaluate changes.

Within the multicultural structure that enables and advances a learning organization (one that knows not only how to acquire and transfer knowledge but can also modify its behavior to reflect new knowledge),[6] the manager-as-role-model has a set of priorities and behaviors:

- *Leadership*: Commitment to the diverse organizational culture is crucial, yet not sufficient. The manager needs to grow and coach champions and change agents at lower organizational

Myth: When it comes down to it, a company is one big family.

This is an outdated way of thinking that glosses over the unique features and challenges of an organization and the realities of business. If an employee is struggling with work-related responsibilities, an organization should try to support that employee overcome his or her challenges and reach full potential, just as a family would help a child struggling in school. But an organization can't support an employee's development for an indefinite period of time. It is after all a business, and underachievement and poor results are costly. Ultimately, if results don't improve, an organization is justified in terminating that employee.

Actors	Strategies
Employees	• Placing a high value on developing vision based on facts and truth • Leading with questions, using informal networks to develop vision • Building consensus rather than imposition or coercion • Using an open or dialogue forum for discussing differences and disagreements • Learning from failed efforts without assigning blame • Understanding and sharing a vision of what the organization does best • Selecting and keeping the best • Earning merit-based (rather than political) rewards, incentives, and promotions • Tapping into strength of cultural diversity
Customers	• Communicating a clear vision of what the organization does best • Opening channels for receiving customer input and feedback • Listening, changing and improving based on feedback
Stakeholders	• Balancing demands of stockholders for profit with concerns for the physical environment • Balancing demands of stockholders for profit with concerns for employees and customers
Leadership	• Empowering and shared leadership functions • Emphasizing principle and values rather than personal charisma • Focusing on leadership identification and development
Organizational structure	• Building a flexible and dynamic structure • Remaining permeable to allow environmental input and scanning

levels, especially key line or front-line managers. At times, it is important to encourage the creation of task forces and advisory committees to address culture or a leadership collective on diversity. The manager needs to constantly feel prevailing and emerging patterns by keeping an open mind and a constant analysis of exogenous factors that have an impact on the organizational fabric of the team or organization.

- *Training*: Constant awareness and sensitization to cultural diversity is not only a starting point but an ongoing development.
- *Knowledge Management*: Collection of information about diversity related issues and how involved actors have been able to overcome, manage, or transform the challenges is key for the learning organization and for the manager to able to share information and good communication.[7]
- *Auditing*: Performance appraisals, regular check-ins, new rituals, and symbols are some components and milestones that can uncover biases and identify ways corporate culture may discriminate or exclude some members.

Strategies and tactics for an effective organizational culture are shown in the chart.

• Conclusion •

As managers, we can create and support a strong and vibrant culture in which values are shared. Employees socialize into a common way of creating meanings and on how to create new pathways to problem solving. At the same time, the workforce becomes more diverse with enough tension to promote creativity and innovation. Though this may sound like a paradox, it is where organizational culture takes place and where the promotion of diversity, inclusion, and equality finds its starting point.

Strong cultures tend to reproduce themselves. New employees are hired because they are a good fit with existing employees. Cultural values and norms are so strong that employees are socialized to accept the company way, with enough space for the individual members of the social structure to accommodate their own preferred values and identities, which then align with the overarching structure. Or these employees leave.

Strong culture inevitably leads to diversity since a cohesive organization can have a constraining effect on the forces of difference and change.

• Endnotes •

1. The Hawthorne effect concerns research participation, the consequent awareness of being studied, and its possible impact on behavior. It is a widely used research term. The original studies that gave rise to the Hawthorne effect were undertaken at Western Electric telephone manufacturing factory at Hawthorne, near Chicago, between 1924 and 1933. Increases in productivity were observed among a selected group of workers

who were supervised intensively by managers under the auspices of a research program. The term was first used in an influential methodology textbook in 1953. A large literature and repeated controversies have evolved over many decades as to the nature of the Hawthorne effect. If there is a Hawthorne effect, studies could be biased in ways we do not under-stand well, with profound implications for research.

2. *Organizational identity* is defined as a set of statements that organization members perceive to be central, distinctive, and enduring to their organization. It widely influences the behavior of both leaders and members/employees of an organization.
3. Social system stability is the degree to which organizational activities emphasize maintaining the status quo in contrast to growth. *Work–life balance* describes the ideal of splitting one's time and energy between work and other important aspects of life. For more, see S. M. Heathfield, "The Importance of Achieving Work-Life Balance and How to Do It," Balance Careers, last updated June 25, 2019, www.thebalancecareers.com/work-life-balance-1918292.
4. D. S. Ana Suzete, M. S. Arnaldo Fernandes, and N. M. Pereira Ribeiro, "Authentic Leadership and Creativity: The Mediating Role of Happiness," *International Journal of Organizational Analysis* 25, no. 3 (2017): 395–412.
5. An early warning mechanism can entail a forecasting component, a process to disseminate warnings, and a collective of members functioning as crisis responders whenever the process of absorbing and adapting to the new organizational culture is hampered by group think or individuals struggling with the adaptation speed.
6. Multiculturalism is a situation in which all the different cultural or racial groups in a society or organizational entity have equal rights and opportunities, and none is ignored or regarded as unimportant.
7. Knowledge management is a collection of systematic approaches to help information and knowledge flow to and between the right people at the right time (and in the right format and at the right cost), so they can act more efficiently and effectively to create value for the organization.

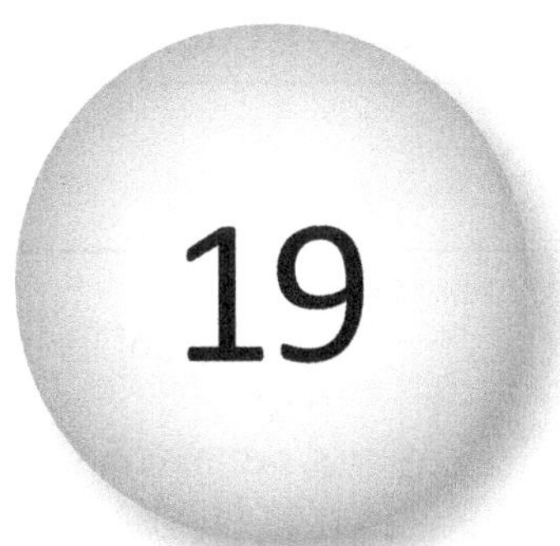

Ethics

LEARNING OBJECTIVES

By the end of this chapter, you will be better equipped to:

- Understand the value of managers' ethical behavior for businesses.
- Recognize specific categories of ethical conduct that are relevant across organizations and professions.
- Recognize the role individual ethical reasoning plays in a manager's day-to-day work.
- Be familiar with the components of individual ethical reasoning.
- Be alert to psychological factors that may inhibit individual ethical reasoning and ethical decision making.
- Understand what motivates ethical actions among managers.

Broadly speaking, business ethics are principles wherein processes should be transparent and guide decision making in all aspects of business above and beyond what the law requires. The principles of business ethics pertain to relations with stockholders as well as stakeholders, including employees and their families, vendors, freelancers, customers, an organization's community, and the environment. While the principles of business ethics reflect values held, such as fairness, most professions and organizations formalize these principles in specific codes of ethics.

For managers, the practice of ethics involves applying their organization's principles to specific situations, including performance management; hiring, promotion, and termination; maintaining a healthy, nonhostile work environment, and resolving disputes.

The process to gain competency in ethical managerial behavior is illustrated in Figure 19-1.

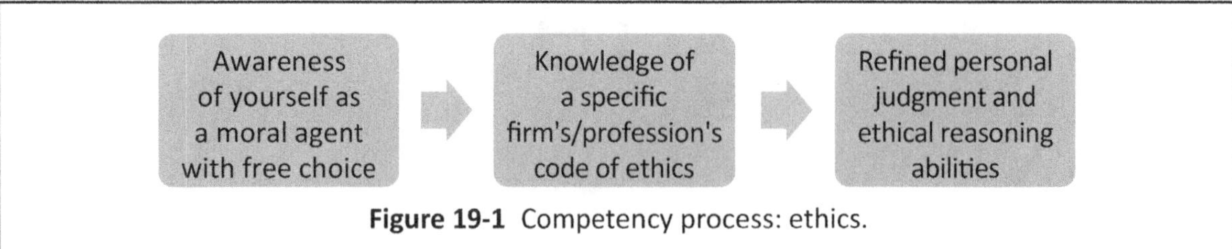

Figure 19-1 Competency process: ethics.

JUSTIFICATION AND STRUCTURE OF BUSINESS ETHICS

Business ethics has evolved from philosophical reflection on different questions about business—for example, Can an organization function as an individual? and Does a corporation have a moral responsibility beyond maximizing profits for stockholders? This chapter draws mainly on the philosophical approach to business ethics but includes insights from other relevant fields.

Business ethics pertains both to specifying types of conduct that are right and wrong in various situations and to examining and explaining the grounds for accepting such specifications of conduct. Business ethics also, therefore, pertains to discussions about the ways that claims specifying right and wrong conduct should be organized and used.

In practice, largely for purposes of liability mitigation, organizations typically create lists of rules outlining behaviors and choices that are acceptable and not acceptable in the eyes of that organization (these rules are above and beyond legal requirements). A different practical approach emphasizes the importance of managers cultivating specific personal virtues, such as courage and honesty. Many initiatives, such as trainings to promote diversity and inclusion, represent efforts to create ethical organizational climates and encourage employees to develop specific personal characteristics and attitudes. Thus, in ad hoc ways, many organizations employ a virtue-based approach as well as a rules-based approach.

Most business ethicists justify specific claims about right and wrong conduct with appeals to what is termed the *common morality*. The common morality is a social institution, largely based on a belief that every individual, in every context, possesses certain inalienable rights simply by virtue of being human. It is composed of norms that extend across different cultures, which individuals begin to learn from infancy.

Pure reason is a European Enlightenment theory that asserts the existence of a transcendent, objective, universal phenomenon—reason—to which all people have access, unaided by any human contrivance (religion, political system, culture). For example, the theory is behind the opening of the U.S. Declaration of Independence, "We hold these truths to be self-evident." To what were the authors referring that makes the truths self-evidence? Pure reason, which any person, unclouded by superstition (today we would say cultural biases) can understand.

As a foundation for business ethics, common morality theory is a pragmatic effort to identify moral norms to which everyone can have equal access, based on the practices shared among different cultures.

Identifying rights as a transcendent feature of the common morality leads most business ethicists to suggest that the structure of business ethics should contain specific moral norms organized into general principles, which are prima facie (at first glance) always relevant and binding but which nonetheless have to be specified and balanced as specific rules and action guides in each particular situation. In a particular situation, certain prima facie principles may conflict, so one will have to override the other. In business ethics there is not a single, absolute principle from which all other action guides derive. However, there is an emphasis on obligations to refrain from certain conduct and sometimes to perform certain actions.

Some ethicists assert that obligation-oriented principles of rights and duties are not robust enough to ensure ethical conduct in organizations. They assert that ethical conduct is a matter of character traits or virtues, which individuals cultivate over time. For example, some argue, possessing the virtue of courage is the only thing that equips someone to blow the whistle on a dangerous process or product—a principle or rule cannot achieve this action. Likewise, some argue, having only the virtue of integrity equips someone to say no to an expensive gift that, if accepted, would give the impression that one's decisions are unduly influenced by a specific party. Virtues and principles are not, however, mutually exclusive, and they can complement each other. Organizations can have composed ethical codes and principles, rules, and the like as well as cultures that foster virtues, such as courage and integrity, and dispose people to implement the principles and rules.

Many organizations use the rhetoric of values rather than ethics and have official values statements. The adjective *values* in the term *values statement* refers to what an individual or group deems to be desirable, worthwhile, obligatory, good, and right. Practically speaking, values statements tend to specify particular kinds of conduct (such as between employees and customers, between direct reports and managers, and between the firm and stockholders), in the same way the prima facie principles do. However, in certain circumstances, such as conveying to customers and the broader community the ethical good standing of an organization, the rhetoric of values is more accessible than the rhetoric of ethics and principles.

PERSONAL JUDGMENT AND ETHICAL REASONING

Most ethicists affirm that a refined sense of moral judgment is essential for understanding how to apply principles in specific situations. In commonsense terms, moral judgment is often referred to as an individual's conscience, and adhering to sound moral judgments is often referred to as conscientiousness. Many would agree that conscientiousness is an essential individual virtue for an ethical manager. Without it, an individual cannot effectively extend, specify, and apply principles and rules to real-life situations. A manager is conscientious when they make every effort to determine what is right in a specific situation, intend to perform the right action, and exert effort to carry out the right action. Conscience, likewise, may be defined as self-reflection undertaken to determine what is right in a given situation. Conscience is a person's judgment about their actions: is an act right or wrong, obligatory or optional, good or bad? In other words, conscience is our awareness of and reflection on our own conduct in relation to our own standards. Consequently, understanding different types of ethical reasoning is important for the practice of business ethics.

The ability to reason ethically allows the individual to recognize the ethical issues in any situation, to identify what principles and norms are relevant to the situation, and to determine whether one principle overrules another. Professions today, as well as most organizations, maintain codes of ethics that outline what is acceptable and unacceptable behavior in various categories, ranging from accounting principles to conduct in meetings. However, no single code can anticipate and address every specific situation that a manager will face. Perhaps more problematically, professional ethical codes frequently specify rules of etiquette and responsibilities professionals have to other members of that profession and thus may focus more on institutional conformity and adherence to group expectations than on broader ethical principles relevant to a range of choices and actions. Therefore, developing ethical reasoning skills and sound personal judgment—to interpret and apply a code to a specific situation and to think more broadly than a code—is essential for effective management.

HISTORICAL CONTEXT

Ethicist Milton Friedman titled a 1970 article in the *New York Times Magazine* "The Social Responsibility of a Firm Is to Increase Its Profits."[1] Friedman articulated an early position in business ethics: A firm has a duty to maximize profits for its stockholders (or stockholders have a right to have their investment maximized), and this is the only principle in business ethics. Otherwise, according to this early view, organizations and the individuals within them must simply stay within the confines of whatever the law happens to be.

This single principle has proven to be inadequate. Individuals within organizations can do many things that are legal yet undermine productivity and thus profitability. For example, investment bankers can put together a deal that ensures them an immediate commission but that may cause the bank as a whole to lose money over the long term. This conduct may be legal, but it is not ethical. Consequently, investment banks have compliance departments to ensure not only that potential deals are legal but also that they uphold the interests of the institution. Moreover, in the past twenty-five years, an organization's pursuit of social responsibility has become an important element of customer loyalty and branding, as well as a criterion for many investors. Even more recently, an organization's pursuit of social responsibility has become an important tool for talent recruitment and retention. A 2013 survey of Wharton School new graduates indicated that the majority would not take jobs at organizations whose products or processes actively harmed or were simply indifferent to society and the environment.[2]

While business ethics as an academic discipline and focus in business schools is nearly a half century old, organizational attention to ethics and compliance dates to the mid-1980s, when a number of scandals occurred within the defense industry. Since that time, many organizations have instituted ethics and compliance officers (ECOs), whose role is to ensure that an organization complies with relevant federal, state, and local laws and regulations and also that it observes relevant principles of business ethics. Given that, in 2012 alone, employee fraud cost U.S. businesses $760 billion, ECOs' primary responsibility, in many cases, is to ensure employees obey the law (in these cases, Friedman's maxim that "The social responsibility of a firm is to increase profits for stockholders" is still relevant).[3]

Beyond ensuring legal compliance, ECOs are frequently responsible for developing values statements and codes of ethics for their organization. In some sense, the practical application of business ethics followed legal requirements; in the wake of the 1980s scandals, federal laws required or incentivized certain types of organizations to institute senior-level roles for compliance and ethics. Likewise, laws related to sexual misconduct had emerged after organizations identified sexual harassment as a profound ethical issue in the workplace.

The issue of blatant, organization-harming conduct, such as embezzlement, aside, ECOs continue to negotiate with the perception that ethics and compliance compete with, rather than advance, business interests. In some for-profit organizations, ethics are seen as encumbering the ability to close an advantageous deal, while in a range of organizations, ethics are viewed as a personal, individual matter, similar to religious belief, which should be off limits at work. In reality, attention to ethics and compliance directly enhances an organization's bottom line in the long run. Sexual misconduct prevention is a case in point. Sexual harassment directly hurts an organization's bottom line, in terms of employee engagement and productivity and in terms of liability. The work of a ECO is to encourage and coordinate the efforts of other chief executives, human resources, and all managers to eliminate sexual misconduct. One's ethical reasoning ability informs management decisions that impact employees. Ethics is, therefore, more than a personal matter. Moreover, as the perceived social responsibility of an organization continues to exert more influence on consumer, investor, and prospective employee choices, the work of ECOs will become even more important for an organization's profitability or sustainability.

MANAGERIAL BEHAVIORS

While organizations may establish a role, such as an ECO, that is formally responsible for ensuring ethical conduct, everyone working in the organization is also responsible, in a day-to-day way, for ensuring ethical decisions and actions. Regardless of their roles or relationships, all people have moral agency.

The Manager As Moral Agent

To say that someone is a moral agent is to say that person has the capacity to engage in ethical reasoning regarding a choice and has the power to act on that reasoning. A realistic understanding of managers as moral agents involves understanding the types of ethical reasoning managers may employ when making decisions and being aware of the different types of motivators that may lead a manager to choose one course of action over another. A more realistic conception of managers as moral agents also involves understanding psychological factors that sometimes inhibit ethical reasoning and rational decision making.

Ethical reasoning entails the conceptual ability to abstract from particular cases to general principles and the ability to reason by analogy when applying existing rules to new situations. In other words, managers need the cognitive ability to see the forest and the trees simultaneously. They need to recognize what general categories a specific situation fits into and they need the ability to recognize what is unique about a specific situation, so they can adapt general principles into particular action guides for decision making.

In addition to the cognitive abilities to abstract and reason by analogy, six specific types of ethical reasoning can inform a manager's view of what counts as the right thing to do in a particular situation. Everyone has some capacity for all six types. Most individuals prefer one or two types of reasoning to the rest, but an effective manager will cultivate facility with all of the following six types:

1. Deontology, or rules-based reasoning
2. Consequentialism, or making a decision based on a particular desired outcome
3. Individualism, or giving the most to each person while taking the least from each person
4. Utilitarianism, or determining the greatest good for the greatest number
5. Burden-benefit analysis (which may sometimes be specifically cost-benefit analysis)
6. Concern for trust and fidelity, or analyzing how a potential decision could impact relationships among colleagues, employees, and stakeholders

Said differently, an effective manager needs know what rules (that is, organizational policies and codes) are in effect and pertain to a specific situation but also needs to be able to recognize an exceptional, perhaps anomalous, situation in which certain rules may not be relevant or for which there is no precedent. An effective manager needs to balance aggregating the greatest good for the greatest number in a particular case while attending to the rights and duties of all the individuals involved in that case. Sometimes, the duty to respect certain individual rights trumps the value of a generalized good outcome, and other times, a generalized good outcome trumps certain individual rights. Finally, making decisions by assessing which course of action has the most benefits and the fewest liabilities needs to include potential impacts on relationships among the possible benefits or liabilities.

Trying to achieve this balance of rights often underlies dilemmas managers face regarding employees who need special accommodations due to extenuating personal circumstances. For example, due to a divorce or illness, one employee may need to work a more flexible schedule, to work remotely, or have a reduced workload, when employees are normally expected to work on-site for specific hours. If accommodating the one employee's special needs causes more work or a stricter schedule for other workers, it may not be fair (ethical) to accommodate the one worker (although emotionally, it may be hard not to accommodate the one worker). In this example, a manager would need to attend to perceptions of fairness as well as ensuring actual fairness.

Managers can strengthen their capacity for ethical reasoning by training themselves to ask certain questions when making decisions, for example:

- What are the relevant rules in this case?
- What is the consequence I hope to see resulting from this decision?
- What are the minority, unpopular, or unlikely perspectives I need to consider?
- Have I looked comprehensively enough at what might be burdens and benefits associated with each alternative course of action?
- How will a particular course of action affect trust among staff, customers, stockholders, and stakeholders?

- While attempting to accomplish an overall good for the group, will I cause undue harm to a particular individual?
- While seeking to honor the preferences of a specific individual, will I cause a larger harm to the group as a whole?

As noted, the ability to reason ethically is learned, not innate, and it can be enhanced through practice. Nonetheless, there are nonrational, psychological factors that often interfere with a manager's ability to reason about a decision. For many, an obstacle to decision making is anticipatory regret, which may delay decision making because of anxiety about the feelings that may emerge if a choice turns out to be wrong. Psychologists have identified four common sources of anticipatory regret:

- Material losses for the self
- Material losses for significant others (in personal relationships and work relations)
- Loss of self-esteem
- Loss of the esteem of colleagues, clients, and others

Anticipatory regret caused by one or more of these fears can lead a manager to stop reasoning about a decision; they may simply refrain from making a decision, becoming preoccupied with the emotions associated with the decision-making process itself. An effective way to overcome this is to discuss fears with a trusted person and assess which fears may be legitimate and which are imaginary. It is also important to remember that putting off a decision will eventually become a decision. The likelihood of making the right choice is normally increased by ethical reflection and deliberate action, rather than by defaulting into an action due to avoidance.[4]

In addition to the challenge of anticipatory regret, research in cognitive psychology points to the existence of biases that cloud ethical reasoning. Cognitive biases in the workplace occur particularly when managers must make decisions under extreme uncertainty, which typically results from a lack of data, ambiguous data (could have more than one meaning), or data that are contradictory. Types of cognitive bias include:

- Belief bias
- Availability heuristic
- Anchoring
- Confirmation bias

Belief bias occurs when an individual makes assumptions about a current situation based on beliefs about reality, which stem from previous experiences. A simple example is if all the football players I know are muscular in appearance, and I see someone muscular in appearance, I may conclude that person is a football player. In reality, I cannot know that the person is a football player without further investigation. My belief about football players, based on my previous experiences, biases me to interpret what I am presently seeing in a particular way, which may not be accurate. Many rules of thumb and intuitive judgments, which often serve a manager well, can become belief biases if a manager loses sight of the fact that they are using rules of thumb to make provisional assumptions about a situation and to compensate for a lack of information.

The availability heuristic refers to a tendency to rely on immediate examples that come to mind when analyzing a particular situation rather than looking more broadly for data that might inform a choice. An example would be using the same vendor over and over again, just because the previous experiences with the vendor seemed to work out. The vendor may not always offer you the best product at the best price.

In a similar way, anchoring refers to a tendency to give precedence to the first piece of information encountered when researching a decision. The first piece of information may not be the most accurate or relevant, but because it is first, it may become the scale by which the accuracy and relevance of all subsequent information is assessed. For example, a company surveys five hundred customers. The first 60 surveys contain many negative comments. The other 440 surveys may contain more neutral or positive comments, but the contents of the first 60 may create a kind of lens through which the remaining survey results will be interpreted. Perhaps negative comments in the remaining 440 surveys will inadvertently receive more weight or attention than the positives ones. This can ultimately lead to using resources to resolve a problem that may not actually exist.

Confirmation bias occurs when an individual becomes attached to a particular course of action when choosing among alternative courses. Rather than collecting information to assess the merits of all possible courses of action, the individual collects information that affirms only the course of action they are predisposed to follow (and sometimes the individual may suppress information that mitigates against the course of the predisposed action). This could occur when a senior leader is selecting a location for an off-site project. For example, if the senior leader enjoyed their experience when working in Orlando for the last project, they may push for that city, even though current data, researched by staff, says a venue in Atlanta would better meet current needs (budget, facilities, and so on).

In essence, each of these biases represents a psychological effort to impose certainty where it does not exist, by importing data that are easy to access but that may not be relevant or reliable.

Often, managers fall prey to these cognitive biases because of an organizational dynamic called *bias for action*. In an organization, the bias for action appears as a preference for doing, rather than thinking. In such organizations, for purposes of advancement, it is better to be seen doing *something*, rather than the best or the right thing. For example, employees may be rewarded for completing a quantity of tasks and not for the quality of their work. If managers believe they will be rewarded simply for taking any action (and may be penalized for seeming to react too slowly), managers may avoid taking the time to research thoroughly and reason ethically.

A final facet of managers' moral agency is their motivations. Much research in behavioral ethics has focused on answering a different question: Why do people do the wrong thing when they know what the right thing is? Psychological research has also focused on a corollary question, Why do people do what they think is right, even when it will undermine their immediate self-interest? There is no definitive answer to either question, but psychological research has provided insights that can enhance a manager's ethical self-awareness.

As noted, conscientiousness is the virtue of making every effort to determine what is right in a specific situation, intending to perform the right action, and exerting effort to carry out the right action.

Ethical reasoning allows a manager to determine what is right in a given situation, while motivation affects intention and effort. In other words, what moves an individual not only to recognize the right thing, but also to do it? One explanation based in psychological research is an individual's sense of satisfaction in being autonomous—of being self-regulating or self-determining. For example, going to work even when one would prefer to stay home is an exercise in self-regulation. In going to work, one overcomes a short-term desire, instead acting in their longer-term interest. Dieting, exercising, saving money, and drinking in moderation are all examples of self-regulating practices. The satisfaction gained through overcoming immediate desires to achieve a greater good drives some people to do the right thing when they recognize it. A manager's self-awareness—that they may in fact be motivated by the satisfaction of self-regulation—can be important in equipping them to do the right thing—for instance, in a situation that requires whistle-blowing (discussed later in this chapter).

Another theory of what motivates people to ethical conduct is that people possess a duty or loyalty orientation, defined as finding satisfaction in serving, supporting, protecting, and advancing the interests of other members of one's group. Some research suggests that a duty or loyalty orientation correlates with managers more consistently acting ethically (such as by ensuring fairness and avoiding favoritism and self-dealing).[5] One inference from this research is that, contrary to the classical economic model, self-interest maximization as a motivation often results in less ethical behavior (that is, thinking short term about how to put oneself in the most advantageous position without regard for duties to others or the future of the organization). Certainly, the assertion that managers possessing a duty orientation tend be more consistently ethical aligns with business ethics' structure of obligation-based prima facie principles. Obligations entail positive and negative duties, so an orientation to duty, like a self-regulation motive, would inherently equip a manager for the practice of business ethics.

SAMPLE CONTEXTUAL SCENARIOS

The following discussion looks more broadly at types of situations managers encounter that require ethical reflection and application of prima facie principles, informed and guided by individual ethical reasoning.

Macro-Business Considerations

That Friedman asserted, in 1970, the social responsibility of a firm is to increase profits for stockholders, reflects the fact that there was already a broader discussion about the ultimate responsibilities of, at least, for-profit organizations. Since 1970, the stakeholder theory of the firm has begun to replace the stockholder theory of the firm in business schools. According to the theory, businesses (and all organizations) must pay attention to a number of parties who support or are impacted by them, not just investors (or those who contribute capital directly to finance the organizations). An organization's stakeholders include its suppliers; its customers, clients, and end users; its employees; the natural environment; its immediate community; and depending on its scale, all of the communities in which it transacts business (see also Chapter 11, Managing Projects).

Mid-level managers, whose role is to implement the strategies of senior managers, increasingly must attend to environmental impacts, consumer protection, and employee relations as they make tactical decisions. As one leader in an ethics and compliance professional group observed, "Before you do something that is, or is perceived as unethical, nobody knows you; as soon as you do something that is, or is perceived as unethical, you are in the *Wall Street Journal*, and everybody knows you."[7]

The well-known situation the adhesive company H. B. Fuller faced in Honduras illustrates the many ethical issues managers must negotiate when making business decisions. According to a newspaper report:

> When it comes to business ethics, few American corporations have a better image than the H. B. Fuller Company of St. Paul, a leading manufacturer of industrial glues, coatings and paints. Awards, honors and inclusion in various socially conscious mutual funds attest to its standing as a good corporate citizen. But that reputation is being clouded by the company's handling of a stubborn image-staining problem: the illegal abuse of its shoemaker's glue by homeless Central American children, who have become addicted to the product's intoxicating but dangerous fumes.[8]

Managers at Fuller had to figure out how to continue selling their product to Central American consumers (shoe manufacturers) and ensure the product was not misused as a drug by underprivileged children. In other words, managers at Fuller had to attend to the needs of stockholders as well as stakeholders (their customers and communities in which their products were consumed). The ultimate solution lay in creating an adhesive that was strong, but did not use any chemicals that could also be intoxicating.

Increasingly, the definition of social responsibility is expanding to include an organization's internal structure: How does an organization share profits or distribute compensation, and what benefits does it provide? A number of associations rate organizations on the quality of their internal cultures, asking whether they are inclusive workplaces where all employees—regardless of race, ethnicity, religion, gender, or sexual orientation—have an equal opportunity to advance. These ratings bear on customer, investor, and prospective employee perceptions. Consequently, managers must consider principles of obligation when hiring, promoting, planning for succession, and structuring compensation plans.

Micro-Interpersonal Interactions

Ethical issues are present not only in strategic and tactical decisions about an organization's direction and purpose. They are also present in interpersonal interactions between individuals. Specific scenarios in which managers need to exercise sound ethical reasoning include recognizing and avoiding conflicts of interest, ensuring fairness, whistle-blowing, and ensuring individuals give informed consent for certain activities.

Recognizing and Avoiding Conflicts of Interest

Generally speaking, a conflict of interest occurs whenever a decision maker is, or appears to be, open to undue influence from someone else. Conflicts of interest may also be described as quid pro quo: party A does *X* for party B, expecting Party B to do *Y* in exchange. For example, if a manager with the authority to purchase services from multiple consultants vacations with one particular consultant, the manager has created a conflict of interest. The manager has indebted themselves, or has given the impression they have, to that particular consultant and thus has compromised their ability to objectively evaluate proposals from other consultants. A compromised manager cannot make decisions with the best interest of the organization in mind. In other words, if a manager takes any action that would give, or seem to give, someone else undue influence over their decisions, that manager creates a conflict of interest and acts unethically.

Clearly, that people influence each other is a basic dynamic of interpersonal relationships. The issue in conflicts of interest is that one party gains a much greater degree of influence over a manager than the other parties with whom the manager engages. Specific manager unethical actions include receiving gifts and perks beyond those available to everyone in the organization and work relationships that become overtly personal and involve spending much out-of-work time together.

Conflicts of interest involve perception as much as reality. A manager's accepting an expensive gift from a vendor or giving one to a wealthy donor or customer or public official gives the impression to others that the manager is now beholden to the vendor and thus will not be able to make objective choices regarding vendors. Even if, in their mind, the manager is able to remain objective, others' perception of compromised objectivity undermines confidence in the manager. This, in turn, can create a climate of mistrust, and a climate in which employees infer from managers' conduct that unethical behavior is acceptable.

To summarize, managers should observe a prima facie principle to avoid being the subject of special treatment. Managers have a positive duty to anticipate what choices could create perceived conflicts of interest as well as a negative duty to avoid actions that constitute conflicts of interest. Commonsense insights from the common morality are helpful in applying this principle. Managers should bear in mind the example they set by their choices and should strive to keep work relationships cordial but transactional and transparent.

Attend to Fairness

Conflicts of interest are unethical partly because they represent instances of unfairness: a manager gives a particular party consideration to which other parties do not have access. Acting fairly is another prima facie principle relevant to managers' interpersonal conduct. The Greek philosopher Aristotle defined fairness as treating like situations the same way. On what criterion is the similarity of situations established? In most organizations, likeness is established in terms of effort or merit: Treat each person according to their effort or what their effort merits. Many cultures have agreed (and often legally require) that individual characteristics of birth, such as race, ethnicity, social class, and physical ability must be avoided as criterion for establishing the similarity of situations. To base treatment of individuals on things they cannot control (characteristics of birth) is unfair and unethical (and often illegal). Said differently, managers have a positive duty to modulate interactions with employees by paying attention to the criteria of effort and merit, and they have a negative duty to avoid interacting with employees based on assessment of employees' personal characteristics, which include both characteristics of birth and personal features, such as personality type, thinking style, and conflict resolution style.

These duties can be specified further. Managers have a positive duty to recognize situations in which they could seem to show favoritism toward a certain employee or employees and a negative duty to avoid favoritism itself. For example, a manager who gives certain individuals access to travel or training opportunities and professional development, but does not make that available to all similarly qualified individuals is showing favoritism and acting unethically. A manager who holds similarly qualified individuals to different standards—for example, letting one person skip meetings while requiring others to attend, without clarifying the rationale for the different requirements—is showing favoritism and acting unethically.

Fairness applies to managerial decisions about promotion, increased compensation, and other benefits. Managers have a positive duty to ensure that procedures are transparent to everyone within reason—for example, employees know the criteria for promotion and they have a clear idea of their status in relation to those criteria. There is also a managerial duty to ensure due process in handling employee complaints, conflicts, discipline, and dismissal. This means managers should ensure that all parties involved know all the steps in a particular grievance process, what the timeline is, and what the possible outcomes are.

Moreover, managers have a positive duty to ensure all employees have equal access to all positions and roles, providing they are qualified for those roles on the criteria of effort or merit or some reasonable accommodation may be made. Managers have a duty to avoid obscuring the steps in a process and criteria for promotion as well as avoid making decisions on promotion and other benefits based on employees' personal characteristics, beyond effort and merit.

Increasingly, academic ethicists and organizational practitioners agree that fairness extends to managers' awareness of cross-cultural differences among employees, and managers' sensitivity to these differences. Fairness requires a duty to avoid privileging one set of cultural norms and expectations over another by subjecting all members of a group to one culture's practices (for a fuller discussion, see Chapter 21, Diversity and Inclusion). For example, publicly celebrating birthdays is valued in some cultures and is insulting in others. Rather than celebrating all birthdays publicly or celebrating no birthdays publicly, managers increasingly have a duty to be familiar with employees' cultural backgrounds and tailor interpersonal activities to align with or accommodate cultural differences. Managers have a duty to ensure that special events, such as for recreation and team building, are accessible to everyone and do not reflect cultural biases or privilege specific cultural traditions.

Whistle-Blowing

Historically, the common morality has indicated that individuals have a right to follow their consciences and abstain from actions that conflict with their personal values. The claim that individuals have a positive duty to attempt to stop others from doing something potentially or actually unethical (that is, whistle-blowing) has been debated. There is now a consensus that managers do have a positive duty at least to report any unethical activities they know of. These activities can range from sexual harassment to cutting corners in a process to create an unfair advantage to suppressing research results that indicate a product is harmful. In other words, whistle-blowing is calling attention to any situation in which a person or group's actions could be or actually are harmful to the organization or are specifically harmful to customers, the environment, or other employees.

An analysis of bureaucracy's influence on personal responsibility published in the *Harvard Business Review*, titled "Moral Mazes: Bureaucracy and Managerial Work," implies that whistle-blowing could be a kind of career suicide.[9] According to research cited in that article, whistle-blowing undermined key elements of a bureaucratic work ethic, such as diffusing responsibility in order to diffuse blame for one's self. Since then, the increased importance of an organization's real and perceived social responsibility (fueled by numerous ethical and legal scandals as well as changing worldviews of different generations of workers and consumers) has transformed whistle-blowing into a positive duty for managers in many organizations. However, whistle-blowing remains a legal land mine, with different rules for different jurisdictions.

In addition, research about the ways unethical behavior undermines productivity and employee engagement supports the view that whistle-blowing, in the long run, can enhance motivational climate, talent retention efforts and ultimately improve the bottom line.[10] Nonetheless, debate continues regarding how far a manager should go, beyond reporting, to stop or remedy an unethical action. While organizations increasing establish mechanisms for anonymous whistle-blowing, managers may not have the scope of authority themselves to stop or minimize the consequences of unethical behavior. Even anonymous reporting, however, sets an example that enhances an organization's ethical climate.

Note: No information in this book should be taken as offering legal advice.

Recognizing Actions That Require Informed Consent

Attending to the amount of knowledge and control individuals have regarding data collected about them is a new area of ethical consideration for managers in many organizations. A prima facie principle of obligation many ethicists locate in the common morality is respect for individual autonomy: Each individual has a right to make their own choices and has a right to adequate information, so they can make informed choices. This principle is often specified as a rule that individuals must give informed consent when they agree to certain things. In the past forty years, the concept of informed consent emerged in the context of patients making healthcare choices and agreeing to participate in medical research. Patients must fully understand all of the risks and benefits of a treatment before they agree to it.

As surveys and other forms of data collection have proliferated, the rule of informed consent is becoming more widely relevant. In an organizational context, when managers ask employees to complete surveys, questionnaires, or on-line personality and style assessments, as well as background checks, or to participate with external consultants, managers likely have a positive duty to inform employees of the reasons for which data are collected, what data are collected, and the ways data will be used and stored. Managers should also recognize the right of employees to decline to participate in initiatives that involve collection of personal data.

Keep in mind special circumstances such as:

- Workplace safety/security
- Heightened professional ethics (lawyers/doctors)
- Financial ethics and criminal statutes
- Workplace bullying (as being different from harassment)
- Bribery

Application Activity

Which ethical dilemma do each of the following situations most clearly illustrate?

Situation 1: A firm depends on recruiting researchers from around the globe. The firm maintains an internal department to process the associated government paperwork. The internal department charges other parts of the organization for this service and is currently behind on processing the paperwork because it is short staffed. When a vice president looks for the root cause of the problem and reviews the ledger for the internal department, she finds that the fees charged for the paperwork processing were not used to defray the costs of the processing or to hire new workers to speed the processing time. Instead, the fees were redirected to pay for the department director's upgrades on flights and hotels related to business trips for the organization. What sort of unethical behavior has the vice president discovered on the director's part?

A. Failure to recognize when informed consent is required
B. Failure to whistle-blow regarding a problem
C. Failure to recognize and avoid a possible conflict of interest
D. Failure to attend to fairness

The best answer is D. The director failed to recognize it was unfair to redirect funds earned by the paperwork processing away from paying the costs associated with the processing and to apply the funds to his personal travel expenses, even though the travel was for the organization.

Situation 2: A business school researcher approaches the CEO of an organization with an offer, saying "If you let me survey and collect data on you senior executives and let me publish research using the data, in exchange, I will provide you with a free longitudinal study of the executives' development as leaders." The CEO see this as a great opportunity for free research and agrees. The researcher is allowed to contact each executive directly and instructs them to complete the survey. The executives receive no information about how the survey results will be used, and they are not given the option to decline the survey. What sort of unethical behavior have the CEO and researcher engaged in?

A. Failure to recognize when informed consent is required
B. Failure to whistle-blow regarding a problem
C. Failure to recognize and avoid a possible conflict of interest
D. Failure to attend to fairness

The best answer is A. The executives should have been told how the survey results would be used and should have been given the option to decline the survey. In this case, the executives have not been able to give informed consent to participate in the researcher's study.

Situation 3: A newly hired contractor had good rapport with a vice president immediately—from the first phone interview to the signing of the contract. Now, the vice president routinely invites the contractor into her office for closed-door discussions; takes the contractor out to lunch several times per week; has, in the last quarter, paid for the contractor to attend three professional conferences at luxury resorts; and most recently, has secured a place for the contractor on the agenda of the annual stockholder's meeting. No other contractors receive this level of attention from the vice president. What sort of unethical behavior have the executive and the contractor engaged in?

A. Failure to recognize when informed consent is required
B. Failure to whistle-blow regarding a problem
C. Failure to recognize and avoid a possible conflict of interest
D. Failure to attend to fairness

The best answer is C. They have failed to recognize that their conduct at least gives the impression of a possible conflict of interest. The conduct suggests that the contractor may have some undue influence over the vice president. Even if this is only an appearance, it would still erode employee's and other contractor's confidence in the vice president.

Situation 4: A county requires that there be one fire station built for every three thousand residences constructed. Developers producing three thousand or more residences are required to pay for a portion of the fire stations that will serve their new communities. A county manager reviewing contracts and permits notices that a particular developer is not being billed for fire station construction, even though the developer is building five thousand new houses. In fact, it looks like there will not be a new fire station constructed to support the new community of five thousand houses. The manager says nothing. Three years later, the houses are completed and a wild fire sweeps through the development. There is no adjacent fire station and two-thirds of the houses are destroyed and several people die. What sort of unethical behavior did the manager participate in?

A. Failure to recognize when informed consent is required
B. Failure to whistle-blow regarding a problem
C. Failure to recognize and avoid a possible conflict of interest
D. Failure to attend to fairness

The best answer is B. The manager discovered a problem—in this case some sort of collusion to break county fire safety laws—and did nothing to report the problem.

SUCCESS FACTORS

Ethical managers will enhance their employees' motivational climate and level of engagement because they will be (and perhaps more important will be perceived) as fair. Ethical managers may experience a reduction in certain forms of psychological stress, such as decision fatigue, regret, or anxiety, because they have more confidence that their decisions are based on the best reasoning possible, given conditions of uncertainty. Good performance of ethical managers is characterized by tolerance for uncertainty, a willingness to acknowledge that a claim about what is right may be provisional until proven or disproven by subsequent experience, and a willingness to reason and ask questions. This often appears to observers as flexibility and willingness to engage in dialogue regarding a situation or decision.

Poor performance of the ethical manager may be characterized by failure to recognize or address an ethical issue, such as a conflict of interest. Conversely, poor performance may also appear to observers as rigidity, oversimplifying complex situations, and a need to be perceived as right all the time (unable to recognize or acknowledge flaws in personal perception and judgment).

COMMON MISCONCEPTIONS

At least three common misconceptions are related to the ethical conduct of managers. First, ethics are often confused with etiquette. While being polite may be a form of respect for others, politeness and other elements of social etiquette (for example, tactful communication) do not exhaust a manager's ethical considerations. A manager can be polite and conduct themselves in a professional way but can still play favorites; fall prey to undue influence from vendors, customers, or clients; and fail to call attention to wrongdoing such as sexual harassment or unsafe products or working conditions.

A second misconception is the assumption that there is only one way to be right. Identifying what should not be done (that is, negative duties, such as not discriminating on the basis of ethnicity, race, or gender) is sometimes easier than identifying what should be done (that is, positive duties, such as when and how much to help another person). In other words, what is positively right in a given circumstance is sometimes hard to identify and may reflect more the consensus of the parties involved than an absolute set of norms and values. Sometimes, the determination of what is right in a specific context, based on ethical reasoning, is an educated guess, the truth of which can only be ascertained in light of subsequent events. Likewise, a choice that is ethically right may have unforeseen negative consequences or double effects. A manager cannot always anticipate these. One reason the virtue of conscientiousness has three aspects—identifying the right thing, willingness to do it, and carrying it out—is that these three elements do not always follow each other. A manager can, will, or intend to do the right thing, but the final action can turn out to be wrong based on a number of variables. In law and ethics, individuals can be exonerated from the negative consequences of a decision if their intentions were to carry out the right action.

A final misconception regarding business ethics involves the failure to recognize the role cultural differences play in determining what is the right action in a particular case. The actual behavior associated with a particular concept, such as lying, may vary from culture to culture. Take into consideration that major cultures around the world all have prohibitions against lying, but cultures differ in the ways they identify specific actions that count as lying. Therefore, just as it is important to be aware of cross-cultural communication patterns in a global context, it is also important to be aware of cultural differences in classifying specific behaviors as ethical or unethical. This is an important topic that will be discussed in greater detail in Chapter 20, Technology.

• Conclusion •

Ethics in business continues to be an ongoing and evolving conversation. As social norms change, the workplace will continue to adapt. As the perception of social responsibility has become increasingly important for branding, customer loyalty, investor confidence, and prospective employee preference, more organizations are making decisions based on the impact of ethics within and around their companies.

• Endnotes •

1. Milton Friedman, "The Social Responsibility of a Firm Is to Increase Its Profits," *New York Times Magazine*, September 13, 1970, pp. 32–33, 122–124.
2. B. Hewitt (preparer), "Wharton Undergraduate Class of 2013 Career Plans Survey Report," University of Pennsylvania, September 2013, www.vpul.upenn.edu/careerservices/files/WHA_2013cp.pdf.
3. Marshall Schminke, James Caldwell, Maureen L. Ambrose, and Sean R. McMahon, "Better Than Ever? Employee Reactions to Ethical Failures in Organizations, and the Ethical Recover Paradox," *Organizational Behavior and Human Decision Processes* 123, no. 2 (2014): 206–219.
4. Recent psychological research regarding ethical decision making has explored what it means to employ ethical reasoning without becoming subject to analysis paralysis. See, Celia Moore and Ann E. Tenbrunsel, " 'Just Think About It'? Cognitive Complexity and Moral Choice," *Organizational Behavior and Human Decision Processes* 123, no 2 (2014): 138–149.
5. Sean T. Hannah, Peter L. Jennings, Dustin Bluhm, Ann Chunyan Peng, and John M. Schaubroeck, "Duty Orientation: Theoretical Development and Preliminary Construct Testing," *Organizational Behavior and Human Decision Processes* 123, no. 2 (2014): 220–238.
6. "The *Wall Street Journal* Workplace-Ethics Quiz," *Wall Street Journal*, October 21, 1999, pp. B1–B4.
7. Linda Klebe Treviño, Niki A. den Nieuwenboer, Glen E. Kreiner, and Derron G. Bishop, "Legitimating the Legitimate: A Grounded Theory Study of Legitimacy Work among Ethics and Compliance Officers," *Organizational Behavior and Human Decision Processes* 123, no. 2 (2014): 186–205.
8. Ibid.

9. Robert Jackall, "Moral Mazes: Bureaucracy and Managerial Work," *Harvard Business Review*, September 1983, https://hbr.org/1983/09/moral-mazes-bureaucracy-and-managerial-work.

10. Treviño et al., "Legitimating the Legitimate."

Managing Technology

LEARNING OBJECTIVES

By the end of this chapter, you will be better equipped to:

- Recall new technologies (in this case, cellphones and cell-phone towers providing fast data speeds).
- Identify location-based services that provide the user's and car's location to a central system.
- Understand an inexpensive set of cloud-computers to scale and manage the data.
- Explore an algorithm that matches drivers to passengers and sets prices (including surge pricing) that both benefits the driver, as well as gets more drivers to swarm popular areas to keep waiting times shorter.

WHY NEW TECHNOLOGY MATTERS TO YOUR ORGANIZATION

Your organization, and every organization that has ever existed, uses technology to increase productivity. Technology ranges from using a rubber stamp with a return address on it so you don't have to write it out every time you send a letter to using printers that can also collate and staple at high speeds to connecting to the newest wireless technologies that let you receive and reply to emails from anywhere on earth.

The bottom line is that companies that adopt new technologies at the right time, and in the right way, are able to increase productivity and will stay ahead of competitors. Failing to recognize the value that new technology creates means a company with a great product or service can be quickly eclipsed by other companies that are using more powerful tools to connect with the marketplace faster and more efficiently.

Consider a company like Uber, which has successfully disrupted the global taxi industry in just a few years. It is a clear example of a company that decided to use:

- New technologies (in this case, cellphones and cellphone towers providing fast data speeds)
- Location-based services that connect the user's and car's location to a central system
- An inexpensive set of cloud computers to scale and manage the data
- An algorithm that matches drivers to passengers and sets prices (including surge pricing) that both benefits the driver and gets more drivers to swarm popular areas to keep waiting times shorter

The technologies that Uber chose were widely accessible at the time, but just a couple of years earlier, they wouldn't have been able to successfully deploy the same product because there weren't enough people using cellphones and not enough of the cellphones that were being used had the ability to report the location of the user.

Of course, it wasn't technology alone that enabled Uber to be successful. There were a number of other factors, including business innovations, dissatisfaction with the traditional method of getting taxis (making a phone call and not knowing where the taxi was traveling from), and the latent need (a need people hadn't explicitly asked for) to have an appropriately priced and reliable alternative to driving a car in instances when calling a cab would have been prohibitive (leaving a professional sports event when thousands of people all need a cab).

Uber leveraged technologies at the right time and was able to innovate in a way that has had a massive impact. And while you may not be developing transformational businesses the size of Uber, you can still use technologies to aid in accelerating your business and enabling your business to grow in new directions, while staying ahead of competition.

WHAT'S DIFFERENT ABOUT TECHNOLOGY NOW?

If people have always transformed companies by bringing in new technology, what's different now? The increased rate of change resulting from broadband Internet and cellular connectivity and the rise of the globalization of goods and services have fundamentally altered how we do business. It used to be that implementing a new communication technology in a large company would be a multiyear process (think: installing a completely new corporate phone network and voice-mail system). Now you can install a superior one using an existing high-speed wireless WiFi network, in just days.

In the past, accessing and receiving services or goods from countries that are literally halfway around the world would take a long time. Now, the items that can't be downloaded (which can take seconds) can be on your doorstep in days. No longer do you have to go to a movie theater in which they have film canisters holding reels of film that were sent from the studio. Now you can pay for and view a movie sent directly to your TV. In the past we owned records, now you listen to almost any piece of recorded music instantly by paying a monthly fee that is less (adjusted for today's dollars) than the cost of a single record back then.

With these radical changes, and an economy that is increasingly relying on data and information instead of only physical goods, there's a new opportunity to leverage technology to push our businesses through traditional boundaries.

Consider just one change that will come in the next few years: moving from the 4G cell phone technologies of today, to 5G technology, which will change the way that people consume, transmit, and manipulate data because of the increase in speed. It's easy to think that increased speed simply means downloading a web page faster or enabling many people to download web pages faster when there are multiple users gathered together (like at a sports event). It's reasonable to think that the speed we have is good enough. It's possible to stream a movie in HD with no reduction in the user's experience.

However, additional speed increases the possibilities for deep, transformational innovations. Yes, with more speed you can download entire movies in 4K resolution in just seconds (but that doesn't sound *radically* transformational, does it?). But when you have 5G, it means that several self-driving cars will be able to communicate with each other, in the few milliseconds before a potentially severe impact and communicate billions of data that will inform decisions among the cars, which will ultimately keep the passengers safe.

In addition, our collective society itself is changing in important ways. Just a few years ago, everyone who used digital technologies like cellphones and computers, had previously used their analog counterparts (for instance, landline phones and typewriters). That group is now called digital immigrants because they have learned to use digital technology after having previously been exposed to analog technology for a long time as children. Contrast that group to the cohort of people who have never used analog technology and grew up with cellphones from a young age. This group is made up of digital natives because they have never depended on analog technologies and are therefore, far more likely to expect any new system to work the way an iPhone (or other brand) does. This radical shift is important to consider as you think about technologies in your workplace and as you see different generations using the same technologies differently.

ADOPTING NEW TECHNOLOGIES IN YOUR WORKPLACE

It can be difficult to determine whether introducing a specific new technology in your workplace is a smart move, particularly when faced with so many choices and a limited amount of time and resources to implement it. It's understandable that you may feel a level of uncertainty about which competing technologies are best and what the best way to implement a change actually is. Figure 20-1 is a simple way to think about the process.

1. Stay aware of new technologies by keeping up to date with business publications that show what successful companies are doing with technology. It will enable you to see significant trends in the world. Likewise, you'll benefit from reading about startup organizations and

learning what tools they use because startups don't have legacy systems that prevent them from trying something new.

2. Quickly assess if a technology could be valuable to the business by doing a brainstorm to see how a new technology might change current behavior and improve productivity.
3. Take a little bet for a technology you think might work and run a small experiment before implementing a big change.
4. Share the results of your experiment, determine if you should implement a larger solution and, if so, what's needed to make the implementation successful.

Stay Aware of New Technologies

It's easy to study how large companies use new technologies because they are generally written about in mainstream business publications. If you read any of the major business publications, like the *Wall Street Journal* or *Harvard Business Review*, you'll note trends in the business landscape. When you see a company, like an Amazon (founded in 1994) or an Uber (founded in 2009), become rather big in a short period of time, you can identify the enabling technologies they are leveraging to provide their service. In doing so, you'll see patterns among the most successful companies and then it's easy to conduct further research. Seeing how the big players are using technologies is how you can be sure you're looking at the best practices of an industry.

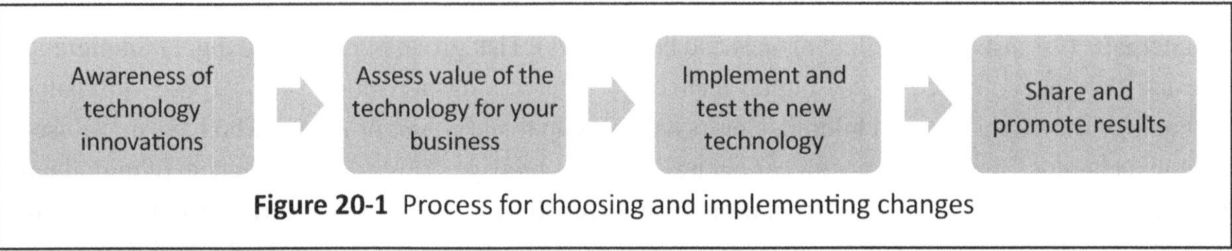

Figure 20-1 Process for choosing and implementing changes

Another great way to see what tools business are adopting is to examine startups. Because startups are so small and typically like to invent new ways of operating, they find the latest technologies and try them out. And since they almost never carry the weight of existing infrastructure that might hold them back, they are generally more willing to try immature technologies that, although in an emergent phase, enable them to do their job in a better way. Be aware, however that a technology solution that's great fit for a startup, may not be appropriate for your company. This is where you have to conduct an assessment to understand if your organization is in a good position to experiment with a new technology. Finally, trade publications (most of which are online now) and companies using technology in new ways are always looking for clients. Invest time in reading the publications in your field, and research the companies that are providing technology solutions. Tech conferences—within your industry as well as other industries—can give you insight into the latest topics being discussed and the companies trying to use technology to help the industry. Local universities are also good resources, and they often have free talks and offer access to experts you can contact for one-on-one discussions.

Assess New Technologies

As you discern trends in technology and observe various companies adopting new technologies, you'll start to identify some technologies you might want to consider for your business. At this point you'll need to consider your options and assess which technology might be valuable to your organization.

In this chapter, we focus on software technologies; however, the process is exactly the same for any technology. Table 20-1 lists important questions you'll want to consider when looking at a new technology. While these questions are extremely valuable to consider and can help you determine which technologies you might want to bring into your organization, there are times when you'll have to decide between competing, similar technologies.

In fact, it's often the case that when a new technology becomes popular, a competing one will soon surface. For example, Dropbox, a technology that helps people store files in the cloud, became popular in a short period of time, primarily with a customer base of small businesses and individuals. Soon, another company called Box, appeared on the scene, emulating elements of the Dropbox solution in a different way because their product was designed specifically for business users.

Table 20-1 Questions to Ask When Reviewing a New Technology

Question	Objective
What's the gap between how we work now and how we will work when we have the new technology in place? What does success look like?	By understanding how things will change when a new technology is introduced, you'll be able to clearly articulate the objectives that will help you identify success metrics. In doing so, you'll be in a better position to articulate to others the compelling reason for adopting the new technology and gain alignment in the organization. Often the vendor will be able to help you through this process because they have a vested interest in educating you about why you should adopt their technology.
Who (people or groups) will be positively affected and who will be negatively affected by the adoption of the new technology?	Draw a map (or make a list) of all the stakeholders that will be affected and how. An important thing to keep in mind is that not everyone will react positively when a new technology is introduced. New technology could place some people's jobs at risk (or they may fear this even if it's not true). An example is when a call center introduces a powerful new automation technology like speech recognition.
What can go wrong? What countermeasures can we put in place to prevent that from happening?	With the introduction of any technology, taking the time to consider the potential problems (and how you can avoid them or at least be aware of them early) will better enable you to ensure that the deployment goes smoothly. Consider the situation in which you introduce a new tool for your team to centrally store files. Things that could go wrong include a loss of data if the technology isn't robust. A countermeasure might be backing up files to the system you've used in the past during the early stages of the deployment.

Table 20-2 Standards Wars	
Factor	**Result**
Low differentiation between the products	Consumers understand both products do almost the same thing, making it confusing to determine which one is best for them.
Buyer unlikely to purchase multiple systems for personal use	Low chance for multihoming (consumers purchasing two similar technologies)—for example, because of cost, a consumer would likely invest in only VHS or Betamax. The cost of today's digital services allows a customer to subscribe to both Hulu and Netflix.
High switching costs	Once a consumer committed to one system (say Betamax), the costs of switching to VHS include selling old equipment, buying new equipment, converting tapes, and learning new technology. The switch from Netflix to Hulu, however, incurs few costs in terms of time, money, and learning the new interface.
Network effects	Consumers who invested in Betamax were restricted to Sony equipment, whereas those who committed to VHS could choose equipment manufactured from several companies that offered various features, because while Sony worked alone, JVC worked with a network of companies, enabling the technology to be widely deployed, improved, and tailored to various users. In the digital world, a company like Netflix or Hulu, which has an online presence and mobile apps that work with both iOS and Android, has a greater distribution and exposure (and thus more ongoing improvements and innovation) than apps linked to only one operating system.
Source: Modified from Annabelle Gawer and Michael A. Cusumano, *Platform Leadership: How Intel, Microsoft, and Cisco Drive Industry Innovation* (Boston: Harvard Business School Publishing, 2002).	

When you have competing products that basically do the same thing it can be hard to decide which technology to choose. Sometimes you'll choose the technology that's easiest to integrate, other times you'll select the one that has the best user experience.

In some scenarios it may be hard to determine which technology to invest in. Sometimes you might simply invest in the wrong one or invest in a solution too soon which could be problematic later on.

An example of this was the VCR. There was a lot of uncertainty about which format to choose when the machines first came out because there were two competing formats. One was developed by Sony which manufactured Betamax, and the other was developed by JVC whose product was called VHS. Both systems did the same basic thing: They enabled people to set up to record TV shows, save them, and play them back. The Sony technology was much higher quality, but the tapes were smaller and could record for only 120 minutes (compared to six or eight hours on VHS).

What resulted was a standards war, with both companies trying to win and dominate the market to become the standard that the vast majority of people chose. This same situation played out more recently when the Blu-ray and HD DVD formats came out.

Four specific factors leading to technology standards wars are presented in Table 20-2.

In a business setting, if you find competing technology solutions, consider the following issues:

- The best technology or solution from the viewpoint of the user does not necessarily win.
- Sometimes the winning technology comes down to the one that can be more widely and inexpensively adopted.
- Determine whether your organization prefers to adopt technology that is more commonly used, making it easier to hire people who already know the technology.
- Determine whether your organization prefers to find the right solution, even if it entails the risk of having to work harder to support it if it doesn't become popular.
- If possible, run experiments to help determine which technology might be best before you commit.
- Take into account which technology is easier to switch to if needed.

Scenario 1: What Users Want Versus What the Organization Wants

Some companies have chosen to use (or support) only Microsoft products. By choosing to commit to the Microsoft set of tools they can get good pricing, ensure the IT department has the knowledge to adequately support users, and be sure everyone is compliant with how they use the tools.

However, in many of those same organizations, people will also use Google Docs, Google Sheets, and Google Slide (which are similar to Microsoft's Word, Excel, and PowerPoint), even if the company explicitly states they're not to do so. The typical reason employees use these alternatives at work is because they use Google applications in their personal lives or have used the Google suite in the past and prefer its features, particularly how easy it is to collaborate with someone else in real time no matter where that person is located.

The problem is that because the Google apps are outside of the normal work systems, some documents might end up in the wrong hands or people might have access to them even after they leave the company. So why do people still use a technology that they aren't supposed to? Here are some common reasons:

- *Low Differentiation*: Perhaps Google Sheets isn't as powerful as Excel but it does everything the users need.
- *Ease of Multihoming*: Employees can have MS Word on their computer and also go to a website for Google Docs; they don't have to choose only one.
- *Low Switching Costs*: Employees can save their Google Docs to MS Word and share it with colleagues.
- *Positive Network Effects*: Employees know many others who also use and prefer the Google suite and collaboration brings even more people to the Google ecosystem.

In this example, the stakeholders include the workers, who want to use Google products; the IT group, who wants to standardize ton Microsoft products; and the operations group, who believe workers want the power of Microsoft without taking into account users' familiarity with Google.

There are times in an organization's life cycle when it's not critical to choose between two (or more) software applications. However, there are other times when the cost of switching (in terms of disruption and various costs) must be considered and weighed because a successful small test doesn't necessarily ensure that a large deployment will also be successful.

Implement New Technologies

When implementing new technologies, experimentation leads to clarity. Here's why: The objective of implementing a new technology is to increase productivity (and, you hope, create a more fulfilling work environment) in order to focus more on the core value of your team or company. Knowing about and testing new technologies is crucial for figuring out which one(s) will benefit your organization. But if you don't have the ability or desire to experiment with new technologies, it becomes incredibly hard to implement something new in a successful way.

If you find a technology you believe will transform your business and you have only one chance to implement it and it has a high associated cost, you're taking on a lot of risk. This approach was commonly practiced many years ago and is why many companies used only tried-and-true (and expensive!) technologies provided by large companies.

Today's world is radically different, and it's often easy to experiment and simulate the incorporation of a new technology. By conducting a number of small experiments, you don't need to pour all your resources into a single opportunity. Small experiments allow you to learn and refine your approach, while encouraging a culture of experimentation within your organization. The knowledge you gain can be shared and used to inform the next experiments.

Here's an example. Your organization makes a lot of PowerPoint presentations, but you think the presentations aren't visually appealing. You find a service that lets you search for and download beautiful, high-resolution images for your presentations, but it's expensive and requires a long process with your legal and finance group to set up. You could make a case for the service, get all the stakeholders onboard, and try to obtain an enterprise-wide license to lower the cost. Or you could make a little bet and work with a small team who is willing to serve as a test group for creating high-impact presentations using the watermarked sample images the service offers for free.

You could pick a group that:

- Doesn't regularly make external presentations (so there won't be copyright issues)
- Doesn't need a high-quality images for printing
- Is willing to try it out for a specific period of time

After the test period, survey the group to measure the impact of the service to see if it's worth paying for. Ask whether the users liked the service and whether they thought the images improved their presentations. Ask if the training was easy and if the service made the group more efficient.

You might discover many things after this experiment, for example:

- The presentations were better, there was measurable positive impact, and the cost was reasonable.
- The positive impact was high, but the actual cost to implement the service cannot be justified.

In the latter case the experiment was still fruitful because you learned the issue would be cost. So now what? You could look for a lower cost provider and determine whether the image quality and range and the service interface would work for your organization.

By conducting an experiment, you haven't used a lot of resources or committed to a single course of action that may or may not have been successful, and the results of the experiment provided you with a powerful tool for figuring out the next steps that may lead to the perfect solution.

FIVE FACTORS THAT HELP ENABLE SUCCESSFUL EXPERIMENTATION

As you bring in new technologies and experiment to see how effective they are, you have to always be thoughtful about managing your risk, understanding what it will take to move from an experiment to a deployment, and be willing to iteratively test and refine your solutions to determine how to be successful. Table 20-3 shows five factors to keep in mind.

UNDERLYING TECHNOLOGIES THAT ARE TRANSFORMING US

An enormous impact technology has recently had on society is the ability for us to grab a resource for just small amounts of time and pay for only that slice of time. This isn't a new concept; however, it's being applied in new ways because of technology enablers.

For example, a car that normally sits idle all day except for the time its driven from a home to an office and back, is now able to be loaned out for the hours it's not needed by the owner, through an app.

Technologies, like mobile phone apps, cloud computing, and software as a service (SaaS) that power many of these technologies can do so affordably because the companies that offer these services are paying for only the time the computer is actually working on their task.

Consider a watch that can detect the motion of falling and then send messages to emergency contacts if the wearer is incapacitated. This is made possible by the machine's ability to characterize a fall (compared to another movement like hitting your hand against a table) by running a set of statistics over a huge set of data gathered from a miniature gyroscope and motion sensor worn by people at risk for

Table 20-3 Evaluating Risk: Five Factors		
Factor	**Explanation**	**Example**
Introduce	Introducing new technologies may pose a risk to business operations; determine whether that risk is high or low. It's critical to contain any risk and alert all relevant people of the potential risks (high or low).	Introducing a system that lets people put ideas in an electronic suggestion box is low risk, as it could be handled internally with existing infrastructure. If the system suddenly stopped working suggestions could simply be emailed to a central address. Introducing a system that manipulates sensitive company-critical data and stores them off site could be high risk (if the providing company were to have a data breach, for example). This is a risky experiment and should be avoided if possible.
Integrate	Some emerging technologies may appear to be useful to your business but difficult to integrate. Don't avoid experimenting with such technology because you may discover the benefits outweigh the complexity of the integration.	A simple technology that can help align the company's goals from the CEO down to the lowest-level employee may be extremely valuable, despite the challenges of integration and companywide training. If you enter into the experimental phase with these challenges in mind, you'll be better able to provide a strong, realistic recommendation.
Experiment	Try out the new technology in a series of short experiments, each lasting only about two weeks (similar to the project management technique known as "agile"). This allows you to make frequent changes, refining the use of the technology for your organization.	You introduce a technology to help a customer service department keep track of end-user problems. A small team tries the system for two weeks, evaluating their experience at the end. You then modify the system based on their feedback, and ask the same group to try again for two weeks. This continues until you have a working system or determine that the new technology will not work for your organization.
Check the culture fit	Each businesses has a unique culture and set of values due to leadership and the composition of the workforce. Help bridge the gaps when you sense a sector of the organization may resist adopting the new technology.	A technology that uses cellphones and social media may be appropriate for a group of young digital natives but may face resistance from older employees who may not be as comfortable with mobile apps.
Advocate	Some experiments provide benefits to employees outside your own business unit. Be sure to position and align the presentation of the experiment's objectives to other teams' values.	To implement a new intranet, you might emphasize the cost savings to your own operations group, but you could also stress the benefits of data management to the human resources group.

falling. The machine learns to differentiate among various actions by running lots of statistics incredibly quickly from data transmitted via components and wireless technologies small enough to be placed in a watch. Table 20-4 documents some of the key technologies that may fundamentally change our future.

WHAT IT MEANS TO BE DISRUPTIVE

When new technologies are introduced, they disrupt the status quo to some degree. Sometimes we think of things that are disruptive as a bad thing. But when technology is disruptive it can be a good thing, at least for some people, and perhaps even for your organization. When a new technology disrupts an entire industry (which has been happening for thousands of years), it provides new opportunities for companies and increases productivity in businesses.

Amazon changed the landscape of retail stores with a mixture of ubiquitous Internet access, powerful search algorithms, and Prime two-day shipping. Amazon disrupted the way people shop, replacing specialized brick-and-mortar stores (such as toy stores) with online browsing and rapid delivery. And while some stores no longer exist because of Amazon's technological and business innovation, others have emerged at the same moment to become more valuable, like Apple Stores, which are designed to be community gathering places, where consumers can experience the Apple brand firsthand, learn about the products, and perfect skills (how to make a better video).

Example of Cloud Technology Enabling Better Business and Better User Experience

Of course, companies like Apple and Amazon innovate in every aspect of their business, but what enables that innovation is how they leverage new technology to provide better experiences for their users. Consider how Apple wants customers to upgrade their phones every year. What enables this process to be smooth is that they use cloud storage to enable customers to keep all their data backed up in the event that they lose a phone and replace it or upgrade to a new phone. In just a short while, the new phone will download everything it needs and the user will be up and running quickly. Before the days of cloud storage, you would have had to keep all your data on a local hard drive. And if you were to damage your hard drive you'd lose all the backups you had. With cloud storage, the data are duplicated and exist in several physical places in a way that protects the information, even if a specific storage device is damaged. And since the cellphone connects by WiFi or by cell tower, data are transferred wirelessly wherever the user is, as long as the user has a connection. And because the process of backing up the data of a phone to cloud storage is done automatically when the user isn't using the phone (usually overnight), the user never has to think about the process. Not only is the solution more reliable than a physical hard drive located in the user's home but it's more convenient as well. The technology provides the ability for Apple to innovate and provide a service that both benefits the company as well as the end user of their products.

Table 20-4 Important Technologies That Are Changing How We Work			
Technology	**Related Terms**	**Working Definition**	**Example Uses**
Machine learning (ML)	Artificial intelligence (AI), expert system (used in the 1980s and 1990s)	A computer system that uses statistics to refine and improve how a computer performs a task; generally done automatically by the machine, but with some human intervention	Speech recognition; weather prediction; assessing compliance with terms of service on social media platforms
Mobile technologies	Wireless, cellular, 3G, 4G, 5G, apps, location-based services, social sharing	A set of technologies that enable cellphones to operate and transmit data, including streaming audio and video data	Text messaging, video on demand, streaming music services, mobile apps, app stores
Software as a service (SaaS)	Platform as a service (PaaS)	A way to sell (or license) software so users pay only for the time they use it or only for the features they use; all users receive updates immediately	Dropbox, Microsoft Office 365, Google apps, DocuSign, Slack
Cloud technologies	Cloud computing, cloud storage	Software that runs in a central data center, enabling small companies to access the same technologies large companies use and allowing them to deploy a small solution that can instantaneously grow to accommodate more users; enables SaaS	Amazon Web Services, Microsoft Azure, VMware
Blockchain	Cryptocurrency, bitcoin, mining, public key, encryption	A public record of a transaction that spreads information over many systems, making it difficult (or impossible) to silently alter the record; although strongly tied to cryptocurrency, it has far-reaching purposes, such as tracking the buying and selling history of artwork	MIT employs blockchain technology for diplomas; IBM and Amazon use it for various services

Example of Software As a Service Enabling Better Business and Better User Experience

Just a few years ago, to acquire software often meant receiving a set of disks and installing them on your computer. If you wanted to use the same software on another computer, you'd have to install it again, assuming you were allowed to use the software on two different computers.

Fast-forward a few years, and now we might download software that can sit on many computers (a desktop, a laptop, and a mobile phone). A person logs into the software and can switch between devices, and the experiences follows that person from device to device in perfect synchronicity, enabled by the business and technology model in which a user is charged not for the software but to use the software. This is called software as a service, and it's transforming every kind of software experience from online versions of business tools like email and spreadsheet applications, to entertainment experiences like Netflix and Spotify.

Spotify sells *access* to millions of songs. Users typically stream the songs, and when they listen to them on their computer, they certainly don't own the song they're listening to. Instead, they purchase only the right to use the Spotify software (either through a web browser or as an app) to stream the music from Spotify's servers at a moment in time. For just a few dollars a month, users get access to an enormous library of music. They can start listening to a song on a laptop, pause it, then pick up their phone and walk out of the house and resume playing the song where they left off. Again, this is enabled by cloud technology that lets all of the devices communicate to a central server with the software enabling the service. Spotify can track users' behaviors and make relevant suggestions to them for additional music they might like. And when a user stops paying for the service, he or she simply loses access to the music.

SaaS has enabled many companies to offer software experiences that are custom tailored to a variety of users. Adobe used to offer only the ability to download and use applications, like Photoshop, for a high fee. In 2011 that program cost $699. In addition, Adobe charged for upgrades as they made new versions. And while many creative professionals needed the software, many could not afford the cost. But now Adobe lets users use the software for as long as they pay for it. For as little as $9.99 a month, users can use Photoshop. And as Adobe improves the software, the user automatically gets the new features without added fees. Now many more people are able to access Photoshop, and a variety of other tools that Adobe makes, and spend far less to do so.

An Example of Machine Learning Enabling Better Business and Better User Experience

As mentioned, Spotify tracks user listening behaviors. They do this by using machine learning (ML) techniques that do incredible things, like analyzing every single track of music to extract a variety of information about a song. They then automatically, for every single user, analyze what the user listens to and attempts to identify songs of a similar style. This ML technique for creating a recommendation engine is extremely valuable for the company because it can better understand each individual customer and provide a better experience for each user. Users love that every week Spotify can curate a unique playlist for them. This feature is a significant reason Spotify users enjoy the service, because it can be hard to discover new music now that people spend less time listening to the radio and there are so many more songs being published than ever before.

FAQS AND COMMON MISUNDERSTANDINGS

Question: How do I bring in new technologies if I don't have authority over the IT department or other related departments?
Answer: It can be difficult to implement new technologies when you depend on other groups for support, but you can influence those groups to help you get buy-in from senior leaders. The best way to do that is to advocate for your experiments by creating a clear vision that shows why they should invest just a little in order to learn a lot.

Question: What's a good way for me to show the vision of my solution?
Answer: Become a storyteller. From Aristotle to Steve Jobs, all people who advocate for their ideas tell a story about a problem, a solution, and a pathway to put that solution in place. In addition to Chapter 3, Presentation, there are plenty of excellent resources that can give you insight into making compelling presentations.

Question: My company is slow to change. How can I accelerate change in my organization?
Answer: Many companies want to be quick to improve, but there can be resistance to change; it's completely normal and expected. So instead of being frustrated with a slow process, use that time to sharpen your experiments, to talk about the results, and to share the success stories and lessons learned. Once you have a few successes, you'll find that people will recognize and prioritize your suggestions and start to move faster. You should also review Chapter 10, Managing Change.

Question: How much of an expert do I need to be at the technology before I experiment with it?
Answer: As you start to experiment with technologies, you'll become more familiar with the language and metrics around the technology. You'll start to acquire a deeper understanding, and when you don't know something, simply Google it, or ask the companies that sell the technology to teach or train you. It's in their best interest to do so, because they want to sell you a solution.

Question: If technology is moving fast, how can I keep ahead of it?
Answer: The underlying technologies don't change that quickly, it's the applications that use the technology that change rapidly. The more you understand about the technologies outlined in this chapter, the more you'll start to see how many applications that appear to be different, are actually using the same technology.

Diversity and Inclusion

LEARNING OBJECTIVES

By the end of this chapter, you will be better equipped to:

- Define diversity, inclusion, and equity.
- Understand and identify your own unconscious bias.
- Understand and coach others on key components of inclusive management.
- Navigate tough dialogue across differences related to performance feedback, coaching, and mentoring.
- Understand unconscious bias.
- Retain and develop talent as a skilled team leader.

As a manager, you have influence on the lives of others. You are asked to meet new challenges and act as part of your organization's leadership. This chapter helps you learn how to tackle these new challenges in an inclusive way. Before we dive in, let's define what we mean by diversity and inclusion. *Diversity* in its broadest context, is understanding that each individual is unique and recognizing our individual differences including, among other things, race, ethnicity, gender, sexual orientation, socioeconomic status, age, physical abilities, religious beliefs, political beliefs, or other ideologies, characteristics or differences that each of us have.

Inclusiveness is best described as creating a welcoming environment that accepts each individual's differences, embraces strengths, encourages involvement, and provides opportunities for all to achieve their full potential. If you have a different identity from the majority in any aspect of your identity, you may sometimes feel like a minority or an outsider. You may be one of a few women, you may be older than most others, you may come from a different part of the country or world, you may be ethnically or racially diverse, or you may have a different sexual orientation or gender expression from the majority. You may have a combination of different dimensions of your identity that make you feel different or actually give you a different set of perspectives from some of your colleagues. Your goal as a manager is to act with objectivity and fairness and to minimize the impact of your own perspectives, in ways that may be influenced by the biases we all have.

When we use the word *bias*, we often think of extreme prejudice and overt acts of discrimination. A bias is defined as a prejudice in favor or against one thing, person, or group compared with another, usually in a way considered to be unfair. However, a great deal of research has been done that reveals that we all have biases, whether we are conscious of them or not. Some are biases in favor, such as favoring your sports team, which isn't normally a concern. Other biases in favor might be driven by stereotypes about others. *Unconscious bias,* for example, is a type of bias that exists outside of a person's consciousness, but can still affect behaviors or emotions.

Neuroscience is the science of the mind. Experts in this field have defined unconscious bias as the phenomenon whereby the mind makes quick, automatic judgments of others. These quick judgments are unconscious and our influenced by our personal histories and experiences. They reveal a bias in favor of or against others. As previously noted earlier, sports fans have an automatic positive response when their team is mentioned. However, unconscious bias frequently leads to negative stereotypes, and our daily decisions and behavior often reflect biases we are totally unaware of.

How can a manager who wants to be fair and equitable at work manage through the challenge of unconscious bias? In what ways do we exclude some and support others without that being our intention?

OVERCOMING UNCONSCIOUS BIAS

As a manager, you will be in a position to give feedback to your team and to other colleagues. Often organizations have formal feedback processes, but feedback can be as simple as, "Great job!" after a presentation. Informal feedback is a key ingredient to learning on the job. You should seek it out yourself and offer it regularly to others.

So where does unconscious bias fit in?

DIVERSITY AND INCLUSION'S IMPACT

Frequently we find ourselves drawn to others like ourselves. But patterns in hiring, advancement, and management reveal that many times, the result is a lack of diversity of thought, experience, and representation of individuals with the characteristics we have defined here as aspects of diversity.

This chapter helps you challenge your own beliefs and perspectives to ensure you are being equitable and fair in your role as a manager. You may share experiences and have common interests with others who initially don't appear similar to you.

One way to do this is to ask questions and build an appropriate, but personal, relationship with your colleagues. Asking others simple questions can help build rapport and form mutual respect. It is understood in business today that when our working environment, culture, policies, procedures, and processes promote diversity and inclusiveness we have higher employee engagement and more effective teams. Being an effective team manager is a valuable skill. As we go through the steps, note the terms introduced and defined in this chapter. They will make up useful language to use as you become more comfortable with the concepts and coach others to be more inclusive.

BRIEF HISTORY OF DIVERSITY AND INCLUSION IN CORPORATE CULTURE

As a manager, you must understand affirmative action and changes in our legal system. These laws and related legislation have emerged as the U.S. workforce has diversified significantly over the last century.

Of critical importance is Title VII of the Civil Rights Act of 1964, which ended segregation in public places, banning employment discrimination on the basis of race, religion, sex, or national origin. Title VII applies to employers with fifteen or more employees and forbids discrimination in any aspect of employment. Title VII applies specifically in decisions affecting the hiring, promotion, or dismissal of employees. As a manager, you should encourage diverse hiring on your team and foster an inclusive environment. Human resource professionals should carefully monitor these practices to prevent legal action being taken against the organization.

In addition to the legal basis for the field, early research responded to employment trends. As white women increasingly entered the workforce in the 1970s the research began with a focus on them.[1] Companies that made a commitment to include other aspects of diversity frequently began to put their emphasis on diversity, recruiting with the goals of hiring black, Latinx, and Asian employees.

Organization goals initially were to diversify a largely white, straight male workforce and recruiting diverse candidates was only to meet a quota. For progressive companies in the 1980s, the goals were often focused on diverse representation of women accompanied often by stretching the company culture toward workplace flexibility. Workplace flexibility in the early years was associated with working mothers and linked to the advancement of married white women with children who were aiming at roles in management.

Early efforts in progressive companies grew concerned at the low numbers of racially and ethnically diverse individuals. Goals were often set to increase the representation of black employees; some were gradually met. These efforts typically expanded to include Latinxs and Asians. Overall the racial and cultural diversity of senior leadership remains lacking and continues to be a challenge in many companies today.

Corporate boards are another area lacking diversity; most rely on membership criteria that drive white male representation.[2]

LET'S GET PRACTICAL: WHAT DO YOU DO?

First, let's unpack how an organization becomes diverse. From a diversity perspective, hiring is the first step (see also Chapter 14, Talent Management). Research shows that we all have unconscious biases, which means when we approach any situation where we are evaluating someone's skills, like a hiring situation, we frequently favor someone who is most similar to ourselves.

Think about going to a party alone when you don't know anyone there. You often feel most at ease with individuals who may have gone to the same school as you, are fans of the same sports teams, or individuals who generally seem like others you already know in your social circle. This kind of thinking impacts hiring practices significantly.

Let's explore some specific experiences you may have and how best to resolve any concerns that can arise related to diversity, using examples related to hiring. What can you, as a manager, do to help your organization be fair, inclusive, and equitable in their hiring practices? You are part of the culture of the organization and, as a manager, have the opportunity to influence it in your role.

Warning: Assumptions Can Be Dangerous!

How can you challenge your assumptions and aim for an objective point of view? You might ask yourself some questions before each interview begins. For example:

- What are my assumptions about who would be best for this role?
- What if this person isn't fitting those assumptions; what can I do to ensure I am being fair?
- Am I giving more weight to characteristics that are the same as those I consider part of my own identity?
- Do I have a bias related to what state they come from, what country they may have been born in, or what their appearance might signal to me about their background or gender?
- As I start to interview as a regular practice, do I see a pattern forming where I tend to favor someone more like me? With similar educational, socioeconomic, or life experiences? Or favoring other dimensions of identity?

Pro tip

Be a change champion as you model self-assessing for bias. You may notice others involved with the interview challenge the candidates based on cultural fit or style. If possible, ask questions to determine if the other interviewers have any biases embedded in their concerns.

Many organizations unintentionally have developed a narrow band of acceptable styles, which shows up in their hiring patterns. This practice can lead to something called *group think*, by which less diverse perspectives lead to mistakes in important decision making. Companies and firms that lack diverse views may fail in international marketing decisions, and in some cases this has led to the closure of large firms. A lack of diversity can put a company at risk. One recent example is IBM. After the CEO felt that the talent in the organization did not reflect the current client base, eight task forces were created to focus on different marginalized groups. These task forces were used to understand the differences of each and appeal to a more employees and customers.

HOW DO YOU BECOME A MORE INCLUSIVE MANAGER?

Creating an Inclusive Environment

Here are some steps you could take:

- Form subteams across what you perceive as the cliques to work on special projects.
- Set aside time for a team discussion possibly an off site location, that has relationship building as its goal. Do this on a regular basis when the team is first assigned to work together.
- As you prepare for these meetings, share your own personal experiences and make sure to demonstrate that you are listening. Ask clarifying questions of others that make clear you are listening and care to hear the answers.
- You could plan a team-building event. Figure out the best times for all to get together for a group discussion to build rapport.
- Make a plan to touch base after an appropriate amount of time to revisit the issues.
- Commit to continue to find ways to ensure all members of the team feel included in team events.

Skills and Behaviors of Inclusive Managers

The following sections offer advice for specific aspects of managing for inclusivity.

Inclusivity

Self-awareness and self-monitoring of unconscious bias are ongoing, fundamental elements for all managers:

- *What*: The inclusive manager is clearly aware of the role of unconscious bias and acts to correct habits that may reveal favoritism.
- *Why*: Self-awareness of unintended bias is a component of the emotional intelligence required in today's business environments, both with one's own teams as well as with customers and clients domestically and within global business environments.
- *How*: Self-monitoring can be a form of measurement.
  - Keep track of who is receiving prime assignments you have influence over.
  - If you see trends or are made aware of trends that favor some individuals over others, assess the situation for fairness.
  - Challenge your ability to offer effective guidance and on-the-job feedback to all.

If you consistently adopt these practices, you, as team manager, will inspire loyalty and motivation from your team members. This in turn will build your own reputation as a manager who has the ability to lead diverse teams effectively. Inclusive team leaders commonly produce higher quality results, and by developing all team members, their teams are ready to successfully cover the needs of clients and customers when voluntary turnover occurs.

Feedback

A critical component of successful performance of your team is providing candid, just-in-time feedback on the job.

- *What*: The ability to deliver effective feedback across race, gender and other identity differences is a key skill for today's managers.
- *Why*: When informal feedback isn't equitably distributed there is a lack of ease in work relationships, leading to uneven performance as it advantages some team members over others.
- *How*: Managers who develop the ability to show genuine interest in their team members learn how to deliver feedback in an environment of trust.
  - Show curiosity about the interests of team members.
  - Share personal experiences relevant to team actions and assignments.
  - Spend even brief amounts of time in nonwork settings. A breakfast, a conversation en route to a client, or a group outing can enhance trust on a team.
  - Give specific feedback and ask the recipient to come to you on a periodic basis to describe his or her progress and remaining challenges.
  - Reflect on how you learned specific skills and share how you developed specific skills from those experiences.
  - Let those you are leading know common pitfalls that occur on the job. Do this when addressing the full group, so everyone can receive the feedback and insights together.

Turnover is common in todays' marketplace and those you have invested in often change jobs. If you haven't offered insights and feedback to everyone on the team, those who leave will create gaps in knowledge and skill.

Mentoring

Mentors and sponsors are critical to career success. Managers who are strong mentors, especially to employees who are in the early years of the job, create productive and successful teams.

- *What*: A good mentor will communicate often and spend time explaining what the unwritten rules of the organizational culture are all about and how they impact the environment.
- *Why*: Successful career development is contingent on true understanding of career and behavioral expectations, both spoken and unspoken. Being viewed as someone who is a good fit for advancement is contingent on knowing the unwritten rules.

- *How*: Coaching is a key component of successful career development. Individual dialogue with members of the team about organizational norms and expectations is critical to their ability to meet those expectations. This kind of dialogue helps the managers contribute to a high-performance culture with coaching as a central element.
  - Mentors describe the common assumptions made by leaders in the organization and identify specific and common expectations. This can be particularly helpful to those who may be from different backgrounds from the majority of the organization and for those who have a different identity or sexual orientation than the majority.
  - Managers who share their experience of learning the do's and don'ts of the work environment effectively mentor across cultural and other identity differences.
  - Coaching is ideally part of most aspects of team leadership.
  - Knowing the unwritten rules can help team members define and model executive presence.
  - Mentoring involves informing new hires of any unspoken dress codes, including standards related to facial hair, shoe style, preferred clothing styles, and hairstyles. These can be difficult signals to read for some employees.

Coaches must also address authenticity and style, which are complex arenas for many and especially for minorities within the organization. An inclusive manager advises and supports team members who are trying to balance their own style with company expectations.

Other areas of mentoring include communication style and body language. Communication style, which is an aspect of executive presence, can vary dramatically across cultural norms and can be essential to success; thus a good mentor address expectations with team members. In addition, issues of body language, personal space, eye contact, and so on can be culturally specific; effective managers coach their hires about these subtle cues.

Mentors should also be aware of *gravitas*, a term that can be hard to pin down. Valued coaches share what they know about a range of common and successful leadership styles.

Finally, mentors should work to create a safe space so team members feel comfortable having conversations with them about their views and observations.

Sponsoring

Business author Sylvia Ann Hewlett, suggests that employees seek out a sponsor instead of a mentor.[9] Why does she offer this advice and what is the difference? Because managers are both supervisors and mentors, it is critical to know the difference and to recognize when mentoring transitions into sponsorship.

- *What*: Mentors offer advice and perspective. The act of positively influencing the advancement of others is called sponsorship. Sponsors have influence and use it on behalf of others.
- *Why*: Managers are expected to achieve their own goals, including development of the individual talents of team members. Sponsors (and successful managers) positively influence the careers of high-potential talent.
- *How*: As a manager matures, his or her ability to influence the career development of others increases.

A primary skill involved in developing talent is spotting others' performance strengths. Managers who give team members a variety of challenging assignments and who share feedback and make observations will know where to find particular skills among those team members.

In a *Fast Company* article, talented women were told they "need more than the advice and encouragement of a professional mentor. The American Bar Association also highlights the critical issues women and minorities face when seeking out sponsorship.

The literature on mentors and sponsors reveals that informal relationships form more routinely between individuals who identify with each other and share similar personal traits. In the United States, this has historically meant that white male leadership sponsors white male employees in terms of business opportunities and promotion.

Observe Behavior and Be Curious

Pro tip

Equity in the delivery of feedback is key. Make a list and monitor yourself to ensure you distributed informal feedback equally. Inform the whole team about upcoming work in group meetings, not in individual exchanges or during nonwork hours.

Sally is new to a team where she is the only woman. One of the team's clients had heavy demands, requiring frequent travel and long hours. Sam, the manager, finds it difficult to find time to spend time with each team member individually. There are group dinners and time spent unwinding in a bar after dinner. Sam finds himself sharing feedback and guidance in bar settings, but Sally isn't spending the time in the bar after dinner.

Sam notices some areas where Sally's performance needs improvement but doesn't feel comfortable speaking with her directly about it. Sam assumes others on the team will fill in the gaps with her performance and help her learn the ropes of the team culture. Moreover, he is unaware that he offers previews of upcoming work in the bar, which she is missing out on. When Sam writes up his midyear feedback review for Sally, Sally is shocked when she gets his negative feedback for the first time in that report. She wonders why Sam hasn't spoken with her about his concerns.

- What kind of coaching would Sam have benefited from in advance?
- How can a manager self-monitor his or her ability to be equitable in interactions with team members?
- Is it effective to share work information in off-hour, nonwork settings?

Sam clearly needed more guidance on the importance of ongoing, informal feedback. Orientation for being a manager needs to include self-awareness. It is natural to fall into patterns like this one, when a manager is new to a certain type of experience, such as working under unfamiliar or heavy work pressures.

WHY MIGHT YOU FEEL UNCOMFORTABLE GIVING FEEDBACK ACROSS DIFFERENCES OF IDENTITY?

A common concern among supervisors giving feedback to those they don't share multiple identity traits with is a fear of being called biased, racist, sexist, or homophobic. Moreover, it isn't easy to give critical feedback under any circumstances (see Chapter 9, Coaching for Performance, and Chapter 14, Talent Management for more ideas on delivering feedback). In regard to diversity, it is important to remind yourself how much relationships rely on intangible feelings.

Don't you sometimes meet someone and instantly hit it off? These instincts we have factor into relationships across differences, despite our ability to define exactly how that might work. The point is, when you approach someone with good intentions, that person can almost always tell.

Pro tip

Take a risk in addressing differences in identity. Demonstrating good intentions goes a long way in developing rapport across dimensions of diversity.

Does this mean you will never get a negative response? No. There might be tears, there might be grumbles or defensiveness. But if you maintain that you are committed to the success of the team member and his or her career development, it is unlikely that your efforts will not be viewed as well intended.

Sometimes it takes a bit of a risk initially to deliver constructive feedback. However, the loyalty you generate if you are known as someone who mentors and offers critical feedback and constructive advice will become part of your brand.

You want to be recognized for your skill at managing *all* members of your team.

WHAT IS THE DIFFERENCE BETWEEN A GENERALIZATION AND A STEREOTYPE?

We have already mentioned the term stereotype. It is a common term but what do we really mean by it? Is it ever a good idea to generalize about a group? Let's explore the difference between the two (see also Chapter 18, Organizational Culture).

A *generalization*, in the context of diversity and inclusion, can refer to common trends that might be observed in a particular country or culture. For example, cultures often have a common value around the sense of time. Some populations embrace a fixed sense of time, which adheres to specific deadlines, what in the United States would be called timeliness. Other cultures value a more fluid sense of time and are less locked into time frames, which appear rigid and inflexible.

A common way that a generalization becomes a stereotype is when a value is placed on one aspect over another. A negative example would be to turn a generalization about time into a negative stereotype.

Here are two examples of stereotyping in relation to a sense of time:

- "She is so uptight and inflexible. I was fifteen minutes late to the meeting, and you would think I had broken the law!"
- "In that country, nothing ever happens when it is supposed to. I hate waiting for my friends who are from there. What is it that they are doing that is so important that it justifies leaving me standing here?"

If one builds a generalization out to become a stereotype, one starts to characterize individuals and projects a negative view of them based on a single cultural value. So as the examples illustrate, someone from a fixed time culture might come to view someone who embraces time in a fluid way as being lazy and disorganized. Looking at it the other way, a person with a fluid time view perceives an individual from a fixed time culture as being overly concerned with details and too rigid.

Either of these stereotypes can lead to comments about all of the people from a particular country, and these can become entrenched biases that are passed along throughout an organization.

As a manager, it is instructive to be aware of your own unconscious biases and to spend time reflecting on what in your background might be influencing the choices you make at work. What kind of values regarding time to do you have? Did you grow up around any overt stereotypes? If yes, how might this continue to impact your decisions and behavior?

A common workplace complaint from minority employees is a sense they are not fitting in. It is unfortunately fairly common for individuals with a minority identity to feel like outsiders when others on the team don't include them.

How Do You Guard against Making Decisions That Aren't Equitable?

There are many subtle ways in which we impact others as managers. The goal isn't to become dreadfully self-conscious or indecisive. Taking time to pause before distributing assignments may slow you down initially, but if you practice being conscious of fairness, it becomes your natural style.

MICROINEQUITIES VERSUS MICROAGGRESSIONS

The following suggestions help you handle microinequities and practice fair coaching for all members of your team.

Exploring the Impact of Microinequities

As a manager, you may be asked to provide formal performance feedback on others, which provides the data for determining the distribution of promotions, bonuses, raises, and terminations. Being aware of potential unconscious bias enables you to make significant steps toward true inclusion and fairness, promoting positive change in the part of the organization you influence as a manager.

Microinequity is a term you are likely to come across as you learn more about diversity and inclusion. Microinequities are defined as small negative actions, such as slights and cutting remarks that align with a biased point of view. On the surface microinequities may seem minor, but their effects are large. Here are some examples:

Pro tip

If your goal is to become an inclusive manager, find time or a process that includes self-reflection. Consider listing inclusive behavior as a performance goal and track your progress over a year.

- A boss fails to say hello to the one member of the team after greeting everyone else.
- A manager repeatedly mispronounces a team member's name.
- A project leader responds to questions only from those with whom she feels comfortable with.
- A supervisor avoids one-on-one conversations with a direct report.

A team member experiencing these kinds of slights might initially bring just one of them to your attention. You might puzzle over why the person reacted so strongly to a seemingly minor slight. However, if you explore further, you will understand how a pattern of micro-inequities can, over time, have a significant negative impact on a person's work experience. When these experiences occur repeatedly, what feels like a *micro* event becomes a full-blown pattern of exclusion. Microinequities can cause people to feel they don't belong in an organization, leading to turnover.

How Can You Coach Others to Avoid Microinequities?

Microinequities can be difficult to identify, even for the individuals who experience them. In addition, those who engage in such slights can become defensive when you identify such behaviors. They may view a microinequity as a minor, one-time event with little significance. This happens because they aren't seeing the pattern of their behaviors and thus don't understand why an individual action even merits a discussion at all.

Even the people being offended may not see an overall pattern clearly. They may feel only the emotions that such patterns raise without objectively identifying the cause. They just know they have had enough.

As a manager, it is your role to help all parties learn from experience, but this takes practice. When working through a microinequity event, keep these issues in mind:

- It is important to avoid taking sides.
- Discourage blame in these circumstances.
- Define what a microinequity is.
- Explain how a pattern of microinequities can lead to a breakdown in communications.

- Explain that the goal isn't to enforce some kind of political correctness; the purpose is to identify behavior that leads to fair outcomes.

Coaching along these lines can help both parties see microinequities in a new light.

Group Coaching

As a manager, you may want to deliver inclusiveness tips to the entire team. Group coaching can be highly effective at establishing team norms. Here are some steps for leading a group discussion:

1. Define the term *microinequities* and give examples.
2. Ask the group to share examples from their own lives from outside your workplace. Give the group time to personalize and discuss the issues.
3. Define the terms *diversity* and *inclusion*. Ask the group to share experiences from their childhood when they felt part of a group and when they felt excluded. Ask them to share what actions changed their experience of exclusion.
4. Provide examples of small acts of inclusion in the discussion, such as inviting everyone to a social event and expressing interest in all team members' past career experiences.

Coaching is an art that will take time to develop for many managers (see Chapter 9, Coaching for Performance, for more guidance). It is wise to speak to each person individually about any sensitive concerns. This allows all members of the team to have a sense that you have heard them and care about their aspirations. Think about experiences you have had with mentors and those who have sponsored your success that you can share with the team members. Personalizing your messages and careful listening are fundamental to being a good mentor.

What Are Microaggressions?

Microaggression is a related term. While microinequities can occur within any context, microaggressions frequently link to racial or gender identity stereotypes. Microaggressions tend to be directly offensive to others and typically are direct stereotypes that insult individuals. An act of microaggression may reveal the perpetrator's lack of knowledge or familiarity with different cultural backgrounds, racial differences and other dimensions of identity. Such acts, however, may also be overt and intentional expressions of bias. Either way, they convey negative bias and beliefs that are offensive to others.

Here are some examples of questions and comments that fall under the umbrella of microaggression:

- Asking an Asian American, "What country are you from?" Many Asian Americans have shared in focus groups that they are often asked this question, even when they have already said they were from Maryland or New Jersey (or another state).
- Saying, "You don't look Jewish."

- Saying—with a surprised tone of voice—to a person of color, "You're so articulate!"
- Saying to a man who actively participates in raising his children, "Isn't it nice that you're helping your wife with the kids."
- Suggesting that a task may be too difficult for a woman co-worker.
- Saying to a co-worker, "I would never have guessed you were gay."

Often the insult lies in what is implied by the comments rather than what is directly said aloud. Microaggressions occur in many other situations and in response to other aspects of identity such as disability, age, and body weight. Inclusive leadership sets a standard where microaggressions are not tolerated. If standards aren't set, you risk legal issues, high turnover, declining morale, and lower productivity.

HANDLING SEVERE OR OVERT BIASES

When you are approached about a conflict that involves severe microaggressions and overt biases, what will you do? If you sense a possible conflict, how do you know when it's time to intervene? When coaching across differences, particularly when the individual you are coaching is part of minority population in your company or firm, you will want to consult your human resources team and other more experienced supervisors. If the situation is complex or can be viewed as extremely challenging, you will need human resource skills and perspectives on your next steps.

There are legal concerns when incidents of overt bias and prejudice become pervasive in a workplace. HR professionals will help you understand if you are dealing with a legal concern referred to as a *hostile work environment*.

Discussing Diversity Issues

Here are some suggestions to keep in mind when initiating a challenging discussion about disagreements related to diverse identities. (For more on this, see Chapter 4, Conflict Management.)

- Don't feel like you have to have all the answers and be candid about not having a solution until you have a better understanding.
- Make clear to the individual that you need to take the time to reflect on the situation.
- Let the offended person know that you are taking his or her concerns seriously and this is why you want time to consider the right response.
- Let the individuals involved know that you have advisers with whom you will consult.
- Discuss confidentiality. There are times when you can maintain confidentiality when consulting others. However, if there are legal concerns, such as potential for sexual harassment, you will not able to provide confidentiality. If someone shares information, you are legally obliged to report it.

You will need advice to determine if the conditions are right for you to host the coaching conversations with the group or individuals involved. If the responsibility is yours, be sure to listen carefully and repeat back what you have heard.

It is helpful to take notes to create a record of incidents that are challenging in this regard. A careful listening process is a baseline for good coaching, and the notes will help you if you need to revisit the situation.

HANDLING IMPOSTER SYNDROME

Imposter syndrome is another useful concept to be aware of as a coach. It is a self-perception or belief that surfaces when an individual continuously doubts his or her own qualifications for a current work role. A person who feels that he couldn't possibly be qualified, despite having obtained educational degrees and other external validation for his job, is experiencing imposter syndrome. In diversity conferences, imposter syndrome is often cited by individuals who have a different identity from the majority.

One common instance of imposter syndrome occurs often among high-ranking women executives. Senior executive women often cite luck as the key to their achievements when speaking in public about their career successes. It is their leadership skills and competencies that have resulted in their success. Yet there is a hesitance to acknowledge achievements.

Other examples include ethnically or racially diverse men and women in a white male–dominated environment who may experience a lot of exclusionary behavior. Over time, this can lead to self-questioning and doubt. Explore the use of this concept when coaching a person who is plagued by self-doubt, despite having all the qualities and qualifications for a position.

How to Recognize and Help an Employee Overcome Imposter Syndrome

If you are coaching a high-performing individual who seems to doubt his or her skills and who attributes success to chance or other people, explore this in a private conversation.

Here are some steps to consider:

1. Ask the individual to describe their achievements and to identify what accomplishments they were given positive recognition for.
2. If the individual was hired after success at a previous employer, ask them to speak in detail about their best achievements in the previous position.
3. Discuss what *imposter syndrome* is and reassure them that their accomplishments are well deserved.

The goal here is to encourage the person to learn how to view their achievements more positively and more realistically in her current role. You will have to revisit this discussion over time. This kind of feedback requires reflection and time to absorb and consider.

HOW TO INCREASE JOB SATISFACTION AND TEAM MEMBER CONFIDENCE

In most United States–based companies, it is rare to see successful careers built by putting one's head down and working hard. While this may be the baseline and focus for early years on the job, relationships are also critical for building one's career success. Most job advice includes a focus on networking. Yet networking for someone who experiences an outsider status can be a daunting task to develop.

How to Respond to Questions about Authenticity

When coaching in the United States across identity differences, it is common to be asked questions related to authenticity. These concerns are often expressed in phrases like "I can't be my true self at work" or "I feel like I have to leave a lot of myself at the door when I come to work." Often individuals feel they have to modify too much of their true personality and natural style.

Team members may ask questions about whether their appearance (including hairstyle, attire, and makeup) is acceptable in the organization's culture or if their communication style is acceptable. They may wonder if they are too direct for the culture and so on. This is common for individuals who are different from most others in a homogenous organization and who are concerned about their status as a minority.

New York University law professor Kenji Yoshino, introduced the term *covering*, which is useful when coaching on this topic.[7] It is a helpful concept for those who are struggling to understand how much of their true selves they can bring to work. It refers to hiding or covering up aspects of oneself that can be viewed as unacceptable in a particular organizational culture. Covering issues can reflect biases in the culture and can be difficult to address for both individuals and managers. Lesbian and gay individuals in particular have identified this covering experience when they don't feel their company culture will support their sexual identity.

In a survey conducted by Yoshino and co-workers, 61 percent of more than three thousand employees surveyed in twenty large U.S. firms found that "they faced overt or implicit pressure to cover in some way" and "fifty-one percent said they perceived demands for covering from leadership affected their view of opportunities within the organization."[8]

THE STAGES OF INCLUSIVE LEADERSHIP

What does it mean to have mastered inclusive management? The manager who is able to fully engage every member of the team will earn a reputation for fairness, and this often yields loyalty as it helps increase the retention of the team members.

The inclusive manager is able to identify the potential of those being supervised and provides helpful just-in-time feedback. Again, this skill set improves the manager's reputation for excellent team leadership.

Table 21-1 The Stages of Inclusive Leadership	
First steps	1. Show curiosity and engage in conversation. 2. Listen well and share back some highlights of what you have heard. 3. Share your experiences and your insights about the work environment and the work-place culture. 4. Work to establish a relationship of trust across differences.
Inclusive management	1. Distribute feedback and assignments to all. 2. Watch for your own unconscious biases and awareness of microinequities and modify your decisions and behaviors. 3. Act as a coach and mentor, sharing advice and understanding differences in perspectives of team members.
Inclusive leadership/ team focus	1. Coach others on inclusive behaviors. 2. Communicate about the value to them as individuals, the value to the team function and the organization for acting inclusively. 3. Intervene when others experience bias or microaggressions. 4. Offer positive descriptions of individual credentials when introducing those in minority populations to leaders and influencers.

It is often the case that senior leaders have not had the benefit of inclusive leadership training and don't easily access inclusive team leadership behaviors. These leaders typically admire newer managers who can be effective in circumstances where perhaps they would not be as successful.

An inclusive work environment means increased employee motivation and productivity. Senior leaders recognize inclusive leadership, seeing newer managers in a positive light when their teams achieve results and when managers are able to retain and develop diverse talent.

The stages of inclusive leadership are outlined in Table 21-1.

GLOBAL DIVERSITY

As mutlicultural business operations increased, the field of diversity grew to include greater emphasis on intercultural diversity and inclusive leadership. A global mind-set involving cross-cultural competencies is viewed as an essential skill set for any organization operating internationally today. Global businesses rely on mutlicultural teams. These teams are expected to work effectively in a global market. This requires new skills and awareness of cultural differences to be able to successfully perform key tasks, such as decision making, setting timelines, and other processes linked to marketing work products and deliverables.

When working across the globe, company leaders are wise to do a local exploration of who is defined in the culture as a minority. Managers must understand the interaction between minority and majority dynamics in the local culture as well as the role of women. Managers must take into account local laws and views toward sexual orientation and gender expression when making important decisions about how to operate inclusively within the company when the external culture espouses conflicting values. It is important as well to explore how visible and invisible disabilities are viewed within the local environment.

• Conclusion •

As this chapter has illustrated managers must be at ease with diversity and inclusivity so all team members have an equal chance to advance and succeed. Inclusive managers help all team members develop their talent, take care to speak about their skills in routine meetings, and highlight their individual talents in formal performance reviews. Some companies refer to this as *credentializing* and it can be used to diminish the impact of stereotypes and bias. In summary, inclusive leadership is a powerful tool for retention and development of talent. If you learn to effective include diverse talent and excel at mentoring and sponsoring individuals, you will build loyal, productive teams and develop a reputation for being an outstanding manager and leader.

• Endnotes •

1. Mitra Toossi, "A Century of Change: The U.S. Labor Force, 1950–2050," *Monthly Labor Review* 125, no. 5 (2002): 15–28, www.bls.gov/opub/mlr/2002/05/art2full.pdf.
2. "2017 Board Diversity Survey: Seeing Is Believing," Deloitte, 2017, www2.deloitte.com/us/en/pages/about-deloitte/articles/board-diversity-survey.html.
3. The founders of Project Implicit were Tony Greenwald (University of Washington), Mahzarin Banaji (Harvard University), and Brian Nosek (University of Virginia). More information about Project Implicit can be found at https://implicit.harvard.edu/implicit.
4. Mahzarin R. Banaji and Anthony G. Greenwald, *Blindspot: Hidden Biases of Good People* (New York: Delacorte Press, 2013).
5. Lori Mackenzie, JoeAnne Wehner, and Shelley Correll, "Why Most Performance Evaluations Are Biased, and How to Fix Them," *Harvard Business Review*, January 11, 2019.
6. Christine Porath, "Give Your Team More Effective Positive Feedback," *Harvard Business Review*, October 25, 2016.
7. Kenji Yoshino, *Covering: The Hidden Assault on Our Civil Rights* (New York: Random House, 2006).
8. Kenji Yoshino and Christie Smith, "Fear of Being Different Stifles Talent," *Harvard Business Review*, March 2014, https://hbr.org/2014/03/fear-of-being-different-stifles-talent.
9. Dan Schawbel, "Sylvia Ann Hewlett: Find a Sponsor Instead of a Mentor," *Forbes*, September 10, 2013.

Glossary

A

Accounting The collection of records of all business transactions and events reported in the form of financial statements.

Accrual method A method of accounting in which revenue is recorded in the time period in which it is earned and an expense is matched to the revenue it helped generate.

Achievement motive The need to accomplish large, inherently valuable goals that benefit large groups of people, an organization, or a community.

Active listening A set of communication techniques (concentrate, understand, respond, remember) and the spirit or intention behind the techniques: sincere curiosity about an employee's perspective and experience.

Adverse impact A rate of selection in employment decisions that may unintentionally work to the disadvantage of a certain race, sex, or ethnic group.

Affiliation motive The need to seek interpersonal relationships more than goal achievement.

Amygdala hijack theory When people perceive a threat, they are motivated by an instinct for fighting, fleeing, or freezing.

Anchoring Tendency to give precedence to the first piece of information encountered when researching a solution or decision.

Anticipatory regret Delaying decision making because of anxiety about the feelings that may emerge if a choice turns out to be wrong.

Argumentation Thinking used to arrive at a logical conclusion.

Artificial Intelligence (AI) A computer system that uses statistics to refine and improve how a computer performs a task.

Assets All things owned by a business.

Assumption An item that we reasonably believe to be true based on prior knowledge, current situational environment, and other factors related to the project.

Atmospheric effect The way in which certain words and grammatical constructions predispose individuals to accept as correct or valid conclusions that may not be so.

Authority An individual's level of power or decision-making rights.

Availability heuristic A tendency to rely on immediate examples that come to mind when analyzing a particular situation rather than looking more broadly for data that might inform a choice.

Average The measure of the center of a distribution of scores for a particular variable.

B

Balance sheet A financial reporting document that describes what an enterprise owns, its debts and obligations, and the shareholder's investment in the company. The balances in the asset accounts must equal the sum of the balances in the liabilities and equity accounts.

Behavioral ethics Principles that motivate an individual to make every effort to determine what is right in a specific situation and to implement that action.

Belief bias When the subject matter of a problem connects to an individual's experiences and opinions in a way that interferes with the ability to think critically about the problem itself.

Bias A prejudice in favor of or against one thing, person, or group compared with another, usually in a way considered to be unfair.

Bias for action A preference for doing rather than thinking.

Blockchain A public record of a transaction that spreads information over many systems, thereby making it difficult to silently alter the record.

Bottom line A company's net income and the clearest measure of success.

Brainstorming Freewheeling discussion in which all ideas are valid, thereby allowing a building of collective ideas and opinions that represent the group or team.

Brainwriting Written ideas created ahead of time, passed around the group or team members for positive/negative comments and including a discussion of the comments.

Break-even point analysis A method of determining the point at which a company stops losing money and begins producing a profit.

Budget The amount of money that has been approved to execute the project according to the project plan.

Budgeting process This is led by the accounting function, but evolves from each manager's statements of purpose and plans for executing the strategic plan of the business.

Burden-benefit analysis Cost-benefit analysis.

Business ethics Principles by which processes should be transparent and guide decision making in all aspects of business above and beyond what the law requires.

C

Capital Expenditure Planning (CAPEX) A broad range of acquisitions, including asset purchases, leasing alternatives, make versus buy alternatives, outsourcing alternatives, and business mergers and acquisitions.

Cash flow A summary of all transactions for a specific period of time.

Cash method An accounting method used for tax purposes for smaller companies in which revenue is recorded in the term period when cash is received and expenses are recorded in the time period when the item or service is paid for.

Cause-effect relationships A necessary cause is something that is required for a particular outcome to occur; a sufficient cause is emoting that could make a particular outcome possible.

Circular reasoning A pattern of weak argument in which a person or group making an assertion responds to requests for elaboration by restating the original assertion with different words.

Cloud technologies Software that runs in a central data center, enabling small companies to access the same technologies as large companies.

Coaching An ongoing, collaborative process of evaluating employee performance, setting goals, providing feedback, identifying development opportunities, and brainstorming plans of action to achieve personal goals in alignment with organizational needs.

Collaboration An activity in which people connect and work together in an interactive, interdependent, unified, cooperative, and synergistic way to achieve a common goal.

Collectivism culture A society in which people expect their needs to be met by others and in which individuals contribute to the betterment of all.

Co-located A designation for team members who are in the same building and can communicate face-to-face without a mediated channel.

Command and control approach An authoritative management style that uses a top-down approach.

Communication The complex and culturally-bound process by which information is imparted or exchanged with the goal of creating shared meaning.

Communication, intercultural The way people communicate across different cultures within an organization.

Communication, interpersonal Communication between people that occurs one-on-one.

Communication, intrapersonal Subvocalized communication with oneself that impacts thought, emotions, physiological responses, attitudes, and verbal and nonverbal communication choices and behaviors.

Communication, mediated Any form of communication that utilizes tools beyond the basic elements found in face-to-face interactions.

Communication, team Communication with and among members of a team who have a shared vision, purpose, and set of goals. This communication is directed toward accomplishment of tasks as well as building and maintaining team relationships and a sense of membership.

Communication style preferences How people prefer to express themselves at work orally or in writing.

Compensation methodology A formal process for determining salaries based on surveys that obtain information on the pay range for all positions and levels in an industry.

Confirmation bias Tendency to look only at evidence that supports an anticipated or hoped for conclusion.

Conflict management approach How people typically navigate and deal with interpersonal challenges and differences of opinion.

Conflict of interest When a decision maker is, or appears to be, open to undue influence from someone else.

Consequentialism Making a decision based on a particular desired outcome.

Contribution margin A product's price after deducting all variable costs that results in the incremental profit earned for each unit sold.

Correlation When two things happen at the same time.

Counterfactual thinking The ability to look at a situation from a variety of perspectives, especially the views of those whose values and frames of reference differ from one's own.

Credibility The trust you gain from others because of your expertise and relationship.

Critical thinking The analysis of an issue in order to form a judgment based on an ability to recognize assumptions, evaluate arguments without bias, and objectively examine all options.

Cross-cultural competencies The knowledge, skills, and motivations that enable individuals to adapt successfully to cross-cultural environments.

Cultural fit Integrating organizational culture criteria with employer brand messaging, job content, and interview processes.

Culture Shared values, beliefs, and behaviors of an organization or a unit within that organization.

Customer centricity An organizational strategy and mindset that places the customer at the center of all decisions and behaviors.

Customer focus The practice of designing an organization's value around the customer's expectations and unmet needs and addressing internal and external customer needs to support business goals.

Customer satisfaction A measure of the customer's evaluation of the quality of the customer experience.

D

Data analysis A process for obtaining raw data and converting it into information useful for decision-making by users.

Data collection and analysis Finding, collecting, and organizing information into a format that can be analyzed as well as examining the data to gain insights and understanding.
Data leveraging Interpretation of the result of data analysis in order to make decisions and influence others to act.
Decision fatigue A form of psychological stress that results in deteriorating quality of decisions after prolonged periods of decision making.
Decision-making approach The process people use to come to a decision and the factors that affect that process.
Deductive reasoning The process of considering a series of givens (data) and drawing a conclusion from them.
Defamation Injury to an individual's character or reputation resulting from another individual's false or malicious statements either orally or in writing.
Delegation The process of assigning some degree of authority and responsibility for specific work to another person.
Deliverable An evident output of a project, usually identified as a requirement throughout the project plan.
Deontology Rules-based reasoning.
Descriptive analysis Collection of large amounts of data to identify clusters, characteristics, and trends that can be used to identify differences between and within groups.
Digital transformation The integration of data into all aspects of behavior and action.
Discounted payback period The number of years it takes to break even from the time of the initial expenditure based on discounting future cash flows and adjusting for the time value of money.
Discretionary effort An individual's willingness to go above and beyond what is specifically required of him or her.
Disparate treatment Rules and policies applied inconsistently, causing a negative impact on protected classes of people.
Disruptive technology New technology that disrupts an entire industry, thereby providing new opportunities and increased productivity for businesses.
Diversity The understanding that each individual is unique and recognition of our differences.

E

Economic value added (EVA) Ratio computed by calculating the difference between the actual rate of return on assets and the cost of capital and then multiplying the result by the net investment in the business.
Emotional courage A willingness to tolerate one's own unpleasant and uncontrollable emotions and physical sensations, which may be triggered by the words and actions of others, and still maintain and open and engaging disposition.
Emotional intelligence (EI) The ability to identify and manage your own emotions and to observe and impact others' emotional states.
Employee engagement An employee's willingness to expend effort on tasks.
Employment-at-will A legal doctrine stating that an employment relationship may be terminated either by the employer or employee at any time for any or no reason.
Engagement assessment matrix A project management grid that determines the current level of stakeholder engagement and projects the desired level of engagement.
Equity The value of shares issued by a company.
Exchange phase The process that uncovers what will create value between the parties to an agreement; it requires the ability to negotiate.

F

Fairness Treating each person according to effort and merit and avoiding assessments based on personal characteristics.
False dichotomy An attempt to create a binary choice, or to suggest a black and white solution to a problem when, in reality, there are a number of viable options and gray areas.

Femininity culture A society that emphasizes cooperation, consensus building, caring, and protection of weaker members.

Finance The analysis of accounting statements to understand how well the business is performing, where problems may be present, and whether continuing investment in the business is advisable.

Fixed costs Costs that do not vary with changes in volume of production.

G

Gambler's fallacy Thinking that because an event has not occurred recently, it probably will not happen anytime soon; or, that because an event has happened recently, it will not repeat any time soon.

Gantt chart A bar chart that illustrates a project schedule, with tasks on the vertical axis and time intervals on the horizontal axis.

Group think A practice in which less diverse perspectives lead to mistakes in important decision making.

Group voting Team members have a set number of points to assign to different ideas, with the most points being the basis for decisions.

GUIDE model A model of managerial coaching that includes gathering data on employee performance, understanding the impact of the data, interviewing employees about recent performance, developing an action plan, and executing the plan and examining progress.

H

Harassment Conduct or actions based on race, religion, sex, national origin, age, disability, military membership or veteran status that are severe enough to create a hostile, abusive, or intimidating work environment.

Healthy conflict Collaborative action that arises from shared and open communication and goals that leads to creativity, innovation, and optimism.

Hostile work environment A culture in which an employee is routinely subjected to some aspect of a work environment that a reasonable person would find severely objectionable or offensive.

Human-centric design (HCD) A design and management framework that places the human perspective at the center of its design process.

Hurdle rate Minimum rate a company expects to earn from a project.

Hypothetical thinking The ability to generate predictions and visualize what consequences are more or less likely to result from particular courses of action.

I

Ideation workshop A process that uses creative tools to reimagine the customer experience.

Illusion of validity A general tendency to use too small a sample, or a nonrepresentative sample, to justify a particular conclusion.

Imposter syndrome A self-perception or belief that surfaces when an individual continuously doubts his or her own qualifications for his or her current role.

Inclusive leadership A management style in which the leader is able to fully engage every member of the team.

Inclusiveness Creation of a welcoming environment that accepts each individual's differences, embraces strengths, encourages involvement, and provides opportunities for all to achieve their full potential.

Income statement A financial reporting document that presents the results of operations by matching revenues earned with expenses related to those revenues and expenses incurred to run the business. Also known as a Statement of Profit and Loss.

Individualism Giving the most to each person while taking the least from each person.

Individualism culture A society in which people are expected to take care of only themselves and their families.
Inductive reasoning The brain's ability to examine a conclusion and determine whether or not it validly follows from the information presented with it.
Indulgence culture A society that encourages gratification, the enjoyment of life, and the pursuit of pleasure.
Influence A process in which one person or group attempts to change the attitudes and thus the behaviors of another person or group for a specific purpose.
Internal rate of return (IRR) A metric used in capital budgeting to estimate the profitability of potential investments.

J

Just cause Guiding principle used by employers when engaged in corrective or disciplinary action with employees.

K

Key Performance Indicators (KPIs) Key financial drivers of business, including ratio analysis, customer service statistics, activity or volume tracking, and scrap rates.
Knowledge management Collection of information about diversity related issues and how involved actors have overcome, manage, or transform the challenges.

L

Liabilities All things owed by a business.
Licensing agreements Legal permission by a licensor that allows a licensee to develop, market, and/or sell specific branded products and services.
Linear ordering Identifying relationships among items based on their characteristics and organizing them relative to each other.
Long-term orientation culture A society that is less tied to tradition and more inclined to prepare for change.

M

Management The art of accomplishing a company's objectives.
Management by objective (MBO) A management style that gives people the autonomy to work toward goals in the ways they identify as best for their own area of responsibility. Members share in planning and are therefore committed to actualizing the plan and achieving their goals.
Management by walking around (MBWA) Physically checking on the status of a project by viewing the work product or talking to staff.
Management style The approach leaders use to provide direction and support, offer feedback, motivate employees, and engage employees in goal accomplishment.
Manager, coaching A manager whose style combines direction, accountability, and the building of independent capability in employees.
Manager, delegating A manager who either does not care how a task is accomplished, as long as it is completed, or who cares but provides no input, guidance, or support.
Manager, directive A manager who issues orders and expects them to be followed to the letter.
Masculinity culture A society that emphasizes achievement, competition, and assertiveness.
Matrixed organizations A structure with more than one line of reporting managers.

Microaggressions Statements or actions that are directly offensive to others and typically are direct stereotypes that insult individuals.
Microinequities Small negative actions, such as slights and cutting remarks, that align with a biased point of view.
Mind mapping Visual brainstorm in which key thoughts are placed on a flip chart and branches of ideas are place around each thought.
Mindset A mental attitude that reflects your emotional perspective on how your results will be accomplished and results in either a closed or open state of mind.
Mobile technologies A set of technologies that enable cellphones to operate and transmit data.
Motivation Internal and external factors that stimulate a person's desire and energy to be continually interested in and committed to an activity, job, role, or subject or to make an effort to attain a goal.
Motivators, external or extrinsic Material things that motivate individuals.
Motivators, internal or intrinsic Nonmaterial things that motivate individuals.
Multihoming The practice of consumers purchasing two similar technologies.
Multisensory listening Intake of and attention to available signs within a communication event, using all sensory systems to better assign meaning.
Mutuality The shared feeling or actions one exhibits toward others.

N
Negative reinforcement Removing a negative consequence when an individual performs a particular behavior.
Negligent hiring A claim made against an employer based on the premise that an employer is obligated not to hire an applicant that the employer knew or should have known was unsuitable and was likely to behave inappropriately toward other employees.
Net present value (NPV) Evaluation of the expected cash flow impacts of a project over its entire estimated useful life that is discounted back to the time period when the project was brought on line using the required rate of return as the discount rate.
Network effects A phenomenon that occurs when an increasing number of people improve the value of a good or service.
Non-falsifiability Dismissing or ignoring all evidence that contradicts a person's theory so that it cannot be disproven.

O
Open door policy An environment in which an employee can report harassment to any level of management and is protected in case his or her manager is the offender.
Operant conditioning The use of reward or punishment after a behavior to either encourage or discourage that behavior.
Operational project management The management of efforts intended to improve operational efficiency that would traditionally be managed as an operational or support function as if they were projects.
Organizational culture The shared values, beliefs, and perceptions held by members of an organization.
Organizational identity A set of statements that organization members perceive to be central, distinctive, and enduring to their organization.
Organizational socialization Learning the values, norms, and behaviors that permit an employee to participate in the organization.
Outlier A data value that falls outside the expected range.

P

Pareto analysis Statistical approach to decision-making used to determine a limited number of functions that will have a significant overall effect.

Pareto principle Eighty percent of the work generates 80% of the benefit of the job.

People flow Treating others with respect, displaying a commitment to them, and letting them know that they make a difference.

Performance management Consists of a diverse set of skills, including the ability to set clear and objective standards, assess employee performance based on those standards, and provide feedback to correct any discrepancies.

Personal influence Building your personal credibility with others by applying empathy as a powerful influencing strategy when coaching and analyzing resistance through the lens of emotional intelligence to identify alternative approaches.

Personality The way that people interact with their world, including how they take in information, relate to others, structure their surroundings, and recharge.

Platform Any technology on which other new technologies are built.

Positive reinforcement Rewarding individuals when they perform a particular behavior.

Power base A source of authority, influence, or support.

Power distance index The degree to which the less powerful members of a society accept and expect power to be distributed unequally.

Power/interest grid A project management tool that helps a team categorize project stakeholders.

Precedence diagram A tool for communicating the plan for a project.

Presentation modality The technologies available to communicate your material beyond in-person presentations.

Prevention motivation The degree to which an individual is intolerant of risk or averse to mistakes.

Prima facie principles The moral norms of business ethics.

Probability judgments Decisions based on the likelihood that something will or will not happen.

Process issue An item that causes a given process to not perform in the way it is intended.

Product-centric companies Businesses that develop products based on the ingenuity of entrepreneurs rather than consumer demand and focus on product, pricing, placement, and promotion.

Pro forma balance sheet Recognizes changes in various categories based on strategic initiatives, cash flows from operations, capital expenditures, divestitures, tax planning, and financing requirements.

Program evaluation and review technique (PERT) A project management tool that takes into consideration the time uncertainty associated with completing the task due to unknown and/or unrelated disturbances.

Progressive discipline The increasingly more severe steps an organization follows when an employee continues to underperform.

Progressive elaboration Adjusting requirements based on new information.

Project lifecycle The consecutive phases that a project typically goes through to achieve its intended benefits.

Project management The management of project stakeholder expectations regarding any factor related to and contained in the project plan.

Project stakeholder Anyone who has an interest in a project, its plan and execution, and its intended benefit(s).

Promotion motivation The degree to which an individual is willing to take risks to test a new idea, innovate, or accomplish a goal.

Prosocial motivators Impulses of concern for the wellbeing of others.

R

Rates of change A linear rate of change remains constant; an exponential rate of change becomes more rapid with time.

Ratio analysis A key performance indicator that measures the impact of events that have already occurred.

Responsibility A person's accountability for a specific outcome.

Responsibility mapping A technique for identifying functional areas where there are process ambiguities, bringing the differences out in the open and resolving them through a cross-functional collaborative effort.

Restraint culture A society that delays gratification and has strict social norms.

Retained earnings A statement of the company's entire history of profits, losses, and dividend payouts to shareholders.

Return on investment (ROI) The return realized on the money invested in a company based on net profit.

Risk An unknown incident that might be anticipated or expected to occur during the execution of a project plan. If the item does occur, it could cause a negative impact to any one of the factors contained in the project plan.

Rule of three Ensure that a persuasive presentations includes only one to three key arguments in support of the ideas.

S

Scope creep Uncontrolled changes or continuous growth in a project's scope and intent.

Self-efficacy An individual's sense that he or she is capable of performing a task and reaching a goal.

Self-referential authority A form of circular reasoning in which the argument restates the original position rather than providing evidence in support of that position.

Sexual harassment Unwelcome sexual advances, requests for sexual favors, and other verbal or physical conduct of a sexual nature when this conduct affects an individual's employment, interferes with work performance, or creates an intimidating work environment.

Shareholders' equity The net worth of the owners of a business.

Short-term orientation culture A society that is suspicious of change and prefers time-honored practices and traditional norms.

Six Sigma A method of management that increases performance and decreases process variation, thereby improving profits, quality, and employee morale.

Skip-level meetings A periodic meeting between an employee and his or her supervisor's boss.

SMART model Documentation of a project's requirements that is specific, measurable, agreed to, realistic, and time bound.

Social system stability The degree to which organizational activities emphasize maintaining the status quo in contrast to growth.

Software as a service (SaaS) A way to sell or license software so users pay only for the time they use it or only for specific features.

Stakeholder management Understanding the business drivers of each stakeholder and how to find common ground between all parties.

Standard deviation A measure of how different the scores for a variable are distributed within a group.

STAR method A structured manner of responding to interview questions by discussing the situation, task, action, and result.

Statement of cash flow A financial reporting document that summarizes all transactions affecting cash for the same period of time.

Sticky notes Written notes posted on a flip chart organized under similarities or general categories.

Structured data Data in numeric form that can be organized into rows and columns.
Student's T-test A tool used to test the null hypothesis that there is no difference between the means of two groups.
Subculture mentality Looking for opportunities within the organizational culture to insert accountability into the way you deal with others.
Succession planning Tools for replacing people who are stepping out of the roles either through retirement or greater opportunities with other companies.
Supplier agreements A binding agreement by which a seller promises to supply goods or services that a buyer needs at an agreed price, that may vary according to quantity, credit terms, etc., and the buyer agrees to purchase such goods or services from the seller during that time.
SWOT A tool for assessing the strengths, weaknesses, opportunities, and threats in a company's environment.
Systematic design process Creation of processes and programs that deliver customer value.
Systemic discrimination A pattern of discrimination that appears neutral on the surface but is discriminatory through its application of policies and practices.

T

Talent alignment Assigning responsibilities to direct reports that match their strengths.
Talent management A set of integrated processes designed to attract, develop, motivate, and retain productive, engaged employees.
Team charter The objectives/goals of the teams tasked with managing a strategic alliance, providing them with a roadmap for how to do business.
Team huddle A round robin discussion in which each person is allowed to speak one at a time.
Team leadership Assessing team performance, stress levels, and mood to remain optimistic and productive.
Threat/asset assessment A project management tool that analyzes stakeholders by categorizing them between those that are, or are perceived to be, a threat or an asset.
Three-point estimating A technique to improve the accuracy of estimates by taking the pessimistic, optimistic, and most likely perspectives into consideration.
Total Quality Management (TQM) A management approach that requires every staff member be committed to high standards of work.
Transparency The openness of information to others so that everyone is able to work from the same set of data.
Tu Quoque Argument An effort to discredit an individual or group's position by asserting that the individual or group is prey to the same issue that the individual or group seeks to address.

U

Uncertainty avoidance index The degree to which people are comfortable with uncertainty and ambiguity.
Unconscious bias A prejudice that exists outside of a person's consciousness that can still affect behaviors or emotions.
Unstructured data Data that can be derived from text, voice, video, graphics, and other media.
Utilitarianism Determining the greatest good for the greatest number.
Values Aspects of work that are most important to employees and their satisfaction with work.

V

Variable A characteristic of something that you measure.
Variable costs Costs that are related to production and are fixed per unit of production. They vary with changes in volume of production.

Vertical analysis Review of related accounts of categories within a reporting period.

Virtual employee A designation for employees who are geographically dispersed.

Virtue-based organizational culture A society in which managers cultivate specific personal virtues, such as courage and honesty.

W

Whistle-blowing Calling attention to any situation in which a person or group's actions could be or actually are harmful to the organization, specifically harmful to customers, the environment, or other employees.

Work preferences How people prefer to structure and manage their work including pace, independent versus collaborative work, organization of work, preferred learning style, level of risk, level of goal clarity, tolerance for change, and preferences around giving and receiving feedback.

Work style The approach an employee takes to work, including how that person thinks, organizes, and completes work.

Z

Zero-tolerance policy Company statement that no harassment of any kind is acceptable and violations can result in serious ramifications.

Made in the USA
Las Vegas, NV
18 March 2025